Street by Street

G000122738

WEST SUSSEX

Enlarged areas BOGNOR REGIS, BRIGHTON, CHICHESTER, CRAWLEY, HORSHAM, WORTHING

Plus Haslemere, Havant, Horley, Hove, Petersfield

2nd edition March 2007
© Automobile Association Developments Limited 2007

Original edition printed May 2001

 This product includes map data licensed from Ordnance Survey® with the permission of the Controller of Her Majesty's Stationery Office. © Crown copyright 2007. All rights reserved. Licence number 100021153.

The copyright in all PAF is owned by Royal Mail Group plc.

Published by AA Publishing (a trading name of Automobile Association Developments Limited, whose registered office is Fanum House, Basing View, Basingstoke, Hampshire RG21 4EA. Registered number 1878835).

Produced by the Mapping Services Department of The Automobile Association. (A03123)

A CIP Catalogue record for this book is available from the British Library.

Printed by Leo, China

The contents of this atlas are believed to be correct at the time of the latest revision. However, the publishers cannot be held responsible or liable for any loss or damage occasioned to any person acting or refraining from action as a result of any use or reliance on any material in this atlas, nor for any errors, omissions or changes in such material. This does not affect your statutory rights. The publishers would welcome information to correct any errors or omissions and to keep this atlas up to date. Please write to Publishing, The Automobile Association, Fanum House (FH12), Basing View, Basingstoke, Hampshire, RG21 4EA.
E-mail: streetbystreet@theaa.com

Ref: MX020z

Key to map pages	ii-iii
Key to map symbols	iv-1
Map pages - 1:10,000	2-13
Map pages - 1:17,500	14-105
Map pages - 1:25,000	106-181
Index – towns & villages	182
Index – streets	183-207
Index – featured places	208-212
Acknowledgements	212

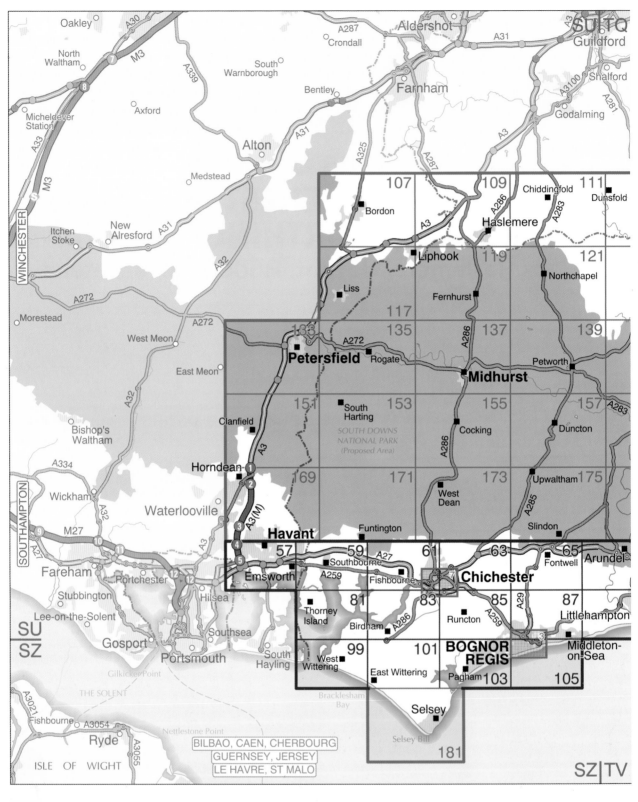

Oakley, North Waltham, Micheldever Station, Axford, Alton, Medstead, Itchen Stoke, New Alresford, Morestead, West Meon, East Meon, Bishop's Waltham, Clanfield, Horndean, Wickham, Waterlooville, Fareham, Portchester, Stubbington, Lee-on-the-Solent, Gosport, Portsmouth, Southsea, Hilsea, Emsworth, Southbourne, Havant, Fishbourne, Birdham, Thorney Island, West Wittering, South Hayling, East Wittering, Selsey, Fishbourne, Ryde, ISLE OF WIGHT, THE SOLENT, Gilkicker Point, Nettlestone Point, Bracklesham Bay, Selsey Bill

Oakley, A30, A287, Crondall, Aldershot, A31, SU TQ, Guildford, M3, South Warnborough, Bentley, Farnham, A3100, Shalford, A281, Axford, A31, Godalming, Alton, A3, Medstead, 107, 109, Chiddingfold, 111, Dunsfold, Bordon, A286, Liphook, Haslemere, A283, 119, 121, Northchapel, Liss, Fernhurst, 117, 135, 137, 139, Petersfield, Rogate, A272, Midhurst, Petworth, 151, South Harting, 153, A286, Cocking, 155, Duncton, 157, A283, SOUTH DOWNS NATIONAL PARK (Proposed Area), 169, 171, West Dean, 173, Upwaltham, 175, A285, Funtington, Slindon, 57, 59, 61, 63, 65, Fontwell, Arundel, Southbourne, A259, Chichester, A29, 81, 83, 85, 87, Littlehampton, Runcton, A259, Middleton-on-Sea, 99, 101, BOGNOR REGIS, 103, 105, Pagham, 181

BILBAO, CAEN, CHERBOURG
GUERNSEY, JERSEY
LE HAVRE, ST MALO

SZ TV

Scale of enlarged map pages 1:10,000 6.3 inches to 1 mile

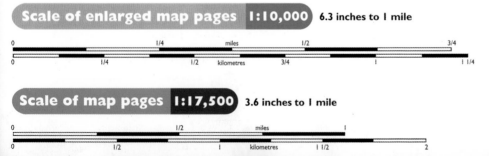

0   1/4   miles   1/2   3/4
0   1/4   1/2   kilometres   3/4   1   1 1/4

Scale of map pages 1:17,500 3.6 inches to 1 mile

0   1/2   miles   1
0   1/2   1   kilometres   1 1/2   2

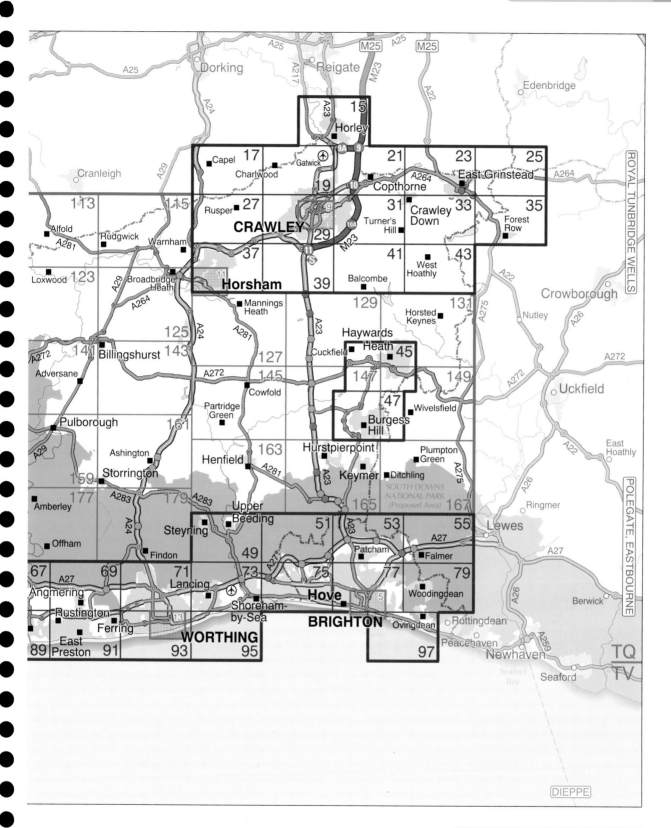

National Grid references are shown on the map frame of each page.
Red figures denote the 100 km square and the blue figures the 1km square.

Example, page 4 : Brighton Station 531 105

The reference can also be written using the National Grid two-letter prefix
shown on this page, where 5 and 1 are replaced by TQ to give TQ3105

2.5 inches to 1 mile   **Scale of map pages 1:25,000**

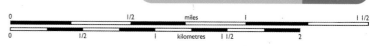

Junction 9	Motorway & junction
Services	Motorway service area
	Primary road single/dual carriageway
Services	Primary road service area
	A road single/dual carriageway
	B road single/dual carriageway
	Other road single/dual carriageway
	Minor/private road, access may be restricted
← ←	One-way street
	Pedestrian area
	Track or footpath
	Road under construction
	Road tunnel
P	Parking
P+	Park & Ride
	Bus/coach station
	Railway & main railway station
	Railway & minor railway station
⊖	Underground station
⊖	Light railway & station
++++++++	Preserved private railway

LC	Level crossing
•—•—•—•—	Tramway
- - - - - - -	Ferry route
··················	Airport runway
— · — · — · —	County, administrative boundary
▾▾▾▾▾▾▾▾▾	Mounds
151	Page continuation 1:25,000
93	Page continuation 1:17,500
7	Page continuation to enlarged scale 1:10,000
	River/canal, lake
	Aqueduct, lock, weir
465 ▲ Winter Hill	Peak (with height in metres)
	Beach
	Woodland
	Park
	Cemetery
	Built-up area
	Industrial/business building
	Leisure building
	Retail building
	Other building

⊓⊔⊓⊔⊓⊔⊓⊔	City wall		♟	Castle
A&E	Hospital with 24-hour A&E department		🏠	Historic house or building
PO	Post Office		Wakehurst Place NT	National Trust property
📖	Public library		🏛	Museum or art gallery
i	Tourist Information Centre		♞	Roman antiquity
i	Seasonal Tourist Information Centre		⍊	Ancient site, battlefield or monument
🔋🔋	Petrol station, 24 hour Major suppliers only		🏭	Industrial interest
†	Church/chapel		❋	Garden
🚻	Public toilets		◉	Garden Centre Garden Centre Association Member
♿	Toilet with disabled facilities		🌷	Garden Centre Wyevale Garden Centre
PH	Public house AA recommended		🌳	Arboretum
🍽	Restaurant AA inspected		🛒	Farm or animal centre
Madeira Hotel	Hotel AA inspected		🦌	Zoological or wildlife collection
🎭	Theatre or performing arts centre		🦜	Bird collection
🎥	Cinema		🦆	Nature reserve
⚑	Golf course		🐠	Aquarium
▲	Camping AA inspected		V	Visitor or heritage centre
🚐	Caravan site AA inspected		♈	Country park
▲🚐	Camping & caravan site AA inspected		◠	Cave
🎡	Theme park		🗼	Windmill
⛪	Abbey, cathedral or priory		🛢	Distillery, brewery or vineyard

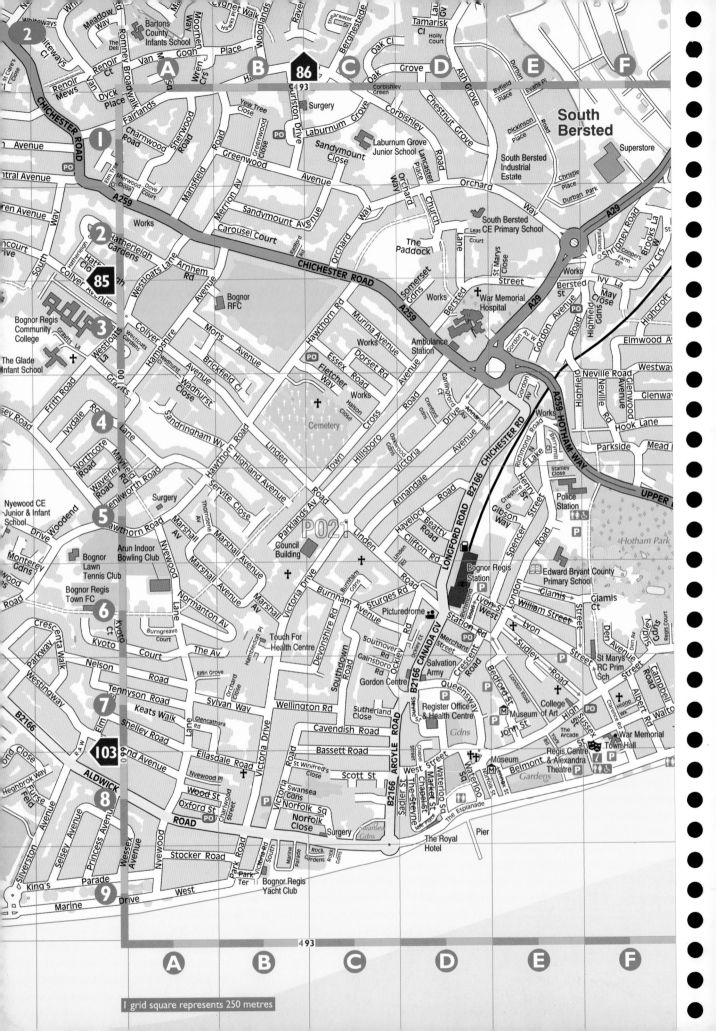

BOGNOR REGIS

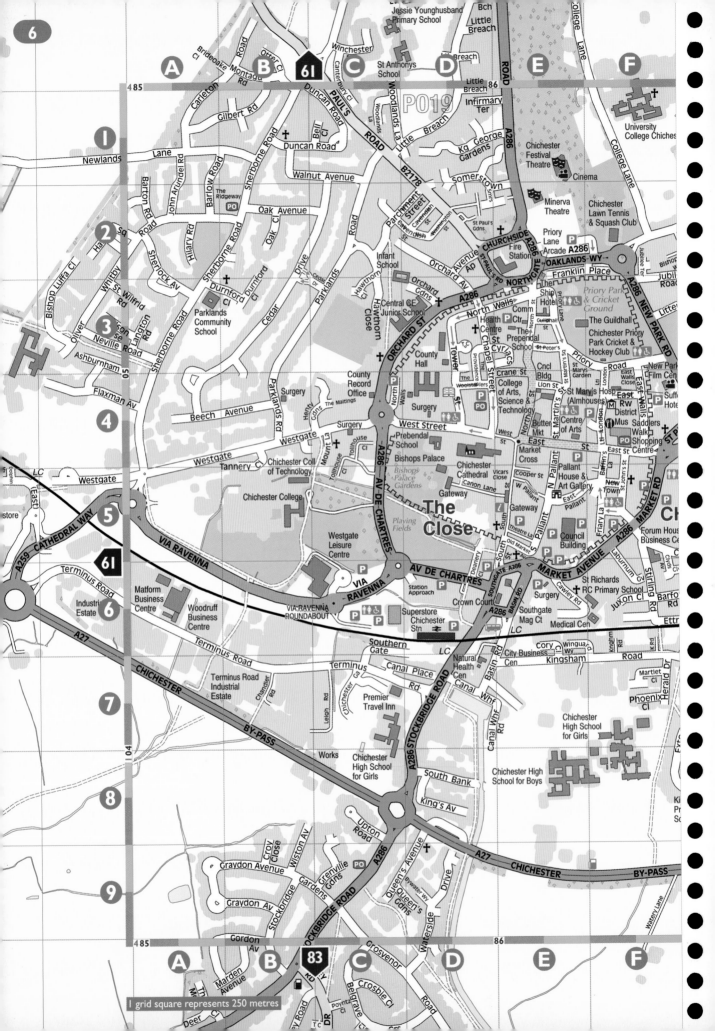

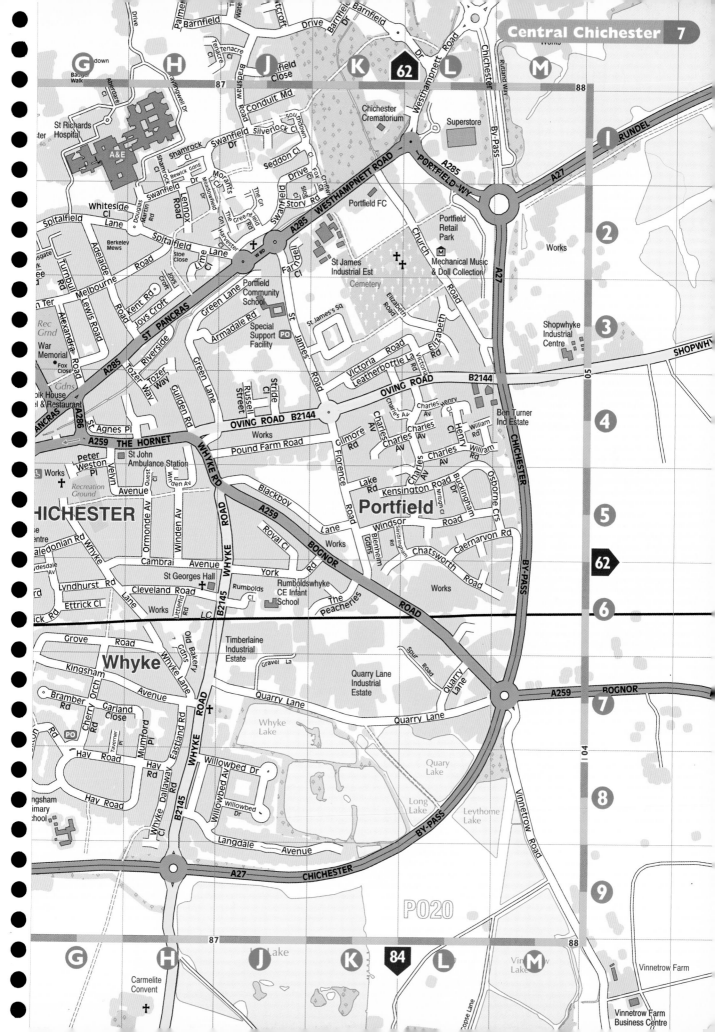

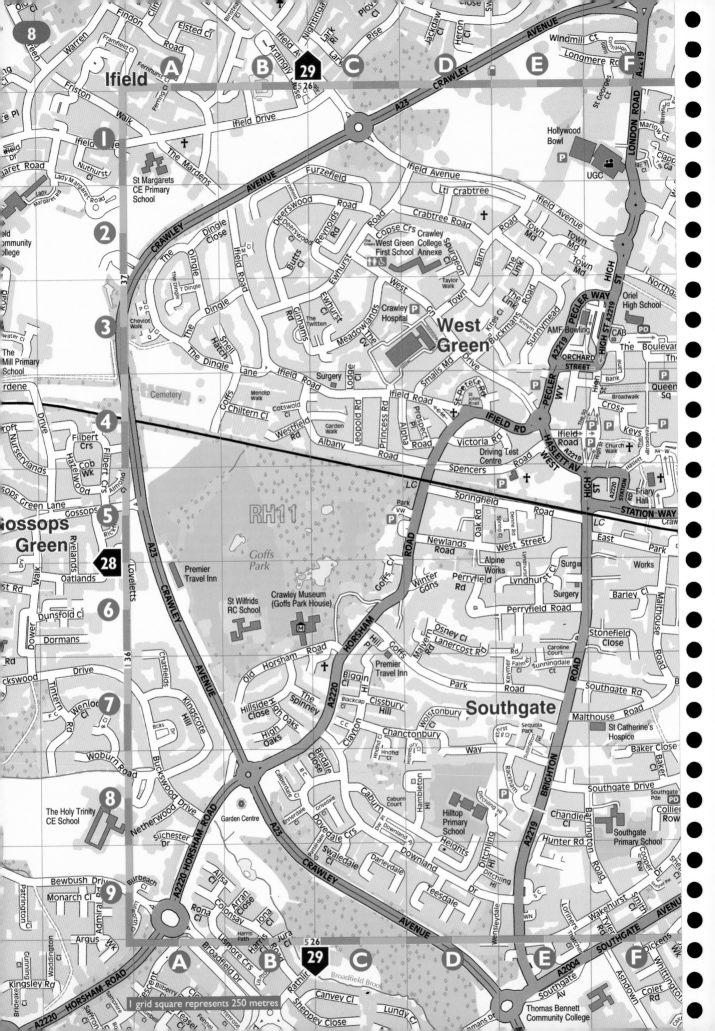

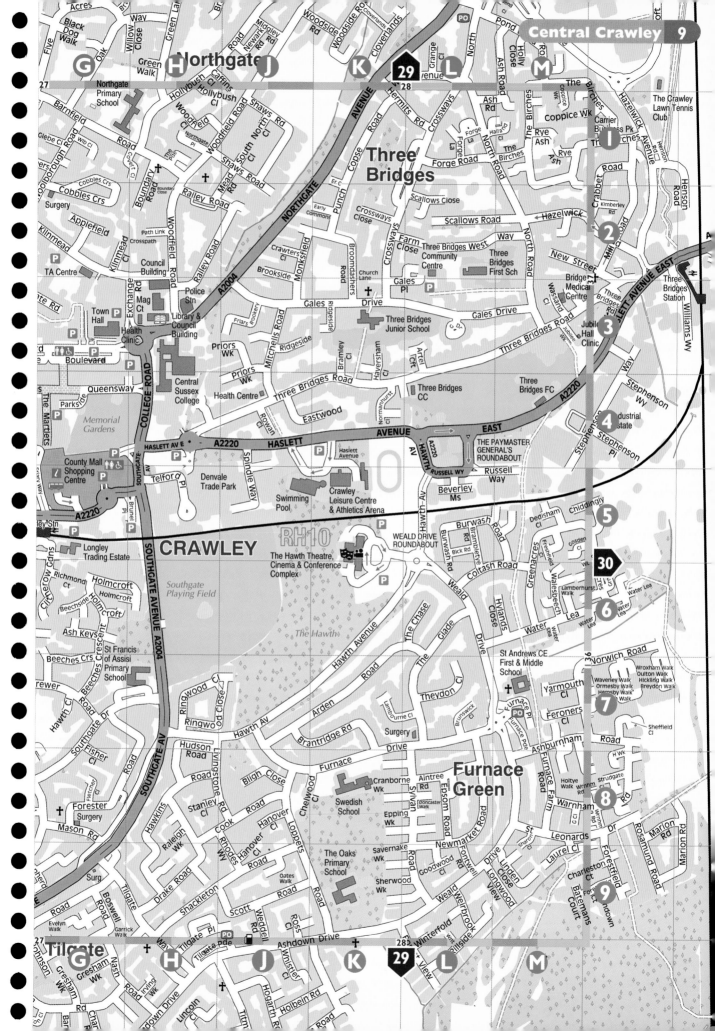

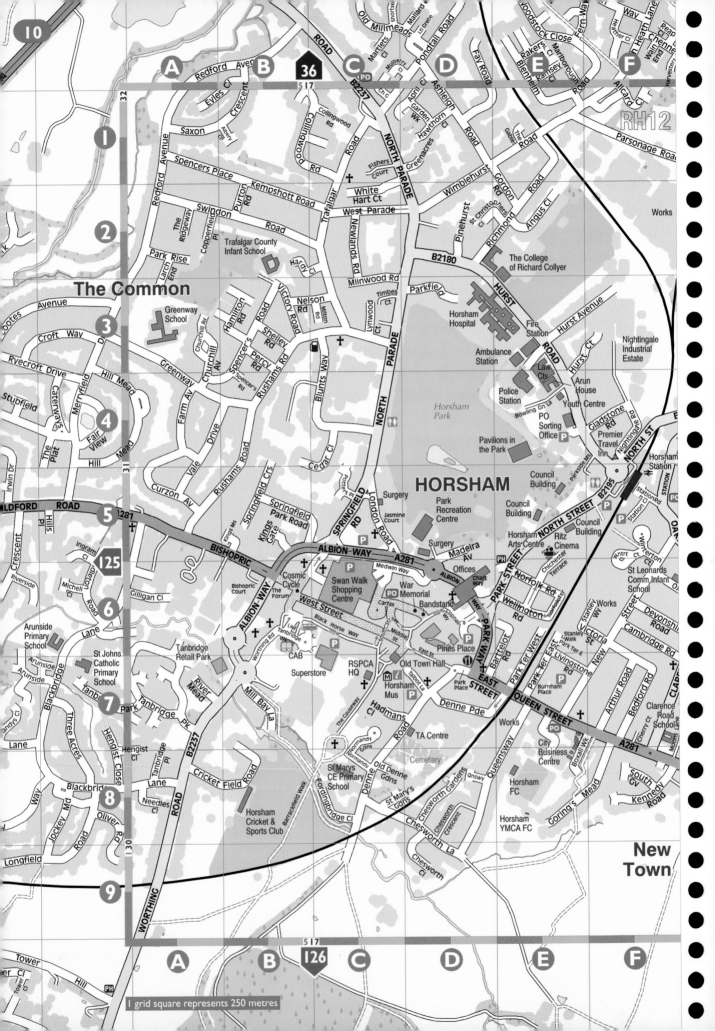

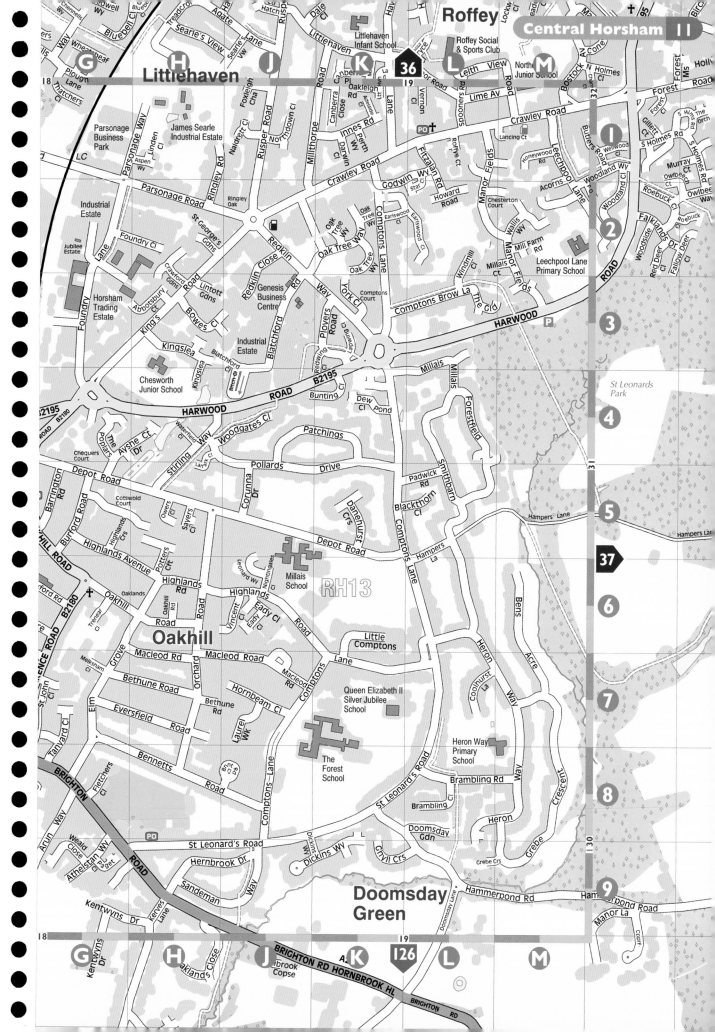

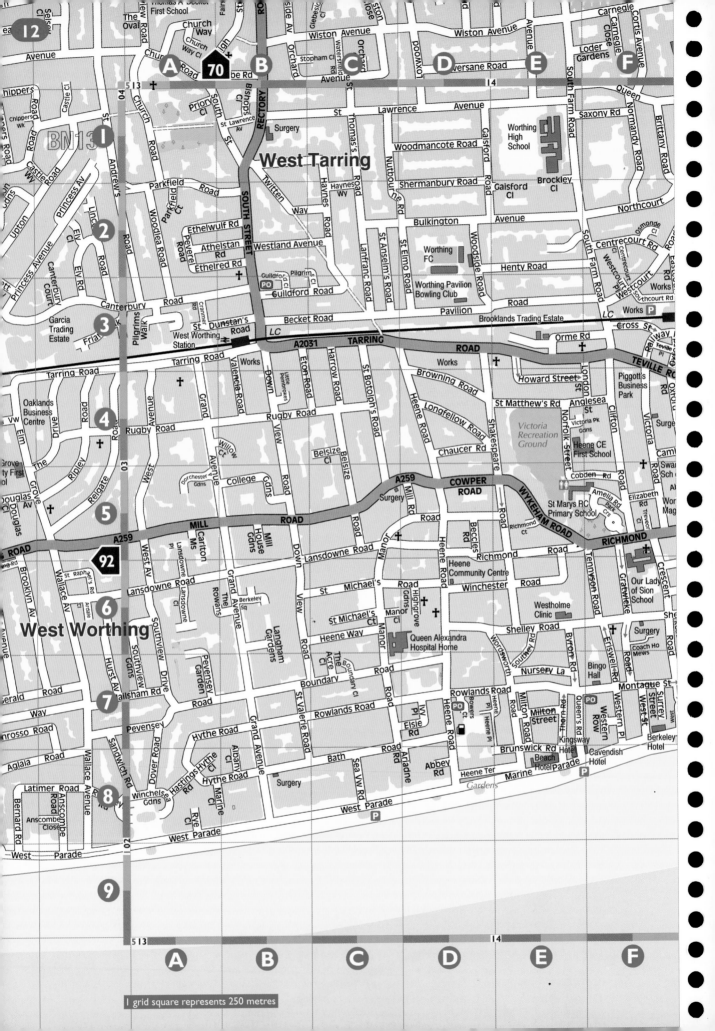

WORTHING

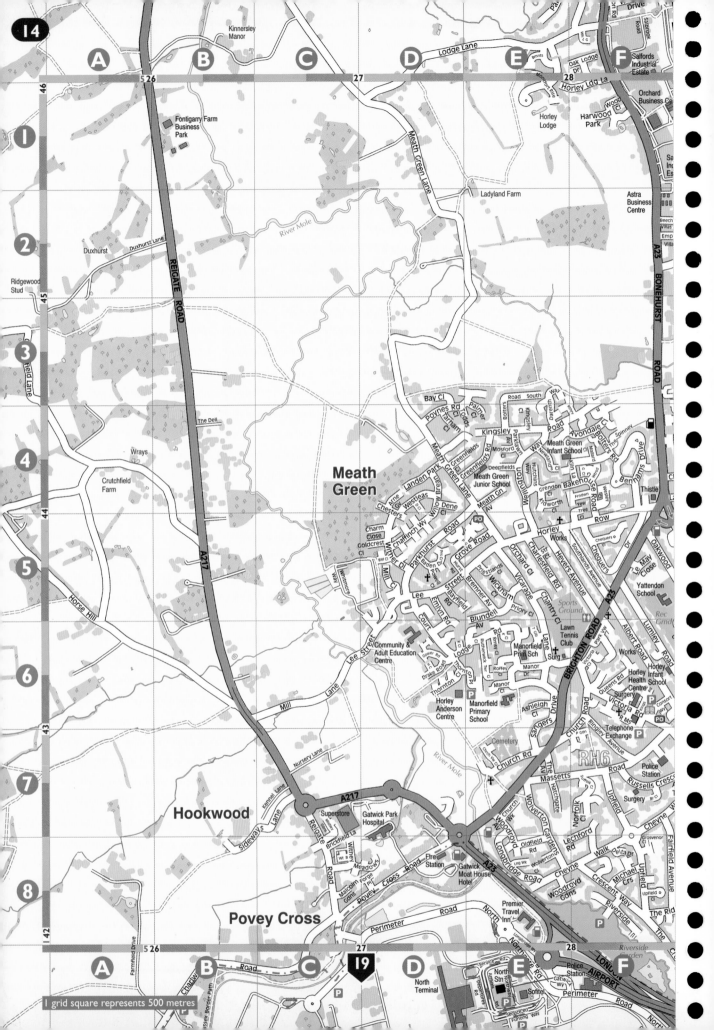

A   B   C   D   E   F

S 26   27   28

I

Kinnersley Manor

Lodge Lane

Fontigarry Farm Business Park

Meath Green Lane

Horley Ldg La

Salfords Industrial Estate

Oak Lodge Dr

Horley Lodge

Harwood Park

Orchard Business Ce

46

2

River Mole

Duxhurst   Duxhurst Lane

Ladyland Farm

Astra Business Centre

45

Ridgewood Stud

BONEHURST ROAD

A23

3

REIGATE ROAD

Shfield Lane

44

4

The Dell

Wrays

Crutchfield Farm

Meath Green

Bay Cl   Road South

Poynes Rd   Palmer   Tarham   Todds   Kingsley

Greenfields Rd   Mosford Cl   Kingsley Av   Parkway   Hutchins Cl   Grendon Cl   Kidworth Cl

Meath Green Infant School

Avondale Cl   Spinney

Bakeho   ROW   Wesley   Yew Tree

Meath Green Junior School

Benhams

Thistle

A217

Deepfields

Meath Gn Av

Landen Park   Breze

Willow Dene   Chesters   Westleas   Arne   Chaffinch Wy

Charm Close   Goldcrest Cl   Billy Dr

PO

Horley Works

Chequers

43

5

Horse Hill

Witker Dr   Mill Cl   Whitmore Way   Parkhurst Road

Grove Road   Orchard Cl   Charlesfield Rd   Vicarage   Heyers Avenue   Southlands Avenue   Chequers Dr

Le May Close   Oakwood

Yattendon School

Rec Grnd

6

Mill Lane

Lee Street

Lee   Emlyn Rd   Bayfield Rd   Court   Street   Baden Powell

Wickham   Bremner Av   Priory Cl   Chantry Cl

Sports Ground

Lawn Tennis Club

Albert Road   Lumley Road

Works

Horley Infant School

Blundell Av   Rd   Manorfield Prim Sch   Surg

BRIGHTON ROAD

A23

Horley Health Centre Surgery

7

Nursery Lane

Kennel Lane

Community & Adult Education Centre

Thornton   Lodge Lane   Thornton Pl   Roffey Cl   Manor Dr   Manor Cl

Horley Anderson Centre

Manorfield Primary School

Ashleigh Cl   Sangers Drive

Cemetery

River Mole

Church Rd

Church Road

RH6

Victoria Rd   Consort

PO

Telephone Exchange

Police Station

Russells Cresce

Surgery

42

8

Sideways Lane

Reigate Road

Hookwood

A217

Superstore

Brickfield La   Withey

Gatwick Park Hospital

Malcolm Gdns   Meadow   Forge

Povey Cross Road

Fire Station

Gatwick Moat House Hotel

North Rd

Longbridge Road   A23

Woodroyd Av   Oldfield Rd   Cheyne Av   Wolverton Gardens   Lechford Rd   Cheyne Walk

Massetts Road   The Hatchgate   Norfolk Cl

Wolverton Rd

Woodroya Gdns

Michael Crs   Crescent Way   Upfield   Delta Dr

Grosvenor   Fairfield Avenue

Povey Cross

Perimeter Road

Premier Travel Inn

Riverside

The Rid

Riverside Garden

A   **B**   Road   **C**   ▼**19**   **D**   North Terminal   **E**   Police Stations   **F**   GATWICK AIRPORT

S 26   27   28   LONDON   Perimeter   North

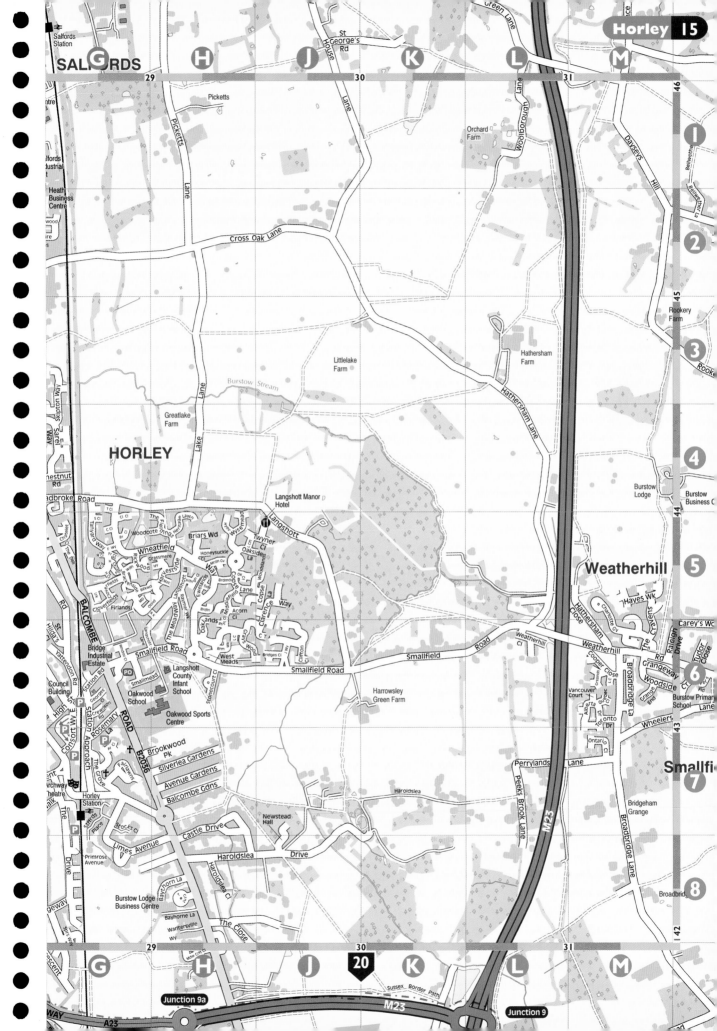

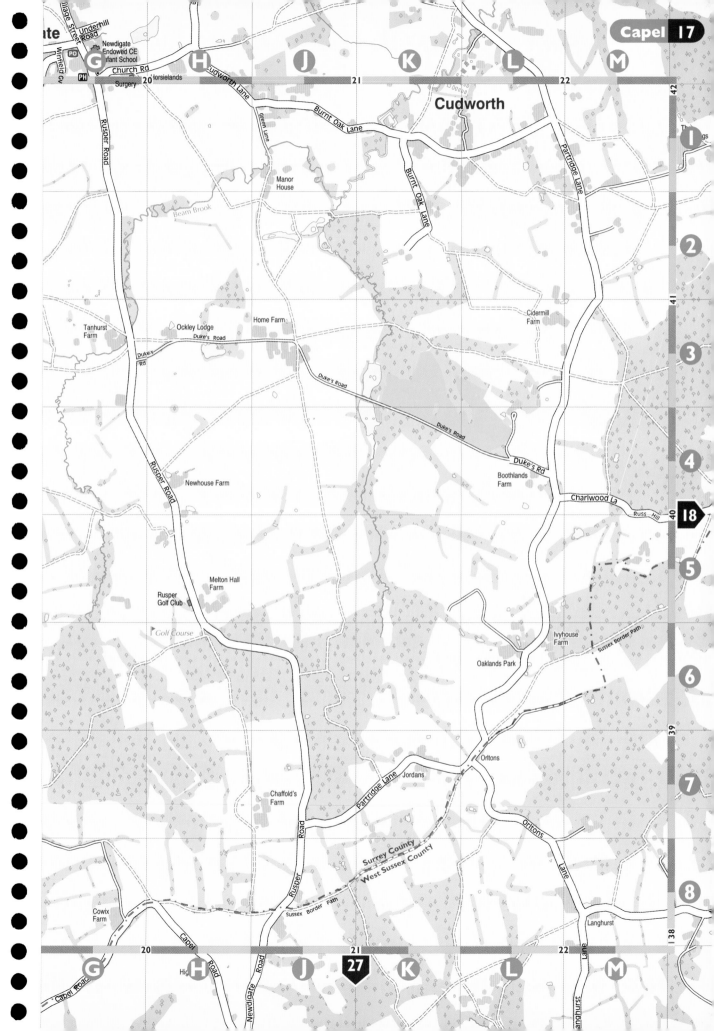

A   B   C   D   E   F

5 23   24   25

Stanhill Court Hotel

I   The Greenings

Beggarshouse Lane

Stan Hill

Charlwood Place

Pudding Lane

2

Charlwood Village Infant School

Swan Lane

Rectory La

Rosemary La

New Tree Rd

Chapel Road

Charlwood

Glover's Rd

The Street

Willow Corner

Perrylands

Lewitt Close

Russ Hill Road

Limes Business Centre

Gatwick Industrial Estate

Glover's Wood

Chalmers Cl

Orchard Farm

3

Works

Lowfield

Russ Hill

Russ Hill

Surrey County

West Sussex County

Heath Road

17   40

4

5

Upper Prestwood Farm

Bonnetts Lane

6

39

Prestwood Lane

Naldretts Farm

7

Lower Prestwood Farm

Charlwood Road

Crawley RFC

Ifieldwood

Ifield Court

8

The Mount

Hillybarn

Ifield Wood

River Mead

Strathmore Road

Tweed Lane

Ifield Green

The Mount

Ifield Avenue

Stafford Road

Burland

1 38

A   B   C   D   E   F

5 23   24   25

Road

Bonwycks Place

28

River

Rectory Lane

Cemetery

Mill La

Surgery

Manor Green

Ifield Green

Old Mnr Close

Hardham

Drive

I grid square represents 500 metres

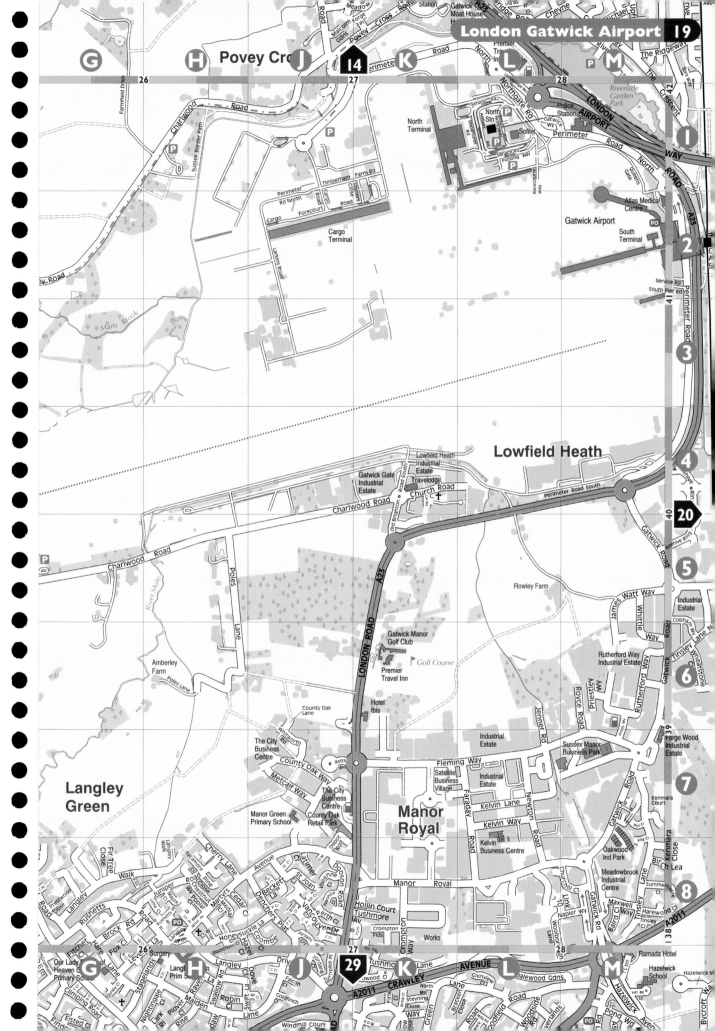

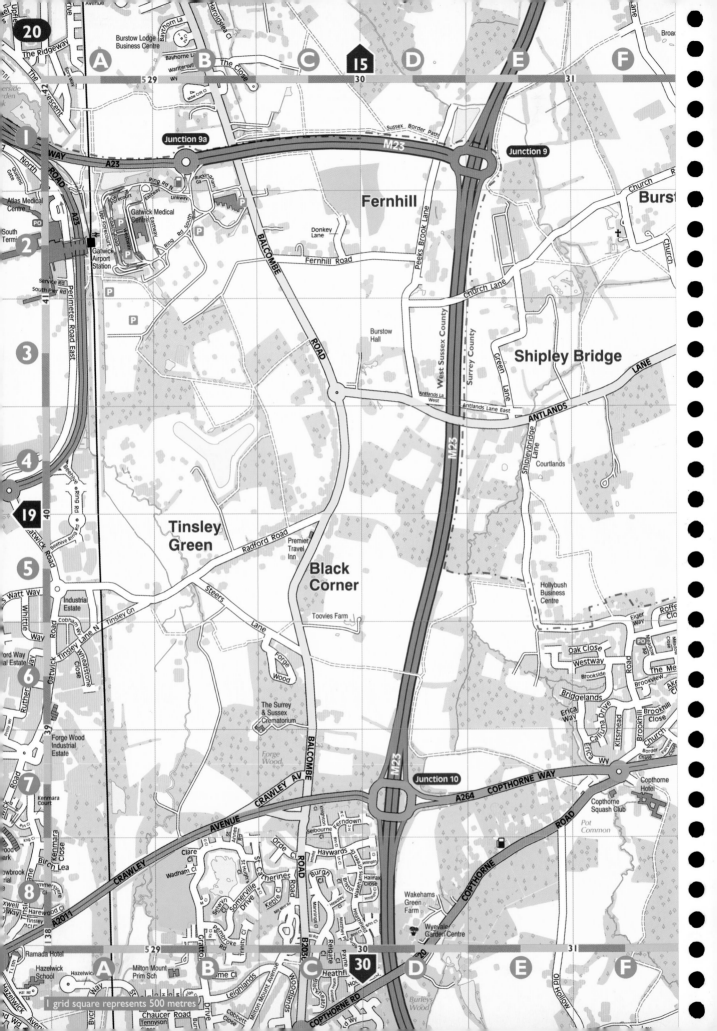

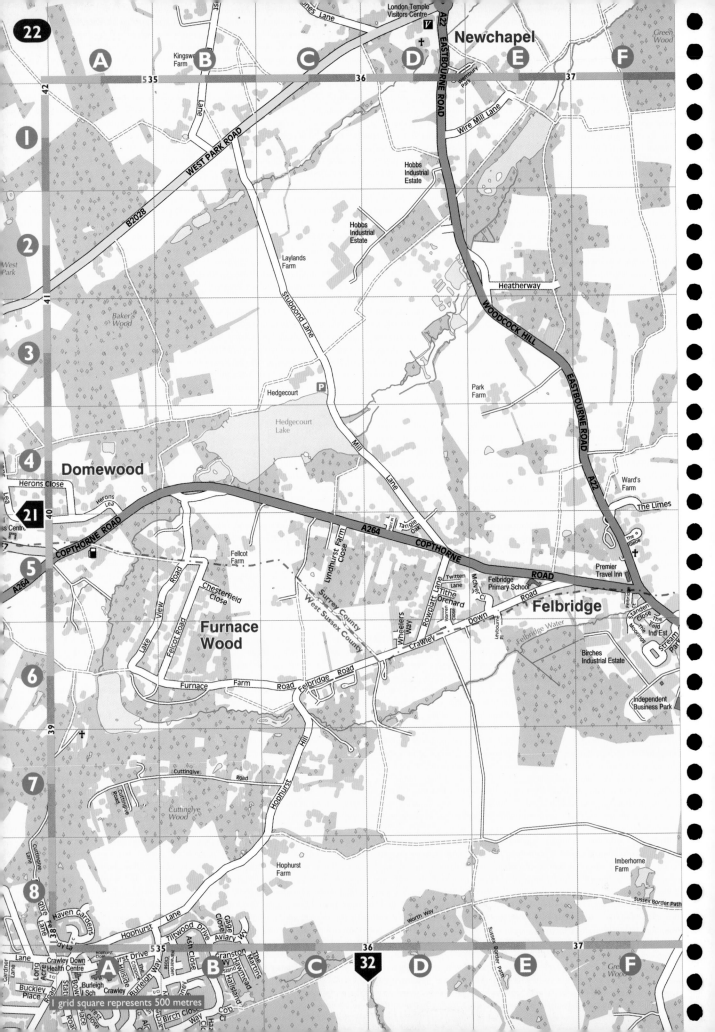

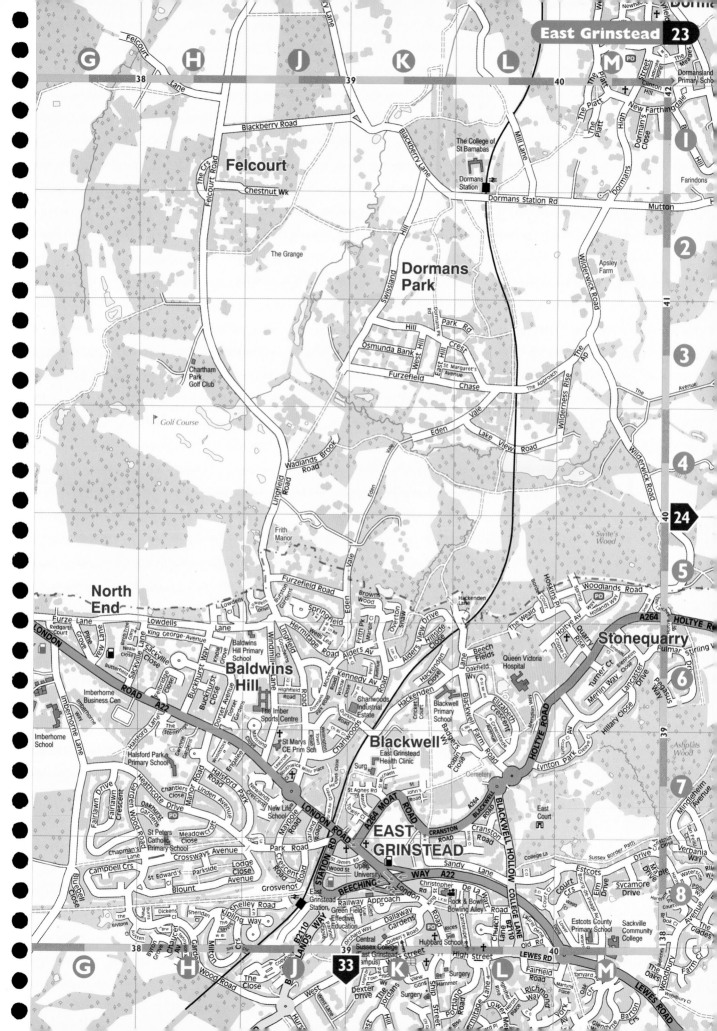

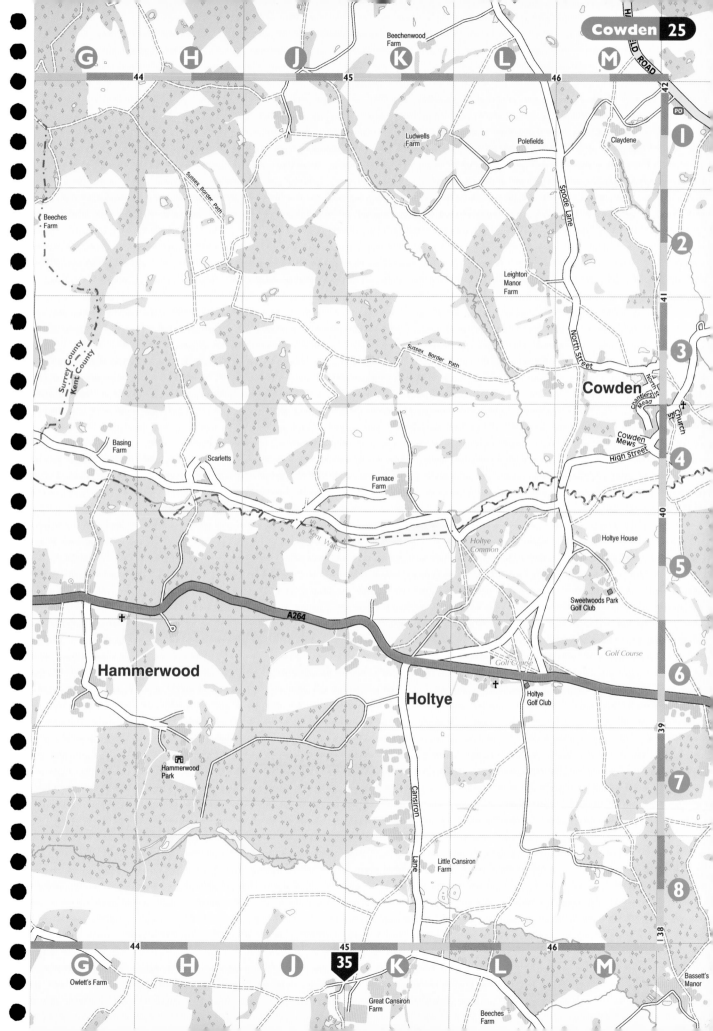

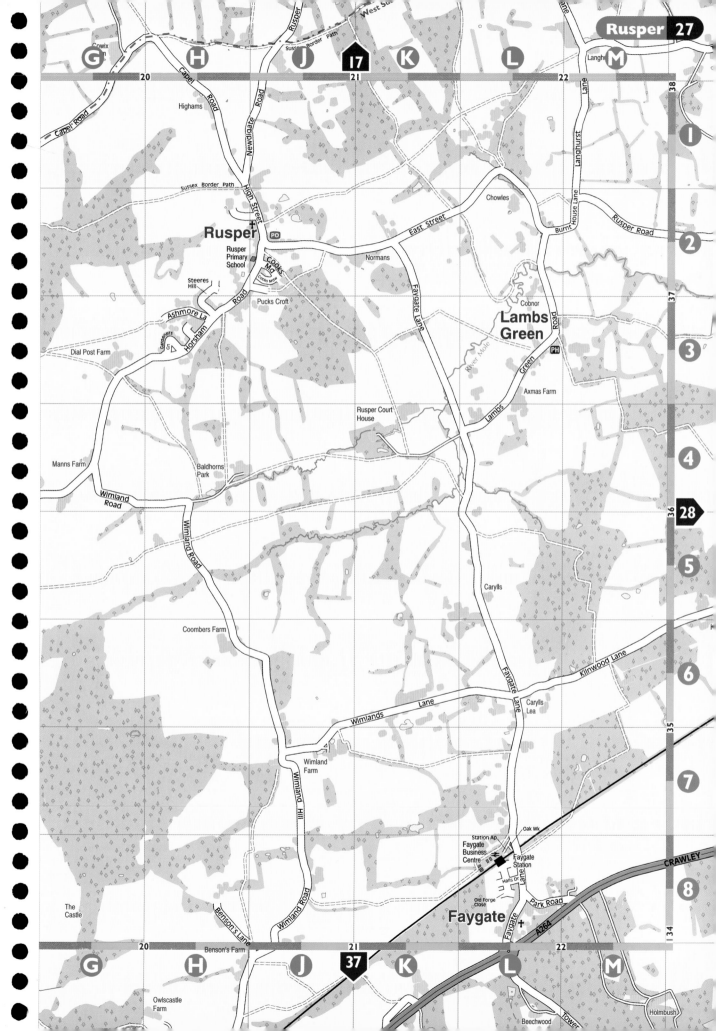

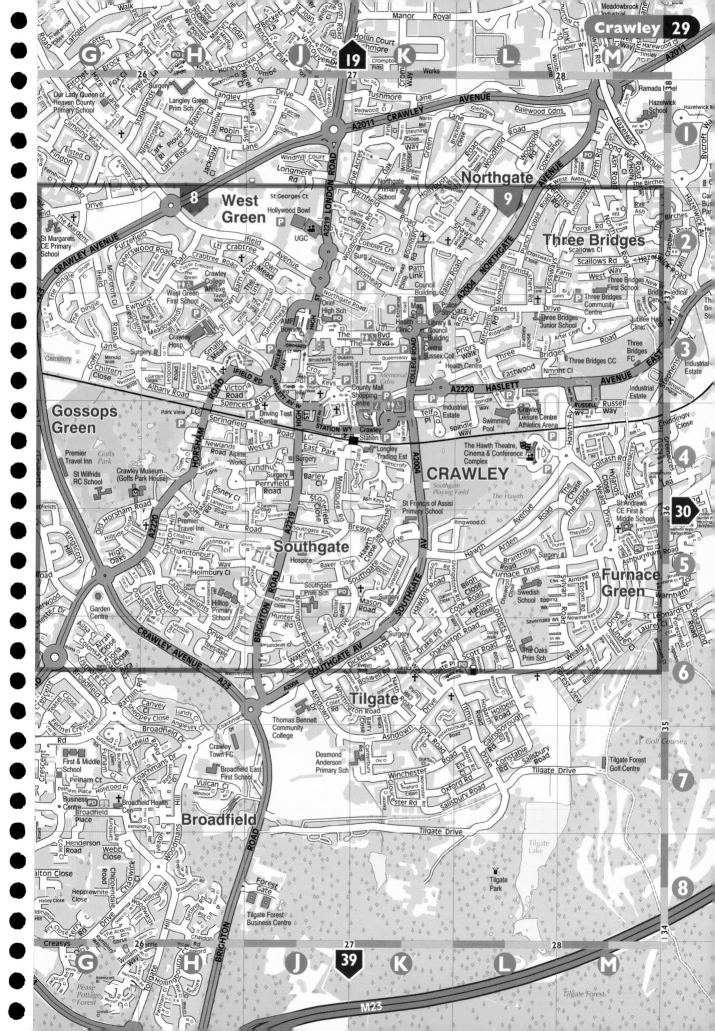

I grid square represents 500 metres

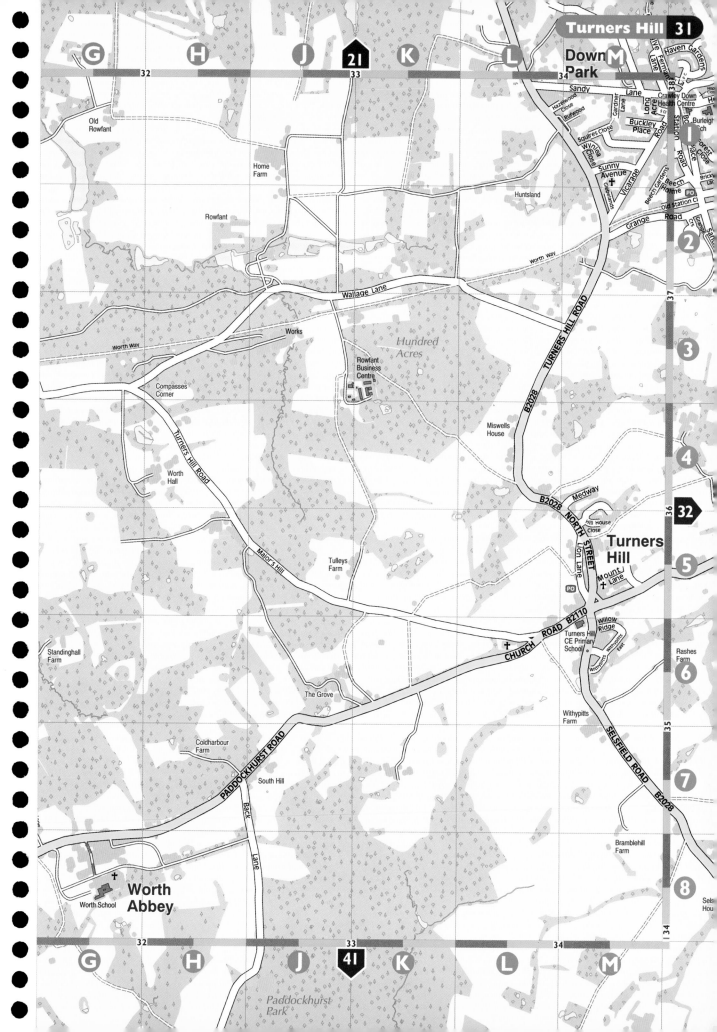

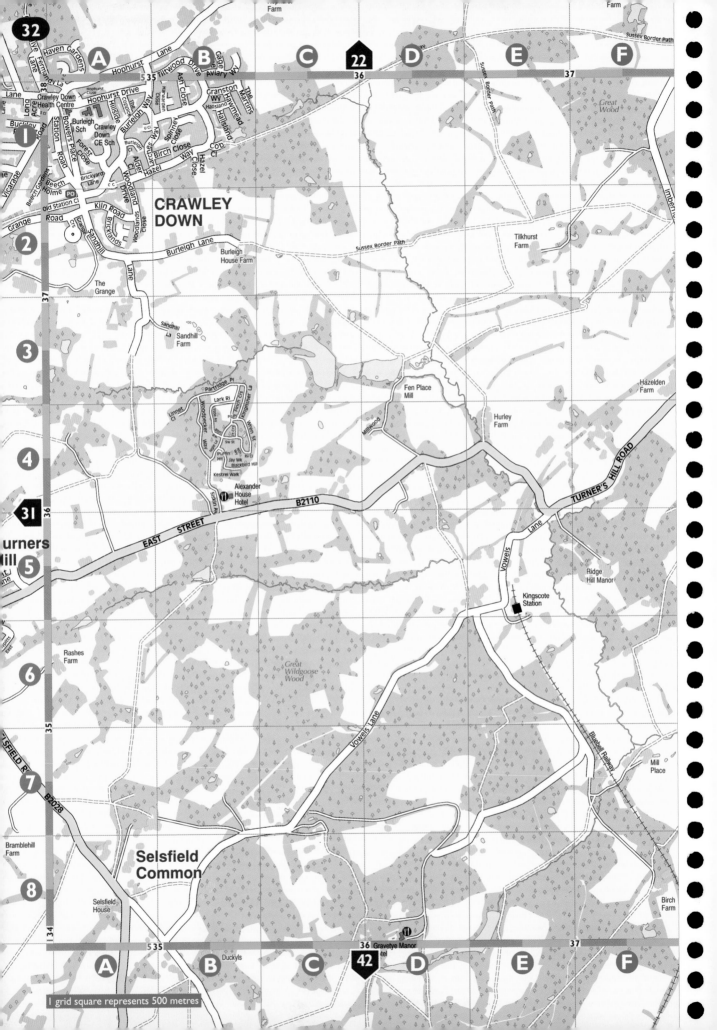

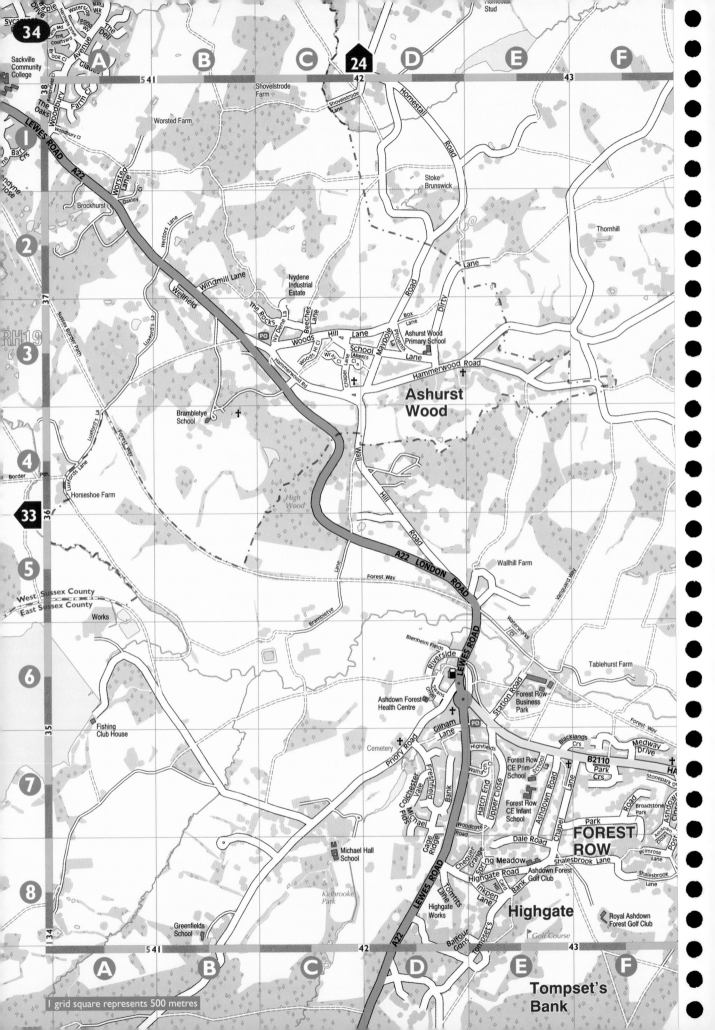

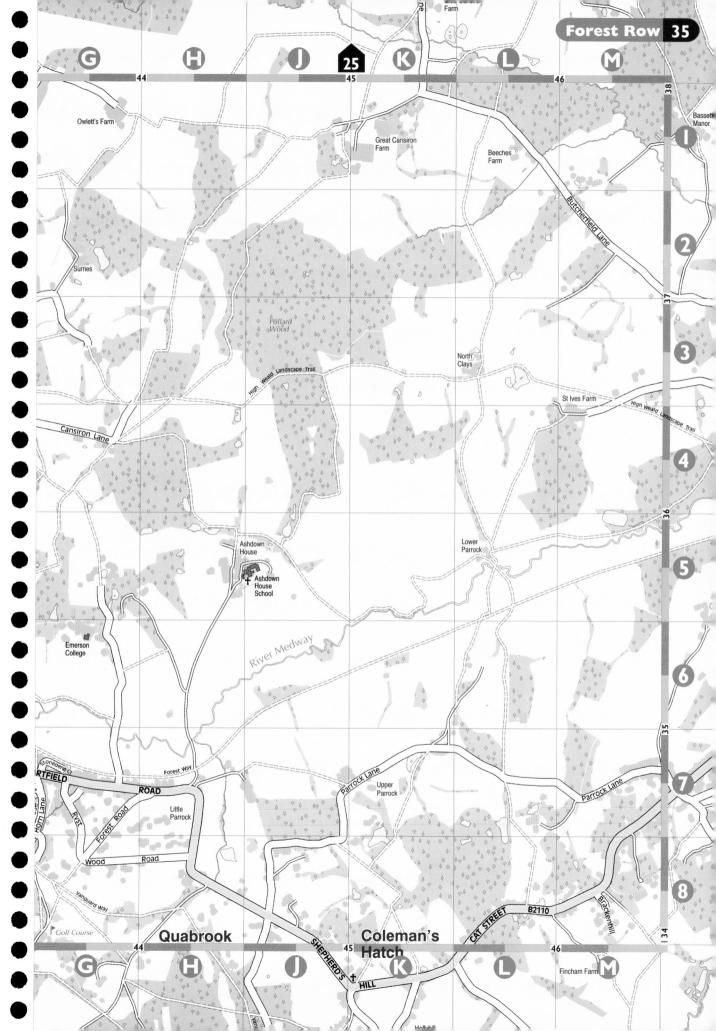

G H J 25 K L M

44 45 46

1

Owlett's Farm

Great Cansiron Farm

Beeches Farm

Bassett Manor

2

Surries

Butcherfield Lane

North Clays

3

Pollard Wood

St Ives Farm

High Weald Landscape Trail

High Weald Landscape Trail

Cansiron Lane

4

Ashdown House

Lower Parrock

5

Ashdown House School

Emerson College

River Medway

6

Stonedene Cl

Forest Way

Parrock Lane

Upper Parrock

7

RTFIELD ROAD

Little Parrock

Parrock Lane

Rvst

Forest Road

Wood Road

Vanguard way

8

Golf Course

Quabrook

Coleman's Hatch

CAT STREET

B2110

Brackenhill

Fincham Farm

SHEPHERD'S HILL

44 45 46

G H J K L M

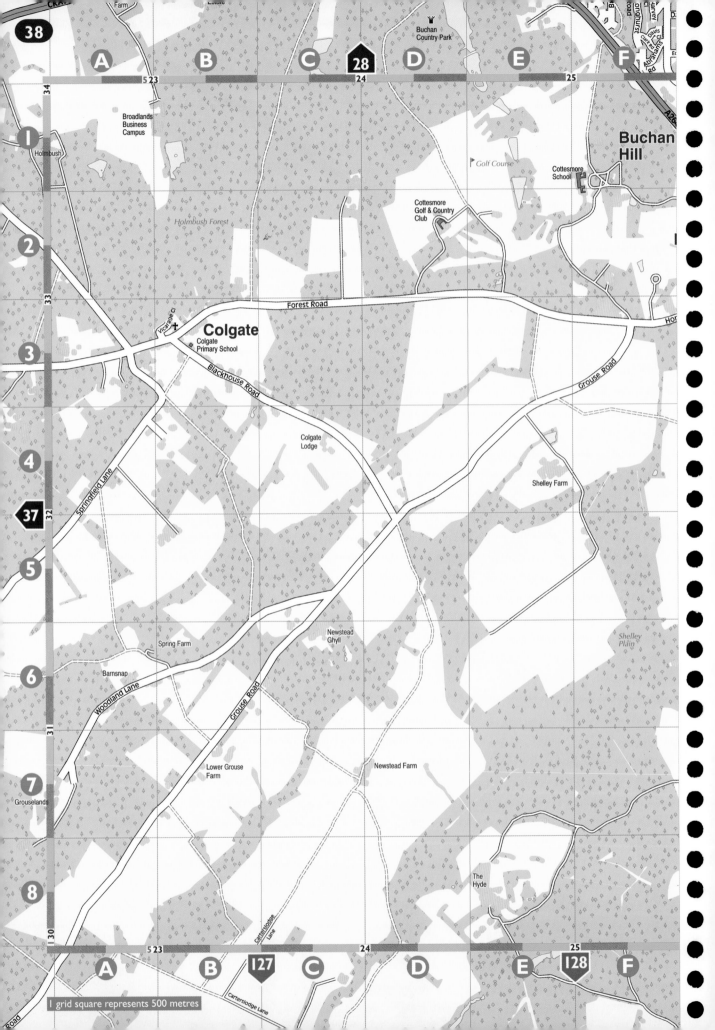

38

A   5 23   B   C   **28**   D   E   25   F

34

Holmbush

Broadlands
Business
Campus

Holmbush Forest

Golf Course

**Buchan
Hill**

Cottesmore
School

Cottesmore
Golf & Country
Club

Buchan Country Park

33

Forest Road

Vicarage Cl

Colgate

Colgate
Primary School

Blackhouse Road

Grouse Road

Colgate
Lodge

Shelley Farm

Springfield Lane

37   32

Shelley
Plain

Spring Farm

Newstead
Ghyll

Barnsnap

Woodland Lane

Grouse Road

Lower Grouse
Farm

Newstead Farm

Grouselands

The
Hyde

1 30

Cartslodge Lane

A   5 23   B   **127**   C   24   D   E   25   **128**   F

Carterslodge Lane

1 grid square represents 500 metres

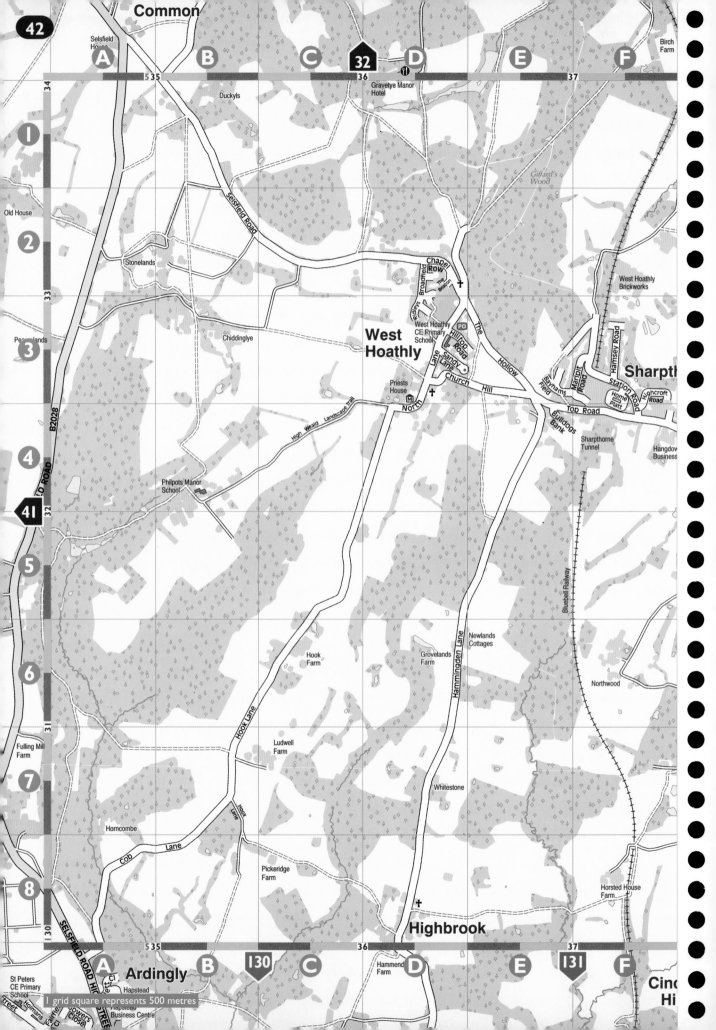

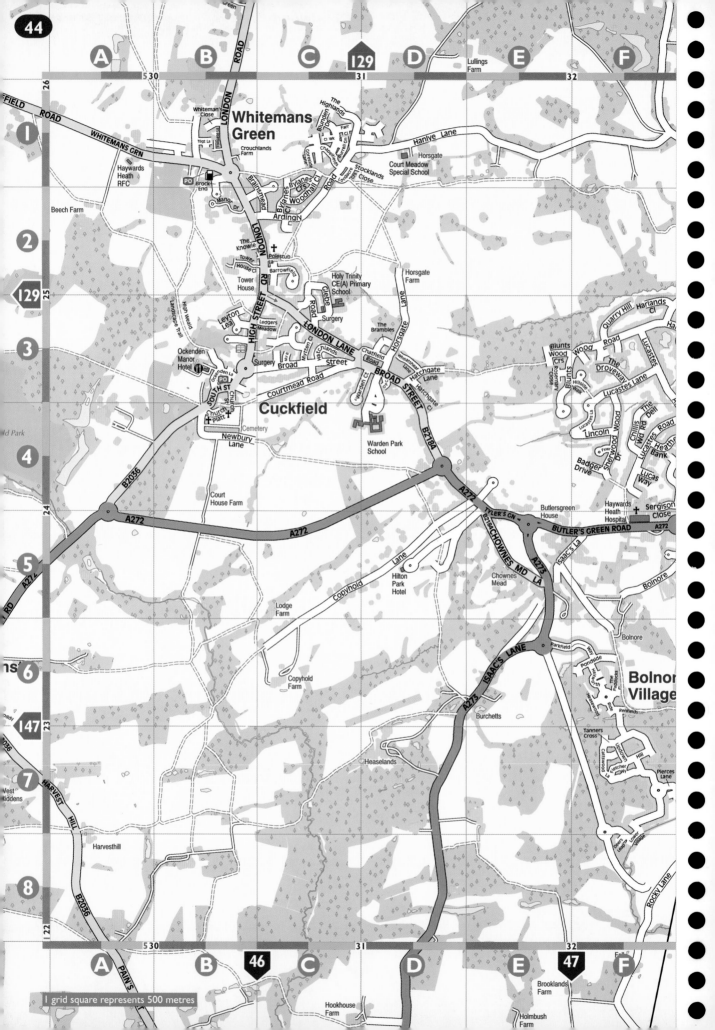

A B 129 C D E F

530 31 32

26

Whitemans Green

FIELD ROAD
WHITEMANS GRN

1

Beech Farm

Haywards Heath RFC

PO Brock End

Whiteman's Close

Crouchlands Farm

Tilgt La

Mano Dr

Brahnsmead

LONDON ROAD

LONDON RD

Bylanes Crs
Woodnall Cl
Arding N

Corsecke Corner

The Highlands
Blunden Dr
Farr
WK

Hanlye Lane

Lullings Farm

Court Meadow Special School

Horsgate

Stocklands Close

2

129

25

The Knowle

Polestub

Tower House Cl
Barrowfield

HIGH STREET

Tower House

Leyton Lea
Ledgers Meadow

Glebe Road

Holy Trinity CE(A) Primary School

Surgery

Horsgate Farm

Horsgate Lane

High Weald
Landscape Trail

3

Ockenden Manor Hotel

Ockenden La

Surgery
Myrten Ct
MW

LONDON LANE

HIGH LANE

Broad Street

Hatchlands

The Brambles

Chatfield Road

Warden Ct

Wheatsheaf Lane

BROAD STREET

Hatchgate Lane
Hatchgate Ct

B2184

Quarry Hill
Harlands Cl

Blunts Wood Crs
Rosemary Close
Blunts Wood

Wood Road

Lucastes Cl
The Droveway

Lucastes Lane

24

SOUTH ST
Church St
Church Platt
Cemetery

Cuckfield

Newbury Lane

B2036

Courtmead Road

Warden Park School

4

Court House Farm

A272

A272

Butlersgreen House

TYLER'S GN

Butlersgreen

The Dell

Lincoln
Lucastes Dr
Sherwood Wood
Lucastes Lane

Badger Drive

Hillside Walk

Heather Bank

Lucas Way

Haywards Heath Hospital

Sergison Close

BUTLER'S GREEN ROAD

A272

5

A272
RD

A273

Copyhold Lane

Hilton Park Hotel

Lodge Farm

CHOWNES MD LA

Chownes Mead

Isaac's La

Bolnore

6

147

23

Copyhold Farm

A273

ISAAC'S LANE

Parkfield
Pondside
Way

Bolnore Village

Burchetts

Tanners Cross

Renfields

7

HARVEST HILL

West Riddens

Harvesthill

Heaselands

Pierces Lane

8

22

B2036

PAIN'S

Hookhouse Farm

Holmbush Farm

Brooklands Farm

530 31 32

A B **46** C D E **47** F

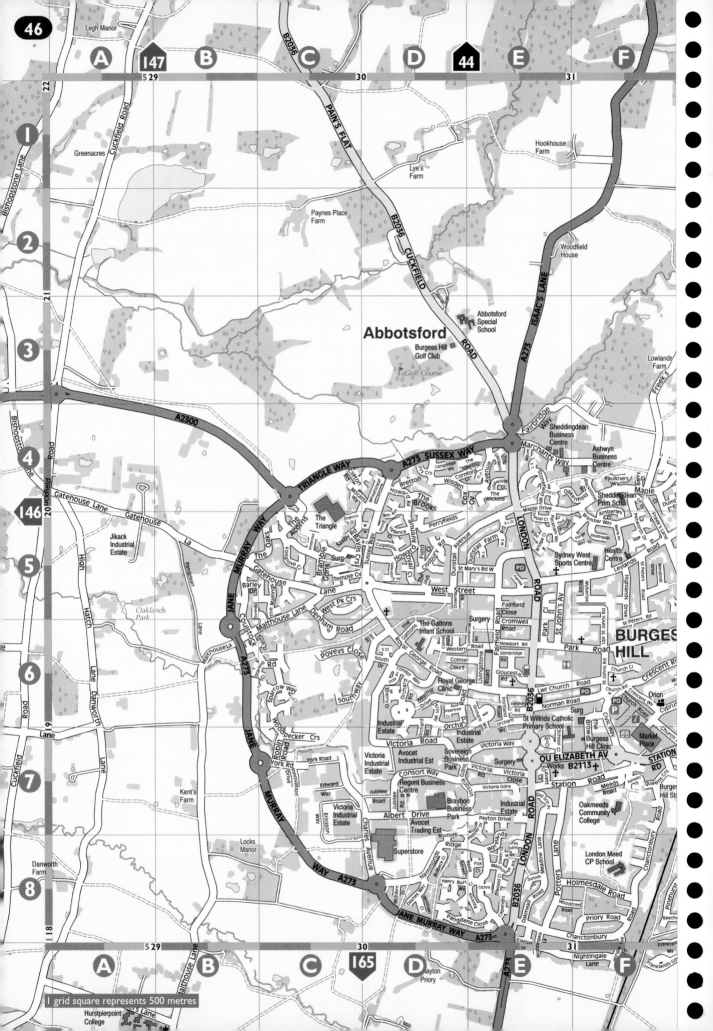

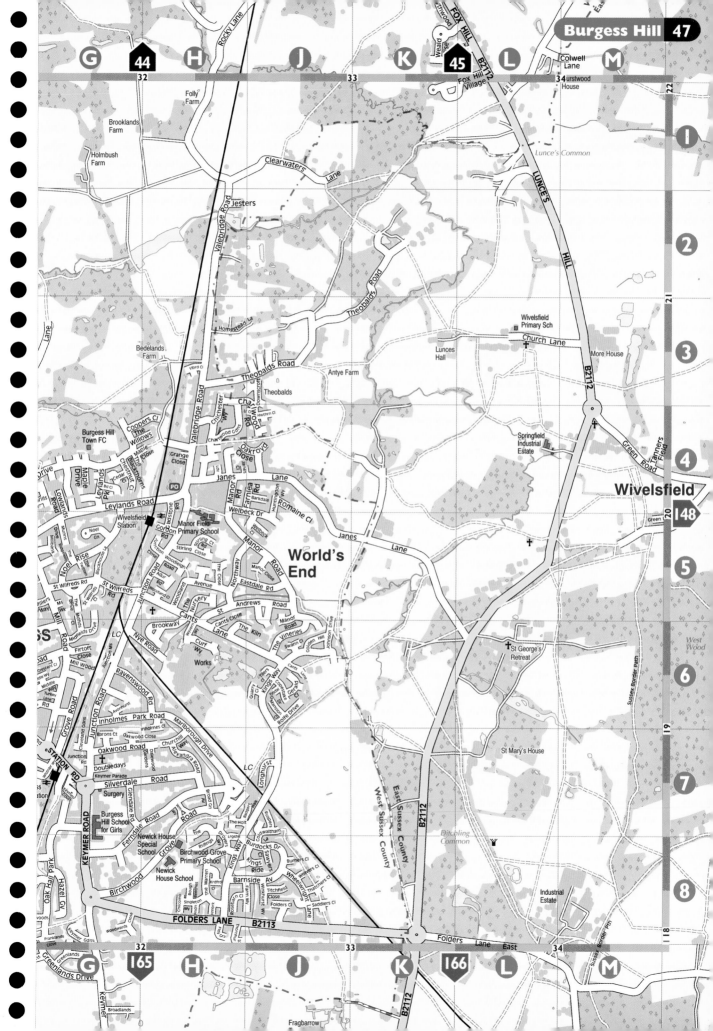

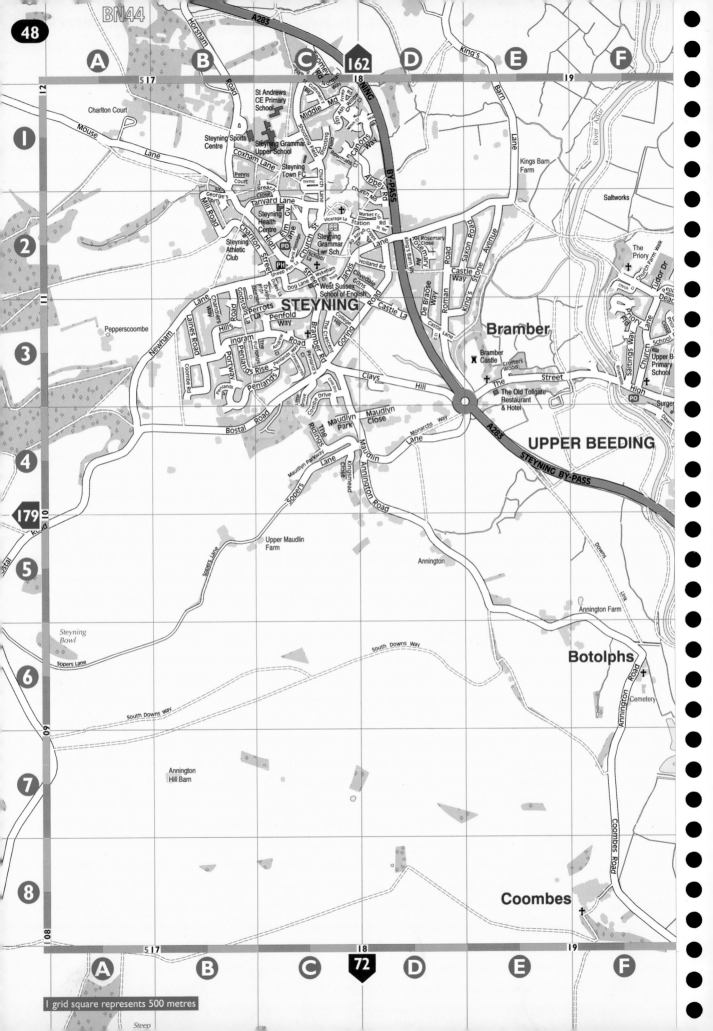

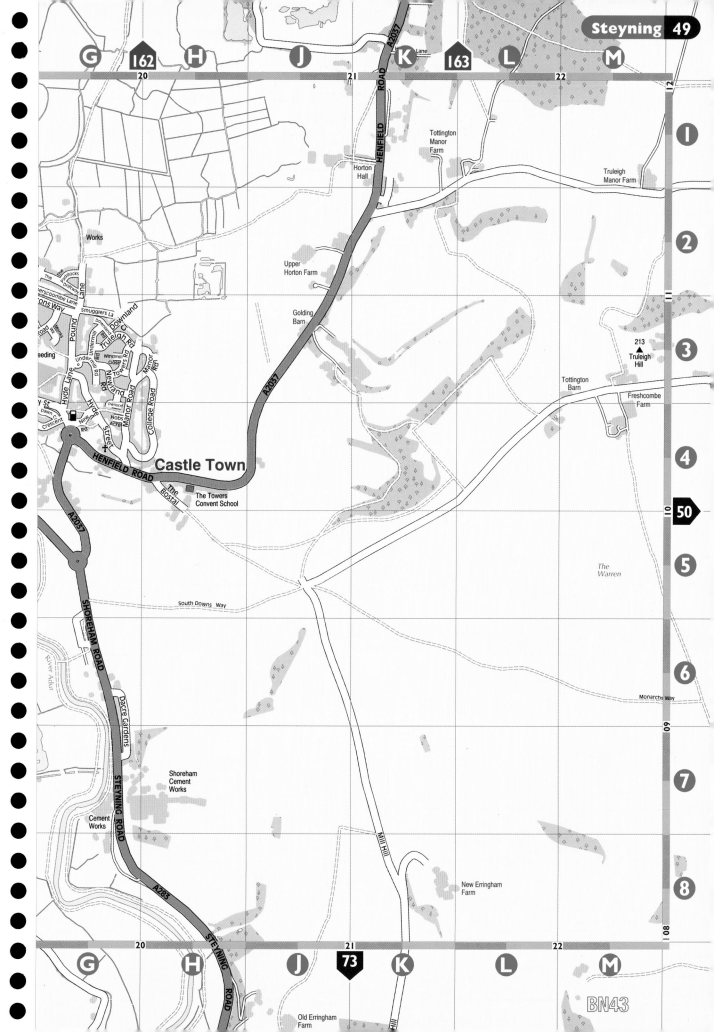

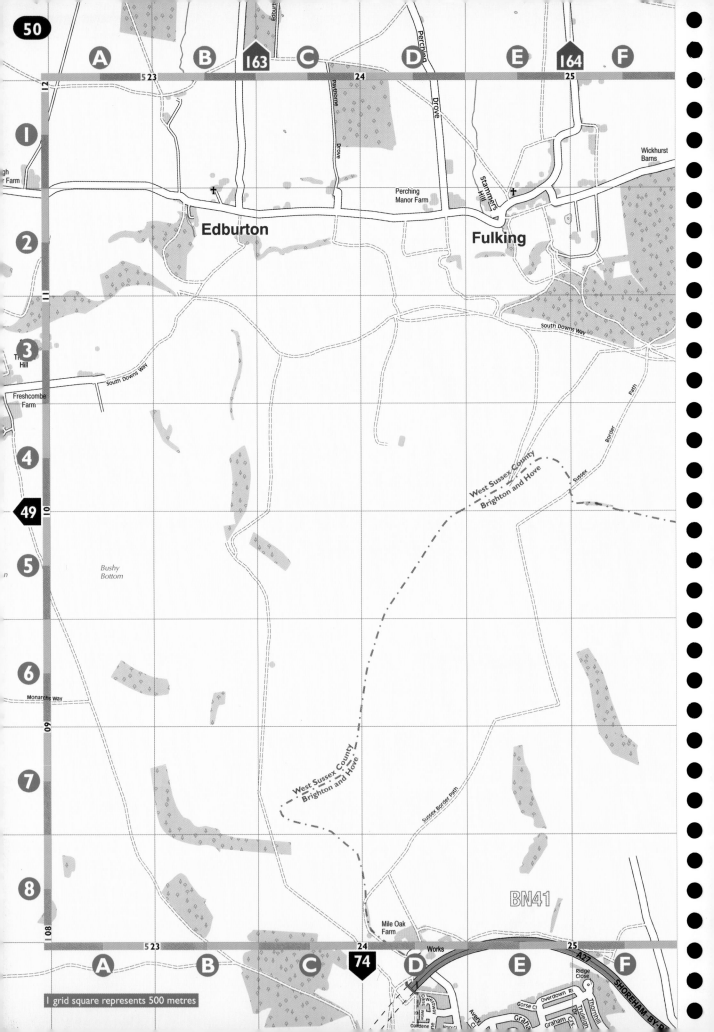

50

A B 163 C D E 164 F

512 523 24 25

1

Wickhurst
Barns

Edburton

Perching
Manor Farm

Fulking

2

South Downs Way

3
Th
Hill

South Downs Way

Freshcombe
Farm

4

West Sussex County
Brighton and Hove

Sussex

49 10

5

Bushy
Bottom

Border

Path

6

Monarchs Way

09

7

West Sussex County
Brighton and Hove

Sussex Border Path

8

BN41

108

Mile Oak
Farm

Works

512 523 24 25

A B C 74 D E F A27

Ridge
Close

SHOREHAM-BY-

1 grid square represents 500 metres

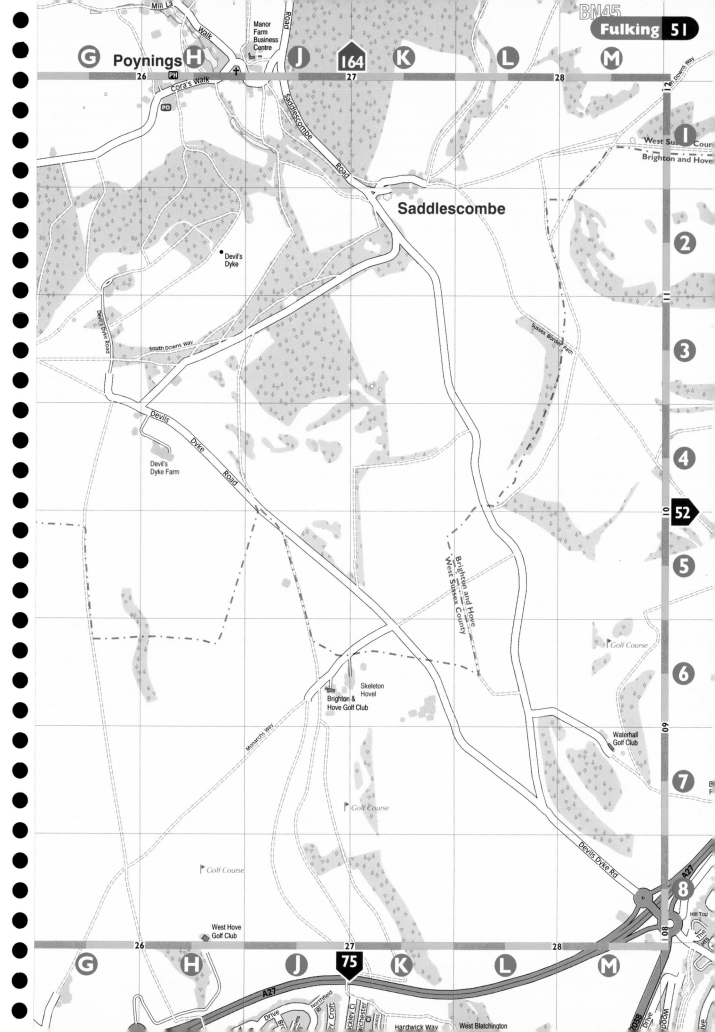

G **Poynings** H

Saddlescombe

52

75

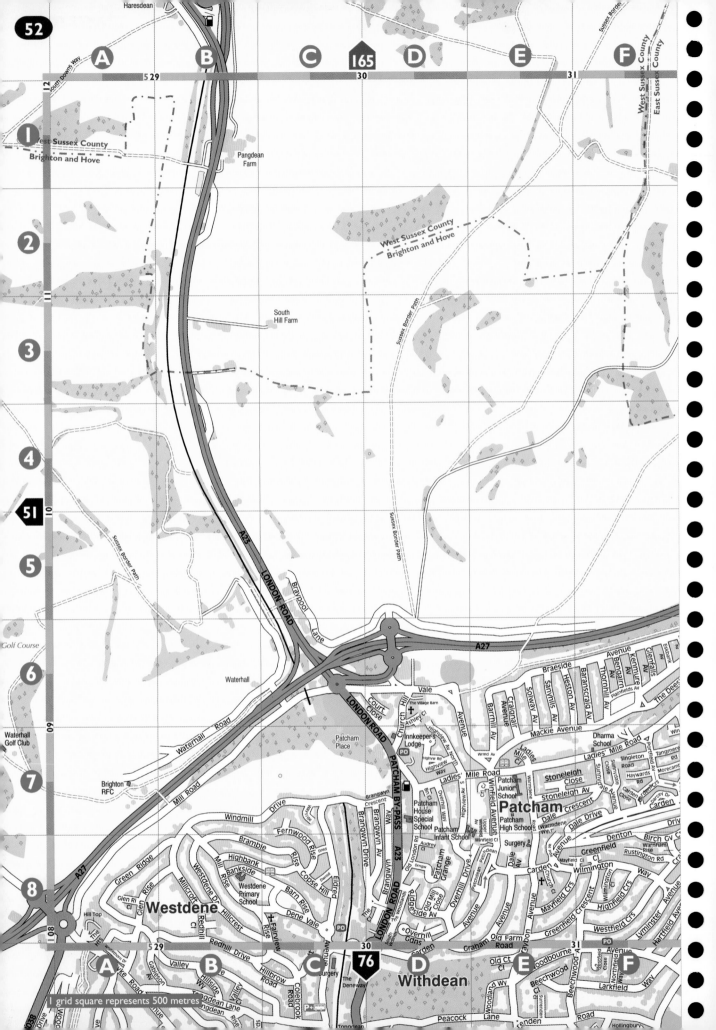

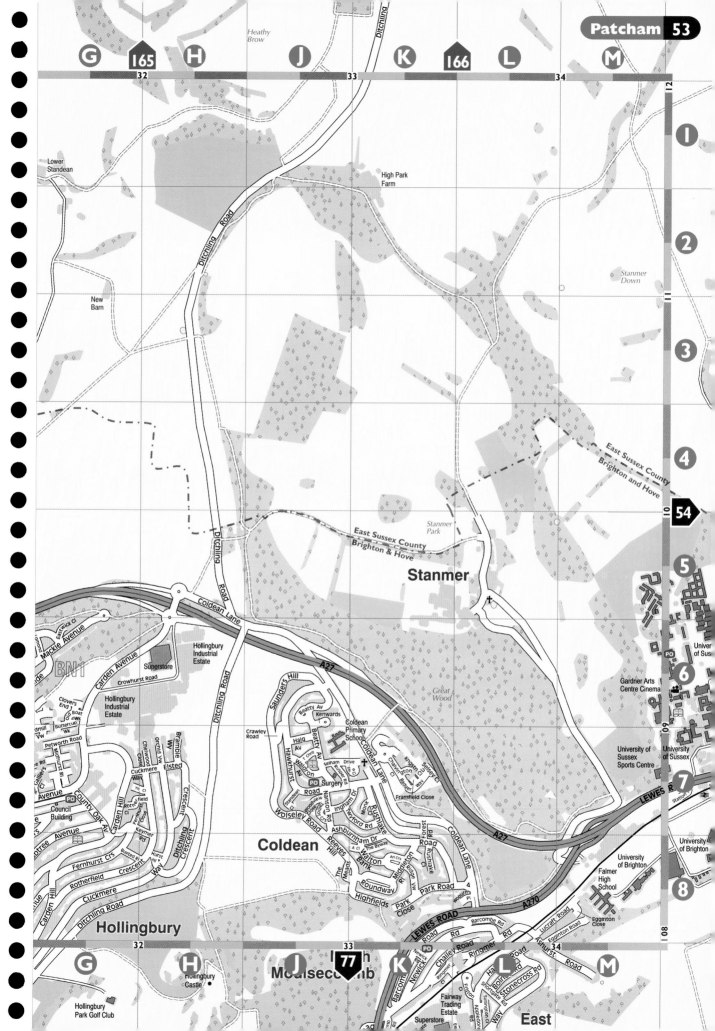

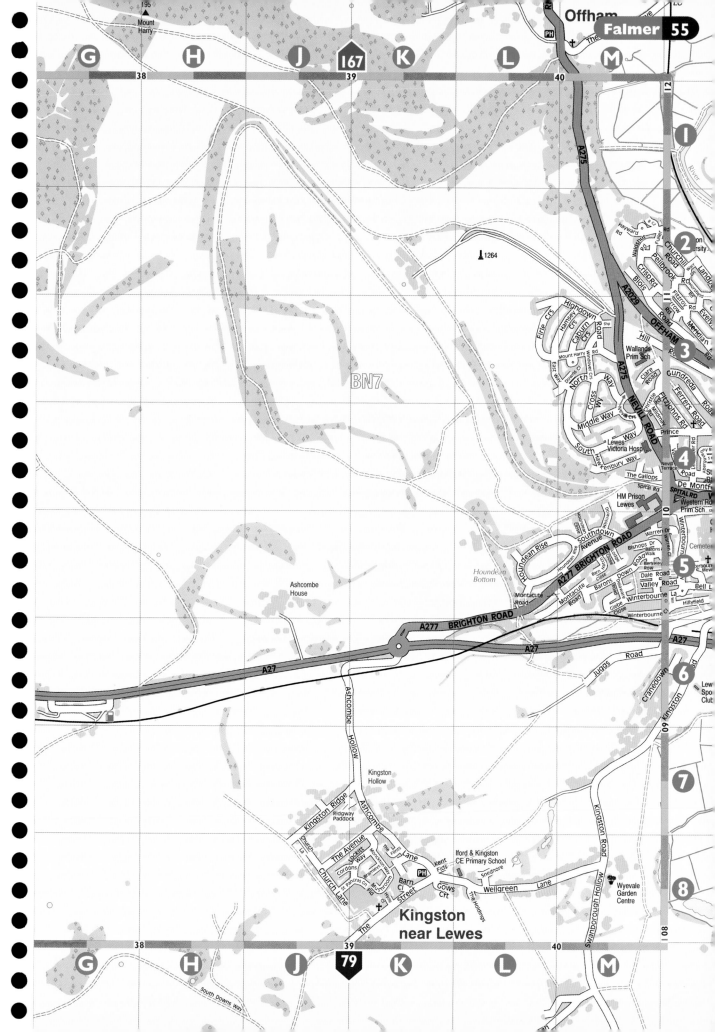

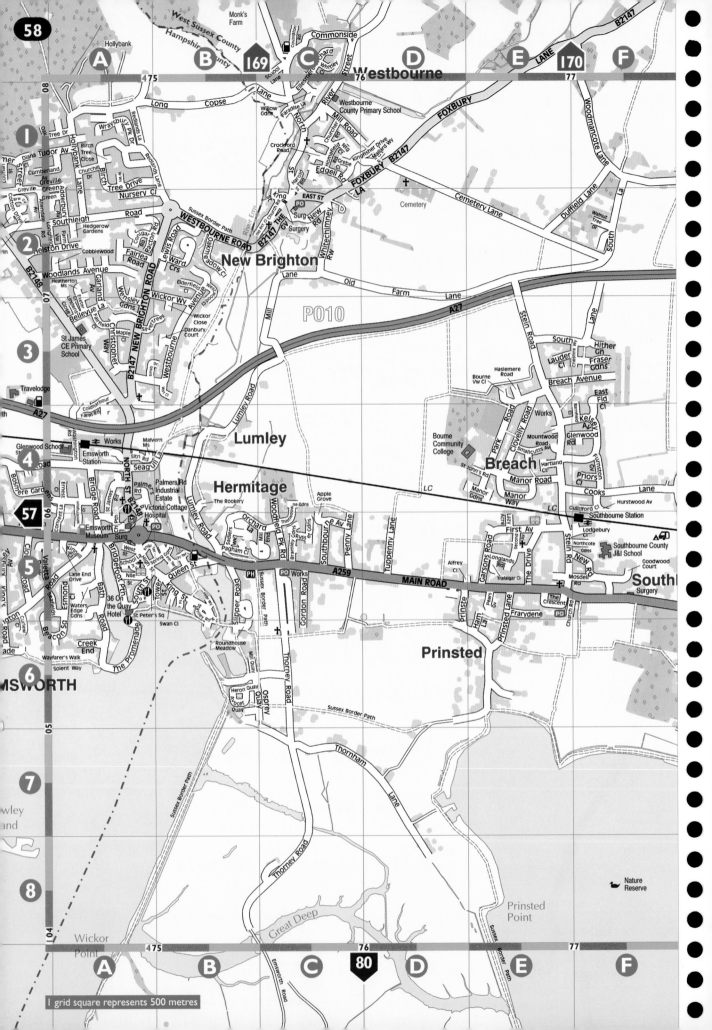

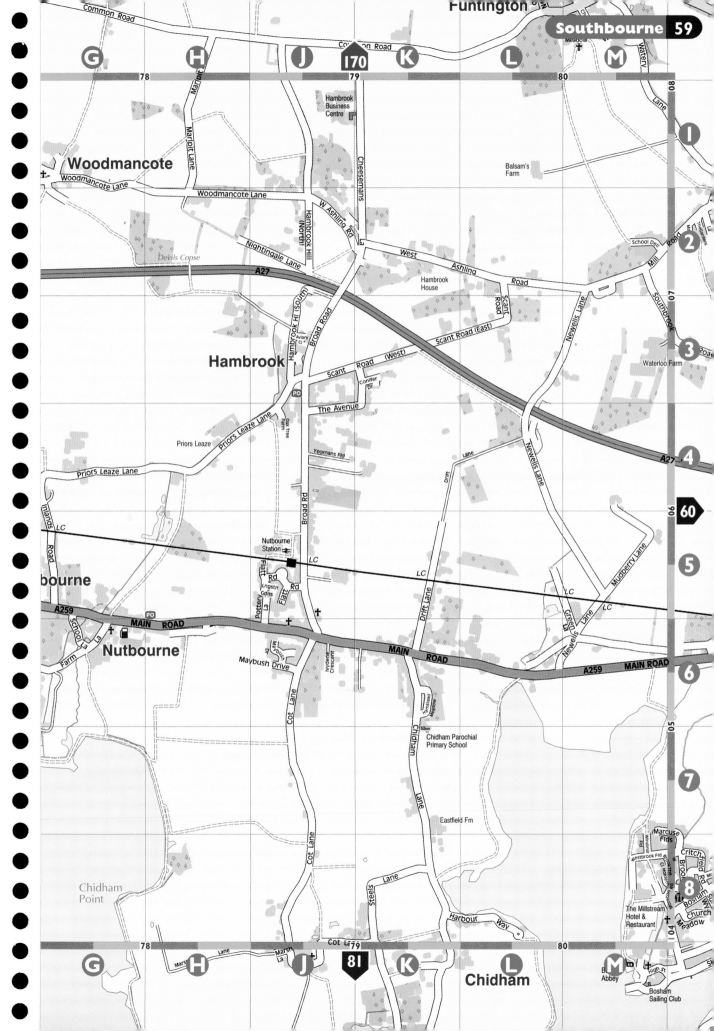

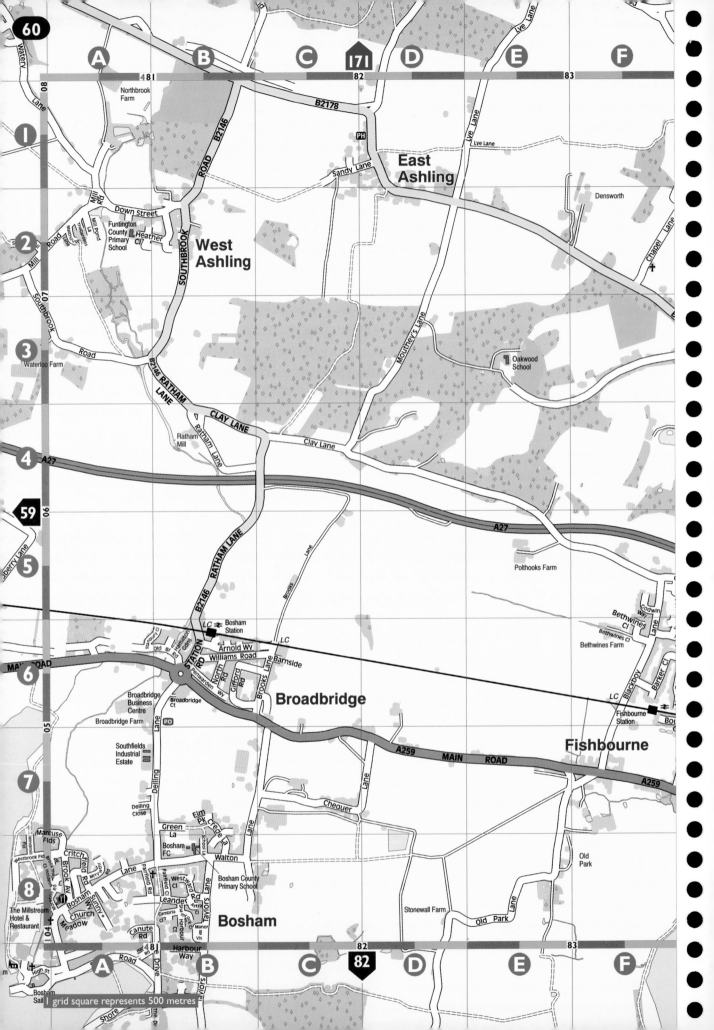

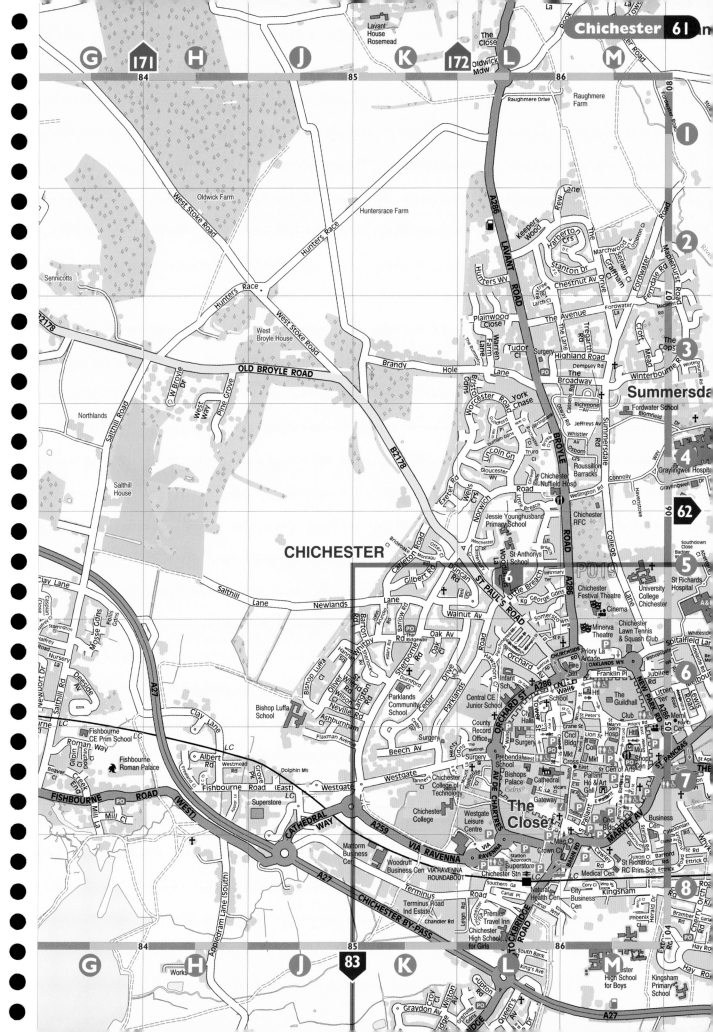

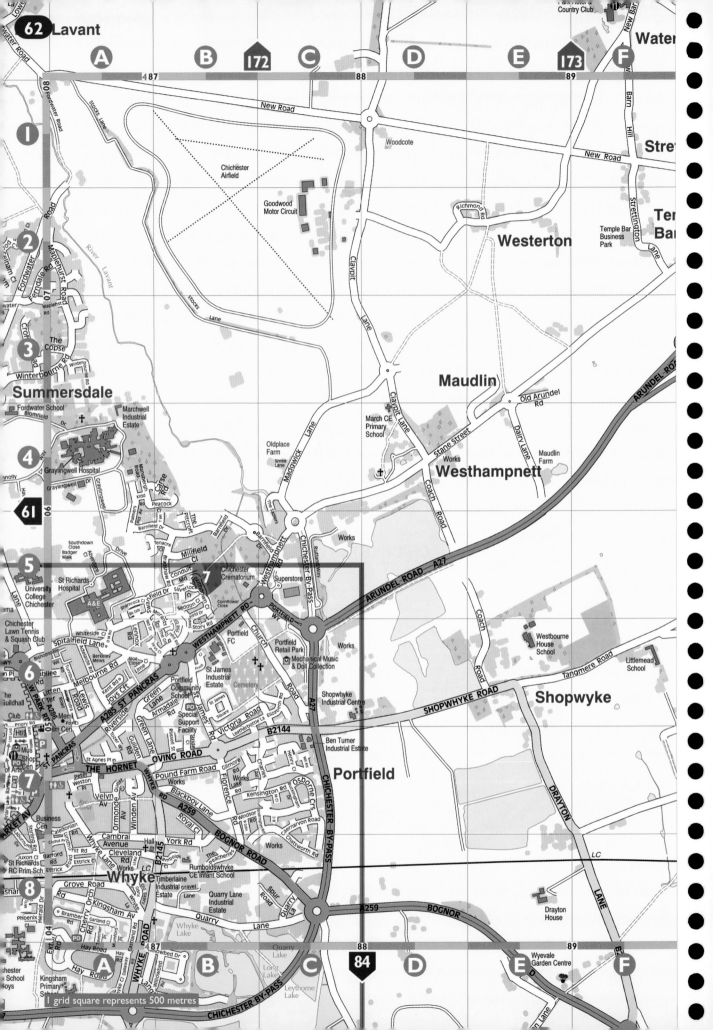

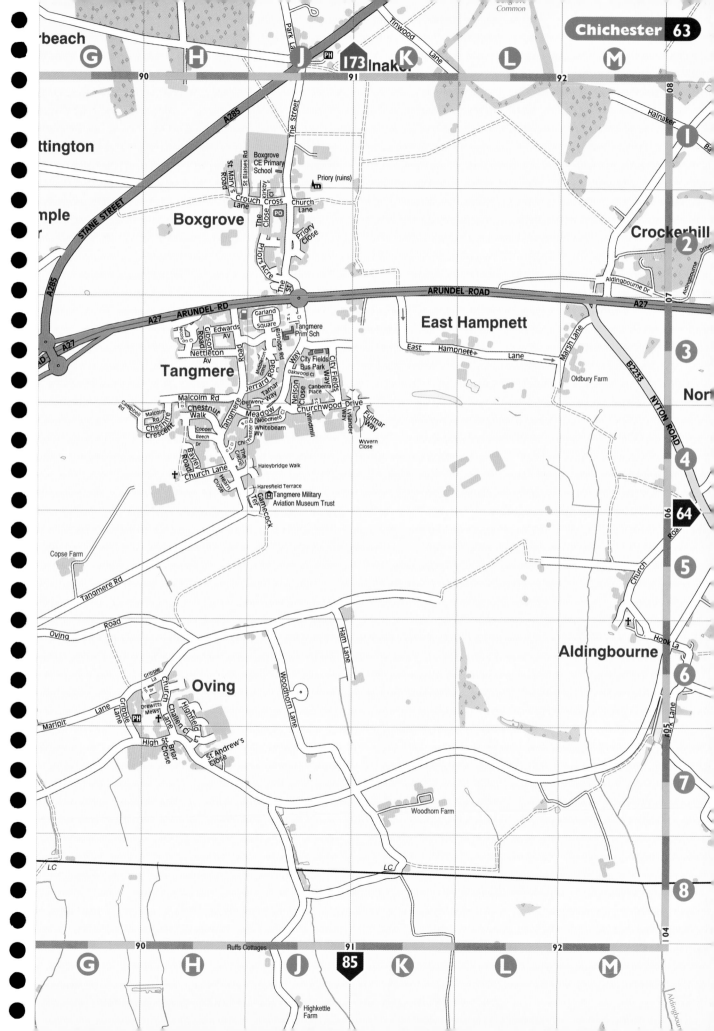

G H J K L M

I

2

3

4

64

5

6

7

8

rbeach

ttington

mple

Boxgrove

Crockerhill

STANE STREET

A285

A285

A27

A27

St Mary's Road

St Blaises Rd

Kirkby Cl

Crouch Cross

The Close

PO

Priory Close

Church Lane

Priors Acre

The St

Park La

The Street

PH

173 lnaker

Tinwood Lane

Common

Hainaker Rd

Boxgrove CE Primary School

Priory (ruins)

ARUNDEL-ROAD

ARUNDEL RD

ARUNDEL-RD

East Hampnett

Aldingbourne Dr

Aldingbourne Drive

East Hampnett Lane

Marsh Lane

Oldbury Farm

NYTON ROAD

B2233

Nor

Garland Square

Tangmere Prim Sch

Edwards Av

Bishops Rd

Nettleton Av

Gibson Road

Acacia Cl

Beacon Cl

Tangmere

Middleton Gdns

Jerrard Road

Derwent

Malcolm Rd

Campbell Rd

Malcolm Rd

Cheshire Crescent

Chestnut Walk

Copper Beech Dr

Bayley Road

Church Lane

Hearn Close

Tamar Way

Tangmere Road

Chichester Dr

The Glebe

Meadow

Woodfield

Whitebeam Wy

Nelson Cl

Mason Cl

City Fields Way

City Fields Bus Park

Oakwood Cl

Canberra Place

Churchwood Drive

Lysander Way

Windmill

Fulmar Way

Wyvern Close

Haleybridge Walk

Haresfield Terrace

Camecock Ter

M Tangmere Military Aviation Museum Trust

Copse Farm

Tangmere Rd

Oving Road

Oving

Road

Ham Lane

Woodhorn Lane

Church Road

Aldingbourne

Hook La

A95 Lane

Marlpit Lane

Gribble Lane

Gribble La

Church Lane

Challen Ct

Highfield Cl

High St

Drewitts Mews

PH

Briar Close

St Andrew's Close

Oving

Woodhorn Farm

LC

LC

Ruffs Cottages

Highkettle Farm

Aldingbour

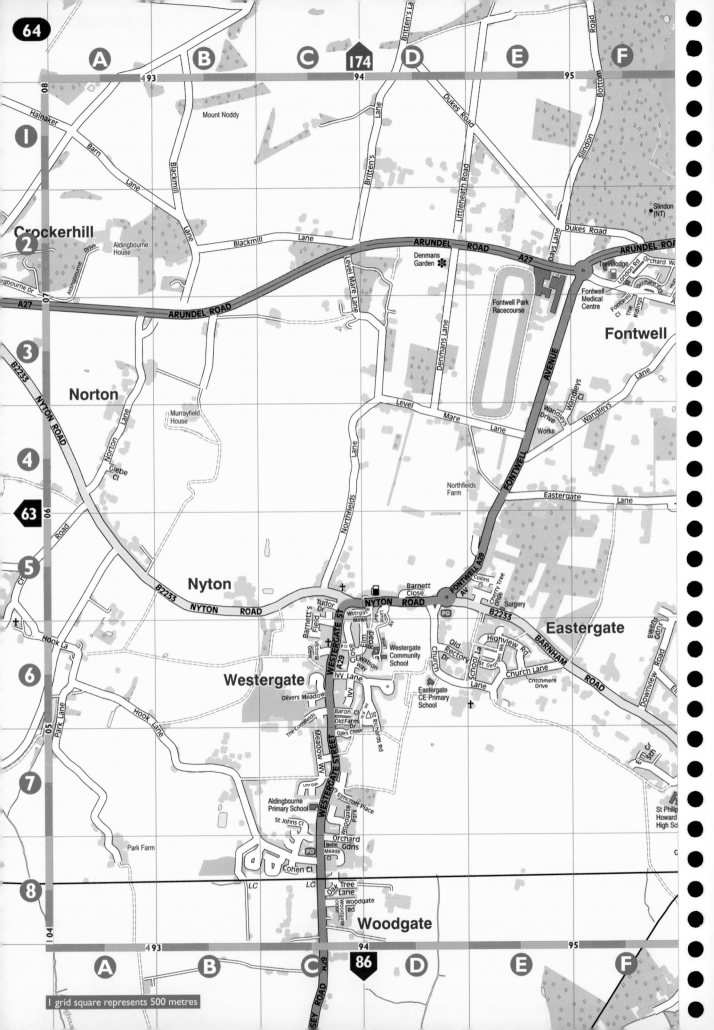

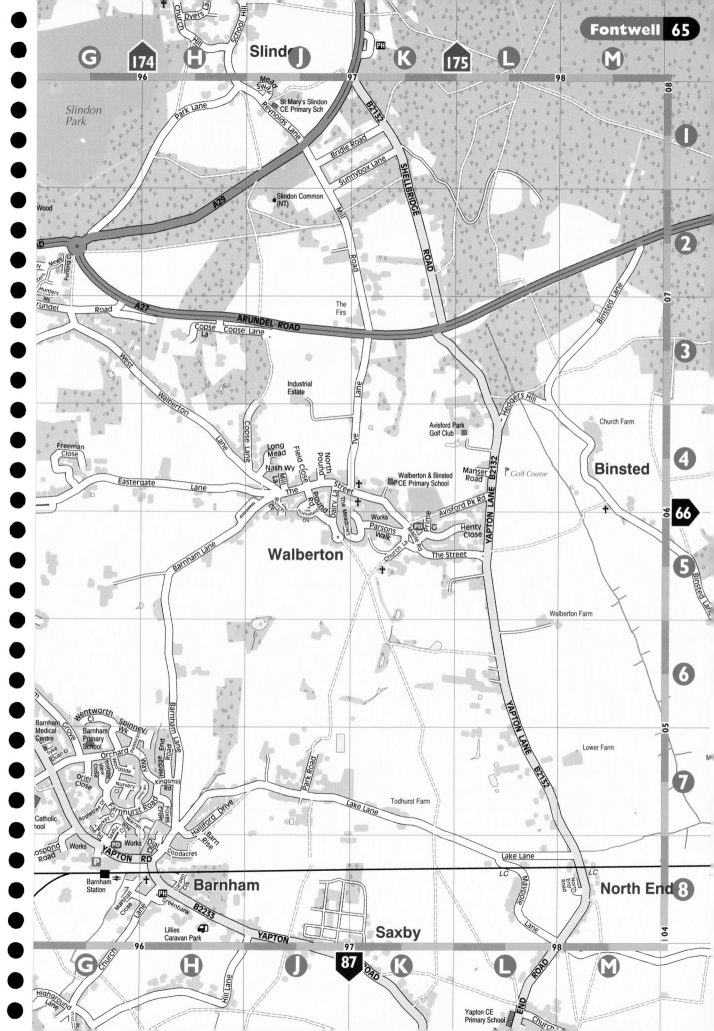

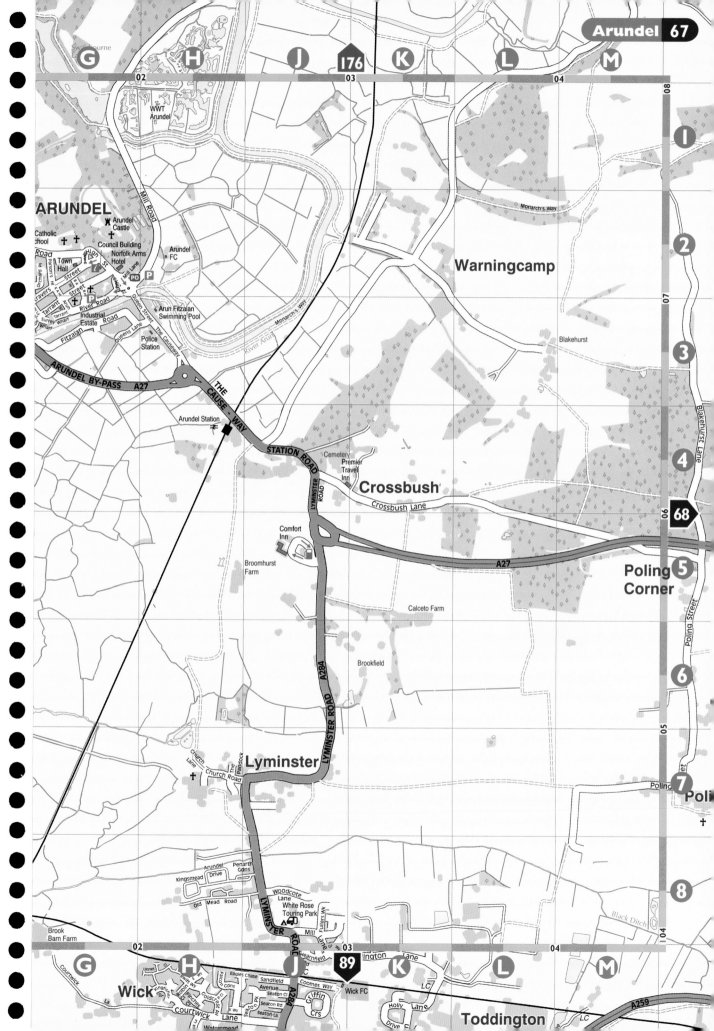

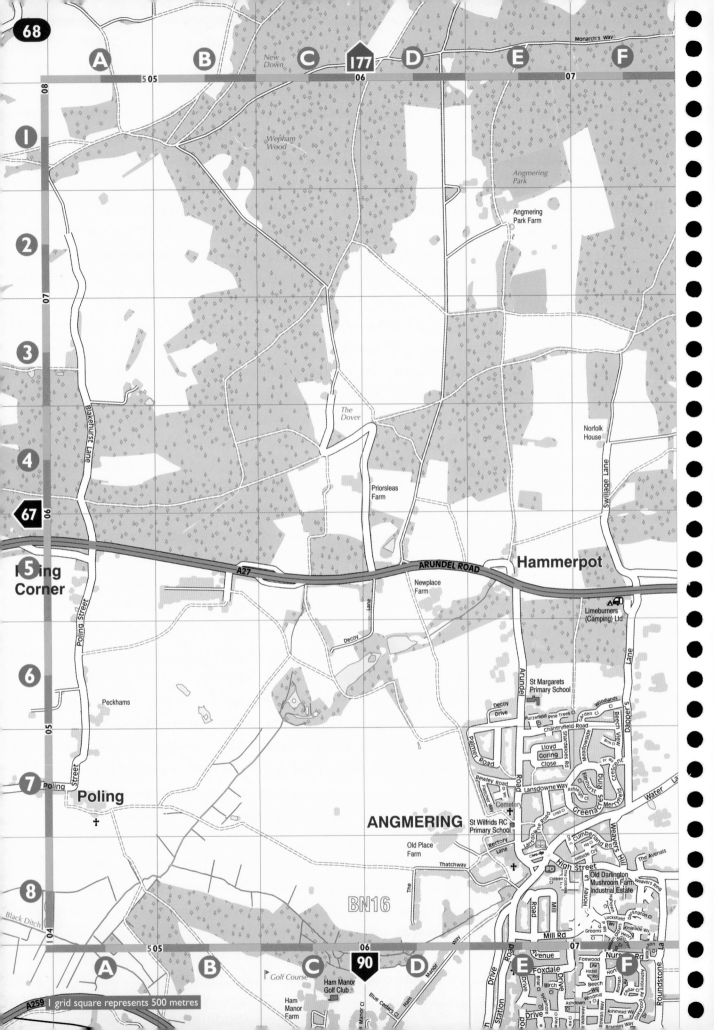

A B C **177** D E F

5 05
06
07

08

I

2

07

3

4

67
06

I5ing Corner
Corner

A27   ARUNDEL ROAD   **Hammerpot**

6

05

Newplace Farm

Limeburners (Camping) Ltd

St Margarets Primary School

Peckhams

7 Poling

Poling

ANGMERING

Old Place Farm

St Wilfrids RC Primary School

Thatchway

8

Black Ditch

04

BN16

5 05
06
07

A B C **90** D E F

Golf Course

Ham Manor Golf Club

Ham Manor Farm

Old Darlington Mushroom Farm Industrial Estate

Foxdale

Wepham Wood

New Down

Angmering Park

Angmering Park Farm

The Dover

Norfolk House

Swillage Lane

Priorsleas Farm

Blakehurst Lane

Poling Street

Poling Street

Decoy

Decoy

Lane

Arundel Road

Palmer Road

Bewley Road

Lansdowne Way

Cemetery

Rectory Lane

High Street

Mill Road

Mill Rd

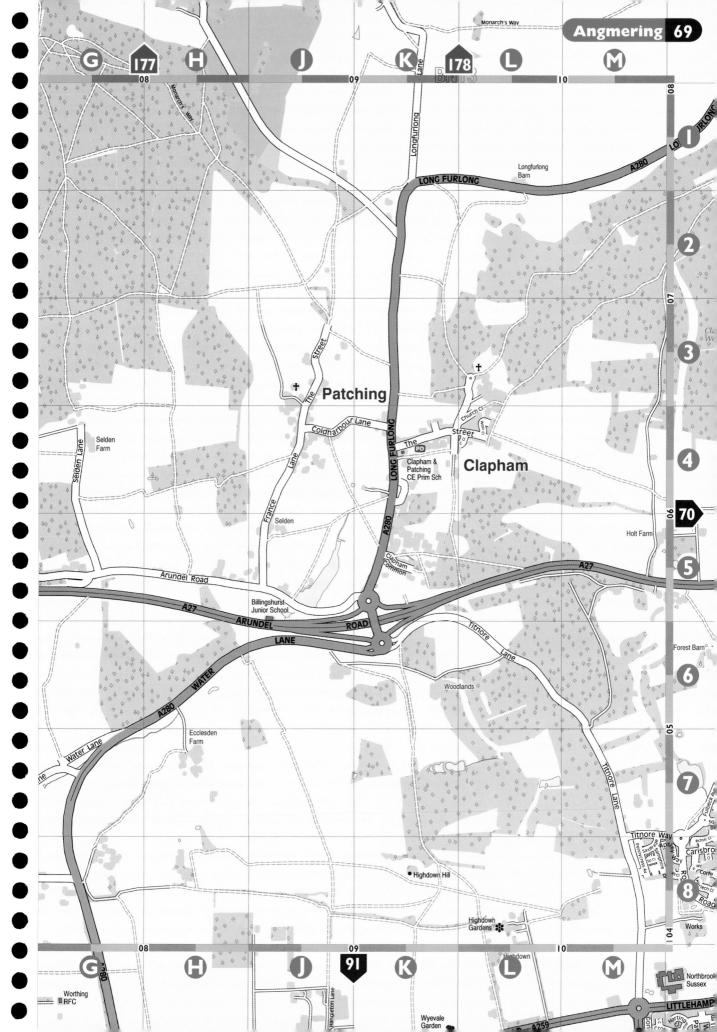

08 09 BRTS 10

I

A280

Monarch's Way

LONG FURLONG

Longfurlong
Barn

Longfurlong

2

07

3

The Street

†

Patching

†

06

Selden
Farm

Selden Lane

Coldharbour Lane

Church Cl

Street

4

France Lane

Selden

LONG FURLONG

The
PO

Clapham &
Patching
CE Prim Sch

Clapham

70

Holt Farm

5

Arundel Road

A280

Clapham
Common

A27

A27

Billingshurst
Junior School

ARUNDEL ROAD

Titnore Lane

Forest Barn

6

LANE

WATER

A280

Woodlands

05

Water Lane

Ecclesden
Farm

7

Titnore Lane

Titnore Way

Carisbro

8

• Highdown Hill

Highdown
Gardens ❈

Highdown

04

Works

08 09 10

Worthing
RFC

Northbrook
Sussex

LITTLEHAMP

Hangleton Lane

Wyevale
Garden

A259

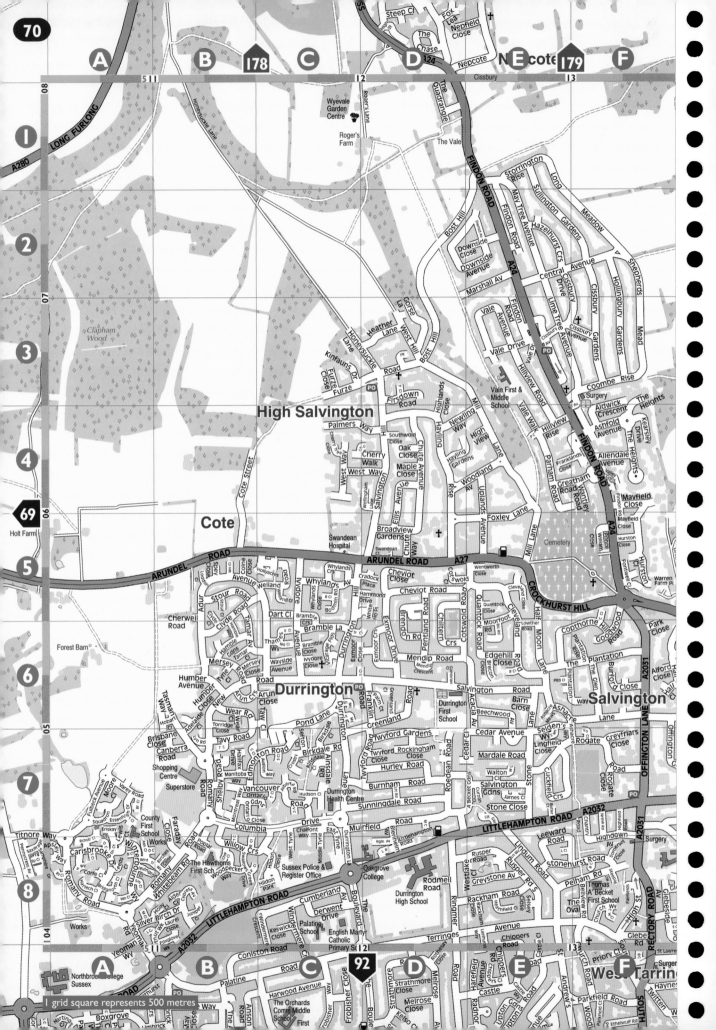

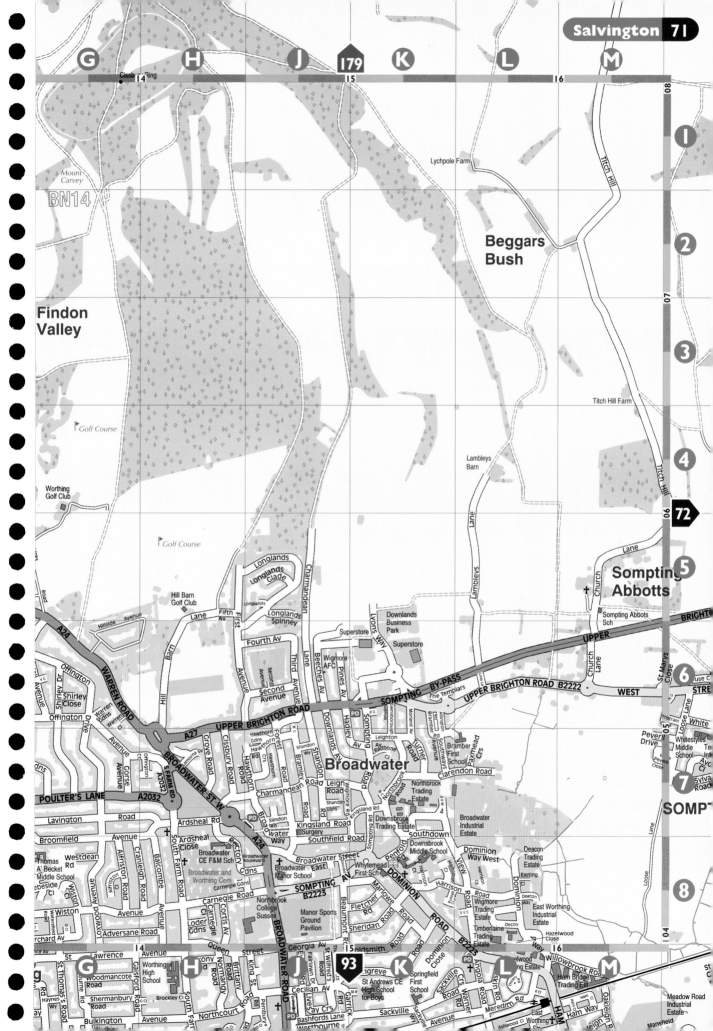

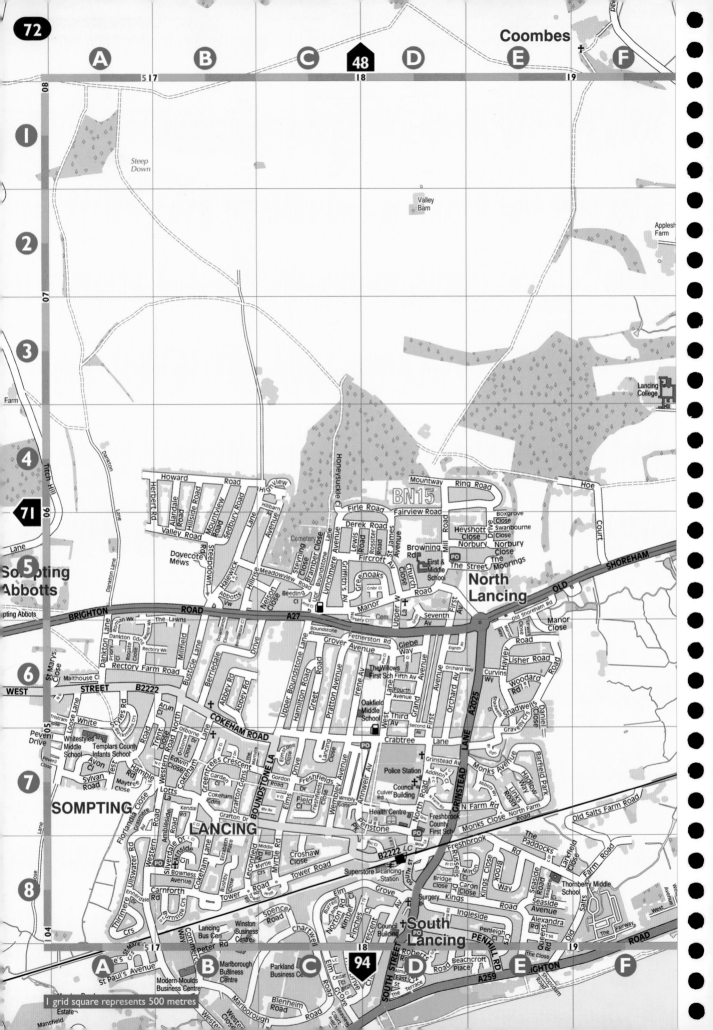

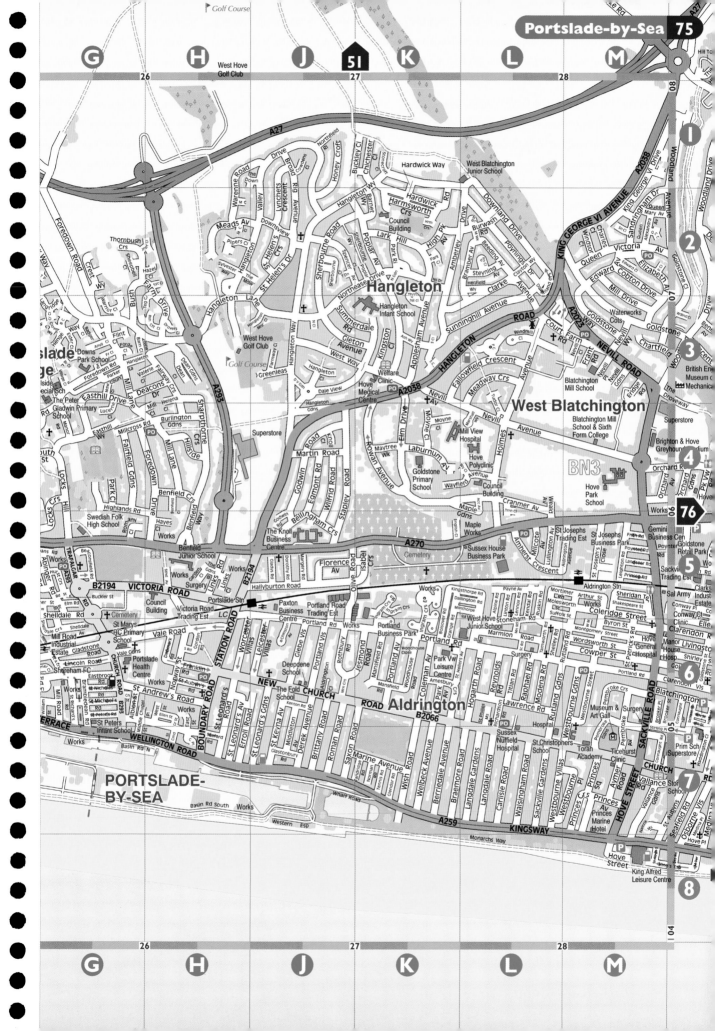

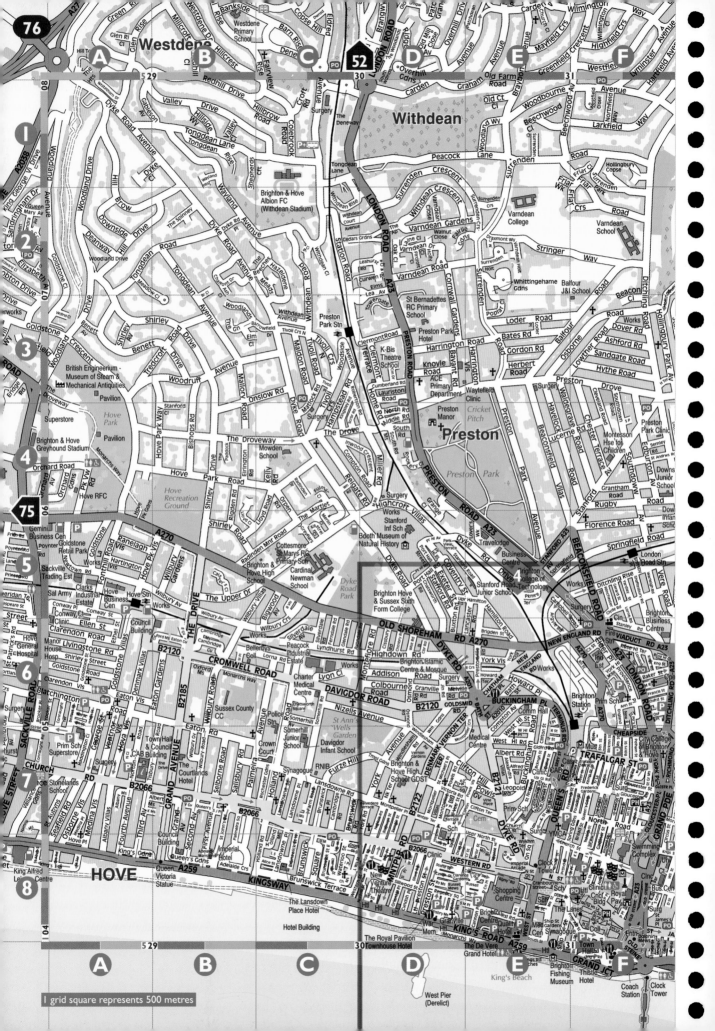

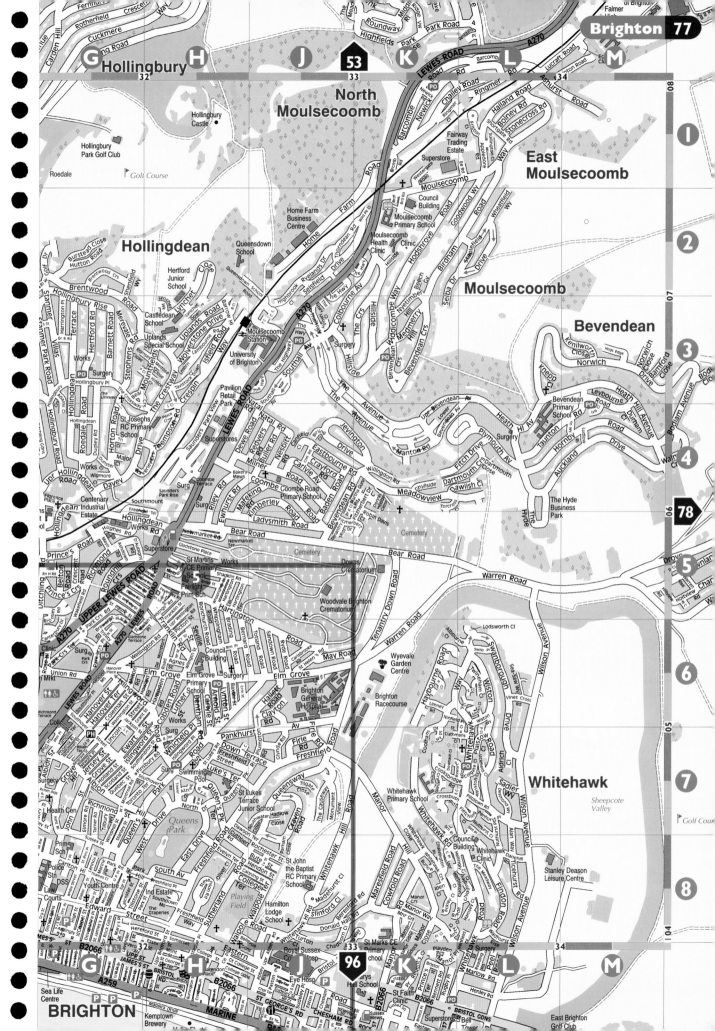

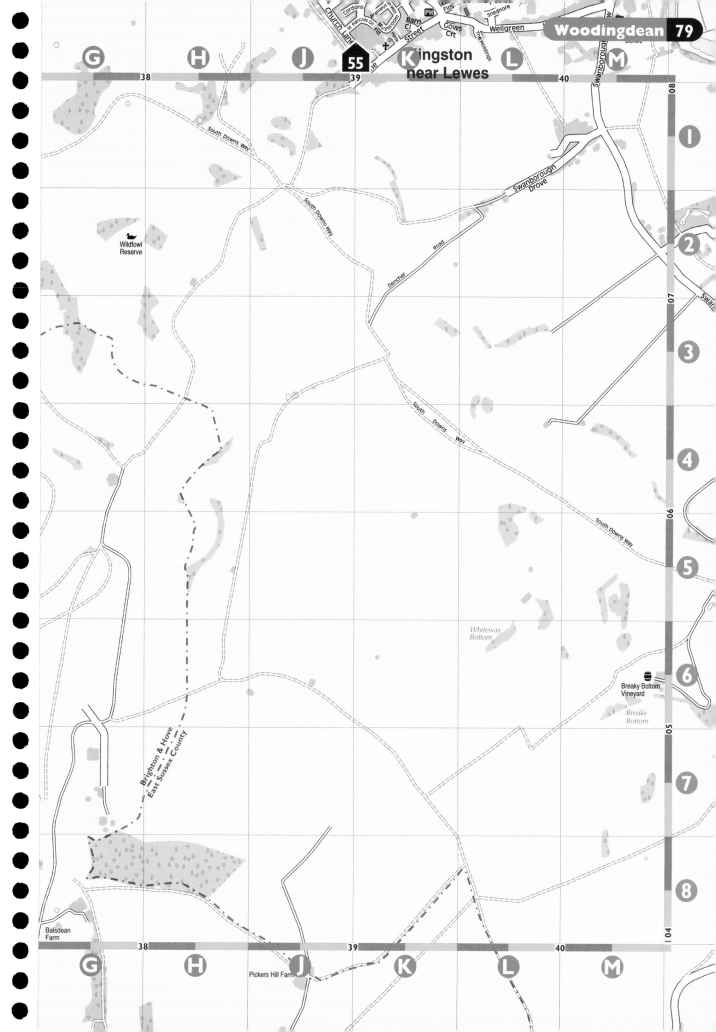

G H J **55** K L M

Kingston
near Lewes

I

2

3

4

5

6

7

8

G H J K L M

Church Lane
St Pancras Cn
Cordons
Bramleys
Mushroom
Barn
Cl
Street
PH
Cows
Cft
snednore
Wellgreen
The Holdings
Centre
Swanborough

South Downs Way

South Downs Way

Wildfowl
Reserve

Swanborough
Drove

Dencher
Road

Swa

South Downs Way

South Downs Way

Whiteway
Bottom

Breaky Bottom
Vineyard

Breaky
Bottom

Brighton & Hove
East Sussex County

Balsdean
Farm

Pickers Hill Farm

38 39 40 08 07 06 05 04

Nature
Reserve

A 475 **B** Great D. **C** 58 **D** Prinsted E. 77 **F**
76

Wickor
Point

West Sussex County

Sussex Border Path

04

I

03

2 Hunter Rd
Swift Road
Spartan Cl
S Bay N Bay
Meteor Road
Canberra Rd
Hornet Road
Emsworth Rd

Thorney Island

Stanbury
Point

Thorney Island
Primary School

3 Barracks

Emsworth Rd

West Thorney

02

Thorney Island
Airfield

Smith Lane

Church
Road
Varsity Road
Vulcan Road
Thorney Old Rd

Thorney
Channel

4 Marker
Point

Pleasant Lane
Victor Rd
Vallant Road
Valetta Road

Sussex Border Path

01

5

6

Sussex Border Path

Longmere
Point

7 Pilsey
Island

00

8 Pilsey
Sand

Chichester Harbour

475 **A** 475 **B** 76 **C** 98 **D** E. 77 **F**
76

Stocker's Lake

West Sussex Count...
Ham...re Cou...

I grid square represents 500 metres

Chidham
Point

G   H   J   59   K   L   M

The Millstream
Hotel &
Restaurant

78   79   Cot Lane   80   04

Marsh   Lane   Marsh   La

Steels   Lane   Harbour

Chidham

Bosham
Abbey

Bosham
Sailing Club

I

Shore Road   2

03   3

New
Barn

Cobnor
Farm

Bosham
Channel

Lowerhone Farm

Hone   Lane

Gerald Daniel
Sailing Club

Cobnor
House

Lower   Lane

Smuggler's Lane   4

02   82

Cobnor
Point   5

B

Chichester Channel

Itchenor
Sailing Club

6

West Itchenor

Street   The

Orchard
Lane
W C

Itchenor   Road

Spinney   Lane   01   7

Itchenor
House   Oldhouse Farm

Itchenor   Road

Chalkdock
Lane   the spinney   Glebe
Field
Road   8

001

78   79   80

G   H   J   99   K   L   M   **Shipton
Green**

Rookwood
Lane   Rook   Sheepwash Lane   Redlands Fm

82
The Millstream
Hotel &
Restaurant

Bosham
Sailing Club

A

B Bosham

C

60
82

D

Old Park Lane

E

F

83

Bosham County
Primary School

Stonewall Farm

Brook Av
field Rd
Bosham
Lane
Fairfield Rd
Leander
Cambria
Church
Meadow
Canute
R 481
The Drive
Shore Road
Harbour Way
Taylors Lane
Stumps Lane
The Dr

Southwood Farm

Old Park Farm

Dell Quay
Sailing Club

Church Farm

Hook Farm

Hook Lane

Old Park Lane

3
hone Farm

Hart's Farm

4
Sm...er's Lane

Hoe Farm

Fletcher's Lane

Oldpark
Wood

81

5

Bosham Hoe

Longmore
Point

Birdham
Pool

Chichester
Yacht Club

Chichester
Harbour

6

Lock Lane

7

Lane

Westlands Farm

The Causeway

Court Barn Lane

Broomers Lane

Birdham

ouse Farm

Westlands
Lane

Oak
Meadow

Martins La

Springfield
Cl

Works

St James's
Crooked La
Church
Lane
KC

Pescott's
Cl

Birdham Primary
School

Cherry

Main Road

Alandale Road

Sidlesham La

8

Glebe
Field
Road

A

B
Lippo...Farm

C

82
100

D

Longmeadow
Gdns
Walwyn
Cl

A286

E

83

F

Works

**Shipton
Green**

Itchenor

1 grid square represents 500 metres

Longmeadow

Farne
Lane

Whitestone
Farm

Florence
Close

Burlow
Crooked

Farne Cl
PO

Main Road

Sidlesham
Lane

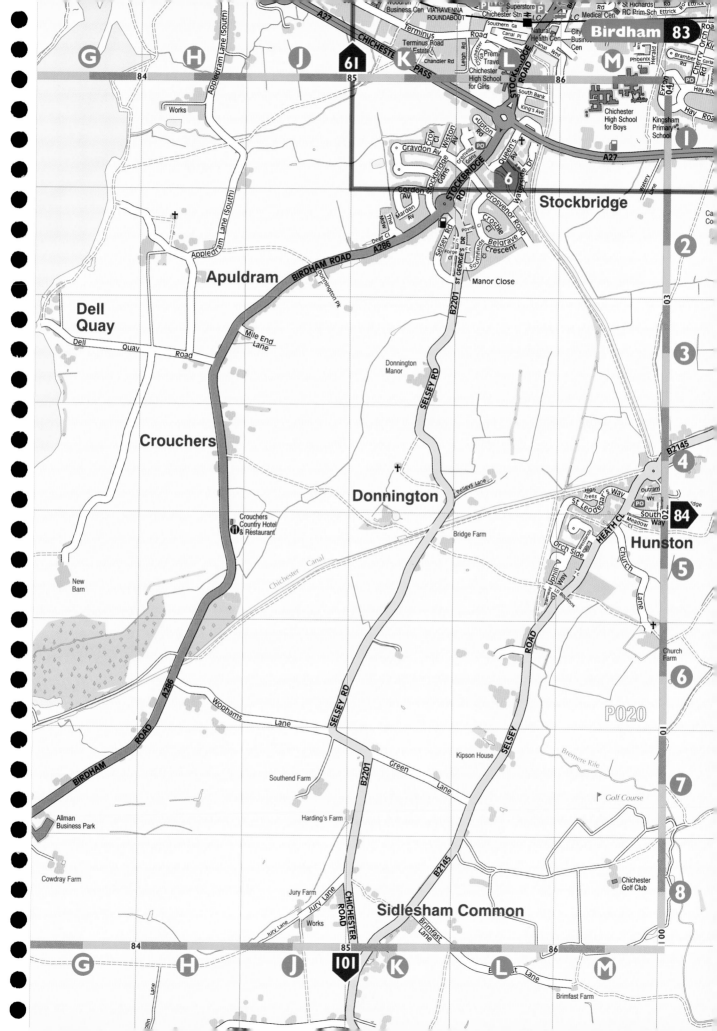

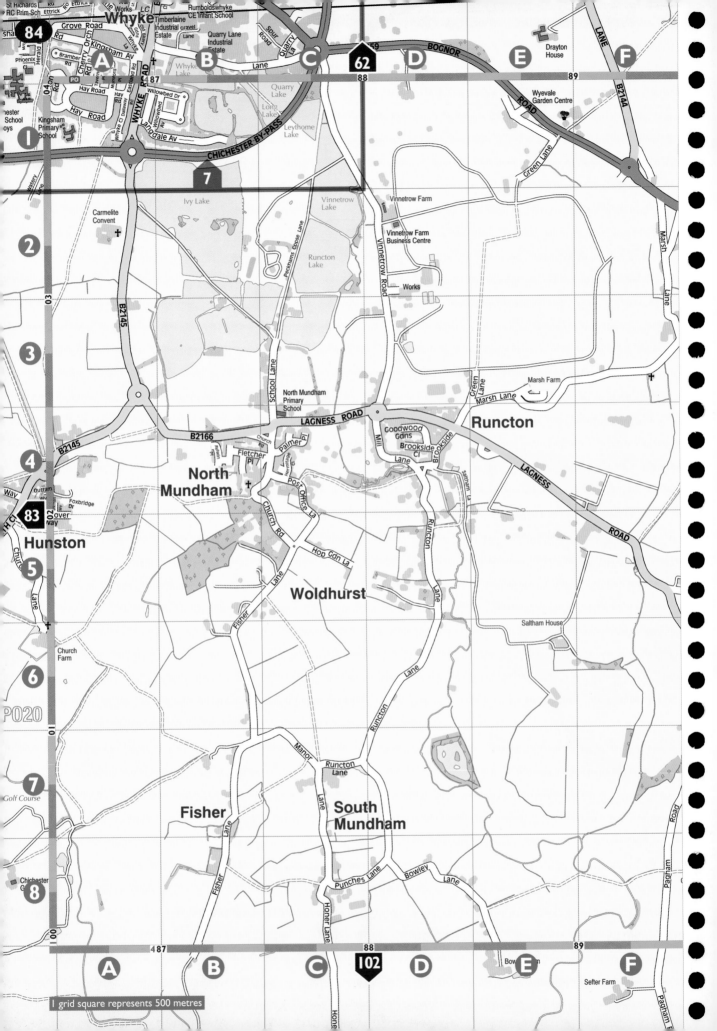

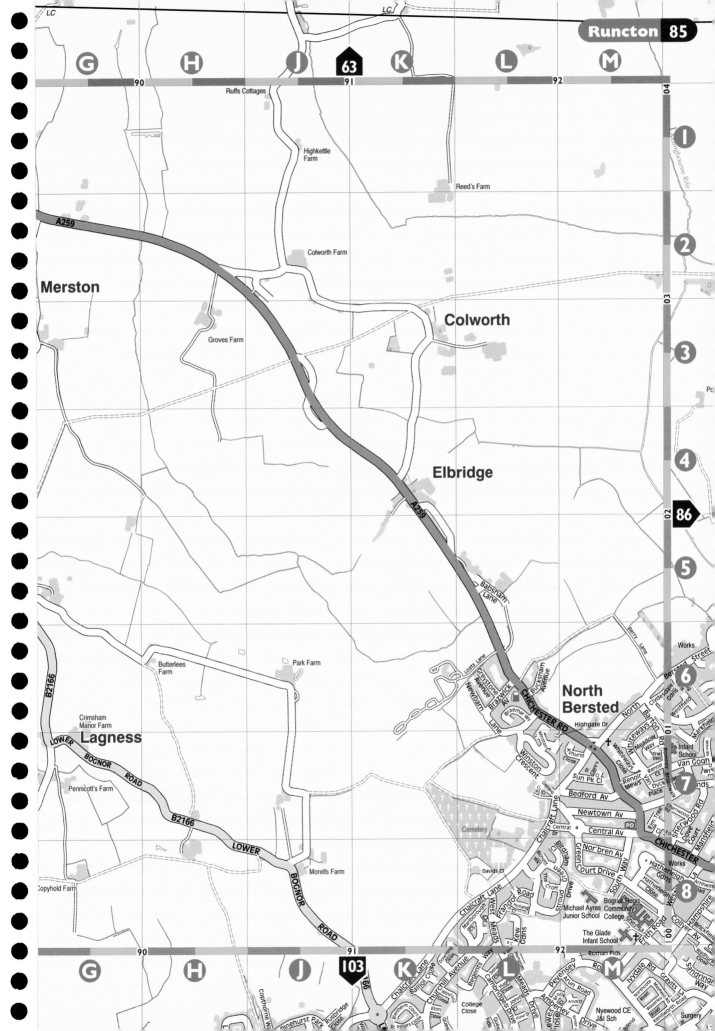

G   H   J   63   K   L   M

90   91   92   04

I

2

Merston

3

Colworth

4

Groves Farm

86

Elbridge

A259

5

Babsham Lane

6

North Bersted

Butterlees Farm

Park Farm

Chichester Rd

Highgate Dr

7

Crimsham Manor Farm

Lagness

Lower Bognor Road

B2166

Winston Crescent

Bedford Av

Newtown Av

Pennicott's Farm

B2166

Central Av

Nor'bren Av

Chichester

8

Lower Bognor Road

Morells Farm

Davids Cl

Cemetery

Green Court Drive

Copyhold Farm

Michael Ayres Junior School

Bognor Regis Community College

The Glade Infant School

Roman Flds

G   H   J   103   K   L   M

90   91   166   92

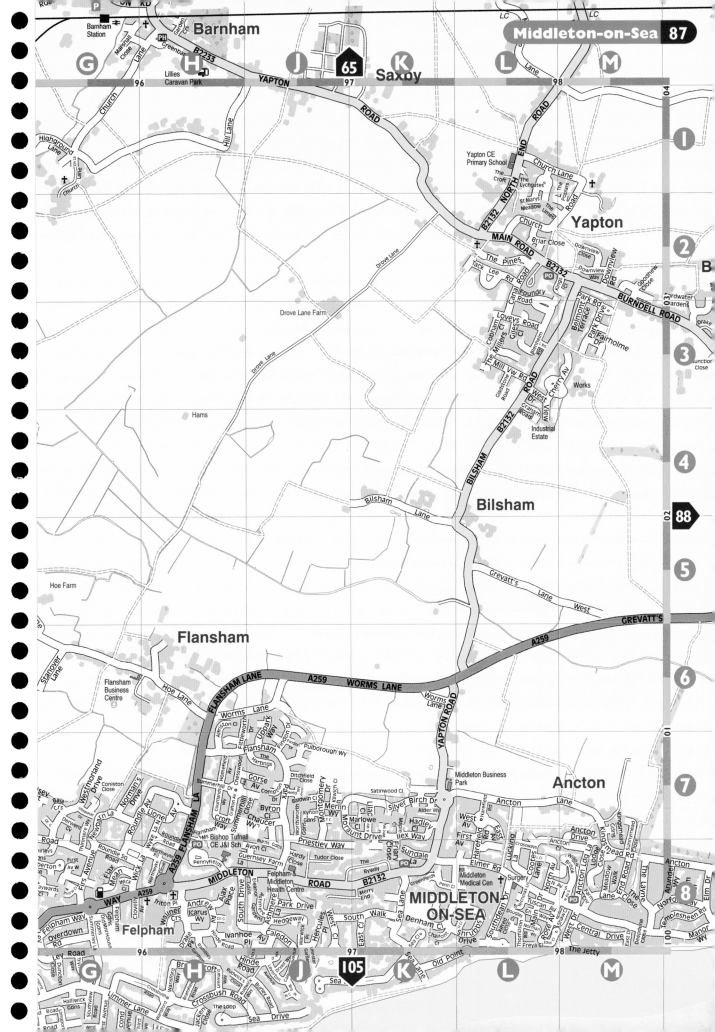

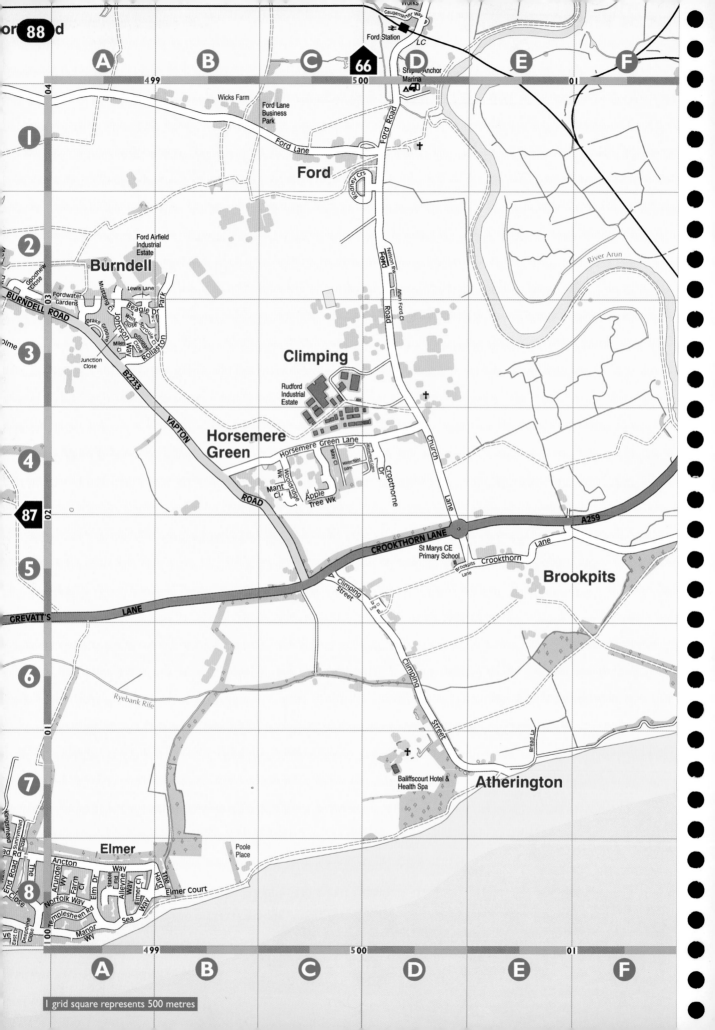

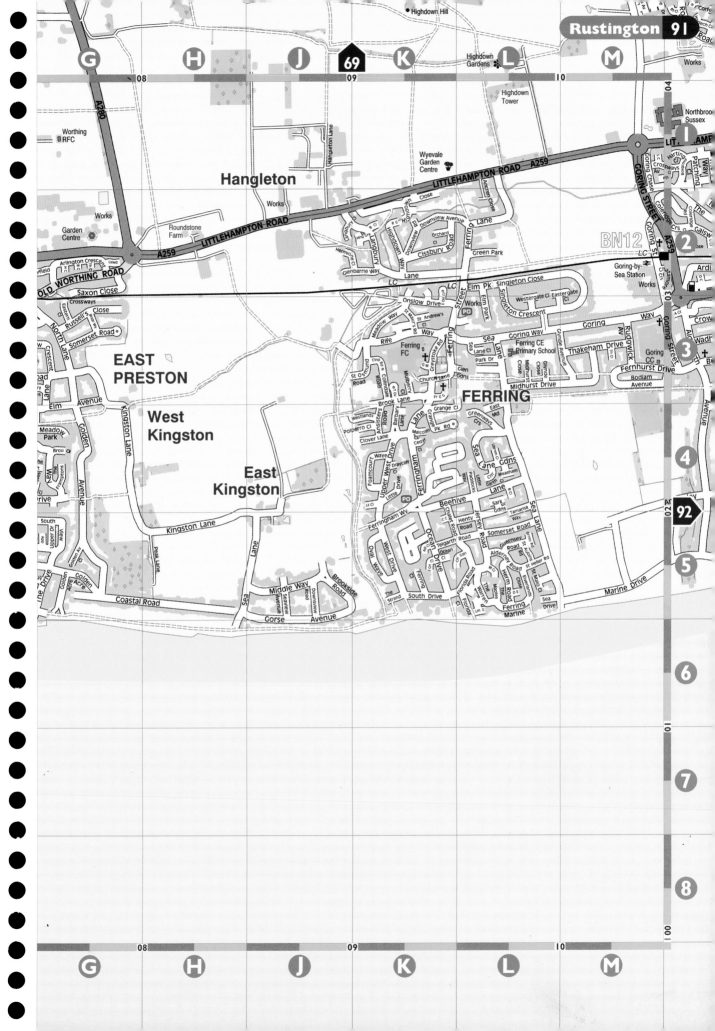

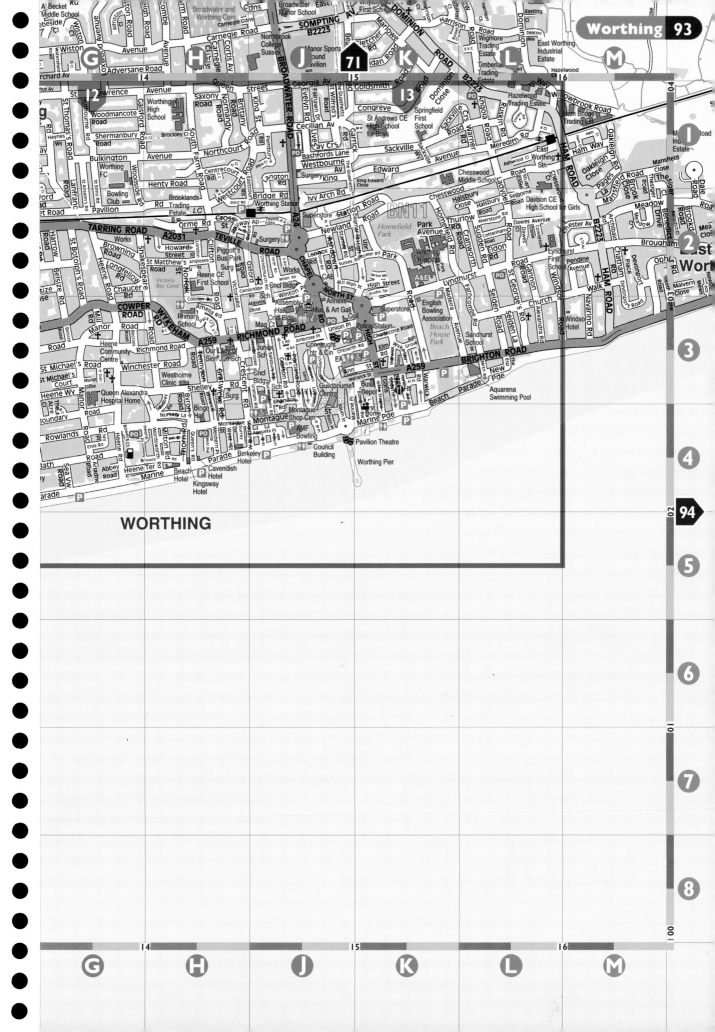

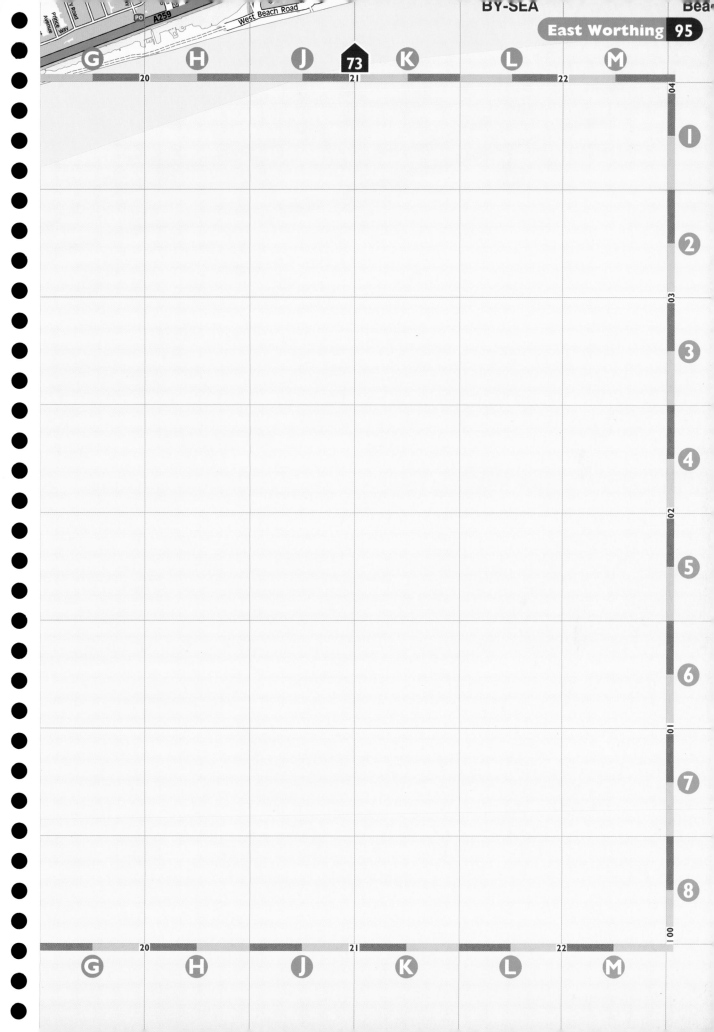

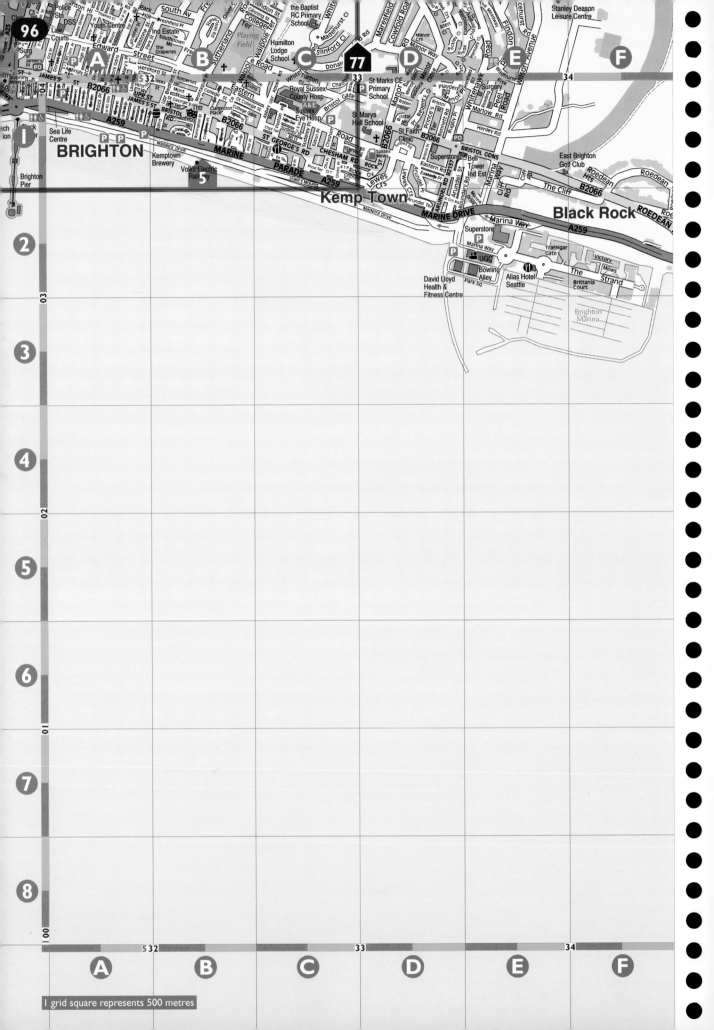

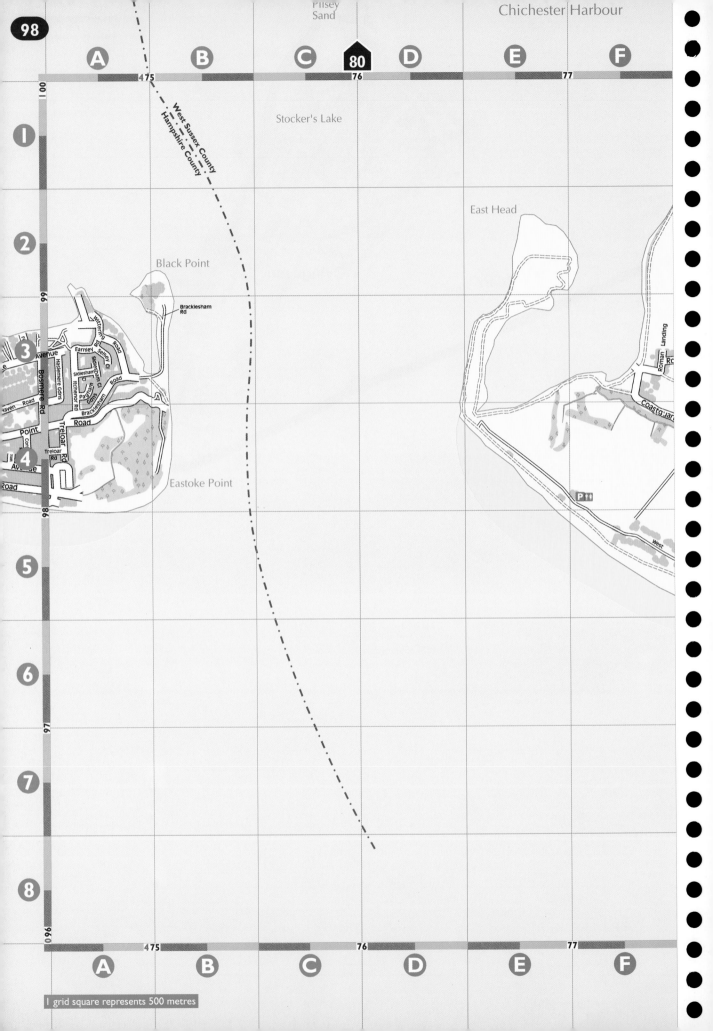

Pilsey
Sand

Chichester Harbour

A B C **80** D E F

475 76 77

Stocker's Lake

West Sussex County
Hampshire County

East Head

Black Point

Brackiesham
Rd

Earnley

Watering
Rd

Selsey Cl

Avenue

Haslemere Gdns

Bosmere Rd

Sidlesham Cl

Pagham Gdns

Itchenor Rd

Road

Road

Roman Landing

Haven Road

Bracklesham

Road

Coastguard

Point

Treloar Rd

Treloar
Rd

Avenue

Road

Eastoke Point

P

West

1 grid square represents 500 metres

A B C D E F

475 76 77

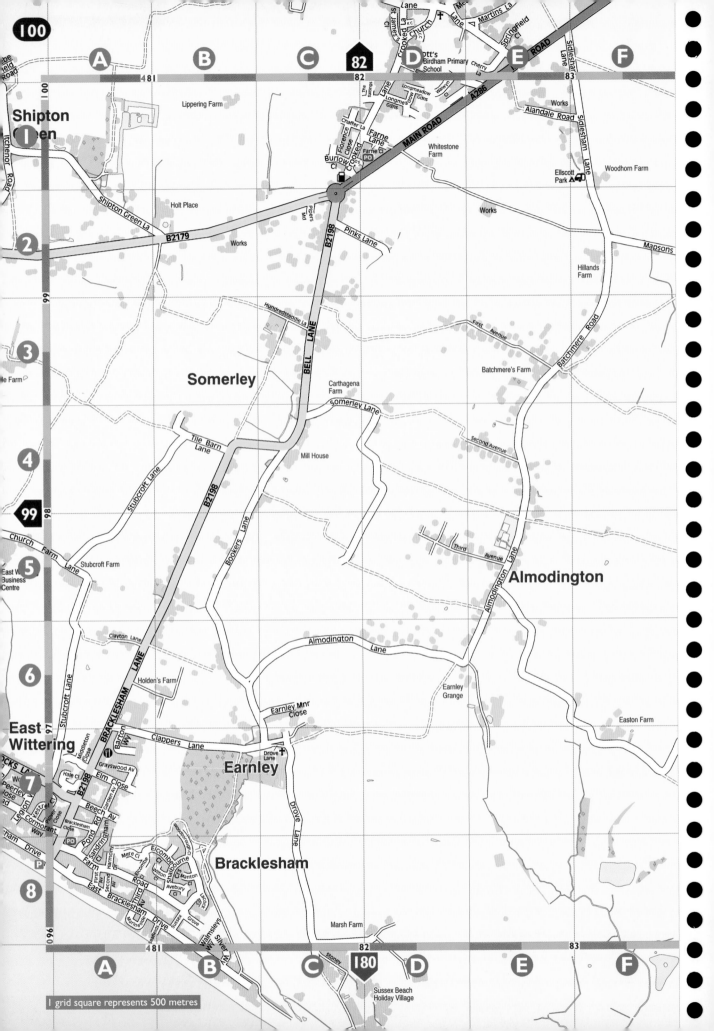

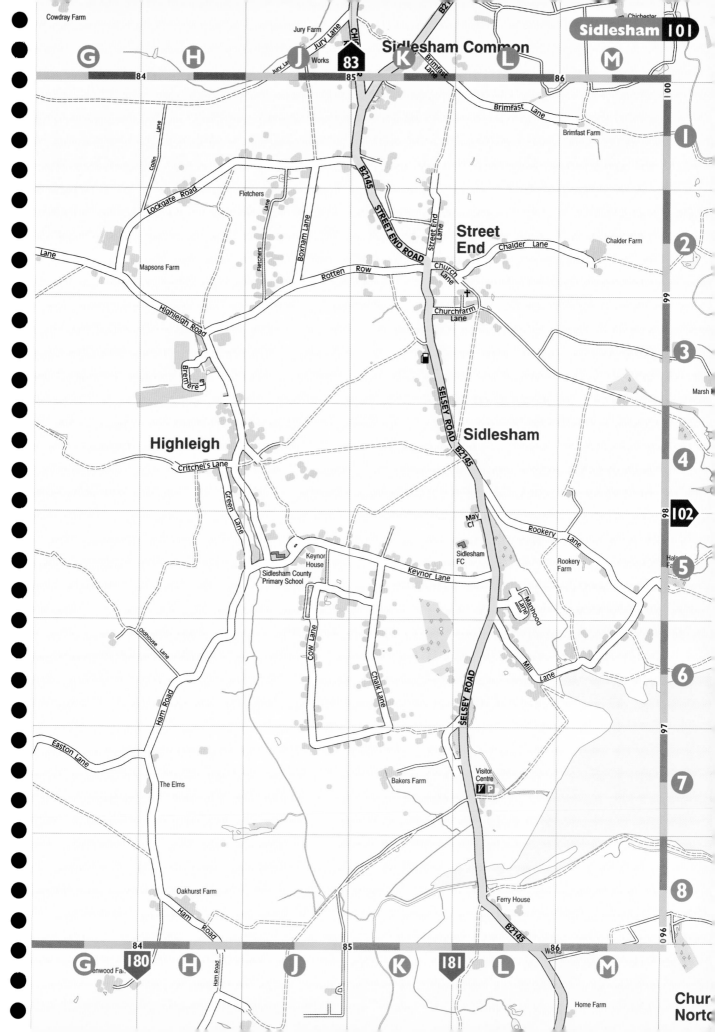

Cowdray Farm

Jury Farm

Jury Lane

G   **H**   **J**   **83**   **K**   **L**   **M**

Works

84   85   86

Sidlesham Common

Chichester

Brimfast Lane

Brimfast Lane

Brimfast Farm

I

100

99

Collin Lane

Lockgate Road

Fletchers

Fletchers Lane

Boxham Lane

B2145

Street End Lane

STREET END ROAD

Street End

Chalder Lane

Chalder Farm

2

Lane

Mapsons Farm

Rotten Row

Church Lane

†

Churchfarm Lane

Highleigh Road

3

Marsh

Bremere

SELSEY ROAD

Sidlesham

B2145

Highleigh

Critchel's Lane

98 **102**

May Cl

Rookery Lane

Rookery Farm

Hale Farm

5

Green Lane

Keynor House

Sidlesham FC

Sidlesham County Primary School

Keynor Lane

Manhood Lane

Cow Lane

Chalk Lane

Mill Lane

6

Oldhouse Lane

97

Ham Road

Easton Lane

The Elms

Bakers Farm

SELSEY ROAD

Visitor Centre

i P

7

Oakhurst Farm

Ham Road

Ferry House

B2145

8

96

84   85   86

G **180**   Glenwood Farm   **H**   **J**   **K**   **181**   **L**   **M**

Works

Home Farm

Church Norton

102

A   B   C   **84**   D   E   F

Chichester

487   88   89

1

Punches Lane   Bowley Lane

Fisher

Honer Lane

Bowley Farm

Sefter Farm

Pagham Road

I

2

Bremer Rife   Bramber Farm

Pagham Rife

Rookery Farm

Commonmead La

Bramble Close   Briar Close

Beech Cl

Honeysuckle Dr

Millview Cl   Barn Close

Downview   Hook

Nyetimber Mill

100

99

3

Marsh Farm

Oaktree Cl   Barley Close

Millfarm Dr

Cordles W

The Inglenook Hotel

The Nyetin

Lion Road

SpringField

Priors

Manor

Nyetimber

Works

PO

Sylvia Cl   Cntr Cl

Pagham CC

Pagham FC

Summer Lane

Barton Cl

98

4

Honer Farm

Horns Lane

Lake Vw   Elm Cl

Harbour View Road

Church

Sussex Drive

Princes Crt

101

The Ct?

The Vw

Bishops

Payne Cl

Aabottsbury

Shirley Cl

East

97

5

Halsey's Farm

Pagham Road

Queensmead

Saxon Cl

Sea Way

The Vw

The Grd

The Gn

Shirley Drive

Silverdale

Pagham

Church Lane

St Thomas Dr

Martlet W

Sea Lane

The Pde

Conway Drive

Church

Venus Lane

Heron Md

Swan Dene

Arthur Griffiths Clinic

Sandy Road

East

Front Road

Mallard Ct

Kestrel Ct.

Well Road

6

Wythering Cl

Lagoon Road

West Front Road

Pagham Yacht Club

Pagham Lagoon

96

7

Pagham Harbour (Nature Reserve)

Lagoon Road   Harbour   West

P

Pagham Harbour

8

487   88   89

A   B   **181**   C   D   E   F

1 grid square represents 500 metres

Norton

P

BOGNOR REGIS

I grid square represents 500 metres

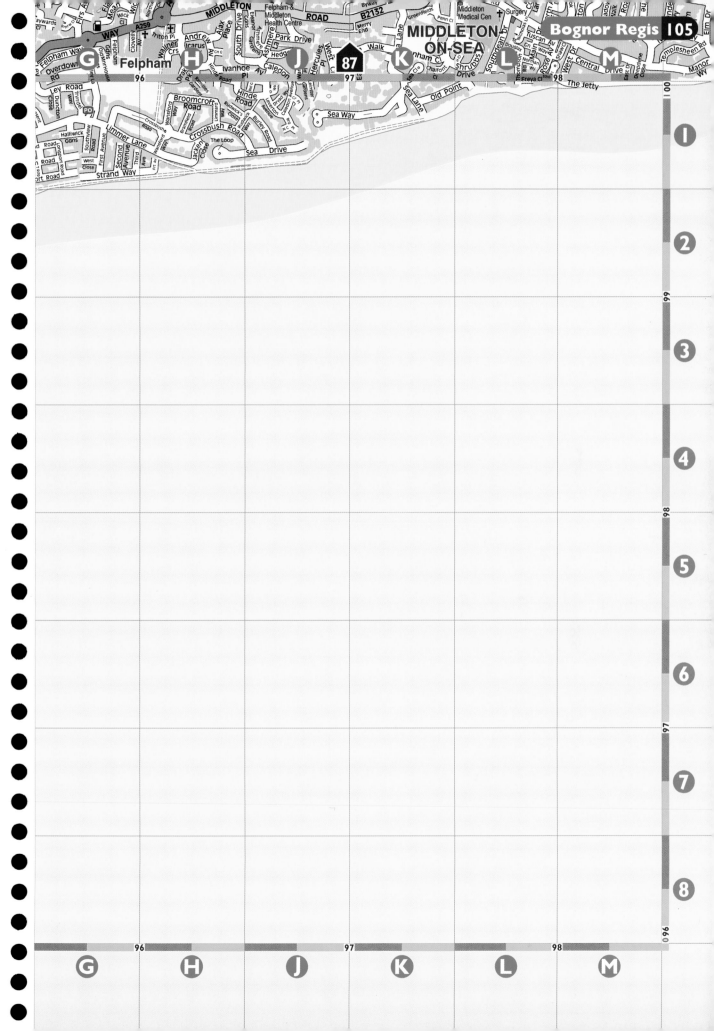

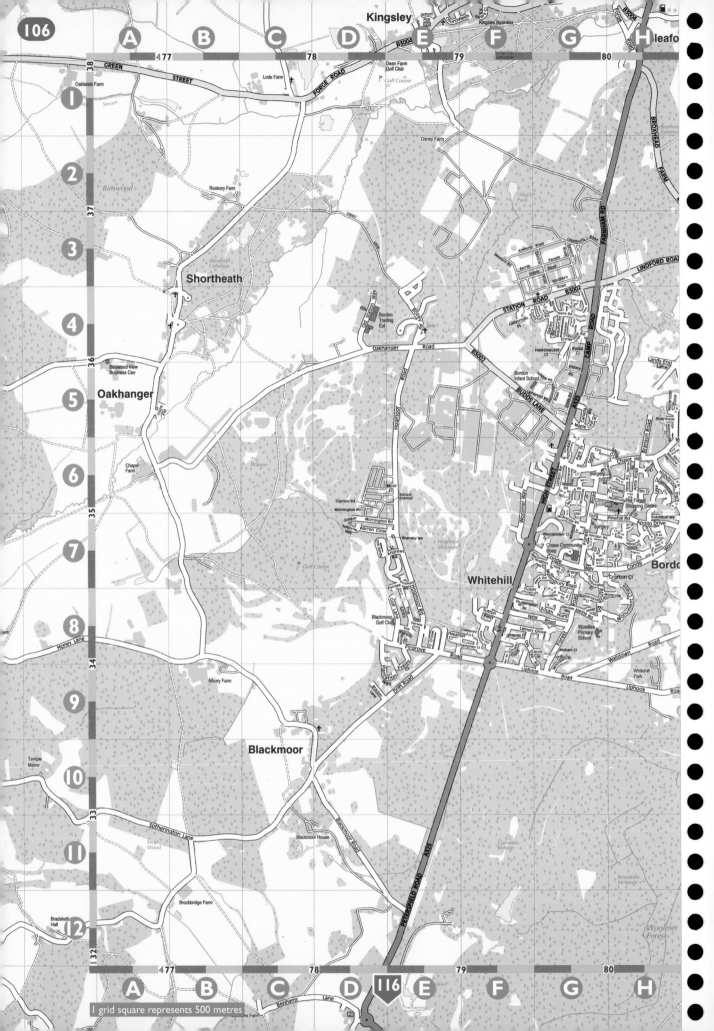

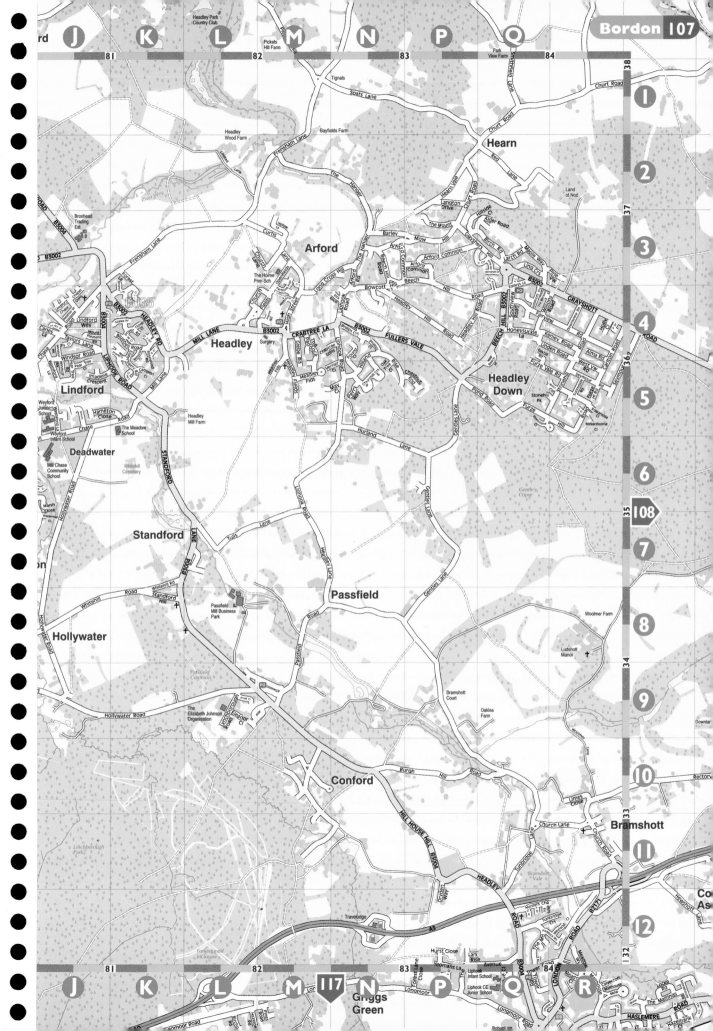

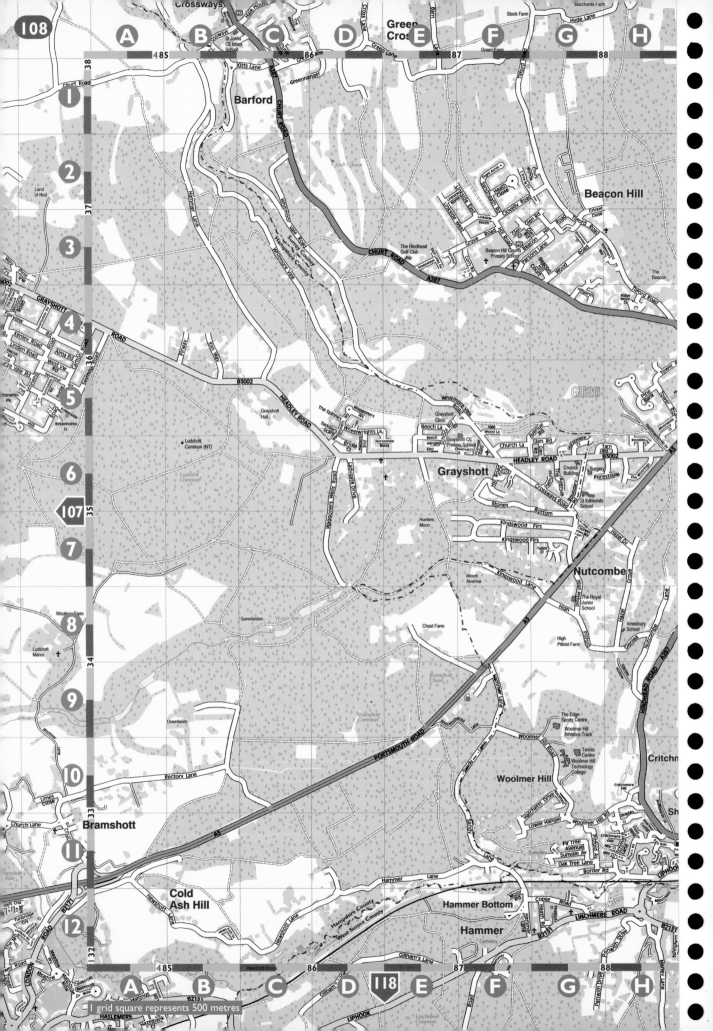

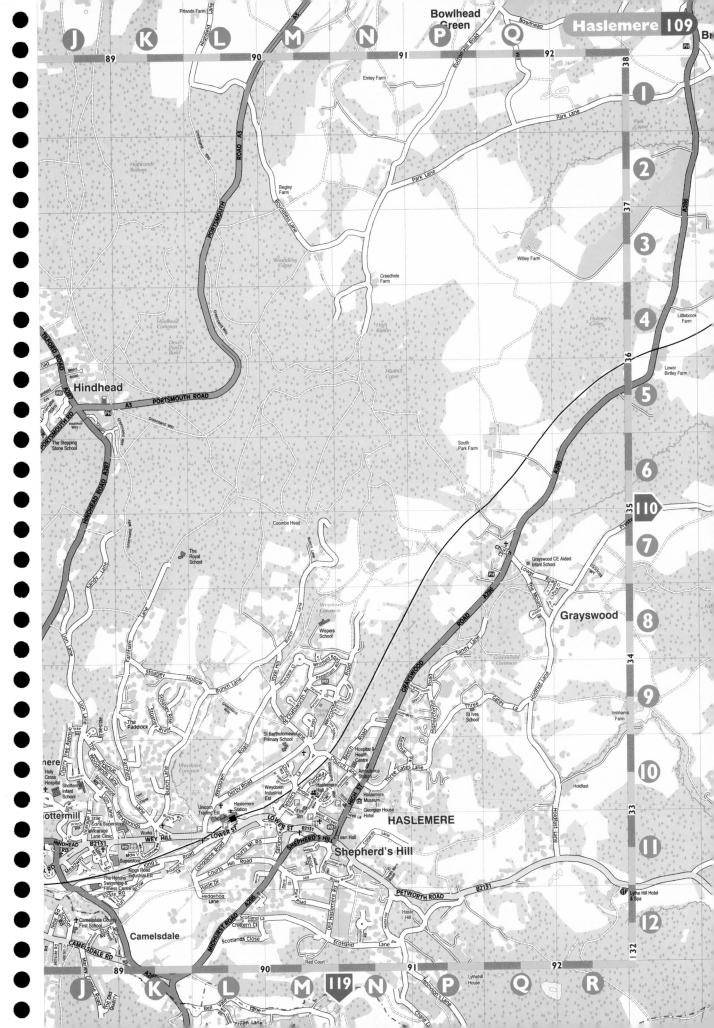

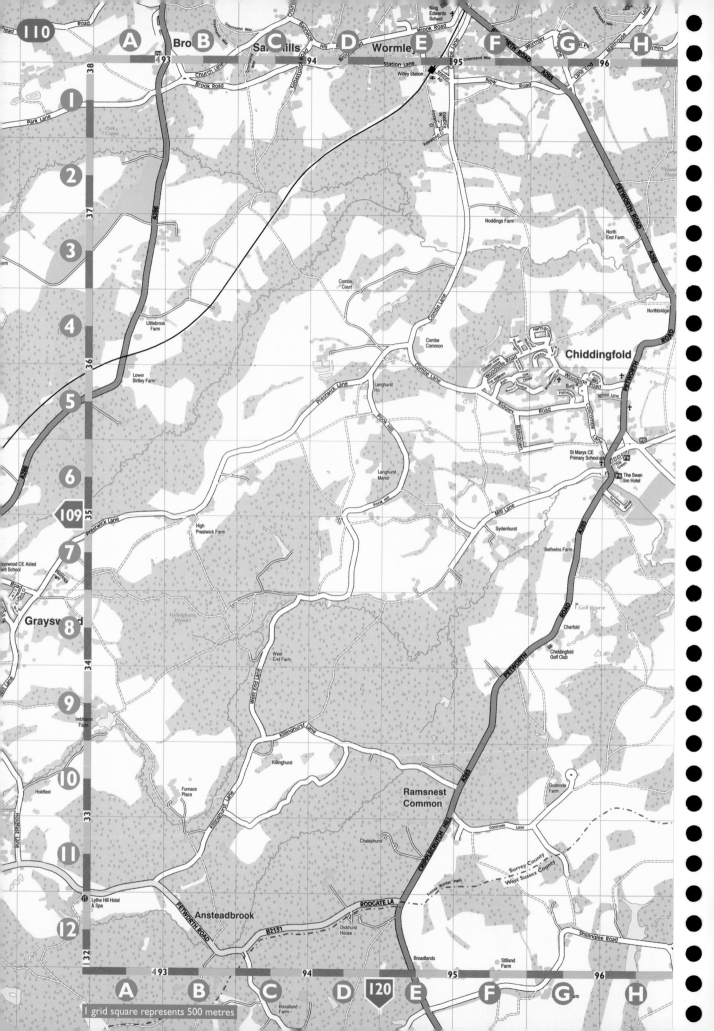

A B C D E F G H

1 grid square represents 500 metres

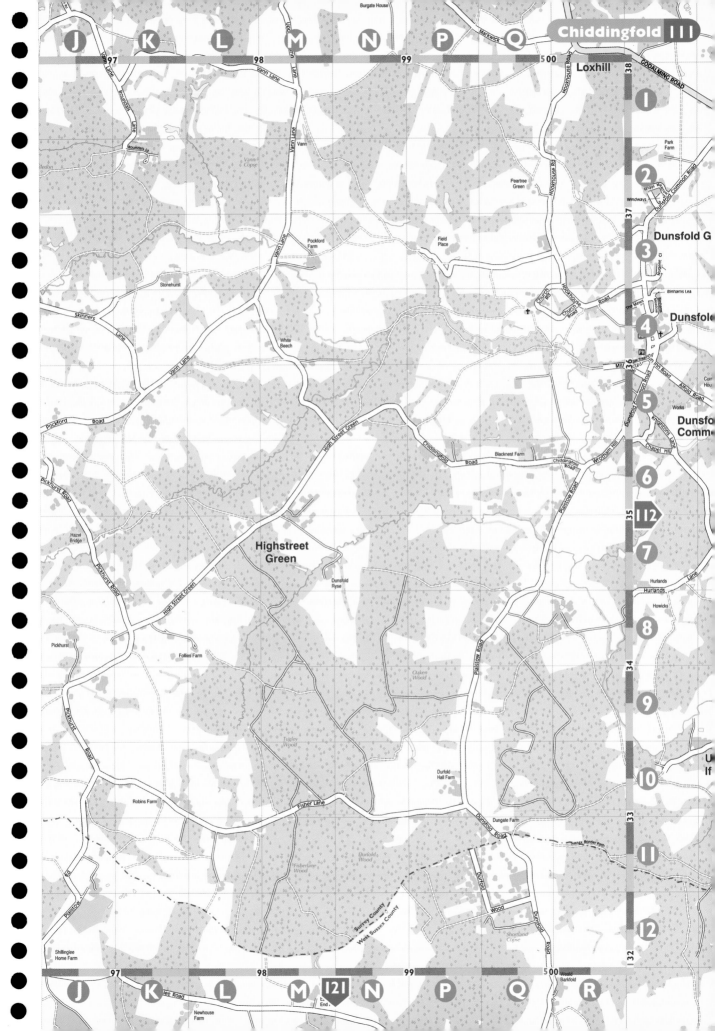

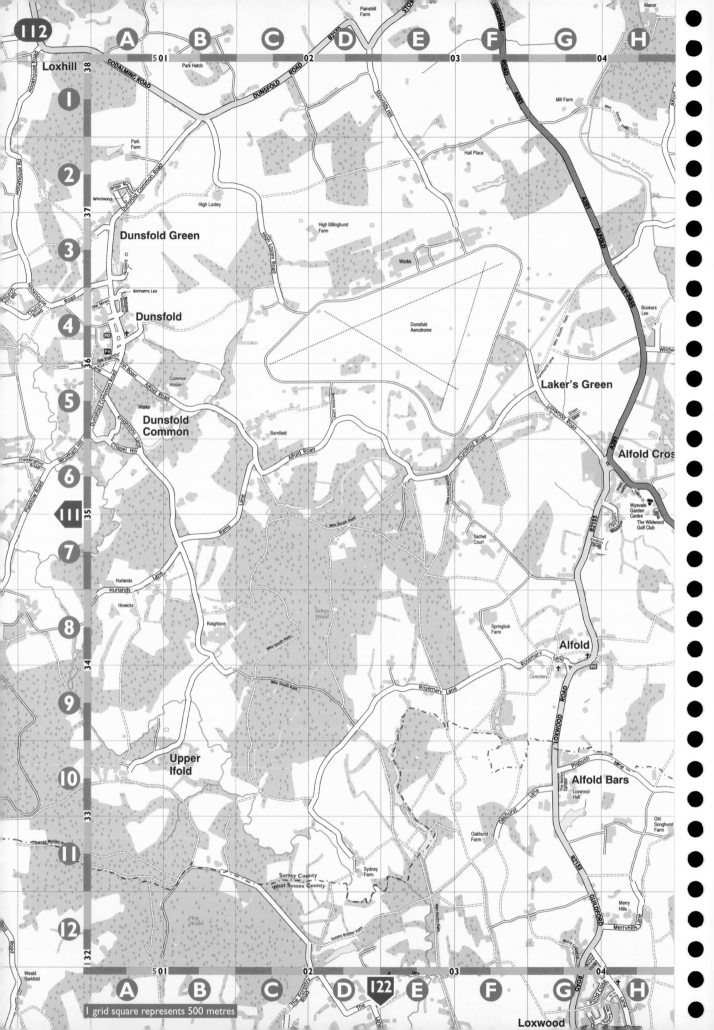

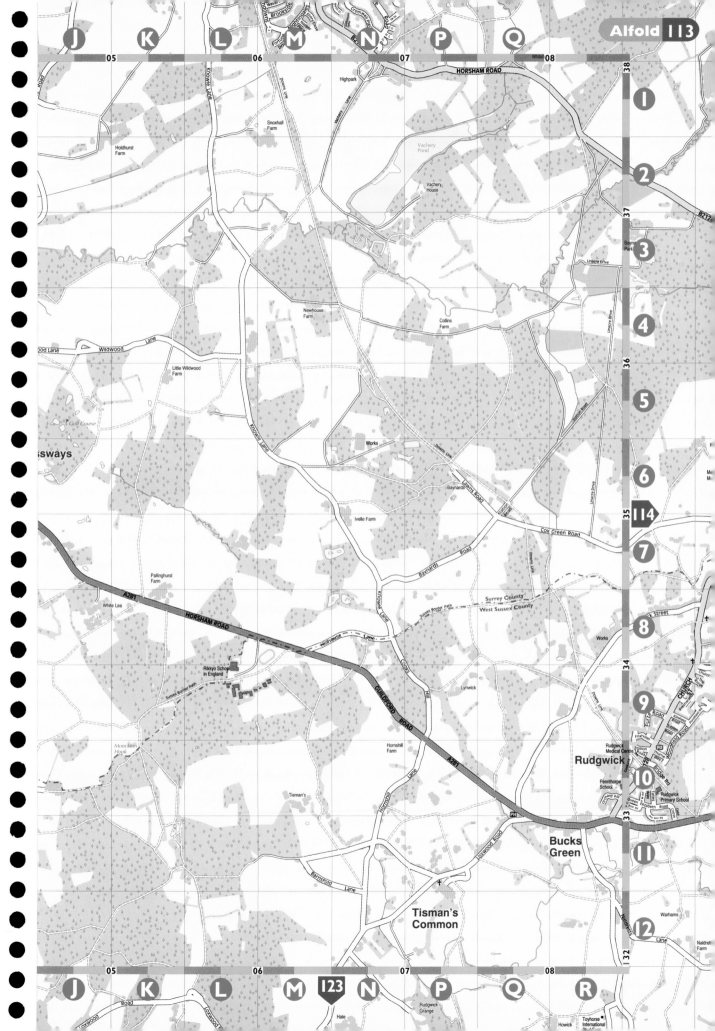

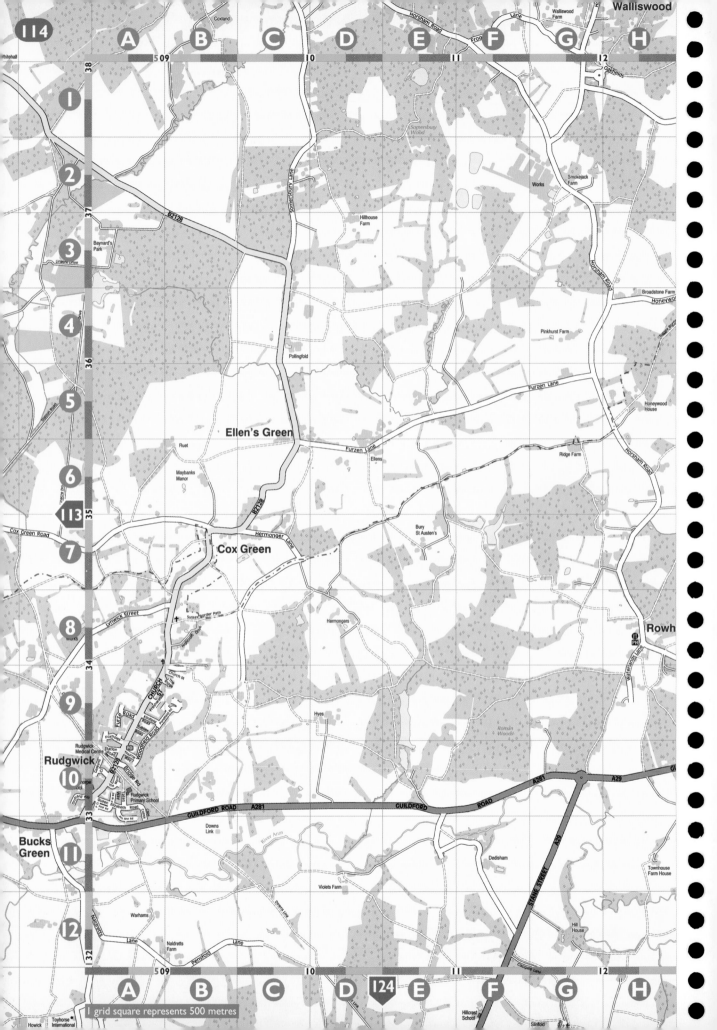

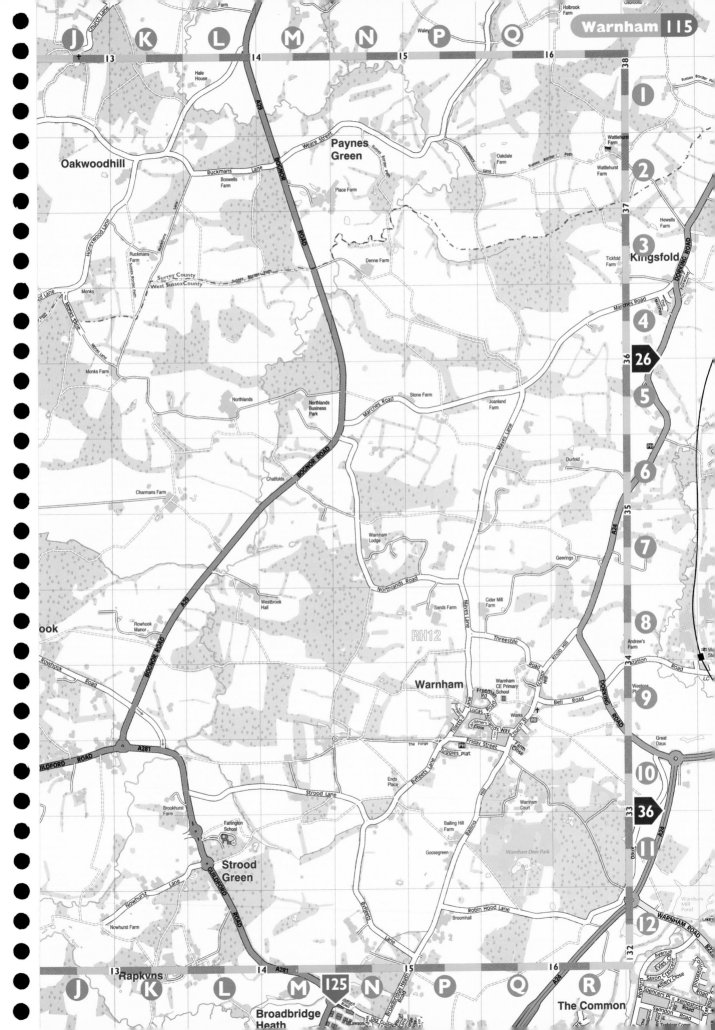

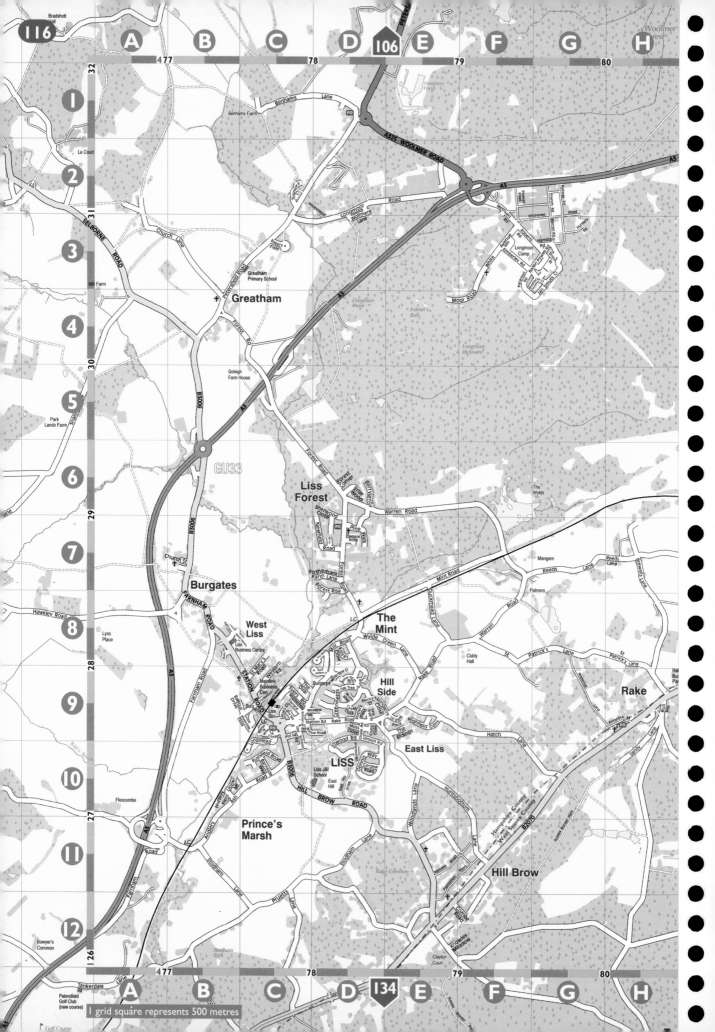

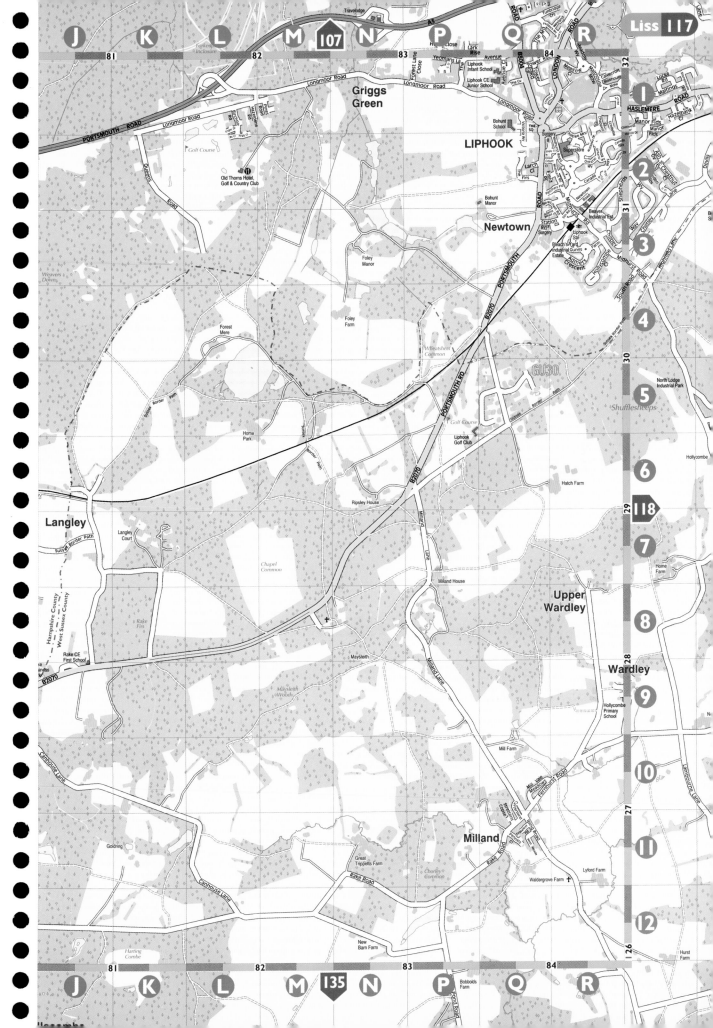

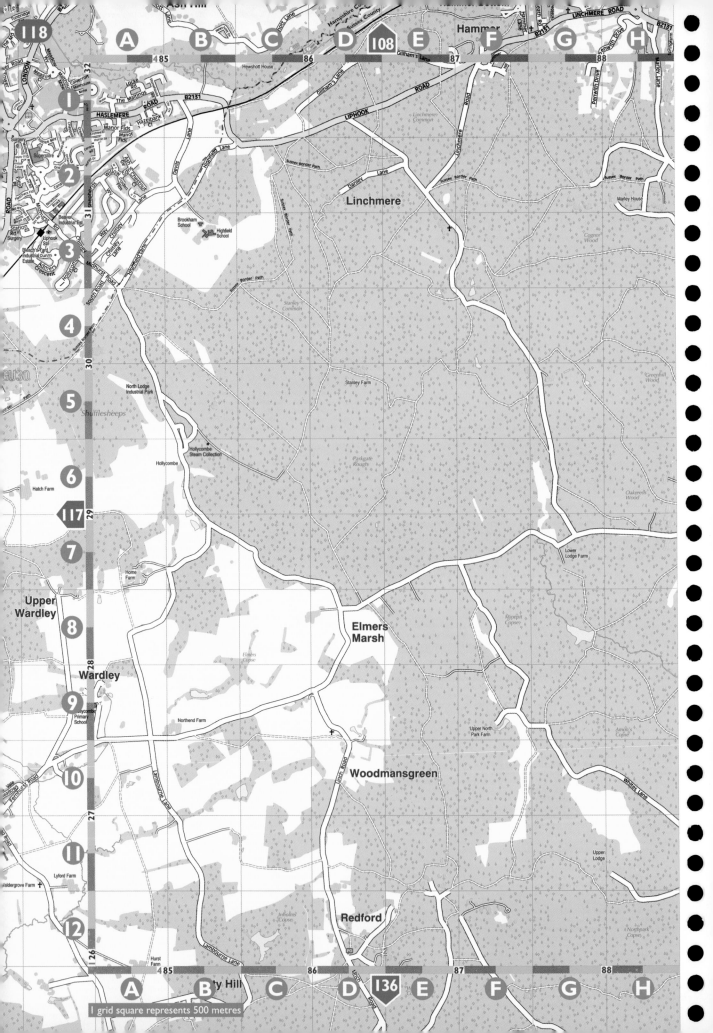

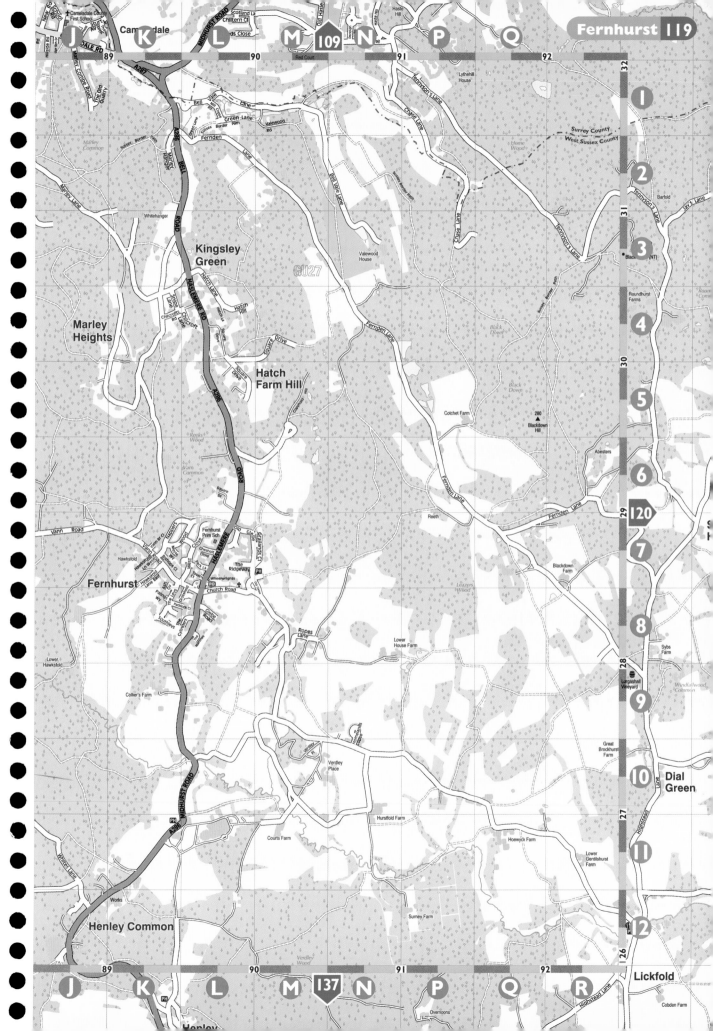

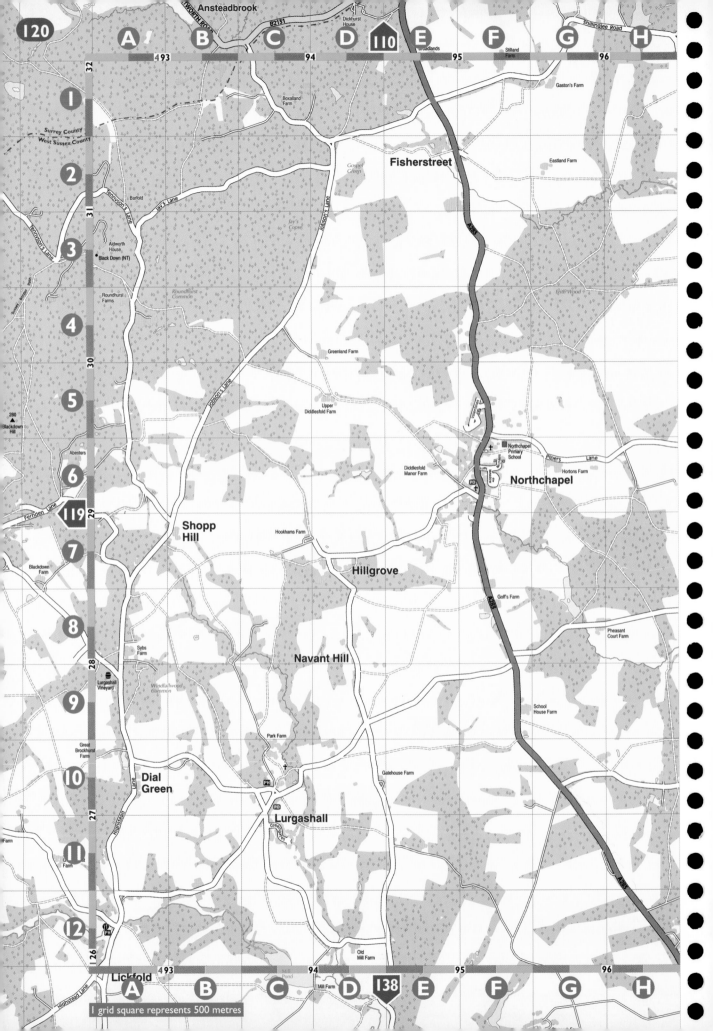

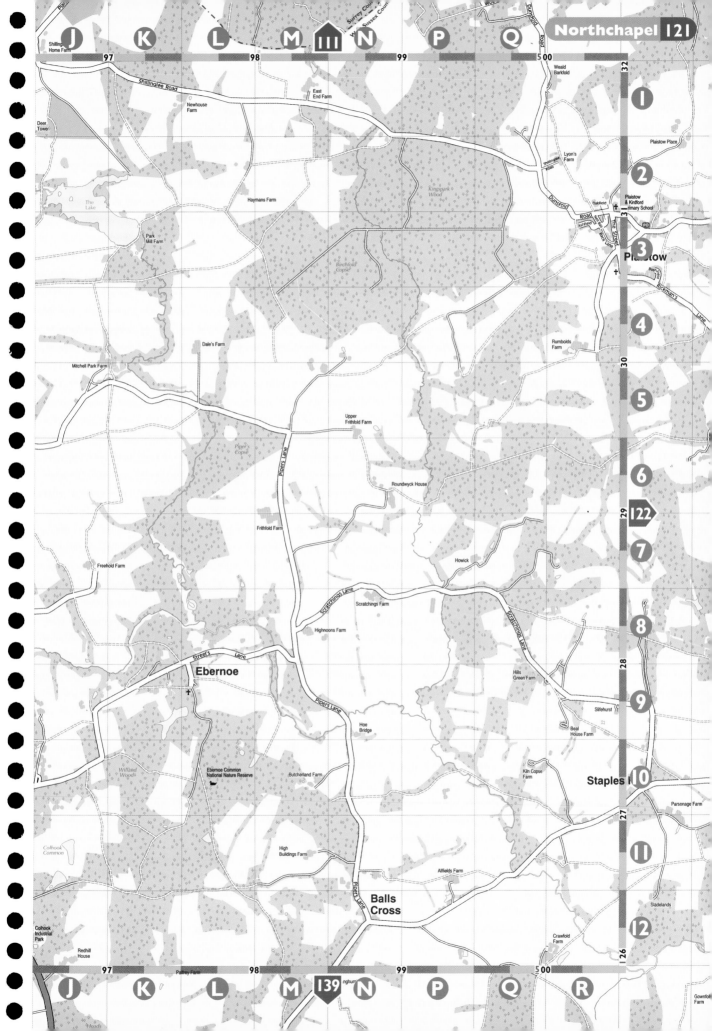

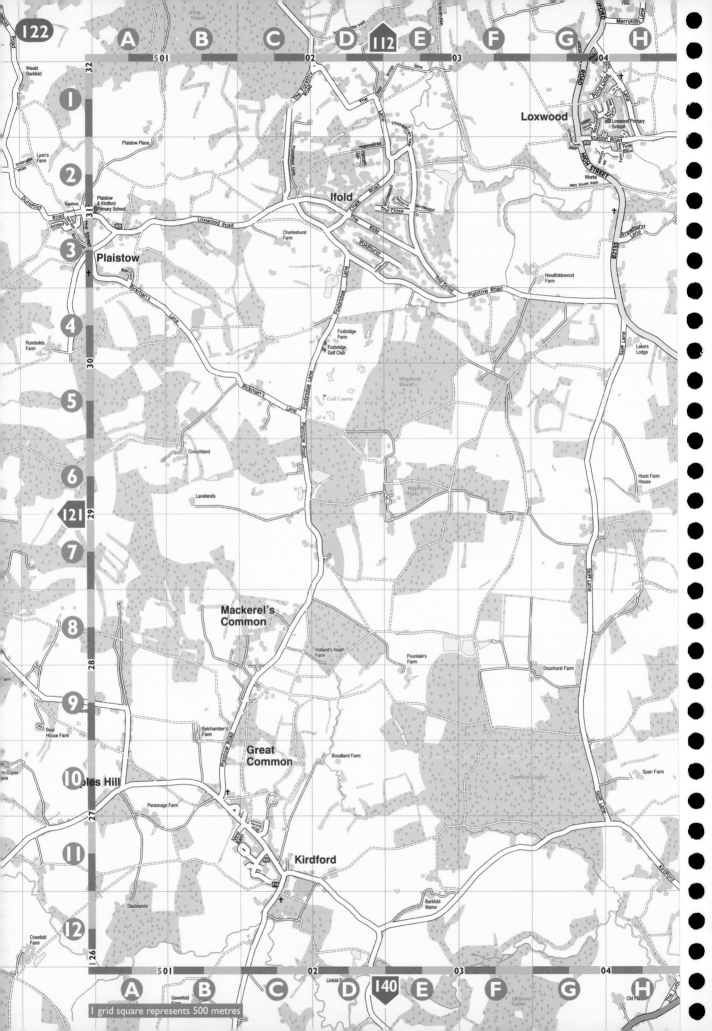

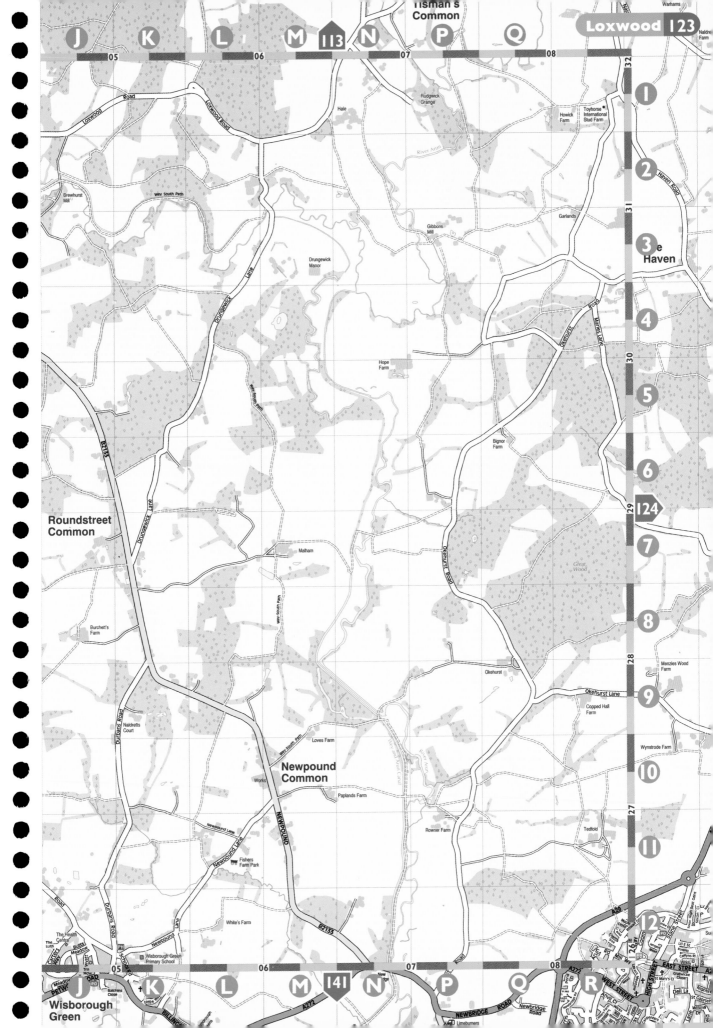

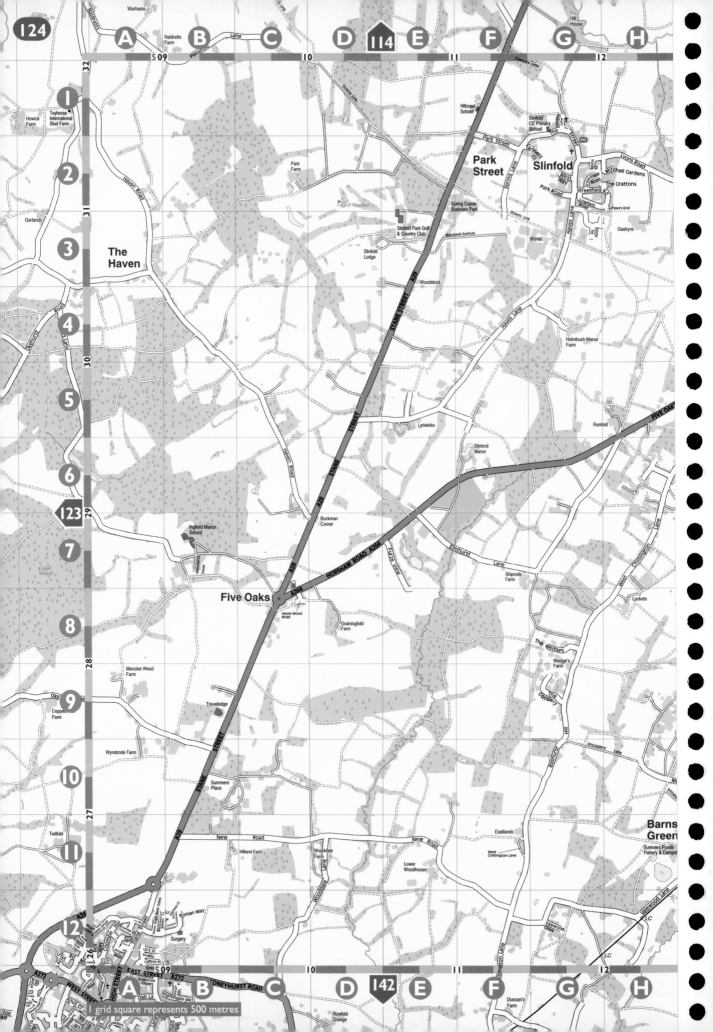

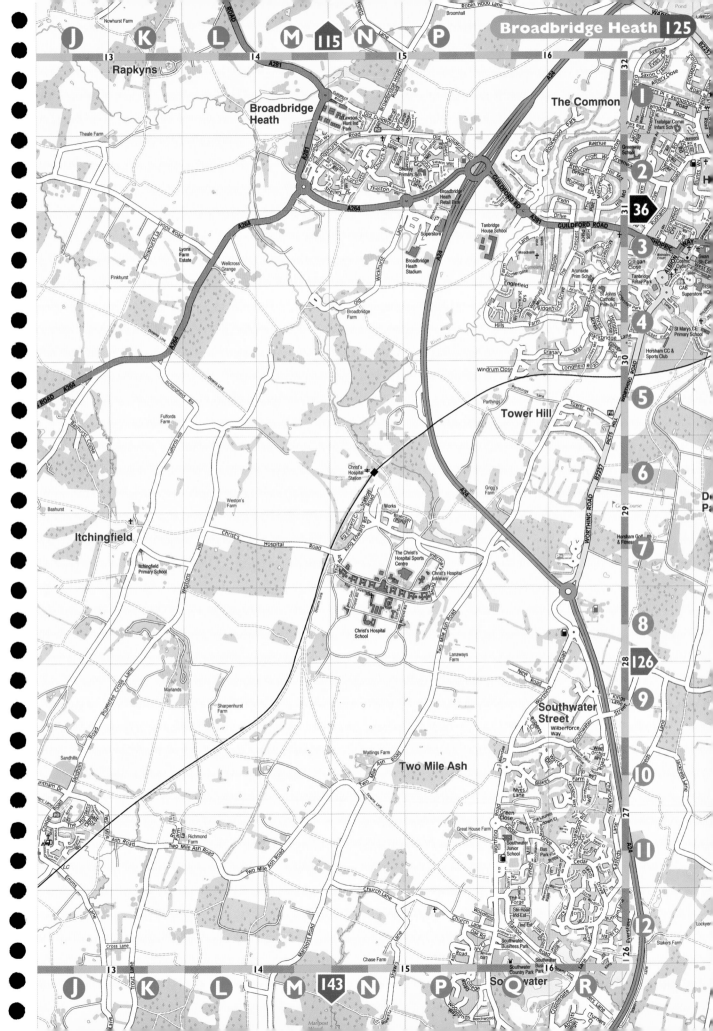

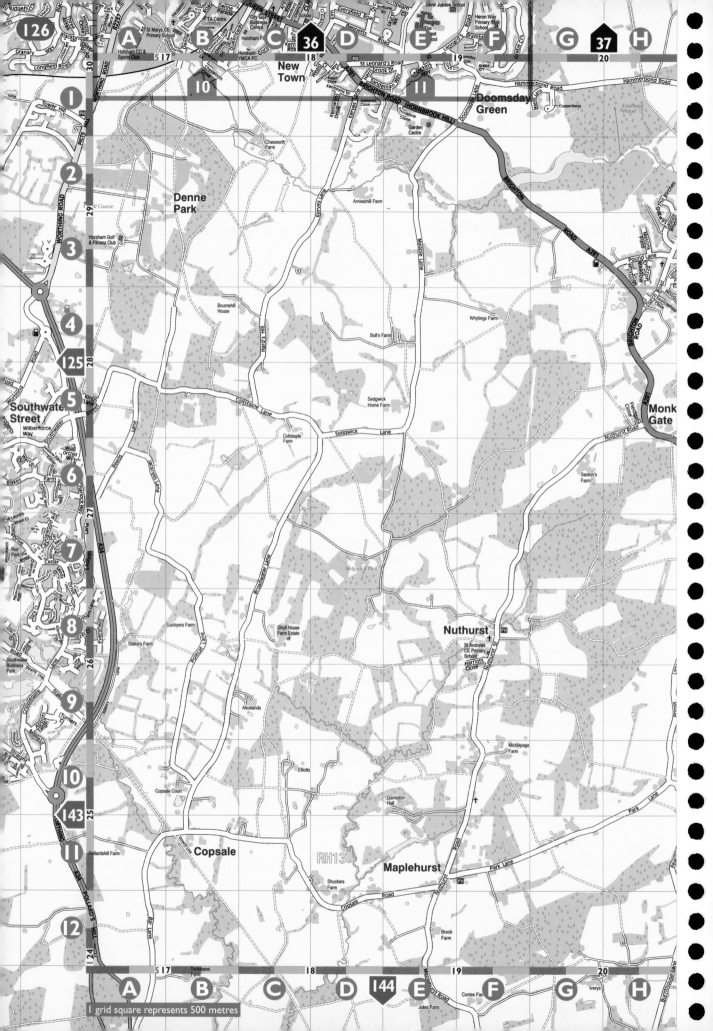

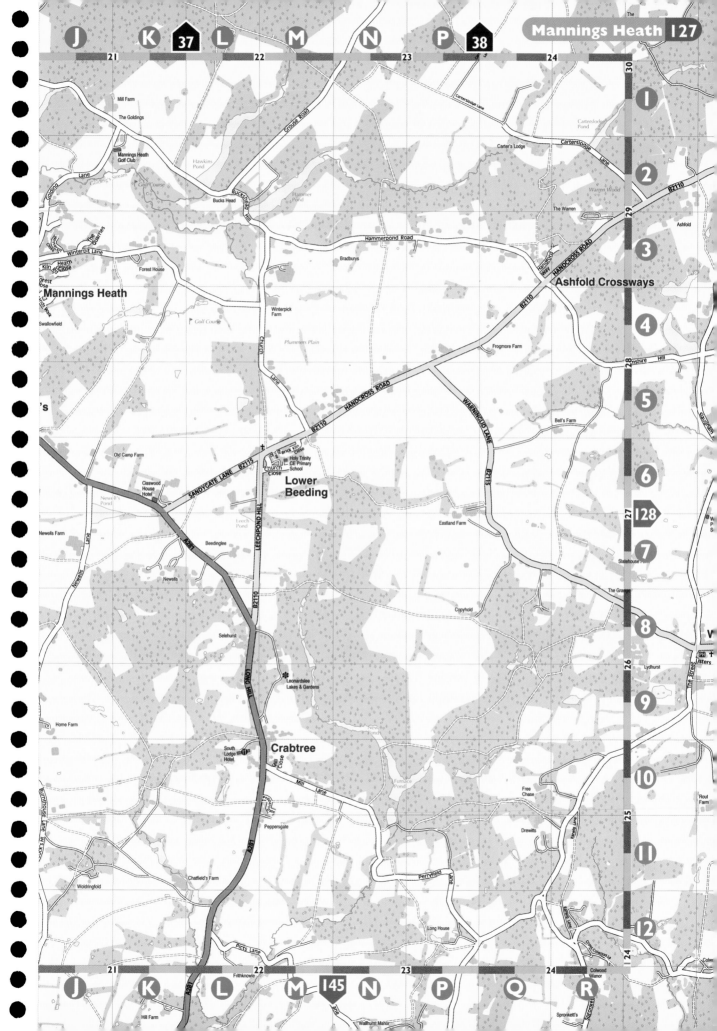

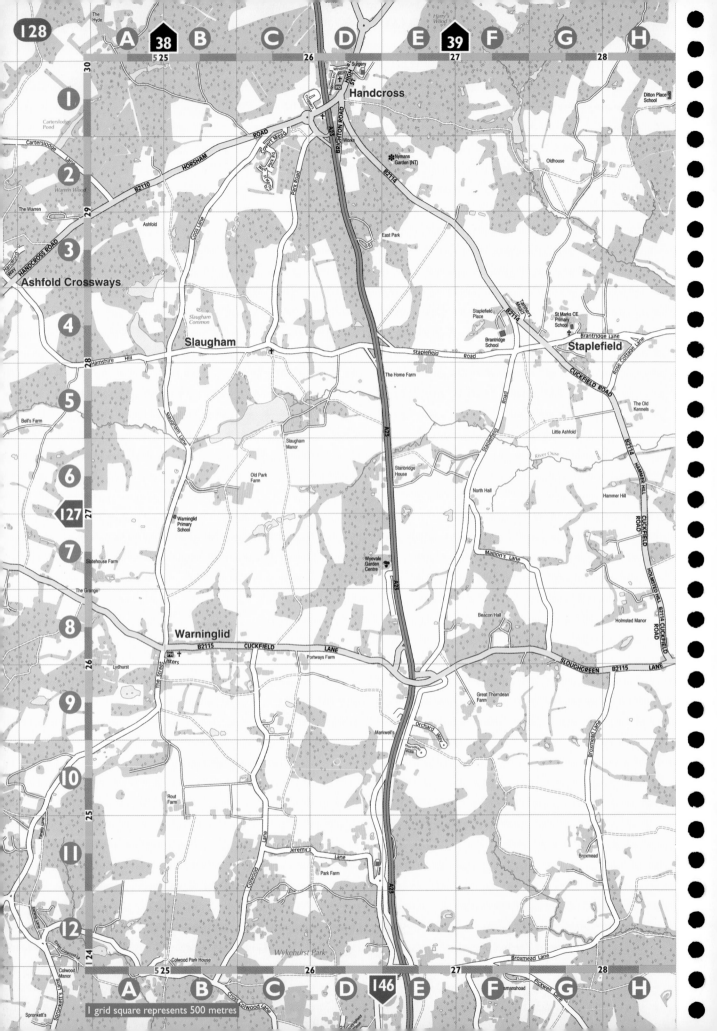

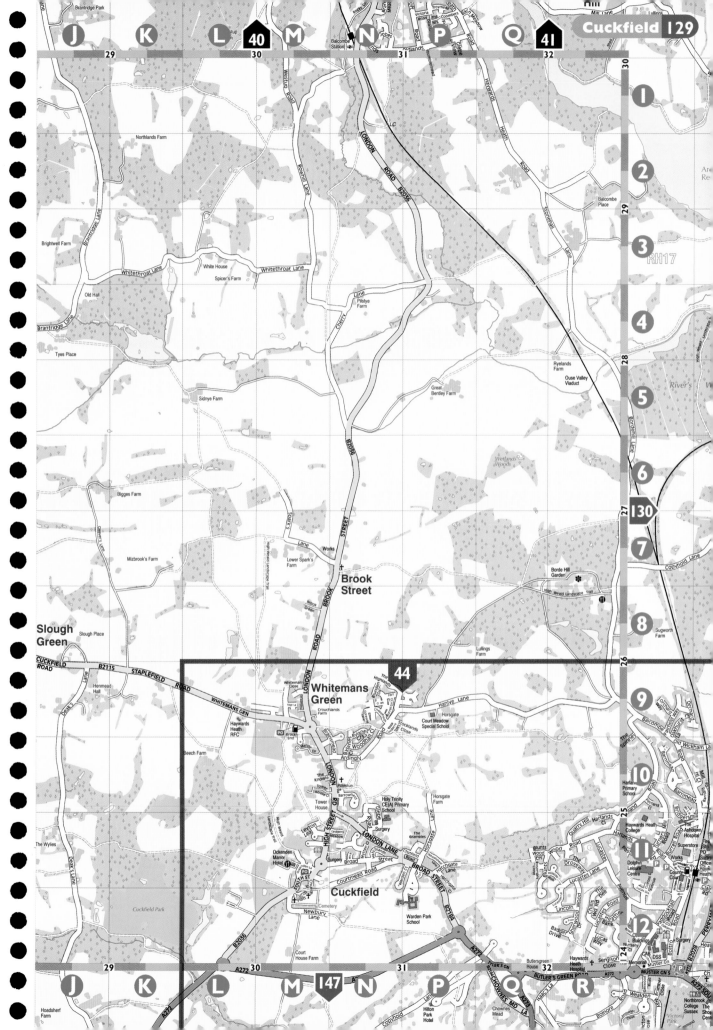

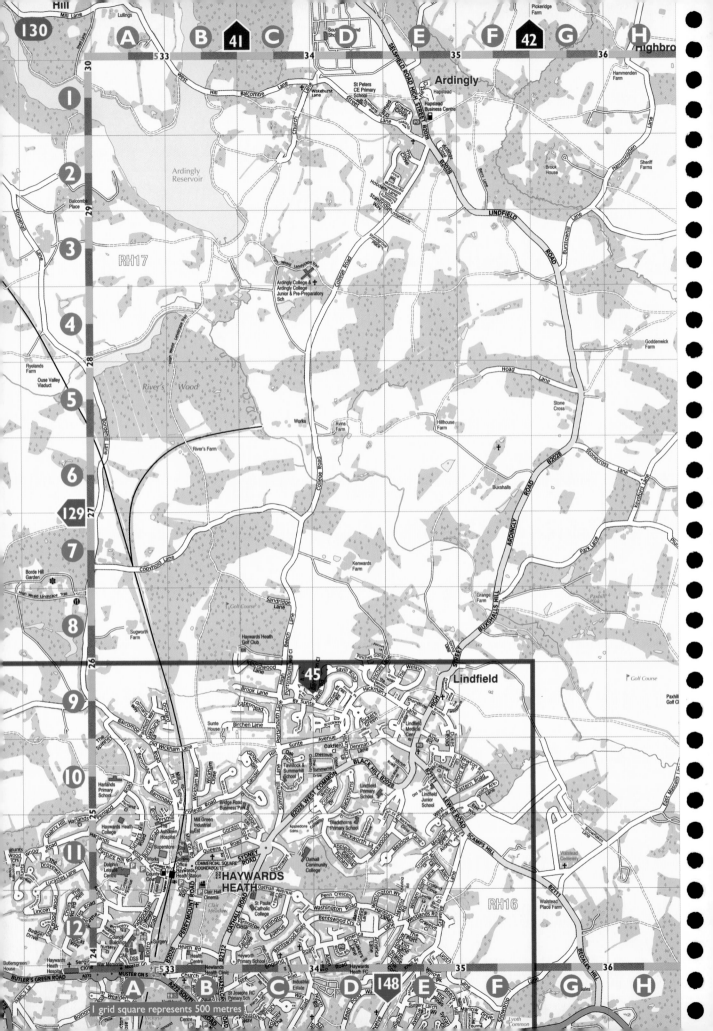

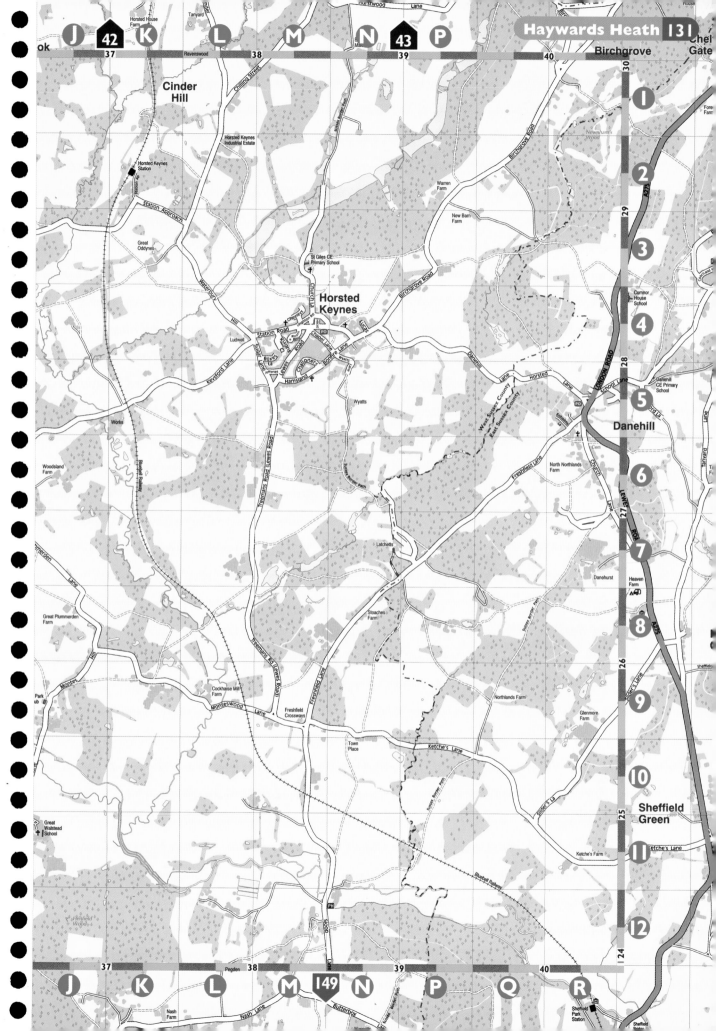

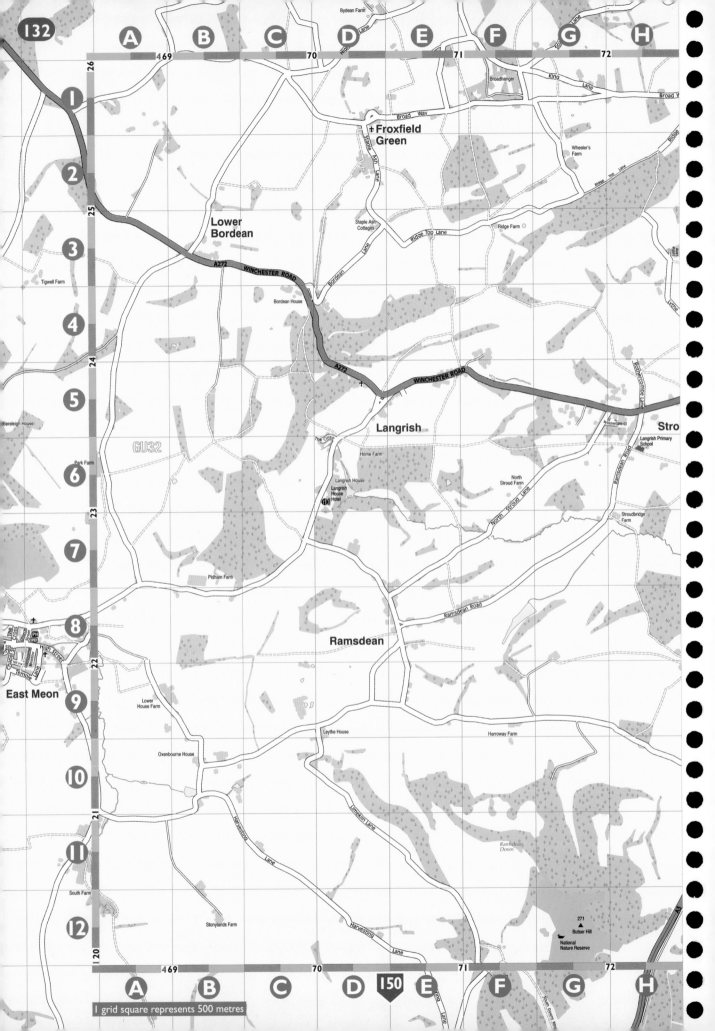

1 grid square represents 500 metres

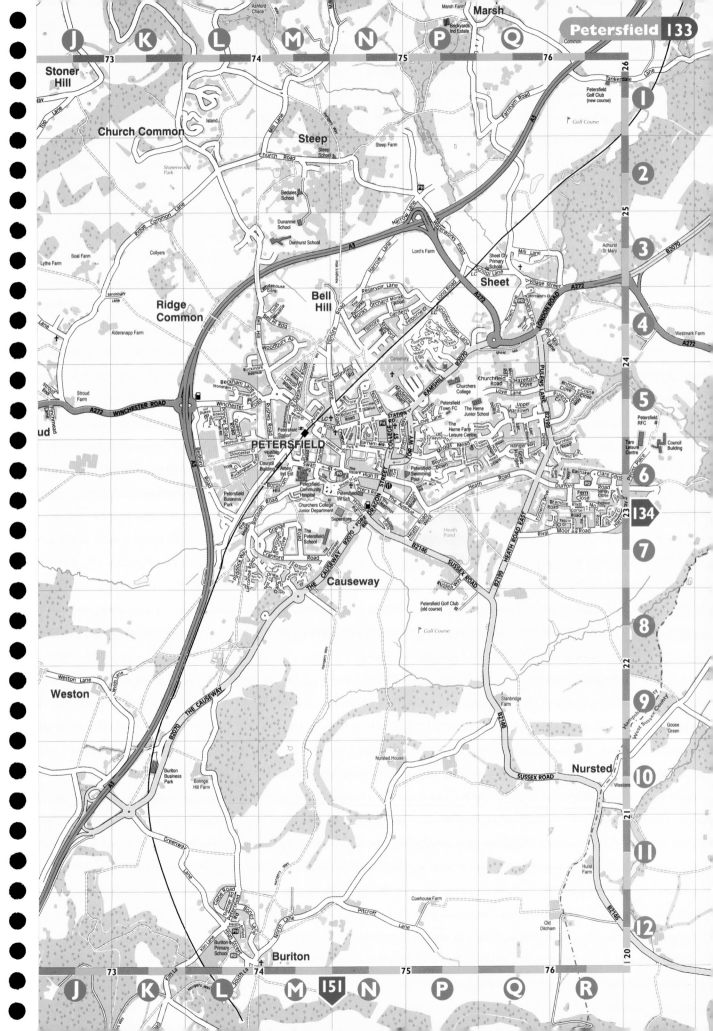

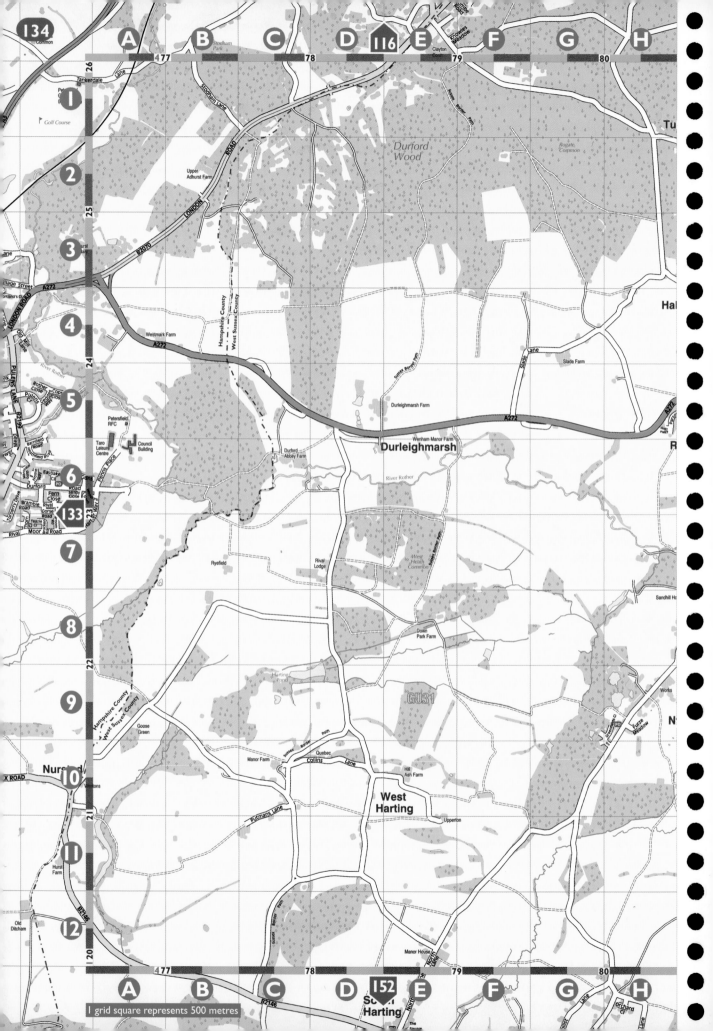

1

Golf Course

Tankerdale

2

Upper Adhurst Farm

3

B2070

Village Street

A272

LONDON ROAD

Hampshire County
West Sussex County

4

Westmark Farm

A272

River Rother

5

Petersfield RFC

Taro Leisure Centre

Council Building

6

Eastlake

Durford

Fern Close

133

7

Ryefield

Rival Lodge

8

Down Park Farm

9

Hampshire County
West Sussex County

Goose Green

Durford Wood

Rogate Common

Durleighmarsh Farm

Wenham Manor Farm

Durleighmarsh

River Rother

West Heath Common

Slade Lane

Slade Farm

A272

Harting Pond

GU31

10

Nursted

X ROAD

B2146

Westons

Putmans Lane

Manor Farm

Sussex Border Path

Quebec

Collins Lane

Hill Ash Farm

11

Hurst Farm

12

Old Ditcham

B2146

West Harting

Upperton

Manor House

North Lane

South Harting

1 grid square represents 500 metres

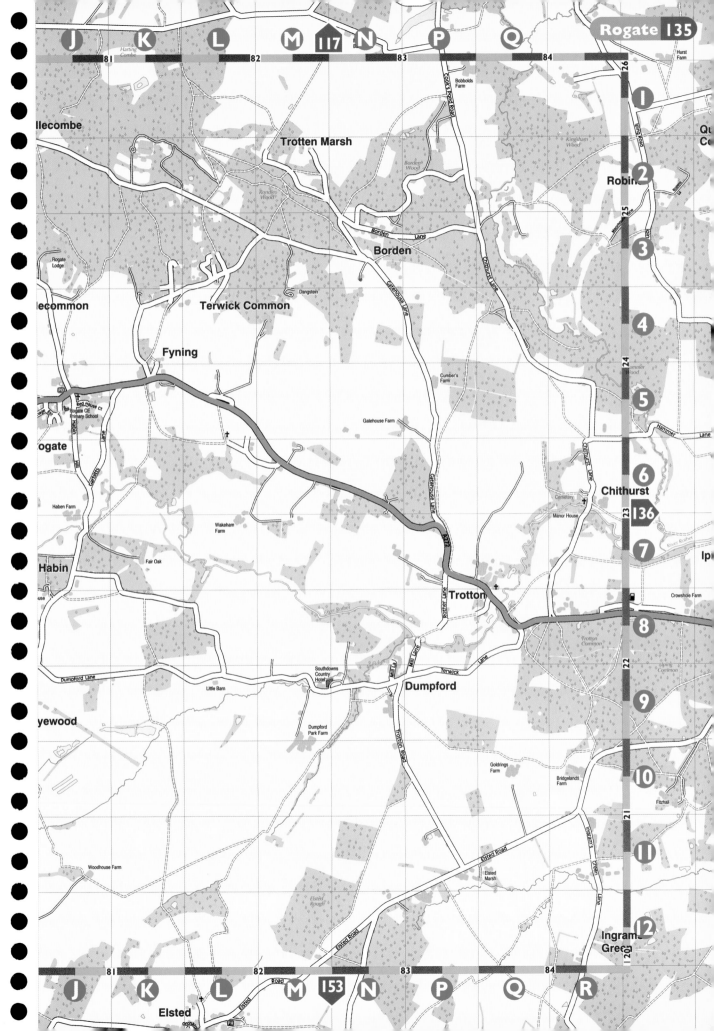

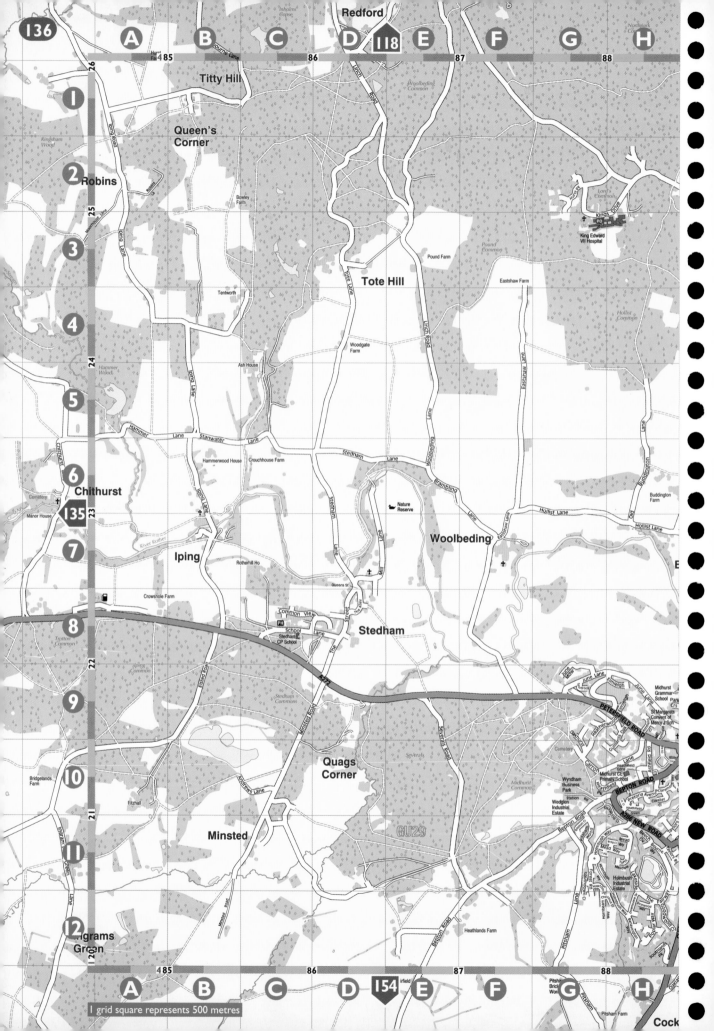

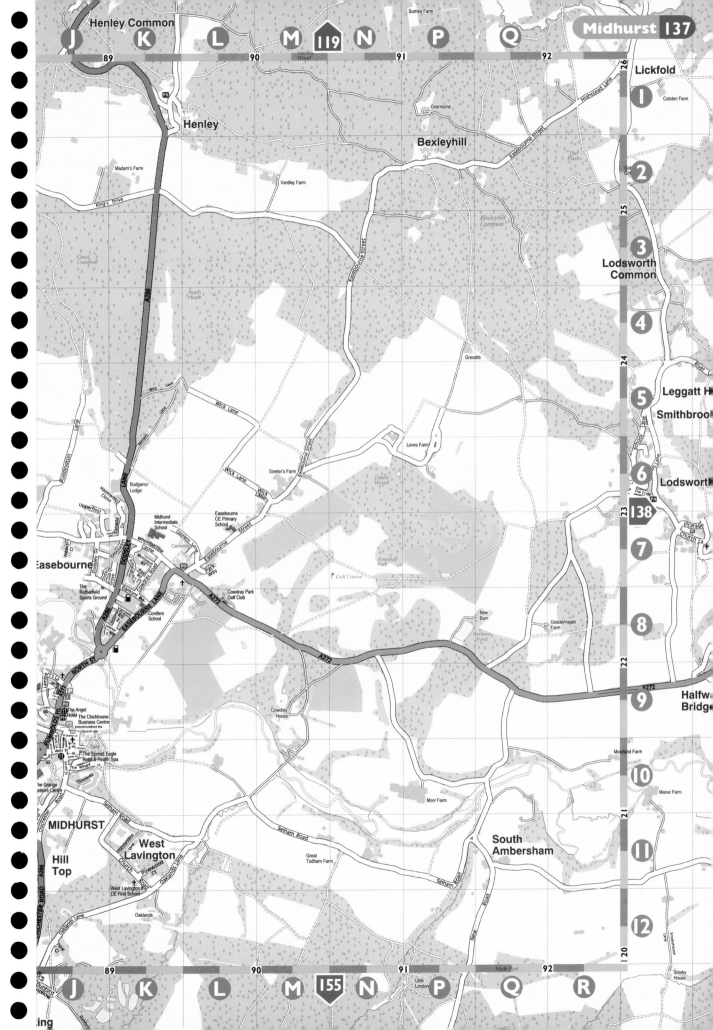

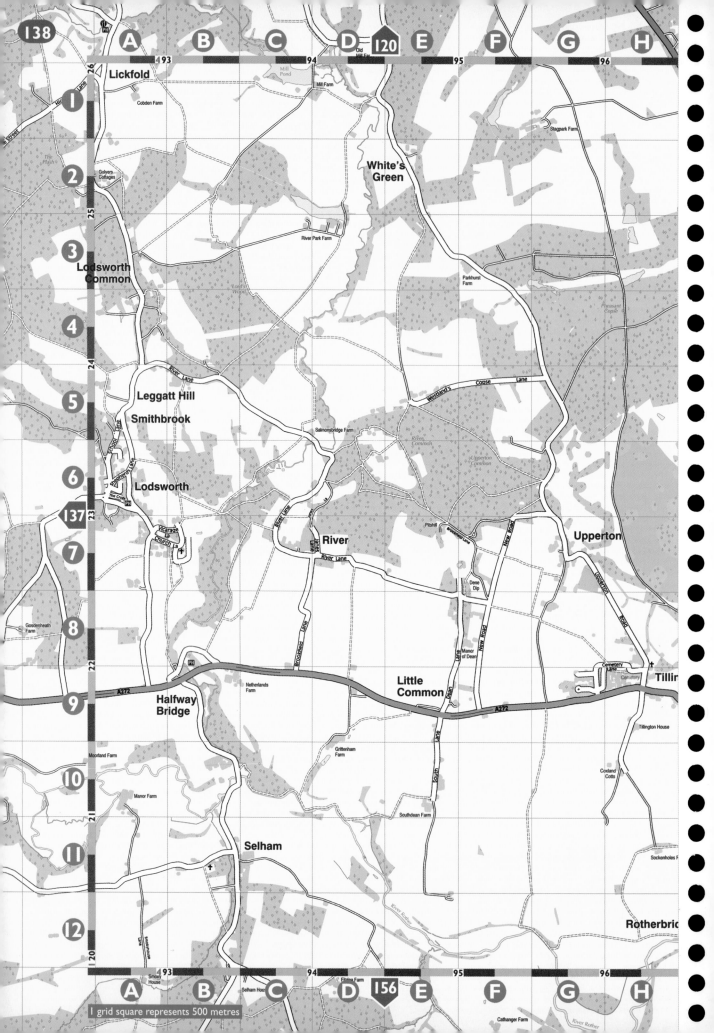

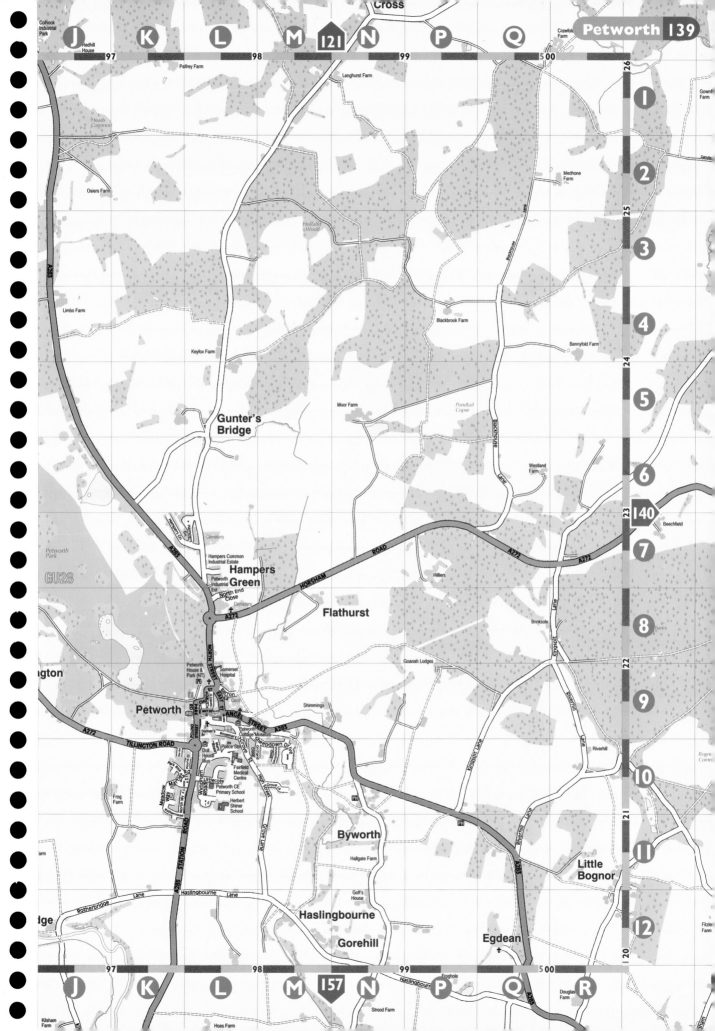

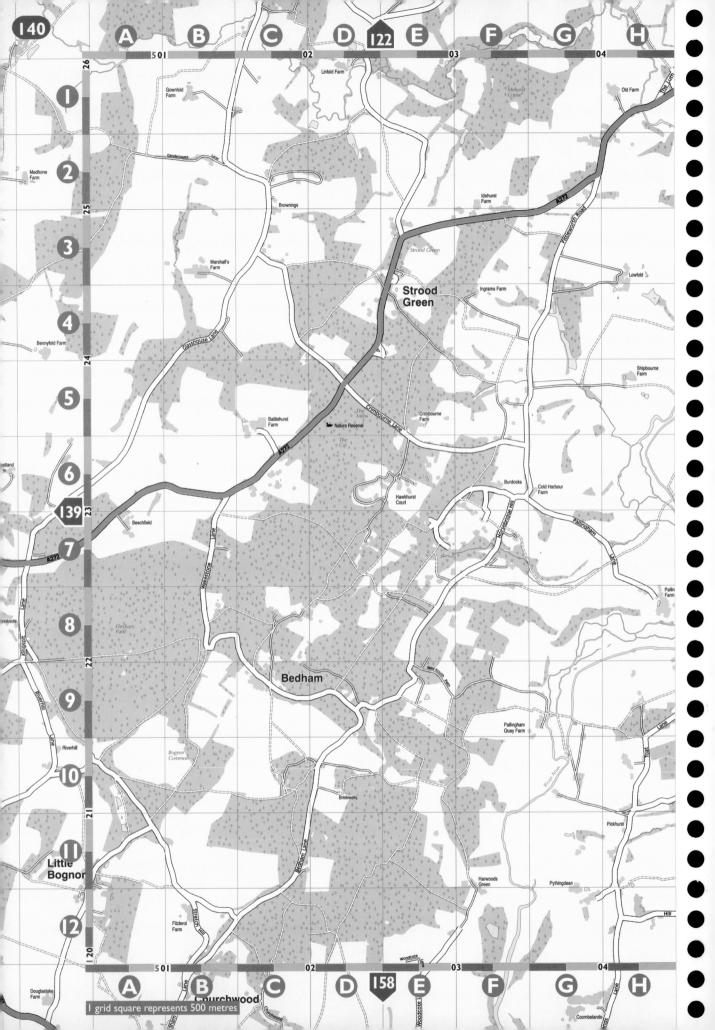

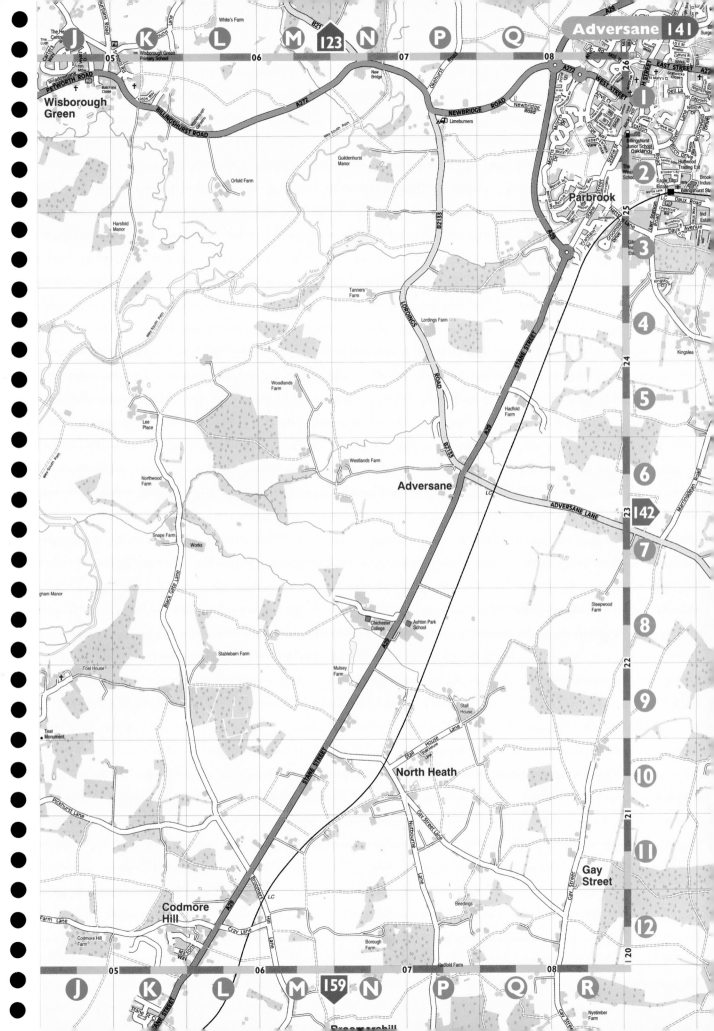

Wisborough Green

Parbrook

Adversane

North Heath

Codmore Hill

Gay Street

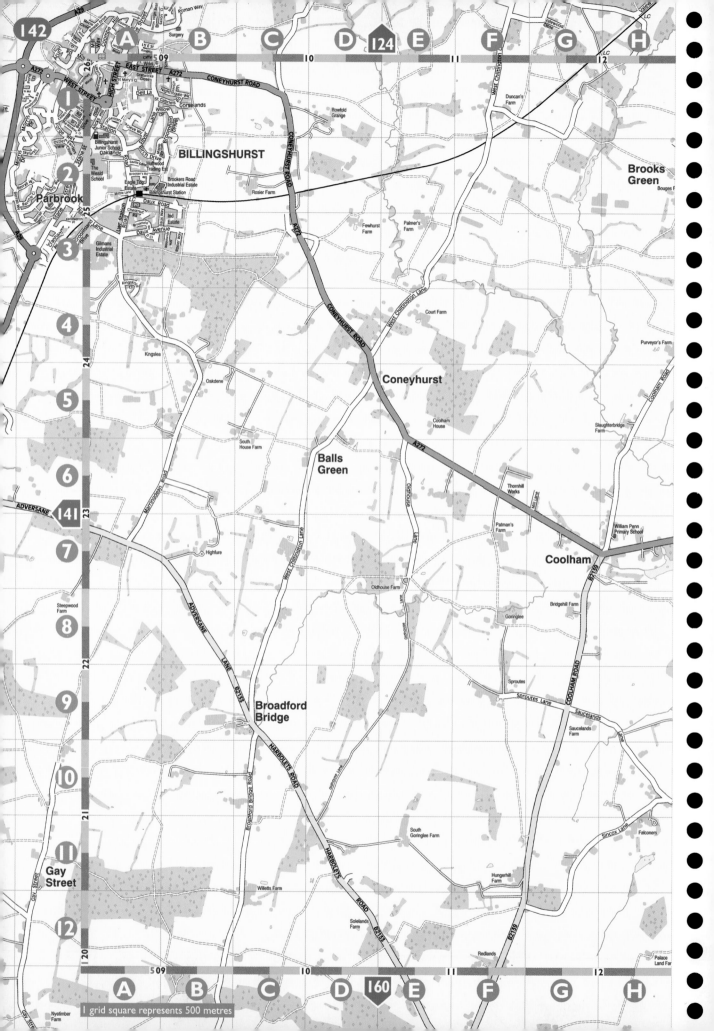

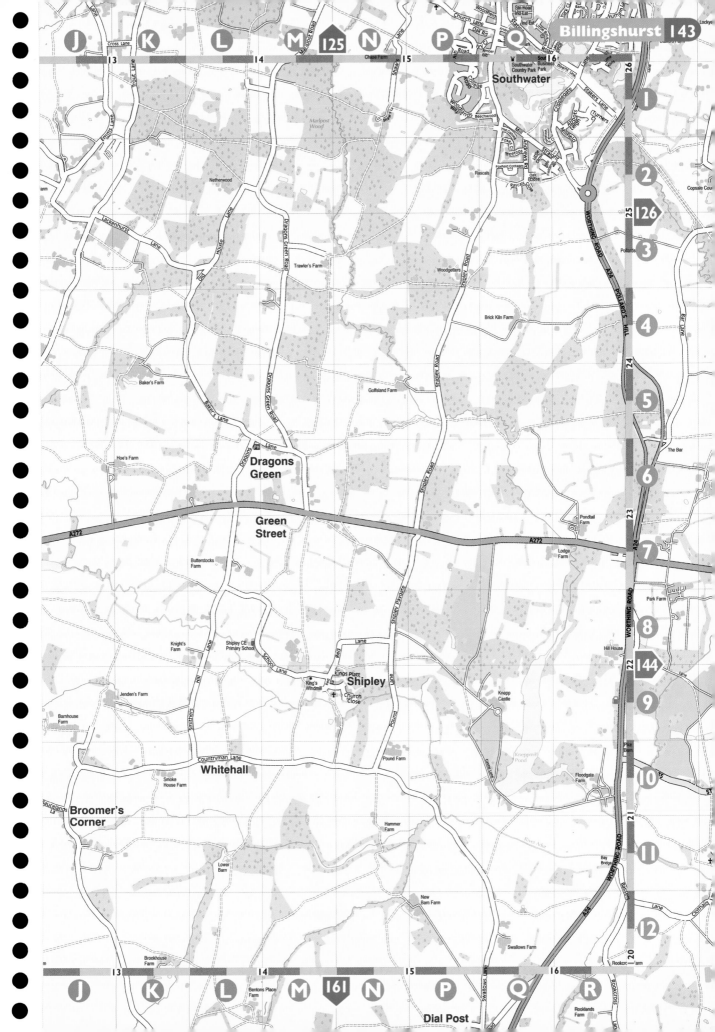

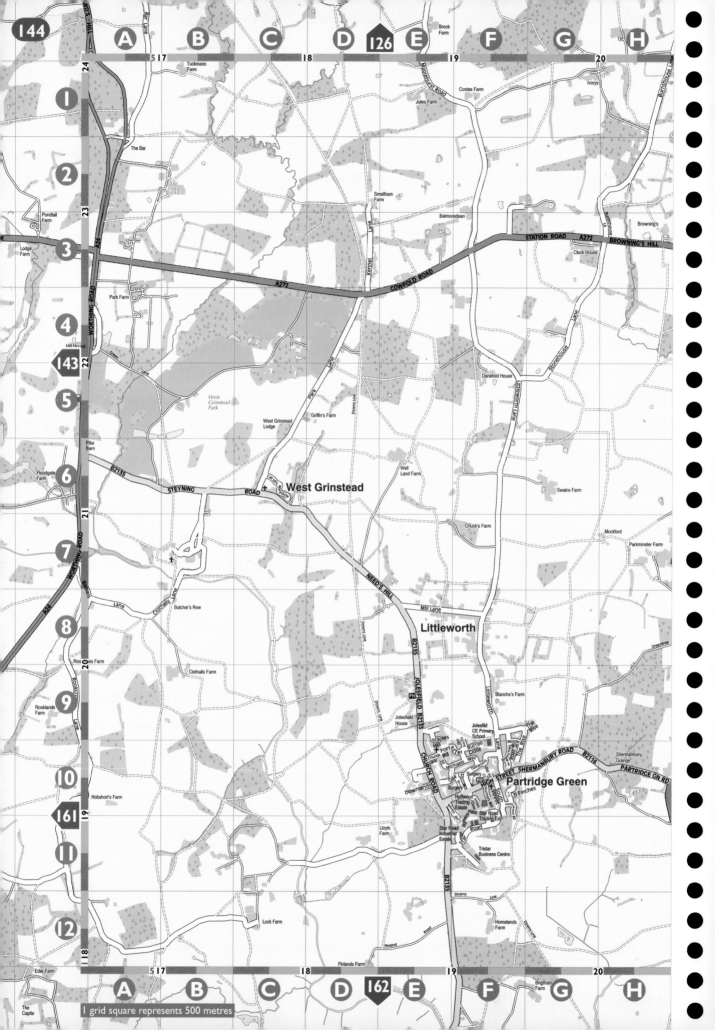

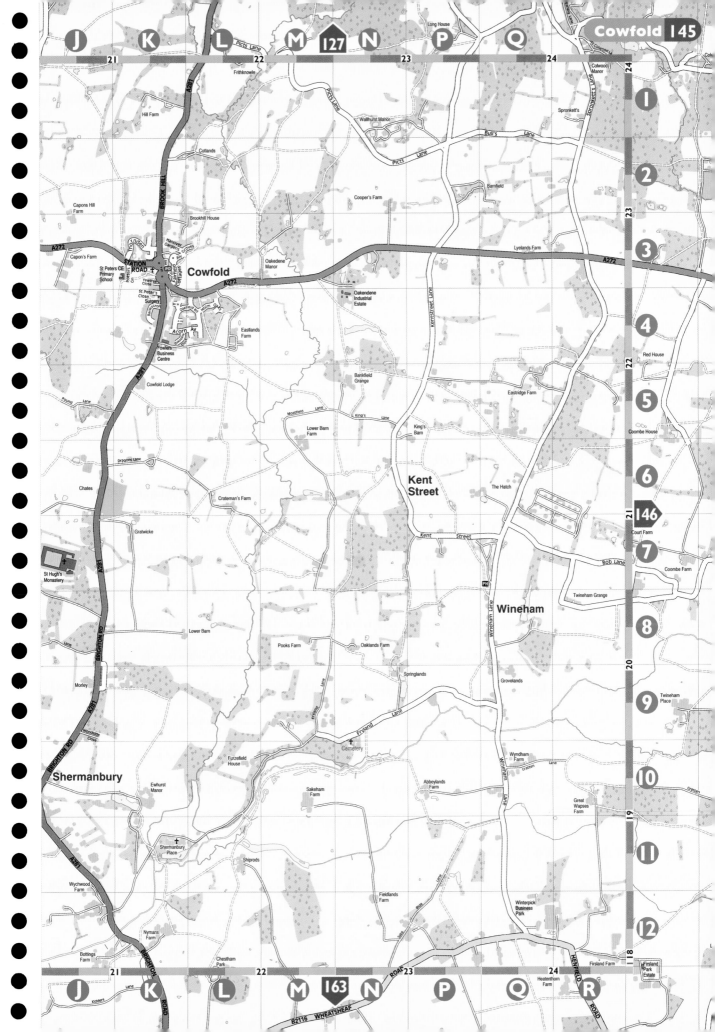

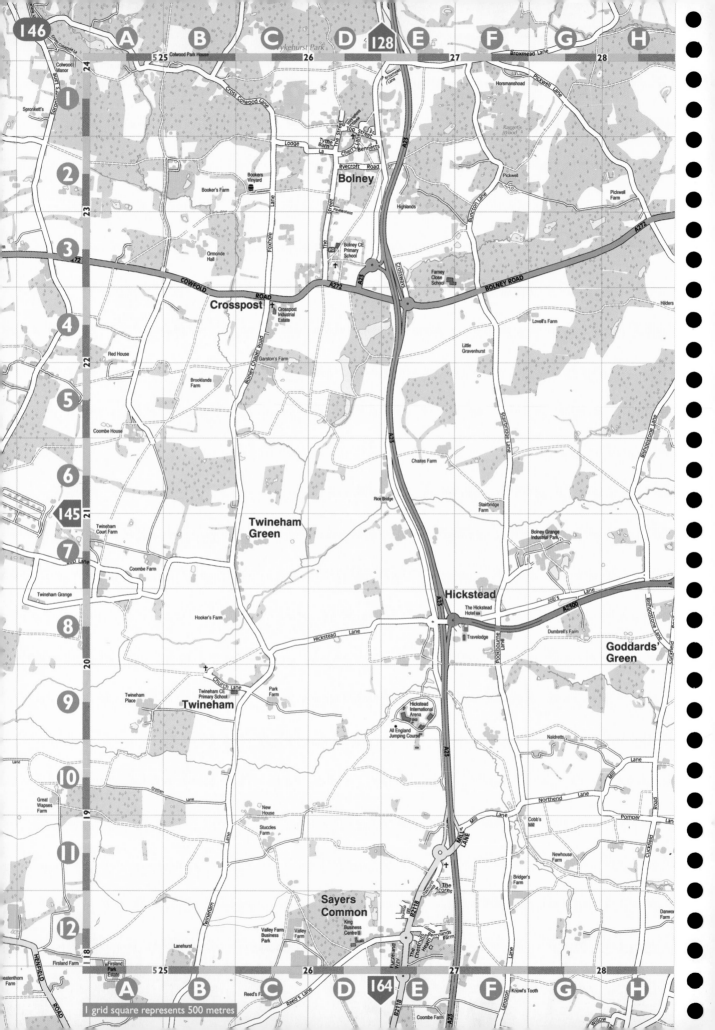

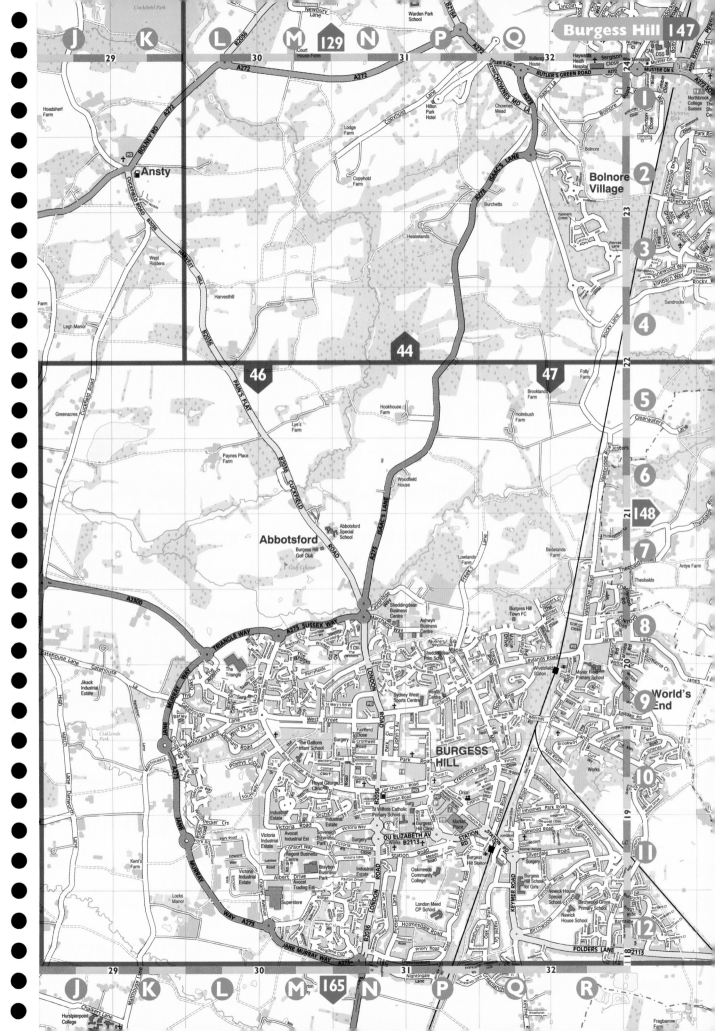

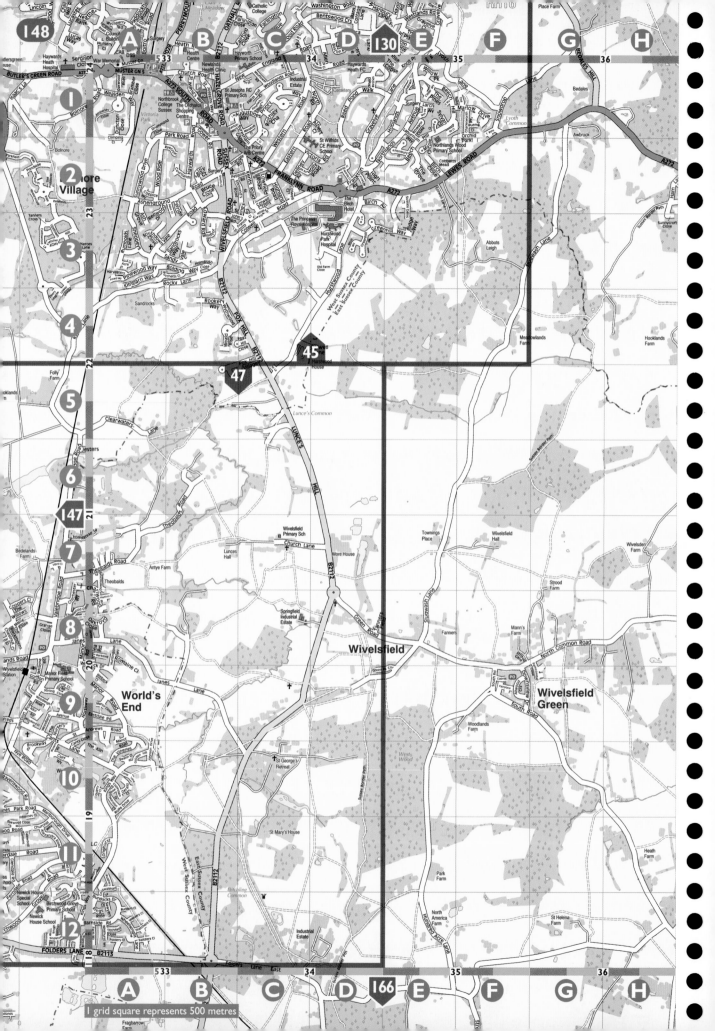

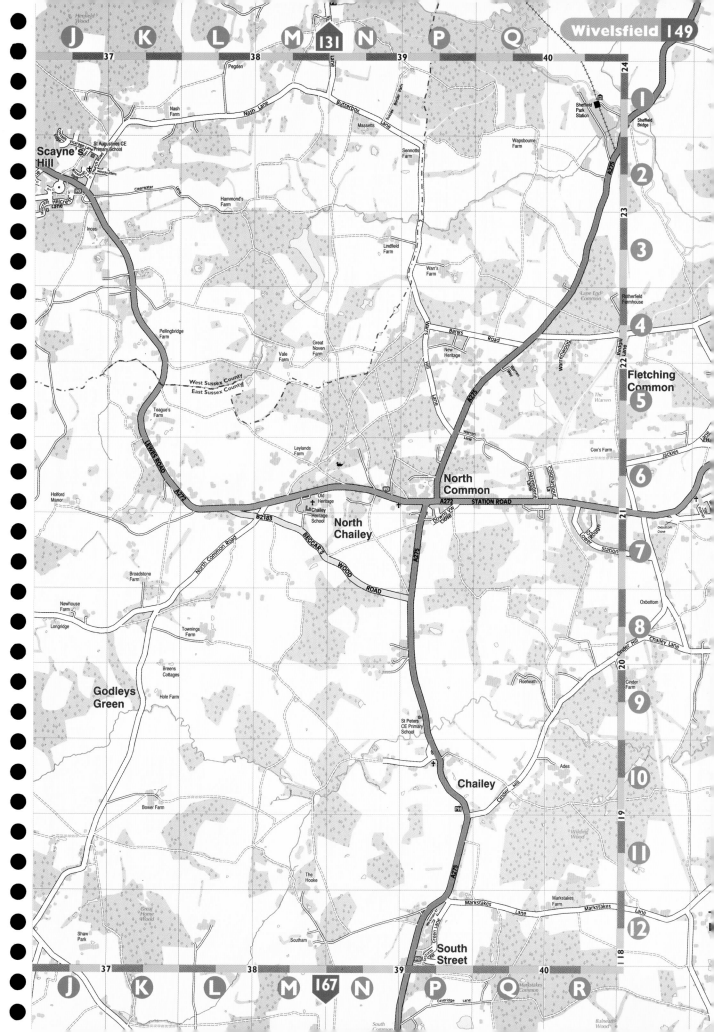

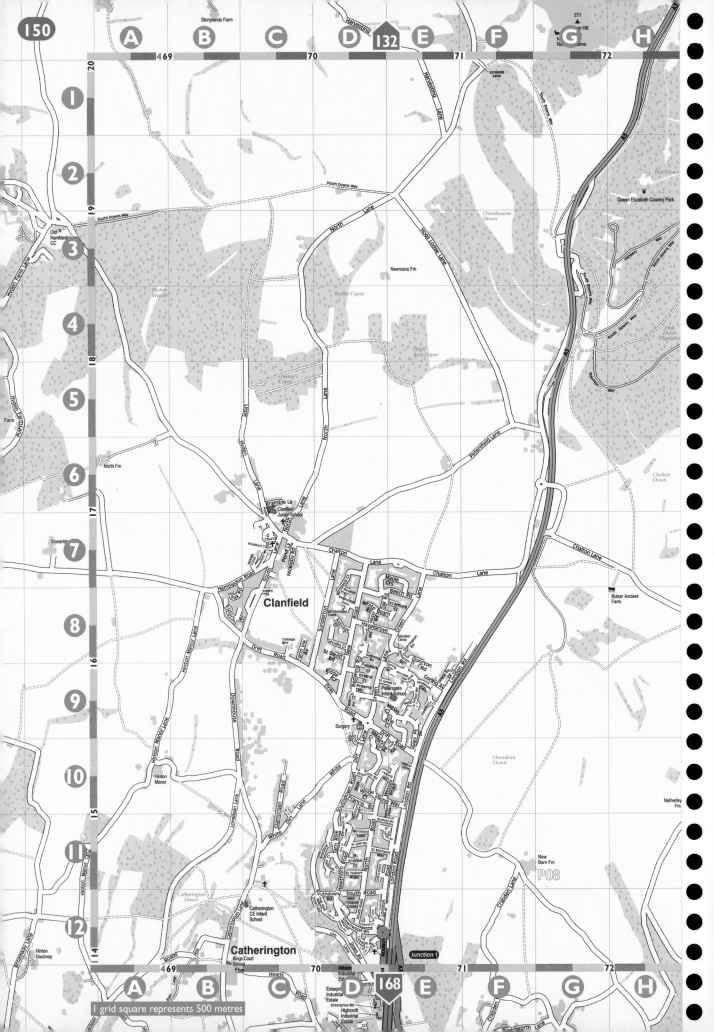

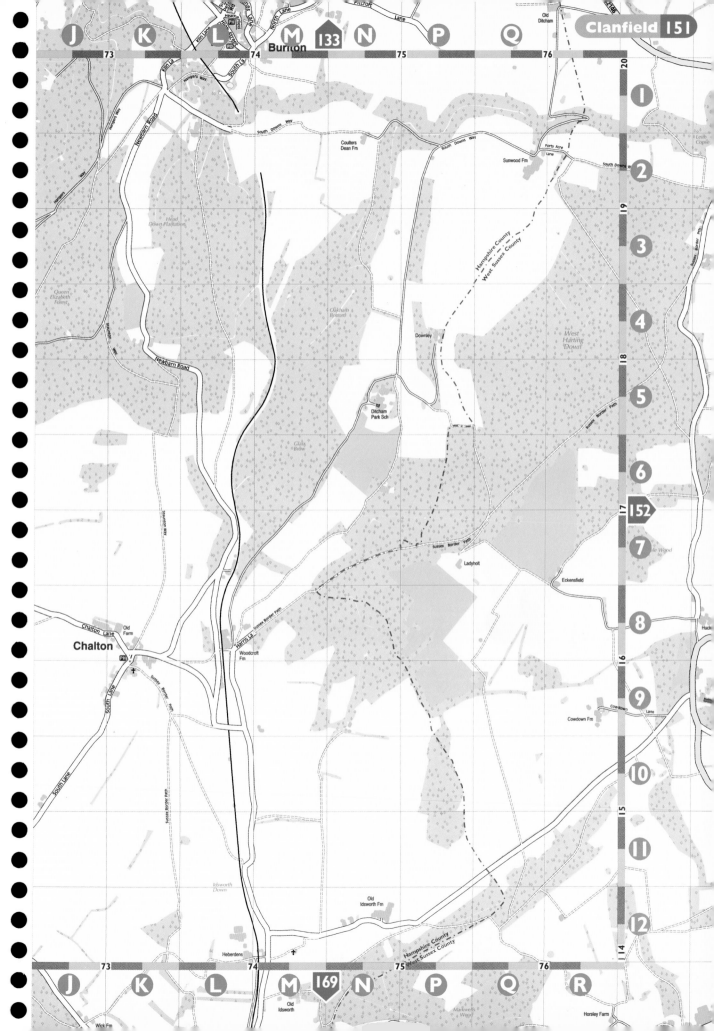

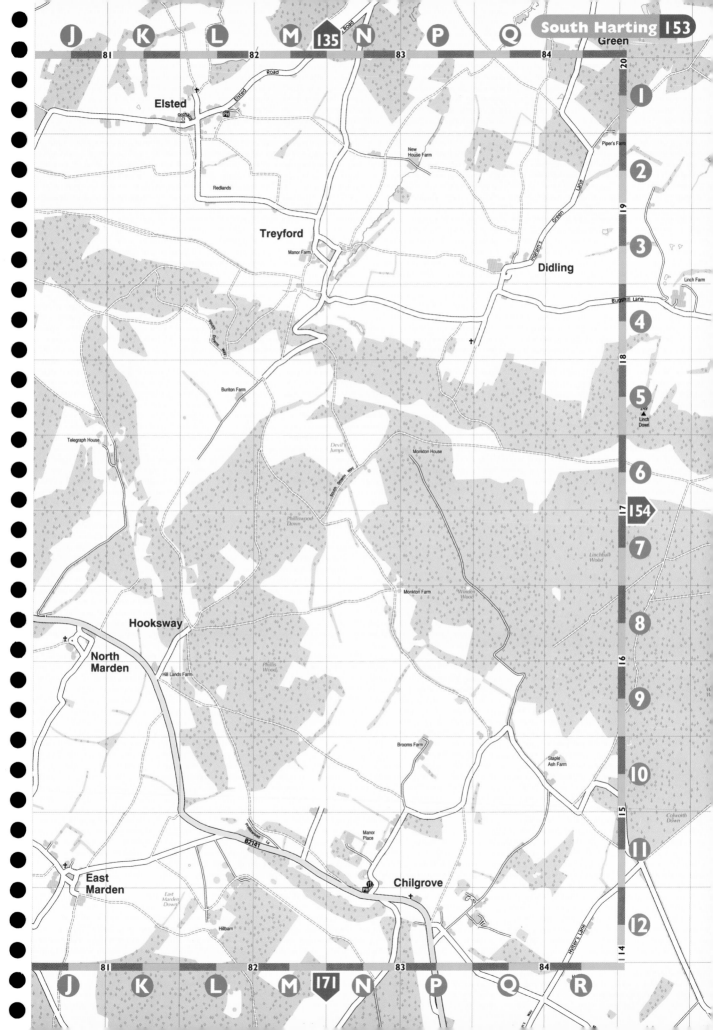

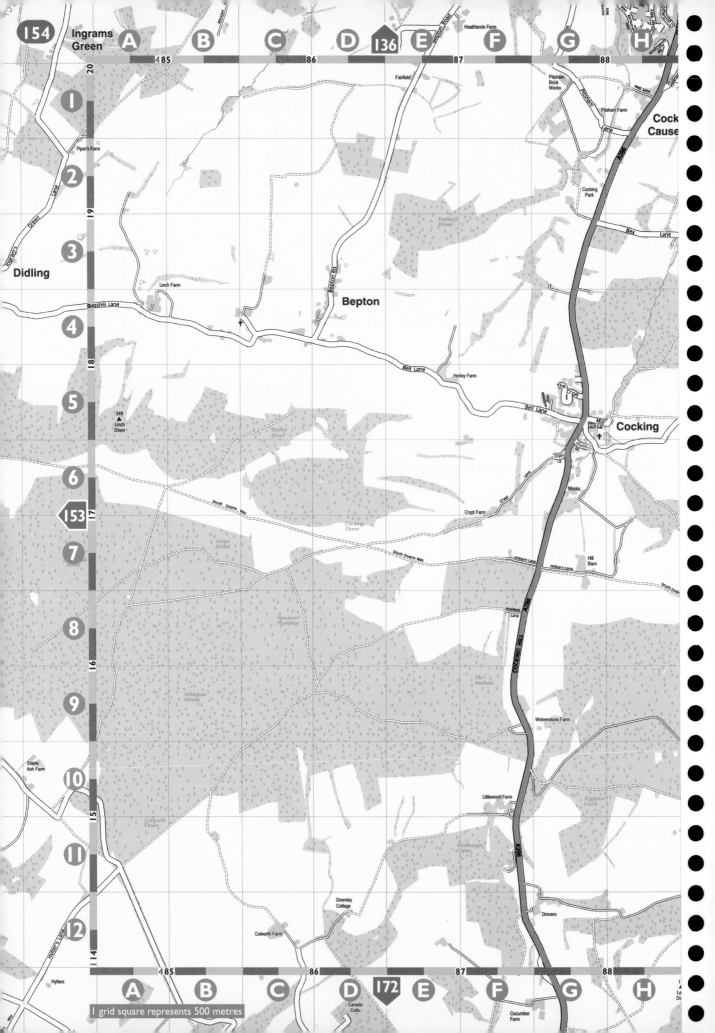

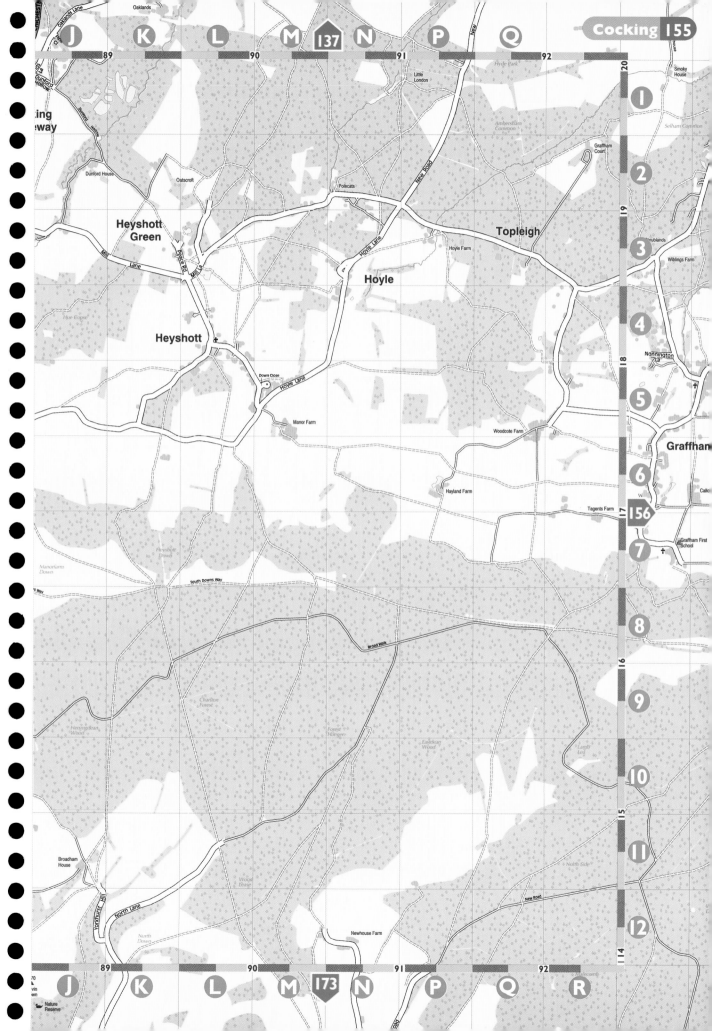

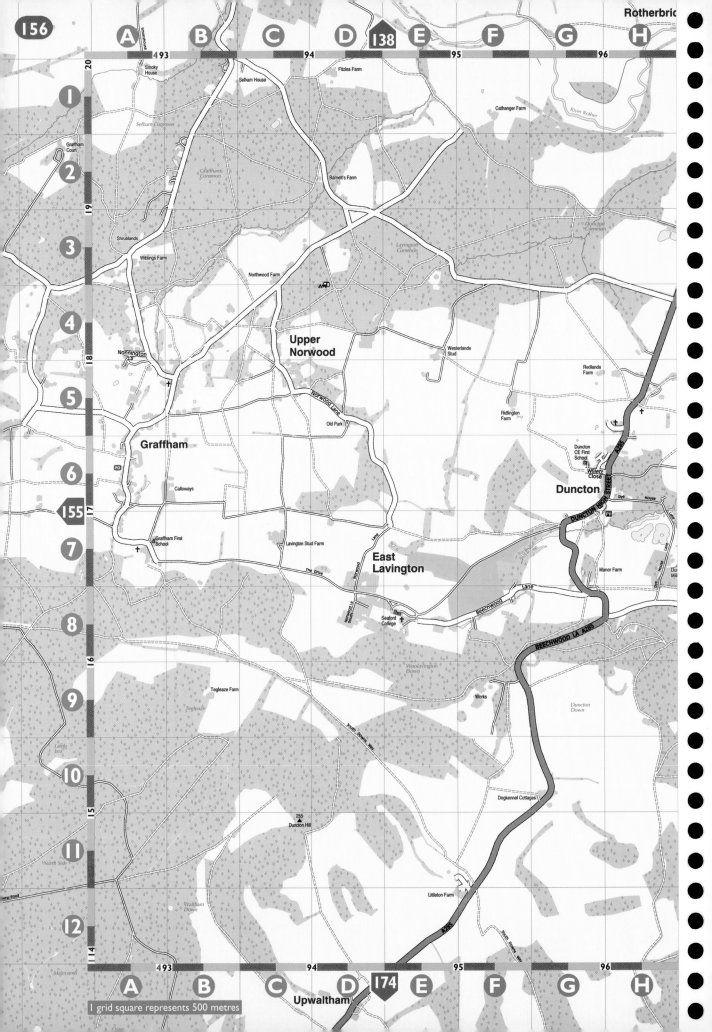

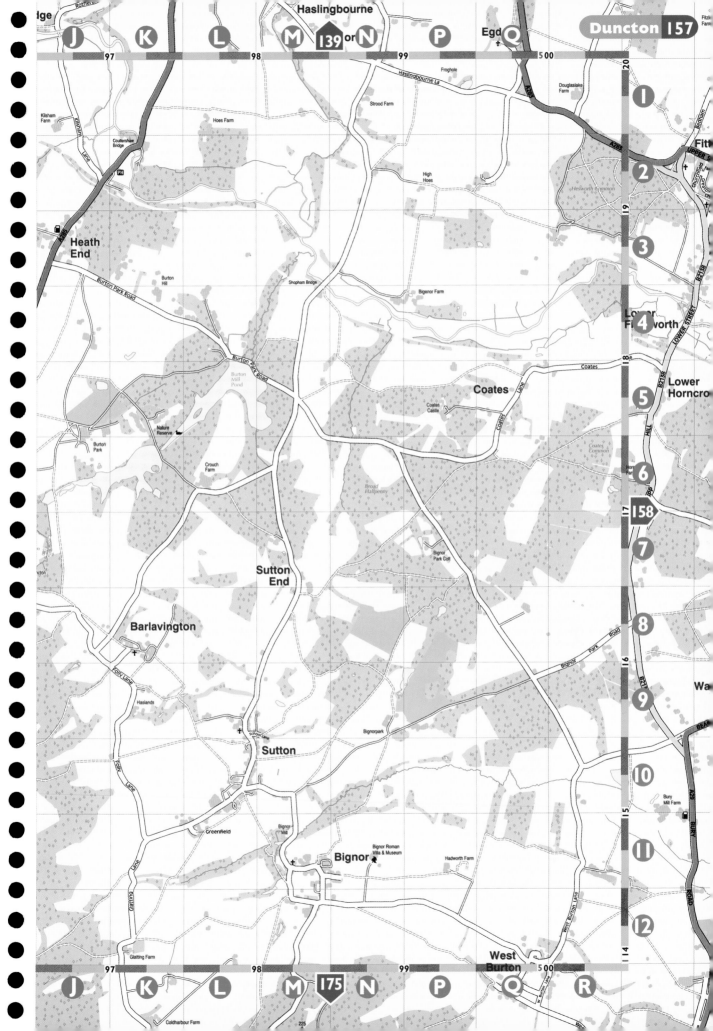

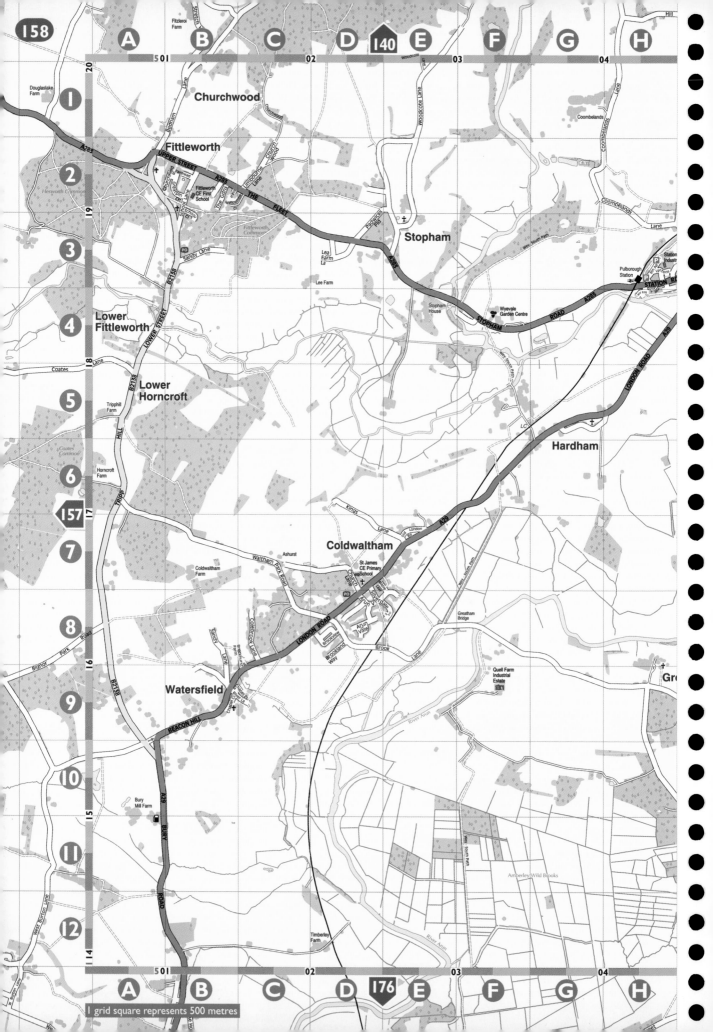

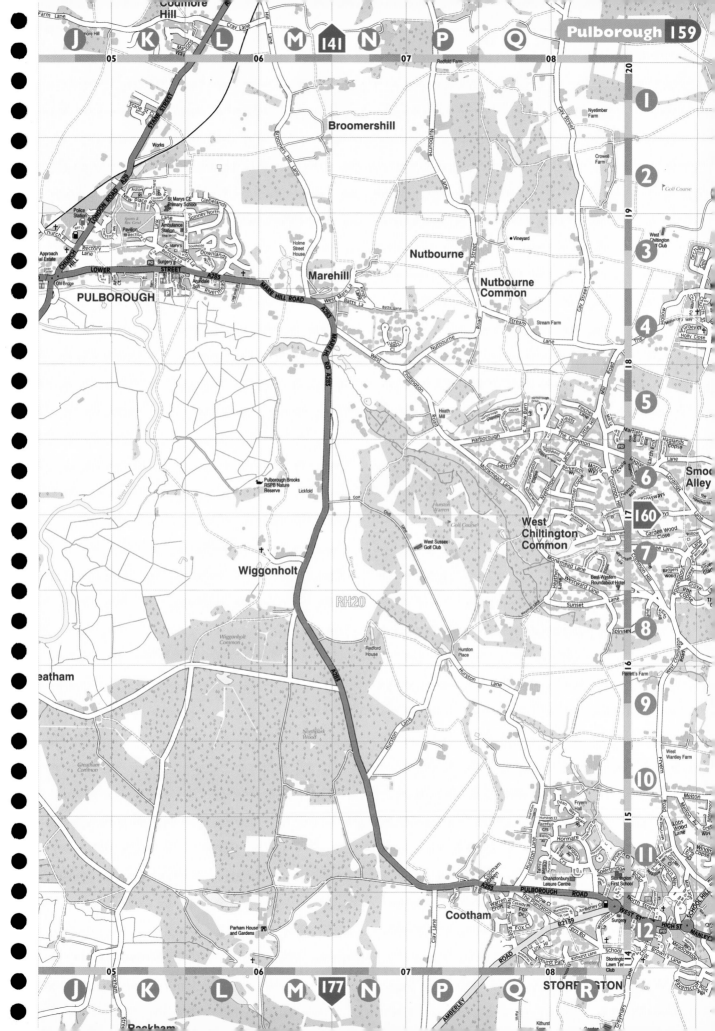

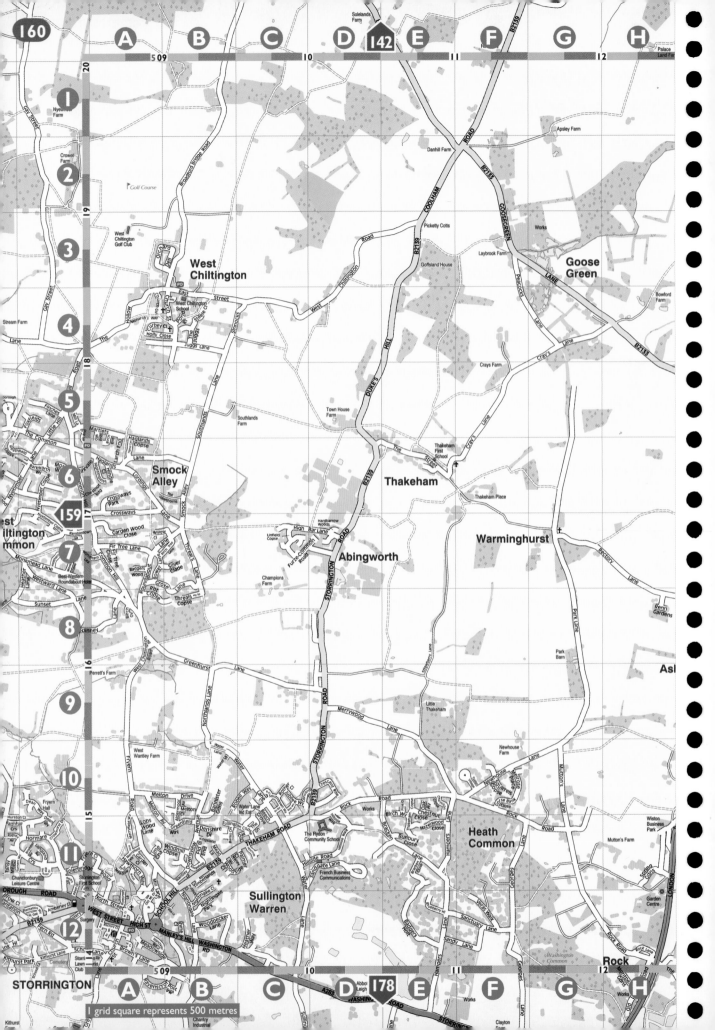

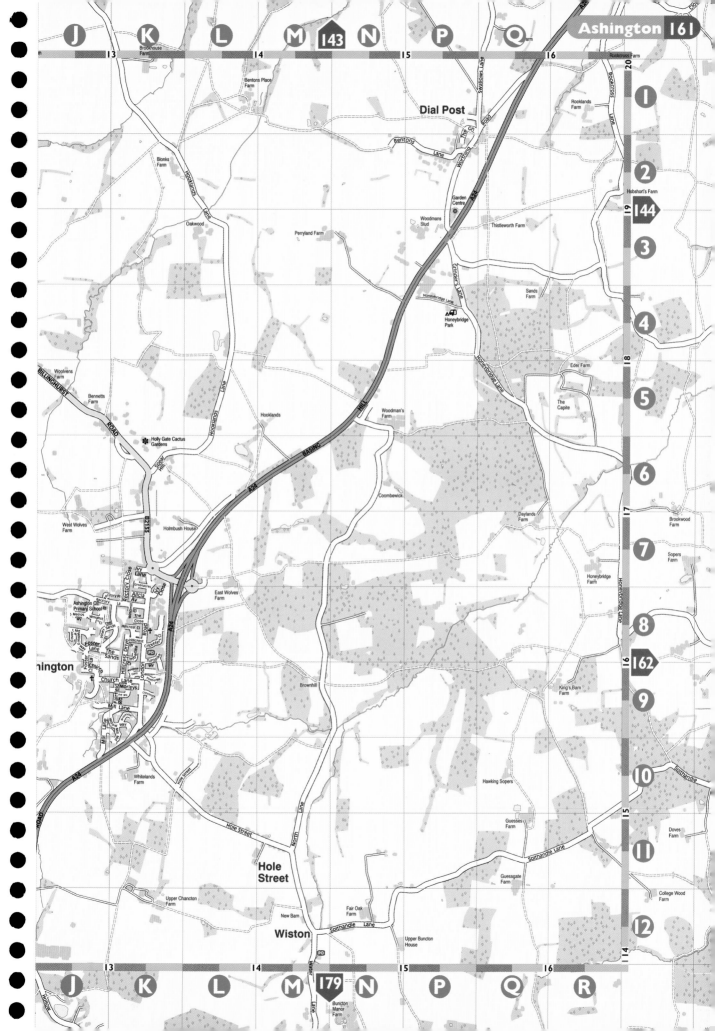

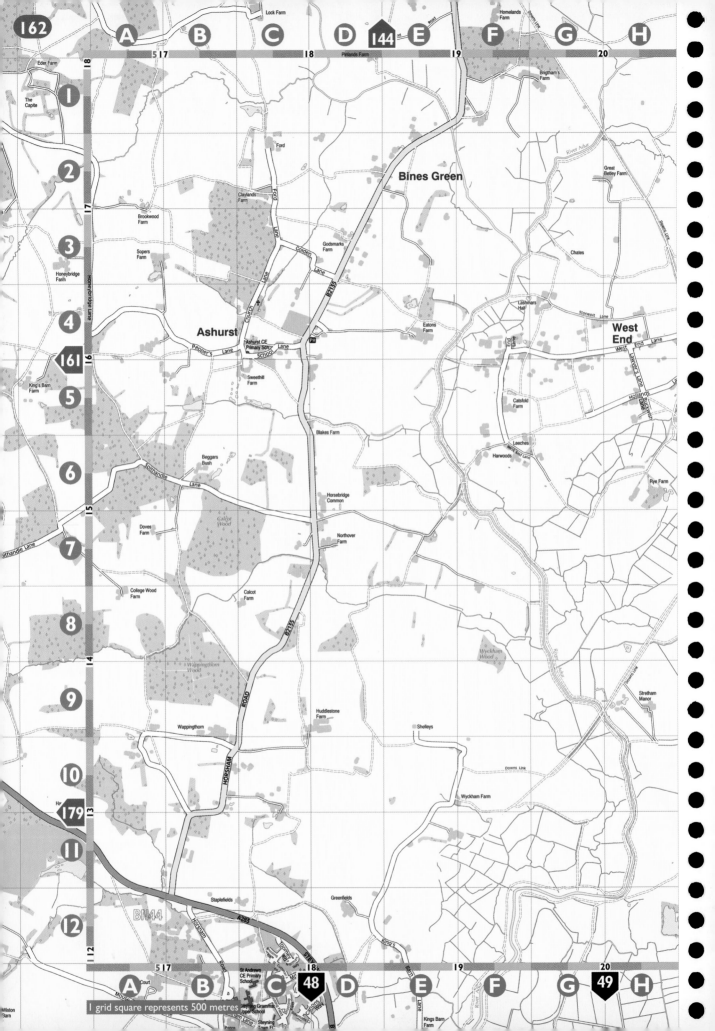

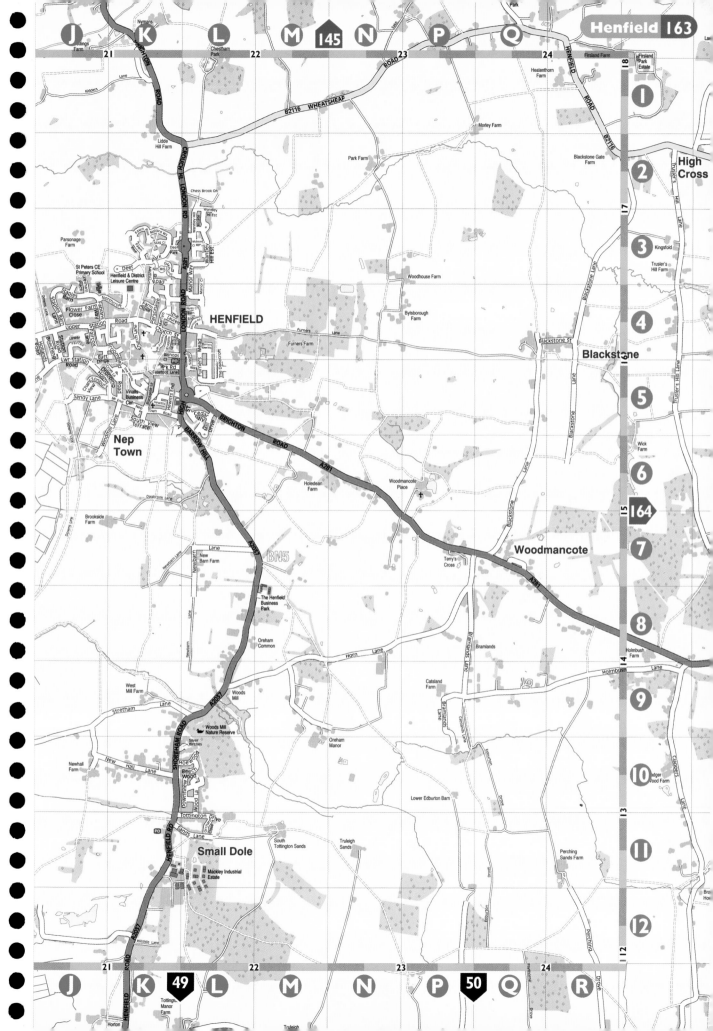

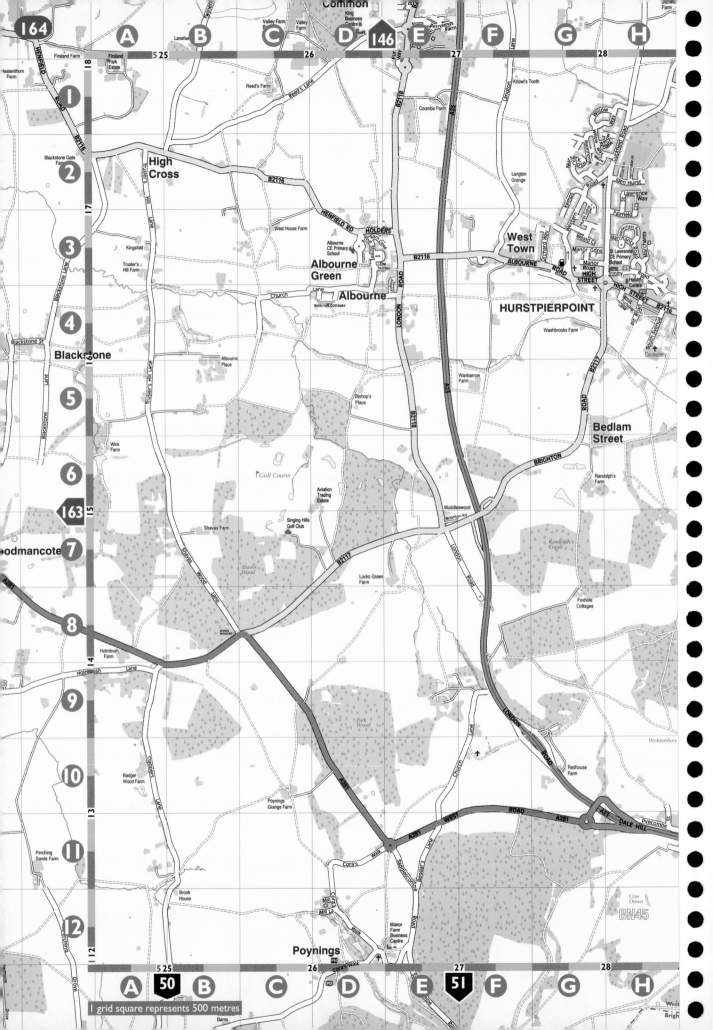

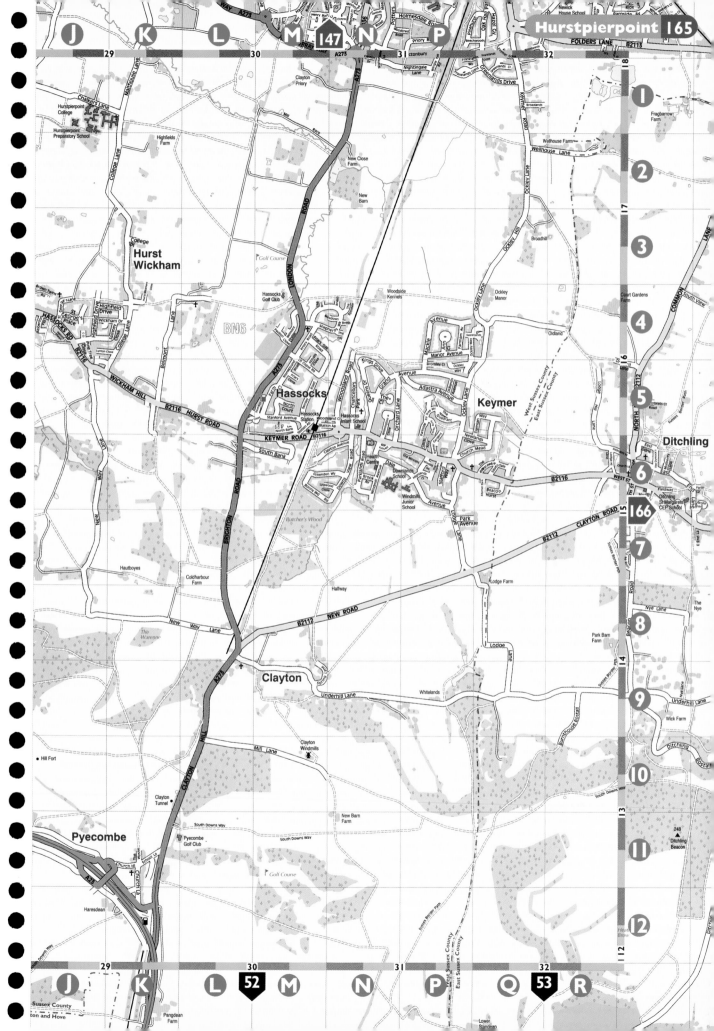

J   K   L   M 147 N   P

29   30   31   32

1

2

3

4

5

6

166

7

8

9

10

11

12

Hurstpierpoint College

Hurstpierpoint Preparatory School

Chalkers Lane

Malthouse Lane

Highfields Farm

College La

College Rd

College Lane

College Lane

Hurst Wickham

Highfield Drive

St George's Place

HASSOCKS RD

Wickham Dr

Highfield Drive

Lynton Close

Belmont

B2116

WICKHAM HILL

B2116 HURST ROAD

Jane Lane

South Bank

New Way Lane

BRIGHTON ROAD

Hautboyes

Coldharbour Farm

The Warenne

A273

Hill Fort

Pyecombe

CLAYTON HILL

Church Hill

School La

Church La

Haresdean

A23

Clayton Tunnel

Mill Lane

Clayton Windmills

Clayton

South Downs Way

Pyecombe Golf Club

Golf Course

New Barn Farm

South Downs Way

South Downs Way

A273 A273 WAY

LONDON ROAD

Clayton Priory

New Close Farm

New Barn

Golf Course

BN6

Hassocks Golf Club

A273

Meadows

Shepherds

Hassocks

North Court

Stanford Avenue

North Bank

Hassocks Station

Station Ap

KEYMER ROAD

B2116

Woodland Lane

Clayton Avenue

Ockenden Wy

Lagwood

Ockley Wy

Brock Rd

Health Centre

Windmills Junior School

Dale Ave

Downlands School

Butcher's Wood

Orchard Lane

Parklands Road

Stafford

Keymer Road

Stamford Ave

Kings Drive

Chancellors Park

Woodsland Road

Grand Avand Manor Avenue

Adastra Avenue

Markle

Keymer

Ockley Lane

Ockley Lane

Church Mead

Newlands Close

Park Avenue

Lower Lane

Tower Lane

B2112 CLAYTON ROAD

B2112 NEW ROAD

New Way Lane

Halfway

Halfway

Lodge Farm

Lodge Lane

Whitelands

Underhill Lane

Woodside Kennels

Ockley Lane

Ockley Lane

Ockley Manor

Oldland

West Sussex County

East Sussex County

B2116

WEST ST

Ditchling

St Margaret's CEP School

East

East

Burnthouse Bostall

Park Barn Farm

Sussex Border Pth

Sussex Border Pth

Underhill Lane

Wick Farm

The Nye

Nye Lane

Ditchling Bostall

South Downs Way

248 Ditchling Beacon

Heath Brow

FOLDERS LANE

B2113

Fragbarrow Farm

Wellhouse Farm

Wellhouse Lane

Broadhill

Court Gardens Farm

South View

COMMON LANE

NORTH

B2112

OCKLEY ROAD

KEYMER ROAD

Newick House School

Holmesdale Rd

Priory Rd

Nightingale Lane

Greenlands Drive

8

17

16

15

14

13

12

J   K 52 L   M   N   P   Q 53 R

29   30   31   32

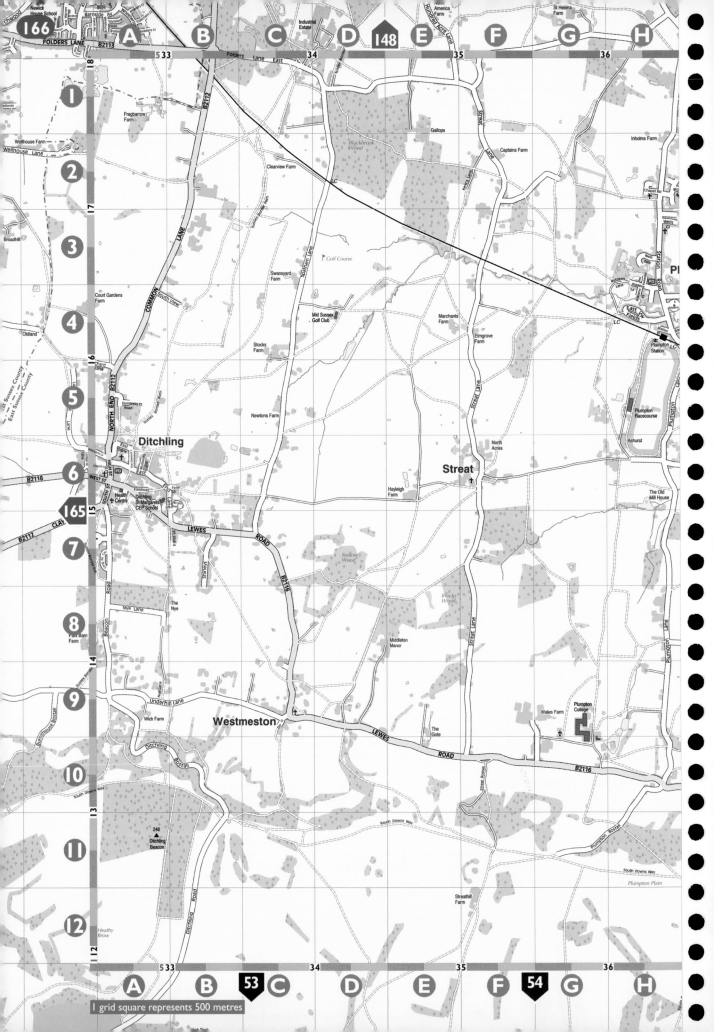

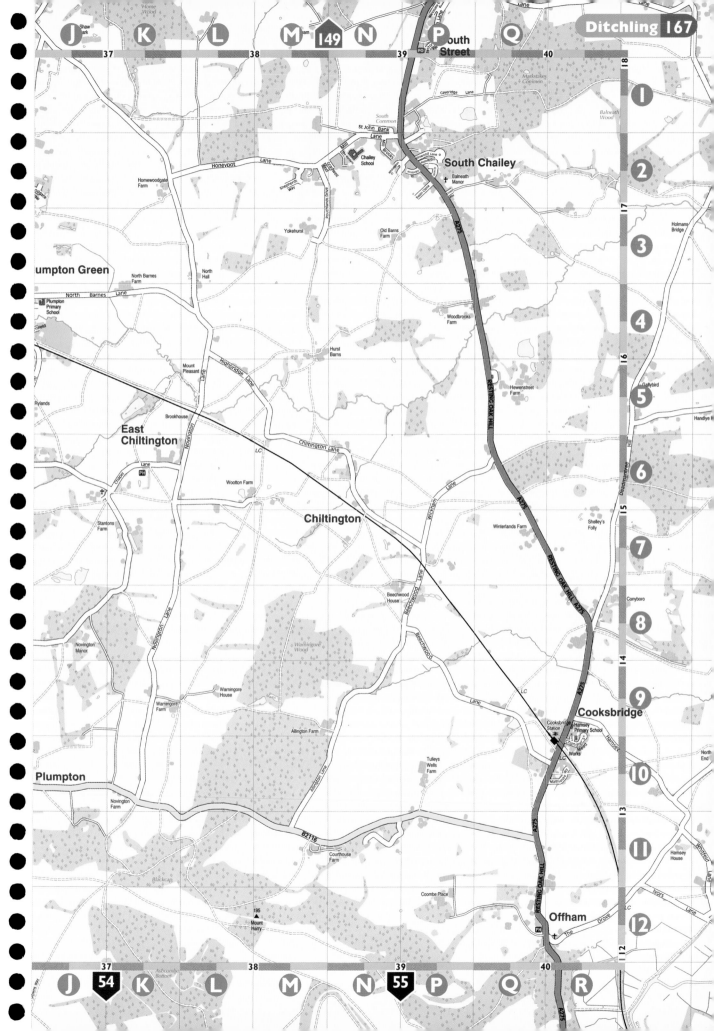

37   38   39   40

South Common

South Chailey

St John   Bank
Lane

Mill

Chailey School

Balneath Manor

Markstakes Common

Balneath Wood

Homewoodgate Farm

Honeypot   Lane

Shepherds   Way

Pouchlands Drive

Yokehurst

Old Barns Farm

Holmans Bridge

Plumpton Green

North Barnes Farm

North Hall

Woodbrooks Farm

Gallybird

Plumpton Primary School

North   Barnes   Lane

Highbridge Lane

Mount Pleasant

Hurst Barns

Hewenstreet Farm

Deadmantree Hill

Handlye

Rylands

Brookhouse

East Chiltington

Chiltington Lane

LC

Novington   Lane

Witchen   Lane

RESTING OAK HILL

A275

Shelley's Folly

Croxton   Lane

PH

Wootton Farm

Chiltington

Winterlands Farm

Stantons Farm

Beechwood House

Conyboro

Warningore Wood

Beechwood

Novington Manor

Warningore House

Warningore Farm

Allington Farm

Lane

LC

A275

Cooksbridge

Plumpton

Allington Lane

Novington Farm

Tulleys Wells Farm

Cooksbridge Station

Hamsey Primary School

Hamsey Works

LC

Malthouse

North End

Hamsey

B2116

Courthouse Farm

Coombe Place

Malthouse

Ivors

Hamsey House

Blackcap

195
Mount Harry

Offham

The   Drove

RESTING OAK HILL

PH

Whitfeld   Lane

LC

Ashcombe Bottom

37   38   39   40

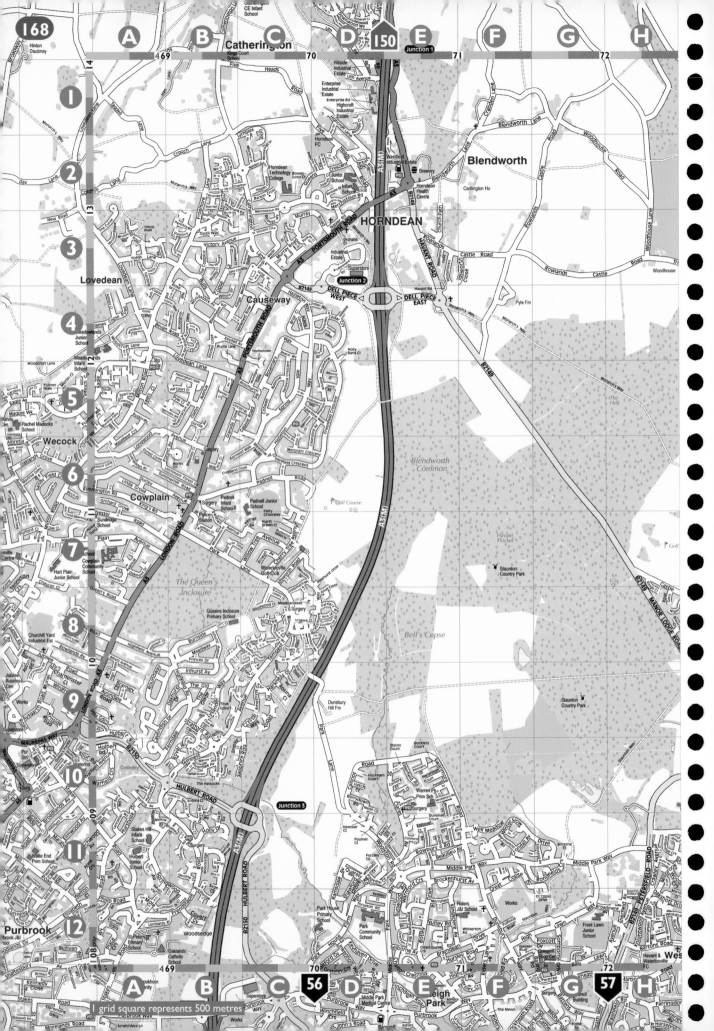

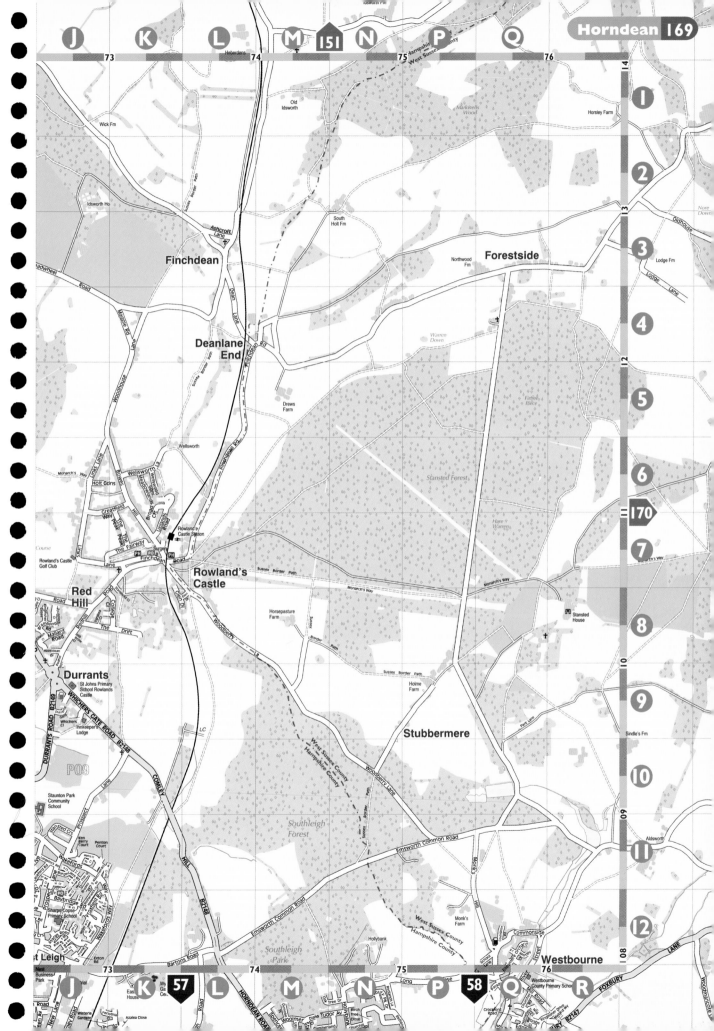

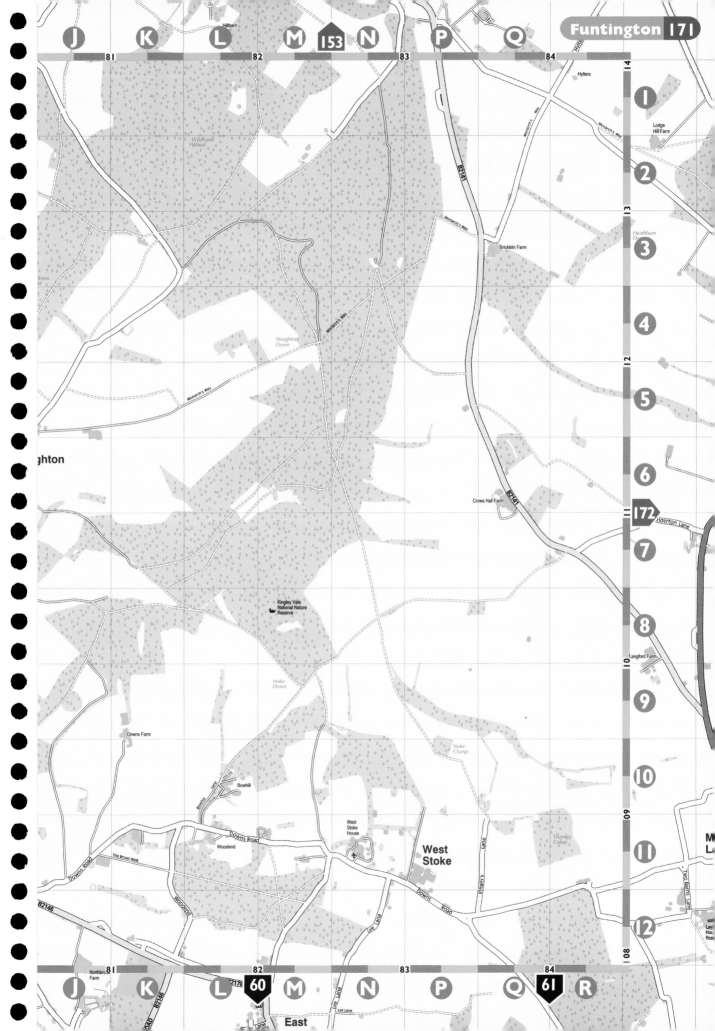

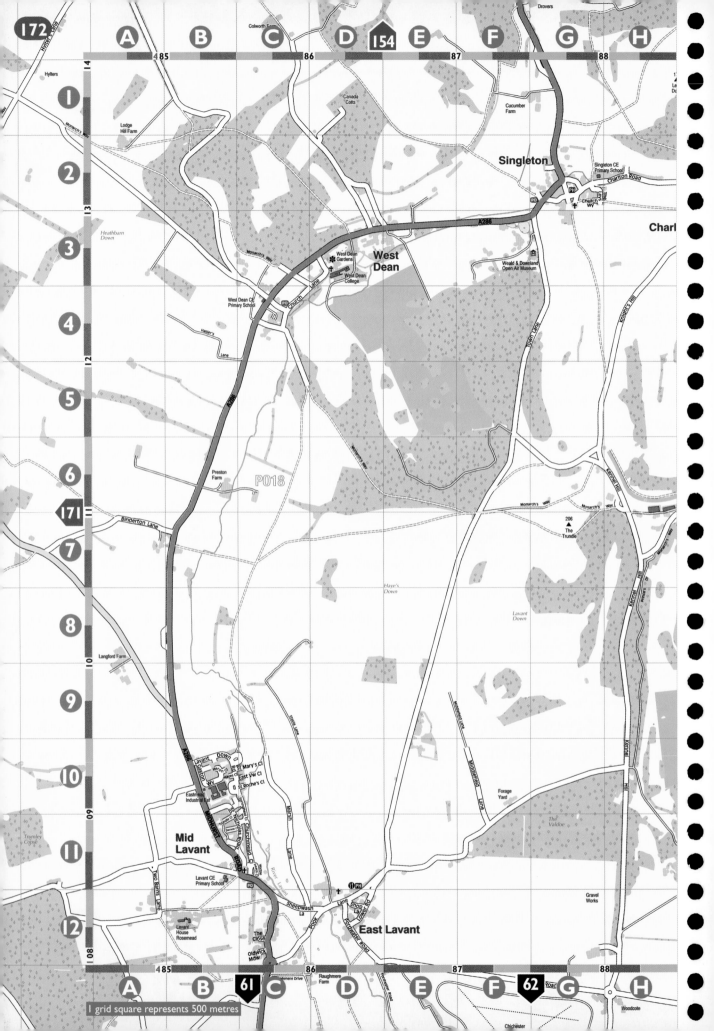

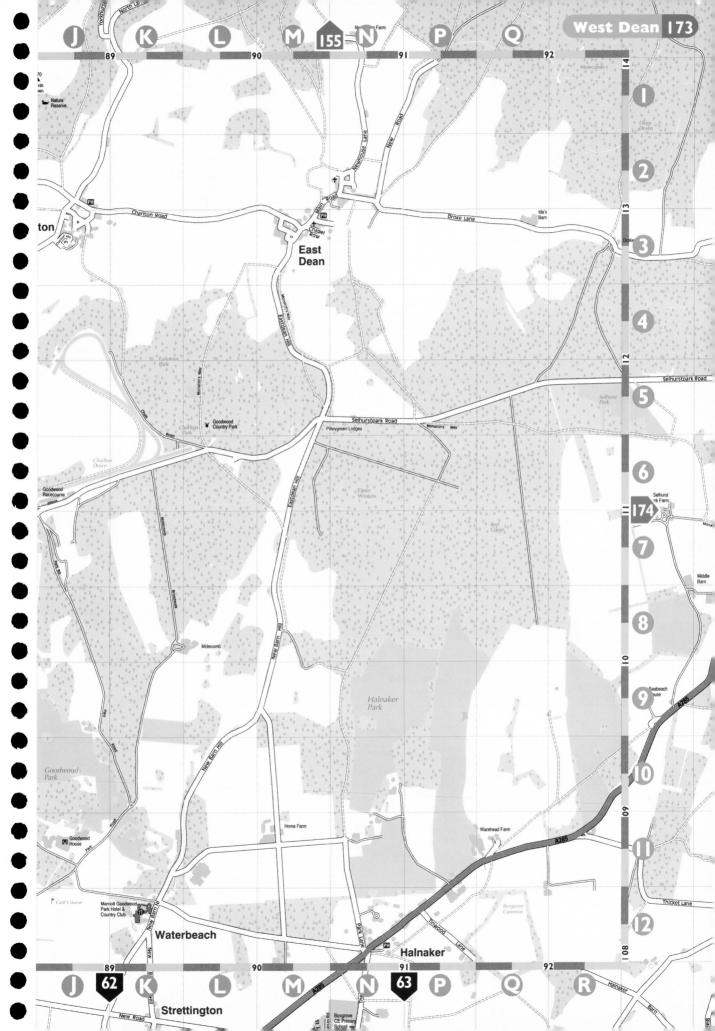

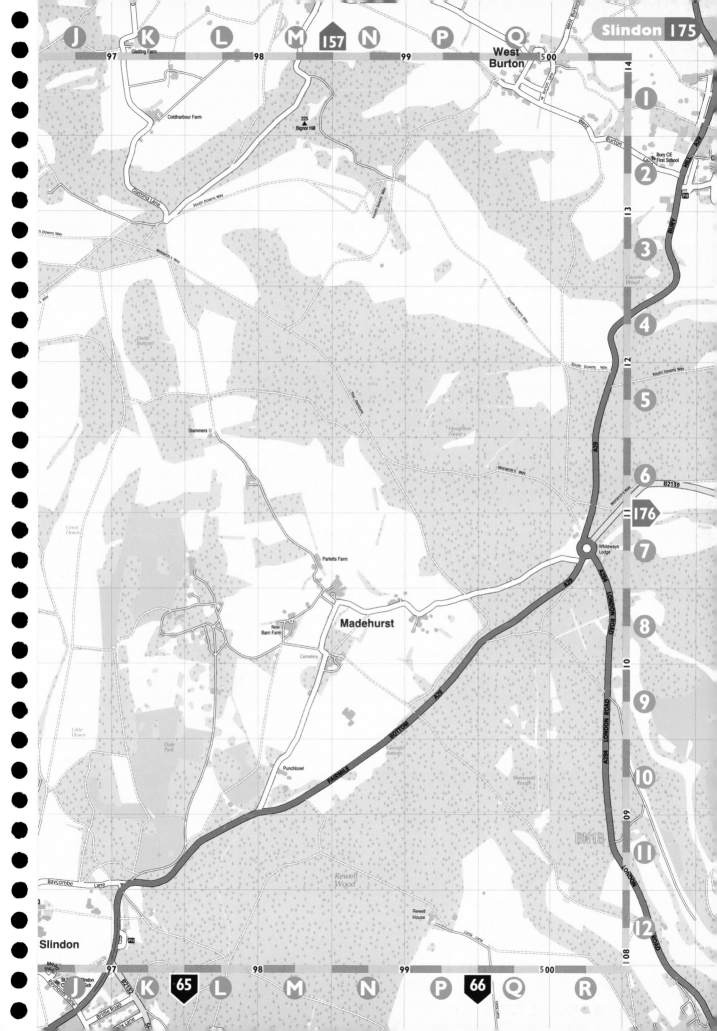

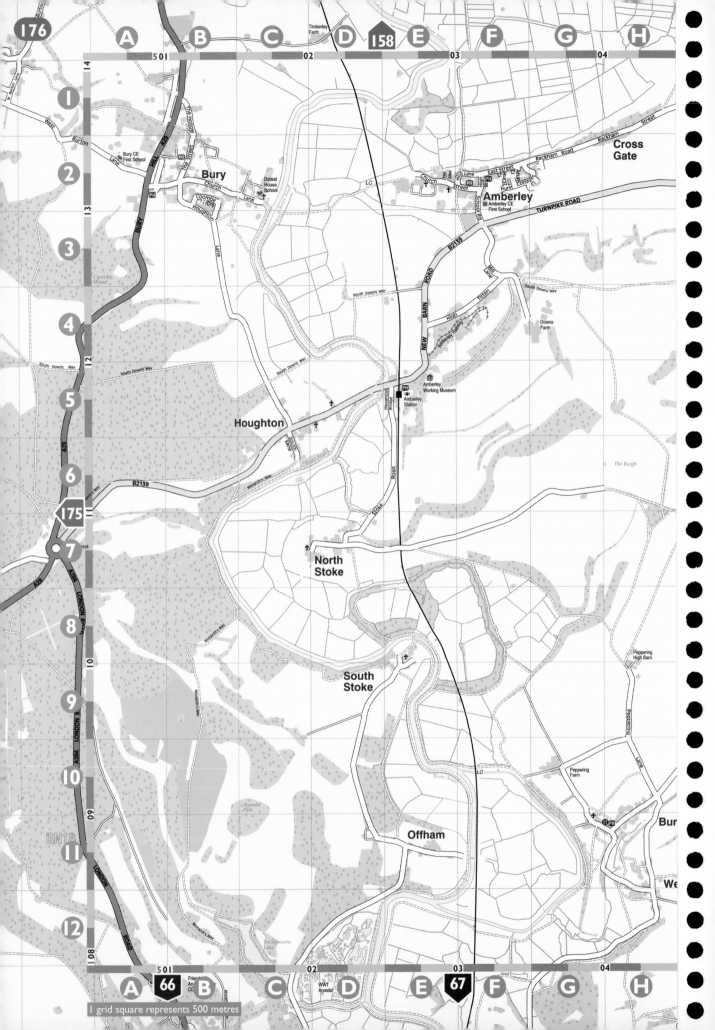

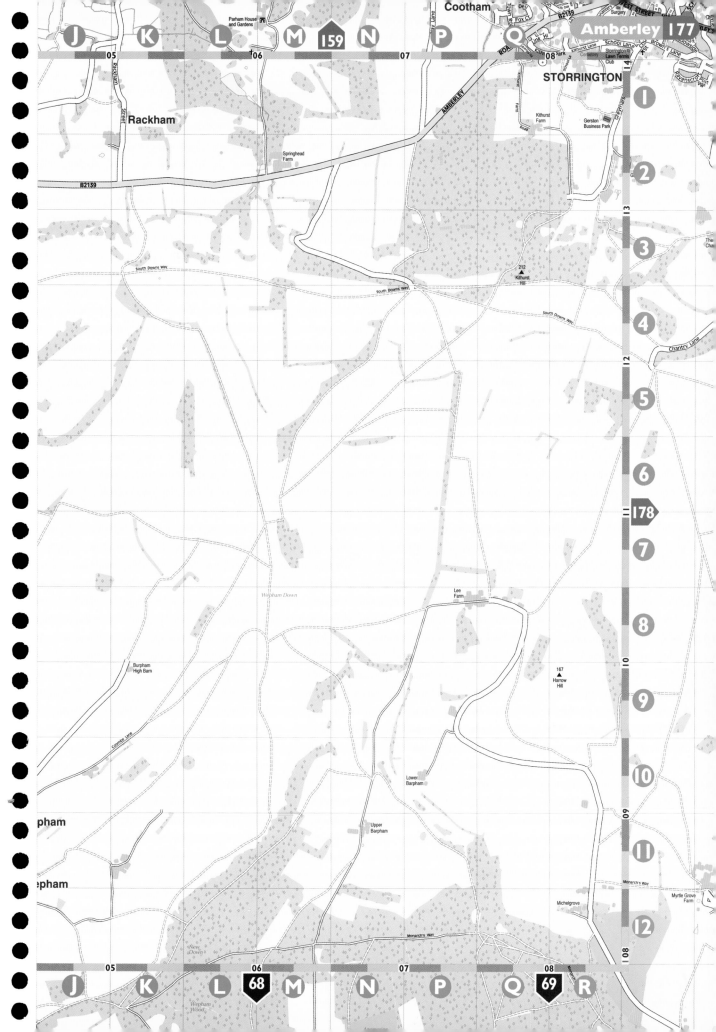

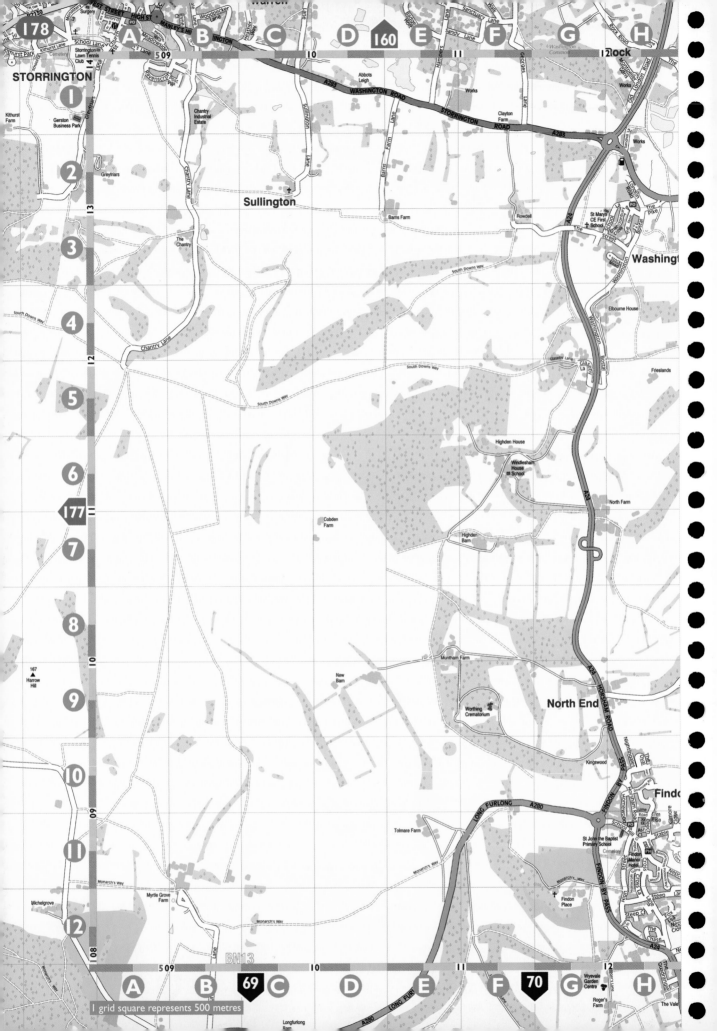

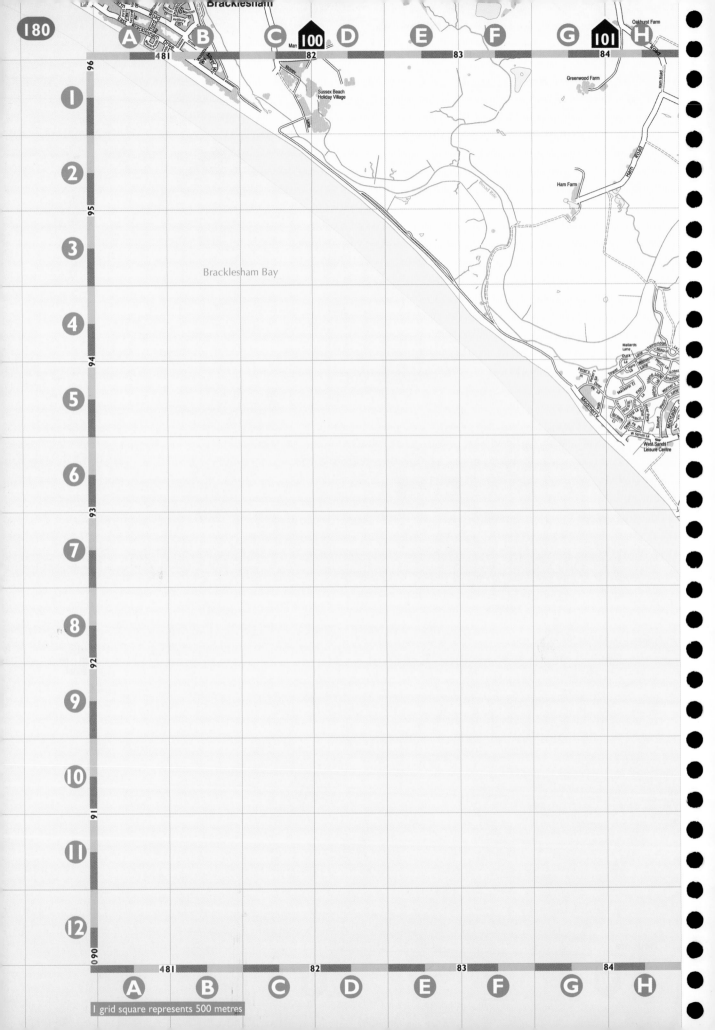

Bracklesham

A B C 100 D E F G 101 H

96
481 82 83 84

1

2
95

3

Bracklesham Bay

4
94

5

6
93

7

8
92

9

10
91

11

12
90
0 90

481 82 83 84

A B C D E F G H

1 grid square represents 500 metres

Sussex Beach
Holiday Village

Ham Farm

Greenwood Farm

Oakhurst Farm

West Sands
Leisure Centre

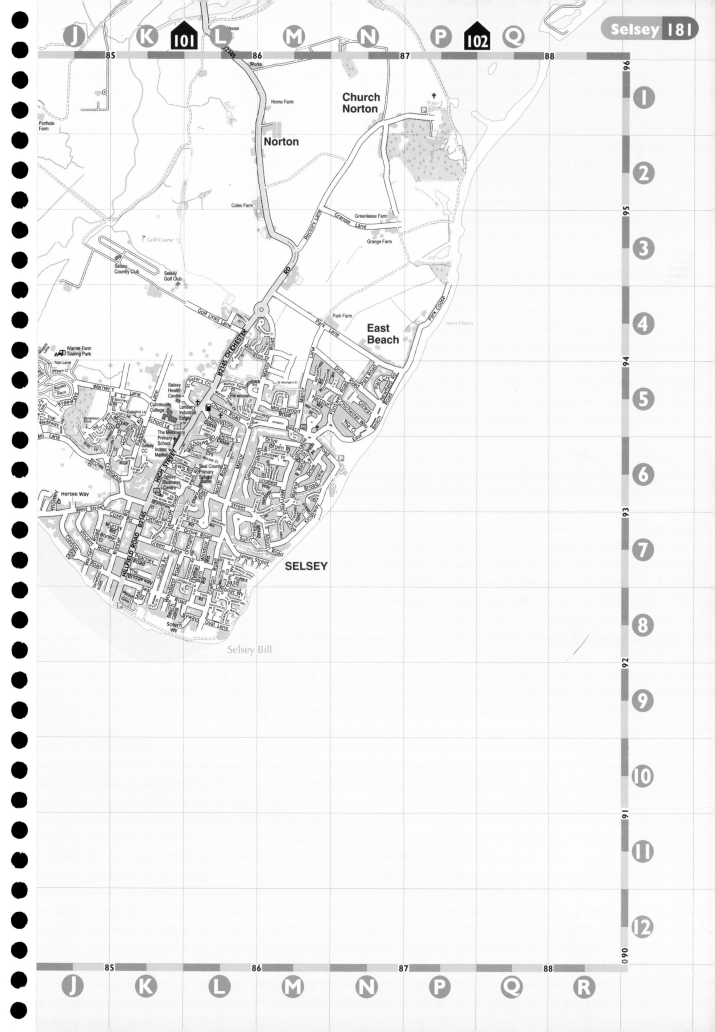

Abbotsford....46 D3
Abingworth....160 D7
Adversane....141 N6
Albourne....63 L6
Albourne Green....164 D3
Aldingbourne....63 L6
Aldrington....75 K6
Aldwick....103 K3
Alfold....112 G8
Alfold Bars....112 G10
Alfold Crossways....112 H6
Almodington....100 E5
Amberley....176 F2
Ancton....87 L7
Angmering....68 D7
Ansteadbrook....110 B12
Ansty....147 K2
Apuldram....83 H2
Ardingly....130 E1
Arford....107 M3
Arundel....67 G2
Ashfold Crossways....127 R3
Ashington....160 H9
Ashurst....162 B4
Ashurst Wood....34 D3
Atherington....88 E7
Balcombe....40 F7
Balcombe Lane....40 F7
Baldwins Hill....23 H6
Balls Cross....121 N12
Balls Green....142 D6
Barford....108 B1
Barlavington....157 K8
Barnham....65 H8
Barns Green....124 H11
Beacon Hill....108 G2
Bedham....140 C9
Bedhampton....56 D4
Bedlam Street....164 G5
Beggars Bush....71 L2
Bell Hill....133 M4
Bepton....154 D4
Bevendean....77 M3
Bewbush....28 E6
Bexleyhill....137 P2
Bignor....157 N11
Billingshurst....142 B2
Bilsham....87 L4
Bines Green....162 E2
Binsted....65 M4
Birchgrove....43 M8
Birdham....82 D7
Black Corner....20 C5
Blackmoor....106 C10
Black Rock....96 E2
Blackstone....163 R4
Blackwell....23 K7
Blendworth....168 F2
Bognor Regis....3 G8
Bolney....146 D2
Bolnore Village....44 F6
Borden....135 N3
Bordon....106 H7
Bosham....60 B8
Bosham Hoe....82 A5
Botolphs....48 E6
Boxgrove....63 H2
Bracklesham....100 B8
Bramber....48 E3
Bramshott....107 R11
Breach....58 E4
Brighton....4 D8
Broadbridge....60 C6
Broadbridge Heath....125 L1
Broadfield....29 H7
Broadford Bridge....142 C9
Broadwater....71 J7
Brockhampton....56 F5
Brookpits....88 E5
Brooks Green....142 H2
Brook Street....129 N7
Broomer's Corner....143 J10
Broomershill....159 M1
Buchan Hill....38 F1
Bucks Green....113 Q11
Burgates....116 B7
Burgess Hill....46 F6
Buriton....133 M12
Burndell....88 A2
Burpham....176 H11
Burstow....20 F2
Bury....176 B2
Byworth....139 N11
Camelsdale....109 K12
Capel....16 C3
Castle Town....49 H4
Catherington....150 B12
Causeway....133 M7
Causeway....168 C4
Chailey....149 P10
Chalton....151 J8
Charlton....172 H3
Charlwood....18 E2
Charlwood....33 K8
Chichester....6 F5
Chichester....61 J5
Chiddingfold....110 G4
Chidham....81 L1
Chilgrove....153 N11
Chiltington....167 M7
Chithurst....135 R6
Church Common....133 J1
Church Norton....181 N1
Churchwood....158 B1
Cinder Hill....131 K1
Clanfield....150 C8
Clapham....69 L4
Clark's Green....16 B5
Clayton....165 M9
Climping....88 C3
The Close....6 D5
Coates....157 P5
Cocking....154 H5
Cocking Causeway....141 H1
Codmore Hill....141 K12
Cold Ash Hill....108 B12
Coldean....53 J8
Coldwaltham....158 D7
Coleman's Hatch....35 K8
Colgate....38 B2
Colworth....85 K3
The Common....125 R1
Compton....152 B11
Coneyhurst....142 E5

Conford....107 N10
Cooksbridge....167 R9
Coolham....142 G7
Coombes....48 E8
Cootham....159 P12
Copsale....126 B11
Copthorne....21 G6
Cote....70 B5
Cowden....25 M3
Cowfold....145 L3
Cowplain....168 A6
Cox Green....114 B7
Crabtree....127 M10
Crawley....9 H5
Crawley Down....32 B2
Critchmere....108 H10
Crockerhill....63 M2
Crossbush....67 K4
Cross Gate....176 H2
Crosspost....146 B4
Crouchers....83 G4
Cuckfield....44 C4
Cudworth....17 K1
Danehill....131 R5
Deadwater....107 J6
Deanlane End....169 L4
Dell Quay....83 G3
Denne Park....126 B2
Denvilles....57 K3
Dial Green....120 A10
Dial Post....161 P1
Didling....153 Q3
Ditchling....166 A6
Domewood....22 A4
Donnington....83 K4
Doomsday Green....11 K9
Doomsday Green....126 F1
Dormans Park....23 K2
Down Park....21 M8
Dragons Green....143 L6
Dumpford....135 P9
Duncton....156 C6
Dunsfold....112 A4
Dunsfold Common....112 A5
Dunsfold....112 A5
Durleighmarsh....134 D6
Durrants....169 J9
Durrington....70 C6
Earnley....100 B7
Eartham....174 C9
Easebourne....136 H7
East Ashling....60 D1
East Beach....181 N4
East Chiltington....167 K5
East Dean....173 M3
East Grinstead....23 K7
East Hampnett....63 J7
East Harting....152 G2
East Kingston....91 H4
East Lavant....172 D12
East Lavington....156 D7
East Liss....116 E10
East Marden....153 J11
East Moulsecoomb....77 L1
East Preston....91 G3
East Wittering....99 M7
East Worthing....94 A2
Ebernoe....121 L9
Edburton....50 B2
Egdean....139 Q12
Elbridge....85 K4
Ellen's Green....114 B5
Elmer....88 A8
Elmers Marsh....118 D6
Elsted....153 K1
Emsworth....57 M6
Falmer....54 C7
Faygate....27 K8
Felbridge....22 E5
Felcourt....23 H1
Felpham....87 G8
Fernhill....20 D2
Fernhurst....119 J7
Ferring....91 L3
Finchdean....169 K3
Findon....178 H10
Findon Valley....71 G3
Fishbourne....60 E7
Fisher....84 B7
Fishersgate....74 E6
Fishersteet....120 E2
Fittleworth....158 B2
Five Oaks....124 B8
Flanshan....87 H6
Flathurst....139 M8
Fontwell....64 F3
Ford....88 C1
Forest Row....34 E8
Forestside....169 Q3
Froxfield Green....132 D1
Fulking....50 E2
Funtington....170 F12
Furnace Green....9 L2
Furnace Wood....22 B6
Fyning....135 K4
Gay Street....141 R11
Goddards' Green....146 H8
Godleys Green....149 J9
Goose Green....160 G3
Gorehill....139 N12
Goring-by-Sea....92 C2
Gossops Green....29 G4
Graffham....156 A6
Grayshott....108 E6
Grayswood....109 R8
Great Common....122 C10
Greatham....116 B4
Greatham....158 H9
Green Street....143 L7
Griggs Green....117 N1
Gunter's Bridge....139 L5
Habin....135 J7
Halecombe....134 H4
Halfway Bridge....138 A9
Halnaker....173 N12
Hambrook....59 H3
Hammer....108 F12
Hammer Bottom....108 E12
Hammerpot....68 E5
Hammerwood....25 G6
Hampers Green....139 L7
Handcross....128 D1
Hangleton....75 K2

Hangleton....91 H1
Hardham....158 C6
Haslemere....109 N11
Haslingbourne....139 M12
Hassocks....165 M5
Hatch Farm Hill....119 M5
Havant....124 A3
The Haven....124 A3
Haywards Heath....45 H3
Headley....107 L4
Headley Down....107 Q5
Hearn....107 Q2
Heath Common....160 F11
Heath End....157 J3
Henfield....163 L4
Henley....137 L1
Henley Common....119 J12
Hermitage....58 A3
Heyshott....155 K4
Heyshott Green....155 K3
Hickstead....146 E8
Highbrook....42 D8
High Cross....164 A2
Highgate....34 E8
Highleigh....101 H4
High Salvington....70 B4
Highstreet Green....111 L7
Hill Brow....116 F11
Hillgrove....120 D7
Hill Side....116 D9
Hill Top....137 J11
Hindhead....109 J5
Hole Street....161 M11
Hollingbury....53 G8
Hollingdean....77 G2
Hollywater....107 J8
Hookwood....14 B7
Horley....15 G4
Horndean....168 D3
Horsemere Green....88 B4
Horsham....10 D5
Horsted Keynes....131 M4
Houghton....176 B5
Hove....76 A8
Hoyle....155 H1
Hunston....83 M5
Hurstpierpoint....164 F4
Hurst Wickham....165 K3
Ifield....28 F1
Ifield Green....18 F8
Ifieldwood....18 C8
Ifold....122 D2
Ingrams Green....135 R12
Iping....136 B7
Itchingfield....125 J7
Kemp Town....96 C2
Kent Street....145 P6
Keymer....165 Q5
Kingsfold....26 A3
Kingsley Green....119 L3
Kingston by Sea....74 B6
Kingston Gorse....90 F6
Kingston near Lewes....55 K8
Kirdford....122 C11
Lagness....85 G7
Laker's Green....112 G5
Lambs Green....27 L3
Lancing....72 B7
Langley....117 J7
Langley Green....19 G7
Langrish....132 D5
Langstone....56 F7
Leggatt Hill....138 A5
Leigh Park....56 E1
Lickfold....138 A1
Lidsey....86 C2
Linchmere....118 D2
Lindfield....45 L1
Lindford....107 J5
Liphook....117 P2
Liss....116 D10
Liss Forest....116 C6
Little Bognor....139 R11
Little Common....138 E9
Littlehampton....89 K4
Littlehaven....36 D4
Littleworth....144 E8
Lodsworth....138 A6
Lodsworth Common....137 R3
Lower Beeding....127 M6
Lower Bordean....132 B3
Lower Fittleworth....158 A4
Lower Horncroft....158 A5
Lowfield Heath....19 L4
Loxhill....111 R1
Loxwood....122 F1
Lumley....58 B4
Lurgashall....120 C11
Lyminster....67 J7
Mackerel's Common....122 B8
Madehurst....175 N8
Maidenbower....30 B5
Mannings Heath....127 J4
Manor Royal....19 K7
Maplehurst....126 E11
Marehill....159 M3
Marley Heights....119 J4
Maudlin....62 D3
Meath Green....14 C4
Merston....85 G2
Middleton-on-Sea....87 K8
Midhurst....137 J11
Mid Lavant....172 B11
Mile Oak....74 E3
Milland....117 P11
Minsted....136 B11
The Mint....116 D8
Monk's Gate....126 H5
Moulsecoomb....77 L2
Navant Hill....120 C8
Nepcote....179 J12
Nep Town....163 K6
New Brighton....58 B2
New Pound Common....123 M10
New Town....10 F9
Newtown....117 Q3
North Bersted....85 M6
North Chailey....149 N7
Northchapel....120 F6
North Common....149 P6
North End....23 G5
North End....65 M8

North End....178 G9
Northgate....29 L1
North Heath....141 N10
North Lancing....72 E5
North Marden....153 J8
North Moulsecoomb....77 J1
North Mundham....84 B4
North Stoke....176 D7
Norton....64 A3
Norton....181 M2
Nursted....133 R10
Nutbourne....59 G6
Nutbourne....159 P3
Nutbourne Common....159 Q3
Nutcombe....108 G7
Nuthurst....126 E8
Nyetimber....102 F3
Nyewood....134 H9
Nyton....64 B5
Oakhanger....106 A5
Oakhill....11 H6
Oakwoodhill....115 J2
Offham....167 R12
Offham....176 E11
Old Shoreham....73 K4
Oving....63 H6
Ovingdean....97 K2
Pagham....102 D5
Parbrook....141 R2
Park Street....124 F2
Partridge Green....144 F10
Passfield....107 N8
Patcham....52 E7
Patching....69 J3
Paynes Green....115 N2
Pease Pottage....38 F2
Petersfield....133 L6
Petworth....139 K9
Plaistow....122 A3
Plumpton....167 J10
Plumpton Green....166 H3
Poling....68 A7
Poling Corner....67 M5
Portfield....7 K5
Portslade-by-Sea....75 G7
Portslade Village....74 F3
Pound Hill....30 B1
Povey Cross....14 B8
Poynings....164 C12
Preston....76 D4
Prince's Marsh....116 C11
Prinsted....58 D6
Pulborough....159 J4
Pyecombe....165 J11
Quabrook....35 H8
Quags Corner....136 D10
Queen's Corner....136 B1
Rackham....177 K1
Rake....116 H9
Ramsdean....132 D8
Ramsnest Common....110 E10
Rapkyns....125 K1
Redford....118 D12
Red Hill....169 J8
Ridge Common....133 K4
River....138 D7
Robins....135 R2
Rock....160 G12
Roedean....97 H2
Roffey....36 F4
Rogate....134 H6
Rose Green....103 H2
Rotherbridge....138 H12
Rottingdean....97 M3
Roundstreet Common....123 J7
Rowhook....114 H8
Rowland's Castle....169 L7
Rudgwick....113 R10
Runcton....84 E4
Rusper....27 L1
Russ Hill....18 B4
Rustington....90 C4
Saddlescombe....51 K2
Saint Hill....33 J5
Salvington....70 F6
Saxby....65 K8
Sayers Common....146 D12
Scayne's Hill....149 J2
Selham....138 C11
Selsey....181 M7
Selsfield Common....32 A8
Sharpthorne....42 F3
Sheet....133 Q3
Shepherd's Hill....109 M11
Shermanbury....145 J10
Shipley....143 N9
Shipley Bridge....20 E3
Shipton Green....99 M1
Shopp Hill....120 B7
Shopwyke....62 E6
Shoreham Beach....74 A8
Shoreham-by-Sea....73 L8
Shortheath....108 H11
Shottermill....108 H11
Shripney....86 C4
Sidlesham....101 L4
Sidlesham Common....83 K8
Singleton....172 F2
Slaugham....128 B4
Slindon....175 J12
Slinfold....124 G2
Slough Green....129 J8
Small Dole....163 L11
Smallfield....15 M7
Smithbrook....138 A5
Smock Alley....160 A6
Somerley....100 B3
Sompting....72 A7
Sompting Abbotts....71 M5
South Ambersham....137 Q11
South Bersted....2 F1
Southbourne....58 F5
South Chailey....167 P2
Southern Cross....74 F5
Southgate....8 D7
South Harting....152 D1
South Lancing....72 C7
South Mundham....84 C7
South Stoke....176 D9
South Street....149 P12
Southwater....143 Q1
Southwater Street....125 Q9
Southwick....74 D5
Standford....107 K7

Stanmer....53 K5
Staplefield....128 G4
Staples Hill....121 R10
Stedham....136 D8
Steep....133 M2
Steyning....48 C3
Stockbridge....83 L2
Stockheath....56 F2
Stonequarry....23 M6
Stoner Hill....133 J1
Stopham....158 E3
Storrington....177 Q1
Stoughton....170 H6
Streat....166 E6
Street End....101 L2
Strettington....62 F1
Strood Green....115 L11
Strood Green....140 E4
Stroud....132 H5
Stubbermere....169 P9
Sullington....178 C2
Sullington Warren....160 C12
Summersdale....61 M3
Sunnyside....33 K3
Sutton....157 M10
Sutton End....157 L7
Tangmere....63 H3
Temple Bar....62 F2
Terwick Common....135 L4
Thakeham....160 E6
Thorney Island....80 D2
Three Bridges....9 K1
Tilgate....34 J4
Tilgate Forest Row....39 H4
Tillington....138 H9
Tinsley Green....20 B5
Tisman's Common....113 P12
Titty Hill....136 B1
Toddington....89 L1
Topleigh....155 Q3
Tortington....66 D6
Tote Hill....136 D3
Tower Hill....125 Q5
Treyford....153 M3
Trotten Marsh....135 M2
Trotton....135 P8
Tullecombe....134 H1
Turners Hill....31 M5
Twineham....146 D6
Twineham Green....146 C7
Two Mile Ash....125 N10
Up Marden....170 G1
Upper Beeding....48 E4
Upper Ifold....112 B10
Upper Norwood....156 C4
Upperton....138 G7
Upper Wardley....117 R8
Upwaltham....174 C1
Walberton....65 J5
Walderton....170 E7
Warblington....57 J5
Wardley....117 R9
Warminghurst....160 F7
Warnham....115 P9
Warningcamp....67 L2
Warninglid....128 B8
Washington....178 H3
Waterbeach....173 K12
Watersfield....158 B9
Weatherhill....15 M5
Wepham....176 H11
West Ashling....60 B2
West Blatchington....75 L4
Westbourne....169 Q12
West Burton....157 Q12
West Chiltington....160 B3
West Chiltington Common....159 Q7
West Dean....172 D3
Westdene....52 A3
West End....162 H4
Westergate....64 B6
Westerton....62 E2
West Green....8 D3
West Grinstead....144 C6
Westhampnett....63 H3
West Harting....134 D10
West Hill....41 H8
West Hoathly....42 D3
West Itchenor....81 K6
West Kingston....91 H4
West Lavington....137 K11
West Leigh....168 H12
West Liss....116 C8
West Marden....170 B1
Westmeston....166 B9
Weston....133 J9
West Stoke....171 P11
West Tarring....12 B1
West Thorney....80 E3
West Town....164 F3
West Wittering....99 H4
West Worthing....92 E3
Whitehall....143 L10
Whitehawk....77 L7
Whitehill....106 F7
Whitemans Green....44 B1
White's Green....138 D2
Whyke....7 G7
Wick....89 G1
Wiggonholt....159 L7
Wineham....145 G8
Wisborough Green....141 J1
Wiston....161 M12
Withdean....76 D1
Wivelsfield....47 M4
Wivelsfield Green....148 Q3
Woldhurst....84 C5
Woodgate....64 C8
Woodingdean....78 B6
Woodmancote....59 G1
Woodmancote....163 Q7
Woodmansgreen....118 D10
Woolbeding....136 E7
Woolmer Hill....108 F10
World's End....47 J5
Worth....30 A1
Worth Abbey....31 G8
Worthing....13 G8
Yapton....87 M2

USING THE STREET INDEX

Street names are listed alphabetically. Each street name is followed by its postal town or area locality, the Postcode District, the page number, and the reference to the square in which the name is found.

Standard index entries are shown as follows:

Abberton Fld *HPPT/KEY* BN6...... **165** *J4*

Street names and selected addresses not shown on the map due to scale restrictions are shown in the index with an asterisk:

Aberdeen Ter *GSHT* GU26 *.......... **108** *G6*

GENERAL ABBREVIATIONS

ACC......ACCESS	CTS......COURTS	HGR......HIGHER	MTN......MOUNTAIN	RP......RAMP
ALY......ALLEY	CTYD......COURTYARD	HL......HILL	MTS......MOUNTAINS	RW......ROW
AP......APPROACH	CUTT......CUTTINGS	HLS......HILLS	MUS......MUSEUM	S......SOUTH
AR......ARCADE	CV......COVE	HO......HOUSE	MWY......MOTORWAY	SCH......SCHOOL
ASS......ASSOCIATION	CYN......CANYON	HOL......HOLLOW	N......NORTH	SE......SOUTH EAST
AV......AVENUE	DEPT......DEPARTMENT	HOSP......HOSPITAL	NE......NORTH EAST	SER......SERVICE AREA
BCH......BEACH	DL......DALE	HRB......HARBOUR	NW......NORTH WEST	SH......SHORE
BLDS......BUILDINGS	DM......DAM	HTH......HEATH	O/P......OVERPASS	SHOP......SHOPPING
BND......BEND	DRO......DROVE	HTS......HEIGHTS	OFF......OFFICE	SKWY......SKYWAY
BNK......BANK	DRY......DRIVEWAY	HVN......HAVEN	ORCH......ORCHARD	SMT......SUMMIT
BR......BRIDGE	DWGS......DWELLINGS	HWY......HIGHWAY	OV......OVAL	SOC......SOCIETY
BRK......BROOK	E......EAST	IMP......IMPERIAL	PAL......PALACE	SP......SPUR
BTM......BOTTOM	EMB......EMBANKMENT	IN......INLET	PAS......PASSAGE	SPR......SPRING
BUS......BUSINESS	EMBY......EMBASSY	IND EST......INDUSTRIAL ESTATE	PAV......PAVILION	SQ......SQUARE
BVD......BOULEVARD	ESP......ESPLANADE	INF......INFIRMARY	PDE......PARADE	ST......STREET
BY......BYPASS	EST......ESTATE	INFO......INFORMATION	PH......PUBLIC HOUSE	STN......STATION
CATH......CATHEDRAL	EX......EXCHANGE	INT......INTERCHANGE	PK......PARK	STR......STREAM
CEM......CEMETERY	EXPY......EXPRESSWAY	IS......ISLAND	PKWY......PARKWAY	STRD......STRAND
CEN......CENTRE	EXT......EXTENSION	JCT......JUNCTION	PL......PLACE	SW......SOUTH WEST
CFT......CROFT	F/O......FLYOVER	JTY......JETTY	PLN......PLAIN	TDG......TRADING
CH......CHURCH	FC......FOOTBALL CLUB	KG......KING	PLNS......PLAINS	TER......TERRACE
CHA......CHASE	FK......FORK	KNL......KNOLL	PLZ......PLAZA	THWY......THROUGHWAY
CHYD......CHURCHYARD	FLD......FIELD	L......LAKE	POL......POLICE STATION	TNL......TUNNEL
CIR......CIRCLE	FLDS......FIELDS	LA......LANE	PR......PRINCE	TOLL......TOLLWAY
CIRC......CIRCUS	FLS......FALLS	LDG......LODGE	PREC......PRECINCT	TPK......TURNPIKE
CL......CLOSE	FM......FARM	LGT......LIGHT	PREP......PREPARATORY	TR......TRACK
CLFS......CLIFFS	FT......FORT	LK......LOCK	PRIM......PRIMARY	TRL......TRAIL
CMP......CAMP	FTS......FLATS	LKS......LAKES	PROM......PROMENADE	TWR......TOWER
CNR......CORNER	FWY......FREEWAY	LNDG......LANDING	PRS......PRINCESS	U/P......UNDERPASS
CO......COUNTY	FY......FERRY	LTL......LITTLE	PRT......PORT	UNI......UNIVERSITY
COLL......COLLEGE	GA......GATE	LWR......LOWER	PT......POINT	UPR......UPPER
COM......COMMON	GAL......GALLERY	MAG......MAGISTRATE	PTH......PATH	V......VALE
COMM......COMMISSION	GDN......GARDEN	MAN......MANSIONS	PZ......PIAZZA	VA......VALLEY
CON......CONVENT	GDNS......GARDENS	MD......MEAD	QD......QUADRANT	VIAD......VIADUCT
COT......COTTAGE	GLD......GLADE	MDW......MEADOWS	QU......QUEEN	VIL......VILLA
COTS......COTTAGES	GLN......GLEN	MEM......MEMORIAL	QY......QUAY	VIS......VISTA
CP......CAPE	GN......GREEN	MI......MILL	R......RIVER	VLG......VILLAGE
CPS......COPSE	GND......GROUND	MKT......MARKET	RBT......ROUNDABOUT	VLS......VILLAS
CR......CREEK	GRA......GRANGE	MKTS......MARKETS	RD......ROAD	VW......VIEW
CREM......CREMATORIUM	GRG......GARAGE	ML......MALL	RDG......RIDGE	W......WEST
CRS......CRESCENT	GT......GREAT	MNR......MANOR	REP......REPUBLIC	WD......WOOD
CSWY......CAUSEWAY	GTWY......GATEWAY	MS......MEWS	RES......RESERVOIR	WHF......WHARF
CT......COURT	GV......GROVE	MSN......MISSION	RFC......RUGBY FOOTBALL CLUB	WK......WALK
CTRL......CENTRAL		MT......MOUNT	RI......RISE	WKS......WALKS

POSTCODE TOWNS AND AREA ABBREVIATIONS

ALTN......Alton	CRAWE......Crawley east	HORL......Horley	MFD/CHID......Milford/Chiddingfold	RFNM......Rural Farnham
ANG/EP......Angmering/East Preston	CRAWW......Crawley west	HORN......Horndean	MIDH......Midhurst	RHWH......Rural Haywards Heath
ARUN......Arundel	EDEN......Edenbridge	HORS......Horsham	MSEA/BNM......Middleton-on-Sea/	RING/NEW......Ringmer/Newick
BIL......Billingshurst	EGRIN......East Grinstead	HOVE......Hove	Barnham	SALV......Salvington
BOGR......Bognor Regis	EMRTH......Emsworth/Southbourne	HPPT/KEY......Hurstpierpoint/Keymer	PETW......Petworth	SELS......Selsey
BOR......Bordon	EPSF......Petersfield east	HRTF......Hartfield	POY/PYE......Poynings/Pyecombe	SHOR......Shoreham
BRI......Brighton	FERR......Ferring	HWH......Haywards Heath	PSF......Petersfield	STEY/UB......Steyning/Upper Beeding
BRIE/ROTT......Brighton east/	FROW......Forest Row	LAN/SOMP......Lancing/Sompting	PTSD......Portslade	STHW......Southwick
Rottingdean	GSHT......Grayshott	LEWES......Lewes	PUL/STOR......Pulborough/Storrington	SWTR......Southwater
BURH......Burgess Hill	HASM......Haslemere	LHPTN......Littlehampton	RCCH......Rural Chichester	UCK......Uckfield
CCH......Chichester	HAV......Havant	LING......Lingfield	RDKG......Rural Dorking	WTHG......Worthing
CHAM......Cosham	HFD......Henfield	LIPH......Liphook	REDH......Redhill	WVILLE......Waterlooville/Denmead
CRAN......Cranleigh	HISD......Hayling Island	LISS......Liss	REIG......Reigate	

Index – streets   Abb – All

A

	HPPT/KEY BN6...... **146** *E11*	**Agate La** *HORS* RH12...... **36** *D4*	*STHW* BN42...... **74** *C7*	**Alexandra Rd** *BURH* RH15...... **47** *H7*
	Acre Cl *ANG/EP* BN16...... **90** *A3*	**Aglaia Rd** *WTHG* BN11...... **92** *E4*	**Albion Wy** *HORS* RH12...... **10** *C5*	*CCH* PO19...... **7** *G3*
Abberton Fld *HPPT/KEY* BN6...... **165** *J4*	*HWH* RH16...... **45** *G7*	**Agnes St** *BRIE/ROTT* BN2...... **5** *J2*	**Alborough Wy** *BOGR* PO21...... **103** *J3*	*LAN/SOMP* BN15...... **72** *E8*
Abbey Cl *LAN/SOMP* BN15...... **73** *G7*	**The Acre Cl** *WTHG* BN11...... **12** *C6*	**Aigburth Av** *BOGR* PO21...... **103** *J2*	**Albourne Cl** *BRIE/ROTT* BN2...... **77** *K6*	*WTHG* BN11...... **13** *M5*
Abbeydore Cl *BOR* GU35...... **107** *M4*	**Acre La** *WVILLE* PO7...... **168** *D8*	**Ailsa Cl** *CRAWW* RH11...... **8** *A9*	**Albourne Rd** *HPPT/KEY* BN6...... **164** *F3*	**Alexandra Ter** *BOGR* PO21 *...... **2** *F7*
Abbey Rd *BRIE/ROTT* BN2...... **5** *L8*	**Acre St** *SELS* PO20...... **99** *L3*	**Ainsdale Cl** *SALV* BN13...... **70** *C7*	**Aldbourne Dr** *BOGR* PO21...... **103** *J3*	**Alexandra Vls** *BRI* BN1 *...... **4** *C4*
LAN/SOMP BN15...... **72** *B4*	**Adams Cl** *BRI* BN1...... **77** *G4*	**Ainsdale Rd** *SALV* BN13...... **70** *C7*	**Alder Cl** *CRAWE* RH10...... **32** *A1*	**Alfold By-Pass** *CRAN* GU6...... **112** *G3*
STEY/UB BN44...... **48** *D1*	**Adams Ms** *LIPH* GU30...... **117** *Q3*	**Ainsworth Av** *BRIE/ROTT* BN2...... **97** *J2*	*SALV* BN13...... **70** *B8*	**Alfold Rd** *MFD/CHID* GU8...... **112** *A5*
WTHG BN11...... **12** *D8*	**Adastra Av** *HPPT/KEY* BN6...... **165** *P5*	**Ainsworth Cl** *BRIE/ROTT* BN2...... **97** *J1*	**Alderman's Wk** *CCH* PO19 *...... **6** *E3*	**Alford Cl** *SALV* BN13...... **70** *F6*
Abbotsbury Ct *SWTR* RH13...... **11** *H3*	**Adderbury Av** *EMRTH* PO10...... **58** *A2*	**Aintree Dr** *WVILLE* PO7...... **168** *C8*	**Aldermoor Av** *PUL/STOR* RH20...... **160** *B11*	*MSEA/BNM* PO22...... **87** *L8*
Abbots Cl *HPPT/KEY* BN6...... **165** *M5*	**Addison Cl** *LAN/SOMP* BN15...... **72** *D7*	**Aintree Rd** *CRAWE* RH10...... **9** *L8*	**Alderney Rd** *FERR* BN12...... **91** *L5*	**Alfred Pl** *WTHG* BN11...... **13** *K6*
Abbotsfield Rd *CRAWW* RH11...... **28** *C4*	**Addison Rd** *HOVE* BN3...... **4** *A3*	**Airport Wy** *HORL* RH6...... **19** *M1*	**Alder Rd** *BOR* GU35...... **107** *Q3*	**Alfred Rd** *BRI* BN1...... **4** *C4*
Abbots Leigh *SWTR* RH13...... **143** *R1*	**Addison Wy** *MSEA/BNM* PO22...... **86** *A6*	**Ajax Pl** *MSEA/BNM* PO22...... **87** *H4*	**Alders Av** *EGRIN* RH19...... **23** *J6*	**Alfrey Cl** *EMRTH* PO10...... **58** *D5*
Abbotstone Av *HAV* PO9...... **57** *H1*	**Adelaide Crs** *HOVE* BN3...... **76** *B8*	**Akehurst Cl** *CRAWE* RH10...... **20** *F6*	**Alders View Dr** *EGRIN* RH19...... **23** *K6*	**Alfriston Cl** *BRIE/ROTT* BN2...... **77** *L7*
Abbots Wy *LAN/SOMP* BN15...... **72** *E7*	**Adelaide Man** *HOVE* BN3...... **76** *B8*	**Alandale Rd** *LAN/SOMP* BN15...... **72** *B5*	**Alder Wy** *MSEA/BNM* PO22...... **87** *K7*	*MSEA/BNM* PO22...... **87** *H7*
Abbotswood Wk *ANG/EP* BN16...... **90** *B5*	**Adelaide Rd** *CCH* PO19...... **7** *G2*	*SELS* PO20...... **100** *E1*	**Alderwood Cl** *HAV* PO9...... **56** *C2*	*SALV* BN13...... **71** *G8*
Abbottsbury *BOGR* PO21...... **102** *F5*	**Adelaide Sq** *SHOR* BN43...... **74** *A6*	**Alan Wy** *BRIE/ROTT* BN2...... **77** *L8*	**Aldingbourne Cl** *CRAWW* RH11...... **28** *E2*	**Alfriston Rd** *SALV* BN13...... **71** *G8*
Abbotts Cl *WTHG* BN11...... **12** *F5*	**Adelphi Cl** *CRAWE* RH10...... **30** *C5*	**Albany Cl** *WTHG* BN11...... **12** *B7*	**Aldingbourne Dr** *RCCH* PO18...... **63** *M2*	**Alice Cl** *HOVE* BN3 *...... **76** *C8*
Abbotts Vw *LAN/SOMP* BN15...... **72** *B5*	**Adhurst Rd** *HAV* PO9...... **57** *H1*	**Albany Ms** *HOVE* BN3...... **76** *A7*	**Aldingbourne Pk** *SELS* PO20 *...... **64** *C8*	**Alice St** *HOVE* BN3...... **76** *C8*
A'Becket Gdns *SALV* BN13...... **70** *E7*	**Admers Crs** *LIPH* GU30...... **117** *R3*	**Albany Rd** *CRAWW* RH11...... **8** *C4*	**Aldrich Cl** *BRIE/ROTT* BN2...... **77** *L7*	**Alicia Av** *CRAWE* RH10...... **30** *A3*
A'Becket's Av *BOGR* PO21...... **103** *G4*	**Admiral Ct** *MSEA/BNM* PO22 *...... **3** *K6*	**Albany Vls** *HOVE* BN3...... **76** *A8*	**Aldridge Cl** *HORN* PO8...... **150** *D8*	*PUL/STOR* RH20...... **161** *K8*
Aberdare Cl *CCH* PO19...... **62** *A5*	**Admiral's Bridge La**	**The Albemarle** *BRIE/ROTT* BN2 *...... **4** *F8*	**Aldrington Av** *HOVE* BN3...... **75** *M5*	**Alicks Hl** *BIL* RH14...... **142** *A1*
Aberdeen Rd *BRIE/ROTT* BN2...... **5** *H1*	*EGRIN* RH19...... **33** *H7*	**Alberta Dr** *HORL* RH6...... **15** *M6*	**Aldrington Cl** *HOVE* BN3...... **75** *J6*	**Alinora Av** *FERR* BN12...... **92** *C3*
Aberdeen Ter *GSHT* GU26 *...... **108** *G6*	**Admirals Wk** *LHPTN* BN17...... **89** *M3*	**Alberta Rd** *SALV* BN13...... **70** *C7*	**Alder Rd** *BOR* GU35...... **107** *Q3*	**Alinora Cl** *FERR* BN12...... **92** *C3*
Abingdon Ldg *ANG/EP* BN16 *...... **90** *C4*	*RCCH* PO18...... **170** *H12*	**Albert Cl** *HWH* RH16...... **45** *K5*		**Alinora Crs** *FERR* BN12...... **92** *C4*
Abinger Rd *BRIE/ROTT* BN2...... **78** *D7*	**Admiralty Gdns**	**Albert Dr** *BURH* RH15...... **46** *D7*	**Aldsworth Av** *FERR* BN12...... **92** *A3*	**Alinora Dr** *FERR* BN12...... **92** *B4*
PTSD BN41...... **75** *G5*	*MSEA/BNM* PO22...... **3** *K5*	**Albert Man** *HOVE* BN3 *...... **76** *B7*	**Aldsworth Ct** *FERR* BN12...... **92** *A3*	**Allandale Cl** *SELS* PO20...... **181** *L5*
Abrahams Rd *CRAWW* RH11...... **28** *F8*	**Admiralty Rd** *MSEA/BNM* PO22 *...... **3** *K5*	**Albert Rd** *ANG/EP* BN16...... **90** *B3*	**Aldwick Av** *BOGR* PO21...... **103** *L4*	**Allangate Dr** *ANG/EP* BN16...... **90** *C3*
Acacia Av *HOVE* BN3...... **75** *L4*	**Adsdean Cl** *HAV* PO9...... **56** *C4*	*BOGR* PO21...... **2** *C7*	**Aldwick Cl** *ANG/EP* BN16...... **90** *A6*	**Allbrook Ct** *HAV* PO9...... **168** *E11*
SALV BN13...... **70** *E6*	**Adur Av** *SALV* BN13...... **70** *B5*	*BRI* BN1...... **4** *C4*	**Aldwick Crs** *SALV* BN13...... **70** *F4*	**Allcard Cl** *HORS* RH12...... **36** *C4*
Acacia Gdns *HORN* PO8...... **168** *C4*	**Adur Cl** *LAN/SOMP* BN15...... **73** *H8*	*CCH* PO19...... **61** *H7*	**Aldwick Felds** *BOGR* PO21...... **103** *L3*	**Allcot Cl** *CRAWW* RH11...... **28** *D6*
Acer Wy *HAV* PO9...... **57** *J1*	**Adur Dr** *SHOR* BN43...... **73** *H4*	*HORL* RH6...... **14** *F6*	**Aldwick Gdns** *BOGR* PO21...... **103** *L2*	**Allee Dr** *LIPH* GU30...... **107** *Q12*
Acorn Av *SWTR* RH13...... **145** *K4*	**Adur Rd** *BURH* RH15...... **47** *H5*	*LHPTN* BN17...... **89** *J4*	**Aldwick Hundred**	**Allendale** *SWTR* RH13...... **125** *Q10*
Acorn Cl *ANG/EP* BN16...... **90** *E1*	**Adur Valley Ct** *STEY/UB* BN44 *...... **49** *G3*	*STHW* BN42...... **74** *C6*	*BOGR* PO21 *...... **103** *K4*	**Allendale Av** *EMRTH* PO10...... **57** *M2*
EGRIN RH19...... **33** *K1*	**Adur Vw** *STEY/UB* BN44 *...... **48** *F3*	**Albery Cl** *HORS* RH12...... **10** *B1*	**Aldwick Pl** *BOGR* PO21...... **103** *K3*	*SALV* BN13...... **70** *F4*
HORL RH6...... **15** *H5*	**Adversane La** *BIL* RH14...... **141** *Q6*	**Albion Cl** *CRAWE* RH10...... **30** *C4*	**Aldwick Rd** *BOGR* PO21...... **103** *J3*	**Allen Rd** *HWH* RH16...... **45** *K4*
SELS PO20...... **181** *K6*	**Adversane Rd** *SALV* BN13...... **71** *G8*	**Albion Ct** *BURH* RH15...... **46** *E7*	**Aldwick St** *BOGR* PO21...... **103** *K3*	**Allen's Cl** *EGRIN* RH19...... **34** *C3*
Acorn End *BOGR* PO21...... **103** *J3*		**Albion Hl** *BRIE/ROTT* BN2...... **5** *H5*	**Alexander Cl** *BOGR* PO21...... **103** *K3*	**Allens Rd** *BRI* BN13...... **145** *K3*
Acorns *BRI* BN1...... **11** *M2*		**Albion Pl** *BRIE/ROTT* BN2...... **5** *L8*	**Alexander Ter** *WTHG* BN11 *...... **13** *H6*	**Allerways Wy** *MSEA/BNM* PO22...... **88** *A8*
The Acorns *BURH* RH15...... **46** *C5*		**Albion Rd** *SELS* PO20...... **181** *M7*	**Alexandra Ct** *BOR* GU35...... **106** *G6*	**The Alley** *ARUN* BN18...... **176** *E2*
CRAWW RH11...... **29** *G8*		**Albion St** *BRIE/ROTT* BN2...... **5** *J2*	*CRAWE* RH10 *...... **8** *F6*	*MIDH* GU29...... **136** *D8*
		PTSD BN41...... **75** *G6*	*FERR* BN12...... **92** *B2*	**Allfreys Whf** *PUL/STOR* RH20...... **159** *J3*

Allington La LEWES BN7 ...... 167 M10
Allington Rd SALV BN13 ...... 71 K6
Allwood Crs RHWH RH17 ...... 148 F9
Allyington Wy RH10 ...... 30 C4
Alma La BOR GU35 ...... 106 H6
  BOR 107 R4
  HWH RH16 ...... 45 L1
Alma St LAN/SOMP BN15 ...... 94 D1
Almodington La SELS PO20 ...... 100 C6
Almond Av SHOR BN43 ...... 73 H5
Almond Cl CRAWW RH11 ...... 28 F4
  HAV PO9 ...... 56 A5
  HORN PO8 ...... 168 D5
Alpha Cottages
  PUL/STOR RH20 * 159 L3
Alpha Rd CRAWW RH11 ...... 8 C4
Alpine Rd BOR GU35 ...... 106 G8
  HOVE BN3 ...... 75 L5
Alresford Rd HAV PO9 ...... 56 F1
Alverstone Rd WTHG BN11 ...... 13 C5
Amber Cl BOR GU35 ...... 106 H7
Amber Gld SWTR RH13 ...... 125 Q12
Amberley Cl BURH RH15 ...... 46 F5
  CRAWE RH10 ...... 30 B3
  HORS RH12 ...... 36 F3
  HWH RH16 ...... 45 G5
  LHPTN BN17 ...... 89 K3
  PUL/STOR RH20 ...... 159 R12
  SHOR BN43 ...... 73 L4
Amberley Ct CRAWW RH11 * 19 J6
Amberley Dr BOGR PO21 ...... 103 L1
  FERR BN12 ...... 92 A4
  HOVE BN3 ...... 75 K2
Amberley Ga PUL/STOR RH20.. 159 Q12
Amberley Rd ANG/EP BN16... 90 B5
  HORN PO8 ...... 150 E8
  HORS RH12 ...... 36 F3
  PUL/STOR RH20 ...... 177 L1
Ambersham Crs ANG/EP BN16... 90 E2
Ambleside Cl CRAWW RH11 ...... 28 C4
  MSEA/BNM PO22 ...... 87 G7
Ambleside Rd LAN/SOMP BN15.. 72 B8
Ambrose Pl WTHG BN11 ...... 13 G5
Amelia Rd WTHG BN11 ...... 12 F5
America La HWH RH16 ...... 45 K4
Amesbury Crs HOVE BN3 ...... 75 K6
Amethyst Gv WVILLE PO7 ...... 168 C9
Amherst Crs HOVE BN3 ...... 75 L5
Amherst Rd BOR GU35 ...... 106 F3
  SWTR RH13 ...... 10 F7
Ampfield Cl HAV PO9 ...... 56 C1
Amport Cl HAV PO9 ...... 168 E11
Amundsen Rd HORS RH12 ...... 36 C3
Anchor Cl SHOR BN43 ...... 73 H7
Anchor Ct FERR BN12 ...... 92 D4
  HORS RH12 * 10 D7
  RCCH PO18 * 59 G6
Anchor Springs LHPTN BN17 ...... 89 J4
Ancren Cl FERR BN12 ...... 91 L1
Ancton Cl MSEA/BNM PO22 ...... 87 L8
Ancton Dr MSEA/BNM PO22 ...... 87 M7
Ancton La MSEA/BNM PO22 ...... 87 L7
Ancton Lodge La
  MSEA/BNM PO22 ...... 87 M8
Ancton Wy MSEA/BNM PO22 ...... 88 A8
Anderson Cl HAV PO9 ...... 57 H2
Andlers Ash La LISS GU33 ...... 116 B11
Andrew Av MSEA/BNM PO22 ...... 87 H8
Andrew Cl ANG/EP BN16 ...... 90 A3
  STEY/UB SN44 ...... 48 C3
Andrews La LHPTN BN17 ...... 89 J4
  SWTR RH13 ...... 125 Q12
Andrews Rd SWTR RH13 ...... 143 Q2
Andromeda Cl CRAWW RH11 ...... 28 D5
Angell Est CCH PO19 * 7 L7
Angelo Cl WVILLE PO7 ...... 168 B9
Angel St PETW GU28 ...... 139 L9
Anglesea St WTHG BN11 ...... 12 F4
Anglesey Cl CRAWW RH11 ...... 29 H6
Angmering La ANG/EP BN16... 90 D5
Angmering Wy ANG/EP BN16.. 90 D2
Angola Rd SALV BN13 ...... 13 L1
Angus Cl HORS RH12 ...... 12 E2
Angus Rd FERR BN12 ...... 92 D3
Anmore Cl HAV PO9 ...... 56 E1
Annandale Av BOOR PO21 ...... 2 D4
Ann Cl HPPT/KEY BN6 ...... 165 P4
Anne Howard Gdns ARUN BN18.. 66 F2
Annington Gdns SHOR BN43 ...... 73 L4
Annington Rd STEY/UB SN44 ...... 48 D4
Ann St BRI BN1 ...... 4 E3
  WTHG BN11 ...... 13 H6
Annweir Av LAN/SOMP BN15... 72 C7
Anscombe Cl WTHG BN11 ...... 92 K4
Anscombe Rd WTHG BN11 ...... 92 K4
Anisters Ct FERR BN12 * 91 K4
Anson Ct FERR BN12 * 92 B1
  FERR BN12 ...... 92 B1
Anson Rd BOGR PO21 ...... 103 C3
  FERR BN12 ...... 92 B1
Anstead MFD/CHID GU8 * 110 H6
Ansty Cl BRIE/ROTT BN2 ...... 77 K8
Anthony Pl GSHT GU26 ...... 109 J8
Antlands La HORL RH6 ...... 20 E4
Antlands La East HORL RH6 ...... 20 D4
Antlands La West HORL RH6 ...... 20 D3
Anvil Cl BIL RH14 ...... 141 R1
  PTSD BN41 ...... 75 G3
  SWTR RH13 ...... 125 Q12
  WVILLE PO7 ...... 168 D3
Apollo Dr BOR GU35 ...... 106 H7
  WVILLE PO7 ...... 56 A2
Appledene Cnr
  RING/NEW BN8 ...... 167 P2
Appledore Cl HWH RH16 ...... 45 K3
Appledore Gdns HWH RH16 ...... 45 K3
Appledore Rd BRIE/ROTT BN2.. 77 L1
Appledram La (North)
  CCH PO19 ...... 61 H7
Appledram La (South)
  SELS PO20 ...... 83 H2
Applefield CRAWE RH10 ...... 9 C4
Applegate Pl HORN PO8 * 168 D4
Apple Gv BOGR PO21 ...... 103 C4
  EMRTH PO10 ...... 58 C4
Applesham Av HOVE BN3 ...... 75 K3
Applesham Wy PTSD BN41 ...... 74 F4
Appleshaw Gn HAV PO9 ...... 56 D1
Appletree Dr MSEA/BNM PO22.. 65 G7
Appletrees SELS PO20 ...... 100 D7
Apple Tree Wk LHPTN BN17 ...... 88 C4
Applewalk BURH RH15 * 46 F6
Applewood HAV PO9 ...... 56 A2
The Approach BRI BN1 ...... 76 D2
  EGRIN RH19 ...... 23 M3
April Cl FERR BN12 ...... 91 K5
  HORS RH12 ...... 10 D1
Apsley Wy SALV BN13 ...... 69 M8

Arcade Buildings WTHG BN11 *... 13 H7
Arcade Rd LHPTN BN17 ...... 89 J4
The Arcade BOGR PO21 ...... 2 E7
  LISS GU33 ...... 116 B8
Archibald Rd WTHG BN11 ...... 93 M2
Arcturus Rd CRAWW RH11 ...... 28 D5
Ardale Cl WTHG BN11 ...... 92 E3
Arden Rd CRAWE RH10 ...... 9 K7
Ardingly Cl CRAWW RH11 ...... 29 G1
Ardingly Ct BRIE/ROTT BN2 * 5 G7
Ardingly Dr FERR BN12 ...... 92 A2
Ardingly Rd HWH RH16 ...... 130 F7
  RHWH RH17 ...... 44 C2
Ardingly St BRIE/ROTT BN2 * 5 G7
Ardingly Cl RHWH RH17 ...... 130 E2
Ardsheal Cl SALV BN13 ...... 71 H8
Ardsheal Rd SALV BN13 ...... 71 H7
Arford Common BOR GU35 ...... 107 N3
Arford Rd BOR GU35 ...... 107 N3
Argus Wk CRAWW RH11 ...... 28 E6
Argyle Circ BOGR PO21 * 2 D7
Argyle La BOR GU35 ...... 106 C7
Argyle Rd BOGR PO21 ...... 2 D7
  BRI BN1 ...... 4 D2
Ariadne Rd WTHG BN11 ...... 12 C8
Arle Cl HORN PO8 ...... 150 D9
Arlington Av BRIE/ROTT BN2... 53 L8
Arlington Ct FERR BN12 ...... 92 A4
Arlington Crs ANG/EP BN16... 91 C2
  BRI BN1 ...... 53 K8
Armadale Rd CCH PO19 ...... 7 H3
Armada Wy LHPTN BN17 ...... 89 M3
Arndale Rd LHPTN BN17 ...... 89 G3
Arne Cl CRAWW RH11 ...... 28 E6
Arne Gv HORL RH6 ...... 14 D4
Arnell Av SELS PO20 ...... 181 L7
Arnfield Cl CRAWW RH11 ...... 28 C4
Arnhem Rd BOGR PO21 ...... 2 A2
Arnold St BRIE/ROTT BN2 ...... 5 K3
Arnold Wy RCCH PO18 ...... 60 B9
Aron Cl EPSF GU31 ...... 133 M7
Arragon Ct WVILLE PO7 ...... 168 B10
Arran Cl CRAWW RH11 ...... 8 B9
Arrivals Rd HORL RH6 ...... 19 L1
Artel Cft CRAWE RH10 ...... 9 L3
Artex Av ANG/EP BN16 ...... 90 D2
Arthur Rd CRAWW RH11 ...... 28 D3
  SWTR RH13 ...... 10 F7
Arthur St HOVE BN3 ...... 75 M5
Arun Cl ANG/EP BN16 ...... 90 B3
  ARUN BN18 ...... 176 F2
  EPSF GU31 ...... 133 M7
  LAN/SOMP BN15 ...... 72 B6
  RCCH PO18 ...... 70 C6
Arun Ct ANG/EP BN16 * 90 F4
  PUL/STOR RH20 ...... 159 K3
Arun Crs SALV BN13 ...... 70 B6
Arundel By-Pass ARUN BN18.. 66 F2
Arundel Cl BOGR PO21 ...... 103 M1
  CRAWE RH10 ...... 30 C8
  LIPH GU30 ...... 107 L9
  SHOR BN43 ...... 74 B5
  SWTR RH13 ...... 125 R12
Arundel Dr LHPTN BN17 ...... 67 H8
Arundel Ms BRIE/ROTT BN2 * .. 96 D1
Arundel Pl BRIE/ROTT BN2 ...... 96 D1
Arundel Rd ANG/EP BN16 ...... 68 D5
  ARUN BN18 ...... 64 D2
  BRIE/ROTT BN2 ...... 96 D2
  LHPTN BN17 ...... 89 J4
  RCCH PO18 ...... 62 F3
  SALV BN13 ...... 69 H5
  SELS PO20 ...... 100 B8
Arundel Ter BRIE/ROTT BN2 ...... 96 D2
Arundel Wy MSEA/BNM PO22.. 88 A8
Arun Ford Cl ARUN BN18 ...... 88 D2
Arun Pde LHPTN BN17 ...... 89 J6
Arun Prospect
  PUL/STOR RH20 * 158 H4
Arun Rd BIL RH14 ...... 123 F12
  BOGR PO21 ...... 103 M1
Arunside HORS RH12 ...... 125 R4
Arun St ARUN BN18 ...... 67 G3
Arun Ter ARUN BN18 * 66 F3
Arun V PUL/STOR RH20 ...... 158 D8
Arun Wy BOGR PO21 ...... 103 C5
  SWTR RH13 ...... 11 G9
Ascot Cl SELS PO20 ...... 99 L5
Ascot Wy ANG/EP BN16 ...... 90 D3
Ashacre La SALV BN13 ...... 70 E6
Ashacre Ms SALV BN13 ...... 70 E6
Ashacre Wy SALV BN13 ...... 70 E7
Ashburnham Cl BRI BN1 ...... 53 K8
  CCH PO19 ...... 61 J4
  SALV BN13 ...... 70 A8
Ashburnham Dr BRI BN1 ...... 53 J7
Ashburnham Rd CRAWE RH10... 9 M8
Ashbury Rd BOR GU35 ...... 106 C7
Ash Cl CRAWE RH10 ...... 22 B8
  HOVE BN3 ...... 76 B2
  SALV BN13 ...... 178 H11
Ash Combe MFD/CHID GU8..... 110 F5
Ashcombe Hollow LEWES BN7.. 55 J6
Ashcombe La LEWES BN7 ...... 55 K7
Ash Copse HORN PO8 ...... 168 A4
Ashcroft Cl SHOR BN43 ...... 74 C6
Ashcroft La HORN PO8 ...... 169 L3
Ashcroft Wy BOGR PO21 ...... 102 F6
Ashdene Gdns
  PUL/STOR RH20 ...... 161 K9
Ashdown Cl ANG/EP BN16... 90 E1
  FROW RH18 ...... 34 E7
  HWH RH16 ...... 45 L5
Ashdown Ct CRAWE RH10 * 29 L6
Ashdown Dr CRAWE RH10 ...... 29 K7
Ashdown Rd BRIE/ROTT BN2... 77 C5
  FROW RH18 ...... 34 E7
  WTHG BN11 ...... 13 H3
Ashdown Vw EGRIN RH19 ...... 33 K4
Ashenground Cl HWH RH16 ...... 45 H6
Ashenground Rd HWH RH16 ...... 45 G6
Ashe Rd HAV PO9 ...... 169 J12
Ashfield BIL RH14 ...... 121 R3
Ashfield Cl MIDH GU29 ...... 136 H9
Ashfield Rd MIDH GU29 ...... 136 H10
Ashfold Av SALV BN13 ...... 70 F4
Ashford Rd BRI BN1 ...... 76 F3
Ash Gv HASM GU27 ...... 119 K8
  HWH RH16 ...... 45 J5
  LIPH GU30 ...... 118 A2
  MSEA/BNM PO22 ...... 86 B6
  WTHG BN11 ...... 13 J5
Ashington Cl HORN PO8 ...... 168 B6
Ash Keys CRAWE RH10 ...... 9 C6

Ash La ANG/EP BN16 ...... 90 B4
Ashleigh Cl ANG/EP BN16 ...... 68 E7
Ashleigh Rd HORS RH12 ...... 36 B4
  HAV PO9 ...... 52 D6
Ashlings Wy HOVE BN3 ...... 75 K3
  SHOR BN43 ...... 74 A4
Ashmead BOR GU35 ...... 106 G6
Ashmead Rd ANG/EP BN16 ...... 90 F1
Ashmere Gdns
  MSEA/BNM PO22 ...... 87 J8
Ashmere La MSEA/BNM PO22.. 87 J8
Ashmore Av HORS RH12 ...... 90 F1
Ashmore Cl HORS RH12 ...... 27 H3
Ash Rd CRAWE RH10 ...... 9 L1
  SWTR RH13 ...... 125 P12
Ashton Gdns ANG/EP BN16... 90 B5
Ashton Ri BRIE/ROTT BN2 ...... 5 J5
Ash Tree Cl HASM GU27 ...... 109 G6
Ashurst Cl BOGR PO21 ...... 85 M7
  FERR BN12 ...... 92 A4
  HORS RH12 ...... 36 F4
Ashurst Dr CRAWE RH10 ...... 30 C5
  FERR BN12 ...... 92 A4
Ashurst Rd BRIE/ROTT BN2... 53 L8
Ashurst Wy ANG/EP BN16 ...... 90 F2
Ash V MFD/CHID GU8 ...... 110 F4
Ashway BURH RH15 ...... 46 F7
Ashwood Cl HAV PO9 ...... 56 C2
  WTHG BN11 ...... 13 M2
Ashwood Dr ANG/EP BN16... 90 F1
Aspen Cl BOR GU35 ...... 106 G8
  HORN PO8 ...... 168 B4
  WTHG BN11 ...... 45 L5
Aspen Ct LAN/SOMP BN15 * 94 B1
Aspen Wy HORN PO8 ...... 168 B4
  HORS RH12 ...... 36 F4
  MSEA/BNM PO22 ...... 87 K7
Aston Ri PUL/STOR RH20 ...... 159 K2
Astra Cl RCCH PO18 ...... 60 B8
Athelstan Cl CRAWE RH10 ...... 30 D3
Athelstan Rd SALV BN13 ...... 12 A2
Athelstan Wy SWTR RH13 ...... 11 G9
Athena Av WVILLE PO7 ...... 56 A2
Atholl Rd BOR GU35 ...... 106 G8
Atkinson Ct HORL RH6 * 15 C7
Atkinson Rd CRAWE RH10 ...... 30 B5
Atlantis Av WVILLE PO7 ...... 56 A3
Atlingworth St BRIE/ROTT BN2.. 5 H8
Attree Dr BRIE/ROTT BN2 ...... 5 J5
Auchinleck Cl CRAWE RH10 * .. 32 A2
Auckland Cl CRAWW RH11 ...... 19 J8
Auckland Dr BRIE/ROTT BN2... 77 L4
Audrey Cl BRI BN1 ...... 52 D8
Augusta Pl WTHG BN11 ...... 13 C7
Augustines Wy HWH RH16 ...... 45 H5
Auriol Dr HAV PO9 ...... 56 B5
Aurum Cl HORL RH6 ...... 15 C7
Austen Cl EGRIN RH19 ...... 23 C8
Avalon Wy SALV BN13 ...... 70 C7
Avebury Cl HORS RH12 ...... 36 F2
  SELS PO20 ...... 100 B8
Aveling Cl BRIE/ROTT BN2 ...... 30 B5
Avenue Ap CCH PO19 * 6 F8
Avenue De Chartres CCH PO19.... 6 D6
Avenue Gdns HORL RH6 ...... 15 H7
Avenue Rd GSHT GU26 ...... 108 C6
The Avenue BOGR PO21 ...... 2 A6
  BRIE/ROTT BN2 ...... 77 J3
  CCH PO19 ...... 61 L3
  EGRIN RH19 ...... 23 M3
  EPSF GU31 ...... 133 N6
  FERR BN12 ...... 92 B1
  GSHT GU26 ...... 108 G6
  HASM GU27 ...... 109 J10
  HORL RH6 ...... 14 E7
  LEWES BN7 ...... 55 J8
  LIPH GU30 ...... 117 P1
  RCCH PO18 ...... 59 J4
  RCCH PO18 ...... 170 F10
  SHOR BN43 ...... 73 K4
  SWTR RH13 ...... 125 N7
Avery Cl SWTR RH13 ...... 74 E1
Avian Gdns BOGR PO21 ...... 103 G3
Aviary Cl RCCH PO18 ...... 59 J3
Aviary Wy CRAWE RH10 ...... 22 B8
Avisford Park Rd ARUN BN18 .. 65 K5
Avisford Ter BOGR PO21 * 103 J2
Avocet Quay EMRTH PO10 ...... 58 C4
Avocet Wy HORN PO8 ...... 168 B2
Avon Cl EPSF GU31 ...... 133 M7
  LAN/SOMP BN15 ...... 72 A7
  MSEA/BNM PO22 ...... 87 H8
Avondale Cl FERR BN12 ...... 92 C2
  HORL RH6 ...... 15 H7
Avondale Rd HOVE BN3 ...... 4 A2
  WVILLE PO7 ...... 168 A9
Avonhurst BURH RH15 ...... 47 G6
Avon Rd LHPTN BN17 ...... 89 J4
Avon Wk CRAWW RH11 ...... 28 E4
Awbridge Rd HAV PO9 ...... 56 F4
Awbrook Cl RHWH RH17 ...... 148 H2
Aylwin Pl SELS PO20 ...... 84 B4
Aymer Rd HOVE BN3 ...... 75 M7
Ayshe Court Dr SWTR RH13 ...... 11 G4
Azalea Av BOR GU35 ...... 107 K4
Azalea Cl HAV PO9 ...... 57 K1
Azalea Dr HASM GU27 ...... 109 J9

B

Babsham La BOGR PO21 ...... 85 L5
Back La BIL RH14 ...... 121 R3
  CRAWE RH10 ...... 31 H7
Backwoods Cl HWH RH16 ...... 45 K3
Backwoods La HWH RH16 ...... 45 K3
Baden Dr HORL RH6 ...... 14 D5
Baden Powell La LISS GU33 ...... 116 C3
Baden Rd BRIE/ROTT BN2 ...... 77 J5
Badger Brow WVILLE PO7 ...... 168 B11
Badger Cl PTSD BN41 ...... 75 F5
Badger Dr HWH RH16 ...... 44 F4
Badgers Cl HORS RH12 ...... 36 E3
Badgers Holt PUL/STOR RH20... 160 E12
Badgers Wk BURH RH15 ...... 47 G7
Badgers Wy BIL RH14 ...... 122 H1
  EGRIN RH19 ...... 23 L5
Badgers Wd PUL/STOR RH20.. 160 A7
Badger Wk CCH PO19 ...... 6 A2
Badger Wy BRI BN1 ...... 53 K7
Baffin's La CCH PO19 ...... 6 F5

Bailey Cl HORS RH12 ...... 36 E2
  LHPTN BN17 ...... 89 M2
Bailing Hl HORS RH12 ...... 115 P11
Baird Cl CRAWE RH10 ...... 19 M8
Bakehouse Barn Cl HORS RH12.. 36 D2
Bakehouse Cl HORL RH6 ...... 14 E4
Baker Cl CRAWE RH10 ...... 8 F8
Bakers Arms Hl ARUN BN18... 67 G2
Bakers Fld LISS GU33 ...... 116 C3
Baker's La SWTR RH13 ...... 143 L5
Baker St BRI BN1 ...... 4 F3
Bakery La BOGR PO21 * 2 C8
Bakery Ms BRIE/ROTT BN2 ...... 77 H4
Bala Crs MSEA/BNM PO22 ...... 87 G7
Balchins Cl BIL RH14 ...... 141 J1
Balcombe Av SALV BN13 ...... 71 H8
Balcombe Gdns HORL RH6 ...... 15 H7
Balcombe La EGRIN RH19 ...... 43 K7
  RHWH RH17 ...... 130 C1
Balcombe Rd CRAWE RH10 ...... 30 D8
  CRAWE RH10 ...... 30 D8
  HORL RH6 ...... 15 C5
  HWH RH16 ...... 45 G1
Baldwin Cl CRAWE RH10 ...... 30 B6
  MSEA/BNM PO22 ...... 87 J7
Baldwins Fld EGRIN RH19 * 23 H5
Balfour Dr LISS GU33 ...... 116 B9
Balfour Rd BRI BN1 ...... 76 E3
Balliol Cl BOGR PO21 ...... 103 K1
  CCH PO19 * 7 L5
Ballsdown MFD/CHID GU8 ...... 110 F5
Balmoral Cl CRAWE RH10 ...... 30 A2
  BOGR PO21 ...... 103 K3
Balmoral Wy PSF GU32 ...... 133 N5
Balsdean Rd BRIE/ROTT BN2... 78 C4
Bamborough Cl SWTR RH13 .. 125 K12
Bamford Cl BRIE/ROTT BN2 ...... 77 M3
Bampfield St PTSD BN41 ...... 75 C5
Bancroft Rd CRAWE RH10 ...... 30 C4
Banjo Rd LHPTN BN17 ...... 89 K6
Bank La CRAWE RH10 ...... 8 F4
Bank Pas STEY/UB SN44 ...... 48 C2
Bank Prec CRAWE RH10 ...... 19 M8
Banks Cft PUL/STOR RH20 ...... 160 E11
Bankside BRI BN1 ...... 52 E8
  HPPT/KEY BN6 ...... 165 N4
Bankside Ct BRI BN1 * 52 E8
Banks Rd CRAWE RH10 ...... 30 B4
  RING/NEW BN8 ...... 149 P4
Bank Ter CRAWE RH10 * 8 E5
Bankview BRI BN1 ...... 53 G5
Bannerman Rd PSF GU32 ...... 133 N5
Bannister Gdns
  PUL/STOR RH20 ...... 160 B10
Bannister Wy HWH RH16 ...... 45 G3
Banstead Cl FERR BN12 ...... 92 B4
Barancraig Av BRI BN1 ...... 52 F6
Barbary La FERR BN12 ...... 91 K4
Barber Cl CRAWE RH10 ...... 30 B7
Barcombe Cl BRI BN1 ...... 53 L8
Barfield Pk LAN/SOMP BN15... 72 E7
Barford Cl CCH PO19 ...... 6 A4
Barham Rd PSF GU32 ...... 133 N6
Barkdale BURH RH15 ...... 47 J4
Barker Cl RCCH PO18 ...... 60 F6
Barkworth Wy
  PUL/STOR RH20 ...... 159 R6
Bar La SWTR RH13 ...... 124 A12
Barlavington Wy MIDH GU29.. 136 H12
Barley Cl BOGR PO21 ...... 102 E3
  CRAWE RH10 ...... 8 F6
Barleycroft SWTR RH13 ...... 145 K4
Barley Dr BURH RH15 ...... 46 F5
Barley Mow Hl BOR GU35 ...... 107 N3
Barlow Rd CCH PO19 ...... 6 A2
  CRAWW RH11 ...... 28 B6
Barnard Ga HWH RH16 ...... 45 H2
Barn Cl CRAWW RH11 ...... 39 G2
  EMRTH PO10 ...... 57 L5
  HPPT/KEY BN6 ...... 164 D3
  LEWES BN7 ...... 55 M8
  LHPTN BN17 ...... 89 K1
  SALV BN13 ...... 70 E6
Barn Cottage La HWH RH16 ...... 45 J8
Barn Ct CRAWE RH10 ...... 21 K7
Barncroft Wy HAV PO9 ...... 56 D1
Barn End HFD BN5 ...... 163 L4
Barnes Cl SELS PO20 ...... 181 L8
Barnes Rd PTSD BN41 ...... 74 F5
Barnes Wy HAV PO9 ...... 56 D2
Barnett Cl SELS PO20 ...... 64 D5
Barnett Rd BRI BN1 ...... 77 G3
Barnett's Fld SELS PO20 ...... 64 D5
Barnet Wy HOVE BN3 ...... 75 K2
Barn Feld MSEA/BNM PO22 ...... 3 H5
Barnfield LEWES BN7 ...... 166 H4
Barnfield Cl EMRTH PO10 ...... 58 F7
Barnfield Dr CCH PO19 ...... 6 B5
Barn Field Gdns BRIE/ROTT BN2.. 5 L1
Barnfield Gdns HPPT/KEY BN6.. 166 B6
Barnfield Rd HWH RH16 ...... 8 F7
  EPSF GU31 ...... 133 N6
Barn Fold WVILLE PO7 * 168 C8
Barnham La ARUN BN18 ...... 65 H6
Barnham Rd SELS PO20 ...... 64 E6
Barn Hatch Cl LEWES BN7 ...... 55 M5
Barnhouse Cl PUL/STOR RH20.. 159 K3
Barn House La
  PUL/STOR RH20 ...... 159 K3
Barn La MSEA/BNM PO22 ...... 86 C4
Barnmead HWH RH16 ...... 45 J2
Barn Meadow RHWH RH17 ...... 40 F8
Barn Ri BRI BN1 ...... 52 D6
  MSEA/BNM PO22 ...... 65 H7
Barn Rd SELS PO20 ...... 99 L6
Barns Farm La
  PUL/STOR RH20 ...... 178 C3
Barnsfold La HORS RH12 ...... 113 M11
Barnside RCCH PO18 ...... 60 C6
Barnside Av BURH RH15 ...... 47 H8
Barnside Cl LISS GU33 ...... 116 C10
Barnsnap Cl HORS RH12 ...... 36 C5
Barn Wk SELS PO20 ...... 99 L7
Barnwood Cl CRAWE RH10 ...... 30 B4
Baron Cl SELS PO20 ...... 64 D5
Barons Ct BURH RH15 ...... 47 G7
Barons Down Rd LEWES BN7... 55 M5
Barons Wk LEWES BN7 ...... 55 M5
Barque Cl LHPTN BN17 ...... 89 M3
Barrackfield Wk HORS RH12.... 10 D7

Barrack La BOGR PO21 ...... 103 J4
Barrack Rw ARUN BN18 * 65 J4
Barrhill Av BRI BN1 ...... 52 E6
Barrington Cl FERR BN12 ...... 92 B5
  HWH RH16 ...... 45 K1
Barrington Rd CRAWE RH10 ...... 8 E8
  HWH RH16 ...... 45 K1
Barrington Wd HWH RH14 ...... 141 R2
Barrow Cl BIL RH14 ...... 141 R2
  BRI BN1 ...... 77 H5
Barrowfield RHWH RH17 ...... 44 C2
Barrowfield Cl HOVE BN3 ...... 76 B3
Barrowfield Dr HOVE BN3 ...... 76 C3
Barrow Hl BRI BN1 ...... 77 H5
  HFD BN5 ...... 163 L5
Barry Cl CRAWE RH10 ...... 29 K6
Barry Wk BRIE/ROTT BN2 ...... 5 J5
Bartholomew CCH PO19 ...... 6 C8
Bartholomew Cl HASM GU27... 109 M9
Bartholomews BRI BN1 * 4 D7
Bartholomew Sq BRI BN1 * 4 D7
Bartholomew Wy HORS RH12... 36 F5
Barton Cl BOGR PO21 ...... 102 F4
  SALV BN13 ...... 70 E8
Barton Crs EGRIN RH19 ...... 33 M1
Barton Cross HORN PO8 ...... 168 C2
Barton La PETW GU28 ...... 139 L9
  RCCH PO19 ...... 6 A1
  MSEA/BNM PO22 ...... 85 M6
Bartons Rd HAV PO9 ...... 57 K1
Barton Wk CRAWE RH10 ...... 30 A5
Barton Wy BOGR PO21 ...... 100 A2
Barttelot Rd HORS RH12 ...... 10 D7
Barwell Gv EMRTH PO10 ...... 57 M2
Barwick Cl ANG/EP BN16 ...... 90 A2
Bashfords La SALV BN13 ...... 13 H2
Bashford Wy CRAWE RH10 ...... 30 C1
Bashurst Copse SWTR RH13.... 125 J5
Bashurst Hl SWTR RH13 ...... 124 G10
Basildon Wy CRAWW RH11 ...... 28 D6
Basing Hl PUL/STOR RH20 ...... 161 M6
Basing Rd HAV PO9 ...... 168 F12
Basin Rd CCH PO19 ...... 6 C6
Basin Rd North PTSD BN41 ...... 75 G7
Basin Rd South PTSD BN41 ...... 74 E7
Bassels La SWTR RH13 ...... 143 R11
Bassenthwaite Gdns
  BOR GU35 ...... 106 G4
Bassett Rd BOGR PO21 ...... 2 C8
  CRAWE RH10 ...... 30 C6
Batchmere Rd SELS PO20 ...... 100 E3
Bateman Ct CRAWE RH10 * 9 M9
Batemans Cl SALV BN13 ...... 70 M9
Batemans Rd BRIE/ROTT BN2.. 78 C3
Bates Rd BRI BN1 ...... 76 E3
Bath Pl WTHG BN11 ...... 13 H7
Bath Rd EMRTH PO10 ...... 58 A5
  WTHG BN11 ...... 12 C8
Bath St BRI BN1 ...... 4 C2
  WTHG BN11 ...... 12 C8
Battens Wy HAV PO9 ...... 57 G1
Batts Dr HFD BN5 ...... 163 J5
Batts La PUL/STOR RH20 ...... 159 N4
Bavant Rd BRI BN1 ...... 76 D3
Baxter Cl CRAWE RH10 ...... 30 A5
Baxter St BRIE/ROTT BN2 ...... 5 K3
Bay Br SWTR RH13 ...... 143 R11
Baybridge Rd HAV PO9 ...... 169 J12
Bay Cl HORL RH6 ...... 14 F7
Baycombe La ARUN BN18 ...... 175 J11
Bayeux Cl HORL RH6 ...... 14 F7
Bayfield Cl HORL RH6 ...... 14 D5
Bayford Rd LHPTN BN17 ...... 89 J5
Bayhams Fld EGRIN RH19 ...... 42 F3
Bayhorne La HORL RH6 ...... 15 H8
Bayley Rd SELS PO20 ...... 63 H4
Baylis Crs BURH RH15 ...... 46 C8
Baylis Wk CRAWW RH11 * 29 C8
Baynards Rd HORS RH12 ...... 113 P7
Baythorn La HORL RH6 ...... 15 J3
Baytree Cl CCH PO19 ...... 61 L3
Bay Tree Cl SHOR BN43 ...... 74 B4
Bay Tree Gdn ANG/EP BN16 * .. 90 E4
Bay Wk BOGR PO21 ...... 103 J4
Baywood Gdns BRIE/ROTT BN2.. 78 B4
Bazehill Rd BRIE/ROTT BN2 ...... 97 M2
Beach Cl BOGR PO21 ...... 103 H4
Beach Crs LHPTN BN17 ...... 89 K6
Beachcroft Pl LAN/SOMP BN15.. 94 D1
Beach Gdns SELS PO20 ...... 181 K8
Beach Gn SHOR BN43 ...... 73 J7
Beach Pde WTHG BN11 ...... 13 K6
Beach Rd BOGR PO21 ...... 102 F6
  EMRTH PO10 ...... 57 M5
  LHPTN BN17 ...... 89 K6
  SELS PO20 ...... 181 M5
  SHOR BN43 ...... 73 M5
Beachside Cl FERR BN12 ...... 92 D4
Beachy Crs CRAWW RH11 ...... 28 F8
Beacon Cl BRI BN1 ...... 76 B2
Beacon Ct SWTR RH13 * 11 M2
Beacon Dr SELS PO20 ...... 181 L7
Beacon Hl BRIE/ROTT BN2 ...... 97 K2
  LING RH7 ...... 24 A1
  PUL/STOR RH20 ...... 158 B9
Beacon Hill Ct GSHT GU26 ...... 108 C3
Beacon Hill Pk GSHT GU26 ...... 108 E4
Beacon Hill Rd GSHT GU26 ...... 108 F3
Beacon Hurst HPPT/KEY BN6.. 165 Q6
Beacon Rd HPPT/KEY BN6 ...... 166 A8
Beaconsfield Cl
  MSEA/BNM PO22 ...... 87 K8
Beaconsfield Pde BRI BN1 * 76 E4
Beaconsfield Rd BRI BN1 * 4 E2
  LHPTN BN17 ...... 89 J2
  PTSD BN41 ...... 75 G5
Beaconsfield Vls BRI BN1 ...... 76 E4
Beacon Vw LHPTN BN17 ...... 89 M3
The Beacon EGRIN RH19 ...... 42 D2
Beagle Dr ARUN BN18 ...... 88 A3
Beal Crs BRI BN1 ...... 77 G3
Beale St BURH RH15 ...... 46 D8
Bear Rd BRIE/ROTT BN2 ...... 77 H5
Bearsden Wy HORS RH12 ...... 125 N2
Beatty Av BRI BN1 ...... 53 J7
Beatty Rd BOGR PO21 ...... 2 D5
Beaufield Cl SELS PO20 ...... 181 K8
Beaufort Rd BOR GU35 ...... 106 G4
  HAV PO9 ...... 56 E3
Beaufort Ter BRIE/ROTT BN2 ...... 5 J4
Beaulieu Av HAV PO9 ...... 168 E11
Beaumont Cl CRAWW RH11 ...... 28 D4
Beaumont Pk LHPTN BN17 ...... 89 M5
Beaumont Rd SALV BN13 ...... 71 J8
Beaver Cl CCH PO19 ...... 61 G7

HORS RH12............................36 D3
Beavers Ms *BOR* GU35............106 H5
Beccles Rd *WTHG* BN11............12 C5
Becket Rd *SALV* BN13............12 B5
Beckett La *CRAWW* RH11............19 J8
Beckford Wy *EGRIN* RH19............33 L1
Beckford Rd *HAV* PO9............30 A8
Beckham La *PSF* GU32............133 L5
Beckley Cl *BRIE/ROTT* BN2............77 K1
SALV BN13............70 A8
Beckworth Cl *HWH* RH16............45 K3
SALV BN13............70 A8
Beckworth La *HWH* RH16............45 K3
Bedale Cl *CRAWW* RH11............8 C3
Bedales Hl *HWH* RH16............130 C12
Bedelands Cl *BURH* RH15............47 G4
Bedenscroft *BOGR* PO21............103 H2
Bedford Av *BOGR* PO21............85 M7
Bedford Cl *BOR* GU35............106 C8
HAV PO9............57 J5
Bedford Pl *BRI* BN1............4 A6
Bedford Rd *PSF* GU32............133 L6
SWTR RH13............10 F7
Bedford Rw *WTHG* BN11............13 J8
Bedford Sq *BRI* BN1............4 A7
Bedford St *BOGR* PO21............2 D7
BRIE/ROTT BN2............5 J8
Bedham La *PUL/STOR* RH20............140 C11
Bedhampton Hl *HAV* PO9............56 C4
Bedhampton Hill Rd *HAV* PO9............56 C4
Bedhampton Rd *HAV* PO9............56 D3
Bedhampton Wy *HAV* PO9............57 G1
Beech Av *CCH* PO19............6 A4
SELS PO20............100 A7
Beech Cl *BOGR* PO21............102 E3
EGRIN RH19 *............23 J7
HORN PO8 *............168 A1
MFD/CHID GU8............110 F5
PTSD BN41............74 E2
SALV BN13............178 H10
SELS PO20............64 C6
Beechcroft Cl *LIPH* GU30............117 L2
Beechers Rd *PTSD* BN41............74 E2
Beeches Av *SALV* BN13............71 J6
Beeches Crs *CRAWE* RH10............9 G7
Beeches La *EGRIN* RH19............34 C3
The Beeches *BRI* BN1............76 C5
Beechey Cl *CRAWE* RH10............21 G6
Beechey Wy *CRAWE* RH10............21 G6
Beechfield Pk *SELS* PO20 *............64 C8
Beech Flds *EGRIN* RH19............23 J6
Beech Gdns *CRAWE* RH10............31 M2
Beech Gv *BRIE/ROTT* BN2............77 K8
LAN/SOMP BN15 *............72 B3
MIDH GU29............136 H11
PUL/STOR RH20............160 C10
Beech Hanger End *GSHT* GU26............108 E6
Beech Hl *BOR* GU35............107 G5
HWH RH16............45 L6
Beech Hill Rd *BOR* GU35............107 N3
Beech Holme *CRAWE* RH10............31 M1
Beech Hurst Cl *HWH* RH16 *............44 F5
Beechings *HFD* BN5............163 J4
Beeching Wy *EGRIN* RH19............23 J8
Beechlands Cl *ANG/EP* BN16............90 F4
Beech La *GSHT* GU26............108 C5
Beech Rd *HASM* GU27............109 N10
HORN PO8............150 E8
HORS RH12............37 G4
SALV BN13............178 H11
Beechside *CRAWE* RH10............9 G6
Beech Tree Cl *CRAWE* RH10............8 F1
Beech Vw *ANG/EP* BN16............68 F6
Beech Wy *ANG/EP* BN16............90 F1
HORN PO8............168 C4
Beechwood *SWTR* RH13............143 P1
Beechwood Av *BRI* BN1............76 C1
SALV BN13............70 A6
Beechwood Cl *BRI* BN1............76 C1
Beechwood Ct *LISS* GU33............116 D7
Beechwood La *LEWES* BN7............167 P7
PETW GU28............156 G8
Beechwoods *BURH* RH15............46 F8
Beechwood Vls *REDH* RH1............14 F2
Beechworth Rd *HAV* PO9............57 H4
Beeding Av *HOVE* BN3............75 L2
Beeding Cl *HORS* RH12............36 F4
LAN/SOMP BN15............72 C6
MSEA/BNM PO22............86 D6
Beedingwood Dr *HORS* RH12............37 K3
Beehive Cl *SELS* PO20............181 M6
Beehive La *FERR* BN12............91 L4
Beehive Ring Rd *HORL* RH6............20 D5
Beggarshouse La *HORL* RH6............18 B1
Beggar's La *POY/PYE* PO45............164 E11
Beggar's Wood Rd
RING/NEW BN8............149 M7
Behenna Cl *CRAWW* RH11............28 D4
Belfast St *HOVE* BN3............76 A6
Belgrave Crs *CCH* PO19............83 P2
Belgrave Pl *BRIE/ROTT* BN2............5 L9
Belgrave St *BRIE/ROTT* BN2............5 G4
Belinus Dr *BIL* RH14............141 R1
Bellair Rd *HAV* PO9............57 H9
Bellamy Rd *CRAWE* RH10............30 B7
Bell Cl *CCH* PO19............6 C1
PUL/STOR RH20............159 J3
Bell Ct *BOGR* PO21............103 H5
RCCH PO18 *............59 C6
Bell Davies Rd *LHPTN* BN17............89 L3
Belle Meade Cl *SELS* PO20............64 C8
Belle Vue *WTHG* BN11 *............13 G5
Bellevue Gdns *BRIE/ROTT* BN2............5 L8
Bellevue La *EMRTH* PO10............58 A7
Bell Hammer *EGRIN* RH19............33 K1
Bell Hl *PSF* GU32............133 M4
Bell Hill Rdg *PSF* GU32............133 M4
Bellingham Crs *HOVE* BN3............75 J5
Bell La *MIDH* GU29............154 E5
SELS PO20............100 C5
Bell Md *HOVE* BN3 *............76 C6
Belloc Cl *CRAWE* RH10............30 A4
Belloc Ct *SWTR* RH13 *............11 M3
Belloc Rd *LHPTN* BN17............89 L2
Bell Rd *HASM* GU27............119 K2
HORS RH12............115 R9
Bellscroft Cl *LHPTN* BN17............89 L3
Bell Vale La *HASM* GU27............119 L1
Bellview Rd *SALV* BN13............70 F8
Belmont *BRI* BN1............4 B2
Belmont Cl *HORN* PO8............150 D11
HPPT/KEY BN6............165 M4
Belmont Gv *HAV* PO9............56 D3
Belmont La *HPPT/KEY* BN6............165 K5
Belmont St *BOGR* PO21............2 E8

BRI BN1............4 F3
Belmont Ter *ARUN* BN18............87 M3
Belsize Cl *WTHG* BN11............12 C4
Belsize Rd *WTHG* BN11............12 C4
Belton Rd *BRIE/ROTT* BN2............5 G1
Belvedere Av *LAN/SOMP* BN15............72 C7
Belverdere Cl *PSF* GU32............133 N5
Belverdere Ter *HOVE* BN3............4 A3
Belynham Ct *LHPTN* BN17............89 J3
Bembridge St *BRIE/ROTT* BN2............5 K1
Benbow Cl *HORN* PO8............168 D2
SHOR BN43............73 L7
Benbow La *MFD/CHID* GU8............112 D5
Benchfield Cl *EGRIN* RH19............34 A1
Benedict Cl *WTHG* BN11............94 A2
Benedict Dr *WTHG* BN11............93 M2
Benett Av *HOVE* BN3............76 A3
Benett Dr *HOVE* BN3............76 A3
Benfield Cl *PTSD* BN41............75 H5
Benfield Crs *PTSD* BN41............75 H4
Benfield Wy *PTSD* BN41............75 H5
Bengairn Av *BRI* BN1............52 F6
Benham Rd *HFD* BN5............163 L4
Benjamin Rd *CRAWE* RH10............30 C5
Bennett Cl *CRAWE* RH10............30 A7
Bennett Rd *BRIE/ROTT* BN2............96 D1
Bennetts Cl *SELS* PO20............99 L6
Bennetts Rd *SWTR* RH13............11 J8
Bennetts Ter *MIDH* GU29 *............136 H10
Bennetts Wd *RDKG* RH5............16 B4
Bens Acre *SWTR* RH13............11 M6
Benson Rd *HFD* BN5............163 L1
Benson's La *HORS* RH12............27 H8
Bentham Rd *BRIE/ROTT* BN2............5 J3
Bentley Cl *HORN* PO8............168 D1
Bentley St *HAV* PO9............169 J12
Bentons La *SWTR* RH13............161 N2
Bentswood Crs *HWH* RH16............45 K4
Bentswood Rd *HWH* RH16............45 J4
Bentworth Cl *HAV* PO9............56 E1
Bepton Cl *MIDH* GU29............136 G11
Bepton Down *EPSF* GU31............133 P6
Bepton Rd *MIDH* GU29............154 D4
Berberis St *SHOR* BN43............74 A4
Beresford Rd *BRIE/ROTT* BN2............5 M7
Bereweeke Rd *MSEA/BNM* PO22............3 L5
Bergamot La *SHOR* BN43............74 B4
Berghestede Rd
MSEA/BNM PO22............86 B7
Berkeley Cl *CRAWW* RH11............28 C7
Berkeley Ms *CCH* PO19............7 G2
Berkeley Rw *LEWES* BN7............55 M5
Berkeley Sq *HAV* PO9............57 J4
WTHG BN11............12 B6
Berkshire Ct *FERR* BN12 *............92 A2
Bernard Pl *BRIE/ROTT* BN2............5 K2
Bernard Rd *ARUN* BN18............66 E3
BRIE/ROTT BN2............5 K2
WTHG BN11............92 E4
Berrall Wy *BIL* RH14............141 R3
Berriedale Av *HOVE* BN3............75 K7
Berriedale Cl *LAN/SOMP* BN15............72 B6
Berriedale Dr *LAN/SOMP* BN15............72 B6
Berrybarn La *SELS* PO20............99 G5
Berry Cl *BURH* RH15............46 F4
Berry Ct *CCH* PO19 *............61 G5
Berrydown Rd *HAV* PO9............168 D10
Berrylands *LISS* GU33............116 D6
Berrylands Farm
HPPT/KEY BN6............146 E12
Berry La *LHPTN* BN17............89 L5
MSEA/BNM PO22............85 M6
Berrymill Cl *BOGR* PO21............2 E4
Bersted Ms *MSEA/BNM* PO22 *............2 E3
Bersted St *MSEA/BNM* PO22............2 E3
Bessborough Ter
LAN/SOMP BN15............94 C1
Betchley Cl *EGRIN* RH19............23 K6
Bethune Cl *CRAWE* RH10............30 C4
Bethune Rd *SWTR* RH13............11 H7
Bethwines Cl *RCCH* PO18............60 C4
Betts Wy *CRAWE* RH10............19 J7
Betula Cl *WVILLE* PO7............168 B11
Bevan Rd *HORN* PO8............168 A4
Bevendean Crs *BRIE/ROTT* BN2............77 K3
Bevendean Rd *BRIE/ROTT* BN2............77 J3
Beverley Cl *SELS* PO20............181 M6
Beverley Gdns *ANG/EP* BN16............90 A4
Beverley Ms *CRAWE* RH10............9 L5
Bewbush Dr *CRAWW* RH11............28 C6
Bewick Gdns *CCH* PO19............7 H1
Bewley Rd *ANG/EP* BN16............68 E7
Bexhill Rd *BRIE/ROTT* BN2............78 C4
Bex La *MIDH* GU29............154 H3
Bidbury La *HAV* PO9............56 D4
Biggin Cl *CRAWW* RH11............8 C7
Bignor Cl *ANG/EP* BN16............90 C3
Bignor Park Rd
PUL/STOR RH20............157 R9
Bigwood Av *HOVE* BN3............76 C6
Bilberry Cl *CRAWW* RH11............29 G5
Billam Ter *BRIE/ROTT* BN2 *............5 G4
Billett Av *WVILLE* PO7............168 A8
Billinghurst Rd
PUL/STOR RH20............160 E5
Billinghurst Rd *BIL* RH14............141 K1
HORS RH12............125 M2
Billinton Dr *CRAWE* RH10............30 A5
Billy Lawn Av *HAV* PO9............57 G1
Bilsham La *ARUN* BN18............87 K4
Bilsham Rd *ARUN* BN18............87 L4
Binderton La *RCCH* PO18............172 A7
Binhams Lea *MFD/CHID* GU8............112 A4
Binhams Meadow
MFD/CHID GU8............112 A4
Binney Ct *CRAWE* RH10............20 D8
Binstead Cl *CRAWW* RH11............29 G1
Binsted Av *MSEA/BNM* PO22............3 M1
Binsted Cl *ANG/EP* BN16............90 A3
Binsted La *ARUN* BN18............65 M3
Birch Av *RHWH* RH17............45 K6
Birch *ANG/EP* BN16............90 D1
ARUN BN18............66 D4
BOGR PO21............103 J2
BOR GU35............106 H7
CRAWE RH10............32 B1
LAN/SOMP BN15............94 C1
LISS GU33............116 D9
RHWH RH17............45 L6
Birch Dr *BIL* RH14............142 A2
Birch End *PUL/STOR* RH20............160 A4
Birchen La *HWH* RH16............45 H1

Birches Cl *SALV* BN13............70 B8
SELS PO20............181 J6
Birches Rd *HORS* RH12............37 C4
The Birches *CRAWE* RH10............9 M1
SWTR RH13............126 H2
Birchfield Est *HORL* RH6 *............18 C8
Birch Gv *BOR* GU35............106 C8
PUL/STOR RH20............160 A8
Birch Grove Crs *BRI* BN1............52 D8
Birchgrove Cl *RHWH* RH17............43 M8
Birchgrove Rd *RHWH* RH17............131 N4
Birch Lea *CRAWE* RH10............19 M8
Bircholt Rd *LIPH* GU30............117 L1
Bircholt Rd *BOR* GU35............107 Q3
Birch Tree Cl *EMRTH* PO10............58 A1
Birch Tree Dr *EMRTH* PO10............58 A1
Birch Tree Gdns *EMRTH* PO10............23 G6
Birch Tree La *PUL/STOR* RH20............160 E11
RHWH RH17............45 J2
Birchwood Cl *BIL* RH14............122 A2
CRAWE RH10............30 B2
HORL RH6............15 C5
Birchwood Grove Rd
BURH RH15............47 H8
CRAWW RH11............29 G1
Birdham Cl *BOGR* PO21............85 J2
Birdham Pl *BRIE/ROTT* BN2 *............77 K2
Birdham Rd *BRIE/ROTT* BN2 *............77 K2
SELS PO20............83 G8
Birdlip Cl *HORN* PO8............168 B3
Birkdale Cl *SALV* BN13............70 C5
Birkdale Dr *CRAWW* RH11............28 C4
Birkdale Rd *SALV* BN13............70 C5
Birkenholme Cl *BOR* GU35............107 R5
Birling Cl *BRIE/ROTT* BN2............77 J4
Biscay Cl *ANG/EP* BN16............90 A3
Bisham Cl *CRAWE* RH10............30 C5
Bishearne Gdns *LISS* GU33............116 A3
Bishop Luffa Cl *CCH* PO19............61 J1
Bishopric *HORS* RH12............10 A5
Bishopric Ct *HORS* RH12............10 A5
Bishops Cl *BOGR* PO21............102 F5
HASM GU27............119 K4
HFD BN5............163 K4
SALV BN13............12 B1
Bishops Ctyd *CCH* PO19 *............7 J2
Bishops Dr *LEWES* BN7............55 M5
Bishopsgate Rd *CCH* PO19............6 F2
Bishops Rd *HOVE* BN3............76 B4
SELS PO20............63 J3
Bishopstoke Rd *HAV* PO9............168 F12
Bishopstone La *RHWH* RH17............146 H6
Bitmead Cl *CRAWW* RH11............28 D4
Bittern Cl *CRAWW* RH11............28 D4
Bitterne Cl *HAV* PO9............168 G11
Black Berry Cl *HORN* PO8............150 E9
Blackberry La *SELS* PO20............181 J5
Blackberry Rd *EGRIN* RH19............23 H1
Blackbird Cl *HORN* PO8............168 A5
Blackbird Hl *CRAWE* RH10............32 B4
Black Boy La *RCCH* PO18 *............60 F7
Blackboy La *CCH* PO19............7 J5
RCCH PO18............60 F7
Blackbridge La *HORS* RH12............125 K4
Blackcap Cl *CRAWW* RH11............8 C7
HAV PO9............168 H8
Black Dog Wk *CRAWE* RH10............29 K1
Blackdown Crs *HAV* PO9............56 F1
Blackdown Rd *SALV* BN13............70 D5
Blackett Rd *CRAWE* RH10............30 B4
Blackfold Rd *CRAWE* RH10............9 L5
Blackgate La *HORS* RH12............163 K5
Black Gate La *PUL/STOR* RH20............141 K8
Blackheath *CRAWE* RH10............30 C1
Black Hl *HWH* RH16............45 K2
Black Horse Wy *HORS* RH12............10 C6
Blackhouse La *BURH* RH15............47 G5
PETW GU28............139 Q3
Blackhouse Rd *SWTR* RH13............38 B3
Blacklands Crs *FROW* RH18............34 E7
Black Lion St *BRI* BN1............4 E6
Blackman St *BRI* BN1............4 F4
Blackman Wy *SELS* PO20............84 A4
Blackmill La *RCCH* PO18............64 B2
Blackmoor Rd *LISS* GU33............106 D11
Blackmores *RHWH* RH17............47 M4
Blacksmiths Cl
PUL/STOR RH20 *............161 K9
Blacksmiths Crs
LAN/SOMP BN15............72 A7
Blackstone La *HFD* BN5............163 Q4
Blackstone La *HFD* BN5............163 Q4
Blackstone Wy *BURH* RH15............46 F4
Black Swan Cl *CRAWW* RH11............39 G2
Blackthorn Cl *BRI* BN1............76 C2
CRAWW RH11............29 H1
PTSD BN41............75 G3
SWTR RH13............11 K5
Blackthorne Cl *BOR* GU35............106 H6
Blackthorns *HPPT/KEY* BN6............164 D2
HWH RH16............45 K2
Blackthorns Cl *HWH* RH16............45 K2
The Blackthorns *BURH* RH15............47 G4
Blackwater La *CRAWE* RH10............30 B4
Blackwater Farm Rd *EGRIN* RH19............23 L7
Blackwell Hollow *EGRIN* RH19............23 L7
Blackwell Rd *EGRIN* RH19............23 L7
Bladon Cl *HAV* PO9............168 B6
Blake Cl *CRAWE* RH10............29 L7
Blakehurst La *ARUN* BN18............66 B4
Blakehurst Wy *LHPTN* BN17............89 J3
Blakemyle *BOGR* PO21............103 J5
Blaker St *BRIE/ROTT* BN2............5 G7
Blakes Farm Rd *SWTR* RH13............125 Q10
Blakes Rd *MSEA/BNM* PO22............3 L5
Blanches Wk *SWTR* RH13............144 F10
Blanches Wk *SWTR* RH13............144 F10
The Blatchen *LHPTN* BN17............89 L5
Blatchford Cl *SWTR* RH13............11 J4
Blatchford Rd *SWTR* RH13............11 J4
Blatchington Rd *HOVE* BN3............75 M6
Blendworth Crs *HAV* PO9............56 F2
Blendworth La *HORN* PO8............168 F1
Blenheim Av *SALV* BN13............70 D7
Blenheim Cl *ANG/EP* BN16............90 A2
CRAWE RH10............20 C7
EGRIN RH19............23 M6
Blenheim Ct *BOGR* PO21............103 K1
ANG/EP BN16............90 A2
SALV BN13............70 A7
Blenheim Flds *CCH* PO19............7 K5
HAV PO9............57 G1
Blenheim Pl *BRI* BN1............4 F5
Blenheim Rd *ARUN* BN18............87 L3
Bourne Wy *MIDH* GU29............136 H11
Blenheim St *HORN* PO8............168 B3

HORS RH12............36 C4
LAN/SOMP BN15............94 C1
Bligh Cl *CRAWE* RH10............9 J3
Blindley Rd *CRAWE* RH10............20 C8
Blissford Cl *HAV* PO9............169 J11
Blois Rd *LEWES* BN7............55 M2
Blomfield Dr *CCH* PO19............61 M4
Blondell Dr *BOGR* PO21............103 J2
Bloomsbury Pl *BRIE/ROTT* BN2............5 J7
Bloomsbury St *BRIE/ROTT* BN2............5 J7
Bloor Cl *HORS* RH12............36 C2
Blount Av *EGRIN* RH19............23 H8
Bluebell Cl *CRAWW* RH11 *............29 G6
EGRIN RH19............23 G8
HORS RH12............36 D4
HWH RH16............45 J5
WVILLE PO7............168 A11
Bluebell Dr *LHPTN* BN17............89 M2
Bluebell Rd *BOR* GU35............107 K4
Blueberry Hl *PUL/STOR* RH20............160 D11
Blue Cedars Cl *ANG/EP* BN16............90 D1
Bluecoat Pond *SWTR* RH13............125 N7
Blundell Av *HORL* RH6............14 G6
Blunden Dr *CRAWE* RH10............44 E3
Blunts Wy *HORS* RH12............10 C4
Blunts Wood Crs *HWH* RH16............44 E3
Blunts Wood Rd *HWH* RH16............44 E3
The Blytons *EGRIN* RH19............23 G8
Boardwalk CCH PO19 *............145 R7
Bob La *RHWH* RH17............145 R7
Boddingtons La
HPPT/KEY BN6............165 R6
Boderton Ms *PETW* GU28 *............157 J5
Bodiam Av *BRIE/ROTT* BN2............78 A4
FERR BN12............91 M3
Bodiam Cl *BRIE/ROTT* BN2............78 A3
CRAWE RH10............30 B3
SWTR RH13............125 R11
Bodmin Cl *SALV* BN13............70 C5
Bodmin Rd *SALV* BN13............70 C5
Bognor Rd *CCH* PO19............7 J5
HORS RH12............115 K9
RDKG RH5............115 M2
SELS PO20............62 D8
Bolding Wy *HWH* RH16............45 G7
Boldre Cl *HAV* PO9............56 D1
Boleyn Cl *CRAWE* RH10............30 C6
Boleyn Dr *BOGR* PO21............103 G4
Bolley Av *BOR* GU35............106 G4
Bolney Av *BRIE/ROTT* BN2............77 L1
Bolney Chapel Rd *RHWH* RH17............146 C5
Bolney Ct *CRAWW* RH11............28 G6
Bolney Rd *BRIE/ROTT* BN2............77 L1
RHWH RH17............146 F4
RHWH RH17............147 K3
Bolnore Rd *HWH* RH16............44 F5
SALV BN13............92 D2
Bolsover Rd *HOVE* BN3............75 K6
SALV BN13............92 D2
Bolters Rd *HORL* RH6............14 E4
Bolters Rd South *HORL* RH6............14 E4
Bolton Rd *CRAWE* RH10............30 A8
Boltro Rd *HWH* RH16............45 G4
Bonchurch Rd *BRIE/ROTT* BN2............5 K1
Bondfields Crs *HAV* PO9............168 G11
Bond St *ARUN* BN18............66 F2
BRI BN1............4 E6
Bonehurst Rd *HORL* RH6............14 F2
Bones La *EPSF* GU31............133 L12
Bonfire La *RHWH* RH17............131 M5
Bonnar Cl *SELS* PO20............181 J7
Bonnar Rd *SELS* PO20............181 K7
Bonnetts La *CRAWW* RH11............18 F6
Bonny Wood Rd
HPPT/KEY BN6............165 M6
Bookers La *SELS* PO20............100 B5
Bookers Yd *MSEA/BNM* PO22 *............2 D6
Booth Rd *CRAWW* RH11............28 F6
Borage Cl *CRAWW* RH11............28 F6
Bordean La *PSF* GU32............132 D4
Bordehill La *HWH* RH16............130 A5
Borden La *LIPH* GU30............135 N3
Border Cha *CRAWE* RH10............20 F7
Border Cl *EGRIN* RH19............23 L5
Border End *HASM* GU27 *............108 G11
Border Rd *HASM* GU27............108 G11
Bordon Rd *HAV* PO9............57 G1
The Boreen *BOR* GU35............107 G4
Borers Arms Rd *CRAWE* RH10............21 G5
Borers Cl *CRAWE* RH10 *............21 H6
Borough Gv *PSF* GU32............133 M7
Borough Hl *PSF* GU32............133 M7
Borough Rd *PSF* GU32............133 L7
Borough St *BRI* BN1............4 A6
Borrowdale Cl *CRAWW* RH11............8 B8
Borrow King Cl *BRIE/ROTT* BN2............77 J5
Bosham La *RCCH* PO18............60 A8
Bosham Rd *CRAWE* RH10............30 A6
Bosmere Gdns *EMRTH* PO10............57 M4
Bostal Rd *STEY/UB* BN44............48 E7
The Bostal *STEY/UB* BN44............49 H4
Bost Hl *SALV* BN13............70 D5
Bostock Av *HORS* RH12............11 M1
Boston Rd *HWH* RH16............45 K6
Boswell Rd *CRAWE* RH10............9 K4
CRAWE RH10............29 K6
Botany Cl *BRIE/ROTT* BN2............90 C5
Botley Dr *HAV* PO9............168 E12
Bottings H *SWTR* RH13 *............143 K1
Bough Beeches *BURH* RH15............47 H8
The Boulevard *CRAWE* RH10............8 F3
SALV BN13............92 D1
Boundary Cl *CRAWE* RH10............9 H2
WTHG BN11............12 C7
Boundary Rd *BRIE/ROTT* BN2............96 D2
CRAWE RH10............9 H2
GSHT GU26............108 C6
LAN/SOMP BN15............73 G8
RHWH RH17............41 G5
WTHG BN11............12 B7
Boundary & Station Roads
HOVE BN3............75 H7
Boundary Wy *ANG/EP* BN16............91 G3
HAV PO9............56 F4
Boundless Cl *MFD/CHID* GU8............109 M2
Boundstone Cl
LAN/SOMP BN15............72 C6
Boundstone La
LAN/SOMP BN15............72 B7
Bourg-de-peage Av
EGRIN RH19............23 M8
Bourne Cl *CCH* PO19............7 G7
HORN PO8............168 C3
SALV BN13............70 A7
The Bourne *HPPT/KEY* BN6............165 M4
Bourne View Cl *EMRTH* PO10............58 E3
Bourne Wy *MIDH* GU29............136 H11
Bowater Rd *CRAWE* RH10............30 B6

Bowcott Hl *BOR* GU35............107 N4
Bower La *PUL/STOR* RH20............160 A7
Bower Ct *HORN* PO8............168 B5
Bowers Cl *WTHG* BN11............12 D7
Bowers Pl *CRAWE* RH10............32 A1
The Bower *HWH* RH16 *............45 G4
Bowers Wy *SWTR* RH13............11 H3
Bowes Hl *HAV* PO9............169 K6
Bowes-lyon Ct *HORN* PO8............168 C2
Bowhill La *RCCH* PO18............171 L10
Bowley La *SELS* PO20............84 D8
Bowling Green La *HORS* RH12............10 E4
Bowman Ct *CRAWE* RH10 *............8 F1
Bowmans La *STEY/UB* BN44............48 C1
Bowness Av *LAN/SOMP* BN15............72 B8
Bowring Wy *BRIE/ROTT* BN2............5 M8
Boxall Wk *SWTR* RH13............10 E8
Box Cl *CRAWW* RH11............29 H8
Boxes La *RHWH* RH17............131 M5
Boxgrove *FERR* BN12............92 A5
Boxgrove Cl *LAN/SOMP* BN15............72 C5
Boxgrove Gdns *BOGR* PO21............103 H3
Boxham La *SELS* PO20............101 J2
Box La *EGRIN* RH19............34 D3
Box Tree Av *ANG/EP* BN16............90 A4
Boyce's St *BRI* BN1............4 D7
Brackenbury Cl *PTSD* BN41............75 G3
Bracken Cl *CRAWE* RH10............21 G7
CRAWE RH10............29 K1
PUL/STOR RH20............160 E11
Bracken Gv *HORS* RH12............37 G4
Bracken Heath *WVILLE* PO7............168 C8
Brackenhill *HRTF* TN7............35 M8
Bracken Rd *BOR* GU35............106 D9
PUL/STOR RH20............160 D11
Bracken Rd *EPSF* GU31............133 R7
Bracklesham Cl *SELS* PO20............100 A7
Bracklesham La *SELS* PO20............100 A7
Bracklesham Rd *HISD* PO11............98 B3
Bracklyn Av *EGRIN* RH19 *............23 M3
Bradbury Rd *CRAWE* RH10............30 B6
Brading Rd *BRIE/ROTT* BN2............5 K2
Bradley Ct *HAV* PO9............169 J12
Bradlond Cl *BOGR* PO21............103 M3
Braemar Wy *BOGR* PO21............85 L5
Braemore Av *HOVE* BN3............75 K7
Braeside Av *BRI* BN1............52 E6
Braeside Cl *HASM* GU27............109 J9
Brainsmead *RHWH* RH17............44 B1
Brainsmead Cl *RHWH* RH17 *............44 B3
Braishfield Rd *HAV* PO9............57 H1
Bramber Av *HOVE* BN3............75 L2
PUL/STOR RH20............159 R11
Bramber Cl *BOGR* PO21............103 M1
CRAWE RH10............29 K1
HAV PO9............57 K2
HWH RH16............45 K6
LAN/SOMP BN15............72 C5
Bramber Rd *CCH* PO19............7 G7
SALV BN13............71 K6
STEY/UB BN44............48 C1
Bramber Wy *BURH* RH15............46 F5
Bramble Cl *BOGR* PO21............102 C2
CRAWE RH10............21 G6
HAV PO9............57 K2
SALV BN13............70 C6
Bramble Crs *SALV* BN13............70 C6
Brambledean Rd *PTSD* BN41............75 C6
Bramble Gdns *BURH* RH15............46 C5
Bramble Hl *RHWH* RH17............40 E8
Bramble La *HORN* PO8............150 C6
PUL/STOR RH20 *............160 C6
SALV BN13............70 C6
Bramble Md *RHWH* RH17............40 E8
Bramble Ri *BRI* BN1............52 B8
Bramble Rd *EPSF* GU31............133 K6
Brambles *HPPT/KEY* BN6............165 N4
The Brambles *RHWH* RH17............44 D3
Brambletye La *FROW* RH18............34 C6
Brambletye Cl *ANG/EP* BN16............68 F7
Bramble Wy *BRI* BN1............53 H7
Brambling Cl *SWTR* RH13............11 L8
Brambling La *MIDH* GU29............136 E6
Brambling Rd *HAV* PO9............169 J8
SALV BN13............11 L8
The Bramblings *ANG/EP* BN16............90 C4
Bramdean Dr *HAV* PO9............168 E12
Bramfield Rd
MSEA/BNM PO22............105 H1
Bramlands Cl *HFD* BN5............163 P9
Bramley Cl *CRAWE* RH10............9 K3
SALV BN13............71 J4
WVILLE PO7............168 A9
Bramley Gdns *EMRTH* PO10............58 C5
MSEA/BNM PO22............86 A7
Bramley Rd *SALV* BN13............71 J7
Bramleys *LEWES* BN7............55 K8
Bramley Wk *BOR* GU35............106 C7
HORL RH6............15 H6
Bramley Wy *ANG/EP* BN16............90 F1
Brampton Cl *SELS* PO20............181 K6
Bramshaw Ct *HAV* PO9............169 J12
Bramshott Ct *LIPH* GU30 *............107 P9
Brandon Cl *CRAWE* RH10............30 C5
Brandy Hole La *CCH* PO19............61 L3
Brangwyn Av *BRI* BN1............52 D7
Brangwyn Cr *BRI* BN1............52 D7
Brangwyn Crs *BRI* BN1............52 C7
Brangwyn Dr *BRI* BN1............52 D8
Brangwyn Wy *BRI* BN1............52 D7
Bransgore Av *HAV* PO9............56 D1
Branson Rd *BOR* GU35............106 H6
Brantridge La *RHWH* RH17............39 M7
Brantridge Rd *CRAWE* RH10............30 B1
Brasslands Dr *PTSD* BN41............74 F4
Braybon Av *BRI* BN1............76 E1
Bray Cl *CRAWE* RH10............30 C5
Braypool La *BRI* BN1............52 B5
Braywick Av *BOGR* PO21............85 L6
Breach Av *EMRTH* PO10............58 D3
Breach Cl *STEY/UB* BN44............48 C2
Bread La *LHPTN* BN17............88 E7
Bread St *BRI* BN1............4 E6
Brean Cl *SELS* PO20............180 H5
Brecon Cl *SALV* BN13............70 B5
Brede Cl *BRIE/ROTT* BN2............77 K8
Breezehurst Dr *CRAWW* RH11............28 E6
Bremere La *SELS* PO20............101 K11
Bremner Av *HORL* RH6............14 E5
Brendon Rd *SALV* BN13............70 D5
Brendon Wy *ANG/EP* BN16............90 A3
Brent Ct *EMRTH* PO10............57 N6
Brent Rd *BOGR* PO21............103 M1
Brentwood Crs *BRI* BN1............77 G2
Brentwood Rd *BRI* BN1............77 G2

Brettingham Cl CRAWW RH11 * 28 D6
Bretton BURH RH15 46 D4
Bretts Orch RHWH RH17 40 F8
Brewells La LISS GU33 116 H7
Brewer Rd CRAWE RH10 8 F7
Brewer St BRIE/ROTT BN2 5 H2
Brewers Yd PUL/STOR RH20 160 A12
Brewery Hl ARUN BN18 67 G2
Brewhurst La BIL RH14 122 H3
Brewster Cl HORN PO8 168 B6
Breydon Wk CRAWE RH10 30 A5
Briar Av SELS PO20 99 L4
Briar Cl ANG/EP BN16 90 E1
ARUN BN18 87 L2
BOGR PO21 102 E2
BRIE/ROTT BN2 78 C5
CRAWW RH11 19 H8
HORN PO8 168 C4
SELS PO20 63 H7
Briarcroft Rd BRIE/ROTT BN2 78 C6
Briarfield Gdns HORN PO8 168 C3
Briars Wd HORL RH6 15 H5
Briarswood Cl CRAWE RH10 30 C1
Briar Wd LISS GU33 116 D6
Brickfield Cl BOGR PO21 2 A3
Brickfield La HORL RH6 14 C8
Brick Kiln Cl SWTR RH13 127 M6
Bricklands CRAWE RH10 32 A2
Brickyard La CRAWE RH10 32 A1
Brideake Cl CRAWW RH11 28 F6
Brideoake Cl CCH PO19 61 K5
Bridge Cl BURH RH15 46 E5
FERR BN12 92 B2
LAN/SOMP BN15 72 D8
Bridgefield Cl MIDH GU29 136 H11
Bridgefoot Pth EMRTH PO10 58 A5
Bridgelands CRAWE RH10 20 E6
Bridge Mdw LISS GU33 116 C9
Bridge Rd EMRTH PO10 58 A4
HASM GU27 109 M10
HORS RH12 114 A10
HWH RH16 45 J2
LHPTN BN17 89 G4
SALV BN13 13 G3
Bridgersmill HWH RH16 45 G2
Bridges Cl HORL RH6 15 J6
Bridget Cl HORN PO8 168 D2
The Bridgeway SELS PO20 181 K7
Bridgnorth Cl SALV BN13 70 A8
Bridle Cl GSHT GU26 108 D6
Bridle Rd ARUN BN18 65 J1
Bridle Wy CRAWE RH10 30 C2
The Bridle Wy SELS PO20 181 K6
Bridorley Cl BOGR PO21 103 G3
Brierley Gdns LAN/SOMP BN15 72 E7
Brigden St BRI BN1 4 C2
Brigham Pl MSEA/BNM PO22 105 J1
Brighton Pl BRI BN1 4 E7
Brighton Rd (Hornbrook Hl)
SWTR RH13 126 E1
Brighton Rd CRAWE RH10 8 E8
CRAWW RH11 39 H2
HFD BN5 145 K12
HFD BN5 163 L5
HORL RH6 14 E6
HPPT/KEY BN6 164 E7
HPPT/KEY BN6 165 L7
LAN/SOMP BN15 94 E1
LEWES BN7 55 K6
RHWH RH17 39 H6
RHWH RH17 128 D2
SHOR BN43 73 J7
SWTR RH13 11 G8
SWTR RH13 126 F2
SWTR RH13 145 J10
WTHG BN11 13 L6
Brighton Sq BRI BN1 * 4 E7
Brills La BRI BN1 4 E8
Brimfast La SELS PO20 83 K8
Brisbane Cl CRAWW RH11 19 J8
SALV BN13 70 A7
Bristol Av LAN/SOMP BN15 73 G8
Bristol Cl CRAWE RH10 20 C8
Bristol Gdns BRIE/ROTT BN2 96 D1
CCH PO19 61 L3
Bristol Ga BRIE/ROTT BN2 5 M8
Bristol Ms BRIE/ROTT BN2 96 D1
Bristol Pl BRIE/ROTT BN2 96 D1
Bristol Rd BRIE/ROTT BN2 5 J8
Bristol St BRIE/ROTT BN2 96 D1
Britannia Cl BOR GU35 106 H6
Britannia St EPSF GU31 133 P4
Brittania Ct BRIE/ROTT BN2 96 F2
Brittany Rd HOVE BN3 75 J7
SALV BN13 12 F1
Britten Cl CRAWW RH11 28 E6
Britten's La ARUN BN18 64 D1
Broadbridge Ct RCCH PO18 60 B6
Broadbridge Heath Rd
HORS RH12 125 N1
Broadbridge La HORL RH6 15 M7
Broadbridge Ml RCCH PO18 * 60 B6
Broad Cft HAV PO9 169 K7
Broadfield EGRIN RH19 42 D2
Broadfield Dr CRAWW RH11 29 H7
Broadfield Pk CRAWW RH11 * 29 J7
Broadfield Pl CRAWW RH11 29 G7
Broadfields BRIE/ROTT BN2 77 K2
Broadfields Rd BRIE/ROTT BN2 77 K2
Broadford Bridge Rd
PUL/STOR RH20 142 C11
Broad Gn BRIE/ROTT BN2 78 D7
Broad Green Av BURH RH15 47 H7
Broadlands BURH RH15 165 Q1
HORL RH6 15 H5
Broadmark Av ANG/EP BN16 90 B5
Broadmark La ANG/EP BN16 90 B5
Broadmark Pde ANG/EP BN16 * 90 B4
Broadmark Wy ANG/EP BN16 90 B5
Broadmead HORL RH6 15 H5
Broadmeadows La
WVILLE PO7 168 B10
Broadmere Av HAV PO9 168 G12
Broad Piece LHPTN BN17 89 G3
Broad Rig Av HOVE BN3 75 J2
Broad Rd RCCH PO18 59 J3
Broadstone Pk FROW RH18 34 F7
Broad Strd ANG/EP BN16 90 C6
Broad St BRIE/ROTT BN2 4 F8
RHWH RH17 44 D3
Broad Vw SELS PO20 181 M6
Broadview Gdns SALV BN13 70 D5
Broadwalk CRAWE RH10 8 F4
Broad Wk PETW GU28 155 N8
The Broad Wk RCCH PO18 171 K11
Broadwater Bvd SALV BN13 71 H8
Broadwater Hall SALV BN13 * 12 E2
Broadwater La SWTR RH13 126 C8
Broadwater Ms SALV BN13 * 71 J8
Broadwater Rd SALV BN13 13 G2
Broadwater St East SALV BN13 71 J8
Broadwater St West SALV BN13 71 H7
Broadwater Wy SALV BN13 71 J8
Broad Wy PSF GU32 132 E1
Broadway SELS PO20 181 J5
Broadway Pk EPSF GU31 133 N8
The Broadway CCH PO19 61 M3
CRAWE RH10 8 F4
LAN/SOMP BN15 73 G8
Broadwood Cl HORS RH12 36 F4
Broadwood Ri CRAWW RH11 28 F8
Brock End RHWH RH17 44 B1
Brockenhurst Av HAV PO9 168 E11
Brockhampton La HAV PO9 56 F4
Brockhampton Rd HAV PO9 56 F4
Brockhurst Cl HORS RH12 125 Q4
Brockhurst Farm
PUL/STOR RH20 158 B8
Brocklands HAV PO9 56 E4
Brockley Cl SALV BN13 12 E2
Brock Rd CRAWW RH11 19 G8
Bromley Cl HPPT/KEY BN6 165 P5
Bromley Rd BRIE/ROTT BN2 5 G1
Brompton Cl BRI BN1 52 D7
The Brontes EGRIN RH19 * 23 J8
Bronze Cl MSEA/BNM PO22 86 B6
Brook Av HPPT/KEY BN6 165 N6
RCCH PO18 60 A8
Brook Barn Wy FERR BN12 92 D4
Brook Cha PUL/STOR RH20 * 159 R7
Brook Cl BOGR PO21 103 M1
EGRIN RH19 24 A8
PUL/STOR RH20 160 C10
WTHG BN11 93 M1
Brookdale Cl WVILLE PO7 168 A9
Brookdean Rd WTHG BN11 94 A2
Brookenbee Cl ANG/EP BN16 90 A2
Brooker Pl HOVE BN3 75 M6
Brooker's Rd BIL RH14 142 A2
Brooker St HOVE BN3 75 M6
Brookfield Cl HAV PO9 56 F3
Brookfield La PETW GU28 138 C9
Brookfield Wy BIL RH14 142 A3
Brook Gdns EMRTH PO10 57 L5
Brook Gn RHWH RH17 129 M8
Brook Hl SWTR RH13 145 K2
Brookhill Cl CRAWE RH10 20 F6
Brookhill Rd CRAWE RH10 20 F7
Brookhurst Fld HORS RH12 * 114 A9
Brooklands BOGR PO21 102 F4
Brooklands Rd CRAWW RH11 29 H8
HAV PO9 56 C3
Brooklands Wy EGRIN RH19 33 J1
Brookland Wy
PUL/STOR RH20 158 D8
Brook La ANG/EP BN16 90 B2
FERR BN12 91 K4
HORS RH12 37 J2
HWH RH16 45 J1
PUL/STOR RH20 158 D8
Brooklyn Av WTHG BN11 92 E3
Brooklyn Chambers
WTHG BN11 * 92 E3
Brooklyn Dr WVILLE PO7 168 A9
Brookmead Wy HAV PO9 57 G6
Brookpits La LHPTN BN17 88 D5
Brook Rd HORS RH12 36 D3
MFD/CHID GU8 110 B1
Brookside CRAWE RH10 9 J2
CRAWE RH10 20 F6
HPPT/KEY BN6 * 165 N6
PUL/STOR RH20 161 K9
SELS PO20 84 D4
Brookside Av ANG/EP BN16 90 B2
Brookside Cl FERR BN12 91 K2
SELS PO20 84 D4
Brookside Rd ANG/EP BN16 91 J5
HAV PO9 56 D3
Brooks La MSEA/BNM PO22 3 G2
RCCH PO18 60 C6
Brooks La West
MSEA/BNM PO22 2 F1
Brooksmead MSEA/BNM PO22 3 H4
The Brooks BURH RH15 46 D4
Brook St RHWH RH17 129 M8
Brooks Wy PUL/STOR RH20 159 K3
The Brook CRAWE RH10 8 F1
SWTR RH13 125 R11
Brookview CRAWE RH10 20 F6
PUL/STOR RH20 158 D8
Brookway BURH RH15 47 H6
HWH RH16 45 K1
Brook Wy LAN/SOMP BN15 72 E8
Brookwood HORL RH6 15 G5
Brookwood Pk HORL RH6 15 G7
Broom Cl WVILLE PO7 168 B12
Broomcroft Rd
MSEA/BNM PO22 105 H1
Broomdashers Rd CRAWE RH10 9 K2
Broome Cl HORS RH12 36 C4
Broomers Hill La
PUL/STOR RH20 141 L11
Broomers Hill Pk
PUL/STOR RH20 * 141 L12
Broomers La SELS PO20 82 E8
Broomfield Av SALV BN13 71 G8
Broomfield Dr BIL RH14 142 B2
PTSD BN41 74 F2
Broomfield Rd BOR GU35 106 E7
HFD BN5 163 J4
SELS PO20 181 M5
Broom Rd EPSF GU31 133 R7
Brou Cl ANG/EP BN16 91 G4
Brougham Rd WTHG BN11 93 M2
Brow Cl PUL/STOR RH20 159 Q12
Browning Cl CRAWE RH10 30 B2
Browning Rd LAN/SOMP BN15 72 D5
WTHG BN11 12 D4
Browning's Hl SWTR RH13 144 H3
The Brownings EGRIN RH19 23 H8
Brownleaf Rd BRIE/ROTT BN2 78 D7
Brown's La PUL/STOR RH20 160 A12
Browns Wd EGRIN RH19 23 K5
Brown Twins Rd
HPPT/KEY BN6 165 J4
The Brow BRIE/ROTT BN2 78 C5
BURH RH15 46 F6
Broxhead Farm Rd BOR GU35 106 H1
Broxhead Rd HAV PO9 168 H11
Broxmead La RHWH RH17 128 F12
Broyle Cl CCH PO19 61 L4
Broyle Rd CCH PO19 61 L4
Bruce Av WTHG BN11 92 E3
Bruce Cl HWH RH16 45 H6
Bruce Vls WTHG BN11 * 92 E2
Bruce Wy WTHG BN11 92 E3
Brunel Pl CRAWE RH10 9 H5
Brunswick Cl CRAWE RH10 9 L7
MSEA/BNM PO22 3 M2
Brunswick Gdns HAV PO9 56 E3
Brunswick Ms HOVE BN3 * 76 C8
Brunswick Pl HOVE BN3 76 C7
Brunswick Rd HOVE BN3 76 C7
SHOR BN43 73 L6
WTHG BN11 12 E8
Brunswick Sq HOVE BN3 76 C8
Brunswick St East HOVE BN3 76 C8
Brunswick St West HOVE BN3 76 C8
Brunswick Ter HOVE BN3 76 C8
Brushes La HWH RH16 45 L1
Brushwood Rd HORS RH12 37 G3
Bryce Cl HORS RH12 36 F4
Bryony Wy WVILLE PO7 168 B11
Buchans Lawn CRAWW RH11 29 G7
Buci Crs SHOR BN43 74 B5
Buckhurst Cl EGRIN RH19 23 H6
Buckhurst Wy EGRIN RH19 23 H6
Buckingham Av SHOR BN43 73 K4
Buckingham Cl BRI BN1 * 4 C3
SHOR BN43 73 M5
Buckingham Dr CCH PO19 7 L5
EGRIN RH19 33 M2
Buckingham Ga HORL RH6 20 B1
Buckingham Ms SHOR BN43 73 L4
Buckingham Pl ANG/EP BN16 90 A2
BRI BN1 4 C3
Buckingham Rd BRI BN1 4 D4
PSF GU32 133 L6
SHOR BN43 73 L6
WTHG BN11 13 G7
Buckingham St SHOR BN43 73 K6
Buckland Dr BOGR PO21 103 G3
Bucklers Ct HAV PO9 168 E10
Buckler St PTSD BN41 75 G5
Buckley Cl HOVE BN3 75 K1
Buckley Pl CRAWE RH10 31 M1
Buckmans Rd CRAWW RH11 8 D3
Buckmore Av PSF GU32 133 L5
Bucknor Cl BOGR PO21 103 H3
Bucksham Av BOGR PO21 85 L6
Buckshead Hl SWTR RH13 127 L2
Buckswood Dr CRAWW RH11 8 A8
CRAWW RH11 28 F5
Buckwell Ct LEWES BN7 55 M2
Buckwish La HFD BN5 162 H5
Buddington La MIDH GU29 137 J6
Budds La BOR GU35 106 F5
Budgen Cl CRAWE RH10 20 C8
Buffbeards La HASM GU27 108 H10
Bugshill La MIDH GU29 153 R4
Bulbeck Cl BURH RH15 46 D8
Bulbeck Rd HAV PO9 57 G4
Bulkington Av SALV BN13 12 D2
Bulldogs Bank EGRIN RH19 42 E4
Buller Rd BRIE/ROTT BN2 77 J4
Bullfinch Cl HORL RH6 14 D5
HORS RH12 36 B2
Bull Hl LISS GU33 116 H9
Bulls Copse La HORN PO8 168 B4
Bull's La SWTR RH13 145 Q1
Bunbury Cl PUL/STOR RH20 160 E11
Bunch La HASM GU27 109 K10
Bunch Wy HASM GU27 109 K11
Buncton La RHWH RH17 146 F3
Bunting Cl SWTR RH13 11 J4
Bunting Gdns HORN PO8 168 A5
Bunyan Cl CRAWW RH11 28 D6
The Burchens SALV BN13 * 71 H7
Burchetts Cl HWH RH16 45 G7
Burchett Wk BOGR PO21 85 L8
Burch Gv ARUN BN18 65 J4
Burdett Cl CRAWE RH10 30 C4
Burdock Cl CRAWW RH11 28 F7
Burdocks Dr BURH RH15 47 H8
Burford Cl SALV BN13 70 F6
Burford Rd SWTR RH13 11 G5
Burgate Cl HAV PO9 56 E2
Burghclere Rd HAV PO9 169 J11
Burgh Cl CRAWE RH10 20 C8
Burgh Hill Rd LIPH GU30 107 N10
Burlands CRAWW RH11 18 F8
Burleigh Cl CRAWE RH10 32 A1
Burleigh La CRAWE RH10 32 B2
Burleigh Wy CRAWE RH10 32 A1
Burley Cl BIL RH14 122 H1
HAV PO9 169 J11
LAN/SOMP BN15 * 72 D7
Burley Rd MSEA/BNM PO22 105 J1
Burleys Rd CRAWE RH10 30 C3
Burlington Gdns PTSD BN41 75 H4
SELS PO20 181 M7
Burlington Rd FERR BN12 92 C2
Burlington St BRIE/ROTT BN2 5 J9
Burlow Cl BRIE/ROTT BN2 77 K8
SELS PO20 100 C1
Burma Cl HWH RH16 45 M5
Burmill Ct ANG/EP BN16 90 D2
Burndell Rd ARUN BN18 87 M2
Burners Cl BURH RH15 47 J8
Burnes V BRIE/ROTT BN2 97 L3
Burngreave Ct BOGR PO21 2 A6
Burnham Av BOGR PO21 2 C6
Burnham Cl BRIE/ROTT BN2 78 E6
Burnham Gdns BOGR PO21 2 C6
Burnham Pl SWTR RH13 10 E7
Burnham Rd SALV BN13 70 D7
Burns Cl HORS RH12 36 D2
Burns Gdns MSEA/BNM PO22 87 J8
Burnside WVILLE PO7 168 B8
Burnside Crs LAN/SOMP BN15 72 B8
Burns Rd CRAWE RH10 30 B1
Burns Wy EGRIN RH19 23 H8
HORS RH12 28 B8
Burnthouse Bostall
HPPT/KEY BN6 165 R10
Burnt House La HORS RH12 27 L2
Burnthouse La SWTR RH13 127 J10
SWTR RH13 144 H2
Burnt Oak La RDKG RH5 17 K1
Burrell Av LAN/SOMP BN15 72 C8
Burrell Buildings
LAN/SOMP BN15 * 72 C8
Burrell Cl SWTR RH13 144 F10
Burrell Gn RHWH RH17 44 C1
Burrell Rd HWH RH16 45 G3
The Burrells SHOR BN43 74 A7
Burrows Cl HAV PO9 57 H2
Bursledon Cl MSEA/BNM PO22 3 M3
Burstead Cl BRI BN1 77 G2
Burston Gdns EGRIN RH19 23 J5
Burstowhill La RHWH RH17 130 G3
Burton Cl HORL RH6 14 F7
Burton Park Rd PETW GU28 157 J3
Burtons Ct HORS RH12 * 10 D6
Burton Vls HOVE BN3 76 C5
Burwash Cl ANG/EP BN16 91 G2
Burwash Rd CRAWE RH10 9 L5
HOVE BN3 75 L2
Bury Dr FERR BN12 92 A3
Bury Hl PUL/STOR RH20 176 A3
Bury Rd PUL/STOR RH20 158 A11
Bushby Av ANG/EP BN16 90 C4
Bushby Cl LAN/SOMP BN15 72 B8
Bush Cl BRIE/ROTT BN2 78 C4
Bush Cottage Cl PTSD BN41 75 H3
Bush Farm Dr PTSD BN41 75 H3
Bushfield BIL RH14 122 A3
Busticle La LAN/SOMP BN15 72 B6
Butcherfield La HRTF TN7 35 M2
Bute St BRIE/ROTT BN2 5 L6
Butler Ct SALV BN13 70 E7
Butler's Green Rd HWH RH16 44 E5
Butlers Rd SWTR RH13 11 M1
Butterbox La RHWH RH17 149 N1
Buttercup Cl BOR GU35 107 K4
Buttercup Wk BRI BN1 53 G7
Buttercup Wy SWTR RH13 125 R11
Butterfield EGRIN RH19 23 G6
Buttermere Cl BOR GU35 106 G4
HORS RH12 37 G3
Buttermere Wy LHPTN BN17 89 M3
Butt La ARUN BN18 174 H11
Button Ct BRIE/ROTT BN2 * 5 G2
Butts Cl CRAWW RH11 8 B2
Butts Meadow BIL RH14 123 J12
Butts Rd STHW BN42 74 D6
Buxshalls Hl HWH RH16 130 F8
Buxted Ri BRI BN1 53 G8
Buxton Rd BRI BN1 4 B2
Bycroft Wy CRAWE RH10 30 A1
Byerley Cl EMRTH PO10 169 Q12
Byerley Wy CRAWE RH10 30 D2
The Bye Wy BOGR PO21 103 H5
The Byeway SELS PO20 99 H4
Byfield Pl MSEA/BNM PO22 2 E1
Byfleets La HORS RH12 115 N12
Bylanes Cl RHWH RH17 44 C2
Bylanes Crs RHWH RH17 44 C2
Byne Cl PUL/STOR RH20 160 B12
Byrd Rd CRAWW RH11 28 E6
Byron Cl CRAWE RH10 30 A2
HORS RH12 36 D3
MSEA/BNM PO22 87 J7
Byron Gv EGRIN RH19 33 H1
Byron Rd ANG/EP BN16 89 M4
WTHG BN11 12 E6
Byron St HOVE BN3 75 M6
By Sunte HWH RH16 45 J1
Bywater Wy CCH PO19 6 C9
Bywaves SELS PO20 * 180 B1
Byways SELS PO20 181 K8
The Byway BRI BN1 53 K8
MSEA/BNM PO22 87 K8
Byworth Cl BRIE/ROTT BN2 77 L7

C

Caburn Ct CRAWW RH11 8 C8
Caburn Crs LEWES BN7 55 M3
Caburn Hts CRAWW RH11 8 D8
Caburn Rd HOVE BN3 4 B2
The Cackstones CRAWE RH10 * 30 C2
Caedwalla Dr SELS PO20 63 H3
Caerleon Cl GSHT GU26 108 F3
Caernarvon Rd CCH PO19 7 L5
Caffins Cl CRAWE RH10 29 K1
Caffyns Ri BIL RH14 124 A12
Cagefoot La HFD BN5 163 K5
Caister's Cl HOVE BN3 76 B5
Cakeham Rd SELS PO20 99 H5
Cakeham Wy SELS PO20 99 K6
Calbourne HWH RH16 45 G4
Calderdale Cl CRAWW RH11 8 B8
Caledon Av MSEA/BNM PO22 87 J8
MSEA/BNM PO22 105 J1
Caledonian Pl WTHG BN11 * 13 G7
Caledonian Rd BRIE/ROTT BN2 5 H1
CCH PO19 6 F5
Caledonian Wy HORL RH6 * 20 A1
Callender Wk RHWH RH17 44 C1
Callisto Cl CRAWW RH11 28 D6
Callon Cl SALV BN13 * 70 A7
Calluna Dr CRAWE RH10 20 F7
Calshot Rd HAV PO9 168 D10
Calvecroft LIPH GU30 117 R1
Camber Cl CRAWE RH10 30 B3
Cambrai Av CCH PO19 7 H6
Cambria Cl RCCH PO18 60 B8
Cambridge Av SELS PO20 99 K5
Cambridge Dr BOGR PO21 103 L1
Cambridge Gv HOVE BN3 76 B6
Cambridge Lodge Pk
HORL RH6 * 14 F3
Cambridge Ms HOVE BN3 76 B6
Cambridge Rd HOVE BN3 76 C7
SWTR RH13 10 F6
WTHG BN11 12 F4
Camden St PTSD BN41 75 H7
Camelford St BRIE/ROTT BN2 5 G8
Camelia Cl HAV PO9 57 K2
LHPTN BN17 89 M2
Camelot Cl SWTR RH13 125 R11
Camelsdale Rd HASM GU27 109 J12
Campbell Ct FERR BN12 * 91 M2
Campbell Crs EGRIN RH19 23 G8
Campbell Dr ANG/EP BN16 90 A3
Campbell Rd BOGR PO21 2 F7
BRI BN1 4 D1
CRAWE RH10 30 B5
SELS PO20 63 G4
Campion Cl BOR GU35 107 K5
WVILLE PO7 168 B11
Camp Rd BOR GU35 106 G4
Canada Gv BOGR PO21 2 D7
MIDH GU29 137 K7
Canada Rd ARUN BN18 66 E2
Canada Wy BOR GU35 106 G5
LIPH GU30 117 R2
Canadian Crs SELS PO20 181 L8
Canal Pl CCH PO19 6 C7
Canal Rd ARUN BN18 87 L3
Canal Whf CCH PO19 6 D7
Canal Wharf Rd CCH PO19 6 E7
Canberra Cl CRAWW RH11 19 J8
HORS RH12 11 K1
Canberra Pl HORS RH12 * 36 E4
SELS PO20 63 J3
Canberra Rd EMRTH PO10 80 B2
SALV BN13 70 B7
Candleford Ga LIPH GU30 * 117 Q1
Canes La BOR GU35 107 J4
Canfield Cl BRIE/ROTT BN2 77 J4
Canfield Rd BRIE/ROTT BN2 77 J4
Canhouse La LISS GU33 117 J10
Canning Rd MSEA/BNM PO22 3 K6
Canning St BRIE/ROTT BN2 5 K6
Cannon Pl BRI BN1 4 C7
Canon La CCH PO19 6 D5
Canon's Cl BOGR PO21 103 J4
Canons Wy STEY/UB BN44 48 D1
Cansiron La EDEN TN8 25 K7
EGRIN RH19 35 G4
Cantelupe Ms EGRIN RH19 * 23 K8
Cantelupe Rd EGRIN RH19 23 L8
Canterbury Cl BOGR PO21 102 F4
CCH PO19 61 L5
Canterbury Ct SALV BN13 92 E2
Canterbury Dr BRIE/ROTT BN2 5 G2
Canterbury Rd ANG/EP BN16 90 C3
CRAWE RH10 29 K7
SALV BN13 92 E2
The Canter CRAWE RH10 30 D2
Cants Cl BURH RH15 47 H6
Cants La BURH RH15 47 J6
Canute Rd RCCH PO18 60 A8
Canvey Cl CRAWW RH11 29 H6
Cape Copse HORS RH12 114 A10
Capel La CRAWW RH11 28 E4
Capel Rd HORS RH12 17 H8
Capenors BURH RH15 46 E8
The Cape LHPTN BN17 89 M4
Capricorn Cl CRAWW RH11 28 D5
Capsey Rd CRAWW RH11 28 D4
Capstan Dr LHPTN BN17 89 M3
Caraway Cl CRAWW RH11 29 G7
Carbery Ct HAV PO9 168 E10
Carden Av BRI BN1 52 E8
Carden Cl BRI BN1 52 F7
Carden Crs BRI BN1 52 F7
Carden Hl BRI BN1 53 G8
Cardew Rd LISS GU33 116 D10
Card Hl FROW RH18 34 E8
Cardinal Dr WVILLE PO7 168 C8
Cardinal's Dr BOGR PO21 102 F4
Carfax HORS RH12 10 C6
Cargo Forecourt Rd HORL RH6 19 J2
Cargo Rd HORL RH6 19 J1
Carisbrooke Cl HAV PO9 57 J3
LAN/SOMP BN15 72 D5
Carisbrooke Dr SALV BN13 70 A8
Carisbrooke Rd BRIE/ROTT BN2 5 L2
Carleton Rd CCH PO19 6 A1
Carlingford Ct BOGR PO21 2 D4
Carlisle Gdns CCH PO19 61 L4
Carlisle Rd HOVE BN3 75 L7
Carlton Av BOGR PO21 103 H2
Carlton Ct HORL RH6 * 15 G4
Carlton Hl BRIE/ROTT BN2 5 G6
Carlton Ms WTHG BN11 12 A5
Carlton Rd BOR GU35 107 R5
Carlton Tye HORL RH6 15 J6
Carlyle Av BRIE/ROTT BN2 77 J4
Carlyle St BRIE/ROTT BN2 5 K3
Carmelstead Cl HWH RH16 * 45 H4
Carmino Ter LIPH GU30 * 117 Q1
Carnation Cl LHPTN BN17 90 A2
Carnegie Cl SALV BN13 71 H8
Carnegie Gdns SALV BN13 71 H8
Carnegie Rd SALV BN13 71 H8
Carnforth Rd LAN/SOMP BN15 72 A8
Carol Cl BRI BN1 52 E7
Caroline Ct CRAWE RH10 8 E6
Caron Cl LAN/SOMP BN15 72 D8
Carousel Ct MSEA/BNM PO22 2 B2
Carpenters BIL RH14 142 A1
Carpenters Meadow
PUL/STOR RH20 159 K3
Carron La MIDH GU29 136 G10
Carse Rd CCH PO19 62 B4
Carter Rd CRAWE RH10 30 C6
Cartersland LIPH GU30 117 Q10
Carterslodge La RHWH RH17 38 B8
RHWH RH17 127 P1
Cartersmead Cl HORL RH6 15 G5
Carters Wy BIL RH14 141 J1
Carvel Wy LHPTN BN17 89 M3
Carylls Meadow SWTR RH13 144 C6
Casher Rd CRAWE RH10 30 B6
Caspian Cl RCCH PO18 60 F5
Cassells Rd CCH PO19 61 M4
Cassidy Pl PUL/STOR RH20 159 Q12
Castle Av HAV PO9 57 J4
Castle Cl SALV BN13 92 E1
STEY/UB BN44 48 D3
Castle Dr HORL RH6 15 H8
Castle Gdns ARUN BN18 * 66 F2
MIDH GU29 * 137 J10
Castlegate PUL/STOR RH20 159 Q6
Castle La STEY/UB BN44 48 D3
SWTR RH13 143 Q10
Castlereagh Gn
MSEA/BNM PO22 3 M2
Castle Rd HAV PO9 168 H7
HORS RH12 125 N2
SALV BN13 92 E1
Castle Sq BRI BN1 4 E7
Castle St BRI BN1 4 B6
The Castle HORS RH12 36 D2
Castleway HAV PO9 57 J4
Castle Wy SALV BN13 92 E1
STEY/UB BN44 48 D2
Castlewood Rd SWTR RH13 125 R11
Caterways HORS RH12 125 R2
Cathedral Ctyd CCH PO19 * 6 D5
Cathedral Gn CCH PO19 * 6 E4
Cathedral Wy CCH PO19 61 J8
Catherine V BRIE/ROTT BN2 78 D5
Catherington La HORN PO8 150 B12
Catherington Wy HAV PO9 57 G1
Catkin Wy HWH RH16 45 L5
Catslands La HFD BN5 163 P9
Cat St HRTF TN7 35 L8
Cattswood La HWH RH16 44 F7
Causeway Farm HORN PO8 168 C3
The Causeway ARUN BN18 67 H3
BOGR PO21 102 F5
BRIE/ROTT BN2 5 M5
EPSF GU31 133 M8

FERR BN12 .... 92 C2
HORS RH12 .... 10 C7
PSF GU32 .... 133 M7
SELS PO20 .... 82 D7
SELS PO20 .... 181 L5
Cavalier Cl MIDH GU29 ...... 136 H10
Cavalier Wy EGRIN RH19 ...... 33 L2
Cavell Wy CRAWE RH10 .... 30 B4
Cavendish Cl FERR BN12 ...... 92 C2
HORS RH12 .... 36 C2
WVILLE PO7 .... 168 A9
Cavendish Dr WVILLE PO7 .... 168 A10
Cavendish Ms HOVE BN3 * 76 C8
WTHG BN11 * 12 E7
Cavendish Pl BRI BN1 .... 4 A7
Cavendish Rd BOGR PO21 .... 2 C7
Cavendish St BRIE/ROTT BN2 ... 5 C8
CCH PO19 .... 6 D2
Caveridge La RING/NEW BN8 ... 167 J1
Cawley Rd CCH PO19 .... 6 E6
Caxton Cl CRAWE RH10 .... 29 J6
Caxton Wy HWH RH16 .... 45 H5
Cecilian Av SALV BN13 .... 13 G1
Cecil Pashley Wy SHOR BN43 ... 73 J5
Cecil Rd LAN/SOMP BN15 ...... 94 D1
Cedar Av SALV BN13 .... 70 E7
Cedar Cl ANG/EP BN16 * 90 F1
BOGR PO21 .... 103 J2
BURH RH15 .... 47 G4
CRAWW RH11 .... 19 H8
FERR BN12 .... 91 K4
HORS RH12 .... 10 B5
LAN/SOMP BN15 .... 94 C1
SALV BN13 .... 70 E7
Cedar Ct HASM GU27 .... 109 M11
Cedar Crs HORN PO8 .... 168 D4
Cedar Dr CCH PO19 .... 6 C2
SWTR RH13 .... 125 K11
Cedar Gdns HAV PO9 .... 57 H3
Cedar Ldg ANG/EP BN16 * 90 B4
HASM GU27 .... 109 P12
Cedars Farm Cl BIL RH14 ...... 141 R1
Cedars Gdns BRI BN1 .... 76 D2
The Cedars ANG/EP BN16 ..... 90 D3
BRI BN1 .... 76 D2
BRIE/ROTT BN2 * 5 G1
HWH RH16 .... 45 G7
Cedar Wy HFD BN5 .... 163 L5
HWH RH16 .... 45 L5
Celandine Av HORN PO8 ...... 168 C6
Celandine Cl CRAWW RH11 * ... 28 F7
Celia Pl WVILLE PO7 .... 168 C9
Cemetery La EMRTH PO10 ...... 58 D1
PETW GU28 .... 138 C8
Centenary Gdns HAV PO9 ...... 57 G3
Central Av ANG/EP BN16 ...... 90 B5
BOGR PO21 .... 85 M7
SALV BN13 .... 70 E2
Central Dr BOGR PO21 .... 85 L7
MSEA/BNM PO22 .... 87 M8
Central Pde HORL RH6 * 14 F4
Central Rd BOR GU35 .... 106 C3
Centrecourt Cl SALV BN13 ..... 12 F2
Centrecourt Rd SALV BN13 ..... 12 F2
Centurion Rd BRI BN1 .... 4 D5
Ceres Pl MSEA/BNM PO22 ..... 105 J1
Chadborn Cl BRIE/ROTT BN2 .... 5 M8
Chadswell Meadow HAV PO9 ... 56 F4
Chadwick Cl CRAWW RH11 ..... 29 G8
Chaffer La SELS PO20 .... 100 C1
Chaffinch Cl BURH RH15 .... 46 C5
CRAWW RH11 .... 29 J1
HORS RH12 .... 36 C2
SALV BN13 .... 70 B8
Chaffinch Wy HORL RH6 .... 14 D5
Chailey Av BRIE/ROTT BN2 .... 97 M4
Chailey Cl CRAWW RH11 .... 28 F6
Chailey Rd BRI BN1 .... 77 K1
Chainbridge La SELS PO20 .... 180 L4
Chalcraft Cl LIPH GU30 .... 117 P1
Chalcraft La BOGR PO21 .... 85 L8
Chalder La SELS PO20 .... 101 L2
Chaldon Rd CRAWW RH11 ..... 29 H8
Chalet Cl FERR BN12 .... 91 K5
Chalet Gdns FERR BN12 .... 91 L5
Chalet Hl BOR GU35 .... 106 H4
Chalet Rd FERR BN12 .... 91 K4
Chalfont Cl MSEA/BNM PO22 ... 87 K8
Chalfont Dr HOVE BN3 .... 76 A3
Chalfont Wy SALV BN13 ...... 70 C8
Chalkdock La SELS PO20 ...... 81 M8
Chalkers La HPPT/KEY BN6 .... 165 J1
Chalkland Ri BRIE/ROTT BN2 .. 78 D3
Chalk La SELS PO20 .... 101 K6
Chalk Rdg HORN PO8 .... 150 E10
Chalk Rd BIL RH14 .... 122 D2
RCCH PO18 .... 173 K5
Chalky Rd PTSD BN41 .... 74 D2
Challen Cl SELS PO20 .... 63 H6
Challoners RHWH RH17 .... 131 M5
Challoners Cl BRIE/ROTT BN2 .. 97 L3
Challoners Ms BRIE/ROTT BN2 .. 97 L3
Challow Cl HPPT/KEY BN6 ..... 165 M5
Chalmers Cl HORL RH6 .... 18 D3
Chaloner Cl HWH RH16 .... 45 L2
Chaloner Rd HWH RH16 .... 45 L2
Chalton Crs HAV PO9 .... 168 E12
Chalton La HORN PO8 .... 150 E7
HORN PO8 .... 151 J8
Chalvington Cl HAV PO9 ...... 53 K7
Champions Rw HOVE BN3 * ... 76 C6
Champney Cl BOR GU35 .... 106 F8
Chancellors Pk HPPT/KEY BN6 . 165 N5
Chanctonbury
PUL/STOR RH20 .... 161 K9
Chanctonbury Cl ANG/EP BN16 . 90 A6
PUL/STOR RH20 .... 178 L3
Chanctonbury Dr SHOR BN43 .. 73 K4
Chanctonbury Ring Rd
STEY/UB BN44 .... 179 L3
Chanctonbury Rd
ANG/EP BN16 .... 90 A5
BURH RH15 .... 46 F8
HOVE BN3 .... 4 A7
Chanctonbury Vw HFD BN5 ... 163 J5
Chanctonbury Wk
PUL/STOR RH20 * 160 A12
Chanctonbury Wy CRAWW RH11 8 E3
Chancton Cl WTHG BN11 ..... 92 E2
Chancton Copse
PUL/STOR RH20 .... 160 E10
Chancton View Rd WTHG BN11 . 11 J2
Chandler Cl CRAWE RH10 ...... 8 E8
Chandler Rd CCH PO19 .... 7 H7
Chandler's Md RING/NEW BN8 . 167 R10

Chandlers Reach SELS PO20 * .. 81 M6
Chandlers Wy STEY/UB BN44 .. 48 B3
Chandos Rd WTHG BN11 ...... 13 G7
Channel Keep LHPTN BN17 * ... 89 K5
Channel Vw BOGR PO21 ...... 102 F5
STHW BN42 * 74 D6
Channel View Rd
BRIE/ROTT BN2 .... 78 A5
Chantlers Cl EGRIN RH19 ..... 23 H7
Chantlers Md EDEN TN8 ...... 25 M4
Chantrey Rd CRAWE RH10 ..... 29 K6
Chantry Cl HFD BN5 .... 163 K3
HORL RH6 .... 14 E5
Chantryfield Rd ANG/EP BN16 . 68 E7
Chantry La PUL/STOR RH20 ... 178 A4
Chantry Rd HORN PO8 .... 168 C1
SALV BN13 .... 70 F1
Chapel Cl BURH RH15 .... 46 E4
LHPTN BN17 .... 89 H3
PUL/STOR RH20 .... 158 B9
Chapelfields RHWH RH17 ...... 44 C1
Chapel Gdns BOR GU35 ...... 107 J4
Chapel Hl MFD/CHID GU8 ..... 112 A6
Chapel La CRAWE RH10 ...... 21 L5
EGRIN RH19 .... 34 C3
FROW RH18 .... 34 E8
LEWES BN7 .... 167 K6
PUL/STOR RH20 .... 159 F12
RCCH PO18 .... 60 F2
RHWH RH17 .... 131 N4
SELS PO20 .... 99 L3
Chapel Ms HOVE BN3 .... 76 C8
Chapel Pl PTSD BN41 .... 75 G6
Chapel Rd HORL RH6 .... 18 D2
LEWES BN7 .... 166 H2
PTSD BN41 .... 74 F6
SWTR RH13 .... 125 J11
WTHG BN11 .... 13 H4
Chapel Rw EGRIN RH19 .... 42 D2
RCCH PO18 .... 173 M3
Chapel St BOGR PO21 .... 2 D8
BRIE/ROTT BN2 * 5 C7
CCH PO19 .... 6 D3
PSF GU32 .... 133 N5
Chapel Ter BRIE/ROTT BN2 * ... 5 L8
Chapman Rd CRAWE RH10 .... 30 A2
Chapman's La EGRIN RH19 .... 23 G8
Chappell Cl LIPH GU30 .... 117 R1
Chappell Cft WTHG BN11 * 12 D5
Charlecote Rd WTHG BN11 .... 13 J5
Charles Av BURH RH15 .... 46 D8
CCH PO19 .... 7 L5
Charles Cl HOVE BN3 .... 75 M2
Charlesfield Rd HORL RH6 ..... 14 C6
Charles St BRIE/ROTT BN2 ..... 4 F8
PSF GU32 .... 133 M6
Charleston Ct CRAWE RH10 .... 9 M9
CRAWE RH10 .... 30 A6
Charlesworth Pk HWH RH16 ... 45 M5
Charlmead SELS PO20 .... 99 L1
Charlock Cl CRAWW RH11 ..... 28 F7
Charlock Wy SWTR RH13 ...... 125 K10
Charlotte Gv HORL RH6 .... 15 M5
Charlotte St BRIE/ROTT BN2 ... 5 H8
Charlton Dr EPSF GU31 .... 133 P4
Charlton Mill Wy RCCH PO18 .. 173 J4
Charlton Rd RCCH PO18 ...... 172 H2
The Charltons BRI BN1 .... 53 J7
Charlton St STEY/UB BN44 .... 48 B2
Charlwood Gdns BURH RH15 ... 47 H4
Charlwood La RDKG RH5 ..... 17 M4
Charlwood Rd BURH RH15 .... 47 H4
CRAWW RH11 .... 18 E7
CRAWW RH11 .... 19 H1
HORL RH6 .... 19 H1
HORL RH6 .... 19 H1
Charlwoods Pl EGRIN RH19 .... 23 K6
Charlwoods Rd EGRIN RH19 ... 23 J7
Charlwood St BOGR PO21 ...... 2 B8
Charlwood Wk CRAWW RH11 .. 18 E7
Charmandean La SALV BN13 .. 71 J5
Charmandean Rd SALV BN13 .. 71 J7
Charmans Ct HORS RH12 * 37 G4
Charm Cl HORL RH6 .... 14 D5
Charnwood Rd MSEA/BNM PO22 2 A1
Charrington Wy HORS RH12 ... 125 M2
Charter Wk HASM GU27 * 109 M11
Chartfield HOVE BN3 .... 75 M3
Chartfield Wy HOVE BN3 * 76 A3
Chart Wy HORS RH12 .... 10 D6
Chartwell Dr HAV PO9 .... 57 K2
Chartwell Rd LAN/SOMP BN15 . 72 C8
Chase Cl LISS GU33 .... 116 D9
Chase La HASM GU27 .... 119 P1
Chase Pln GSHT GU26 * 108 J4
Chase Rd BOR GU35 .... 107 J4
LISS GU33 .... 116 D9
The Chase CRAWE RH10 .... 9 L6
SALV BN13 .... 178 H12
Chatburn Av HORN PO8 ...... 168 A4
Chatelet Cl HORL RH6 .... 15 G5
Chatfield Rd RHWH RH17 ..... 44 D3
Chatfields CRAWW RH11 ...... 8 A6
Chatham Pl BRI BN1 .... 4 C3
Chatsmore Crs FERR BN12 .... 91 M2
Chatsworth Av HASM GU27 ... 109 M9
Chatsworth Cl ANG/EP BN16 .. 90 A2
Chatsworth Dr ANG/EP BN16 .. 90 A2
Chatsworth Rd BRI BN1 .... 4 B3
CCH PO19 .... 7 L5
WTHG BN11 .... 13 H4
Chatsworth Sq HOVE BN3 .... 76 C6
Chaucer Av ANG/EP BN16 .... 90 A4
EGRIN RH19 .... 33 H1
Chaucer Dr SELS PO20 .... 99 L5
Chaucer Rd CRAWE RH10 .... 30 A1
WTHG BN11 .... 13 H4
Chaucer Wy MSEA/BNM PO22 . 87 H7
Chaucer Av ANG/EP BN16 .... 90 A4
Chawkmare Coppice
BOGR PO21 .... 103 L3
Cheal Cl SHOR BN43 .... 73 M7
Cheam Rd ANG/EP BN16 ...... 90 C5
Cheapside BRI BN1 .... 4 F4
Cheeleys RHWH RH17 .... 131 M4
Cheesemans La RCCH PO18 ... 59 K4
Chelsea Ar HWH RH16 * 45 G5
Chelston Av HOVE BN3 .... 75 J6
Cheltenham Rd HORN PO8 .... 169 J11
Chelwood Av FERR BN12 ...... 92 B4
Chelwood Dr BRI BN1 .... 53 H7
CRAWE RH10 .... 9 J8
Chennells Brook Cottages
HORS RH12 * 36 E2

Chennells Wy HORS RH12 ..... 36 C4
Chepstow Cl CRAWE RH10 .... 30 D3
Chepstow Ct BRI BN1 * 53 L8
WVILLE PO7 .... 168 A4
Chequer Gra FROW RH18 ..... 34 D8
Chequer La RCCH PO18 .... 60 C7
Chequer Rd CCH PO19 .... 6 C2
Chequers Cl HORL RH6 .... 14 F5
Chequers Ct SWTR RH13 ..... 11 L4
Chequers Dr HORL RH6 .... 14 F5
Cherington Cl HPPT/KEY BN6 . 165 J4
Cheriton Cl HAV PO9 .... 168 E12
HORN PO8 .... 168 B2
Cherrimans Orch HASM GU27 . 109 J11
Cherry Av BRIE/ROTT BN2 ..... 87 L3
Cherry Cl BOGR PO21 .... 103 J3
BURH RH15 .... 46 D6
Cherry Ct SWTR RH13 .... 10 F7
Cherry Cft LHPTN BN17 ...... 89 J2
SELS PO20 .... 181 M3
Cherrylands Cl HASM GU27 ... 119 J5
Cherry La CRAWW RH11 ...... 19 H8
RHWH RH17 .... 129 N4
RHWH RH17 .... 146 D2
SELS PO20 .... 82 D3
CRAWE RH10 .... 30 C1
SALV BN13 .... 70 C4
Cherry Tree Av HASM GU27 ... 109 J10
HORN PO8 .... 168 C7
Cherry Tree Cl BIL RH14 ..... 123 R12
CRAWE RH10 .... 30 C1
SALV BN13 .... 70 C4
Cherry Tree Dr SELS PO20 .... 64 E5
Cherry Wk SALV BN13 .... 70 D4
Chervil Cl HORN PO8 .... 150 D12
Cherwell Rd SALV BN13 ...... 70 B5
Cherwell Wk CRAWW RH11 ... 28 C4
Chesham Cl BRIE/ROTT BN2 ... 92 D3
Chesham Pl BRIE/ROTT BN2 * .. 5 M9
Chesham Rd BRIE/ROTT BN2 * .. 5 M9
Cheshire Cl BOGR PO21 .... 2 E5
Cheshire Crs SELS PO20 ...... 63 H4
Cheshire Wy EMRTH PO10 .... 58 F3
Chesholt Cl HASM GU27 ...... 119 L7
Chesley Cl SALV BN13 .... 70 B7
Chess Brook Gn HFD BN5 .... 163 L2
Chesswood Av
MSEA/BNM PO22 .... 87 H7
Chesswood Cl WTHG BN11 .... 13 M2
Chesswood Rd WTHG BN11 ... 13 K3
WTHG BN11 .... 13 M3
Chester Av LAN/SOMP BN15 .. 94 D1
WTHG BN11 .... 13 M3
Chesterfield Rd EGRIN RH19 .. 22 B5
Chesterfield Rd FERR BN12 ... 92 C2
Chesters RD HWH RH16 ...... 24 D4
Chester Ter BRI BN1 .... 76 F4
Chesterton Cl EGRIN RH19 .... 33 L2
Chesterton Ct SWTR RH13 .... 11 L2
Chestnut Av CCH PO19 .... 61 L2
HASM GU27 .... 109 M10
HAV PO9 .... 56 C2
HORN PO8 .... 168 C7
Chestnut Cl ANG/EP BN16 * .. 90 F4
BURH RH15 .... 47 H5
EGRIN RH19 .... 23 M8
GSHT GU26 .... 108 E6
LIPH GU30 .... 118 A2
MIDH GU29 .... 136 G12
PUL/STOR RH20 .... 160 E11
Chestnut Ct ANG/EP BN16 ... 90 F4
BOR GU35 .... 106 H7
Chestnut End BOR GU35 ..... 107 N5
Chestnut Gdns HORS RH12 ... 10 C1
HPPT/KEY BN6 .... 164 G2
Chestnut Gv MSEA/BNM PO22 . 2 D1
Chestnut Rdg PUL/STOR RH20 .159 R6
Chestnut Rd BIL RH14 .... 142 A2
HORL RH6 .... 14 F4
Chestnuts Cl HWH RH16 ...... 45 K2
The Chestnuts BRIE/ROTT BN2 * 5 G1
HPPT/KEY BN6 .... 146 E12
HWH RH16 .... 45 J2
SELS PO20 .... 83 M5
Chestnut Wk CRAWW RH11 ... 19 H8
EGRIN RH19 .... 23 H2
PUL/STOR RH20 .... 159 J3
SALV BN13 .... 92 A1
SELS PO20 .... 63 H4
Chestnut Wy HFD BN5 .... 163 K4
Chesworth Cl SWTR RH13 .... 10 D9
Chesworth Crs SWTR RH13 ... 10 D8
Chesworth Gdns SWTR RH13 .. 10 D8
Chesworth La SWTR RH13 .... 10 D8
Chetwood Rd CRAWW RH11 .. 28 C7
Cheveley Gdns BOGR PO21 ... 103 J3
Chevening Cl CRAWW RH11 ... 29 H8
Cheviot Cl ANG/EP BN16 * 90 F3
SALV BN13 .... 70 D5
Cheviot Rd SALV BN13 .... 70 D5
Cheviot Wk CRAWW RH11 ..... 8 A3
Cheyne Wk HORL RH6 .... 14 F7
Chichester By-Pass CCH PO19 . 6 A7
Chichester Cl BRIE/ROTT BN2 * 5 M9
CRAWE RH10 .... 29 K7
HOVE BN3 .... 75 K1
Chichester Ct WTHG BN11 * .. 12 A7
Chichester Dr SELS PO20 ..... 63 H4
Chichester Ga CCH PO19 ...... 6 C7
Chichester Pl BRIE/ROTT BN2 .. 5 M9
Chichester Rd ARUN BN18 .... 66 B2
BOGR PO21 .... 2 B2
BOGR PO21 .... 85 L6
MIDH GU29 .... 137 J12
SELS PO20 .... 83 J8
SELS PO20 .... 181 M3
Chichester Ter HORS RH12 ... 10 E6
Chichester Wy BURH RH15 ... 47 H4
SELS PO20 .... 181 N5
Chiddingfold Rd
MFD/CHID GU8 .... 111 P6
Chiddingley Cl BRIE/ROTT BN2 77 L8
Chiddingly Cl CRAWE RH10 .... 9 M5
Chidham Cl HAV PO9 .... 56 F3
Chidham Dr HAV PO9 .... 56 F3
Chidham Rd HAV PO9 .... 56 K6
Chidham Sq HAV PO9 .... 56 F3
Chidham Wk HAV PO9 .... 56 F3
Chilbolton Av CCH PO19 ..... 6 D6
Chilcomb Cl HAV PO9 .... 56 F2
Chilcroft La HASM GU27 ..... 119 L4
Chilcroft Rd HASM GU27 ..... 109 J10
Chilcrofts Rd HASM GU27 .... 119 K4
Childerstone Cl LIPH GU30 ... 117 Q1

Chilgrove Cl FERR BN12 ...... 92 A2
Chilgrove Pl ARUN BN18 * 87 M3
Chilling St EGRIN RH19 ...... 43 J5
RHWH RH17 .... 131 L1
Chillis Wood Rd HWH RH16 ... 44 F4
Chilmark Ct LISS GU33 ...... 116 C9
Chiltern Cl ANG/EP BN16 ..... 90 F3
CRAWW RH11 .... 8 B3
HASM GU27 .... 109 L12
SHOR BN43 .... 74 B5
Chiltern Crs SALV BN13 ...... 70 D5
Chiltington Cl BURH RH15 .... 46 E4
Chiltington Ct BRI BN1 ...... 52 E8
Chiltington La LEWES BN7 .... 167 M6
Chiltlee Cl LIPH GU30 .... 117 R1
Chiltlee Mnr LIPH GU30 ...... 117 R1
Chiltley La LIPH GU30 .... 118 A3
Chiltley Wy LIPH GU30 ...... 117 R3
Chilton Cl CRAN GU6 .... 112 G7
Chilworth Gdns HORN PO8 * .. 150 D9
The Chine LHPTN BN17 ...... 89 M5
Chippendale Rd CRAWW RH11 . 29 G8
Chippers Cl SALV BN13 ...... 92 E1
Chippers Rd SALV BN13 ...... 70 E8
Chippers Wk SALV BN13 * 92 E1
Chithurst La CRAWW RH11 .... 21 K2
Chorley Av BRIE/ROTT BN2 ... 87 H2
Chownes Mead La HWH RH16 . 44 E5
Chrisdory Rd PTSD BN41 ..... 74 D2
Christchurch Crs BOGR PO21 . 103 K2
Christchurch Rd WTHG BN11 . 13 G4
Christie Pl MSEA/BNM PO22 ... 2 E1
Christie Rd LEWES BN7 ...... 55 M4
Christopher Rd EGRIN RH19 .. 23 K6
Christopher Wy EMRTH PO10 . 58 A3
Christ's Hospital Rd
SWTR RH13 .... 125 L7
Church Ap LHPTN BN17 ...... 89 K5
Church Av HWH RH16 .... 45 H4
Church Cl BOGR PO21 .... 102 D6
BRI BN1 .... 52 E8
BURH RH15 .... 46 F6
HASM GU27 .... 109 Q7
HORN PO8 .... 150 C7
LAN/SOMP BN15 .... 72 D5
PUL/STOR RH20 .... 161 J9
SALV BN13 .... 69 L4
STEY/UB BN44 .... 48 F2
SWTR RH13 .... 127 M6
SWTR RH13 .... 143 N9
Churcher Rd EMRTH PO10 .... 58 C1
Church Farm Ct SELS PO20 * .. 99 M5
Church Farm La SELS PO20 ... 99 M5
Churchfarm La SELS PO20 .... 101 K3
Church Farm Wk
STEY/UB BN44 .... 48 F2
Churchfield PUL/STOR RH20 .. 158 B2
Churchfield Rd EPSF GU31 .... 133 Q5
Church Flds BOR GU35 ...... 107 M4
Church Gn SHOR BN43 .... 74 B6
Church Green Cottages
HASM GU27 * 109 M10
Church Gv PUL/STOR RH20 .. 160 A4
Church Hl ARUN BN18 ...... 174 H12
BRI BN1 .... 52 D7
EGRIN RH19 .... 42 D3
MIDH GU29 .... 137 J9
POY/PYE BN45 .... 165 K11
PUL/STOR RH20 .... 159 J3
Church House Cl STHW BN42 .. 74 D4
Church House Ms
MSEA/BNM PO22 * 3 L4
Churchill Av BOGR PO21 ..... 103 K1
HORS RH12 .... 10 A4
Churchill Ct CRAWE RH10 .... 19 L8
Churchill Pde ANG/EP BN16 * . 90 F5
Churchill Sq BRI BN1 * 4 C6
Churchill Wy BURH RH15 .... 47 H7
Church La ARUN BN18 .... 65 K5
ARUN BN18 .... 87 L1
BOGR PO21 .... 102 C5
BOR GU35 .... 107 L3
CRAWE RH10 .... 9 K2
CRAWE RH10 .... 20 F7
EGRIN RH19 .... 23 L8
FERR BN12 .... 91 K3
GSHT GU26 .... 108 H10
HASM GU27 .... 109 M10
HAV PO9 .... 57 J5
HFD BN5 .... 163 K4
HORL RH6 .... 20 D3
HORS RH12 .... 125 N2
HPPT/KEY BN6 .... 164 C4
HPPT/KEY BN6 .... 164 E10
HPPT/KEY BN6 .... 165 R6
LAN/SOMP BN15 .... 71 M6
LEWES BN7 .... 55 M4
LHPTN BN17 .... 67 H7
LHPTN BN17 .... 88 D4
LIPH GU30 .... 107 Q11
LISS GU33 .... 116 A3
MFD/CHID GU8 .... 110 B1
MIDH GU29 .... 154 C6
MSEA/BNM PO22 .... 2 D3
PETW GU28 .... 138 A7
POY/PYE BN45 .... 165 K11
PUL/STOR RH20 .... 158 D7
PUL/STOR RH20 .... 161 J9
PUL/STOR RH20 .... 176 B2
RCCH PO18 .... 63 J2
RCCH PO18 .... 170 H12
RCCH PO18 .... 172 C4
RHWH RH17 .... 47 L3
RHWH RH17 .... 130 C1
RHWH RH17 .... 131 M3
RHWH RH17 .... 131 R6
RHWH RH17 .... 146 D3
SELS PO20 .... 63 H4
SELS PO20 .... 64 D3
SELS PO20 .... 82 D8
SELS PO20 .... 83 M5
SELS PO20 .... 101 K2
STEY/UB BN44 .... 48 C2
STEY/UB BN44 .... 48 B2
STEY/UB BN44 .... 162 C4
STHW BN42 .... 74 D6
SWTR RH13 .... 125 N12
SWTR RH13 .... 127 M4
SWTR RH13 .... 144 E10
Church Md HPPT/KEY BN6 ... 165 P6
STEY/UB BN44 .... 48 C1

Churchmead Cl RCCH PO18 ... 172 C11
Church Meadow RCCH PO18 .. 60 A8
Church Pk CRAWW RH11 * 28 F2
Church Pth EMRTH PO10 ..... 58 A5
HORN PO8 .... 168 C3
RCCH PO18 .... 170 H5
Church Pl BRIE/ROTT BN2 .... 159 J3
Church Platt RHWH RH17 .... 44 B4
Church Rd ANG/EP BN16 ..... 68 E8
ANG/EP BN16 .... 90 B4
ARUN BN18 .... 87 L2
BURH RH15 .... 46 F7
CCH PO19 .... 7 L2
CRAWE RH10 .... 21 G6
CRAWE RH10 .... 30 D3
CRAWE RH10 .... 31 L6
EMRTH PO10 .... 58 C2
EMRTH PO10 .... 58 E6
EMRTH PO10 .... 80 E4
HASM GU27 .... 109 M10
HASM GU27 .... 119 L8
HORL RH6 .... 14 E7
HORL RH6 .... 19 K4
HORL RH6 .... 20 E7
HORS RH12 .... 37 G4
HORS RH12 .... 125 N2
HOVE BN3 .... 75 M7
HWH RH16 .... 45 H5
LHPTN BN17 .... 67 H7
LIPH GU30 .... 107 R11
MFD/CHID GU8 .... 111 R4
MIDH GU29 .... 137 K11
PSF GU32 .... 133 M2
PTSD BN41 .... 75 G6
RHWH RH17 .... 149 J11
SALV BN13 .... 70 F8
SELS PO20 .... 63 H5
SELS PO20 .... 84 C4
SELS PO20 .... 99 L6
SELS PO20 .... 181 L5
SWTR RH13 .... 126 H4
SWTR RH13 .... 144 E10
Churchside CCH PO19 .... 6 D2
Church St ARUN BN18 .... 176 E2
BRI BN1 .... 4 D6
CRAWW RH11 .... 8 D4
HFD BN5 .... 163 K4
HORS RH12 .... 114 B9
HORS RH12 .... 115 Q10
LHPTN BN17 .... 89 K4
LISS GU33 .... 116 A7
PETW GU28 .... 139 L9
PTSD BN41 .... 75 G6
PUL/STOR RH20 .... 160 A12
PUL/STOR RH20 .... 160 B3
RHWH RH17 .... 44 B3
SHOR BN43 .... 73 L6
STEY/UB BN44 .... 48 C2
Church Vw EMRTH PO10 * 58 C2
Church View Cl HORL RH6 .... 14 E7
Church Wk CRAWE RH10 ..... 8 E7
HORL RH6 .... 14 E7
WTHG BN11 .... 13 M5
Church Wy BOGR PO21 ...... 102 F4
RCCH PO18 .... 172 C2
SALV BN13 .... 70 F8
Church Way Cl SALV BN13 ... 70 F8
Churchwood PUL/STOR RH20 . 158 C1
Church Wd PUL/STOR RH20 .. 158 C2
Churchwood Dr SELS PO20 ... 63 J4
Churt Rd BOR GU35 .... 107 Q1
RFNM GU10 .... 108 C1
Churt Wynde GSHT GU26 .... 108 G2
Chute Av SALV BN13 .... 70 D4
Chute Wy SALV BN13 .... 70 D5
Cinder Hl EGRIN RH19 .... 43 G9
RING/NEW BN8 .... 149 Q10
The Circle ANG/EP BN16 ..... 90 F5
Circus St BRIE/ROTT BN2 ..... 4 F6
Cissbury Av SALV BN13 ...... 70 E3
Cissbury Cl HORS RH12 ...... 36 F3
Cissbury Dr SALV BN13 ...... 70 E3
Cissbury Gdns SALV BN13 .... 70 F2
Cissbury Hl CRAWW RH11 ..... 8 C7
Cissbury Rd BURH RH15 ..... 46 D5
FERR BN12 .... 91 K2
HOVE BN3 .... 4 A2
SALV BN13 .... 71 H7
City Fields Wy SELS PO20 .... 63 J3
Civic Cere Rd HAV PO9 ...... 57 H2
Civic Wy BURH RH15 .... 46 F6
Claigmar Rd ANG/EP BN16 ... 90 B4
Claire Gdns HORN PO8 ...... 150 D11
Clair Rd HWH RH16 .... 45 J4
Clairgate La SWTR RH13 .... 114 F12
Clapham Cl SALV BN13 ...... 69 L4
Clapham Common SALV BN13 . 69 K5
Clappers Ga CRAWE RH10 ..... 8 F1
Clappers La HFD BN5 .... 164 A10
SELS PO20 .... 100 A7
Clappers Meadow CRAN GU6 . 112 H7
Clappers Orch CRAN GU6 * .. 112 G6
Clare Ct CRAWE RH10 .... 20 B8
Clare Gdns EPSF GU31 ...... 133 R6
Clare Ldg ANG/EP BN16 * 90 A4
Claremont Wy MIDH GU29 ... 136 H10
Clarence Av LHPTN BN17 ..... 89 H2
Clarence Ct HORL RH6 * 15 J5
Clarence Dr ANG/EP BN16 ... 90 E3
EGRIN RH19 .... 33 L2
Clarence Gdns BRI BN1 .... 4 B6
Clarence Rd BOGR PO21 ...... 2 F7
SWTR RH13 .... 10 F7
Clarence Sq BRI BN1 .... 4 C6
Clarence Ter HFD BN5 * 163 K5
Clarence Wy HORL RH6 ...... 15 J6
Clarendon Pl BRIE/ROTT BN2 * . 5 K8
PTSD BN41 .... 56 H7
Clarendon Rd HAV PO9 ...... 76 A6
HOVE BN3 .... 76 A6
SALV BN13 .... 71 K7
SHOR BN43 .... 74 B5
Clarendon Ter BRIE/ROTT BN2 .. 5 M9
Clarendon Vls HOVE BN3 .... 75 M6
Clare Rd LEWES BN7 .... 55 M3
Clarke Av HOVE BN3 .... 75 L2
Clark Rd CRAWW RH11 ...... 28 F8
Clay Hall La CRAWE RH10 ... 21 H5
Clay La CCH PO19 .... 61 H7
PUL/STOR RH20 .... 159 P12
RCCH PO18 .... 60 C4
Claypit La RCCH PO18 .... 62 D3
Clays Cl EGRIN RH19 .... 33 K1
Clays Hl STEY/UB BN44 ...... 48 D3
Clayton Av HPPT/KEY BN6 ... 165 N6

Clayton Dr BURH RH15....46 E8
Clayton Hl CRAWW RH11....8 C7
POY/PYE RH45....165 L10
Clayton La SELS PO20....100 A6
Clayton Rd BRIE/ROTT BN2....5 L3
HPPT/KEY BN6....165 R7
SELS PO20....181 L8
Claytons Cnr SELS PO20....82 D8
Clayton Wy HOVE BN3....75 L4
Clearwater La RHWH RH17....149 K6
Clearwaters La HWH RH16....47 J1
Cleaver's La RHWH RH17....129 J7
Cleeves Wy ANG/EP BN16....90 C3
Clerks Acre HPPT/KEY BN6....165 P6
Clermont Rd BRI BN1....76 D3
Clermont Ter BRI BN1....76 D3
Cleveland Cl SWTR RH13....70 E5
Cleveland Gdns BURH RH15....47 G1
Cleveland Rd BRI BN1....76 F3
CCH PO19....7 H6
SALV BN13....70 E5
Clevelands HWH RH16....45 H3
Cleve Wy BIL RH14....142 F4
Cliff Ap BRIE/ROTT BN2....96 E1
Cliff Rd BRIE/ROTT BN2....96 E2
The Cliff BRIE/ROTT BN2....96 E1
Clifton Cl HORL RH6....15 J6
Clifton Ct WTHG BN11 *....12 F4
Clifton Gdns WTHG BN11 *....12 F4
Clifton Hl BRI BN1 *....4 B4
Clifton Ms BRI BN1 *....4 C5
Clifton Pl BRI BN1....4 C5
Clifton Rd BOGR PO21....2 D5
BRI BN1....4 C4
BURH RH15....46 C4
CRAWE RH10....30 B4
LHPTN BN17....89 J5
WTHG BN11....12 F5
Clifton St BRI BN1....4 C4
Clifton Ter BRI BN1....4 C5
Climping Pk LHPTN BN17 *....88 E5
Climping Pl CRAWW RH11....29 G1
Climping St LHPTN BN17....88 D6
Clitherow Gdns CRAWE RH10....9 G6
Clive Av FERR BN12....92 C3
Clivedale Gdns STEY/UB BN44....48 C2
Clive Wy CRAWE RH10....30 B3
Clock House La HASM GU27....109 M11
Clock Pk MSEA/BNM PO22....86 D7
The Cloisters LHPTN BN17....89 L5
The Close ANG/EP BN16....90 C5
BIL RH14....122 D2
BOGR PO21....103 H4
BRI BN1....52 C8
BURH RH15....47 H5
EGRIN RH19....33 J1
HORL RH6....15 H8
HPPT/KEY BN6....165 N5
LAN/SOMP BN15....94 E1
MSEA/BNM PO22....87 M8
PSF GU32....132 C6
PUL/STOR RH20....161 K8
RCCH PO18....63 J2
RCCH PO18....172 C12
RHWH RH17....130 E2
SELS PO20....181 N5
SHOR BN43....73 L7
Closewalks MIDH GU29....137 J10
Clothalls La SWTR RH13....144 E4
Clovelly Av MSEA/BNM PO22....87 G8
Clovelly Dr GSHT GU26....108 F2
Clovelly Rd EMRTH PO10....57 M5
EMRTH PO10....58 E4
GSHT GU26....108 F3
Clover Cl BOGR PO21....107 K4
Clover Ct HWH RH16....45 H5
Cloverfields HORL RH6....15 G5
Cloverlands CRAWE RH10....29 L1
Clover La FERR BN12....91 K4
Clovers End BRI BN1....53 G6
HORS RH12....36 F4
Clovers Wy HORS RH12....37 J2
Clover Wy PTSD BN41....75 G3
Club Wk ANG/EP BN16....90 F7
Clun Rd LHPTN BN17....89 G3
Clyde Cl SALV BN13....70 B6
Clyde Rd BRI BN1....4 E1
MSEA/BNM PO22....3 K6
SALV BN13....70 B6
Clydesdale Av CCH PO19....6 C5
Clydesdale Gdns
MSEA/BNM PO22....85 M6
Clyde Ter STEY/UB BN44 *....48 C2
Coach House Cl SELS PO20....181 L6
Coach House Ms WTHG BN11....12 F6
Coachmans Dr CRAWW RH11....29 G7
Coach Rd HORL RH6....20 A2
RCCH PO18....62 D4
Coastal Av LAN/SOMP BN15....91 G5
Coastguard La SELS PO20....98 C4
Coastguard Pde BOGR PO21....103 J4
Coastguard Rd LHPTN BN17....89 J6
Coates La PUL/STOR RH20....157 R5
Cobbett Cl CRAWE RH10....30 B1
Cobbetts Md RHWH RH17....45 L6
Cobbles Crs CRAWE RH10....9 G2
Cobblewood EMRTH PO10....58 A2
Cob Cl CRAWE RH10....30 B1
Cobden La HASM GU27....109 N10
Cobden Rd BRIE/ROTT BN2....5 J3
MIDH GU29....136 H10
WTHG BN11....12 F5
Cobham Cl ARUN BN18....87 L3
Cobham Wy CRAWE RH10....20 A5
Cob La RHWH RH17....42 A8
Cobnor Cl CRAWW RH11....28 E5
Cobton Dr HOVE BN3....75 M2
Cob Wk CRAWW RH11....28 F4
Cocking Hl RCCH PO18....154 F9
Cohen Cl SELS PO20....64 C8
Cokeham Gdns
LAN/SOMP BN15....72 B7
Cokeham La LAN/SOMP BN15....72 B8
Cokeham Rd LAN/SOMP BN15....72 B6
Colbourne Av BRIE/ROTT BN2....77 J3
Colbourne Rd HOVE BN3....4 A3
Colbury Gv HAV PO9....56 D1
Colchester V FROW RH18....34 D7
Colchins CRAWW RH11....46 B8
Coldean La BRI BN1....53 H5
Coldharbour Farm Rd
EMRTH PO10....58 A4
Coldharbour La
RING/NEW BN8....149 R6
SALV BN13....69 J4

Coldwaltham La BURH RH15....47 J8
Colebrook Cl WTHG BN11....13 M3
Colebrook La PUL/STOR RH20....158 C6
Colebrook Rd BRI BN1....76 C1
LHPTN BN17....89 H2
STHW BN42....74 E6
Cole Cl CRAWW RH11....29 G8
Coleman Av HOVE BN3....75 K6
Coleman St BRIE/ROTT BN2....5 H3
Colemore Sq HAV PO9....57 H1
Coleridge Cl FERR BN12....92 A2
HORS RH12....36 D3
Coleridge Crs BRIE/ROTT BN2....91 M2
Coleridge Gdns HORN PO08....168 A5
Coleridge Rd FERR BN12....92 A2
Coleridge St HOVE BN3....75 M5
Coles La RDKG RH5....16 A4
Colet Rd CRAWW RH10....29 J6
Colgate Cl BRIE/ROTT BN2....77 L7
CRAWW RH11....29 G1
Colindale Rd FERR BN12....91 K3
Colindale Rd North FERR BN12....91 K3
Collards Ga HASM GU27....109 N11
Collards La HASM GU27....109 N11
Collard Wy LISS GU33....116 C9
College Cl BOGR PO21....103 L1
EGRIN RH19....23 L8
HAV PO9....169 K8
PTSD BN41....74 E2
RHWH RH17....39 H7
College Gdns BRIE/ROTT BN2....5 L8
WTHG BN11....12 B5
College Hl HASM GU27....109 M11
STEY/UB BN44....48 C3
College Hill Ter HASM GU27....109 M11
College La CCH PO19....61 M5
EGRIN RH19....23 L8
HPPT/KEY BN6....165 L8
College Pl BRIE/ROTT BN2....5 L8
CRAWE RH10....9 H4
HPPT/KEY BN6....165 K3
College Rd BRIE/ROTT BN2....5 L8
CRAWE RH10....9 H4
HWH RH16....45 H3
STEY/UB BN44....49 H4
SWTR RH13....143 P1
EPSF GU31....133 N6
Collier Rw CRAWE RH10....8 F8
Collingwood Pl PUL/STOR RH20....159 K2
HORL RH6....15 G5
Collingwood Ct SHOR BN43....73 L7
Collingwood Rd CRAWE RH10....30 C4
FERR BN12....92 B1
HORS RH12....10 C1
Collingwood Wy EPSF GU31....133 P4
Collins Cl SELS PO20....64 E5
Collins La EPSF GU31....134 C10
Collins Rd CRAWW RH11....28 D5
Collyer Av BOGR PO21....2 A3
Collyers Crs LIPH GU30....118 B1
Colmer Ct BURH RH15....46 D6
Colmer Rd BURH RH15....46 D6
Colnsay Rd CRAWW RH11....8 A9
Coltash Rd CRAWE RH10....9 L6
Colt's Bay BOGR PO21....103 H4
Coltsfoot Dr HORS RH12....36 D4
WVILLE PO7....168 B12
Colts Foot Rd BOR GU35....107 K4
Coltstaple La SWTR RH13....126 B5
Colt St SELS PO20....181 L6
Columbia Dr SALV BN13....70 B7
Colville Av SHOR BN43....73 J5
Colwell Cl HWH RH16....45 J8
Colwell Gdns HWH RH16....45 J6
Colwell La RHWH RH17....45 J8
RHWH RH17....45 L6
Colwell Rd HWH RH16....45 J6
Colwood La RHWH RH17....128 C11
Colwyn Cl CRAWW RH11....28 D5
Combe Dr STEY/UB BN44....48 C4
Combe La MFD/CHID GU8....110 E4
Combe Rd LISS GU33....116 E12
Combe Vw MFD/CHID GU8....110 F5
Comfrey Cl HORN PO08....150 D12
Comley Hl HAV PO9....169 K10
Commerce Wy
LAN/SOMP BN15....72 B8
Commercial Rd BURH RH15....46 E6
Commercial Square Rbt
HWH RH16....45 H3
Common La PUL/STOR RH20....159 R6
Common La HPPT/KEY BN6....166 A4
Commonmead La BOGR PO21....102 F3
Common Rd EMRTH PO10....170 C12
RCCH PO18....170 C12
Common Vw MIDH GU29....136 C8
Compass Cl LHPTN BN17....89 M3
Compass Ct PTSD BN41 *....74 E2
Compassion La CRAWW RH11....28 D5
Compeer Cl CRAWW RH11....28 D5
Compton Av BRI BN1....4 C4
FERR BN12....92 A3
Compton Cl CCH PO19....61 M2
HAV PO9....57 J7
Compton Dr MSEA/BNM PO22....87 J7
Compton Rd BRI BN1....76 D4
HWH RH16....45 L1
Comptons Brow La SWTR RH13....11 K3
Comptons Cl SWTR RH13....11 K3
Comptons La SWTR RH13....11 J8
Conbar Av ANG/EP BN16....90 B3
Concorde Cl PUL/STOR RH20....160 D10
Conde Wy BOR GU35....106 H7
Conde Wy BURH RH15....46 E6
Conduit Md CCH PO19....7 J1
Coney Cl CRAWW RH11....29 G1
SELS PO20....99 L1
Coney Cft HORS RH12....11 K3
Coneyhurst La BIL RH14....142 B6
Coney Six SELS PO20....99 L2
Conge Rd SALV BN13....13 J1
Conifer Cl BOR GU35....106 F8
HORN PO08 *....168 B7
Conifer Dr RCCH PO18....59 K3
Conifers Cl HORS RH12....37 G3
Conifer Wy BOGR PO21....102 E3

Conigar Rd EMRTH PO10....58 A2
Coniston Cl CRAWW RH11....28 C5
HORL RH6....37 G4
LAN/SOMP BN15....72 B7
MSEA/BNM PO22....87 G7
Coniston Rd BOR GU35....106 F4
Coniston Wy LHPTN BN17....89 M2
Connaught Av MSEA/BNM PO22....73 K5
Connaught Cl BOR GU35....106 G8
Connaught Gdns CRAWE RH10....29 J1
Connaught Rd HAV PO9....57 H4
HOVE BN3....75 M7
LHPTN BN17....89 M7
Connaught Ter HOVE BN3....76 A6
Connell Dr BRIE/ROTT BN2....78 D6
Connolly Wy BURH RH15....46 D7
Consort Wy BURH RH15....46 D7
Consort Wy East HORL RH6....15 G7
Constable Dr SELS PO20....181 M6
Constable Rd CRAWE RH10....29 L7
Convent Gdns SALV BN13....178 H11
Convent La EMRTH PO10....58 A5
Conway Dr BOGR PO21....102 F5
Conway Pl HOVE BN3....76 A5
Conway St HOVE BN3....76 A5
Cooksbridge Rd
BRIE/ROTT BN2....77 K7
Cooks Hl HORS RH12....113 N8
Cooks La EMRTH PO10....58 F4
RCCH PO18....170 E7
Cooks Mead HORS RH12....27 J2
Cook's Pond Rd LIPH GU30....135 P1
Coolham Dr BRIE/ROTT BN2....77 K7
Coolham Rd PUL/STOR RH20....160 E3
SWTR RH13....142 G9
Coolhurst La SWTR RH13....11 L7
Coombe Cl BIL RH14....124 A12
CRAWW RH11....19 J8
Coombe Crs PUL/STOR RH20....176 B2
Coombe Dro STEY/UB BN44....48 C3
Coombe La BIL RH14....124 A12
EGRIN RH19....33 H3
Coombelands La
PUL/STOR RH20....158 H2
Coombe La ARUN BN18....177 K10
Coombe Lea BRIE/ROTT BN2 *....76 B7
Coombe Ri SALV BN13....70 F3
Coombe Rd BRIE/ROTT BN2....77 J4
BRI BN1....77 J4
STEY/UB BN44....48 B3
Coombers RHWH RH17....40 F8
Coombes La HWH RH16....45 L4
Coombes Rd LAN/SOMP BN15....48 H8
Coombe Ter BRIE/ROTT BN2....77 H4
Coombes Cl HORN PO08....150 D12
Coomes Wy LHPTN BN17....89 J1
Cooper Cl HORL RH6....15 M6
Cooper Rw CRAWE RH10....8 F9
Coopers Cl BURH RH15....47 G4
Coopers Farm Cl
MSEA/BNM PO22....2 F2
Cooper St CCH PO19....6 E5
Coopers Wy HFD BN5....163 L4
Coos La RHWH RH17....128 B3
Cootes Av HORS RH12....125 R2
Cootes La MSEA/BNM PO22....87 L8
Cootham Gn PUL/STOR RH20....159 Q11
Copeland Rd MSEA/BNM PO22....3 M4
Copestake Dr BURH RH15....47 J6
Copnall Wy HORS RH12....10 D6
Coppards Cl RHWH RH17....148 F9
Copper Beech Dr SELS PO20....63 H4
Copper Cl HORL RH6....15 M6
Copperfield Pl HORS RH12....10 A2
Copperfields SWTR RH13....126 C1
Copper Hall Cl ANG/EP BN16....90 D3
Coppetts Wd ANG/EP BN16 *....90 A5
Coppice La SELS PO20....181 K5
Coppice Pl HORS RH12....36 F4
The Coppice CRAWE RH10....32 A1
HORN PO08....168 B3
RHWH RH17....149 J2
Coppice Wk CRAWE RH10....9 M1
Coppice Wy HWH RH16....45 G6
Copsale Rd SWTR RH13....126 D12
Copse Cl CRAWE RH10....32 A1
EGRIN RH19....23 R5
EPSF GU31....133 N6
HORS RH12 *....10 C4
LISS GU33....116 D9
Copse Crs CRAWW RH11....8 C2
Copse Gn PETW GU28 *....120 F10
Copse Hl BRI BN1....52 C8
Copse La ARUN BN18....65 H4
Copse Rd HASM GU27....108 G12
The Copse CCH PO19....61 N3
HWH RH16....45 L4
Copse Vw ANG/EP BN16....90 E3
Copthorne Bank CRAWE RH10....21 H3
HORL RH6....21 H3
Copthorne Common Rd
CRAWE RH10....21 H6
Copthorne Hl SALV BN13....70 E6
Copthorne Rd CRAWE RH10....20 D8
CRAWE RH10....22 A5
EGRIN RH19....22 D5
Copthorne Wy BOGR PO21....103 J1
Copyhold Hl HASM GU27....119 M5
Copyhold La HWH RH16....130 A7
RHWH RH17....44 C3
Copyhold Rd EGRIN RH19....33 J1
Coral Cl SELS PO20....180 H5
Coralin Gv WVILLE PO7....168 C8
Coral La SELS PO20....180 H5
Cora's Wy SELS PO20....51 H1
Corbishley Gn MSEA/BNM PO22....86 B7
Corbishley Rd MSEA/BNM PO22....2 C1
Corbyn Crs SHOR BN43....73 M6
Cordal Cl ANG/EP BN16....90 A6
Cordons LEWES BN7....55 J8
Corfe Cl SALV BN13....70 A8
SWTR RH13....125 R12
Cormorant Wy SELS PO20....99 M7
Cornbrook Gv WVILLE PO7....168 D8
Cornelius Dr WVILLE PO7....168 D8
Corner Garth FERR BN12....91 L4

Cornfield Cl LHPTN BN17....89 K2
The Cornfields SELS PO20....64 C7
Cornflower Cl CCH PO19....7 K1
Cornflower Wy SWTR RH13....125 R10
Cornford Cl BURH RH15....46 D7
PTSD BN41....75 G3
Cornwall Gdns BRI BN1....76 D2
EGRIN RH19....33 L1
LHPTN BN17....89 J4
Cornwall Rd BOR GU35....106 G8
LHPTN BN17....89 J3
Cornwood BIL RH14 *....122 C11
Coronation Rd EGRIN RH19....33 K2
Coronation St BRIE/ROTT BN2....5 J2
The Coronet HORL RH6....15 H8
Corry Rd GSHT GU26....108 F3
Corsletts Av HORS RH12....125 K2
Cortis Av SALV BN13....71 H8
Corunna Dr SWTR RH13....11 J3
Cory Cl CCH PO19....6 E6
Costells Edge RHWH RH17....149 J1
Cote St SALV BN13....70 B4
Cotland Rd BRIE/ROTT BN2....181 M7
Cot La RCCH PO18....59 J2
Cotsford CRAWW RH11....39 G3
Cotswold Cl CRAWW RH11....8 B4
HAV PO9....168 F11
SALV BN13....70 D5
Cotswold Pl BRIE/ROTT BN2 *....77 L8
Cotswold Rd SALV BN13....70 D5
The Cotswolds STHW BN42....74 D6
Cotswold Wy ANG/EP BN16....90 F7
Cottage Cl BOGR PO21....103 H3
HORS RH12....37 G3
Cottage Pl CRAWE RH10....21 K6
Cottenham Rd WTHG BN11....13 L3
Cottingham Av HORS RH12....36 C2
Cotton Dr EMRTH PO10....57 M2
Cottrell Cl ANG/EP BN16....68 A3
The Cottrells LAN/SOMP BN15....68 A6
Cotwell Av HORN PO08....168 C5
Coulstock Rd BURH RH15....46 B8
Coultershaw Br PETW GU28....157 K2
Countisbury Cl BOGR PO21....103 L2
Countryman La SWTR RH13....143 L10
Countryside Farm Pk
STEY/UB BN44....48 F2
County Oak Av BRI BN1....53 G7
County Oak La CRAWE RH10....19 J4
County Oak Wy CRAWW RH11....19 J7
Court Barn La SELS PO20....82 D8
Court Cl BRI BN1....52 D6
EGRIN RH19....23 L8
LIPH GU30....117 G2
Court Crs EGRIN RH19....23 M8
Court Farm Rd BRIE/ROTT BN2 *....97 K2
HOVE BN3....75 L3
Courtfields LAN/SOMP BN15 *....12 C4
Courtlands HWH RH16....45 H6
Courtlands Cl FERR BN12....92 B1
Courtlands Ter HORN PO08 *....168 B5
Courtlands Wy FERR BN12....92 B1
MSEA/BNM PO22....87 H7
Court Lodge Rd HORL RH6....14 F8
Courtmead Rd RHWH RH17....44 C3
Court Ord Rd BRIE/ROTT BN2....97 K2
Courts Hill Rd HASM GU27....109 L11
Courts Mount Rd HASM GU27....109 L11
The Court BOGR PO21....102 F4
Courtwick La LHPTN BN17....89 H2
Courtwick Rd LHPTN BN17....89 H1
The Courtyard CRAWE RH10 *....8 F7
EGRIN RH19....24 A8
EPSF GU31....133 N6
HORS RH12 *....10 C4
WTHG BN11 *....12 C4
Cousins Wy PUL/STOR RH20....159 K2
Coventry Cl BOGR PO21....103 J1
Coventry Ct WTHG BN11 *....12 A6
Coventry St BRI BN1....4 E2
Cove Rd ANG/EP BN16....90 A5
Covert Cl CRAWE RH10....30 B4
Covert Gv WVILLE PO7....168 B12
Covert Md PUL/STOR RH20....161 J8
RHWH RH17....128 C2
The Covey CRAWE RH10....30 D1
Covington Rd EMRTH PO10....169 Q12
Cowden Ms EDEN TN8....25 M4
Cowdens Cl HOVE BN3....75 J1
Cowdown La RCCH PO18....151 R9
Cowdray Cl ANG/EP BN16....90 A5
CRAWW RH10....30 B4
FERR BN12....92 C4
Cowdray Ct BRIE/ROTT BN2 *....92 A5
MIDH GU29....137 J9
Cowdray Dr ANG/EP BN16....90 A2
FERR BN12....92 C4
Cowdray Rd MIDH GU29....137 K8
Cowfold Cl CRAWW RH11....28 E6
Cowfold Rd BRIE/ROTT BN2....77 K8
RHWH RH17....148 B3
SWTR RH13....144 E4
Cow La EPSF GU31....152 D2
SELS PO20....101 J6
Cowley Dr BRIE/ROTT BN2....78 E6
LAN/SOMP BN15....72 E8
Cowper Rd WTHG BN11....12 A8
Cowper St HOVE BN3....75 M6
Cowslip Cl BOR GU35....107 K5
SWTR RH13....125 R11
Coxcombe La MFD/CHID GU8....110 G5
Coxes Gn PETW GU28 *....133 M4
Coxes Rd SELS PO20....181 J7
Cox Green Rd HORS RH12....113 Q5
Cox Gv BURH RH15....46 D4
Coxham La STEY/UB BN44....48 B1
Coxswain Wy SELS PO20....181 L8
Crabbet Rd CRAWE RH10....30 A4
Crabden La HORN PO08....168 F1
Crablands SELS PO20....181 J5
Crablands Cl SELS PO20....181 K6
Crabtree Ar LAN/SOMP BN15 *....72 D7
Crabtree Av BRI BN1....52 F6
Crabtree Gdns BOR GU35....107 M4
Crabtree La BOR GU35....107 M4
LAN/SOMP BN15....72 D7
Crabtree Rd CRAWW RH11....8 C2
Crabwood Ct HAV PO9....168 E10
Cradock Pl SELS PO20....181 J7
Crafts La EPSF GU31....133 P4
Craggits La HFD BN5....163 K4
Craigans CRAWW RH11....28 F3
Craignair Av BRI BN1....53 H7
Craigwell La BOGR PO21....103 K4
Craigwell Mnr BOGR PO21....103 J4

Cranborne Wk CRAWE RH10....9 K8
Cranbourne Cl HORL RH6....15 G4
Cranbourne St BRI BN1....4 D6
Cranedown LEWES BN7....55 M6
Crane St CCH PO19....6 E4
Cranford Gdns BOGR PO21....2 D4
Cranford Rd PSF GU32....133 M7
Cranham Av BIL RH14....141 R3
Cranleigh Rd SALV BN13....71 G8
Cranmer Av HOVE BN3....75 L4
Cranmer Rd SALV BN13....12 A3
Cranston Rd EGRIN RH19....23 L7
Cranworth Rd WTHG BN11....13 L3
Craven Pl BRIE/ROTT BN2....5 L6
Craven Rd BRIE/ROTT BN2....5 L6
CRAWE RH10....30 A4
The Cravens HORL RH6....15 M6
Crawford Gdns SWTR RH13....11 H2
Crawfurd Wy EGRIN RH19....23 L7
Crawley Av CRAWE RH10....29 K1
CRAWE RH10....29 K1
CRAWW RH11....A6
HAV PO9....168 F11
Crawley Down Rd EGRIN RH19....22 D6
Crawley La CRAWE RH10....30 B2
RHWH RH17....40 D5
Crawley Rd BRI BN1....53 J7
HORS RH12....11 K2
HORS RH12....11 K2
Crawters CRAWE RH10....9 J2
Crayford Rd BRIE/ROTT BN2....77 J4
Cray La PUL/STOR RH20....141 L12
Cray's La PUL/STOR RH20....160 D10
Creasys Dr CRAWW RH11....39 G1
Crede La RCCH PO18....60 B7
Creek End CCH PO19....61 G7
EMRTH PO10....58 A6
Cremorne Pl PSF GU32....133 N5
Crescenta Wk BOGR PO21....103 N2
Crescent Cl BRIE/ROTT BN2....78 D5
BURH RH15....47 G6
Crescent Cl HORL RH6....14 F8
Crescent Dr North
BRIE/ROTT BN2....78 E6
Crescent Dr South
BRIE/ROTT BN2....78 E6
Crescent Pl BRIE/ROTT BN2....5 K9
Crescent Ri PUL/STOR RH20....160 D10
Crescent Rd BOGR PO21....2 D7
BRIE/ROTT BN2....5 G1
BURH RH15....46 F6
EGRIN RH19....23 J8
WTHG BN11....12 F6
The Crescent ANG/EP BN16....89 M5
ANG/EP BN16 *....90 A5
BOGR PO21....102 F5
BRIE/ROTT BN2....77 K3
EGRIN RH19....23 H1
EMRTH PO10....58 E5
HORL RH6....14 F8
HORS RH12....125 R3
HPPT/KEY BN6....165 G6
LAN/SOMP BN15....94 D1
MSEA/BNM PO22....3 M4
PUL/STOR RH20....159 P12
SELS PO20....99 K6
STEY/UB BN44....48 C3
STHW BN42....74 E5
Crescent Wy BURH RH15....46 F6
HORL RH6....14 F8
Crespin Wy BRI BN1....77 H4
Crestland Cl HORN PO08....168 B6
Crest Wy PTSD BN41....75 G2
Crestway Pde BRI BN1 *....77 H3
The Crestway BRI BN1....77 H4
Crewdson Rd HORL RH6....15 G6
Cricket Ct EGRIN RH19....23 K6
Cricket Dr HORN PO08....168 B4
Cricket Field Rd HORS RH12....10 A8
Cricket Lea BOR GU35....107 J4
Crimbourne La BIL RH14....140 D5
Cripland Cl HORN PO08....168 A5
Cripplecrutch Hl
MFD/CHID GU8....110 E11
Cripplegate La SWTR RH13....143 R1
Cripps La STEY/UB BN44....48 D2
Crisp Rd LEWES BN7....55 M2
Crisspyn Cl HORN PO08....168 C3
Critchel's La SELS PO20....101 H4
Critchfield Rd RCCH PO18....60 A8
Critchmere Dr SELS PO20....64 E6
Critchmere Hl HASM GU27....108 H10
Critchmere La HASM GU27....108 H11
Critchmere V HASM GU27....108 G11
Cricket Cl GSHT GU26....108 G3
Crockford Rd EMRTH PO10....58 C1
Crockham Cl CRAWW RH11....28 E5
Crockhurst SWTR RH13....125 R11
Crockhurst Hl SALV BN13....70 E5
Croft Av STHW BN42....74 E6
Croft Dr PTSD BN41....74 F2
Crofters St STEY/UB BN44....48 E3
Croft La HFD BN5....163 J5
Croft Md CCH PO19....61 M3
Croft Rd BRI BN1....76 C1
SELS PO20....181 K7
Crofts Cl MFD/CHID GU8....110 G4
The Croft HORS RH12....90 F4
ARUN BN18....87 L1
BOGR PO21....1 L8
BRI BN1 *....4 B3
CRAWW RH11....28 F3
HPPT/KEY BN6....165 N4
MIDH GU29....54 G5
PETW GU28....138 A6
Croft Vls HFD BN5 *....163 L4
Croft Wy HORS RH12....125 R2
MSEA/BNM PO22....87 H7
SELS PO20....181 K6
Crombie Cl HORN PO08....168 A5
Cromleigh Wy STHW BN42....74 D3
Crompton Flds CRAWE RH10....19 K8
Crompton Wy CRAWE RH10....29 K1
Cromwell Pl EGRIN RH19....33 L1
Cromwell Rd BURH RH15....46 C6
HOVE BN3....76 B6
Cromwell St BRIE/ROTT BN2....5 J3
HOVE BN3....76 B6
Crondall Av HAV PO9....168 F11
Crooked La SELS PO20....82 D8
Crookham Cl HAV PO9....56 D1
Crookthorn La LHPTN BN17....88 E5
Crosbie Cl CCH PO19....83 L2
Crosby Cl SALV BN13....70 C7
Croshaw Cl LAN/SOMP BN15....72 C8

Crossbill Cl HORN PO8 * 168 B2
Crossbush La ARUN BN18.... 67 K4
Crossbush Rd BRIE/ROTT BN2.... 77 K7
  MSEA/BNM.... 105 H1
Cross Colwood La RHWH RH17..127 R12
Crossfield HASM GU27.... 119 K8
Crosshaven LHPTN BN17.... 89 M3
Cross Keys CRAWE RH10.... 8 F4
Crossland Dr HAV PO9.... 57 H2
Cross La HORL RH6.... 21 H1
  HORN PO8.... 168 B4
  SALV BN13.... 178 H11
  SWTR RH13.... 125 J12
Cross Oak La REDH RH1.... 15 K2
Crosspath CRAWE RH10.... 9 K4
Cross Rd ANG/EP BN16.... 90 D4
  STHW BN42.... 74 C5
Crossroad Cl STHW BN42.... 74 C5
Cross St BRI BN1.... 4 D7
  HOVE BN3.... 76 C8
  WTHG BN11.... 12 F1
Cross Wy HAV PO9.... 56 F3
  LEWES BN7.... 55 M4
Crossways ANG/EP BN16.... 91 G3
  CRAWE RH10.... 9 L1
  MIDH GU29.... 137 K9
  MSEA/BNM PO22.... 87 L8
  PUL/STOR BN20.... 160 A7
  RHWH RH17.... 146 E3
Crossways Av EGRIN RH19.... 23 H8
  FERR BN12.... 91 M1
Crossways Cl CRAWE RH10.... 9 L2
Crossways Pk PUL/STOR BN20..160 A6
Crossways Rd GSHT GU26.... 108 G6
The Crossways LHPTN BN17.... 89 H4
The Crossway BRI BN1.... 77 G3
  PTSD BN41.... 74 B3
Crouch Cross La RCCH PO18.... 63 H2
Crouch HI HFD BN5.... 163 L5
Crouchlands Farm RHWH RH17.. 44 B1
Crouch La HORN PO8.... 168 B3
Crowberry Cl CRAWW RH11.... 28 F7
Crowborough Dr FERR BN12.... 92 B4
Crowhurst Cl CRAWE RH10.... 30 D3
Crowhurst Crs PUL/STOR RH20....159 R11
Crowhurst Rd BN1.... 53 G6
Crown Buildings
  LAN/SOMP BN15 *....94 B1
Crown Cl HOVE BN3 *.... 76 C7
Crown Gdns BRI BN1 *.... 4 D5
Crown Rd PTSD BN41.... 74 F5
  SHOR BN43.... 74 A3
Crown St BRI BN1.... 4 C6
Crowsbury Cl EMRTH PO10.... 57 M2
Croxton La HWH RH16.... 45 L3
Croy Cl CCH PO19.... 6 B9
Crundens Cnr ANG/EP BN16.... 90 D3
Crundles EPSF GU31.... 133 P4
Crypt La MIDH GU29.... 154 G6
Crystal Wy WVILLE PO7.... 168 G8
Cubitt Ter BRIE/ROTT BN2 *.... 5 M7
Cuckfield Cl CRAWW RH11.... 28 E6
Cuckfield Cl SALV BN13.... 70 E7
Cuckfield La RHWH RH17.... 128 C8
Cuckfield Rd BURH RH15.... 46 D2
  HPPT/KEY BN6.... 46 D2
  RHWH RH17.... 46 A1
  RHWH RH17....
Cuckmere Cl CRAWW RH11.... 28 E4
Cuckmere Wy BRI BN1.... 53 G6
Cudlow Av ANG/EP BN16.... 90 B4
Cudlow Gdn ANG/EP BN16.... 90 B5
Cudworth Pk RDKG RH5 *.... 17 K1
Cuffs HI CRAWE RH10.... 30 D7
Culimore Cl SELS PO20.... 99 K6
Culimore Rd SELS PO20.... 99 G5
Culpepper Rd SELS PO20.... 46 D5
Culpepper Cl BRIE/ROTT BN2.... 77 K4
Culross Av HWH RH16.... 45 C4
Culver Rd LAN/SOMP BN15.... 72 D7
  MSEA/BNM PO22.... 3 C5
Culvers EPSF GU31.... 152 B4
Cumberland Av EMRTH PO10.... 57 M1
  FERR BN12.... 70
Cumberland Crs ANG/EP BN16.. 68 G3
Cumberland Dr BRI BN1.... 76 D3
Cumberland Rd ANG/EP BN16.... 68 G4
  BRI BN1.... 76 D3
Cumbrian Cl SALV BN13.... 70 C4
Cunliffe Cl SELS PO20.... 99 H4
Cunningham Gdns
  MSEA/BNM PO22.... 87 H8
Cunningham Rd HORN PO8.... 168 D2
Curbey Cl PUL/STOR RH20.... 160 A4
Curdridge Cl HAV PO9.... 168 H12
Curf Wy BURH RH15.... 47 H6
Curlescroft Rd BOGR PO21.... 103 L3
Curlew Cl EMRTH PO10.... 57 M6
Curlew Gdns HORN PO8.... 73 M5
The Curlews SHOR BN43.... 73 M3
Curtis Cl BOR GU35.... 107 M3
Curtis La BOR GU35.... 107 R5
The Curve HORN PO8.... 168 A3
Curvins Wy LAN/SOMP BN15.... 72 C6
Curzon Pl BRI BN1.... 76 D2
Curzon Av HORN RH12.... 10 A5
Curzon Cl SALV BN13.... 70 E7
Cutfield Cl CCH PO19.... 83 L2
Cuthbert Rd BRIE/ROTT BN2.... 5 K6
Cuttinglye La CRAWE RH10.... 21 M8
Cuttinglye Rd CRAWE RH10.... 22 B7
Cygnet Rd CHAM PO6.... 56 A6
The Cygnets SHOR BN43.... 73 L5
Cygnet Wk MSEA/BNM PO22.... 86 A7
The Cylinders HASM GU27.... 119 K8
Cypress Av SALV BN13.... 70 C8
Cypress Cl SHOR BN43.... 73 C4
Cypress Crs HORN PO8.... 168 B4
Cypress Rd BOR GU35.... 106 D6
Cypress Wy BOGR PO21.... 103 G3
  GSHT GU26.... 108 G7
Cyprus Rd BURH RH15.... 46 F6
Cyprus Vls LHPTN BN17 *.... 89 H4

D

Dacre Gdns STEY/UB BN44.... 49 G6
Dagbrook La HFD BN5.... 163 K6
Dagmar St WTHG BN11.... 13 H3
Dairyfields CRAWW RH11.... 28 F4
Dairy La ARUN BN18.... 65 J5
  RCCH PO18.... 62 E4

The Daisycroft HFD BN5.... 163 L5
Daisy Md WVILLE PO7.... 168 B11
Dakin Cl CRAWE RH10.... 30 B7
The Dakins EGRIN RH19.... 33 K1
Dale Av BRI BN1.... 52 E8
Dale Cl HORS RH12.... 36 E4
Dale Crs BRI BN1.... 52 E7
Dale Dr BRI BN1.... 52 F7
Dale HI POY/PYE BN45.... 164 H11
Dale Rd FROW RH18.... 34 E8
  LEWES BN7.... 55 M5
  WTHG BN11.... 94 A1
Dale Vw BRI BN1.... 52 C8
Dale V BRI BN1.... 52 C8
Dale View Gdns HOVE BN3.... 75 J3
Dalewood Gdns BURH RH15.... 47 H7
  CRAWE RH10.... 29 L1
Dallaway Gdns EGRIN RH19.... 23 K8
Dallaway Rd CCH PO19.... 7 H8
Dallington Rd HOVE BN3.... 75 L5
Dalloway Rd ARUN BN18.... 66 D4
Dalton Cl CRAWW RH11.... 28 F8
Daltons Pl ARUN BN18.... 66 F3
Damask Gdns WVILLE PO7.... 168 C8
Damer's Br PETW GU28.... 139 L9
Damian Wy HPPT/KEY BN6.... 165 Q5
Danbury Rd HORL RH6.... 14 M4
Dancton La HORN PO8.... 58 B3
Danebury Cl HAV PO9.... 168 F11
Danefield Rd SELS PO20.... 181 J6
Danehill La RHWH RH17.... 131 P4
Danehill Rd BRIE/ROTT BN2.... 77 L8
Danehurst Crs SWTR RH13.... 11 K5
Danesbrook La WVILLE PO7.... 168 B10
Daniel Cl LAN/SOMP BN15.... 72 A5
Dankton Gdns LAN/SOMP BN15..72 A4
Dankton La LAN/SOMP BN15.... 72 A4
Danley La HASM GU27.... 118 D2
Danworth La HPPT/KEY BN6.... 46 M1
Dapper's La ANG/EP BN16.... 68 F7
Darcey Dr BRI BN1.... 52 F7
Darenth Wy HORL RH6.... 14 L4
Dark La BOGR PO21.... 103 K3
Darleydale CRAWW RH11.... 8 C9
Darlington Cl ANG/EP BN16.... 68 F3
The Darlingtons ANG/EP BN16.. 90 D2
Dart Cl SALV BN13.... 70 C3
Dartmouth Cl BRIE/ROTT BN2.. 77 K4
Dartmouth Crs BRIE/ROTT BN2..77 K4
Darton Cl HORS RH12.... 11 K1
Daux Av BIL RH14.... 142 A3
Daux HI HORS RH12.... 36 A3
Daux Wy BIL RH14.... 142 A2
Dauxwood Cl BIL RH14.... 142 A2
Davey Dr BRI BN1.... 77 G4
Davids Cl BOGR PO21.... 85 L8
Davigdor Rd HOVE BN3.... 76 C6
Davis Cl CRAWW RH11.... 28 F4
Dawes Av LAN/SOMP BN15.... 94 G4
Dawes Cl WTHG BN11.... 13 M3
Dawlish Cl BRIE/ROTT BN2.... 77 K4
Dawn Cl STEY/UB BN44.... 49 G4
Dawn Crs STEY/UB BN44.... 48 F4
Dawson Ter BRIE/ROTT BN2.... 5 M3
Dawtrey Cl ANG/EP BN16.... 90 D3
Dawtrey Rd PETW GU28 *.... 139 L10
Daynes Wy BURH RH15.... 46 D3
Dayseys HI REDH RH1.... 15 M1
Days La ARUN BN18.... 64 E2
Deacons Dr PTSD BN41.... 75 G3
Deacons Wy STEY/UB BN44.... 48 F3
Deacon Wy SALV BN13.... 71 L1
Deak's La RHWH RH17.... 129 J11
Dean Cl LHPTN BN17.... 89 H3
  PTSD BN41.... 75 H3
Dean Court Rd BRIE/ROTT BN2..97 M3
Deane Cl HAV PO9 *.... 169 J12
Deanery Cl CCH PO19.... 6 D6
Dean Gdns PTSD BN41.... 75 H3
Deanland Rd RHWH RH17.... 40 F8
Dean La HORN PO8.... 169 L4
  PETW GU28.... 138 E9
Deans Cl BRIE/ROTT BN2.... 78 D5
Dean St BRI BN1.... 4 B6
Deans Yd ARUN BN18 *.... 64 F2
Deanway HOVE BN3.... 76 A2
Dean Wy PUL/STOR RH20.... 159 R11
De Braose Wy STEY/UB BN44.... 48 D3
De Courcel Rd BRIE/ROTT BN2.. 96 D2
Decoy Dr ANG/EP BN16.... 68 G6
Decoy La ARUN BN18.... 66 D5
Decoy Rd SALV BN13.... 71 L1
Dedisham Cl CRAWE RH10.... 9 M3
Deep Dene HASM GU27.... 108 H11
Deepdene Cl MSEA/BNM PO22.. 87 M8
Deepfields HORL RH6.... 14 E4
Deeping Ga WVILLE PO7.... 168 B10
Deer Cl CCH PO19.... 83 K2
Deerleap BOR GU35 *.... 107 R5
Deer Pk Cl SELS PO20.... 180 H5
Deer Park Cl SELS PO20.... 180 H5
Deer Park Dr SELS PO20.... 180 H5
Deer Park La SELS PO20.... 180 H5
Deers Leap HWH RH16.... 44 F8
Deerswood Cl CRAWW RH11.... 8 A8
  SALV BN13.... 70 A8
Deerswood Rd CRAWW RH11.... 8 B7
Deeside Av CCH PO19.... 61 G6
The Deeside BRI BN1.... 52 F6
Defiance Pl MSEA/BNM PO22 *..105 H1
Delaware Rd LEWES BN7.... 55 M5
De La Warr Rd EGRIN RH19.... 23 L8
Delfont Cl CRAWE RH10.... 30 C5
Delius Gdns SWTR RH13.... 37 G5
Dell Cl HASM GU27.... 109 K10
Dell Dr CRAWE RH11.... 90 A7
Delling Cl RCCH PO18.... 60 A7
Delling La BIL RH14.... 142 A1
Dellney Av HWH RH16.... 45 L4
Dell Piece East HORN PO8.... 168 E4
Dell Piece West HORN PO8.... 168 D4
Dell Quay Rd SELS PO20.... 83 D3
The Dell EGRIN RH19.... 24 A8
  HAV PO9.... 56 A5
  HORL RH6.... 14 B4
  HORL RH6.... 15 C5
  HWH RH16.... 44 F4
  MSEA/BNM PO22.... 85 M7
Delphi Wy WVILLE PO7.... 56 M3

Delta Dr HORL RH6.... 14 F8
De Montfort Rd BRIE/ROTT BN2.. 5 J2
Dempsey Rd BOGR PO21.... 2 F6
Den Av BOGR PO21.... 2 F6
Denbigh Rd HASM GU27.... 109 N12
Dencher Rd LEWES BN7.... 79 K3
Denchers Plat CRAWW RH11.... 19 J8
Dene Cl BOR GU35.... 106 G7
  HASM GU27.... 109 M11
Deneside BRI BN1.... 52 C8
The Dene HOVE BN3.... 75 J2
Dorrita Av HORN PO8.... 168 B5
Deneway BRI BN1.... 76 C1
  LAN/SOMP BN15.... 72 C7
Denham Cl MSEA/BNM PO22.... 87 K8
Denham Rd BURH RH15.... 46 C5
Denmans CRAWE RH10.... 30 C2
Denman's Cl HWH RH16.... 45 K1
Denman's La HWH RH16.... 45 K2
  SELS PO20.... 64 D3
Denmark Rd PTSD BN41.... 75 H6
Denmark Ter BRI BN1.... 4 A6
Denmark Vls HOVE BN3.... 76 A6
Denne Pde HORS RH12.... 11 M8
Denne Rd CRAWW RH11.... 8 E5
  HORS RH12.... 11 M8
Dennis Hobden Cl
  BRIE/ROTT BN2.... 77 K4
Dennis Wy LISS GU33.... 116 D10
Denny's Cl SELS PO20.... 181 L6
Denshare Rd SELS PO20.... 181 L5
Denshire Dr PUL/STOR RH20.. 160 B11
Densihale BOGR PO21.... 103 C3
Denton Cl FERR BN12.... 92 A2
Denton Dr BRI BN1.... 52 F8
The Denture ARUN BN18.... 175 N5
Denville Av CHAM PO6.... 56 A5
Denvilles Cl HAV PO9.... 57 J3
Departures Rd CRAWW RH11.... 19 L10
Depot Rd CRAWW RH11.... 11 G5
  SWTR RH13.... 11 J5
Derby Rd HAV PO9.... 109 L10
Derek Av HOVE BN3.... 75 J7
Derek Rd LAN/SOMP BN15.... 72 C5
Derwent Av BOR GU35.... 106 G4
  CRAWW RH11.... 28 E4
  HORN PO8.... 150 D11
  HORS RH12.... 37 G3
  LAN/SOMP BN15.... 72 B8
  LHPTN BN17.... 89 M3
  SELS PO20.... 63 H4
Derwent Dr FERR BN12.... 70 C8
Derwent Gv MSEA/BNM PO22.. 87 G7
Desmond Wy BRIE/ROTT BN2.. 77 L7
Detling Rd CRAWW RH11.... 29 H8
Devils Dyke Rd BRI BN1.... 51 H4
  HOVE BN3.... 51 M8
Devils La LIPH GU30.... 118 B2
Devonia Cl BRIE/ROTT BN2 *.... 5 L2
Devonport Pl WTHG BN11.... 93 M2
Devonport Rd WTHG BN11.... 93 M2
Devon Rd BOR GU35.... 106 G6
Devonshire Ct HOVE BN3 *.... 76 B5
Devonshire Pl BRIE/ROTT BN2.. 5 K5
Devonshire Rd BOGR PO21.... 2 C7
Devas St BRI BN1.... 10 F6
Dewar Cl CRAWW RH11 *.... 28 D4
Dew Pond Cl SWTR RH13.... 11 K4
Dexter Dr EGRIN RH19.... 33 K1
Dial Cl MSEA/BNM PO22.... 105 M1
Diana Cl EMRTH PO10.... 57 M1
Dibden Cl HAV PO9.... 56 D7
Dickens Cl CRAWE RH10.... 9 M3
Dickins La EPSF GU31.... 133 P4
Dickinson Pl MSEA/BNM PO22.. 2 E4
Dickins Wy SWTR RH13.... 11 J9
Dingle Cl CRAWW RH11.... 8 A3
The Dingle CRAWW RH11.... 8 A3
Dingley Rd ANG/EP BN16.... 90 A4
Dinsdale Gdns ANG/EP BN16.... 90 B3
Dirty La EGRIN RH19.... 34 D3
Ditcham Crs HAV PO9.... 56 F1
Ditchfield Cl MSEA/BNM PO22.. 87 M7
Ditchling Bostall
  HPPT/KEY BN6.... 166 A10
Ditchling Cl FERR BN12.... 92 A1
Ditchling Crs BRI BN1.... 53 H8
Ditchling Gdns BRI BN1.... 76 F4
Ditchling HI CRAWW RH11.... 8 D9
Ditchling Ri BRI BN1.... 4 E1
Ditchling Rd BRI BN1.... 4 E1
  BRI BN1.... 53 H2
Dobbins Pl CRAWW RH11.... 28 D4
Dobson Rd CRAWW RH11.... 19 J8
Dockenfield Cl HAV PO9 *.... 56 D1
Dodsley Gv EPSF GU31.... 137 K7
Dodsley La MIDH GU29.... 137 K7
Dog La STEY/UB BN44.... 48 C2
Dogwood Dell WVILLE PO7.... 168 A12
Dolby Ter HORL RH6.... 18 D3
Dollis Cl CRAWE RH10.... 30 B4
Dolphin Cl CCH PO19.... 61 G7
  HASM GU27.... 108 H11
Dolphin Ms BRI BN1 *.... 4 F8
  CCH PO19.... 61 J7
  SHOR BN43.... 73 M6
Dolphin Rd SHOR BN43.... 73 M6
Dolphin Wy ANG/EP BN16.... 90 C5
  SHOR BN43.... 74 A6
Domehouse Cl SELS PO20.... 181 L8
Dominion Buildings
  SALV BN13 *.... 13 L1
Dominion Ct SALV BN13.... 13 L1
Dominion Rd SALV BN13.... 71 K6
Dominion Wy ANG/EP BN16.... 90 B2
  SALV BN13.... 71 L8
Dominion Wy West SALV BN13.. 71 L7
Donald Hall Rd BRIE/ROTT BN2.. 5 M7
Donaldson Cl SELS PO20.... 181 J5
Doncaster Wk CRAWE RH10.... 9 L8
Donkey La HORL RH6.... 20 C7
Donkey Ms HORN PO8.... 58 C8
Donne Cl CRAWE RH10.... 30 A1
Donnington Ct CRAWW RH11.. 28 E6
Donnington Pk SELS PO20.... 83 D2
Donnington Rd ANG/EP BN16 *.. 90 B3
Donnington Rd BRIE/ROTT BN2.. 78 D7
Doomsday Gdn SWTR RH13.... 11 L9
Doomsday La SWTR RH13.... 11 L9
Doone End FERR BN12.... 91 L5
Dorcas Cl WVILLE PO7.... 168 B8
Dorchester Gdns WTHG BN11.. 12 A5

Dorking Rd HORS RH12.... 26 A3
  HORS RH12.... 115 R9
Dormans CRAWW RH11.... 28 F4
Dormans High St LING RH7.... 23 M2
Dormans Park Rd EGRIN RH19.. 23 J6
  EGRIN RH19.... 23 K3
Dormans Station Rd LING RH7.. 23 L2
Dormermere La WVILLE PO7.... 168 B10
Dorothy Rd HOVE BN3.... 75 J5
Dorset Av EGRIN RH19.... 23 H8
Dorset Cl BRIE/ROTT BN2 *.... 4 E7
Dorset Gdns BRIE/ROTT BN2 *.. 5 G7
  EGRIN RH19.... 23 G7
Dorset Ms BRIE/ROTT BN2 *.... 5 G7
  SALV BN13.... 70 E8
Dorset Pl BRIE/ROTT BN2 *.... 5 G7
Dorset Rd BOGR PO21.... 2 C3
Dorset St BRIE/ROTT BN2 *.... 4 F7
Doubledays BURH RH15.... 47 H6
Douglas Cl ARUN BN18.... 88 A3
  MSEA/BNM PO22.... 87 L8
  WTHG BN11.... 92 B3
Douglas Gdns HAV PO9.... 57 H1
Douglas Martin Rd CCH PO19.. 7 K5
Dove Cl CRAWW RH11.... 29 J1
  HORN PO8.... 168 B3
Dovecote Ms LAN/SOMP BN15..72 B5
Dove Ct MSEA/BNM PO22.... 2 A2
Dovedale Crs CRAWW RH11.... 8 B8
Dover Cl SWTR RH13.... 125 Q11
Dover Rd BRI BN1.... 76 F3
  WTHG BN11.... 12 A4
Dower Cl MSEA/BNM PO22.... 97 J2
Dower Wk CRAWW RH11.... 28 F4
Downash Cl BRIE/ROTT BN2.... 77 K7
Down Cl MIDH GU29.... 155 M5
Downe Cl HORL RH6.... 14 D4
Down Farm Pl HORN PO8.... 150 D12
Downham Cl HORN PO8.... 168 A6
Downhill Vw BRIE/ROTT BN2.... 78 D6
Downhouse Rd HORN PO8.... 150 B9
Downing Cl BOGR PO21.... 103 K1
Downland Av STHW BN42.... 74 E5
Downland Cl CRAWE RH11.... 8 A5
  SALV BN13.... 178 H11
  STEY/UB BN44.... 49 G3
  STHW BN42.... 74 E5
Downland Ct PTSD BN41.... 74 E2
Downland Crs HOVE BN3.... 75 L2
Downland Dr CRAWE RH10.... 8 C9
  HOVE BN3.... 75 L2
Downland Pl CRAWW RH11 *.... 8 A5
Downland Rd BRIE/ROTT BN2.. 78 A5
  STEY/UB BN44.... 49 G3
Downlands Cl BOGR PO21.... 102 F3
  LAN/SOMP BN15.... 72 B6
Downlands Gdns SALV BN13.... 71 K6
Downlands Pde SALV BN13.... 71 K6
Downley Point HORN PO8.... 57 J1
Downley Rd HAV PO9.... 57 J1
Down Rd HORN PO8.... 150 D12
Downs Cl LAN/SOMP BN15.... 73 C7
  LEWES BN7.... 55 M3
  WVILLE PO7.... 56 A2
Downscroft BURH RH15.... 47 J4
  STEY/UB BN44.... 49 G4
Downshire Ter RHWH RH17 *.. 130 D1
Downside BRI BN1.... 52 E8
  GSHT GU26.... 108 G2
  HOVE BN3.... 76 A2
  LEWES BN7.... 55 M4
  SHOR BN43.... 73 H4
Downside Av SALV BN13.... 70 E2
Downside Cl SALV BN13.... 70 D3
  SHOR BN43.... 73 L4
Downs Link HFD BN5.... 162 H9
  HORS RH12.... 113 R9
  STEY/UB BN44.... 48 F5
  SWTR RH13.... 124 D1
  SWTR RH13.... 125 L5
  SWTR RH13.... 144 D1
Downs Md LAN/SOMP BN15 *.. 72 B5
Downs Rd BURH RH15.... 46 D5
  RCCH PO18.... 171 J11
Down St RCCH PO18.... 60 A2
Downs Valley Rd
  BRIE/ROTT BN2.... 78 D5
Downsview HFD BN5.... 163 L10
  HOVE BN3.... 75 J2
Downs Vw STEY/UB BN44 *.... 162 G14
Downsview Av BRIE/ROTT BN2.. 78 B4
  PUL/STOR BN20.... 160 B11
Downsview Dr MIDH GU29.... 136 H12
  RHWH RH17.... 148 F9
Downs View Wy
  HPPT/KEY BN6.... 165 N6
Downsview Rd ANG/EP BN16.... 91 G3
  BOR GU35.... 107 R4
  HORS RH12.... 37 G3
  PTSD BN41.... 74 G3
Downsway BRIE/ROTT BN2.... 78 C5
  SHOR BN43.... 73 L4
  STHW BN42.... 74 E5
Down Ter BRIE/ROTT BN2.... 5 M4
The Down HOVE BN3.... 75 J2
Downview Av FERR BN12.... 91 K2
Downview Cl ARUN BN18.... 87 K2
  GSHT GU26.... 108 G3
  RCCH PO18.... 172 B3
  SELS PO20.... 99 M7
Downview Rd ARUN BN18.... 87 K2
  FERR BN12.... 91 K2
  MSEA/BNM PO22.... 3 G1
  PETW GU28.... 139 K10
  SALV BN13.... 178 H11
Down View Rd WTHG BN11.... 12 B3
Downview Wy ANG/EP BN16.... 91 G3
Downwood Wy HORN PO8.... 150 D12
Dragons Green Rd SWTR RH13..143 M3
Dragons Green SWTR RH13.... 143 L6
Dragon St EPSF GU31.... 133 N7
Drake Av FERR BN12.... 92 C1
Drake Cl HORS RH12.... 36 D3
Drake Gv ARUN BN18.... 88 A3

Drakeleys Fld LIPH GU30.... 117 Q11
Drake Pk MSEA/BNM PO22.... 105 H1
Drake Rd CRAWE RH10.... 9 H9
  HORL RH6.... 14 D6
Drakes Cl LAN/SOMP BN15.... 73 G7
Draxmont Wy BRI BN1.... 76 B2
Draycliff Cl FERR BN12.... 91 K4
Draycote Rd HORN PO8.... 150 D10
Drayton La SELS PO20.... 62 G7
Drayton Pk SELS PO20 *.... 84 F1
Drewetts Cl ANG/EP BN16.... 90 A2
Drewitts Ms SELS PO20.... 63 G6
Drift La RCCH PO18.... 59 K4
  SELS PO20.... 181 J6
Drift Rd BOGR PO21.... 103 C3
  BOR GU35.... 106 E9
  HORN PO8.... 150 D5
  SELS PO20.... 181 N5
The Drift HAV PO9.... 169 J8
The Driftway ANG/EP BN16.... 90 A2
  STEY/UB BN44.... 49 G2
The Drills ANG/EP BN16 *.... 68 E8
The Drive ANG/EP BN16.... 91 G5
  BIL RH14.... 122 H3
  BOGR PO21.... 103 J4
  BURH RH15.... 47 G5
  CCH PO19.... 61 M2
  CRAWE RH10.... 21 H6
  EMRTH PO10.... 58 E5
  HAV PO9.... 57 G2
  HORL RH6.... 15 C7
  HOVE BN3.... 76 B7
  LAN/SOMP BN15.... 73 C4
  LAN/SOMP BN15.... 94 C1
  PETW GU28.... 156 C7
  RCCH PO18.... 60 A8
  SHOR BN45.... 73 L4
  STHW BN42.... 74 D4
  WTHG BN11.... 92 B2
The Driveway SHOR BN43.... 73 L5
Droke Cl RCCH PO18.... 173 P3
Dropping Holms HFD BN5.... 163 J5
Drove Av BRIE/ROTT BN2.... 78 C3
Drove Crs PTSD BN41.... 74 F3
Drove La ARUN BN18.... 87 J3
  SELS PO20.... 100 C7
Drove Rd BRIE/ROTT BN2.... 77 M5
  PTSD BN41.... 74 F4
Drovers RHWH RH17.... 146 D2
Drovers Cl PTSD BN41.... 75 H3
Drovers Wy BURH RH15.... 47 H5
The Drove BRI BN1.... 54 B8
  LEWES BN7.... 167 K12
The Droveway HOVE BN3.... 75 M3
  HWH RH16.... 44 F3
Drum Md PSF GU32.... 133 N6
Drummond Cl HWH RH16.... 45 C5
Drummond Ct FERR BN12.... 92 C4
  HWH RH16 *.... 45 C5
Drummond Rd CRAWW RH11.. 28 C4
  FERR BN12.... 92 D4
Drungewick La BIL RH14.... 123 K7
Drury Cl CRAWE RH10.... 30 C5
Dryad Wk MSEA/BNM PO22.... 105 J1
Dryad Wy MSEA/BNM PO22.... 105 J1
Dryden Wy LIPH GU30.... 107 P12
Drygrounds La MSEA/BNM PO22.. 3 K3
Ducklands BOR GU35.... 106 F4
Duck La MIDH GU29.... 137 J9
Duckmead La LISS GU33.... 116 E7
Dudleston Heath Dr
  HORN PO8.... 168 C7
Dudley Cl BOR GU35.... 106 F9
Dudley Rd BRI BN1.... 77 G4
Dudwell Rd BRIE/ROTT BN2.... 78 D6
Duffield La EMRTH PO10.... 58 E2
Duke Cl CRAWE RH10.... 30 B7
Dukes Cl ARUN BN18.... 66 E3
  PSF GU32.... 133 L5
Dukes Ct CCH PO19 *.... 7 L6
Duke's HI PUL/STOR RH20.... 160 D5
Dukes La BRI BN1 *.... 4 D7
  STEY/UB BN44.... 48 C2
Dukes Meadow BOGR PO21.... 103 G2
Duke's Mound BRIE/ROTT BN2.. 5 L3
Dukes Rd ARUN BN18.... 64 C1
  HWH RH16.... 45 L1
  RDKG RH5.... 17 K3
  RDKG RH5.... 17 L4
Duke St BRI BN1.... 4 D7
  LHPTN BN17.... 89 H4
Dukes Yd STEY/UB BN44.... 48 C2
Duke Ter HAV PO9.... 56 E1
Dumbrells Cottages
  RHWH RH17 *.... 47 M4
Dumbrells Court Rd
  HPPT/KEY BN6.... 166 A5
Dumbrills Cl BURH RH15.... 46 F4
Dummer Ct HAV PO9.... 168 E12
Dumpford La EPSF GU31.... 135 J9
Duncan Rd CCH PO19.... 6 C1
Duncton Cl HWH RH16.... 45 L2
  MSEA/BNM PO22.... 105 L1
Duncton High St PETW GU28.. 156 H6
Duncton Rd ANG/EP BN16.... 90 B3
  HORN PO8.... 150 B9
The Dunes BOGR PO21.... 103 G5
Dunford Hollow MIDH GU29.... 154 H1
Dunhurst Cl HAV PO9.... 57 H2
Dunlop Cl HPPT/KEY BN6.... 146 E12
Dunnings Rd EGRIN RH19.... 33 K3
Dunnock Cl HAV PO9.... 169 J8
Dunsbury Wy HAV PO9.... 168 F12
Dunsfold Cl CRAWW RH11.... 28 F4
Dunsfold Common Rd
  MFD/CHID GU8.... 112 A2
  CRAN GU6.... 112 F6
  MFD/CHID GU8.... 111 P10
  MFD/CHID GU8.... 112 C1
Dunstall Av BURH RH15.... 46 D5
Dunstall Farm Rd BURH RH15.. 46 C5
Dunster Cl BRI BN1.... 77 C8
Durban Pk MSEA/BNM PO22.... 2 A2
Durban Rd MSEA/BNM PO22.... 86 B7
Durford Cl BIL RH14.... 123 J12
Durford Ct HAV PO9.... 168 E11
Durford Rd EPSF GU31.... 133 K6
Durham Cl BOGR PO21.... 102 F5
  BRIE/ROTT BN2.... 77 M4

CRAWE RH10 29 K7
Durham Gdns CCH PO19 61 L4
WVILLE PO7 168 A12
Durkins Rd EGRIN RH19 23 J6
Durlands Rd HORN PO8 168 D1
Durley Av HORN PO8 168 A6
Durlston Dr MSEA/BNM PO22 86 A7
Durlston Pde MSEA/BNM PO22 * 2 B1
Durnford Cl CCH PO19 6 B3
Durrants Gdns HAV PO9 169 J9
Durrants Rd HAV PO9 169 J10
Durrington Gdns FERR BN12 * 92 C2
Durrington Hl SALV BN13 70 C6
Durrington La SALV BN13 70 C6
Dutchells Copse HORS RH12 36 D3
Duxhurst La REIG RH2 14 A2
Dyall Cl BURH RH15 46 D5
Dye House La PETW GU28 156 H6
Dyers La ARUN BN18 174 H12
Dyke Cl HOVE BN3 76 A1
Dyke Rd BRI BN1 4 B2
HOVE BN3 4 B2
Dyke Road Av BRI BN1 76 A1
Dyke Road Dr BRI BN1 4 C1
Dyke Road Pl BRI BN1 76 B2
The Dymock's HPPT/KEY BN6 166 A6
Dymoke St EMRTH PO10 57 M1
Dyson Wk CRAWW RH11 * 29 G8

E

Eady Cl SWTR RH13 11 J6
Eagles Cha LHPTN BN17 89 H1
Earles Meadow HORS RH12 37 G3
Earlswood Cl SWTR RH13 11 L2
Early Commons CRAWE RH10 9 K2
Earnley Manor Cl SELS PO20 100 C6
Earnley Rd HISD PO11 98 A3
Earwig La RHWH RH17 127 R11
Easebourne La MIDH GU29 137 K8
Easebourne St MIDH GU29 137 M6
PETW GU28 137 Q2
East Av FERR BN12 92 E4
MSEA/BNM PO22 87 L7
East Bank ARUN BN18 * 65 M8
SELS PO20 181 M6
Eastbank STHW BN42 74 E4
East Beach Rd SELS PO20 181 N6
Eastbourne Rd BRIE/ROTT BN2 77 J4
EGRIN RH19 22 E3
East Bracklesham Dr
SELS PO20 100 A8
Eastbrook Rd PTSD BN41 75 G6
Eastbrook Wy PTSD BN41 74 F6
East Cl MSEA/BNM PO22 87 K8
East Ct EGRIN RH19 * 23 L7
Eastcourt Rd SALV BN13 12 F2
East Court Wy ANG/EP BN16 90 C3
Eastdale Rd BURH RH15 47 H5
Eastdean Hl RCCH PO18 173 M4
East Dr ANG/EP BN16 90 D1
BRIE/ROTT BN2 5 J6
MSEA/BNM PO22 87 M8
Easteds La SWTR RH13 125 R11
East End La HPPT/KEY BN6 166 B7
Eastergate Cl FERR BN12 91 M3
Eastergate La ARUN BN18 65 G4
SELS PO20 64 E4
Eastergate Rd BRIE/ROTT BN2 77 L1
Eastern Av SHOR BN43 73 M6
Eastern Cl ANG/EP BN16 91 G3
SHOR BN43 73 M6
Eastern Pl BRIE/ROTT BN2 96 D1
Eastern Rd BOR GU35 106 G3
BRIE/ROTT BN2 5 H7
BRIE/ROTT BN2 96 D1
HAV PO9 57 H3
HWH RH16 45 J6
HWH RH16 45 L2
Eastern Ter BRIE/ROTT BN2 5 L9
Eastern Terrace Ms
BRIE/ROTT BN2 5 L9
East Field Cl EMRTH PO10 58 F3
Eastfield La EPSF GU31 152 H2
East Front Rd BOGR PO21 102 F6
East Gdns HPPT/KEY BN6 166 A6
Eastgate Sq CCH PO19 * 6 F4
East Gun Copse Rd
SWTR RH13 125 N8
East Hampnett La RCCH PO18 63 K3
East Ham Rd LHPTN BN17 89 H4
East Harting St EPSF GU31 152 G2
East Hl EGRIN RH19 23 K3
East Hill Dr LISS GU33 116 D10
Easthill Dr PTSD BN41 75 G3
East Hill La CRAWE RH10 21 J3
Easthill Wy PTSD BN41 75 G4
Easting Cl SALV BN13 71 L8
East Lake BOGR PO21 2 E5
Eastlake Cl EPSF GU31 133 R6
Eastland Rd CCH PO19 7 H8
East Leigh Rd HAV PO9 57 L1
East Lodge Pk CHAM PO6 56 A5
East Mascalls La HWH RH16 130 H10
East Md BOGR PO21 102 F5
FERR BN12 91 L4
East Meadway SHOR BN43 73 M7
East Ms HORS RH12 * 10 D6
Easton Crs BIL RH14 142 B1
Easton La SELS PO20 101 G7
East Onslow Cl FERR BN12 91 K3
Eastover Ct HAV PO9 168 E11
Eastover Wy MSEA/BNM PO22 3 K5
East Pallant CCH PO19 6 E5
East Pk CRAWE RH10 8 F5
East Rw CCH PO19 6 F4
Eastshaw La MIDH GU29 136 F5
East Strd SELS PO20 99 G5
East St ARUN BN18 176 F2
BIL RH14 142 A1
BRI BN1 4 E7
BRI BN1 54 B7
CCH PO19 6 F4
CRAWE RH10 32 A5
EMRTH PO10 58 C2
HAV PO9 57 G4
HORS RH12 10 D7
HORS RH12 27 K2
LAN/SOMP BN15 94 D1
LHPTN BN17 89 K4
PETW GU28 139 L9
PTSD BN41 75 H7
PUL/STOR RH20 160 B4
SELS PO20 181 L6
SHOR BN43 73 L6
East Tyne SALV BN13 70 C7
East View Cl RCCH PO18 172 C10
East View Flds LEWES BN7 166 H4
East Walls CCH PO19 6 F4
East Walls Cl CCH PO19 6 F4
Eastway HORL RH6 20 A2
East Wy LEWES BN7 55 L3
SELS PO20 181 M6
East Wick HWH RH16 45 M2
Eastwick Cl BRI BN1 53 G6
Eastwood CRAWE RH10 9 J4
Eaton Gdns HOVE BN3 76 B6
Eaton Gv HOVE BN3 76 B6
Eaton Mnr HOVE BN3 * 76 B6
Eaton Pl BRIE/ROTT BN2 5 M9
Eaton Rd HOVE BN3 76 B7
Eaton Vls HOVE BN3 76 A6
Edburton Av BRI BN1 76 F4
Edburton Dro HFD BN5 163 Q10
Edburton Gdns SHOR BN43 73 L4
Eddeys Cl BOR GU35 107 Q3
Eddeys La BOR GU35 107 Q4
Eddington Hl CRAWW RH11 28 F8
Eden Rd CRAWW RH11 28 E5
Eden V EGRIN RH19 23 K5
Edgar Cl CRAWE RH10 30 D4
Edgefield Gv WVILLE PO7 168 D8
Edgehill Cl SALV BN13 70 E6
Edgehill Wy PTSD BN41 74 E3
Edgell Rd EMRTH PO10 58 C1
Edinburgh Cl BOGR PO21 103 K3
SWTR RH13 125 R12
Edinburgh Rd BRIE/ROTT BN2 5 H1
Edinburgh Sq MIDH GU29 137 J10
Edinburgh Wy EGRIN RH19 33 L2
Edmonton Rd SALV BN13 70 B7
Edrich Rd CRAWW RH11 28 F8
Edward Av HOVE BN3 75 M2
Edward Cl HOVE BN3 75 M2
Edward Gdns HAV PO9 56 D4
Edward Rd HWH RH16 45 H6
Edwards Av SELS PO20 63 H3
Edwards Cl HORN PO8 168 A7
Edwards Ter LAN/SOMP BN15 * 71 L6
Edward St BRIE/ROTT BN2 5 G7
Edwards Wy LHPTN BN17 89 H1
Edward Wy BURH RH15 46 C7
Edwen Cl BOGR PO21 103 G2
Edwin Cl LAN/SOMP BN15 72 B7
Effingham La CRAWE RH10 21 K4
Effingham Rd HORL RH6 21 H3
Egan Wy LHPTN BN17 89 G3
Egginton Cl BRIE/ROTT BN2 53 M8
Egginton Rd BRIE/ROTT BN2 77 L1
Eglantine Cl HORN PO8 168 C5
Eglantine Wk HORN PO8 168 C5
Egmont Rd HOVE BN3 75 J4
MIDH GU29 137 K7
Egremont Pl BRIE/ROTT BN2 5 H7
Egremont Rw PETW GU28 * 139 L9
Eight Acres GSHT GU26 108 F2
Eighth Av LAN/SOMP BN15 72 D6
Eirene Av FERR BN12 92 E4
Eirene Rd FERR BN12 92 D4
Elaine Gdns HORN PO8 168 A4
Elbridge Crs BOGR PO21 103 H3
Elcombe Cl SELS PO20 100 A8
Elderberry Cl HORN PO8 150 E9
Elderberry Rd BOR GU35 107 K4
Elderberry Wy HORN PO8 168 C5
Elder Cl PTSD BN41 75 G3
Elderfield Cl EMRTH PO10 58 B2
Elderfield Rd HAV PO9 168 E10
Elder Pl BRI BN1 4 E2
Elder Rd HAV PO9 57 J2
Eldon Rd WTHG BN11 13 L4
Eldon Wy LHPTN BN17 89 G3
Eldred Av BRI BN1 52 C8
Eleanor Cl LIPH GU30 107 L9
Eleanor Gdns MSEA/BNM PO22 87 J8
Eley Crs BRIE/ROTT BN2 97 K2
Eley Dr BRIE/ROTT BN2 97 K1
Elfin Gv BOGR PO21 2 A7
Elgar Wk WVILLE PO7 56 A1
Elgar Wy SWTR RH13 37 G5
Elger Wy CRAWE RH10 20 F5
Elgin Rd FERR BN12 92 C3
Eling Ct HAV PO9 168 E11
Eliot Dr HASM GU27 108 H11
Elizabethan Wy CRAWE RH10 30 B4
Elizabeth Av BOGR PO21 103 H2
HOVE BN3 75 M2
Elizabeth Cl BOGR PO21 103 H2
HOVE BN3 75 M2
Elizabeth Ct HORL RH6 * 14 F6
Elizabeth Crs EGRIN RH19 23 L6
Elizabeth Pl LAN/SOMP BN15 72 B8
Elizabeth Rd CCH PO19 7 L3
SHOR BN43 74 B5
WTHG BN11 12 F5
WVILLE PO7 168 A11
Ella Cl SELS PO20 99 K6
Ellanore La SELS PO20 99 G3
Ellasdale Rd BOGR PO21 2 A8
Ellen St HOVE BN3 76 A6
PTSD BN41 75 H6
Ellesmere Orch EMRTH PO10 58 C1
Elliot Cl CRAWE RH10 30 B4
Ellis Av SALV BN13 70 D5
Ellis Cl ARUN BN18 66 E3
Ellisfield Rd HAV PO9 56 F1
Ellis Wy BOGR PO21 102 F5
Ellman Rd CRAWW RH11 28 E5
Ellson Cl CRAWE RH10 30 B5
Ellwood Pl CRAWW RH11 * 28 E3
Elm Av ANG/EP BN16 91 G4
Elm Cl BOGR PO21 102 F4
BOR GU35 106 H6
HOVE BN3 76 B3
SELS PO20 100 A7
SHOR BN43 73 L4
Elmcroft Pl SELS PO20 64 C7
Elm Dr EGRIN RH19 23 M8
HOVE BN3 75 K4
MSEA/BNM PO22 88 A8
Elmer Cl MSEA/BNM PO22 88 A8
Elmer Ct MSEA/BNM PO22 88 B8
Elmer Rd MSEA/BNM PO22 87 L8
Elmeswelle Rd HORN PO8 168 B3
Elm Gv BOGR PO21 103 M2
BRIE/ROTT BN2 5 J3
LAN/SOMP BN15 72 C8
MSEA/BNM PO22 64 F6
SELS PO20 181 K6
SWTR RH13 11 G7
WTHG BN11 92 E2
Elm Grove La STEY/UB BN44 48 C2
Elmgrove Rd LHPTN BN17 89 L3
Elm Gv South MSEA/BNM PO22 64 F7
Elmhurst Cl ANG/EP BN16 68 F7
Elmhurst La SWTR RH13 124 E7
Elm La HAV PO9 57 G4
Elmleigh MIDH GU29 136 H9
Elmleigh Ct MIDH GU29 * 136 H9
Elmleigh Rd HAV PO9 57 G3
Elmore Rd BRIE/ROTT BN2 5 G5
Elm Pk FERR BN12 91 L2
RCCH PO18 60 B7
Elm Park Rd HAV PO9 57 G3
Elm Pl ANG/EP BN16 90 C4
Elm Ri SALV BN13 178 H11
Elm Rd HAV PO9 57 H5
PTSD BN41 75 G5
SELS PO20 64 D6
WTHG BN11 13 J6
Elms Dr LAN/SOMP BN15 72 C7
Elmsfield SELS PO20 181 L6
Elms La SELS PO20 99 H4
Elms Lea Av BRI BN1 76 D3
Elms Ride SELS PO20 99 H4
Elmstead Gdns SELS PO20 99 H3
Elmstead Park Rd SELS PO20 99 H3
Elmstone Cl LAN/SOMP BN15 72 C7
Elms Wy SELS PO20 99 H3
Elm Ter LISS GU33 116 B8
Elm Tree Cl BOGR PO21 85 M7
HORL RH6 * 14 F5
SELS PO20 181 L5
Elmwood Av MSEA/BNM PO22 2 F3
Elrington Rd HOVE BN3 76 B4
Elsie Rd WTHG BN11 12 D7
Elsted Cl CRAWW RH11 29 G1
Elsted Crs BRI BN1 53 H7
Elsted Rd MIDH GU29 135 N12
Elverlands Cl FERR BN12 91 L5
Elvin Crs BRIE/ROTT BN2 97 K1
Elwood Cl BURH RH15 46 E8
Ely Cl CRAWE RH10 29 L7
SALV BN13 92 E1
SELS PO20 99 L5
Ely Gdns BOGR PO21 103 J2
Ely Rd SALV BN13 92 E1
Emberwood CRAWW RH11 * 29 J1
Embleton Rd BOR GU35 107 Q3
Emerald Cl WVILLE PO7 168 B10
Emerald Quay SHOR BN43 73 M7
Emlyn Rd HORL RH6 14 D5
Emms La SWTR RH13 125 J11
Empire Vls REDH RH1 14 F2
Emsbrook Dr EMRTH PO10 58 A3
Emsworth Cl CRAWE RH10 * 30 B6
Emsworth Common Rd
HAV PO9 169 L12
Emsworth House Cl
EMRTH PO10 57 M4
Emsworth Rd EMRTH PO10 80 C1
HAV PO9 57 J4
End La HFD BN5 162 F4
Ends Pl HORS RH12 * 115 M10
Enfield Rd CRAWW RH11 29 G7
Engalee EGRIN RH19 23 H7
Englefield HORS RH12 125 Q3
English Cl HOVE BN3 75 K5
Enholms La RHWH RH17 131 R5
Ennerdale Cl CRAWW RH11 8 B8
HORN PO8 150 D11
Ennerdale Dr LAN/SOMP BN15 72 A8
Ennerdale Rd BOR GU35 106 G4
Ensign Wy LHPTN BN17 89 M3
Enterprise Ct FERR BN12 * 92 B2
Enterprise Rd HORN PO8 168 D1
Epping Wk CRAWE RH10 9 K8
Epsom Rd CRAWE RH10 9 L8
Erica Cl HORN PO8 168 C6
Erica Wy CRAWE RH10 20 F7
HORN PO8 168 C6
HORS RH12 36 C4
Ericsson Wy BURH RH15 46 C7
Eridge Cl CRAWE RH10 30 B3
Eridge Rd HOVE BN3 75 M3
Erin Wy BURH RH15 46 D6
Eriskay Ct SALV BN13 70 A8
Eriswell Rd WTHG BN11 12 F6
Erles Rd LIPH GU30 117 R1
Ernest Cl EMRTH PO10 58 A4
Ernest Rd HAV PO9 56 D1
Erringham Rd SHOR BN43 73 K5
Erroll Rd HOVE BN3 75 H7
Erskine Cl CRAWW RH11 28 D7
Esher Cl BOGR PO21 103 G3
Esher Dr LHPTN BN17 89 L4
Eskbank Av BRI BN1 52 F6
Eskdale Cl HORN PO8 150 D11
Esmond Cl EMRTH PO10 58 A5
Esmonde Cl LHPTN BN17 89 L3
Esplanade Ct WTHG BN11 * 13 M6
The Esplanade BOGR PO21 2 D8
WTHG BN11 13 L6
Essenhigh Dr SALV BN13 70 A7
Essex Pl BRIE/ROTT BN2 * 5 J8
Essex Rd BOGR PO21 2 C3
BOR GU35 106 G5
Essex St BRIE/ROTT BN2 5 H7
Estcots Dr EGRIN RH19 23 M8
The Estuary LHPTN BN17 89 L5
Ethelred Rd SALV BN13 12 A2
Ethel St HOVE BN3 76 A6
Ethelwulf Rd SALV BN13 12 A2
Eton Cl BOGR PO21 103 K1
Eton Dr SELS PO20 99 L5
Eton Rd WTHG BN11 12 B3
Ettrick Cl CCH PO19 7 G6
Ettrick Rd CCH PO19 6 F6
Evans Cl CRAWE RH10 30 C4
Evans Pl MSEA/BNM PO22 2 E1
Eveley Cl BOR GU35 106 E9
Evelyn Av ANG/EP BN16 90 C5
Evelyn Rd SALV BN13 13 H1
Evelyn Ter BRIE/ROTT BN2 5 K6
Evelyn Wk CRAWE RH10 9 G9
Everglades Av HORN PO8 168 A6
Eversfield SWTR RH13 126 A8
Eversfield Rd SWTR RH13 11 G7
Evershed Wy SHOR BN43 74 A6
Eversley Crs HAV PO9 56 E1
Ewart St BRIE/ROTT BN2 5 H4
Ewelands HORL RH6 15 H5
Ewens Gdns MSEA/BNM PO22 64 F6
Ewhurst Cl CRAWW RH11 8 C3
HAV PO9 56 E1
Ewhurst Rd BRIE/ROTT BN2 77 H5
CRAWW RH11 8 C3
Exbury Rd HAV PO9 168 H12
Excalibur Cl CRAWW RH11 28 D3
Exceat Cl BRIE/ROTT BN2 77 K7
The Excelsior BRI BN1 * 76 C1
Exchange Rd CRAWE RH10 9 H3
Exeter Cl BOGR PO21 103 L2
CRAWE RH10 29 K7
EMRTH PO10 58 A2
Exeter Ct WTHG BN11 * 12 A7
Exeter Rd CCH PO19 61 K4
Exeter St BRI BN1 4 B1
Exmoor Cl SALV BN13 70 C6
Exmoor Crs SALV BN13 70 D6
Exmoor Dr SALV BN13 70 D5
Exton Rd CCH PO19 7 G8
HAV PO9 169 J12
Eyles Cl HORS RH12 10 A1

F

Faber Cl HAV PO9 57 H1
Fabian Cl WVILLE PO7 168 B9
Fabians Wy HFD BN5 163 J4
Fairbanks HWH RH16 45 H5
Fairbridge Wy BURH RH15 46 E4
Faircox La HFD BN5 163 J4
Fairdene STHW BN42 74 E4
Fairfield Av HORL RH6 14 F8
Fairfield Cl BURH RH15 46 E5
EMRTH PO10 58 A3
RCCH PO18 60 B8
RHWH RH17 130 D1
SHOR BN43 74 A4
Fairfield Cottages SWTR RH13 145 K3
Fairfield Crs HPPT/KEY BN6 164 H3
Fairfield Gdns PTSD BN41 75 G4
Fairfield Ms PUL/STOR RH20 * 161 J9
Fairfield Ri PETW GU28 139 L10
Fairfield Rd BURH RH15 46 E6
EGRIN RH19 33 L1
HAV PO9 57 G4
PUL/STOR RH20 161 K9
RCCH PO18 60 A8
Fairfields SALV BN13 70 F8
Fairfield Ter HAV PO9 * 57 G4
Fairfield Wy HWH RH16 45 G1
PUL/STOR RH20 161 K9
Fairford Cl HWH RH16 45 H4
Fairholme Dr ARUN BN18 87 M3
Fairlands ANG/EP BN16 90 E4
MSEA/BNM PO22 86 A7
Fairlawn ANG/EP BN16 90 B3
Fairlawn Crs EGRIN RH19 23 G7
Fairlawn Dr EGRIN RH19 23 G7
SALV BN13 13 H1
Fairlawns HORL RH6 15 G7
SHOR BN43 73 M5
Fairlea Cl BURH RH15 46 E5
Fairlead LHPTN BN17 89 L5
Fairlea Rd EMRTH PO10 58 A2
Fairlie Gdns BRI BN1 76 D2
Fairlight Pl BRIE/ROTT BN2 5 J1
Fairmead Cl PUL/STOR RH20 158 B2
Fairmead Wk HORN PO8 168 B6
Fairmile Bottom ARUN BN18 175 M10
Fair Oak Dr HAV PO9 57 G2
Fair Pl RHWH RH17 * 148 F9
Fairplace RHWH RH17 148 F9
Fairstone Ct HORL RH6 15 G5
Fair Vw HORS RH12 125 R2
Fairview Av FERR BN12 92 B4
Fairview Ri BRI BN1 52 C8
Fairview Rd BOR GU35 107 Q4
LAN/SOMP BN15 72 D5
Fairview Ter BOR GU35 * 107 P3
Fairway CRAWE RH10 21 G7
CRAWW RH11 28 C4
LHPTN BN17 89 L5
Fairway Cl CRAWE RH10 20 F7
LIPH GU30 117 L2
Fairway Crs PTSD BN41 75 H3
Fairways GSHT GU26 108 E3
The Fairway BOGR PO21 103 H5
BOR GU35 106 E8
HAV PO9 169 K7
LAN/SOMP BN15 72 F8
MIDH GU29 136 H12
Fairy Crossway HORN PO8 168 C7
Faithfull Crs PUL/STOR RH20 159 Q11
Falcon Cl CRAWW RH11 29 J1
SHOR BN43 74 B7
Falcon Gdns LHPTN BN17 89 H1
Falcon Rd HORN PO8 168 B2
Falkland Av LHPTN BN17 89 L3
Falklands Cl MSEA/BNM PO22 2 F2
Falklands Dr SWTR RH13 37 G5
Fallow Deer Cl SWTR RH13 37 G6
Fallowfield Cl HOVE BN3 75 L3
Fallowfield Crs HOVE BN3 75 K3
Fallowfield Wy HORL RH6 15 G5
Falmer Av FERR BN12 92 A4
Falmer Cl CRAWW RH11 8 E7
FERR BN12 92 B4
Falmer Gdns BRIE/ROTT BN2 78 C5
Falmer House Rd BRI BN1 54 A6
Falmer Rd BRIE/ROTT BN2 78 C3
Falmouth Ms SWTR RH13 * 125 R12
Faraday Av EGRIN RH19 33 L3
Faraday Cl SALV BN13 70 B7
Faraday Rd CRAWE RH10 19 L7
Farebrothers HORS RH12 * 115 Q9
Faresmead BOGR PO21 103 L3
Farhalls Crs HORS RH12 36 E3
Farleigh Cl HAV PO9 168 E12
Farlington Av HWH RH16 45 J4
Farlington Cl HWH RH16 45 H4
Farm Acre ANG/EP BN16 * 90 E3
Farman St HOVE BN3 * 76 C8
Farm Av HORS RH12 10 A4
Farm Cl BIL RH14 122 H2
CRAWE RH10 9 K2
EGRIN RH19 34 A1
HFD BN5 163 K4
HORS RH12 115 Q10
HPPT/KEY BN6 165 M5
MSEA/BNM PO22 88 A8
PTSD BN41 74 F3
Farm Cnr MSEA/BNM PO22 87 M8
Far Meadow Wy EMRTH PO10 57 L5
Farmfield Dr HORL RH6 19 G1
Farm Hl BRIE/ROTT BN2 78 B5
Farmhouse Wy HORN PO8 168 B4
Farm La HPPT/KEY BN6 166 B6
RCCH PO18 59 G6
Farmleigh Cl CRAWE RH10 30 B1
Farm Ms HOVE BN3 * 76 C7
Farm Rd HOVE BN3 76 C7
SELS PO20 100 A8
Farm Vw EMRTH PO10 58 A2
Farm View Av HORN PO8 150 C8
Farm Wy ANG/EP BN16 90 A4
BURH RH15 47 J8
STHW BN42 74 F6
Farmway Cl HOVE BN3 75 J3
Farncombe Cl RHWH RH17 148 G8
Farncombe Rd WTHG BN11 13 L5
Farndell Cl CCH PO19 7 J3
Farne Cl SELS PO20 100 D1
Farnefold Rd STEY/UB BN44 48 C1
Farne La SELS PO20 100 D1
Farnham Av HPPT/KEY BN6 165 P4
Farnham Cl CRAWW RH11 39 H1
Farnham La HASM GU27 109 K8
Farnham Rd BOR GU35 106 G3
LISS GU33 116 B9
PSF GU32 133 Q1
Farnhurst La CRAN GU6 112 G5
Farnhurst Rd MSEA/BNM PO22 65 G7
Farnlea Rd BURH RH15 47 J4
The Faroes LHPTN BN17 89 M3
Farr Cl RHWH RH17 44 C1
Farriers Cl BIL RH14 141 R2
Farriers Wy WVILLE PO7 168 D8
Farringdon Rd HAV PO9 57 H1
Farthing Flds BOR GU35 107 M4
Farthings Hl HORS RH12 * 10 A7
Farthings Wk HORS RH12 125 Q2
Fastnet Wy LHPTN BN17 89 M4
Faulkner Cl CRAWW RH11 39 H1
Faulkners Wy BURH RH15 46 F4
Fawley Ct HAV PO9 169 J12
Fawn Ri HFD BN5 163 K3
Faygate La HORS RH12 27 K2
Felbridge Av CRAWE RH10 30 C2
Felbridge Cl EGRIN RH19 23 H6
Felbridge Ct EGRIN RH19 22 F5
Felbridge Pl EGRIN RH19 * 22 F5
Felbridge Rd EGRIN RH19 22 C6
Felcot Rd EGRIN RH19 22 B6
Felcourt Rd EGRIN RH19 23 H2
The Feld EGRIN RH19 22 F6
Fellcott Wy HORS RH12 125 Q4
Felpham Gdns
MSEA/BNM PO22 87 G8
Felpham Rd MSEA/BNM PO22 3 K5
Felpham Wy MSEA/BNM PO22 3 J5
Felride HWH RH16 45 H6
Fenby Cl SWTR RH13 37 G5
Fenchurch Rd CRAWE RH10 30 A5
Fenhurst Cl HORS RH12 125 Q4
Fennel Crs CRAWW RH11 29 G6
Fereday Cl LAN/SOMP BN15 72 D7
Fermandy La CRAWE RH10 21 M8
Fern Cl EPSF GU31 133 R6
Ferncote Rd BOR GU35 106 H6
Ferndale WVILLE PO7 168 A10
Ferndale Rd BURH RH15 47 G8
CCH PO19 61 M3
HOVE BN3 76 C6
Ferndale Wk ANG/EP BN16 68 F7
Fernden La HASM GU27 119 M2
Ferndown CRAWE RH10 20 C7
HORL RH6 14 F4
Ferndown Gdns
MSEA/BNM PO22 3 M3
Fern Dr HAV PO9 57 H3
Fernhill Cl CRAWE RH10 22 A8
Fernhill Rd HORL RH6 20 C2
Fernhurst Cl BRI BN1 53 H7
CRAWW RH11 29 G1
Fernhurst Crs BRI BN1 53 G8
Fernhurst Dr FERR BN12 91 M3
Fernhurst Gdns BOGR PO21 103 J3
Fernhurst Rd LIPH GU30 117 Q10
Fernlea BOR GU35 106 E8
Fern Rd PUL/STOR RH20 159 R12
Fern Wy HORS RH12 36 C4
Fernwood Ri BRI BN1 52 C8
Feroners Cl CRAWE RH10 9 M7
Ferring Cl CRAWW RH11 8 A1
FERR BN12 91 K5
Ferring Gdns MSEA/BNM PO22 3 L3
Ferring Grange Gdns
FERR BN12 91 K3
Ferringham La FERR BN12 91 K4
Ferringham Wy FERR BN12 91 K5
Ferring La FERR BN12 91 L2
Ferring Marine FERR BN12 91 L5
Ferring St FERR BN12 91 K3
Ferry Rd LHPTN BN17 89 G5
SHOR BN43 73 L7
Fetherston Rd LAN/SOMP BN15 72 D6
Feversham Cl SHOR BN43 74 A7
Fidler Cl SELS PO20 181 M4
Field Cl ARUN BN18 65 J4
BURH RH15 46 D5
LAN/SOMP BN15 72 C7
Fieldend HORS RH12 37 G4
Field End PUL/STOR RH20 160 B11
Fieldfare Cl HORN PO8 150 D9
Fieldgate Cl SWTR RH13 126 H5
The Fieldings HORL RH6 15 G5
SWTR RH13 143 Q2
Field Pl LHPTN BN17 89 J4
LIPH GU30 117 Q2
Field Place Pde FERR BN12 * 92 D2
Field Rd SELS PO20 99 L6
Field Rw WTHG BN11 13 G6
Fields End Cl HWH RH16 45 J5
The Fields SELS PO20 * 64 C7
Fieldview HORL RH6 15 G5
Fieldway HASM GU27 109 M10
HPPT/KEY BN6 166 A6
HWH RH16 45 J1
Fifth Av HAV PO9 57 J3
LAN/SOMP BN15 72 D6
SALV BN13 71 H5
Filbert Crs CRAWW RH11 28 F3
Filey Cl CRAWW RH11 28 E5
Fincham Cl ANG/EP BN16 90 E4
Finch Crs CRAWE RH10 32 B4
Finchdean Rd HAV PO9 56 E1
HAV PO9 169 L6
Finches Cl LAN/SOMP BN15 72 C8
LHPTN BN17 89 H1
SWTR RH13 144 F10
Finches Gdns HWH RH16 130 D8
Finches La HWH RH16 45 K1
PUL/STOR RH20 159 R5

Finches Park Rd HWH RH16 — 45 K1
The Finches SHOR BN43 — 73 M5
Finch Gdns MSEA/BNM PO22 — 86 A6
Finchmead La PSF GU32 — 133 J5
Findon By-Pass SALV BN13 — 178 G11
Findon CI HOVE BN3 — 75 L2
Findon Dr MSEA/BNM PO22 — 87 J7
Findon Rd BRIE/ROTT BN2 — 77 L8
　CRAWW RH11 — 29 C1
　SALV BN13 — 70 E2
Findon Wy HORS RH12 — 125 N2
Finisterre Wy LHPTN BN17 — 89 M5
Finsbury CI CRAWW RH11 — 29 H7
Finsbury Rd BRIE/ROTT BN2 — 5 H4
Fir CI BRIE/ROTT BN2 — 78 E6
Fircroft Av LAN/SOMP BN15 — 72 C5
Fircroft CI BRI BN1 — 76 D2
Fircroft Crs ANG/EP BN16 — 90 C3
Fir Gv BOR GU35 — 106 E8
Firgrove Rd BOR GU35 — 106 E8
Firlands HORL RH6 — 15 G5
　HWH RH16 — 45 J5
Firlands Ri HAV PO9 — 56 B4
Firle CI CRAWE RH10 — 29 K1
Firle Crs LEWES BN7 — 55 L3
Firle Rd BRIE/ROTT BN2 — 5 M3
　LAN/SOMP BN15 — 72 C4
Firs Av HORN PO8 — 168 A7
Firs Av West MSEA/BNM PO22 — 87 G8
Firsdown CI SALV BN13 — 70 D3
Firsdown Rd SALV BN13 — 70 D4
First Av EMRTH PO10 — 58 E5
　HAV PO9 — 57 J3
　HORN PO8 — 150 D10
　HOVE BN3 — 76 B8
　LAN/SOMP BN15 — 72 D5
　MSEA/BNM PO22 — 87 K7
　MSEA/BNM PO22 — 105 G1
　SALV BN13 — 71 H5
　SELS PO20 — 100 A8
The Firs LIPH GU30 — 117 Q2
Firtoft CI BURH RH15 — 47 G6
Fir Tree Av HASM GU27 — 108 C11
Fir Tree CI CRAWW RH11 — 19 G8
　PUL/STOR RH20 — 160 A7
　SWTR RH13 — 127 M6
Firtree Gdns HORN PO8 — 168 D4
Fir Tree La PUL/STOR RH20 — 160 A7
Fir Tree Wy HPPT/KEY BN6 — 165 J5
　MSEA/BNM PO22 — 86 B6
Firway GSHT GU26 — 108 B4
Fishbourne Rd (East) CCH PO19 — 61 J7
Fishbourne Rd (West)
　CCH PO19 — 61 H7
Fisher CI CRAWE RH10 — 9 G8
Fisher La MFD/CHID GU8 — 111 M10
　SELS PO20 — 84 B6
The Fishermans EMRTH PO10 — 58 B5
Fisherman's Wk BOGR PO21 — 103 J4
　SELS PO20 — 181 M7
　SHOR BN43 — 73 J7
Fishers CI LHPTN BN17 — 89 M5
Fishers Ct HORS RH12 — 10 C1
Fishersgate CI PTSD BN41 — 74 F6
Fishersgate Ter PTSD BN41 — 74 F6
Fish La BOGR PO21 — 103 L3
　SELS PO20 — 180 H5
Fitch Dr BRIE/ROTT BN2 — 77 K4
Fitchet CI CRAWW RH11 — 29 G1
Fittleworth CI FERR BN12 — 91 M1
Fittleworth Dr
　MSEA/BNM PO22 — 87 J7
Fittleworth Rd BIL RH14 — 140 G3
Fitzalan Rd ARUN BN18 — 66 F4
　LHPTN BN17 — 89 K5
　SWTR RH13 — 11 L1
Fitzherbert Dr BRIE/ROTT BN2 — 77 K5
Fitzjohns Rd LEWES BN7 — 55 H5
Fitzwilliam CI BOGR PO21 — 103 L1
Fitzwygram Crs HAV PO9 — 57 G2
Five Acres CRAWE RH10 — 29 K1
　RCCH PO18 — 170 H12
Five Acres CI BOR GU35 — 107 J4
Five Heads Rd HORN PO8 — 168 B1
Five Oaks Rd SWTR RH13 — 124 H5
Fixcroft HFD BN5 * — 145 Q9
Flag Sq SHOR BN43 — 73 L7
Flag Wk HORN PO8 — 168 A5
Flamsteed Hts CRAWW RH11 * — 29 G8
Flansham La MSEA/BNM PO22 — 87 H6
Flansham Ms MSEA/BNM PO22 — 87 H7
Flansham Pk MSEA/BNM PO22 — 87 H5
Flatt Rd RCCH PO18 — 59 J5
Flaxman Av CCH PO19 — 61 J7
Flax Mean MSEA/BNM PO22 — 87 G8
Fleet CI LHPTN BN17 — 89 M3
Fleetend CI HAV PO9 — 58 F11
The Fleet PUL/STOR RH20 — 158 C2
Fleming CI BOGR PO21 — 102 F4
Fleming Wy CRAWE RH10 — 19 K7
Fletcher CI BOGR PO21 — 103 G3
　CRAWE RH10 — 9 G8
Fletcher PI SELS PO20 — 84 B4
Fletcher Rd SALV BN13 — 71 K8
Fletchers SWTR RH13 — 125 Q10
Fletchers CI SWTR RH13 — 11 G8
Fletchers Fld LIPH GU30 — 117 Q2
Fletcher's La RCCH PO18 — 82 C4
　SELS PO20 — 101 J2
Fletcher Wy ANG/EP BN16 — 68 E7
　BOGR PO21 — 2 C1
　HWH RH16 — 44 F7
Fletching CI BRIE/ROTT BN2 — 77 L7
Flexford Gdns HAV PO9 — 57 H2
Flimwell CI BRIE/ROTT BN2 — 77 K8
Flint CI ANG/EP BN16 — 90 C3
　CRAWE RH10 — 30 A6
　PTSD BN41 — 75 G3
The Flints LEWES BN7 — 55 K8
Florence Av HOVE BN3 — 75 J5
Florence CI SELS PO20 — 100 C1
Florence PI BRI BN1 — 77 G4
Florence Rd BRI BN1 — 76 F5
　CCH PO19 — 7 K4
Florentine Wy WVILLE PO7 — 168 B9
The Florets STEY/UB BN44 * — 49 G4
Florida CI FERR BN12 — 91 L5
Florida Gdns FERR BN12 * — 91 L5
Florida Rd FERR BN12 — 91 L5
Florlandia CI LAN/SOMP BN15 — 72 A8
Flower Farm CI HFD BN5 — 163 J4
Foamcourt Waye FERR BN12 — 91 K4
Folders CI BURH RH15 — 47 J8
Folders Gra BURH RH15 — 47 H8

Folders La BURH RH15 — 47 H8
Folders La East BURH RH15 — 47 K8
Follett CI CRAWE RH10 — 103 K4
Follis Gdns CCH PO19 — 61 C6
Folly La EPSF GU31 — 133 N6
　PETW GU28 — 157 K10
Fontana CI CRAWE RH10 — 30 C4
Fonthill Rd HOVE BN3 — 76 A5
Fontwell Av SELS PO20 — 64 E4
Fontwell CI ANG/EP BN16 — 90 A3
　ARUN BN18 — 64 E3
　SALV BN13 — 70 F5
Fontwell Ms WVILLE PO7 — 168 C8
Fontwell Rd CRAWE RH10 — 9 L9
　SELS PO20 — 181 N5
Forbes CI CRAWE RH10 — 30 A4
Fordingbridge CI HORS RH12 — 10 C8
Fordingbridge Site
　MSEA/BNM PO22 * — 87 F6
Ford La ARUN BN18 — 88 D1
　STEY/UB BN44 — 162 C2
Ford Rd ARUN BN18 — 88 D2
Fordwater Gdns ARUN BN18 — 88 A2
Fordwater La CCH PO19 — 61 M3
　RCCH PO18 — 61 M1
Fore Br EPSF GU31 — 133 N7
Foredown CI BRIE/ROTT BN2 — 75 G4
Foredown Dr PTSD BN41 — 75 G4
Foredown Rd PTSD BN41 — 75 G3
Forest Av HORN PO8 — 168 A6
Forest CI CRAWE RH10 — 32 A1
　HORN PO8 — 168 A6
　SWTR RH13 — 37 G5
　SWTR RH13 — 126 H3
Forest Cnr LISS GU33 — 116 D6
Forestdale GSHT GU26 — 108 C6
Forester CI CRAWE RH10 — 9 C8
Forestfield CRAWE RH10 — 33 J5
　SWTR RH13 — 11 L4
Forest Ga CRAWW RH11 — 37 K5
Forest Gra HORS RH12 * — 37 K5
Forest La BOR GU35 — 107 K3
Forest Lane CI LIPH GU30 — 117 P1
Forest Ms HORS RH12 — 37 G4
Forest Oaks SWTR RH13 — 11 M2
Forest Pk SWTR RH13 — 127 K3
Forest Ri LISS GU33 — 116 D7
Forest Rd BOR GU35 — 107 K3
　BRI BN1 — 53 K8
　FROW RH18 — 35 G8
　HORS RH12 — 37 G5
　LISS GU33 — 116 B4
　MIDH GU29 — 136 G11
　SALV BN13 — 71 J7
The Forestry Rd BIL RH14 — 122 C1
Forestside Av HAV PO9 — 168 H12
Forest Vw CRAWE RH10 — 9 L9
Forest View Rd EGRIN RH19 — 33 K3
Forest Wy EGRIN RH19 — 34 A4
Forge CI ANG/EP BN16 — 90 E3
　CCH PO19 — 83 K2
　HORS RH12 — 125 P1
　PTSD BN41 — 75 G3
Forge La CRAWE RH10 — 9 L1
　HORS RH12 — 125 N1
Forge PI HORL RH6 — 14 D8
Forge Rd BOR GU35 — 106 D1
　CRAWE RH10 — 9 L1
The Forge HORL RH6 * — 18 D2
　HORS RH12 — 115 P10
　RHWH RH17 — 128 D1
　SELS PO20 * — 181 K6
　SWTR RH13 — 125 Q12
Forge Wy BIL RH14 — 141 R1
　BURH RH15 — 46 F5
Forge Wd CRAWE RH10 — 20 C6
Forrester Av SWTR RH13 — 144 E10
Forsters Yd LHPTN BN17 * — 89 G4
Forsythia CI HAV PO9 — 57 J1
Fort Hvn SHOR BN43 — 74 F1
Fort Rd LHPTN BN17 — 89 H3
Fortunes Wy HAV PO9 — 56 D4
Forty Acre La EPSF GU31 — 151 Q2
The Forum HORS RH12 — 10 B6
Foster La PUL/STOR RH20 — 161 J9
Fosters CI ANG/EP BN16 — 90 D5
Foundry CI SWTR RH13 — 11 G2
Foundry La HASM GU27 — 109 K11
　SWTR RH13 — 11 L3
Foundry Rd ARUN BN18 — 87 L2
Foundry St BRI BN1 — 4 E5
Fountains CI BRI BN1 — 77 G3
　CRAWW RH11 — 28 F5
Fourth Av HAV PO9 — 57 J3
　HOVE BN3 — 76 A8
　LAN/SOMP BN15 — 72 D6
　MSEA/BNM PO22 — 105 H1
　SALV BN13 — 71 J6
Fowey CI SHOR BN43 — 74 A7
Fowler CI CRAWE RH10 — 30 B7
Foxbridge Dr SELS PO20 — 84 A4
Foxbridge La BIL RH14 — 122 D4
Foxbury La EMRTH PO10 — 58 D1
Fox CI BURH RH15 — 46 E8
　CCH PO19 — 7 G3
　CCH PO19 — 7 G3
　CRAWW RH11 — 29 G1
Foxcott Gv HAV PO9 — 168 G12
Fox Ct PUL/STOR RH20 — 159 Q12
Foxdale Dr ANG/EP BN16 — 90 E1
Fox Dell PUL/STOR RH20 — 159 Q12
Foxdown Rd BRIE/ROTT BN2 — 78 E6
Foxes CI ANG/EP BN16 — 90 A1
　SWTR RH13 — 143 G2
Foxes Cft MSEA/BNM PO22 — 65 H7
Foxfield Cottages SWTR RH13 — 143 G2
Foxfields PUL/STOR RH20 — 159 R5
Foxglove Av HORS RH12 — 36 C3
Foxglove CI BURH RH15 — 46 C5
Foxglove Dr BOR GU35 — 106 H7
Foxglove Wk SALV BN13 — 92 K4
Foxglove Wy LHPTN BN17 — 89 M2
Fox HI HWH RH16 — 45 H8
Fox Hill CI HWH RH16 — 45 H8
Foxhill CI HWH RH16 — 45 H6
Fox Hill Village HWH RH16 — 47 H8
Foxhole La RHWH RH17 — 146 C3
Foxholes RHWH RH12 — 114 A9
Foxhunters Rd PTSD BN41 — 163 H4
Fox Lea SALV BN13 — 178 H12
Foxleigh Cha RHWH RH12 — 11 J1
Foxley La SALV BN13 — 70 E5
Fox Rd HASM GU27 — 108 H11
　MIDH GU29 — 137 K7
Foxwarren HWH RH16 — 44 F4

Foxwarren CI SELS PO20 — 99 L6
Fox Wy PTSD BN41 — 74 F2
Foxwells RHWH RH17 — 40 F5
Foxwood AV MFD/CHID GU8 — 110 B6
Foxwood Av ANG/EP BN16 — 90 F1
Foxwood La MFD/CHID GU8 — 110 C8
Framfield CI BRI BN1 — 53 K7
　CRAWW RH11 — 28 F1
Frampton Ct FERR BN12 * — 92 B3
Frampton PI SHOR BN43 — 73 K5
The Framptons ANG/EP BN16 — 91 G4
France La SALV BN13 — 69 J3
Franciscan Wy LHPTN BN17 — 89 J4
Francis Edwards Wy
　CRAWW RH11 — 8 E1
Francis Rd HORN PO8 — 150 D10
　HWH RH16 — 45 L1
Francis St BRI BN1 — 4 F1
Frandor Rd BOGR PO21 — 85 L8
Frankland Md PUL/STOR RH20 — 178 H3
Franklands CI BURH RH15 — 47 G8
　BURH RH15 — 165 G1
　SALV BN13 — 70 E4
Franklands Gdns BURH RH15 — 165 G1
Franklands Wy BURH RH15 — 165 G1
Frankland Ter EMRTH PO10 — 58 B5
Franklin PI CCH PO19 — 6 E3
Franklin Rd BRIE/ROTT BN2 — 5 J2
　CRAWE RH10 — 30 B4
　PTSD BN41 — 75 H6
　SALV BN13 — 70 D6
　SHOR BN43 — 74 B5
Franklin St BRIE/ROTT BN2 — 5 J2
Franklynn Rd HWH RH16 — 45 J3
Frankton Av HWH RH16 — 45 K6
Frant Rd HOVE BN3 — 75 M3
Frarydene EMRTH PO10 — 58 A5
Fraser CI SELS PO20 — 181 M6
Fraser Gdns EMRTH PO10 — 58 F3
Fraser Rd HAV PO9 — 56 E3
Frederick CI BRI BN1 * — 4 D5
Frederick PI BRI BN1 — 4 D5
Frederick Rd CCH PO19 * — 61 H7
Frederick St BRI BN1 — 4 D5
Frederick Ter BRI BN1 * — 4 D5
Freehold St BRIE/ROTT BN2 — 77 G4
Freek's La BURH RH15 — 46 F3
Freeland CI CCH PO19 — 61 H7
Freeman CI ARUN BN18 — 65 G4
Freeman Rd HORS RH12 — 115 P9
Freemans CI BIL RH14 — 141 R5
Freemans Rd PTSD BN41 — 74 F5
Freeways SELS PO20 — 181 M5
Frenches PUL/STOR RH20 — 160 A11
Frenches Md BIL RH14 — 141 R5
French Gdns HWH RH16 — 45 J3
Frenchmans Rd PSF GU32 — 133 M5
French Rd LISS GU33 — 116 C2
Frendstaple Rd WVILLE PO7 — 168 B12
Frensham La BOR GU35 — 107 K3
Freshbrook CI LAN/SOMP BN15 — 72 D8
Freshbrook Rd
　LAN/SOMP BN15 — 72 E8
　LAN/SOMP BN15 — 72 D7
　PTSD BN41 — 75 H5
　SHOR BN43 — 74 A4
Freshfield Bank FROW RH18 — 34 D7
Freshfield CI CRAWE RH10 — 9 M5
Freshfield La RHWH RH17 — 131 M9
Freshfield PI BRIE/ROTT BN2 — 5 J5
Freshfields CI LAN/SOMP BN15 — 72 C7
Freshfields Dr LAN/SOMP BN15 — 72 C7
Freshfield St BRIE/ROTT BN2 — 5 K4
Freshfield Wy BRIE/ROTT BN2 — 5 J5
Freshwater Pde HORS RH12 * — 10 B6
Freshwoods RHWH RH12 — 114 A9
Freya CI MSEA/BNM PO22 — 105 L1
Friar CI BRI BN1 — 76 F1
Friar Crs BRI BN1 — 76 E2
Friar Rd BRI BN1 — 76 F1
Friars CI HPPT/KEY BN6 — 165 J4
Friars Oak Rd HPPT/KEY BN6 — 165 M4
Friars Rookery CRAWE RH10 — 9 J3
Friar Wk BRI BN1 — 76 E1
　SALV BN13 — 92 E1
Friary CI MSEA/BNM PO22 — 87 A8
Friary La CCH PO19 — 6 C5
Friary Wy CRAWE RH10 — 8 F5
Friday St HORS RH12 — 26 D4
　HORS RH12 — 115 P10
Friends CI CRAWW RH11 — 19 J8
Frimley CI BRIE/ROTT BN2 — 78 D6
Friston CI BRIE/ROTT BN2 — 77 L1
Friston Wk CRAWW RH11 — 28 F2
Frith Pk EGRIN RH19 — 23 K6
Frith Rd BOGR PO21 — 85 M8
　HOVE BN3 — 75 M5
Frobisher CI FERR BN12 — 92 C1
Frobisher Gdns EMRTH PO10 — 58 A5
Frobisher Rd BOGR PO21 — 103 H3
Frobisher Wy ANG/EP BN16 — 90 D5
　FERR BN12 — 92 C1
Frogmore La HORN PO8 — 168 B3
Froxfield Rd HAV PO9 — 169 L12
Froyle Ct HAV PO9 — 169 L12
Fry CI CRAWW RH11 — 29 G8
Fry Crs BURH RH15 — 46 D4
Fryern CI PUL/STOR RH20 — 159 R11
Fryern Rd PUL/STOR RH20 — 160 A10
Fryland La HFD BN5 — 145 N9
Fulbeck Av SALV BN13 — 70 A7
Fulflood Rd HAV PO9 — 168 F12
Fulfords HI SWTR RH13 — 125 K6
Fulham CI CRAWW RH11 — 29 G7
Fuller Rd LEWES BN7 — 55 M2
Fullers Wk LHPTN BN17 — 67 J8
Fullerton CI HAV PO9 — 169 J12
Fulmar CI CRAWW RH11 * — 28 F2
　HOVE BN3 — 76 C4
Fulmar Dr EGRIN RH19 — 23 M6
Fulmar Wy SELS PO20 — 63 K4
Furlong CI ARUN BN18 — 66 C3
The Furlongs STEY/UB BN44 — 49 L1
Furlong Wy HORL RH6 — 19 L1
Furnace Dr CRAWE RH10 — 9 K8
Furnace Farm Rd CRAWE RH10 — 9 M8
　EGRIN RH19 — 22 B6
Furnace Pde CRAWE RH10 — 9 M7
Furnace PI CRAWE RH10 — 9 M7
Furners La HFD BN5 — 163 H4
Furners Md HFD BN5 — 163 L5
Furnston Gv EMRTH PO10 — 58 F4
Furse Feld BOGR PO21 — 103 M3
Furze CI SALV BN13 — 70 C3
Furze Common Rd
　PUL/STOR RH20 — 160 C7

Furzedown LHPTN BN17 — 89 K5
Furzedown Crs HAV PO9 — 168 H12
Furzefield CRAWW RH11 — 8 B1
　SELS PO20 — 99 L4
Furzefield Cha EGRIN RH19 — 23 K3
Furzefield CI ANG/EP BN16 — 68 E6
Furzefield Rd EGRIN RH19 — 23 K3
　HORS RH12 — 37 G4
Furze Hill HOVE BN3 — 76 C7
Furze Hill Rd BOR GU35 — 107 R5
Furzeholme SALV BN13 — 70 D3
Furzeland Wy HPPT/KEY BN6 — 164 E1
Furze La EGRIN RH19 — 23 G6
Furze Meadow EPSF GU31 — 134 H9
Furzen La HORS RH12 — 114 D6
Furze Rd HORS RH12 — 114 A9
　SALV BN13 — 70 C3
Furze Vale Rd BOR GU35 — 107 Q5
Furze Vw SWTR RH13 — 124 E7
Furze Wy HORN PO8 — 168 C5
Furzley CI HAV PO9 — 168 D11
Fushia CI HAV PO9 — 57 K1

G

Gableson Av BRI BN1 — 76 A1
The Gables HORS RH12 — 10 E1
　PUL/STOR RH20 * — 160 B12
　SWTR RH13 — 143 Q1
Gabriel Rd CRAWE RH10 — 30 C1
Gage CI CRAWE RH10 — 22 B8
Gage Rdg FROW RH18 — 34 D8
Gaggle Wd SWTR RH13 — 126 H3
Gainsboro Rd BOGR PO21 — 2 C7
Gainsborough Av SALV BN13 — 71 K6
Gainsborough Dr SELS PO20 — 181 L6
Gainsborough Ldg SALV BN13 * — 12 J7
Gainsborough Rd CRAWE RH10 — 29 L7
Gaisford CI SALV BN13 — 12 E2
Gaisford Rd SALV BN13 — 12 D1
Galahad Rd CRAWW RH11 — 28 D3
Galaxie Rd HORN PO8 — 168 C5
Gales Dr CRAWE RH10 — 9 L3
　CRAWE RH10 — 9 L3
Gales PI CRAWE RH10 — 9 K3
Galliers CI BRI BN1 — 53 J2
The Gallops LEWES BN7 — 55 M4
Galsworthy CI FERR BN12 — 92 A2
Galsworthy Rd FERR BN12 — 92 A2
Gamecock Ter SELS PO20 — 63 J4
Gammon CI EPSF GU31 — 133 P4
Gander CI BURH RH15 — 46 F4
Gander Gn HWH RH16 — 45 J2
Gander HI HWH RH16 — 45 J2
Gandersgate CI HFD BN5 * — 163 J4
Gandersgate La BIL RH14 — 140 B7
Gannon Rd WTHG BN11 — 13 M4
Garbitts La EPSF GU31 — 135 J6
Garden CI ANG/EP BN16 — 68 F6
　EGRIN RH19 — 33 L2
　LAN/SOMP BN15 — 72 D6
　PTSD BN41 — 75 H5
　PUL/STOR RH20 — 160 A11
　SHOR BN43 — 74 A4
Garden Ct BOGR PO21 — 103 K3
Garden Crs MSEA/BNM PO22 — 65 H8
Gardeners CI HORS RH12 — 115 P9
Gardeners Gn HORS RH12 — 27 H3
Gardener St PTSD BN41 — 74 F5
Garden House La EGRIN RH19 — 33 L2
The Gardens HAV PO9 — 57 J5
　PTSD BN41 — 75 H5
　PUL/STOR RH20 — 158 B2
　RCCH PO18 — 60 A2
　STHW BN42 — 74 E6
Garden Wk CRAWW RH11 — 8 C4
　HORS RH12 — 10 D1
Garden Wood CI
　PUL/STOR RH20 — 160 A7
Garden Wood Rd EGRIN RH19 — 23 J2
Gardner La CRAWW RH11 — 31 N1
Gardner Rd PTSD BN41 — 74 F5
Gardner St BRI BN1 — 4 E6
Garland Av EMRTH PO10 — 58 A4
Garland CI CCH PO19 — 7 G7
Garland Rd EGRIN RH19 — 23 J8
Garland Rd EGRIN RH19 — 23 J8
Garland Sq SELS PO20 — 63 J4
Garnet Rd BOR GU35 — 106 H7
Garratt CI CRAWE RH10 — 30 B5
Garrick Rd SALV BN13 — 13 H1
Garrick Wk CRAWE RH10 — 9 C9
The Garrones CRAWE RH10 * — 30 D2
Garsons Rd EMRTH PO10 — 58 E5
Garton CI CRAWW RH11 — 28 D4
Gaskyns CI HORS RH12 — 114 A10
Gasson Wood Rd CRAWW RH11 — 28 D5
Gaston PY RCCH PO18 — 172 B10
Gatcombe CI SALV BN13 — 70 A4
Gateford Dr HORS RH12 — 36 E3
Gatehouse La BURH RH15 — 46 B5
　EPSF GU31 — 135 N3
Gates CI CRAWE RH10 — 30 B7
Gatesmead HWH RH16 — 45 H1
Gatewycke Ter STEY/UB BN44 * — 48 D7
The Gattons BURH RH15 — 46 D6
Gatwick Rd CRAWE RH10 — 20 A6
　HORL RH6 — 19 M5
Gatwick Wy HORL RH6 — 19 L1
Gaugemaster Wy ARUN BN18 — 66 D3
Gaulter CI HAV PO9 — 57 H2
Gay St PUL/STOR RH20 — 141 R12
Gay Street La PUL/STOR RH20 — 141 P10
Geddes Wy EPSF GU31 — 133 R5
Gemini CI CRAWW RH11 — 28 C5
George Denyer CI HASM GU27 — 109 M10
George Iv Wk MSEA/BNM PO22 — 3 L2
George St BRIE/ROTT BN2 — 5 K8
　CCH PO19 * — 6 E2
　HOVE BN3 — 75 H6
　PTSD BN41 — 75 H6
George V Av LAN/SOMP BN15 — 73 G8
　WTHG BN11 — 12 D1
Georgia Av SALV BN13 — 13 G1
Georgian CI CRAWE RH10 — 30 C4
Georgian Gdns ANG/EP BN16 — 90 D3
Gerald CI BURH RH15 — 47 J6
Gerald Rd WTHG BN11 — 92 F4

Gerard St BRI BN1 — 4 E1
Ghyll Ct SWTR RH13 * — 125 Q12
Ghyll Crs SWTR RH13 — 11 K3
Ghyllside BRIE/ROTT BN2 — 77 K4
Gibbons CI CRAWE RH10 * — 30 B6
Gibbs' La EPSF GU35 — 106 D3
Giblets La HWH RH16 — 36 E2
Giblets Wy HORS RH12 — 36 E3
Gibson Rd SELS PO20 — 63 H3
Gibson Wy BOGR PO21 — 2 E5
Giffards CI EGRIN RH19 — 23 L8
Gifford Rd RCCH PO18 — 60 B6
Gilbert Rd CCH PO19 — 6 A1
The Gilberts ANG/EP BN16 — 90 A6
Giles CI ARUN BN18 — 87 L3
Gilham La FROW RH18 — 34 D7
Gillet CI SWTR RH13 * — 37 G5
Gillett Ct SWTR RH13 — 37 G5
Gillham's La HASM GU27 — 118 C5
Gilligans BURH RH15 — 46 E4
Gillway SELS PO20 — 181 N5
Gilmore Rd CCH PO19 — 7 K4
Gilpin CI CCH PO19 — 7 K4
Gilwynes BOGR PO21 — 103 L3
Ginhams Rd CRAWW RH11 — 28 C2
The Glades EGRIN RH19 — 24 A8
The Glade BOGR PO21 — 102 F5
　CRAWE RH10 — 9 L7
　SWTR RH13 — 11 L3
　WVILLE PO7 — 168 B9
Gladonian Rd LHPTN BN17 * — 89 J2
Gladstone PI BRIE/ROTT BN2 — 77 H5
Gladstone Rd ARUN BN18 — 87 L3
　BURH RH15 — 47 H4
　HORS RH12 — 10 F7
　PTSD BN41 — 75 G6
Gladstone Ter BRIE/ROTT BN2 * — 5 J2
　LHPTN BN17 — 89 J2
Gladys Av HORN PO8 — 168 B3
Gladys Rd HOVE BN3 — 75 J5
Glamis CI WVILLE PO7 — 168 B3
Glamis Ct BOGR PO21 — 2 F6
Glamis St BOGR PO21 — 2 F6
Glamorgan Rd HORN PO8 — 150 C11
Glaseby La PUL/STOR RH20 — 178 G5
Glasshouse La BIL RH14 — 140 B4
Glastonbury Rd HOVE BN3 — 75 J7
Glatting La PUL/STOR RH20 — 157 K12
Glayshers HI BOR GU35 — 107 P3
Glaziers La MIDH GU29 — 137 K7
Gleave CI EGRIN RH19 — 23 M7
Glebe CI CRAWE RH10 — 8 F1
　LAN/SOMP BN15 — 72 D6
　LEWES BN7 — 55 M5
　SELS PO20 — 64 A4
　STHW BN42 — 74 E6
Glebe Field Rd SELS PO20 — 81 M8
Glebelands BIL RH14 — 122 C4
　CRAWE RH10 — 31 N1
　PUL/STOR RH20 — 159 L2
Glebelands Meadow
　CRAN GU6 * — 112 G8
Glebe Park Av HAV PO9 — 56 B4
Glebe Rd BOR GU35 — 107 M4
　EPSF GU31 — 133 L12
　HASM GU27 — 119 L8
　RHWH RH17 — 44 C3
　SALV BN13 — 70 F8
Glebeside Av SALV BN13 — 70 F8
Glebeside CI SALV BN13 — 70 F8
The Glebe CRAWE RH10 — 21 G6
　EGRIN RH19 — 33 L3
　HORL RH6 — 14 E6
　HPPT/KEY BN6 * — 164 H1
　HWH RH16 — 45 K1
　SELS PO20 — 63 H4
Glebe Twitten RHWH RH17 * — 44 C3
Glebe Vw RHWH RH17 — 40 F8
Glebe Vls BN3 — 75 J6
Glebe Wy BIL RH14 — 141 K1
　LAN/SOMP BN15 — 72 D6
Glenbarrie Wy FERR BN12 — 91 K2
Glencathara Rd BOGR PO21 — 2 A7
Glen CI GSHT GU26 — 108 F3
Glen Crs SELS PO20 — 181 L6
Glen DI HAV PO9 — 169 L8
Glendale CI HORS RH12 — 36 F3
Glendale Rd BURH RH15 — 47 G5
　HOVE BN3 — 76 C6
Glendor Rd HOVE BN3 — 75 J5
Glendyne CI EGRIN RH19 — 33 M1
Glendyne Wy EGRIN RH19 — 33 M1
Gleneagles Ct CRAWE RH10 * — 8 F6
Gleneagles Dr HORN PO8 — 168 C2
Glenelg CI BOGR PO21 — 85 L7
Glenfalls Av BRI BN1 — 52 F6
Glenfergus HWH RH16 — 45 H3
Glen Gdns FERR BN12 — 91 L3
Glenlea GSHT GU26 — 108 H8
Glenlea Hollow GSHT GU26 — 108 H9
Glenleigh Pk HAV PO9 — 57 J3
Glen Ri BRI BN1 — 52 A8
Glen Rise CI BRI BN1 — 52 A8
Glen Rd GSHT GU26 — 108 F3
The Glen SALV BN13 — 70 F6
　SWTR RH13 — 125 R11
Glenview CI CRAWE RH10 — 29 L1
Glenville Gdns GSHT GU26 — 109 J3
Glenville Rd ANG/EP BN16 — 90 B5
Glen Vue EGRIN RH19 — 23 K8
Glenway MSEA/BNM PO22 — 2 F4
Glenwood Av MSEA/BNM PO22 — 2 F4
Glenwood Gdns HORN PO8 — 168 A7
Glenwood Rd EMRTH PO10 — 58 A4
Gleton Av HOVE BN3 — 75 J3
Globe PI LHPTN BN17 — 89 J2
Gloster Dr BOGR PO21 — 103 G3
Gloucester La PSF GU32 — 133 L6
Gloucester La LHPTN BN17 — 89 J4
Gloucester Ms BRI BN1 — 4 F5
Gloucester Pas BRI BN1 — 4 F5
Gloucester PI BRI BN1 — 4 F5
　LHPTN BN17 — 89 G7
Gloucester Rd BOGR PO21 — 3 G7
　BRI BN1 — 4 F5
　BURH RH15 — 46 E6
　CRAWE RH10 — 29 K7
　LHPTN BN17 — 89 G7
　WVILLE PO7 — 168 A11
Gloucester St BRI BN1 — 4 F5
Gloucester Wy CCH PO19 — 61 L4
Glover's Rd HORL RH6 — 18 C2
Glynde Av FERR BN12 — 91 L3
Glynde CI SWTR RH13 — 91 L3
Glynde Crs MSEA/BNM PO22 — 3 L2

Glynde Pl HORS RH12 * 10 C6
Glynde Rd BRIE/ROTT BN2 5 L4
Glynn House SELS PO20 181 K6
Goda Rd LHPTN BN17 89 K4
Goddard Cl CRAWE RH10 30 A6
Godman Cl BOGR PO21 103 J3
Godolphin Ct CRAWE RH10 * 8 F6
Godstalls La STEY/UB BN44 48 B2
Godwin Cl EMRTH PO10 57 M2
Godwin Crs HORN PO8 150 D9
Godwin Rd HOVE BN3 75 J5
Godwin Wy RCCH PO18 60 F5
SWTR RH13 11 K2
Goffs Cl CRAWW RH11 8 C6
Goffs La CRAWW RH11 8 B4
Goffs Park Rd CRAWW RH11 8 C6
Goldcrest Av LHPTN BN17 89 H1
Goldcrest Cl HORL RH6 14 C5
HORN PO8 168 B2
Golden Acre ANG/EP BN16 91 G5
BOGR PO21 102 F5
Golden Av ANG/EP BN16 91 G4
Golden Avenue Cl
ANG/EP BN16 91 G5
Goldenfield Cl LIPH GU30 118 A2
Golden Flds LIPH GU30 118 A2
Golden Hl BURH RH15 47 J6
Golden La HOVE BN3 * 76 C8
STEY/UB BN44 162 C3
Goldfinch Cl CRAWW RH11 29 J1
HORS RH12 36 B2
Golding Cl CRAWE RH10 30 B4
Golding La SWTR RH13 127 J2
Goldsmid Rd BRI BN1 4 B3
Goldsmith Rd SALV BN13 13 J1
Goldstone Cl HOVE BN3 76 A2
Goldstone Crs HOVE BN3 75 M3
Goldstone La HOVE BN3 76 A5
Goldstone Rd HOVE BN3 76 A6
Goldstone St HOVE BN3 76 A6
Goldstone Vls HOVE BN3 76 A6
Goldstone Wy HOVE BN3 75 M3
Golf Club La PUL/STOR RH20 159 N7
Golf Dr BRI BN1 77 G2
Golf La BOR GU35 106 E8
Golf Links Av GSHT GU26 108 E3
Golf Links La SELS PO20 181 L4
Golf Links Rd MSEA/BNM PO22 86 F7
Goodacres MSEA/BNM PO22 65 H8
Goodhew Cl ARUN BN18 87 M2
Goodwin Cl CRAWW RH11 28 D6
Goodwins Cl EGRIN RH19 23 J6
Goodwood Av MSEA/BNM PO22 3 L2
Goodwood Cl ANG/EP BN16 90 D3
CRAWE RH10 9 L9
HORN PO8 168 C8
MIDH GU29 136 H12
Goodwood Ct EMRTH PO10 58 F5
Goodwood Gdns SELS PO20 84 D4
Goodwood Pl BOGR PO21 * 2 D8
Goodwood Rd SALV BN13 70 F6
Goodwood Wy BRIE/ROTT BN2 77 K2
Goose Green Cl HORS RH12 36 C4
Goosegreen La
PUL/STOR RH20 160 F2
Gordon Av BOGR PO21 2 E4
CCH PO19 83 K2
MSEA/BNM PO22 2 E3
SHOR BN43 73 M6
Gordon Av West
MSEA/BNM PO22 2 E3
Gordon Cl HWH RH16 45 H3
Gordon Rd BRI BN1 76 E3
BURH RH15 47 H5
EMRTH PO10 58 C6
HORS RH12 10 E1
HWH RH16 45 J3
LAN/SOMP BN15 72 C7
PTSD BN41 75 H6
SHOR BN43 73 L6
WTHG BN11 13 H4
Goreside La RHWH RH17 44 C1
Gorham Av BRIE/ROTT BN2 97 M3
Gorham Cl BRIE/ROTT BN2 97 M3
Goring Av HORN PO8 150 E9
Goring Cha FERR BN12 91 M1
Goring Rd FERR BN12 92 C3
STEY/UB BN44 48 C3
WTHG BN11 92 E3
Goring's Md SWTR RH13 10 E8
Goring St FERR BN12 91 M1
Goring Wy FERR BN12 91 M3
SWTR RH13 144 F9
Gorley Ct HAV PO9 168 E11
Gorling Cl CRAWW RH11 28 D4
Gorringe Cl SHOR BN43 74 C6
Gorringes Brook HORS RH12 36 C3
Gorse Av ANG/EP BN16 91 J6
MSEA/BNM PO22 87 J7
SALV BN13 71 G7
Gorse Bank Cl PUL/STOR RH20 160 F10
Gorse Cl CRAWE RH10 21 G7
CRAWW RH11 39 G1
PTSD BN41 74 E1
Gorsedown Cl BOR GU35 106 E8
Gorse End HORS RH12 36 C4
Gorselands BIL RH14 142 B1
Gorselands Cl BOR GU35 107 R5
Gorse La SALV BN13 70 D3
Gorse Rd EPSF GU31 133 R6
Gorse Vw ANG/EP BN16 * 91 H5
Gosden Cl CRAWE RH10 9 M5
Gosden Rd LHPTN BN17 89 L3
Gospond Rd MSEA/BNM PO22 64 F8
Gossamer La BOGR PO21 103 J2
Gossops Dr CRAWW RH11 28 F4
Gossops Green La
CRAWW RH11 28 F4
Gostrode La MFD/CHID GU8 110 F11
Goudhurst Cl CRAWE RH10 30 D3
Goverlands Cl BURH RH15 46 E8
Gower Rd HORL RH6 14 D6
HWH RH16 45 H5
Gowers Cl RHWH RH17 130 E1
Gows Cft LEWES BN7 55 K8
Gowscroft LEWES BN7 * 55 K8
Grace Rd CRAWW RH11 28 F8
Gradwell End RING/NEW BN8 167 M2
Graffham Cl BRIE/ROTT BN2 77 K7
CCH PO19 61 M2
CRAWW RH11 29 G1
Grafton Av MSEA/BNM PO22 87 H7
Grafton Cl ANG/EP BN16 90 B3
BOR GU35 106 H7
Grafton Dr LAN/SOMP BN15 72 B7
Grafton Gdns LAN/SOMP BN15 72 B7
Grafton Pl WTHG BN11 13 G6
Grafton Rd SELS PO20 181 L8
WTHG BN11 13 G6
Grafton St BRIE/ROTT BN2 5 H8
Graham Av BRI BN1 76 D1
PTSD BN41 74 E1
Graham Crs PTSD BN41 74 E1
Graham Rd ARUN BN18 87 L4
WTHG BN11 12 F6
Grailands Cl HASM GU27 119 M7
Granada Cl HORN PO8 168 B6
Granary Cl HORL RH6 14 F4
Granary La SELS PO20 181 K5
Granary Wy HORS RH12 125 Q4
LHPTN BN17 89 J1
Grand Av HOVE BN3 76 B7
HPPT/KEY BN6 165 N5
LAN/SOMP BN15 72 D6
LHPTN BN17 89 H2
WTHG BN11 12 A4
Grand Crs BRIE/ROTT BN2 97 M4
Grand Junction Rd BRI BN1 4 E8
Grand Pde BRIE/ROTT BN2 4 F5
CRAWE RH10 * 8 E4
Grand Parade Ms
BRIE/ROTT BN2 4 F6
Grange Cl BRI BN1 76 D4
BURH RH15 47 H4
CRAWE RH10 29 M1
FERR BN12 91 K4
HAV PO9 57 J3
Grange Ct BOGR PO21 103 K4
FERR BN12 * 91 K3
Grange Crs CRAWE RH10 32 A2
Grange End HORL RH6 15 M6
Grange Field Wy BOGR PO21 103 J4
Grange La SELS PO20 181 N3
Grange Park Rd FERR BN12 91 K4
Grange Rd CRAWE RH10 31 M2
HOVE BN3 75 K6
MIDH GU29 137 J10
PSF GU32 133 M7
STHW BN42 74 D6
Grangeway HORL RH6 15 M6
Grange Wy SWTR RH13 125 Q11
Grangeways BRI BN1 52 D8
The Grangeway ANG/EP BN16 90 B4
Grangewood Dr BOGR PO21 103 J3
Granston Wy CRAWE RH10 32 B1
Grant Cl SELS PO20 181 K6
Grantham Cl RING/NEW BN8 167 P2
Grantham Rd BRI BN1 76 F4
Grantsmead LAN/SOMP BN15 72 D6
Grant St BRIE/ROTT BN2 5 H3
Granville Cl HAV PO9 57 J5
Granville Rd HOVE BN3 4 A3
LHPTN BN17 89 K5
The Graperies BRIE/ROTT BN2 5 J7
Grasmere Av LAN/SOMP BN15 72 A7
Grasmere Cl BOR GU35 106 G4
Grasmere Gdns HORS RH12 37 G3
Grasslands HORL RH6 15 M6
Grassmere HORL RH6 15 G5
Grassmere Cl LHPTN BN17 89 M2
MSEA/BNM PO22 3 K4
Grassmere Wy WVILLE PO7 168 C8
Grateley Crs HAV PO9 56 D1
Gratten La HFD BN5 145 Q10
RHWH RH17 146 B10
Grattons Dr CRAWE RH10 20 B8
The Grattons SWTR RH13 124 H2
Gratwicke Cl BIL RH14 142 A1
Gratwicke Rd WTHG BN11 12 F7
Gravel La CCH PO19 7 J7
Gravelly Crs LAN/SOMP BN15 72 E7
Gravelye Cl HWH RH16 45 L4
Gravelye La HWH RH16 45 L4
Graveney Rd CRAWE RH10 30 B4
Gravett Ct BURH RH15 46 E7
Gravetye Cl CRAWE RH10 9 M8
Gravits La BOGR PO21 85 M8
Graydon Av CCH PO19 6 B9
Graylingwell Dr CCH PO19 61 M4
Grays Cl HASM GU27 109 P9
Grayshott Laurels BOR GU35 107 K3
Grayshott Rd BOR GU35 107 R4
Grays Wd HORL RH6 15 H6
Grayswood Av SELS PO20 100 A7
Grayswood Ms HASM GU27 * 109 Q7
Grayswood Rd HASM GU27 109 N9
Great College St BRIE/ROTT BN2 5 K8
Great Copse Dr HAV PO9 168 G12
Greatfield Wy HAV PO9 169 J7
Greatham Br PUL/STOR RH20 158 F8
Greatham Rd CRAWE RH10 30 B6
SALV BN13 70 E4
Great Hanger EPSF GU31 133 Q6
Great House Ct EGRIN RH19 * 33 L1
Greatlake Ct HORL RH6 15 G5
Great Lime Kilns SWTR RH13 125 R12
Greatpin Cft PUL/STOR RH20 158 B2
Great Rough RING/NEW BN8 149 R7
Grebe Cl EMRTH PO10 58 C1
Grebe Crs SWTR RH13 11 M9
Greenacre Cl
PUL/STOR RH20 * 159 Q12
Greenacres BOR GU35 107 J5
BRI BN1 * 76 E4
CRAWE RH10 9 M6
HORS RH12 10 D1
PUL/STOR RH20 161 K7
SHOR BN43 73 K5
STEY/UB BN44 48 C3
Greenacres Ring ANG/EP BN16 68 F7
Greenbank MSEA/BNM PO22 65 H8
Green Bushes Cl ANG/EP BN16 90 A5
Green Cl STHW BN42 74 D6
SWTR RH13 125 Q11
Green Ct STHW BN42 * 74 D6
Greencourt Dr BOGR PO21 85 M8
Greenfield PUL/STOR RH20 157 L11
Greenfield Cl BRI BN1 52 F8
LIPH GU30 107 R12
Green Field Cl STHW BN42 74 D5
Greenfield Crs BRI BN1 52 E8
HORN PO8 168 D5
Greenfield Ri HORN PO8 168 C6
Greenfield Rd CCH PO19 7 J2
SWTR RH13 124 G2
Greenfields EPSF GU31 134 H10
LHPTN BN17 89 G2
LISS GU33 116 D9
MSEA/BNM PO22 87 K8
Greenfields Cl EPSF GU31 134 H9
HORL RH6 14 D4
HORS RH12 36 F3
Greenfields Rd HORL RH6 14 D4
HORS RH12 36 F4
Greenfields Wy HORS RH12 36 F3
Greenfield Wy
PUL/STOR RH20 160 B11
Greenfinch Wy HORS RH12 36 C2
Greengates PETW GU28 120 C11
Greenhanger RFNM GU10 108 C1
Green Hedges Av EGRIN RH19 23 J7
Green Hedges Cl EGRIN RH19 23 J7
Greenhill Pk RHWH RH17 45 K7
Greenhill Wy RHWH RH17 45 K7
Greenhurst La PUL/STOR RH20 160 B8
Greening Wd GSHT GU26 * 109 J4
Greenland Cl SALV BN13 70 D6
Greenland Rd SALV BN13 70 D7
Greenlands Cl BURH RH15 165 Q1
Greenlands Dr BURH RH15 165 Q1
Green La BRIE/ROTT BN2 78 D7
CCH PO19 7 H3
CRAN GU6 112 G5
CRAWE RH10 21 L5
CRAWE RH10 29 K1
CRAWE RH10 30 C3
HASM GU27 119 L2
HORL RH6 20 E3
HORN PO8 150 E8
HORS RH12 26 D5
RCCH PO18 59 M5
RCCH PO18 60 B8
RDKG RH5 17 J1
RFNM GU10 108 C1
RING/NEW BN8 149 P12
SELS PO20 83 K7
SELS PO20 84 E1
SELS PO20 101 H4
SELS PO20 181 K7
SWTR RH13 144 A4
Green Lane Cl ARUN BN18 66 E3
Greenlea Av BOGR PO21 103 G3
Greenleas HOVE BN3 75 J3
Green Mdw HWH RH16 45 L1
Greenoaks LAN/SOMP BN15 72 C5
Green Pk FERR BN12 91 L2
Green Park Cnr RHWH RH17 47 M5
RHWH RH17 148 E9
Green Pond Cnr HAV PO9 * 57 J4
Green Rdg BRI BN1 52 A8
Green Rd RHWH RH17 47 M4
Greensand Wy GSHT GU26 109 K7
HASM GU27 109 M10
Greens La SWTR RH13 127 J2
Greenstede Av EGRIN RH19 23 L6
Green St ALTN GU34 106 A1
The Green BOGR PO21 102 F5
BRIE/ROTT BN2 97 L3
CCH PO19 7 J2
CRAWE RH10 21 G6
CRAWW RH11 8 C2
HOVE BN3 76 B3
LISS GU33 116 B8
MFD/CHID GU8 110 H6
PUL/STOR RH20 * 159 K1
PUL/STOR RH20 160 C11
SWTR RH13 161 P2
Greentree La SWTR RH13 144 H8
Greentrees LAN/SOMP BN15 * 72 B7
Greentrees Cl LAN/SOMP BN15 72 B7
Greentrees Crs
LAN/SOMP BN15 72 B7
Green Wk CRAWE RH10 29 K1
Greenway HORS RH12 10 A3
Green Wy MSEA/BNM PO22 87 L8
Greenway La EPSF GU31 133 K11
Greenways BOGR PO21 103 G4
BRIE/ROTT BN2 97 J2
HWH RH16 45 J3
PTSD BN41 * 75 G4
STHW BN42 74 E4
Greenways Cnr
BRIE/ROTT BN2 * 97 J1
Greenways Crs FERR BN12 91 L4
SHOR BN43 74 A4
The Green Wy FERR BN12 92 A1
Greenwich Cl CRAWW RH11 29 H7
Greenwood Av MSEA/BNM PO22 2 B1
Greenwood Cl MSEA/BNM PO22 2 B1
Greenwood Ct CRAWW RH11 * 29 G8
Greenwood Dr ANG/EP BN16 90 E2
Greet Rd LAN/SOMP BN15 72 C6
Gregory Cl CRAWE RH10 30 B7
Gregsons HORS RH12 115 P9
Grendon Cl HORL RH6 14 E4
Grenehurst Wy EPSF GU31 133 N6
Grenville Av FERR BN12 92 C2
Grenville Cl FERR BN12 92 B2
LIPH GU30 117 R1
Grenville Gdns CCH PO19 6 C9
Gresham Pl HFD BN5 163 J3
Gresham Wk CRAWE RH10 29 K6
Grevatt's La ARUN BN18 87 M6
Grevatt's La West ARUN BN18 87 L5
Greville Gn EMRTH PO10 57 M2
Grey Alders HWH RH16 45 L3
Greyfiars HOVE BN3 76 C5
Greyfriars Cl BOGR PO21 103 L2
SALV BN13 70 F7
Greyfriars La PUL/STOR RH20 177 R1
Greyhound Slip CRAWE RH10 30 C2
Greynville Cl BOGR PO21 103 H3
Greystoke Ms FERR BN12 91 K3
Greystoke Rd FERR BN12 91 K3
Greystone Av BOGR PO21 85 L6
SALV BN13 70 E8
Greywell Rd HAV PO9 168 F12
Gribble La SELS PO20 63 H6
Grier Cl CRAWW RH11 28 D4
Griffin Crs LHPTN BN17 89 J1
Griffith's Av LAN/SOMP BN15 72 C5
Griggs Meadow
MFD/CHID GU8 112 A2
Grinder's La SWTR RH13 161 P3
Grinstead Av LAN/SOMP BN15 72 D7
Grinstead La EGRIN RH19 43 H1
LAN/SOMP BN15 72 D7
Grinstead Mt BRIE/ROTT BN2 * 77 L8
Grisedale Cl CRAWW RH11 8 C8
Groombridge Wy HORS RH12 125 Q4
Grooms Cl ANG/EP BN16 68 F8
Groomsland Dr BIL RH14 141 R3
The Grooms CRAWE RH10 30 C1
Grosvenor Cl HORL RH6 14 F8
Grosvenor Gdns BOGR PO21 103 H2
Grosvenor Rd CCH PO19 83 L2
EGRIN RH19 23 J8
WTHG BN11 13 G5
Grosvenor St BRIE/ROTT BN2 5 H7
Grosvenor Wy BOGR PO21 103 H2
Grouse Rd SWTR RH13 38 B6
SWTR RH13 127 M1
Grove Bank BRIE/ROTT BN2 * 5 G5
Grove Crs LHPTN BN17 89 K3
Grove Hl BRIE/ROTT BN2 5 G5
Grovelands Cottages
BURH RH15 * 46 E8
The Grovelands
LAN/SOMP BN15 94 D1
Grove La PETW GU28 139 M11
PUL/STOR RH20 160 A7
Grove Pk CCH PO19 61 J7
Grover Av LAN/SOMP BN15 72 C6
Grove Rd BURH RH15 47 G7
CCH PO19 7 G6
GSHT GU26 108 F3
HAV PO9 57 G4
HORL RH6 14 D5
SALV BN13 71 H7
SELS PO20 181 K7
Grove St BRIE/ROTT BN2 5 H4
PETW GU28 139 L10
The Grove CRAWW RH11 8 C3
EMRTH PO10 58 C2
FERR BN12 91 K3
HORL RH6 15 G7
HWH RH16 45 L6
LIPH GU30 117 Q1
MSEA/BNM PO22 3 M4
Guernsey Cl CRAWW RH11 28 F7
Guernsey Farm La
MSEA/BNM PO22 87 H8
Guernsey Rd FERR BN12 91 L5
Guilden Rd CCH PO19 7 H4
Guildford Cl EMRTH PO10 58 E4
SALV BN13 12 B3
Guildford Pl CCH PO19 61 L4
Guildford Rd ANG/EP BN16 90 D3
BIL RH14 112 G12
BRI BN1 4 D4
HORS RH12 113 N9
HORS RH12 125 R3
SALV BN13 12 B3
SWTR RH13 114 E10
Guildford St BRI BN1 4 D4
Guildhall St CCH PO19 6 E3
Guillards Oak MIDH GU29 136 H10
Guinevere Rd CRAWW RH11 28 D3
Gunning Cl CRAWW RH11 28 F6
Gunns Farm LIPH GU30 117 R3
Gunwin Ct BOGR PO21 103 J3
Gwatkin Cl HAV PO9 56 D2
Gwynne Gdns EGRIN RH19 23 H7
Gypsy La HORN PO8 168 A4

H

Habin Hl EPSF GU31 135 J5
Hackenden Cl EGRIN RH19 23 K6
Hackenden Cottages
EGRIN RH19 * 23 K6
Hackenden La EGRIN RH19 23 L5
Hacketts La HFD BN5 * 163 K4
Haddington Cl HOVE BN3 76 A7
Haddington St HOVE BN3 76 A6
Hadlands BOGR PO21 102 F4
Hadley Av SALV BN13 71 J6
Hadley Cl MSEA/BNM PO22 87 K7
Hadlow Cl BRIE/ROTT BN2 5 L5
Hadlow Wy LAN/SOMP BN15 72 E7
Hadmans Cl HORS RH12 10 C7
Hadrian Av STHW BN42 74 E5
Haglands Copse
PUL/STOR RH20 160 A6
Haglands La PUL/STOR RH20 160 A6
Haig Av BRI BN1 53 J7
Haigh Cl LAN/SOMP BN15 73 G8
Hailsham Cl ANG/EP BN16 91 G2
Hailsham Rd WTHG BN11 92 E4
Hale Cl SELS PO20 100 A7
Hales Fld HASM GU27 109 M11
Halewick Cl LAN/SOMP BN15 72 B5
Halewick La LAN/SOMP BN15 72 B5
Haleybridge Wk SELS PO20 63 J4
Half Moon Hl HASM GU27 109 M11
Half Moon La SALV BN13 70 E6
Half Moon Pde SALV BN13 * 70 E6
Halfrey Cl RCCH PO18 60 F6
Halfrey Rd RCCH PO18 60 F6
Halifax Cl CRAWE RH10 20 D8
Halifax Dr SALV BN13 70 B7
Halifax Ri WVILLE PO7 168 A10
Halland Cl CRAWE RH10 9 L1
Halland Rd BRIE/ROTT BN2 77 L1
Hall Av SALV BN13 70 F6
Hall Cl SALV BN13 70 F6
Hallett Rd BRIE/ROTT BN2 5 L3
HAV PO9 57 J3
Halley Cl CRAWW RH11 29 G8
Halliford Dr MSEA/BNM PO22 65 H8
Halliwick Gdns
MSEA/BNM PO22 105 G1
Halls Dr HORS RH12 27 L8
Hallsland CRAWE RH10 32 B1
Hallyburton Rd HOVE BN3 75 J5
Halnaker Barn La RCCH PO18 63 M1
Halnaker Gdns BOGR PO21 103 H3
Halnaker Wk CRAWW RH11 * 28 E6
Halsbury Cl WTHG BN11 13 K3
Halsbury Rd WTHG BN11 13 L3
Halsford La EGRIN RH19 23 G7
Halsford Park Rd EGRIN RH19 23 H7
Halson Cl BOGR PO21 2 C4
Halters End GSHT GU26 108 D6
Halton Shaws HPPT/KEY BN6 165 J4
Hambledon Pl BOGR PO21 2 B7
Hambledon Rd HORN PO8 150 B8
Hamble Gdns SALV BN13 70 B6
Hamble Rd LAN/SOMP BN15 72 A7
Hambleton Hl CRAWW RH11 8 D8
Hamble Wy SALV BN13 70 B6
Hambrook BURH RH15 47 H8
Hambrook Hl (North)
RCCH PO18 59 J2
Hambrook Hl (South)
RCCH PO18 59 J3
Ham Cl WTHG BN11 93 M1
Hamilton Cl ANG/EP BN16 90 A1
BOR GU35 107 J5
HAV PO9 57 G5
PTSD BN41 74 F2
SALV BN13 71 K8
Hamilton Ct FERR BN12 92 C2
Hamilton Dr ANG/EP BN16 90 A1
Hamilton Gdns BOGR PO21 103 J3
RCCH PO18 60 B6
Hamilton Ms LAN/SOMP BN15 * 72 B6
Hamilton Rd BRI BN1 4 C1
HORS RH12 10 B3
LAN/SOMP BN15 72 C6
LISS GU33 116 G3
Ham La EMRTH PO10 58 E6
HORN PO8 168 A1
RHWH RH17 148 H2
SELS PO20 63 J6
Ham Manor Cl ANG/EP BN16 90 C1
Ham Manor Wy ANG/EP BN16 90 D1
Hammer Hl HASM GU27 118 F1
RHWH RH17 128 H6
Hammer La GSHT GU26 108 B2
GSHT GU26 108 F9
HASM GU27 108 D11
MIDH GU29 136 A5
Hammerpond Rd SWTR RH13 11 L9
SWTR RH13 126 H1
SWTR RH13 127 N3
Hammerwood Copse
HASM GU27 108 G12
Hammerwood Rd EGRIN RH19 34 D3
Hammer Yd CRAWE RH10 * 8 E5
Hammingden La EGRIN RH19 42 D6
RHWH RH17 130 H2
Hammond Dr SALV BN13 70 C5
Hammond Pl
PUL/STOR RH20 * 160 A12
Hammond Rd CRAWW RH11 39 G1
Hammonds Gdns BURH RH15 46 E8
Hammonds Rdg BURH RH15 46 D8
Hammy Cl SHOR BN43 74 A5
Hammy La SHOR BN43 74 A5
Hammy Wy SHOR BN43 74 A5
Hampden Cl CRAWE RH10 20 D8
MSEA/BNM PO22 87 L8
Hampden Rd BRIE/ROTT BN2 5 J3
Hampers Gn PETW GU28 139 L7
Hampers La PUL/STOR RH20 178 E1
SWTR RH13 11 M5
SWTR RH13 37 H7
Hampshire Av BOGR PO21 2 A3
Hampshire Ct BRIE/ROTT BN2 * 5 H8
Hampshire Rd BOR GU35 106 G5
Hampstead Rd BRI BN1 76 C4
Hampstead Wk CRAWW RH11 * 29 H7
Hampton Cl WVILLE PO7 168 B10
Hampton Ct BOGR PO21 103 L1
Hampton Flds LHPTN BN17 89 J3
Hampton Pl BRI BN1 4 B6
Hampton St BRI BN1 4 B6
Hampton Ter BRI BN1 4 B5
Hampton Wy EGRIN RH19 33 L2
Ham Rd SELS PO20 101 H8
SHOR BN43 73 L6
WTHG BN11 93 M2
Hamsey Cl BRIE/ROTT BN2 77 L8
Hamsey Crs LEWES BN7 55 M3
Hamsey La RING/NEW BN8 167 R10
Hamsey Rd EGRIN RH19 42 F3
Hamshire Hl RHWH RH17 128 A5
Hamsland RHWH RH17 131 M5
Hamstead Meadow RCCH PO18 59 K6
Ham Wy WTHG BN11 93 M1
Hanbury La HWH RH16 45 K4
Hanbury Rd CRAWW RH11 28 D4
Hancock Wy SHOR BN43 74 A7
Handcross Rd RHWH RH17 40 B6
SWTR RH13 127 N5
Handford Wy SWTR RH13 127 Q3
Hangers Wy EPSF GU31 133 M11
EPSF GU31 151 K1
HORN PO8 150 H3
The Hanger BOR GU35 107 M2
Hanger Wy EPSF GU31 133 Q6
Hangleton Cl HOVE BN3 75 J3
Hangleton Gdns HOVE BN3 75 J4
Hangleton Gra FERR BN12 91 K2
Hangleton La FERR BN12 91 J1
HOVE BN3 75 H3
Hangleton Manor Cl HOVE BN3 75 J3
Hangleton Rd HOVE BN3 75 K3
Hangleton Valley Dr HOVE BN3 75 J2
Hangleton Wy HOVE BN3 75 J3
Hanlye La RHWH RH17 44 D1
Hannah Gdns WVILLE PO7 168 A9
Hannah Sq CCH PO19 61 J6
Hannington Pl HPPT/KEY BN6 164 H2
Hannington Rd HAV PO9 168 E10
Hanover Cl CRAWE RH10 9 J9
PUL/STOR RH20 176 B2
SELS PO20 181 M6
Hanover Ct MIDH GU29 137 K7
Hanover Crs BRIE/ROTT BN2 5 H3
Hanover Gdns SWTR RH13 145 K3
Hanover Ms BRIE/ROTT BN2 5 H3
Hanover Pl BRIE/ROTT BN2 5 H2
Hanover St BRIE/ROTT BN2 5 H3
Hanover Ter BRIE/ROTT BN2 5 H3
Hanover Wk PUL/STOR RH20 160 A12
Harberton Crs CCH PO19 61 M2
Harbolets Rd BIL RH14 142 C10
Harborough Cl
PUL/STOR RH20 159 Q5
Harborough Dr
PUL/STOR RH20 159 Q5
Harborough Gorse
PUL/STOR RH20 159 Q5
Harborough Hl
PUL/STOR RH20 159 P6
Harborough Meadow
PUL/STOR RH20 159 Q5
Harbour Ct RCCH PO18 60 B8
Harbour Rd BOGR PO21 102 E7
RCCH PO18 82 A1
Harbourside HAV PO9 57 G7
Harbour View Rd BOGR PO21 102 F5
Harbour Wy EMRTH PO10 58 B5
RCCH PO18 82 B1
SHOR BN43 73 M7
Harbridge Ct HAV PO9 168 E10
Harcourt Cl HORN PO8 168 B5
Harcourt Wy SELS PO20 181 M5
Hardbarrow Woods
PUL/STOR RH20 160 D7
Hardham Cl ANG/EP BN16 90 A5
CRAWW RH11 28 F1
Hardham Rd CCH PO19 * 7 G8
Hard's Hl SWTR RH13 126 C4
The Hard MSEA/BNM PO22 88 B8
Hardwick Rd HOVE BN3 75 K2

Hardwick Wy HOVE BN3 ... 75 K1
Hardy Av EPSF GU31 ... 133 P4
Hardy Cl CRAWE RH10 ... 30 B2
  HORL RH6 ... 14 D6
  HORS RH12 ... 10 B2
  MSEA/BNM PO22 ... 87 J8
  SHOR BN43 ... 73 L7
Harebell Cl LHPTN BN17 ... 90 A2
Harebell Dr PTSD BN41 ... 74 F2
Harefield Av SALV BN13 ... 92 E1
Harefield Rd MSEA/BNM PO22 ... 87 L8
Hare La CRAWW RH11 ... 19 G8
  SELS PO20 ... 180 H5
Haresfield Ter SELS PO20 ... 63 J4
Haresfoot Cl RCCH PO18 ... 170 G12
Hares La RCCH PO18 ... 170 E10
Harestock Rd HAV PO9 ... 56 E2
Harewood Cl CRAWE RH10 ... 19 M8
Harkness Dr WVILLE PO7 ... 168 C9
Harlands Cl HWH RH16 ... 44 F3
Harlands Rd HWH RH16 ... 44 F3
Harlech Cl SALV BN13 ... 70 A8
Harmans Dr EGRIN RH19 ... 24 A8
Harmans Md EGRIN RH19 ... 23 M8
Harmony Cl CRAWW RH11 ... 28 D5
Harmony Dr SELS PO20 ... 100 A8
Harmsworth Crs HOVE BN3 ... 75 K2
Harold Cl BOGR PO21 ... 85 L2
Harold Rd CRAWE RH10 ... 30 D4
  EMRTH PO10 ... 58 C1
Haroldslea Cl HORL RH6 ... 15 H8
Haroldslea Dr HORL RH6 ... 15 H8
Harper Dr CRAWE RH10 ... 30 B7
Harrier Cl HORN PO8 ... 168 B3
Harrier Wy EPSF GU31 ... 133 R7
Harrington Pl BRI BN1 ... 77 L4
Harrington Rd BRI BN1 ... 76 D3
Harrington Vls BRI BN1 ... 76 E3
Harriots Cl CRAWW RH11 ... 29 C6
Harris La HORN PO8 ... 151 L8
Harrison Ct SALV BN13 ... 71 L8
Harrison Rd SELS PO20 ... 71 K8
Harrow Dr SELS PO20 ... 99 L6
Harrow La PSF GU32 ... 133 N3
Harrow Rd WTHG BN11 ... 12 C1
Harrowsley Ct HORL RH6 ... 15 C5
Harsfold Cl ANG/EP BN16 ... 89 M5
Harsfold Rd ANG/EP BN16 ... 90 D4
Hartfield Av BRI BN1 ... 76 F1
Hartfield Rd FROW RH18 ... 34 F7
  HORN PO8 ... 150 D11
Harting Cl FERR BN12 ... 92 A1
Harting Ct CRAWW RH11 ... 28 E6
Harting Down EPSF GU31 ... 133 Q6
Harting Rd LHPTN BN17 ... 89 J2
The Hartings MSEA/BNM PO22 ... 87 J7
Hartington Pl BRIE/ROTT BN2 ... 5 K1
Hartington Rd BRIE/ROTT BN2 ... 5 K1
Hartington Ter BRIE/ROTT BN2 ... 5 K1
Hartington Vls HOVE BN3 ... 76 A5
Hartland Ct EMRTH PO10 ... 58 E4
Hart Plain Av HORN PO8 ... 168 A4
Harts Farm Wy HAV PO9 ... 56 E5
Hartsgrove Cl MFD/CHID GU8 ... 110 C8
Harvest Cl HWH RH16 ... 45 L2
Harvester Cl CCH PO19 ... 7 H2
Harvesters HORS RH12 ... 10 F1
  HWH RH16 ... 45 G7
Harvest Hl EGRIN RH19 ... 33 K1
  RHWH RH17 ... 147 K3
Harvesting La PSF GU32 ... 132 B11
  PSF GU32 ... 150 E1
Harvest Rd CRAWE RH10 ... 30 B5
Harvestside HORL RH6 ... 15 H5
Harvey Cl CRAWW RH11 ... 28 F8
Harvey Rd FERR BN12 ... 92 D4
Harwarden Cl CRAWE RH10 ... 32 B1
Harwood Av FERR BN12 ... 92 C1
Harwood Pk REDH RH1 ... 14 F1
Harwood Rd LHPTN BN17 ... 89 J3
  SWTR RH13 ... 11 H4
Harwoods Cl EGRIN RH19 ... 33 L2
Harwood's La EGRIN RH19 ... 33 L1
Hasle Dr HASM GU27 ... 109 L12
Haslemere Gdns HISD PO11 ... 98 A3
Haslemere Rd EMRTH PO10 ... 58 E3
  HASM GU27 ... 119 L3
  LIPH GU30 ... 118 A1
Hasler's Cl RCCH PO18 ... 172 B4
Haslett Av CRAWE RH10 ... 9 K4
Haslett Av East CRAWE RH10 ... 9 L4
Haslett Av West CRAWE RH10 ... 8 F5
Haslingbourne La PETW GU28 ... 139 K12
Hassocks Ct CRAWW RH11 ... 28 E6
Hassocks Rd HPPT/KEY BN6 ... 165 J4
The Hassocks WVILLE PO7 ... 168 B10
Haste Hl HASM GU27 ... 109 N12
Haste Hill Top HASM GU27 * ... 109 N12
Hastings Cl BOGR PO21 ... 103 L1
Hastings Rd BRIE/ROTT BN2 ... 5 J1
  CRAWE RH10 ... 30 A3
  WTHG BN11 ... 12 A8
Hatch Cl CRAN GU6 ... 112 H6
Hatch Ct HAV PO9 ... 168 D10
Hatch End FROW RH18 ... 34 E7
Hatchetts Dr HASM GU27 ... 108 F11
Hatchgate HORL RH6 ... 14 C7
Hatchgate La RHWH RH17 ... 44 D3
Hatchgate La RHWH RH17 ... 44 D3
Hatch Hl HASM GU27 ... 119 L4
Hatchlands HORS RH12 ... 36 F2
  RHWH RH17 ... 44 C3
Hatch La HASM GU27 ... 119 L4
  LISS GU33 ... 116 F9
Hathaway Rd WVILLE PO7 ... 168 C8
Hatherleigh Cl BOGR PO21 ... 85 M8
Hatherleigh Gdns BOGR PO21 ... 85 M8
Hathersham Cl HORL RH6 ... 15 M5
Hathersham La HORL RH6 ... 15 L3
Havant Farm Cl HAV PO9 ... 57 J7
Havant Rd EMRTH PO10 ... 57 L5
  HAV PO9 ... 56 B5
  HAV PO9 ... 56 B5
  HORN PO8 ... 168 E4
Havelock Cl MSEA/BNM PO22 ... 3 K6
Havelock Rd BOGR PO21 ... 2 D5
  BRI BN1 ... 76 E4
Haven Gdns CRAWE RH10 ... 21 M8
Havengate HORS RH12 ... 36 E4
Haven Rd BIL RH14 ... 124 A2
Havenside SHOR BN43 ... 73 J8
Havenstoke Cl CCH PO19 ... 61 M4
The Haven LAN/SOMP BN15 * ... 94 E1

LHPTN BN17 ... 89 M4
Haversham Cl CRAWE RH10 ... 9 K4
Haveswater Cl BOR GU35 ... 106 C4
Hawke Cl ANG/EP BN16 ... 90 D4
Hawkenbury Wy LEWES BN7 ... 55 M4
Hawker Close. SELS PO20 ... 63 J3
Hawkesbourne Rd HORS RH12 ... 36 E4
Hawkesmoor Rd CRAWW RH11 ... 28 D5
Hawkhurst Pl BRI BN1 * ... 53 J7
Hawkhurst Rd BRI BN1 ... 53 J7
Hawkhurst Wk CRAWE RH10 ... 30 A5
Hawkins Cl BOGR PO21 ... 103 G3
  SHOR BN43 ... 74 C4
Hawkins Crs SALV BN13 ... 71 L8
Hawkins Rd CRAWE RH10 ... 30 B1
  SHOR BN43 ... 74 C4
Hawkley Cl HAV PO9 ... 168 F11
Hawksfold La East
  HASM GU27 ... 119 K7
Hawksfold La West
  HASM GU27 ... 119 K7
Hawkshaw Cl LIPH GU30 ... 118 A1
Hawks Pl MSEA/BNM PO22 ... 86 A7
Hawley Rd ANG/EP BN16 ... 90 A5
Hawmead CRAWE RH10 ... 32 B1
Haworth Rd CRAWE RH10 ... 30 A4
Hawth Av CRAWE RH10 ... 9 J7
Hawth Cl CRAWE RH10 ... 9 G7
Hawthorn Bank
  BRIE/ROTT BN2 * ... 77 L1
  CCH PO19 ... 6 C3
  CRAWW RH11 ... 19 H8
  HORS RH12 ... 10 D1
  MIDH GU29 ... 136 C11
Hawthorn Cl BURH RH15 ... 47 J4
Hawthorn Crs SALV BN13 ... 71 L8
Hawthorn Gdns SALV BN13 ... 71 L7
Hawthorn Rd BOGR PO21 ... 103 M2
  HORN PO8 ... 150 D12
  LHPTN BN17 ... 89 J1
Hawthorn Wy PTSD BN41 ... 74 F2
  SHOR BN43 ... 160 A11
Haybarn Dr HORS RH12 ... 36 D2
Haybourne Cl BRIE/ROTT BN2 ... 77 K6
Haybourne Rd BRIE/ROTT BN2 ... 77 K6
Haydock Ms WVILLE PO7 ... 168 C8
Haydon Cl BOGR PO21 ... 103 H4
Hayes Cl PTSD BN41 ... 75 H5
  RCCH PO18 ... 172 B10
Hayes La SWTR RH13 ... 124 F4
Hayes Wk HORL RH6 ... 15 M5
Hayes Wood Rd BIL RH14 ... 124 C8
Hayfields HORL RH6 ... 15 H5
Hayley's Gdns MSEA/BNM PO22 ... 3 L4
Hayland Rd HWH RH16 ... 45 H4
Hayling Gdns SALV BN13 ... 70 D4
Hayling Ri SALV BN13 ... 70 D4
Haynes Cl SALV BN13 ... 12 C1
Haynes Wy SALV BN13 ... 12 C1
Hay Rd CCH PO19 ... 7 H8
Hayward Rd LEWES BN7 ... 55 M2
Haywards CRAWE RH10 ... 20 C8
Haywards Cl MSEA/BNM PO22 ... 3 M2
Haywards Heath Rd
  RHWH RH17 ... 40 F7
Haywards Rd BRI BN1 ... 52 F7
  LIPH GU30 ... 118 A1
Hazelbank Cl EPSF GU31 ... 133 Q5
Hazel Cl CRAWE RH10 ... 32 B1
  CRAWW RH11 ... 19 H8
  PTSD BN41 ... 75 H2
  SWTR RH13 ... 125 F12
Hazeldean Dr HAV PO9 ... 169 J8
Hazeldene Meads BRI BN1 ... 76 C2
Hazeldene La LIPH GU30 ... 117 L1
Hazeledene La RING/NEW BN8 ... 149 Q6
Hazel Gv ARUN BN18 ... 66 D3
  BURH RH15 ... 47 G8
  GSHT GU26 ... 108 E7
Hazelgrove HORN PO8 ... 150 D8
Hazelgrove Rd HWH RH16 ... 45 H5
Hazelholt Dr HAV PO9 ... 56 D2
Hazelhurst HORL RH6 ... 15 H5
Hazelhurst Crs HORS RH12 ... 125 Q4
  SALV BN13 ... 70 E1
Hazelhurst Dr CRAWE RH10 ... 30 D3
Hazel Ldg ANG/EP BN16 * ... 90 B5
Hazelmead Dr ANG/EP BN16 ... 90 F1
Hazel Rd ANG/EP BN16 ... 90 F1
  HORN PO8 ... 150 D8
  MSEA/BNM PO22 ... 86 A7
Hazel Wy CRAWE RH10 ... 32 A1
Hazelwick Av CRAWE RH10 ... 29 M1
Hazelwick Mill La CRAWE RH10 ... 29 M1
Hazelwick Rd CRAWE RH10 ... 9 M2
Hazelwood CRAWW RH11 ... 28 F3
Hazelwood Av HAV PO9 ... 56 C2
Hazelwood Cl CRAWE RH10 ... 31 L1
  MIDH GU29 ... 137 J6
  PUL/STOR RH20 ... 160 A11
  SALV BN13 ... 13 M1
Hazelwood Rd SWTR RH13 ... 144 F10
Hazleton Int HORN PO8 * ... 168 D3
Hazleton Wy HORN PO8 ... 168 C4
Head Down EPSF GU31 ... 133 Q6
Headley Cl CRAWE RH10 ... 20 C8
Headley Flds BOR GU35 ... 107 M5
Headley Hill Rd BOR GU35 ... 107 N4
Headley La LIPH GU30 ... 107 M7
Headley Rd BOR GU35 ... 107 K4
  GSHT GU26 ... 108 C3
  GSHT GU26 ... 107 P11
Hearn Cl SELS PO20 ... 63 H4
Hearn Cl LHPTN BN17 ... 89 J1
Hearn V BOR GU35 ... 107 P2
Heasewood HWH RH16 ... 44 F6
Heath Cl GSHT GU26 ... 108 F7
  HORN PO8 ... 168 C2
  HORS RH12 ... 125 P2
  HPPT/KEY BN6 ... 146 E12
  HWH RH16 * ... 45 H5
  SELS PO20 ... 83 M5
  SWTR RH13 ... 127 J3
Heathcote Dr EGRIN RH19 ... 23 C7
Heathcote Rd BOR GU35 ... 106 H6
Heath Cottages GSHT GU26 * ... 108 C3
Heather Bank HWH RH16 ... 44 F4
Heather Cl BOR GU35 ... 106 E8
  CRAWE RH10 ... 21 M4
  HORS RH12 ... 36 C4

RCCH PO18 ... 60 A2
  WVILLE PO7 ... 168 A11
Heather Dr BOR GU35 ... 107 J4
Heatherfield EPSF GU31 ... 133 L12
Heatherlands HORL RH6 * ... 15 H5
Heather La PUL/STOR RH20 ... 159 R7
  SALV BN13 ... 70 D3
Heathermead PUL/STOR RH20 ... 159 R7
Heather Rd EPSF GU31 ... 133 R6
The Heathers ANG/EP BN16 * ... 68 D7
Heatherton Ms EMRTH PO10 ... 58 A4
Heatherway EGRIN RH19 ... 22 E2
Heather Wy GSHT GU26 ... 109 J5
  PUL/STOR RH20 ... 160 C12
Heathfield CRAWE RH10 ... 20 C8
Heathfield Av ANG/EP BN16 ... 90 E2
Heathfield Cl MIDH GU29 ... 136 H10
  SALV BN13 ... 70 E8
Heathfield Copse
  PUL/STOR RH20 ... 159 Q6
Heathfield Crs PTSD BN41 ... 74 E1
Heathfield Dr PTSD BN41 ... 74 E2
Heathfield Gdns MIDH GU29 ... 136 H10
Heathfield Gn MIDH GU29 ... 136 H10
Heathfield Pk MIDH GU29 ... 136 G10
Heathfield Rd EPSF GU31 ... 133 R6
Heath Hill Av BRIE/ROTT BN2 ... 77 M4
Heath Pl MSEA/BNM PO22 ... 86 C5
Heath Rd EPSF GU31 ... 133 P6
  HASM GU27 ... 108 G12
  HWH RH16 ... 45 H4
Heath Rd East EPSF GU31 ... 133 Q7
Heath Rd West EPSF GU31 ... 133 P7
Heathside La GSHT GU26 ... 108 G3
Heath Sq HWH RH16 * ... 45 G4
Heath Wy HORS RH12 ... 36 C4
Hebe Rd SHOR BN43 ... 73 K6
Hechle Wd BOGR PO21 ... 105 L3
Heckfield Cl HAV PO9 ... 169 J12
Hectors La EGRIN RH19 ... 34 E8
Hedgecourt Pl EGRIN RH19 ... 22 D5
Hedge End Rd
  MSEA/BNM PO22 ... 65 H7
Hedgehog La HASM GU27 ... 109 L12
Hedgerow Gdns EMRTH PO10 ... 58 A2
Hedgers Hl ARUN BN18 ... 65 L4
Hedgeside CRAWW RH11 ... 29 H8
Hedgeway MSEA/BNM PO22 ... 87 J8
Hedingham Cl HORL RH6 ... 15 H5
Heene Pl WTHG BN11 ... 12 D7
Heene Rd WTHG BN11 ... 12 D4
Heene Ter WTHG BN11 ... 12 D8
Heene Wy WTHG BN11 ... 12 C6
Heghbrok Wy BOGR PO21 ... 103 M3
The Heights BRI BN1 ... 76 A1
  SALV BN13 ... 70 F4
Helena Cl PTSD BN41 ... 75 H4
Helena Rd BRIE/ROTT BN2 ... 78 B4
Hellingly Cl BRIE/ROTT BN2 ... 77 K8
Helston Dr EMRTH PO10 ... 57 M2
Helyer's Gn LHPTN BN17 ... 89 H3
Hemsby Wk CRAWE RH10 ... 30 A5
Hemsley Wk HORN PO8 ... 168 A5
Henderson Cl CRAWW RH11 ... 29 G8
Henderson Wk STEY/UB BN44 ... 48 D1
Hendon Av ANG/EP BN16 ... 89 M6
Hendon Rd BOR GU35 ... 106 H7
Hendon St BRIE/ROTT BN2 ... 5 L6
Henfield Cl BRIE/ROTT BN2 ... 96 E1
  FERR BN12 ... 92 A1
Henfield Rd HFD BN5 ... 49 K1
  HPPT/KEY BN6 ... 145 R12
  HPPT/KEY BN6 ... 164 D3
  STEY/UB BN44 ... 75 G4
Henfield Wy HOVE BN3 ... 75 L2
  MSEA/BNM PO22 ... 87 J7
Henge Wy PTSD BN41 ... 75 G3
Hengist Cl HORS RH12 ... 125 R4
Henley Cl CRAWE RH10 ... 30 C6
Henley Rd BRIE/ROTT BN2 ... 96 E1
Henry Av LHPTN BN17 ... 89 M4
Henry Burt Wy BURH RH15 ... 46 D8
Henry Cl CCH PO19 ... 7 L4
Henry Fletcher Cl
  ANG/EP BN16 ... 68 F3
Henry St BOGR PO21 ... 2 E5
Henshaw Cl CRAWW RH11 ... 28 E5
Henson Rd CRAWE RH10 ... 30 A5
Henty Cl ARUN BN18 ... 65 L5
  CRAWW RH11 ... 28 D6
Henty Gdns CCH PO19 ... 6 C5
Henty Rd FERR BN12 ... 91 L5
  SALV BN13 ... 12 E2
Henwood Down EPSF GU31 ... 133 P6
Hepplewhite Cl CRAWW RH11 ... 29 G8
Herald Dr CCH PO19 ... 6 F7
Herbert Rd BRI BN1 ... 76 E3
  LAN/SOMP BN15 ... 72 A4
Hercules Pl MSEA/BNM PO22 ... 87 L4
Hereford Cl CCH PO19 ... 61 L4
  CRAWE RH10 ... 29 K7
Hereford St BRIE/ROTT BN2 ... 5 L6
Herington Rd ARUN BN18 ... 66 E3
Heritage Lawn HORL RH6 ... 15 H5
Herm Cl CRAWW RH11 * ... 28 F7
Hermione Cl FERR BN12 ... 91 J2
Hermitage Cl HAV PO9 ... 56 F1
  SELS PO20 ... 84 C4
Hermitage La EGRIN RH19 ... 33 L1
Hermitage Rd CRAWE RH10 ... 9 L1
Hermits Rd CRAWE RH10 ... 9 L1
Hermongers La HORS RH12 ... 114 C7
Herm Rd FERR BN12 ... 91 L5
Hernbrook Dr SWTR RH13 ... 11 H9
Herne Ct ANG/EP BN16 * ... 90 C3
Herne Gdns ANG/EP BN16 ... 90 C3
Herne La ANG/EP BN16 ... 90 C3
Herne Rd EPSF GU31 ... 133 P6
Heron Cl CRAWW RH11 ... 29 H1
  MSEA/BNM PO22 ... 86 A6
  RCCH PO18 ... 172 B10
Herondale CRAWE RH10 ... 21 M4
Heron La SELS PO20 ... 180 H11
Heron Md BOGR PO21 ... 102 E6
Heron Pl EGRIN RH19 ... 33 L1
Heron Quay EMRTH PO10 ... 58 B6
Herons Cl BIL RH14 ... 122 C11
The Herons LAN/SOMP BN15 * ... 94 E1

Heronswood Cl HORL RH6 ... 15 G5
Herons Wood Ct HORL RH6 * ... 15 G5
Heron Tye HPPT/KEY BN6 * ... 165 N6
Herontye Dr EGRIN RH19 ... 33 L1
Heron Wy SWTR RH13 ... 11 L6
Herrick Cl CRAWE RH10 ... 30 B1
Herriott Cl HORN PO8 ... 168 B4
Hersee Wy SELS PO20 ... 181 J6
Hersham Cl CRAWW RH11 * ... 29 G8
Herschel Wk CRAWW RH11 * ... 29 G8
Hertford Cl EMRTH PO10 ... 103 L2
Hertford Rd BRI BN1 ... 77 G3
  WTHG BN11 ... 13 G4
Heston Av BRI BN1 ... 52 E6
Heston Gv BOGR PO21 ... 103 H4
Hett Cl RHWH RH17 ... 130 E1
Hevers Av HORL RH6 ... 14 E5
Hewart's La BOGR PO21 ... 103 G9
Hewitts HFD BN5 ... 163 K5
Hewitts Rd HFD BN5 ... 163 K5
Hewshott Cv LIPH GU30 ... 108 A12
Hewshott La LIPH GU30 ... 108 A12
Hexham Cl CRAWE RH10 ... 30 D3
Heyshott Cl LAN/SOMP BN15 ... 72 D5
Heyworth Cl BRIE/ROTT BN2 ... 78 E5
Heyworth Ride CRAWE RH10 ... 44 F6
Hibiscus Gv BOR GU35 ... 106 H7
Hickling Wk CRAWE RH10 ... 30 A5
Hickman's La HWH RH16 ... 45 L1
Hickman's La HWH RH16 ... 45 K1
Hickstead La RHWH RH17 ... 146 D8
Hickstead Pk HPPT/KEY BN6 * ... 146 F11
Hide Gdns ANG/EP BN16 ... 90 A3
Highams Hl CRAWW RH11 ... 28 E4
Highbank BRI BN1 ... 52 B8
High Bar La PUL/STOR RH20 ... 160 C7
Highbarn SALV BN13 ... 178 H10
High Beeches La RHWH RH17 ... 39 J7
Highbridge La LEWES BN7 ... 167 L5
Highbrook Cl BRIE/ROTT BN2 ... 77 J3
Highbrook Pl
  PUL/STOR RH20 * ... 160 A12
Highbury Gv HASM GU27 ... 109 M9
Highclere Av HAV PO9 ... 56 F1
Highclere Wy SALV BN13 ... 70 A8
Highcroft Av MSEA/BNM PO22 ... 2 F3
Highcroft Crs MSEA/BNM PO22 ... 3 G2
Highcroft Dr HORS RH12 ... 114 D8
Highcroft La HORN PO8 ... 168 D1
Highcroft Rd EGRIN RH19 ... 42 F3
Highcroft Vls BRI BN1 ... 76 D3
Highdown BRI BN1 ... 52 C5
Highdown Av SALV BN13 ... 70 A8
Highdown Cl ANG/EP BN16 ... 68 F3
  FERR BN12 ... 91 K2
Highdown Ct CRAWE RH10 ... 30 A6
Highdown Dr LHPTN BN17 ... 89 K3
Highdown Rd HOVE BN3 ... 4 A2
  LEWES BN7 ... 55 M3
Highdown Wy FERR BN12 ... 91 K2
  HORS RH12 ... 36 E2
Highfield LHPTN BN17 ... 89 G2
Highfield Av WVILLE PO7 ... 168 B9
Highfield Cl ANG/EP BN16 ... 68 E8
  MIDH GU29 ... 137 K7
  WVILLE PO7 ... 168 A8
Highfield Crs BRI BN1 ... 52 F8
  GSHT GU26 ... 108 H5
Highfield Dr HPPT/KEY BN6 ... 165 J4
Highfield Gdns ANG/EP BN16 ... 90 A5
  LISS GU33 ... 116 E9
  MSEA/BNM PO22 ... 2 F3
Highfield La LIPH GU30 ... 118 A3
  SELS PO20 ... 63 H7
Highfield Rd EGRIN RH19 ... 23 J6
  MSEA/BNM PO22 ... 2 F4
  PSF GU32 ... 133 N5
  SALV BN13 ... 70 F7
Highfields BRI BN1 ... 53 H8
  FROW RH18 ... 34 E7
Highgate Dr BOGR PO21 ... 85 M6
Highgate Rd FROW RH18 ... 34 E8
Highground La
  MSEA/BNM PO22 ... 87 G1
Highgrove Gdns WTHG BN11 ... 12 D6
High Hatch La HPPT/KEY BN6 ... 46 A5
Highland Av HPPT/KEY BN6 ... 2 C5
Highland Cl EMRTH PO10 ... 57 M5
Highland Ct HWH RH16 ... 45 H5
Highland Rd CCH PO19 ... 61 L3
  EMRTH PO10 ... 57 M5
  HWH RH16 ... 45 J6
Highlands RHWH RH17 ... 44 C1
Highlands Cl HPPT/KEY BN6 ... 165 P6
  SALV BN13 ... 70 D4
Highlands Crs SWTR RH13 ... 11 J6
Highlands Dr BURH RH15 ... 46 F5
Highlands Rd PTSD BN41 ... 75 G4
  SWTR RH13 ... 11 J6
The Highlands RHWH RH17 ... 44 C1
High La HASM GU27 ... 109 M9
High Lawn Wy HAV PO9 ... 168 G12
Highleigh Rd SELS PO20 ... 101 H3
High Loxley Rd
  MFD/CHID GU8 ... 112 C3
High Meadow MIDH GU29 ... 154 C5
High Oaks CRAWW RH11 ... 8 B7
High Park Av HOVE BN3 ... 75 K2
High Pitfold GSHT GU26 ... 108 G8
High Point HWH RH16 ... 45 K6
High Ridge Cl ARUN BN18 ... 66 E4
High Seat Gdns BIL RH14 ... 124 A12
High Spinney PUL/STOR RH20 ... 160 B8
Highstanding La MIDH GU29 ... 137 K11
Highstead La PETW GU28 ... 137 K11
High St ANG/EP BN16 ... 68 E4
  ARUN BN18 ... 67 G2
  ARUN BN18 ... 176 C2
  BIL RH14 ... 122 G2
  BIL RH14 ... 142 A1
  BOGR PO21 ... 2 D5
  BOR GU35 ... 106 G5
  BOR GU35 ... 107 M4
  BRIE/ROTT BN2 ... 6 E3
  BRIE/ROTT BN2 ... 97 G2
  CCH PO19 * ... 6 D3
  CRAWE RH10 ... 21 M4
  EDEN TN8 ... 25 M4
  EGRIN RH19 ... 33 L1
  EMRTH PO10 ... 58 A5
  EPSF GU31 ... 133 L12

HASM GU27 ... 109 N11
HFD BN5 ... 163 L5
HORL RH6 ... 15 G6
HORS RH12 ... 27 H1
HPPT/KEY BN6 ... 164 H4
HPPT/KEY BN6 ... 166 A6
LEWES BN7 ... 45 L1
LHPTN BN17 ... 89 J3
PETW GU28 ... 139 M10
PSF GU32 ... 133 N6
PTSD BN41 ... 74 F2
PUL/STOR RH20 ... 160 A12
RCCH PO18 ... 81 M1
RHWH RH17 ... 40 A5
RHWH RH17 ... 44 B3
RHWH RH17 ... 128 D5
RHWH RH17 ... 130 E1
SALV BN13 ... 70 E4
SELS PO20 ... 63 H7
SELS PO20 ... 181 K6
SHOR BN43 ... 73 K6
STEY/UB BN44 ... 48 C2
STEY/UB BN44 ... 48 F3
SWTR RH13 ... 144 F10
WTHG BN11 ... 13 J5
High Street Gn MFD/CHID GU8 ... 11 K8
High Titten ARUN BN18 ... 176 F4
High Trees BOGR PO21 ... 103 L3
  HWH RH16 ... 45 J4
  SELS PO20 ... 83 M4
  WVILLE PO7 ... 168 A9
Highview LAN/SOMP BN15 ... 72 C4
High Vw PSF GU32 ... 133 N5
  SALV BN13 ... 70 E4
Highview Av North BRI BN1 ... 52 D7
Highview Av South BRI BN1 ... 52 D7
Highview Rd BRI BN1 ... 52 D7
  SELS PO20 ... 52 D7
Highview Wy BRI BN1 ... 52 D7
Highway Cl BRIE/ROTT BN2 ... 77 J3
Highways PTSD BN41 ... 75 G3
The Highway BRIE/ROTT BN2 ... 77 K2
High Weald Landscape Trail
  EGRIN RH19 ... 33 J2
  EGRIN RH19 ... 42 J4
  FROW RH18 ... 35 J3
  HWH RH16 ... 129 Q8
Highworth SWTR RH13 * ... 11 K7
Hilary Rd CCH PO19 ... 6 J2
Hildon Cl SALV BN13 ... 70 C8
Hildon Pk FERR BN12 ... 70 C8
Hilland Ri BOR GU35 ... 107 N5
Hillary Cl EGRIN RH19 ... 23 M7
Hillbank Cl PTSD BN41 ... 74 E2
Hillbarn Av LAN/SOMP BN15 ... 72 C5
Hill Barn La MIDH GU29 ... 154 F7
Hill Barn La SALV BN13 ... 71 H6
Hill Brow HOVE BN3 ... 76 A1
Hill Brow Cl HAV PO9 ... 169 J4
Hillbrow BRI BN1 ... 76 B1
Hill Brow Rd LISS GU33 ... 116 C10
Hill Crest EGRIN RH19 ... 23 K3
Hillcrest BRI BN1 ... 52 B8
  HASM GU27 * ... 119 L8
  RHWH RH17 ... 131 M4
Hillcrest Cl CRAWE RH10 ... 30 C3
  PUL/STOR RH20 ... 161 K8
  RHWH RH17 ... 149 J3
Hillcrest Dr PUL/STOR RH20 ... 161 K9
Hillcrest La RHWH RH17 ... 149 J3
Hillcrest Pk PUL/STOR RH20 ... 159 L3
Hillcroft PTSD BN41 ... 74 E3
Hill Dr HOVE BN3 ... 76 A2
Hillside HOVE BN3 ... 76 A4
Hill Farm Cl HASM GU27 * ... 109 J12
Hill Farm La PUL/STOR RH20 ... 140 H12
Hill Farm Wy STHW BN42 ... 74 C3
Hillfield Rd SELS PO20 ... 181 K7
Hillgarth GSHT GU26 ... 108 G4
Hill House Cl CRAWE RH10 ... 31 M5
Hill House Hl LIPH GU30 ... 107 N10
Hillhouse La HAV PO9 ... 113 M8
Hillingdale CRAWW RH11 ... 29 H8
Hill La EPSF GU31 ... 152 F3
  MSEA/BNM PO22 ... 87 H1
Hillmead CRAWW RH11 ... 28 E3
Hillmead Gdns HAV PO9 ... 56 C3
Hill Pl CRAWW RH11 ... 8 C6
Hillrise LAN/SOMP BN15 ... 72 B5
Hill Rd GSHT GU26 ... 108 F3
  HASM GU27 ... 109 M11
  LEWES BN7 ... 55 M3
  LHPTN BN17 ... 89 K3
Hillsboro Rd BOGR PO21 ... 2 C4
Hills Farm La HORS RH12 ... 125 G4
Hillside BRIE/ROTT BN2 ... 77 K3
  CRAWE RH10 ... 32 A1
  HORS RH12 ... 125 P4
  PTSD BN41 ... 75 H4
  STHW BN42 ... 74 E4
Hillside Av SALV BN13 ... 71 G6
Hillside Cl BOR GU35 ... 107 P3
  CRAWW RH11 ... 23 A1
  EGRIN RH19 ... 23 K6
Hillside Crs ANG/EP BN16 ... 68 F8
Hillside Rd HFD BN5 ... 163 L9
Hillside Rd HASM GU27 ... 109 J12
  LAN/SOMP BN15 ... 72 B5
  PUL/STOR RH20 ... 160 D11
  PUL/STOR RH20 ... 160 D11
Hillside Wk BRI BN1 ... 76 B3
Hillside Wy BRI BN1 ... 76 B3
Hills Pl HORS RH12 ... 125 R3
Hills Rd STEY/UB BN44 ... 48 F3
Hill Ter ARUN BN18 ... 66 E3
Hill Top BRI BN1 ... 52 A8
Hill Top Cl PTSD BN41 ... 74 E3
Hilltop Gdns HORN PO8 ... 150 E10
Hilltop Rd EGRIN RH19 ... 42 D3
Hill Vw HFD BN5 * ... 163 L10
Hillview HORN PO8 ... 168 D4
Hillview Crs ANG/EP BN16 ... 90 C3
Hillview Gdns CRAWW RH11 ... 39 H1
Hillview Ri SALV BN13 ... 70 E4
Hillview Rd BRIE/ROTT BN2 ... 77 M5
  SALV BN13 ... 70 E4
Hillybarn Rd CRAWW RH11 ... 18 B8
Hiltingbury Rd HAV PO9 ... 168 H11
Hilton Pk SELS PO20 ... 99 M5
Hinde Rd MSEA/BNM PO22 ... 105 H1
Hindhead Cl CRAWW RH11 ... 8 C6
Hindhead Rd HASM GU27 ... 108 H9
  HASM GU27 ... 109 J11
Hindle Cl PUL/STOR RH20 ... 160 A6
Hinton Cl BRI BN1 ... 77 H3

HAV PO9 56 D1
Hinton Manor La HORN PO8 150 A10
Hipley Rd HAV PO9 57 H2
Hislop Wk BOGR PO21 2 F7
Hither Gn EMRTH PO10 58 F3
Hitherwood Cl WVILLE PO7 168 C8
Hoadlands EPSF GU31 133 P5
Hoad La HWH RH16 130 F5
Hobart Cl SALV BN13 70 B7
Hobbs Rd CRAWW RH11 28 F8
Hobbs Sq EPSF GU31 133 P4
Hobbs Wy ANG/EP BN16 90 B4
Hobdens La RHWH RH17 130 D2
Hoblands HWH RH16 45 L5
Hobs Acre STEY/UB BN44 49 G4
Hocken Md CRAWE RH10 30 C1
Hockham Ct HAV PO9 168 D10
Hodges Cl HAV PO9 57 H2
Hodgkin Cl CRAWE RH10 30 A4
Hodshrove Pl BRIE/ROTT BN2 * 77 K2
Hodshrove Rd BRIE/ROTT BN2 77 K2
Hoe Ct LAN/SOMP BN15 72 F4
Hoefield La MIDH GU29 154 F8
Hoe La ARUN BN18 66 B6
MSEA/BNM PO22 86 F5
RCCH PO18 82 B4
Hoewood HFD BN5 163 K10
Hogarth Rd CRAWE RH10 29 L6
HOVE BN3 75 L6
Hoggarth Cl EPSF GU31 133 P4
Hog La ARUN BN18 176 F2
Hogmoor Rd BOR GU35 106 E5
Hogs Edge BRIE/ROTT BN2 77 M3
Hogs Lodge La HORN PO8 150 E3
Hogwood Rd BIL RH14 122 D2
Holbein Rd CRAWE RH10 29 L6
Holbrook School La HORS RH12 36 C2
Holbury Ct HAV PO9 169 J12
Holdenhurst Cl HORN PO8 150 D12
The Holdens RCCH PO18 59 M8
Holder Rd CRAWE RH10 30 A6
Holders HPPT/KEY BN6 164 D3
Holdfast La HASM GU27 109 Q9
The Holdings LEWES BN7 55 L8
Hole St PUL/STOR RH20 161 K10
Holford Gn SELS PO20 181 M5
Holland Cl BOGR PO21 85 L8
Holland Ms HOVE BN3 76 C8
Holland Rd HOVE BN3 76 C6
STEY/UB BN44 48 C2
Hollands Fld HORS RH12 125 P1
Hollands La HFD BN5 162 H5
Hollands Rd HFD BN5 163 J4
Holland St BRIE/ROTT BN2 5 H5
Hollands Wy EGRIN RH19 23 M5
HORS RH12 115 Q9
The Hollies BOGR PO21 * 85 L8
Hollin Ct CRAWE RH10 19 K8
Hollingbourne Crs
CRAWW RH11 39 H1
Hollingbury Copse BRI BN1 76 F1
Hollingbury Crs BRI BN1 77 G4
Hollingbury Gdns SALV BN13 70 F2
Hollingbury Park Av BRI BN1 76 F3
Hollingbury Pl BRI BN1 77 G3
Hollingbury Ri BRI BN1 77 G2
Hollingbury Ri West BRI BN1 76 F3
Hollingbury Rd BRI BN1 77 G4
Hollingbury Ter BRI BN1 76 F3
Hollingdean La BRI BN1 77 G5
Hollingdean Rd BRIE/ROTT BN2 77 H5
Hollingdean St BRI BN1 77 G4
Hollingdean Ter BRI BN1 77 G4
Hollist La EPSF GU31 152 G1
MIDH GU29 136 G6
Hollow La BOR GU35 107 M3
LING RH7 24 A1
The Hollow CRAWW RH11 28 E4
EGRIN RH19 42 E3
HWH RH16 45 L4
PUL/STOR RH20 160 A4
PUL/STOR RH20 176 B1
PUL/STOR RH20 178 H1
Hollyacres SALV BN13 70 B5
Holly Bank Cl HORN PO8 168 D4
Hollybank La EMRTH PO10 58 A1
Hollybrook Pk BOR GU35 106 H6
Hollybush Cl CRAWE RH10 9 H1
Hollybush Rd CRAWE RH10 9 H1
Holly Cl BOR GU35 107 R4
BRI BN1 76 D2
CRAWE RH10 29 M1
HORS RH12 36 F4
PUL/STOR RH20 159 R12
PUL/STOR RH20 160 A4
SALV BN13 70 B8
Hollycombe Cl LIPH GU30 117 R3
Holly Ct MSEA/BNM PO22 86 B7
PUL/STOR RH20 159 R11
Holly Dr LHPTN BN17 89 K1
WVILLE PO7 168 B11
Hollyhock Wy LHPTN BN17 89 M2
Holly Ms HPPT/KEY BN6 * 165 J4
Hollyridge HASM GU27 109 M11
Holly Rd HWH RH16 45 J6
Hollywater Rd LIPH GU30 107 J9
Holman Cl CRAWW RH11 39 G1
HORN PO8 168 B7
Holmans RHWH RH17 130 D1
Holmbury Cl CRAWW RH11 8 D8
Holmbush Cl HWH RH16 45 H7
SHOR BN43 74 C3
Holmbush Ct HORS RH12 * 28 A8
Holmbush La HFD BN5 163 R9
Holmbush Wy MIDH GU29 136 H12
STHW BN42 74 C4
Holmcroft CRAWE RH10 9 G6
Holmcroft Gdns SALV BN13 178 H12
Holmdale Est SELS PO20 * 64 E4
Holmes Av HOVE BN3 75 L4
Holmesdale Rd BURH RH15 46 E8
Holmes Foundation
ARUN BN18 * 67 G3
Holmes La ANG/EP BN16 90 A5
Holmfield Cl ANG/EP BN16 90 B3
Holming End HORS RH12 37 G4
Holm Oak PUL/STOR RH20 159 R12
Holm Oaks SWTR RH13 145 L4
Holmsted Hl RHWH RH17 128 H7
Holst Wy WVILLE PO7 168 A12
Holt Down EPSF GU31 133 Q6
Holt Gdns HAV PO9 169 J6
Holton Hl BRIE/ROTT BN2 78 D6
The Holt BURH RH15 47 H7
PUL/STOR RH20 178 H3
Holtview Rd BRIE/ROTT BN2 78 A5
Holtye Av EGRIN RH19 23 M6
Holtye Pl EGRIN RH19 24 A6
Holtye Rd EGRIN RH19 23 L7
EGRIN RH19 24 D6
Holtye Wk CRAWE RH10 9 M8
Holybourne Rd HAV PO9 57 G2
Holyrood Cl WVILLE PO7 168 B10
Holyrood Pl CRAWW RH11 29 G7
Home Cl CRAWE RH10 30 B1
Home Farm Rd BRI BN1 77 K1
Homefield Av MSEA/BNM PO22 87 H7
Homefield Cl HORL RH6 15 G5
Homefield Crs ARUN BN18 65 J5
Homefield Rd EMRTH PO10 58 C1
WTHG BN11 13 K3
Homefield Wy HORN PO8 150 C7
Homelands Av ANG/EP BN16 90 F5
Homelands Copse HASM GU27 119 N10
Home Platt EGRIN RH19 42 F3
Home Rd BRI BN1 76 D3
Homestall Rd EGRIN RH19 34 D1
Homestead La BURH RH15 47 H3
Home Wy EPSF GU31 133 R6
Homewell HAV PO9 57 G4
Homewood SALV BN13 178 H10
Homing Gdns MSEA/BNM PO22 86 A6
Honer La SELS PO20 102 C1
Honeybridge La SWTR RH13 161 P4
Honey Cft HOVE BN3 75 J1
Honey La ANG/EP BN16 68 F8
Honeypot La LEWES BN7 167 L2
Honeysuckle Cl HORL RH6 15 H5
LAN/SOMP BN15 72 C4
LHPTN BN17 89 M2
Honeysuckle Ct WVILLE PO7 168 A12
Honeysuckle Dr BOGR PO21 102 E3
Honeysuckle La BOR GU35 107 Q4
CRAWW RH11 19 H8
SALV BN13 70 B1
SELS PO20 181 J5
Honeysuckle Wk HORS RH12 36 F4
Honeywood La RDKG RH5 114 H4
Honeywood Rd SWTR RH13 11 M1
The Hooe LHPTN BN17 89 M4
Hookhouse Rd MFD/CHID GU8 111 R3
Hooklands La SWTR RH13 161 K2
Hook La BOGR PO21 102 F3
EGRIN RH19 42 B7
MSEA/BNM PO22 2 F4
RCCH PO18 82 E3
RHWH RH17 42 B7
SELS PO20 63 M6
Hook Lane Cl BOGR PO21 103 G2
Hook's Farm Wy HAV PO9 56 E2
Hook's La HAV PO9 56 E3
The Hooks HFD BN5 163 K5
Hope Ct CRAWW RH11 * 29 G8
Hopeswood LISS GU33 116 C2
Hop Garden La SELS PO20 84 C5
The Hop Gdn EPSF GU31 152 E2
The Hopgarton BOGR PO21 * 103 K2
Hophurst Cl CRAWE RH10 32 A1
Hophurst Dr CRAWE RH10 32 A1
Hophurst Hl CRAWE RH10 22 C7
Hophurst La CRAWE RH10 22 A8
Hopkins Ct CRAWW RH11 * 29 G8
The Hordens SWTR RH13 125 J11
Hordle Rd HAV PO9 56 D1
Horley Lodge La REDH RH1 14 E1
Horley Pl BRIE/ROTT BN2 77 K7
Horley Rd HORL RH6 18 F2
Horley Rw HORL RH6 14 E5
Hormare Crs PUL/STOR RH20 159 R11
Hornbeam Cl BOGR PO21 103 L4
SWTR RH13 11 J7
Hornbeam Rd HAV PO9 57 J2
Hornbeam Wy MIDH GU29 136 G12
Hornbrook Copse SWTR RH13 126 E1
Hornbuckles Cl
RING/NEW BN8 167 P2
Hornby Pl BRIE/ROTT BN2 * 77 M4
Hornby Rd BRIE/ROTT BN2 77 L4
Horndean Cl CRAWE RH10 20 C7
Horndean Prec HORN PO8 * 168 E2
Horndean Rd EMRTH PO10 57 L1
Hornet Rd EMRTH PO10 80 B2
The Hornet CCH PO19 7 G4
Horn La HFD BN5 163 N8
Hornshill La HORS RH12 113 N10
Horns La BOGR PO21 102 E4
Horsebridge Hl BIL RH14 140 F7
Horsebridge Rd HAV PO9 57 H1
Horsefield Rd SELS PO20 181 K6
Horse Hl HORL RH6 14 A5
Horsemere Green La
LHPTN BN17 88 D4
Horseshoe Bend GSHT GU26 108 D6
Horseshoe Cl CRAWE RH10 30 D2
Horseshoe Crs BOR GU35 106 H6
The Horse Shoe SELS PO20 181 K6
Horsgate La RHWH RH17 44 D3
Horsham Cl BRIE/ROTT BN2 77 L7
Horsham Gates SWTR RH13 * 11 G4
Horsham Rd BIL RH14 124 D7
CRAN GU6 113 P1
CRAWW RH11 8 C6
HORS RH12 26 F5
HORS RH12 113 L8
LHPTN BN17 89 L3
PETW GU28 139 M8
RDKG RH5 16 B7
RDKG RH5 114 G3
RHWH RH17 128 B2
SALV BN13 178 G9
STEY/UB BN44 162 B10
Horsham Rd West LHPTN BN17 89 L3
Horsted La EGRIN RH19 43 G5
RHWH RH17 131 R5
Horton Pl ANG/EP BN16 90 F1
Horton Rd BRI BN1 77 G4
Hoskins Pl EGRIN RH19 23 L5
Hospital Vls HWH RH16 45 J4
Hotham Gdns MSEA/BNM PO22 3 G4
Hotham Wy BOGR PO21 2 E4
Houghton Br ARUN BN18 176 E5
Houghton Cl HAV PO9 * 169 J11
Houghton La PUL/STOR RH20 176 B2
Houghton Rd CRAWE RH10 * 30 B6
Houndean Cl LEWES BN7 55 M5
Houndean Ri LEWES BN7 55 M5
Hova Vls HOVE BN3 76 A7
Hove Park Gdns HOVE BN3 76 A5
Hove Park Rd HOVE BN3 76 B4
Hove Park Vls HOVE BN3 76 A5
Hove Park Wy HOVE BN3 76 B4
Hove Pl HOVE BN3 76 A8
Hove St HOVE BN3 75 M8
Howard Av BURH RH15 46 D5
SELS PO20 99 J6
Howard Ct HOVE BN3 * 75 L3
Howard Pl BRI BN1 4 C3
LHPTN BN17 89 J4
Howard Rd ARUN BN18 66 F3
BRIE/ROTT BN2 5 J3
CRAWW RH11 28 C7
LAN/SOMP BN15 72 B4
LHPTN BN17 89 H4
SWTR RH13 11 L2
Howard St WTHG BN11 12 E4
Howards Wy ANG/EP BN16 90 A6
Howard Ter BRI BN1 4 C3
Hoylake Cl CRAWW RH11 28 C4
Hoyle La MIDH GU29 155 M5
Hudson Cl LIPH GU30 117 R2
SALV BN13 70 C7
Hudson Dr ANG/EP BN16 90 C5
Hudson Rd CRAWE RH10 9 H7
Hughes Cl BOGR PO21 103 L1
Hughes Rd BRIE/ROTT BN2 77 G5
Hugo Platt EPSF GU31 134 H5
Hulbert Rd HAV PO9 56 D2
WVILLE PO7 168 A10
Humber Av SALV BN13 70 B6
Humber Cl LHPTN BN17 89 L5
SALV BN13 70 B6
Humphrey's Gap SHOR BN43 73 M7
Humphrys Rd WTHG BN11 13 G6
Hundred Acre La
HPPT/KEY BN6 148 E12
Hundredsteddle La SELS PO20 100 C3
Hunnisett Cl SELS PO20 181 M4
Hunstanton Cl CRAWW RH11 28 C4
Hunston Cl BRIE/ROTT BN2 78 E6
Hunter Rd CRAWE RH10 8 E9
EMRTH PO10 80 B2
Hunters Cha LIPH GU30 107 Q12
Hunters Cl BOGR PO21 103 H4
Hunters Ga SELS PO20 * 63 H4
Hunters Md HPPT/KEY BN6 * 164 E3
SWTR RH13 144 F10
Hunters Ms ARUN BN18 64 F2
Hunters Race CCH PO19 61 J2
Hunters Rd LISS GU33 116 G3
Hunters Wy CCH PO19 61 L2
Huntingdon House Dr
GSHT GU26 108 H5
Huntingdon Wy BURH RH15 47 J4
Huntingford Cl GSHT GU26 * 108 F2
Huntsbottom La LISS GU33 116 E10
Hurland La BOR GU35 107 N5
Hurlands La MFD/CHID GU8 112 A8
Hurley Rd SALV BN13 70 D7
Hurn Ct HAV PO9 169 J11
Huron Dr LIPH GU30 117 R2
Hursley Rd HAV PO9 168 E12
Hurst Av HORS RH12 10 E3
WTHG BN11 92 E3
Hurstbourne Cl HAV PO9 * 168 E11
Hurst Cl ARUN BN18 176 F2
CRAWW RH11 28 E5
LIPH GU30 107 P12
Hurst Cottages ARUN BN18 176 F2
Hurst Ct HORS RH12 10 E4
Hurst Crs PTSD BN41 75 G5
Hurst Farm Rd EGRIN RH19 33 J1
Hurstfield LAN/SOMP BN15 72 C8
Hurstfield Cl RHWH RH17 45 K7
Hurst Gdns HPPT/KEY BN6 164 G3
Hurst Green Cl HORN PO8 168 C7
Hurst Hl BRI BN1 53 H8
Hurstlands BIL RH14 141 R2
Hurstmere Cl GSHT GU26 108 G6
Hurston Cl PUL/STOR RH20 159 Q11
SALV BN13 70 F5
Hurston Gv PUL/STOR RH20 159 Q11
Hurston La PUL/STOR RH20 159 N10
Hurst Pk MIDH GU29 136 G2
Hurst Rd ANG/EP BN16 90 D3
HORL RH6 14 D5
HORS RH12 10 E3
HPPT/KEY BN6 165 L5
Hurstville Dr WVILLE PO7 168 A11
Hurst Wickham Cl
HPPT/KEY BN6 165 K4
Hurstwood Av EMRTH PO10 58 F4
Hurstwood La EGRIN RH19 43 J8
RHWH RH17 45 K8
RHWH RH17 47 L1
Hutchinson Cl LHPTN BN17 90 A2
Hutchins Wy HORL RH6 14 E4
Hutton Rd BRI BN1 77 G2
Hyde Cl LEWES BN7 55 K8
Hyde Dr CRAWW RH11 28 D4
Hyde La STEY/UB BN44 49 G4
Hyde Sq STEY/UB BN44 * 49 G3
Hyde St STEY/UB BN44 49 G3
The Hyde BRIE/ROTT BN2 77 L4
Hylands Cl CRAWE RH10 9 M6
Hylden Cl BRIE/ROTT BN2 78 A5
Hylter's La RCCH PO18 153 R12
Hylton Rd PSF GU32 133 N6
Hyndman Cl CRAWW RH11 39 G1
Hyperion Ct CRAWW RH11 28 D5
Hythe Cl WTHG BN11 12 A8
Hythe Rd BRI BN1 76 F3
WTHG BN11 12 A7

I

Ibsley Gv HAV PO9 56 E2
Icarus Pl WVILLE PO7 56 A3
Icarus Wy MSEA/BNM PO22 87 H8
Iden Cl BRIE/ROTT BN2 77 K8
Iden Hurst HPPT/KEY BN6 164 H2
Idsworth Cl HORN PO8 168 F3
Idsworth Rd HORN PO8 168 D2
Ifield Av CRAWW RH11 8 D1
Ifield Dr CRAWW RH11 28 F2
Ifield Gn CRAWW RH11 18 F8
Ifield Pk CRAWW RH11 * 28 E3
Ifield Rd CRAWW RH11 8 B2
HORL RH6 18 D4
Ifield St CRAWW RH11 28 E1
Ifield Wd CRAWW RH11 18 C8
Ifold Bridge La BIL RH14 122 D1
Ifoldhurst BIL RH14 122 D3
Iford Ct HAV PO9 169 J11
Ilex Cl ANG/EP BN16 90 A5
Ilex Ct FERR BN12 * 92 A3
Ilex Wy FERR BN12 92 A3
MSEA/BNM PO22 87 K7
Imadene Crs BOR GU35 107 J5
Imberhorne La EGRIN RH19 23 G6
EGRIN RH19 32 F2
Imberhorne Wy EGRIN RH19 23 G6
Infirmary Dr SWTR RH13 125 P7
Infirmary Ter CCH PO19 6 D1
Ingham Dr BRI BN1 53 J7
Inglecroft Ct LAN/SOMP BN15 * 72 B6
Ingledene Cl HAV PO9 56 E3
Ingle Green Cl FERR BN12 91 K5
Ingleside Crs LAN/SOMP BN15 72 D8
Ingleside Rd LAN/SOMP BN15 72 D8
Inglewood Dr BOGR PO21 103 G4
Ingram Cl ANG/EP BN16 90 A4
HORS RH12 125 R3
Ingram Crs HOVE BN3 75 K5
Ingram Crs East HOVE BN3 75 K6
Ingram Crs West HOVE BN3 75 K6
Ingram Rd STEY/UB BN44 48 B3
Ingram's Green La MIDH GU29 135 R11
MIDH GU29 153 R3
Inham's La RCCH PO18 171 Q12
Inholmes Cl BURH RH15 47 H7
Inholmes Park Rd BURH RH15 47 H6
Inhurst Av WVILLE PO7 168 B9
Inkpen La FROW RH18 34 E8
Inlands Rd RCCH PO18 59 G4
Inmans La PSF GU32 133 Q4
Innerwyke Cl MSEA/BNM PO22 87 G8
Innes Rd HORS RH12 11 K1
Innovation Dr BURH RH15 46 C7
Inval Hl HASM GU27 109 M9
Inverness Rd BRIE/ROTT BN2 5 J1
Inwood Crs BRI BN1 76 C4
Inwood Rd LISS GU33 116 D10
Iona Cl CRAWW RH11 8 B9
Iona Wy HWH RH16 45 H5
Iping Av HAV PO9 168 E12
Iping La MIDH GU29 136 A3
Iping Rd LIPH GU30 117 Q11
MIDH GU29 136 A1
Irene Av LAN/SOMP BN15 72 C6
Iris Cl LHPTN BN17 90 A2
Irvine Rd LHPTN BN17 89 K5
Irving Wk CRAWE RH10 29 K6
Irwin Dr HORS RH12 125 R3
Isaac's La BURH RH15 46 E3
HWH RH16 44 E6
Isabel Crs HOVE BN3 75 K5
Isfield Rd BRI BN1 77 H3
Island La SELS PO20 180 H5
Island Loop SELS PO20 180 H5
Islingword Pl BRIE/ROTT BN2 5 J4
Islingword Rd BRIE/ROTT BN2 5 H3
Islingword St BRIE/ROTT BN2 5 H4
Itchen Cl EPSF GU31 133 M7
Itchenor Rd HISD PO11 98 A3
SELS PO20 99 M1
Itchen Rd HAV PO9 169 J11
Itchingfield Rd SWTR RH13 125 K5
Ivanhoe Cl CRAWW RH11 19 J8
Ivanhoe Pl MSEA/BNM PO22 87 H8
Iveagh Cl CRAWW RH11 29 H8
Ivor Rd BRIE/ROTT BN2 78 B4
Ivory Pl BRIE/ROTT BN2 5 G5
Ivory Wk CRAWW RH11 28 D6
Ivy Arch Cl SALV BN13 179 J11
Ivy Arch Rd SALV BN13 13 H3
Ivy Cl PUL/STOR RH20 161 K8
SELS PO20 64 C6
SWTR RH13 125 P12
Ivy Crs MSEA/BNM PO22 2 F2
Ivydale Rd BOGR PO21 103 M1
Ivydene Crs RCCH PO18 59 J6
Ivydene Gdns HORN PO8 168 B5
Ivy Dene La EGRIN RH19 34 C3
Ivydore Av SALV BN13 70 C5
Ivydore Cl SALV BN13 70 C6
Ivy La MSEA/BNM PO22 2 F3
PUL/STOR RH20 161 K7
SELS PO20 64 C6
Ivy Ms HOVE BN3 * 76 C8
Ivy Pl HOVE BN3 76 C8
WTHG BN11 12 D7

J

Jacaranda Rd BOR GU35 106 G7
Jackdaw Cl CRAWW RH11 29 H1
Jackdaw La HORS RH12 36 D4
Jacken Cl MSEA/BNM PO22 105 H1
Jackrells La SWTR RH13 126 A6
Jackson Rd CRAWW RH11 39 G1
Jacksons Pl HRTF TN7 * 35 J8
Jackson St BRIE/ROTT BN2 5 H4
Jacobean Cl CRAWE RH10 30 B4
Jacobs Cl HORN PO8 150 D8
James Cl SALV BN13 70 E7
James Copse Rd HORN PO8 168 A4
James Rd HAV PO9 56 E3
James St SELS PO20 181 L7
James Watt Wy CRAWE RH10 19 M5
Jane Murray Wy BURH RH15 46 B5
Janes Cl BURH RH15 47 H4
Janes La BURH RH15 47 J5
PETW GU28 138 D7
Jan Smuts Cl LISS GU33 116 G4
Japonica Cl SHOR BN43 74 A4
Japonica Wy HAV PO9 57 K1
Jarvis La STEY/UB BN44 48 C2
Jarvis Rd ARUN BN18 66 E3
Jasmine Cl LHPTN BN17 89 M2
Jasmine Ct HORS RH12 10 C5
Jasmine Gv WVILLE PO7 168 B11
Jasmine Wy BOR GU35 106 H7
HORN PO8 150 D8
Javelin Rd EMRTH PO10 80 B2
Jay Cl HORN PO8 168 B2
SWTR RH13 125 R11
Jays Cl LHPTN BN17 89 J3
Jay's La HASM GU27 120 A2
The Jays BURH RH15 46 D5
Jay Wk CRAWE RH10 32 B4
Jefferies RHWH RH17 131 M5
Jefferies La FERR BN12 92 B4
Jeffreys Av CCH PO19 61 M4
Jengers Md BIL RH14 124 A12
Jenner Rd CRAWE RH10 19 L6
Jennings Wy HORL RH6 15 J6
Jeremy's La RHWH RH17 128 C11
Jerrard Rd SELS PO20 63 J3
Jersey Rd CRAWW RH11 28 F7
FERR BN12 91 L4
Jersey St BRIE/ROTT BN2 5 G4
Jervis Av ANG/EP BN16 90 C4
Jesmond Rd HOVE BN3 75 K6
Jessica Cl WVILLE PO7 168 C8
Jessie Rd HAV PO9 56 D2
Jesters HWH RH16 47 H2
The Jetty MSEA/BNM PO22 105 M1
Jevington Cl SALV BN13 70 A8
Jevington Dr BRIE/ROTT BN2 77 J4
Jew St BRI BN1 4 E6
Jib Cl LHPTN BN17 89 M2
Jobes RHWH RH17 40 E8
Job's La HPPT/KEY BN6 146 G8
Jobson's La HASM GU27 120 B5
Jockey Md HORS RH12 125 R4
Jodrell Cl HORN PO8 168 D2
John Arundel Rd CCH PO19 6 A2
John Howard Cottages
BRIE/ROTT BN2 * 96 E1
Johnson Bank
BRIE/ROTT BN2 * 5 J2
Johnson Dr BURH RH15 47 J6
Johnson Wk CRAWE RH10 29 J6
Johnson Wy ARUN BN18 88 A3
John St BOGR PO21 2 E7
BRIE/ROTT BN2 5 G6
SHOR BN43 73 K6
Jolesfield CRAWW RH11 28 E6
SWTR RH13 144 E9
Jolliffe Rd SELS PO20 99 J6
Jones Sq SELS PO20 181 L7
Jordans Cl CRAWW RH11 29 J1
Jordans Crs CRAWW RH11 19 J8
The Jordans EGRIN RH19 33 K1
Joyce Cl LHPTN BN17 89 H2
Joys Cft CCH PO19 7 H3
Jubilee Av ANG/EP BN16 90 B3
Jubilee Cl HWH RH16 45 K5
Jubilee Ct BRIE/ROTT BN2 * 77 K3
Jubilee Est SWTR RH13 11 G2
Jubilee La GSHT GU26 108 F6
Jubilee Rd BURH RH15 46 D7
CCH PO19 6 F3
HORS RH12 114 A9
STHW BN42 74 F5
Jubilee St BRI BN1 4 E6
Jubilee Ter CCH PO19 6 F2
Jubilee Wk CRAWE RH10 9 M3
Jubilee Wy PUL/STOR RH20 160 C10
Judges Ter EGRIN RH19 33 K1
Juggs La PUL/STOR RH20 160 B4
Juggs Rd LEWES BN7 55 M6
The Juggs PUL/STOR RH20 160 B4
Julian Rd HOVE BN3 4 B3
Juliet Ct WVILLE PO7 * 168 B9
Junction Cl ARUN BN18 88 A3
BURH RH15 47 H5
Junction Ms BURH RH15 47 G6
Junction Rd BRI BN1 4 D4
BURH RH15 47 G5
June Cl BOGR PO21 102 E5
June La MIDH GU29 136 G9
June Mdw MIDH GU29 136 G9
Juniper Cl BOR GU35 106 D7
MSEA/BNM PO22 * 87 K7
PTSD BN41 75 G2
SALV BN13 70 B8
Juniper Rd CRAWW RH11 19 H8
HORN PO8 * 150 D12
Juniper Sq HAV PO9 57 G5
Juno Cl FERR BN12 92 B3
Jupp's La FERR BN12 92 A2
Jura Cl CRAWW RH11 29 G6
Jury La SELS PO20 83 J8
Juventu Cl HAV PO9 57 H2
Juxon Cl CCH PO19 6 F6
CRAWW RH11 28 E5

K

Kassel Cl WVILLE PO7 168 C8
Kay Crs BOR GU35 107 Q3
Kearsley Dr SALV BN13 70 F4
Keats Cl HORN PO8 168 A4
HORS RH12 36 D2
Keats Pl EGRIN RH19 23 J8
Keats Wk BOGR PO21 2 A7
Keble Cl BOGR PO21 103 L2
CRAWE RH10 20 C8
Keelson Wy LHPTN BN17 89 M3
Keepers Wd CCH PO19 61 L2
Kefford Cl HORN PO8 * 168 C3
Kelly Rd HOVE BN3 76 C4
Kelmscott Ri CRAWW RH11 39 G1
Kelsey Av EMRTH PO10 58 F4
Kelsey Cl HORL RH6 14 E6
LISS GU33 116 D8
Kelso Cl CRAWE RH10 30 D2
SALV BN13 92 D1
Kelvin La CRAWE RH10 19 L7
Kelvin Wy CRAWE RH10 19 L7
Kemnal Pk HASM GU27 109 N9
Kemps HPPT/KEY BN6 164 G3
Kempshott Rd HORS RH12 10 B2
Kemp St BRI BN1 4 E5
Kempton Pk WVILLE PO7 168 C8
Kemptown Ms
BRIE/ROTT BN2 * 96 D1
Kemp Town Pl BRIE/ROTT BN2 5 M9
Kemshott Ct HAV PO9 168 E11
Ken Berry Ct HAV PO9 169 J11
Kendal Cl HORN PO8 168 B5
LHPTN BN17 89 M2
Kendale Cl CRAWE RH10 30 B7
Kendal Rd HOVE BN3 75 L5
LAN/SOMP BN15 72 B7
Kenilworth Cl BRIE/ROTT BN2 77 M3
CRAWW RH11 29 G7
Kenilworth Pl BIL RH14 141 R3
Kenilworth Rd BOGR PO21 103 M1
Kenlegh BOGR PO21 103 L3
Kenley Rd BOR GU35 107 Q4
Kenmara Cl CRAWE RH10 20 A8
Kenmara Ct CRAWE RH10 19 M7
Kenmure Av BRI BN1 52 F6
Kennard Ct FROW RH18 * 34 D6
Kennedy Av EGRIN RH19 23 J6
Kennedy Rd SWTR RH13 10 F8
Kennel Hl RCCH PO18 172 H10
Kennel La HORL RH6 14 C7
SWTR RH13 144 D3
Kennet Cl CRAWW RH11 28 E4
SALV BN13 70 C6
Kennet Rd EPSF GU31 133 M7

Kensington Cl
  PUL/STOR RH20 * ... 159 R6
Kensington Gdns *BRI* BN1 ... 4 E5
Kensington Pl *BRI* BN1 ... 4 E5
Kensington Rd *CCH* PO19 ... 7 J3
  CRAWW RH11 ... 29 G7
Kensington St *BRI* BN1 ... 4 E5
Kent Cl *SHOR* BN43 ... 74 B6
Kent Flds *LEWES* BN7 ... 55 H4
Kenton Rd *HOVE* BN3 ... 75 J6
Kent Rd *BOR* GU35 ... 106 G7
  CCH PO19 ... 7 H3
  LHPTN BN17 ... 89 J3
Kent's La *RHWH* RH17 ... 131 P10
Kents Rd *HWH* RH16 ... 45 J6
Kent St *SWTR* RH13 ... 145 P7
Kentstreet La *SWTR* RH13 ... 145 P4
Kentwyns Dr *SWTR* RH13 ... 11 G9
Kenwards *BRI* BN1 ... 53 J6
Kenya Ct *HORL* RH6 * ... 14 E5
Kerry Gdns *ANG/EP* BN16 ... 90 F3
Kerves La *SWTR* RH13 ... 11 H9
Kestrel Cl *CRAWW* RH11 ... 29 H1
  HORN PO8 ... 150 D9
  HORS RH12 ... 36 D4
  HOVE BN3 ... 76 C5
  SELS PO20 ... 99 M7
Kestrel Ct *BOGR* PO21 ... 102 E6
Kestrel Cl *CHAM* PO6 ... 56 A6
Kestrel Rd *CRAWW* RH10 ... 32 B6
Kestrel Wk *CRAWW* RH10 ... 32 B6
Kestrel Wy *LHPTN* BN17 ... 89 H1
Keswick Cl *CRAWW* RH11 ... 28 C5
  FERR BN12 ... 70 C8
Ketche's La *RHWH* RH17 ... 131 P10
Ketch Rd *LHPTN* BN17 ... 89 M5
Kevin Gdns *BRIE/ROTT* BN2 ... 78 D5
Kewell's Cnr *SELS* PO20 ... 82 D8
Kew Gdns *BOGR* PO21 ... 85 L3
Kew St *BRI* BN1 ... 4 D5
Keydell Av *HORN* PO8 ... 168 B4
Keydell Cl *HORN* PO8 ... 168 B4
Keyhaven Dr *HAV* PO9 ... 168 D12
Keymer Ct *BURH* RH15 ... 47 C3
Keymer Crs *FERR* BN12 ... 92 B4
Keymer End *HWH* RH16 * ... 45 G6
Keymer Gdns *BURH* RH15 ... 47 G8
Keymer Pde *BURH* RH15 ... 47 G7
Keymer Pk *HPPT/KEY* BN6 ... 165 Q6
Keymer Rd *BRI* BN1 ... 53 G8
  BURH RH15 ... 47 G8
  CRAWW RH11 ... 8 E7
  HPPT/KEY BN6 ... 165 N6
Keymer Ter *HPPT/KEY* BN6 * ... 165 P6
Keymer Wy *FERR* BN12 ... 92 B4
Keynor La *SELS* PO20 ... 101 K5
Keysford La *HWH* RH16 ... 130 H6
Keystone Cl *FERR* BN12 ... 92 B2
Khandala Gdns *WVILLE* PO7 ... 56 A1
Kidborough Rd *CRAWW* RH11 ... 28 E5
Kidbrook *HWH* RH16 ... 45 L3
Kidders La *HFD* BN5 ... 163 K1
Kidd Rd *CCH* PO19 ... 62 A4
Kidmans Cl *HORS* RH12 ... 36 E4
Kidworth Cl *HORL* RH6 ... 14 E4
Kildare Rd *BOR* GU35 ... 106 G5
Killinghurst La *HASM* GU27 ... 110 B13
Kilmore Cl *SALV* BN13 ... 178 H11
Kilnbarn Ct *HWH* RH16 * ... 45 G7
Kilnbarn Wy *HWH* RH16 ... 45 G7
Kiln Fld *LISS* GU33 ... 116 D3
Kilnfield Rd *HORS* RH12 ... 114 A9
Kiln Flds *HASM* GU27 ... 109 M9
Kiln La *EPSF* GU31 ... 151 K1
  HORL RH6 ... 14 L4
  HWH RH16 ... 45 L4
Kilnmead *CRAWE* RH10 ... 9 G2
Kilnmead Cl *CRAWE* RH10 ... 9 G2
Kiln Rd *CRAWE* RH10 ... 32 A2
The Kiln *BURH* RH15 ... 47 J6
Kiln Wy *GSHT* GU26 ... 108 B4
Kilnwood Cl *SELS* PO20 ... 181 L6
Kilnwood La *HORS* RH12 ... 27 M6
  RING/NEW BN8 ... 167 F7
Kilsham La *PETW* GU28 ... 157 J1
Kilwich Cl *MSEA/BNM* PO22 ... 87 J7
Kimber Cl *LAN/SOMP* BN15 ... 72 C3
Kimberley Cl *HORL* RH6 ... 14 D6
Kimberley Rd *BRIE/ROTT* BN2 ... 77 J5
  CRAWE RH10 ... 30 C4
  LISS GU33 ... 116 F3
Kimbers *PSF* GU32 ... 133 M5
Kimbridge Crs *HAV* PO9 ... 168 H11
Kimbridge Rd *SELS* PO20 ... 99 M7
Kimpton Ct *HAV* PO9 * ... 169 J11
Kindersley Cl *EGRIN* RH19 ... 24 A6
Kinfauns Dr *SALV* BN13 ... 13 C2
King Alfred Cl *STEY/UB* BN44 ... 48 C3
King Edward Av *SALV* BN13 ... 13 J2
King Edward Cl *SALV* BN13 ... 13 J2
  SWTR RH13 ... 125 N7
King Edward Rd *SWTR* RH13 ... 125 N7
Kingfisher Cl *BOR* GU35 ... 106 H7
  CRAWE RH10 ... 19 M8
  HAV PO9 ... 169 J8
  SALV BN13 ... 70 B8
Kingfisher Dr *EMRTH* PO10 ... 58 C1
  LHPTN BN17 ... 89 H1
Kingfisher La *CRAWE* RH10 ... 32 B4
Kingfisher Ri *EGRIN* RH19 ... 33 L1
Kingfisher Wy *HORS* RH12 ... 36 B4
  PSF GU32 ... 133 N5
King George Av *EGRIN* RH19 ... 23 H6
King George Gdns *CCH* PO19 ... 6 D3
King George Ms *PSF* GU32 ... 133 N5
King George Rd *SHOR* BN43 ... 74 B4
King George VI Av *HOVE* BN3 ... 75 M2
King George VI Dr *HOVE* BN3 ... 75 M2
King George VI Man
  HOVE BN3 ... 75 L3
King La *PSF* GU32 ... 132 G1
King Pl *BRI* BN1 ... 4 D6
King's Arms Hl *ARUN* BN18 ... 67 G2
King's Av *CCH* PO19 ... 6 D8
Kings Barn End
  STEY/UB BN44 * ... 48 E2
King's Barn La *STEY/UB* BN44 ... 162 D12
King's Barn Vls *STEY/UB* BN44 ... 48 E2
Kingsbridge Ms *SALV* BN13 ... 70 C6
Kingsbury Dr *HORN* PO8 ... 150 D9
Kingsbury Rd *BRI* BN1 ... 4 F3
Kingsclere Av *HAV* PO9 ... 168 E12
Kings Cl *ARUN* BN18 ... 87 M2
  HAV PO9 ... 168 H7
  LAN/SOMP BN15 ... 72 G4
Kings Copse *EGRIN* RH19 ... 33 L1
Kingscote Hl *CRAWW* RH11 ... 8 A7

Kings Ct *SELS* PO20 ... 181 L5
  SWTR RH13 ... 11 G4
Kings Crs *BN43* ... 73 J8
Kingscroft Ct *HAV* PO9 ... 56 K5
King's Croft La *HAV* PO9 ... 56 D4
Kings Dr *BOGR* PO21 ... 103 G5
  HPPT/KEY BN6 ... 165 N5
  MIDH GU29 ... 137 J2
  SHOR BN43 ... 73 J7
King's Esp *HOVE* BN3 ... 75 M8
Kingsey Av *EMRTH* PO10 ... 57 M5
Kingsfernsden La *PSF* GU32 ... 133 P4
Kingsfield *PUL/STOR* RH20 ... 160 B11
Kingsfold Cl *BIL* RH14 ... 142 A3
Kingsfold Ct *HORS* RH12 * ... 26 A4
Kings Gap *SHOR* BN43 ... 73 J8
King's Gdns *HOVE* BN3 ... 76 A8
Kingsgate *CRAWW* RH10 * ... 9 G3
Kings Ga *HAV* PO9 ... 10 B5
Kingsham Av *CCH* PO19 ... 7 G5
Kingsham Rd *CCH* PO19 ... 7 G5
Kings Head Ms *EPSF* GU31 * ... 135 L2
Kingsland Cl *PUL/STOR* RH20 ... 160 B11
  SHOR BN43 ... 74 B6
Kingsland Ct *CRAWW* RH10 * ... 9 M3
Kingsland Rd *SALV* BN13 ... 71 K1
Kings La *PUL/STOR* RH20 ... 158 D6
  PUL/STOR RH20 ... 159 N4
  SWTR RH13 ... 125 R9
  SWTR RH13 ... 145 K1
Kingslea *SWTR* RH13 ... 11 H4
Kingslea Ms *BIL* RH14 * ... 142 A3
Kingsley Cl *HORL* RH6 ... 14 E4
  SALV BN13 ... 13 M1
Kingsley Rd *BRI* BN1 ... 76 C4
  CRAWW RH11 ... 28 F6
  HORL RH6 ... 14 E4
Kingsmead *LHPTN* BN17 ... 67 H8
  MSEA/BNM PO22 ... 3 J1
Kingsmead Cl *STEY/UB* BN44 ... 48 C5
Kingsmead Pl *HORS* RH12 ... 125 M2
Kingsmead Rd *HORS* RH12 ... 125 M2
  MSEA/BNM PO22 ... 87 M7
Kings Mede *HORN* PO8 ... 168 C3
Kingsmere *BRI* BN1 * ... 76 D5
Kings Ms *HORS* RH12 ... 36 A7
  SHOR BN43 ... 74 A7
Kingsmill Rd *MSEA/BNM* PO22 ... 65 H7
King's Pde *BOGR* PO21 ... 103 M5
  BRI BN1 * ... 76 F3
The Kings Peace *GSHT* GU26 * ... 108 F6
Kingspit La *PETW* GU28 ... 139 D7
Kings Platt *SWTR* RH13 ... 143 M9
Kings Ride *BURH* RH15 ... 47 J3
King's Rd *BRI* BN1 ... 4 B7
  EMRTH PO10 ... 57 M5
  HASM GU27 ... 109 K11
  HORL RH6 ... 14
  HORN PO8 ... 168 A6
  HWH RH16 ... 45 J7
  LAN/SOMP BN15 ... 72 D8
  PSF GU32 ... 133 L8
  STHW BN42 ... 74 C4
  SWTR RH13 ... 11 H3
Kings Rd Arches *BRI* BN1 ... 4 D8
King's Stone Av *STEY/UB* BN44 ... 48 C5
King's Ter *EMRTH* PO10 ... 58 A5
Kingsthorpe Rd *HOVE* BN3 ... 75 K5
Kingston Bay Rd *SHOR* BN43 ... 74 B7
Kingston Broadway
  SHOR BN43 ... 74 B4
Kingston Cl *BRI* BN1 ... 53 K7
  HOVE BN3 ... 75 K3
  SHOR BN43 ... 74 B5
Kingston La *ANG/EP* BN16 ... 91 G4
  STHW BN42 ... 74 C6
Kingston Rdg *LEWES* BN7 ... 55 J7
Kingston Rd *LEWES* BN7 ... 55 M7
Kingston Wy *SHOR* BN43 ... 74 B4
King St *ARUN* BN18 ... 66 F2
  BRI BN1 ... 4 E6
  EGRIN RH19 ... 23 K3
  EMRTH PO10 ... 58 B5
  EMRTH PO10 ... 58 C2
  SALV BN13 ... 13 J1
Kings Wk *SHOR* BN43 ... 73 J8
Kings Wy *BURH* RH15 ... 47 J3
Kingsway *BOGR* PO21 ... 103 J4
  HOVE BN3 ... 75 J7
  SELS PO20 ... 181 M7
  WTHW BN11 * ... 92 E3
Kingswood Cl *PUL/STOR* RH20 ... 159 Q6
Kingswood Firs *GSHT* GU26 ... 108 F7
Kingswood La *GSHT* GU26 ... 108 F7
Kingswood St *BRIE/ROTT* BN2 ... 4 F7
Kingsworthy Rd *HAV* PO9 ... 57 G2
Kinleside Wy *ANG/EP* BN16 ... 68 F4
Kinnell Cl *EMRTH* PO10 ... 58 A5
Kipling Av *BRIE/ROTT* BN2 ... 78 D5
  FERR BN12 ... 92 A2
Kipling Cl *CRAWE* RH10 ... 30 B1
Kipling Ct *SWTR* RH13 * ... 11 M2
Kipling Wy *EGRIN* RH19 ... 23 H9
Kippens La *SWTR* RH13 * ... 144 A3
Kirdford Cl *ANG/EP* BN16 ... 90 A5
  BURH RH15 ... 47 H8
  CRAWW RH11 ... 28 F1
Kirdford Rd *ARUN* BN18 ... 66 F3
  BIL RH14 ... 122 H11
Kirkby Cl *RCCH* PO18 ... 63 J2
Kirk Knoll *BOR* GU35 ... 107 N4
Kirkland Cl *HAV* PO9 ... 90 A4
Kitchener Rd *LISS* GU33 ... 116 F3
Kites Cl *CRAWW* RH11 ... 8 D3
Kithurst Cl *ANG/EP* BN16 ... 90 D5
  CRAWW RH11 ... 8 E7
  FERR BN12 ... 92 A1
Kithurst Crs *FERR* BN12 ... 92 A1
Kithurst Farm Rd
  PUL/STOR RH20 ... 177 Q1
Kithurst La *PUL/STOR* RH20 ... 159 R12
Kithurst Pk *PUL/STOR* RH20 ... 159 Q12
Kitsmead *CRAWE* RH10 ... 20 F7
Kittiwake Cl *CRAWW* RH11 ... 28 C5
Kitts La *RFNM* GU10 ... 108 A1
Kitwood Gn *HAV* PO9 * ... 169 J12
Knepp Cl *BRIE/ROTT* BN2 ... 77 L3
  CRAWE RH10 ... 30 B3
Knighton Cl *CRAWE* RH10 ... 20 C7
Knightons La *MFD/CHID* GU8 ... 112 A5
Knightscroft Av *ANG/EP* BN16 ... 90 B5
Knightscroft Ct *ANG/EP* BN16 ... 90 A5
Knight's Hl *RCCH* PO18 ... 172 H4
Knightwood Av *HAV* PO9 ... 168 H12
Knob Hl *HORS* RH12 ... 115 R4
Knockhundred La *GSHT* GU26 ... 108 E9

Knockhundred Rw
  MIDH GU29 ... 137 J9
Knole Cl *CRAWE* RH10 ... 30 C2
Knole Gv *EGRIN* RH19 ... 23 H6
Knole Rd *BRIE/ROTT* BN2 ... 97 M4
Knoll Cl *HOVE* BN3 ... 75 J4
Knoll Rd *HWH* RH16 ... 45 L5
  HWH RH16 * ... 130 E8
Knowle Cl *CRAWE* RH10 ... 21 H6
Knowle Dr *CRAWW* RH11 ... 21 G6
Knowle La *CRAN* GU6 ... 113 L1
  HORS RH12 ... 113 N8
Knowles Meadow *LISS* GU33 ... 116 E12
The Knowle *BOR* GU35 ... 107 Q3
  RHWH RH17 ... 44 B2
Knowsley Ter
  MFD/CHID GU8 * ... 110 H5
Knox Rd *HAV* PO9 ... 56 E4
Knoyle Rd *BRI* BN1 ... 76 D3
Kymer Gdns *HPPT/KEY* BN6 ... 165 P6
Kynon Gdns *MSEA/BNM* PO22 ... 87 J3
Kyoto Ct *BOGR* PO21 ... 103 M2

L

Laburnum Av *HOVE* BN3 ... 75 K4
Laburnum Cl *FERR* BN12 ... 91 L4
  LAN/SOMP BN15 ... 94 C1
Laburnum Gv *BRI* BN1 * ... 77 G2
  CCH PO19 ... 6 F5
  MSEA/BNM PO22 ... 2 C1
Laburnum Ms *BOGR* PO21 * ... 2 E6
Laburnum Wy *HWH* RH16 ... 45 L5
Lackenhurst La *SWTR* RH13 ... 143 J3
Lacock Cl *SELS* PO20 ... 100 B8
Ladbroke Rd *HORL* RH6 ... 14 C4
Ladies Mile Rd *BRI* BN1 ... 52 E7
Ladies' Mile Rd *BRI* BN1 ... 52 D7
Ladydell Rd *WTHW* BN11 ... 13 L3
Ladygate Dr *GSHT* GU26 ... 108 D6
Lady Margaret Rd
  CRAWW RH11 ... 28 F2
Ladymead Cl *CRAWE* RH10 ... 30 B4
Ladysmith Pl *BOR* GU35 ... 106 F4
Ladysmith Rd *BRIE/ROTT* BN2 ... 77 J5
Lagness Rd *BOGR* PO21 ... 84 C4
Lagoon Rd *BOGR* PO21 ... 102 E4
Lagwood Cl *HPPT/KEY* BN6 ... 165 M6
Laine Cl *BRI* BN1 ... 76 D2
Laines Rd *STEY/UB* BN44 ... 48 B3
Lake Dr *BOR* GU35 ... 106 H6
Lake La *ARUN* BN18 ... 65 L8
  HORL RH6 ... 15 H4
  MSEA/BNM PO22 ... 65 J7
Lake Rd *CCH* PO19 ... 7 K5
Lakers Meadow *BIL* RH14 ... 142 A1
Lakeside *HORS* RH12 ... 36 B4
  MIDH GU29 ... 136 H11
Lakeside Dr *SWTR* RH13 ... 125 R12
Lakeside Gdns *HAV* PO9 ... 57 H3
Lakesmere Rd *HORN* PO8 ... 168 D3
Lake Vw *BOGR* PO21 ... 102 F4
Lake View Rd *EGRIN* RH19 ... 22 A6
  EGRIN RH19 ... 23 H6
Lamberhurst Wk *CRAWE* RH10 * ... 9 M6
Lambert's La *MIDH* GU29 ... 137 J3
Lambeth Cl *CRAWW* RH11 ... 29 G7
Lambeth Wk *CRAWW* RH11 * ... 29 G7
Lambleys La *SALV* BN13 ... 71 K3
Lambourn Cl *EGRIN* RH19 ... 23 K6
Lambourne La *BRI* BN1 ... 77 H3
  CRAWE RH10 ... 30 C4
Lambourne Rd *BRI* BN1 ... 77 H3
Lambs Crs *HORS* RH12 ... 36 E4
Lambs Farm Cl *HORS* RH12 ... 36 F4
Lambs Farm Rd *HORS* RH12 ... 36 E4
Lambs Green Rd *HORS* RH12 ... 27 L4
Lambyn Cft *HORL* RH6 ... 15 H5
Lamerton Rd *BOR* GU35 ... 106 F5
Lammas Cl *LHPTN* BN17 ... 89 K2
Lamorna Gdns *FERR* BN12 ... 91 L5
  SELS PO20 ... 64 C7
Lamorna Gv *SALV* BN13 ... 71 H7
Lanark Ct *SWTR* RH13 ... 11 L6
Lancaster Cl *CRAWE* RH10 ... 20 C8
Lancaster Dr *EGRIN* RH19 ... 23 M6
Lancaster Pl *MSEA/BNM* PO22 ... 2 D1
Lancaster Rd *BRI* BN1 ... 76 D3
  FERR BN12 ... 92 D4
Lancaster Wy *WVILLE* PO7 ... 168 A11
Lancastrian Gra *CCH* PO19 * ... 6 D3
Lancelot Cl *CRAWW* RH11 ... 28 D3
Lancing Cl *CRAWW* RH11 ... 28 F2
  LAN/SOMP BN15 ... 72 C7
Lancing Ct *HORS* RH12 ... 11 M1
Lancing Pk *LAN/SOMP* BN15 ... 94 C1
Landen Pk *HORL* RH6 ... 14 D4
Landseer Dr *SELS* PO20 ... 181 M6
Landseer Rd *HOVE* BN3 ... 75 M5
Lands End La *BOR* GU35 ... 106 H4
Lane End *MFD/CHID* GU8 ... 110 G1
Lane End Dr *EMRTH* PO10 ... 58 A5
Lane End Rd *MSEA/BNM* PO22 ... 87 M8
Lanercost Rd *CRAWW* RH11 ... 8 D2
The Lane *BIL* RH14 ... 122 D1
  CCH PO19 ... 61 L3
Lanfranc Rd *SALV* BN13 ... 12 C3
Langbrook Cl *HAV* PO9 ... 57 G5
Langbury Cl *FERR* BN12 ... 91 K2
Langbury La *FERR* BN12 ... 91 K2
Langdale Av *CCH* PO19 ... 7 J3
Langdale Cl *LAN/SOMP* BN15 ... 72 D8
Langdale Gdns *HOVE* BN3 ... 75 L7
Langdale Rd *CRAWW* RH11 ... 28 F2
  HOVE BN3 ... 75 L7
Langham Gdns *WTHG* BN11 ... 12 B6
Langhurst Cl *HORS* RH12 ... 26 C5
Langhurst La *CRAWW* RH11 ... 27 M1
Langhurstwood Rd *HORS* RH12 ... 26 D5
Langley Cl *LHPTN* BN17 ... 88 D5
Langley Gv *BOGR* PO21 ... 103 H4
Langley La *CRAWW* RH11 ... 28 F1
Langley Pde *CRAWW* RH11 ... 19 H6
Langley Wk *CRAWW* RH11 ... 19 H6
Langmead Cl *LHPTN* BN17 ... 88 D5
Langridge Dr *EGRIN* RH19 ... 33 K1
  PTSD BN41 ... 74 F3
Langridge La *HWH* RH16 ... 45 J4
Langridge Wy *BURH* RH15 ... 46 D4

Langrish Cl *HAV* PO9 ... 168 H11
Langshott *HORL* RH6 ... 15 J5
Langshott La *HORL* RH6 ... 15 H5
Langstone Av *HAV* PO9 ... 57 G6
Langstone Br *HAV* PO9 ... 57 H8
Langstone Gdns *RCCH* PO18 ... 59 J5
Langstone High St *HAV* PO9 ... 57 G7
Langstone Rd *HAV* PO9 ... 57 G6
Langton Cl *SELS* PO20 ... 181 K7
Langton Dr *BOR* GU35 ... 107 P2
Langton La *HPPT/KEY* BN6 ... 164 F1
Langton Pl *PUL/STOR* RH20 * ... 160 A12
Langton Rd *CCH* PO19 ... 6 A3
  SALV BN13 ... 13 G2
Lansbury Rd *CRAWW* RH11 ... 29 G8
Lansdown Cl *HORS* RH12 ... 37 G3
  WTHG BN11 ... 12 A6
Lansdowne Ms *HOVE* BN3 ... 76 C7
Lansdowne Pl *HOVE* BN3 ... 76 C7
  WTHG BN11 ... 12 A5
Lansdowne Rd *ANG/EP* BN16 ... 68 E7
  HOVE BN3 ... 76 C7
  LHPTN BN17 ... 89 J2
Lansdowne Sq *HOVE* BN3 ... 76 C7
Lansdowne St *HOVE* BN3 ... 76 C7
Lansdowne Wy *ANG/EP* BN16 ... 68 E7
Lantana Cl *WVILLE* PO7 ... 168 A11
Lanyards *LHPTN* BN17 ... 89 M2
Lanyon Cl *HORS* RH12 ... 36 F3
Lanyon Ms *HORS* RH12 * ... 36 F3
Lapwing Cl *HORN* PO8 ... 168 B2
  SWTR RH13 ... 11 K3
Larch Cl *ANG/EP* BN16 ... 90 C4
  BRIE/ROTT BN2 ... 78 E6
  CCH PO19 ... 61 L3
  LIPH GU30 ... 117 Q2
  MSEA/BNM PO22 ... 86 B7
Larch End *HORS* RH12 ... 10 A3
  PUL/STOR RH20 ... 160 A6
The Larches *EGRIN* RH19 ... 23 M5
  HORS RH12 ... 37 H3
Larches Wy *CRAWE* RH10 ... 32 B1
Larchfield Cl *BOGR* PO21 ... 103 J4
Larchfield Wy *HORN* PO8 ... 168 D4
Larch Rd *BOR* GU35 ... 107 Q3
Larch Wy *HWH* RH16 ... 45 L5
Larchwood Av *HAV* PO9 ... 56 C1
Larcombe Rd *PSF* GU32 ... 133 L8
Large Acres *SELS* PO20 ... 181 K6
Larke Cl *SHOR* BN43 ... 74 B6
Larkfield Cl *LAN/SOMP* BN15 ... 72 E8
  HORL RH6 ... 15 M6
Larkfield Wy *BRI* BN1 ... 76 F1
Lark Hl *HOVE* BN3 ... 75 K2
Larkins Rd *HORL* RH6 ... 19 J2
Lark Ri *CRAWE* RH10 ... 32 B3
  CRAWW RH11 ... 29 H1
  LIPH GU30 ... 107 P12
Larksfield *HORL* RH6 ... 15 G5
Larkspur Cl *LHPTN* BN17 ... 89 H1
Larkspur Wy *SWTR* RH13 ... 125 R10
Larks Vw *BIL* RH14 ... 141 R1
Lasham Gn *HAV* PO9 * ... 169 J12
Lashmar Rd *ANG/EP* BN16 ... 90 F4
Lashmere *CRAWW* RH11 ... 21 J6
Latchmore Forest Gv
  HORN PO8 ... 168 A6
Latchmore Gdns *HORN* PO8 ... 168 A6
Latham Cl *LHPTN* BN17 ... 89 G3
Latham Rd *SELS* PO20 ... 181 K7
Latimer Cl *CRAWW* RH11 ... 19 J8
Latimer Rd *WTHG* BN11 ... 92 E4
Laud Dr *CRAWE* RH10 ... 30 C4
Lauder Cl *EMRTH* PO10 ... 58 E3
Laughton Rd *BRIE/ROTT* BN2 ... 78 E5
  HORS RH12 ... 36 E2
Laundry Wy *RDKG* RH5 ... 16 B4
Laurel Cl *BURH* RH15 ... 47 H4
  CRAWE RH10 ... 9 M8
  SALV BN13 ... 70 B8
Laurel Dene *EGRIN* RH19 ... 23 L8
Laurel Gv *MSEA/BNM* PO22 ... 86 B7
Laurel Mt *PUL/STOR* RH20 ... 159 K3
Laurel Rd *HORN* PO8 ... 168 D5
The Laurels *BRIE/ROTT* BN2 * ... 5 L5
  CRAWE RH10 ... 19 M8
  HFD BN5 ... 163 K4
  SWTR RH13 ... 125 Q11
Laurel Wk *SWTR* RH13 ... 11 J7
Lauriston Rd *BRI* BN1 ... 76 D3
Laurus Cl *WVILLE* PO7 ... 168 B12
Lavant Cl *CRAWW* RH11 ... 28 E4
  FERR BN12 ... 91 M1
  HORN PO8 ... 168 C8
Lavant Down Rd *RCCH* PO18 ... 172 B10
Lavant Dr *HAV* PO9 ... 57 G2
Lavant Rd *CCH* PO19 ... 61 L2
Lavant St *PSF* GU32 ... 133 M6
Lavender Cl *BOR* GU35 ... 106 G7
Lavender Hl *SHOR* BN43 ... 74 A4
Lavender Rd *WVILLE* PO7 ... 168 B11
Lavender St *BRIE/ROTT* BN2 ... 5 H8
Lavington Cl *CRAWW* RH11 ... 28 E2
Lavington Rd *SALV* BN13 ... 71 H7
Lavinia Ct *FERR* BN12 ... 92 B2
Lavinia Wy *ANG/EP* BN16 ... 90 F4
Lawns Rd *HORS* RH12 ... 113 P6
The Lawns *ANG/EP* BN16 ... 90 F6
  LAN/SOMP BN15 ... 72 B6
Lawnswood Cl *HORN* PO8 ... 168 A6
The Lawn *BOGR* PO21 ... 103 K3
  LAN/SOMP BN15 ... 94 C1
Lawrence Av *ANG/EP* BN16 ... 90 C5
Lawrence Cl *SELS* PO20 ... 181 L7
Lawrence Rd *HOVE* BN3 ... 75 L4
Lawrie La *HWH* RH16 ... 45 L4
Laws Cl *CRAWW* RH11 ... 28 C4
Lawyer's La *HFD* BN5 ... 162 H4
Laylands Rd *PTSD* BN41 ... 74 F3
The Layne *MSEA/BNM* PO22 ... 87 M8
Lazy Acre *EMRTH* PO10 ... 58 E5
Lea Cl *CRAWW* RH11 ... 28 E4
Leacroft *EGRIN* RH19 ... 23 J7
Lea Farm La *PUL/STOR* RH20 ... 158 D3
Leahurst Court Rd *BRI* BN1 ... 76 D2
Leaman Cl *MSEA/BNM* PO22 ... 87 L3
Leander Rd *RCCH* PO18 ... 60 B8
Lea Rd *MSEA/BNM* PO22 ... 2 D2
The Leas *ANG/EP* BN16 ... 90 D2
  BURH RH15 ... 46 E5
Leatherbottle La *CCH* PO19 ... 7 K4
Lechford Rd *HORL* RH6 ... 14 C4
Leckford Rd *HAV* PO9 ... 169 J11
Leconfield Rd *LAN/SOMP* BN15 ... 72 C4

Ledbury Wy *BOGR* PO21 ... 103 G3
Ledgers Meadow *RHWH* RH17 ... 44 C3
Ledra Dr *BOGR* PO21 ... 103 G5
Leechpond Hl *SWTR* RH13 ... 127 M1
Leechpool La *SWTR* RH13 ... 11 M1
Leecroft *BOGR* PO21 ... 103 K3
Leeds Cl *SALV* BN13 ... 70 A8
  SWTR RH13 ... 125 P13
Leeside *HORS* RH12 * ... 27 H3
Lee St *HORL* RH6 ... 14 D5
Leeward Cl *SALV* BN13 ... 70 E8
Leeward Rd *LHPTN* BN17 ... 89 L4
  SALV BN13 ... 70 E8
Legion Wy *SELS* PO20 ... 99 M9
Legsheath La *EGRIN* RH19 ... 33 J8
Leicester St *BRIE/ROTT* BN2 ... 5 H7
Leicester Vls *HOVE* BN3 ... 75 J6
Leighlands *CRAWE* RH10 ... 30 B1
Leigh Rd *CCH* PO19 ... 6 C7
  HAV PO9 ... 57 G3
  SALV BN13 ... 71 J7
Leighton Av *SALV* BN13 ... 71 J7
Leighton Rd *HOVE* BN3 ... 75 M5
  RHWH RH17 ... 131 M8
Leinster Gdns *MSEA/BNM* PO22 ... 87 J3
Leith View Rd *HORS* RH12 ... 36 F4
Le May Cl *HORL* RH6 ... 14 F5
Lemmington Wy *HORS* RH12 ... 36 F4
Lemon Gv *BOR* GU35 ... 106 F8
Lenham Rd West
  BRIE/ROTT BN2 ... 97 M4
Lenhurst Wy *SALV* BN13 ... 70 E8
Lennox Rd *CCH* PO19 ... 7 F2
  HOVE BN3 ... 75 L5
  SHOR BN43 ... 74 A5
  WTHG BN11 ... 13 H3
Lennox St *BOGR* PO21 ... 2 E8
  BRIE/ROTT BN2 ... 5 J8
Lensyd Gdns *HORN* PO8 ... 168 A3
Leonardslee Ct *CRAWE* RH10 * ... 30 A4
Leonard Wy *SWTR* RH13 ... 11 J6
Leonora Dr *BOGR* PO21 ... 103 H4
Leopold Cl *MSEA/BNM* PO22 ... 3 M2
Leopold Rd *BRI* BN1 ... 4 C5
  CRAWW RH11 ... 8 C4
Lesser Foxholes *SHOR* BN43 ... 73 J4
Lester Av *HAV* PO9 ... 56 D3
Letchworth Cl *FERR* BN12 ... 91 K4
Level Mare La *SELS* PO20 ... 64 C2
Leveret La *CRAWW* RH11 ... 29 G1
Leverton Av *MSEA/BNM* PO22 ... 105 J1
Lewes Rd *BOGR* PO21 ... 103 J3
  CRAWE RH10 ... 30 D2
Lewes Crs *BRIE/ROTT* BN2 ... 96 D2
Lewes Ms *BRIE/ROTT* BN2 * ... 96 D2
Lewes Rd *BRI* BN1 ... 53 M7
  BRIE/ROTT BN2 ... 96 D2
  EGRIN RH19 ... 33 M1
  FROW RH18 ... 34 D6
  HPPT/KEY BN6 ... 166 D2
  HWH RH16 ... 45 L2
  RHWH RH17 ... 45 L2
  RHWH RH17 ... 131 M5
Lewes St *BRIE/ROTT* BN2 ... 5 L4
Lewin Cl *LAN/SOMP* BN15 ... 72 F2
Lewis Ct *SALV* BN13 ... 70 A8
Lewisham Cl *CRAWW* RH11 ... 29 H7
Lewis La *ARUN* BN18 ... 88 A2
Lewis Rd *CCH* PO19 ... 7 G3
  EMRTH PO10 ... 58 B2
  SELS PO20 ... 181 K6
Leybourne Cl *BRIE/ROTT* BN2 * ... 77 M4
  CRAWW RH11 ... 29 H1
Leybourne Pl *EGRIN* RH19 ... 22 E6
Leybourne Rd *BRIE/ROTT* BN2 ... 77 M3
Leyfield *HPPT/KEY* BN6 ... 164 E4
Leylands Pk *BURH* RH15 ... 47 G4
Leylands Rd *BURH* RH15 ... 46 F5
Ley Rd *MSEA/BNM* PO22 ... 105 J2
The Leys *HASM* GU27 ... 119 K8
  RCCH PO18 ... 172 H2
Leyton Lea *RHWH* RH17 ... 44 C3
Liam Cl *HAV* PO9 ... 57 H1
Library Gdns *HAV* PO9 ... 56 F2
Library Pl *WTHG* BN11 ... 13 H4
Lichfield Ct *WTHG* BN11 * ... 13 K2
Lichfield Gdns *BOGR* PO21 ... 103 K2
Lidsey Cl *CRAWW* RH11 ... 29 H1
Lidsey Rd *MSEA/BNM* PO22 ... 86 C2
Lifeboat Wy *SELS* PO20 ... 181 L8
Lilac Cl *BOR* GU35 ... 106 G7
  HAV PO9 ... 57 G3
  MSEA/BNM PO22 ... 87 K7
  SALV BN13 ... 70 B8
Lillywhite Cl *BURH* RH15 ... 46 E4
Limbourne La *PUL/STOR* RH20 ... 158 C2
Limbrick Cl *FERR* BN12 ... 92 B2
Limbrick Cnr *FERR* BN12 ... 92 B2
Limbrick La *FERR* BN12 ... 92 B2
Limbrick Wy *FERR* BN12 ... 92 B1
Lime Av *HORS* RH12 ... 11 L1
  SELS PO20 ... 64 D8
Lime Cha *PUL/STOR* RH20 ... 160 A11
Lime Cl *CCH* PO19 ... 7 H2
  CRAWE RH10 ... 21 G6
  HAV PO9 ... 19 H8
Lime Kiln La *PSF* GU32 ... 132 D10
  PSF GU32 ... 150 F1
Lime Kiln Rd *SWTR* RH13 ... 126 H3
Lime Rd *SALV* BN13 ... 178 H11
Limes Av *HORL* RH6 ... 15 G8
Limes Cl *LIPH* GU30 ... 107 R10
  LISS GU33 ... 116 C9
The Limes *ARUN* BN18 ... 87 L2
  BRIE/ROTT BN2 * ... 5 G1
  EGRIN RH19 ... 22 F4
  SALV BN13 ... 178 H10
Lime Tree Av *SALV* BN13 ... 70 E8
Lime Tree Cl *ANG/EP* BN16 * ... 90 E3
Limmard Wy *SALV* BN13 ... 70 D8
Limmer La *MSEA/BNM* PO22 ... 3 L4
Limney Rd *BRIE/ROTT* BN2 ... 5 L4
Linacre Dr *CRAN* GU6 ... 113 R3
  HORS RH12 ... 113 R6
Lincett Av *SALV* BN13 ... 92 E2
Linchmere Pl *CRAWW* RH11 ... 28 F2
Linchmere Rd *HASM* GU27 ... 118 F2
Linch Rd *LIPH* GU30 ... 118 D10
  MIDH GU29 ... 136 D1
Lincoln Av *BOGR* PO21 ... 103 H1
Lincoln Cl *CRAWE* RH10 ... 30 K6
Lincoln Cottages
  BRIE/ROTT BN2 * ... 5 H4
Lincoln Gn *CCH* PO19 ... 61 L4

Lincoln Ri *HORN* PO8 .....168 C5
Lincoln Rd *PTSD* BN41 .....75 G6
  SALV BN13 .....92 E1
Lincoln St *BRIE/ROTT* BN2 .....5 H4
Lincoln Wd *HWH* RH16 .....44 F4
Lindale Rd *PUL/STOR* RH20 * 160 A12
Lind Cl *WVILLE* PO7 .....56 A2
Linden Av *EGRIN* RH19 .....23 H7
  HORS RH12 .....11 H1
Linden Cl *CRAWE* RH10 .....9 M9
  HORS RH12 .....11 H1
Linden Dr *LISS* GU33 .....116 C9
Linden Gv *HWH* RH16 .....45 K3
Linden Pk *LHPTN* BN17 .....89 H1
Linden Rd *BOGR* PO21 .....2 C5
  BOR GU35 .....107 Q4
  LHPTN BN17 .....89 H4
Lindens Cl *EMRTH* PO10 .....58 A2
The Lindens *BRIE/ROTT* BN2 * 5 G2
  CRAWE RH10 .....21 G6
Linden Wy *HAV* PO9 * 57 G2
  HORN PO8 .....168 C4
Lindfield *PTSD* BN41 .....74 F4
Lindfield Rd *RHWH* RH17 .....130 F3
Lindford Cha *BOR* GU35 .....107 J4
Lindford Rd *BOR* GU35 .....106 H3
Lindford Wey *BOR* GU35 .....107 J4
Lindgren Wk *CRAWW* RH11 * 29 G8
Lindsey Ct *MSEA/BNM* PO22 .....3 M1
Lindum Rd *SALV* BN13 .....70 E8
Lindum Wy *SALV* BN13 .....70 E8
Lineside Wy *LHPTN* BN17 .....89 G3
Linfield Copse *PUL/STOR* RH20 .....160 C7
The Linfields *PUL/STOR* RH20 * 160 C7
Linford Cl *HAV* PO9 .....168 G10
Ling Crs *BOR* GU35 .....107 Q3
Lingfield Cl *SALV* BN13 .....70 E7
Lingfield Dr *CRAWE* RH10 .....30 D2
Lingfield Rd *EGRIN* RH19 .....23 J4
Lingfield Wy *SELS* PO20 .....181 M6
Link 10 *CRAWE* RH10 .....19 M8
Linkenholt Wy *HAV* PO9 .....168 D12
Link Hl *PUL/STOR* RH20 .....159 Q12
Link La *PUL/STOR* RH20 .....159 K3
Links Av *MSEA/BNM* PO22 .....3 J3
Links Cl *PTSD* BN41 .....75 H5
Linkside East *GSHT* GU26 .....108 E2
Linkside North *GSHT* GU26 .....108 E2
Linkside South *GSHT* GU26 .....108 E3
Linkside West *GSHT* GU26 .....108 E2
Links La *HAV* PO9 .....169 J6
Links Rd *LAN/SOMP* BN15 .....72 C5
  PTSD BN41 .....75 H5
  SALV BN13 .....70 F5
The Links *BOR* GU35 .....106 E8
The Link *CRAWW* RH11 .....8 E3
  WVILLE PO7 .....168 B8
Link Wy *BOGR* PO21 .....102 F4
Linkway *HORL* RH6 .....20 B2
The Linkway *BRI* BN1 .....77 G3
  WTHG BN11 .....12 K4
Linnell Cl *CRAWW* RH11 * 39 G1
Linnet Cl *CRAWE* RH10 .....32 B4
  EPSF GU31 .....133 R7
  LHPTN BN17 .....89 H1
Linnett Cl *CRAWE* RH10 * 32 B4
Linsted La *BOR* GU35 .....107 L2
Linton Rd *HOVE* BN3 .....75 L5
Lintott Gdns *SWTR* RH13 .....11 H3
Lionel Av *MSEA/BNM* PO22 .....87 H7
Lion La *CRAWE* RH10 .....31 M5
  GSHT GU26 .....109 J8
Lion Md *HASM* GU27 .....109 J11
Lion Rd *BOGR* PO21 .....102 F4
Lions Ct *BRIE/ROTT* BN2 * 77 K8
Lions Fld *BOGR* PO21 .....106 C4
Lion St *CCH* PO19 .....6 E4
Liphook Cl *BRI* BN1 .....77 H4
Liphook Rd *BOR* GU35 .....106 F9
  BOR GU35 .....107 J4
  HASM GU27 .....108 H11
  HASM GU27 .....118 D1
Lisher Rd *LAN/SOMP* BN15 .....72 E6
Lisle Wy *EMRTH* PO10 .....57 M2
Lismore Crs *CRAWW* RH11 * 8 A4
Lister Av *EGRIN* RH19 .....33 K3
Listers *RHWH* RH17 .....128 A8
Lith Av *HORN* PO8 .....168 D1
Lith La *HORN* PO8 .....150 D12
Litle Hyden La *HORN* PO8 .....150 C6
Litten Ter *CCH* PO19 .....6 F3
Little Ashfield *MIDH* GU29 .....136 H9
Little Babbsham *BOGR* PO21 .....103 K3
Little Barn Pl *LISS* GU33 .....116 E9
Little Bentswood *HWH* RH16 .....45 J4
Little Black Hl *HWH* RH16 .....45 L2
Little Boultons *SELS* PO20 .....85 L5
Little Breach *CCH* PO19 .....6 C1
Little Bridges Cl *SWTR* RH13 .....125 Q12
Little Cl *SWTR* RH13 .....143 Q2
Little Comptons *SWTR* RH13 .....11 K6
Little Copse Rd *HPPT/KEY* BN6 .....165 M5
Littlecote *CRAWE* GU28 .....139 L10
Little Court *CRAWW* RH11 * 7 J4
Little Crabtree *CRAWW* RH11 * 7 J4
Little Crs *BRIE/ROTT* BN2 .....97 M4
Little Dipper's *PUL/STOR* RH20 * 159 K4
Little Dro *FERR* BN12 * 91 K4
Little Dro *STEY/UB* BN44 .....48 C4
Little East St *BIL* RH14 .....124 A12
  BRI BN1 * 4 E8
Littlefield Cl *SELS* PO20 .....181 L5
Littlefield Rd *CCH* PO19 .....7 H6
Little Finches *SWTR* RH13 .....144 F10
Little Gables *SALV* BN13 .....70 E7
Little Grebe *HORS* RH12 .....56 J1
Littlegreen Av *HAV* PO9 .....57 J1
Littlehampton Rd *FERR* BN12 * 91 H2
  SALV BN13 .....70 E7
Little Hatch *HORS* RH12 .....56 J1
Little Haven La *HORS* RH12 .....11 K1
Littleheath Rd *ARUN* BN18 .....66 A4
Little High St *BOGR* PO21 * 2 D8
  SHOR BN43 .....73 K6
  WTHG BN11 .....13 H4
Litle Hyden La *HORN* PO8 .....150 D6
Little King St *EGRIN* RH19 .....23 K5
Little Ledgers *RHWH* RH17 * 44 C3
Little London *CCH* PO19 .....6 D3
Little Md *FERR* BN12 * 92 B3
  RING/NEW BN8 .....R10
Little Paddocks Wy *FERR* BN12 * 91 L4
Littlepark Av *HAV* PO9 * 56 C2
Little Pembrokes *WTHG* BN11 * 12 A4
Little Preston St *BRI* BN1 * 4 B7

Littlestone Rd *SALV* BN13 .....70 D7
Littleton Gv *HAV* PO9 .....57 G1
Little Western St *BRI* BN1 .....76 C8
Littleworth Cl *BRIE/ROTT* BN2 .....78 E6
Littleworth La *SWTR* RH13 .....144 F5
Liverpool Gdns *WTHG* BN11 .....13 H6
Liverpool Rd *CRAWE* RH10 .....13 H6
Liverpool Ter *WTHG* BN11 .....13 H5
Livesay Crs *SALV* BN13 .....13 H1
Livingstone Rd *BURH* RH15 .....46 E6
  CRAWE RH10 .....9 H7
  HOVE BN3 .....76 A6
  SWTR BN43 .....10 E7
Livingstone St *BRIE/ROTT* BN2 .....5 L6
Lizard Head *LHPTN* BN17 .....89 M3
Lloyd Cl *HOVE* BN3 .....76 B5
Lloyd Goring Cl *ANG/EP* BN16 .....68 C3
Lloyd Rd *HOVE* BN3 .....76 C5
Lloyds Ct *CRAWE* RH10 * 19 K8
Loats La *SELS* PO20 .....180 H5
Lobster La *SELS* PO20 .....180 H5
Lobs Wood La *PUL/STOR* RH20 * 160 A11
Lockerley Rd *HAV* PO9 .....57 H2
Locke Rd *LIPH* GU30 .....118 A1
Lockgate Rd *SELS* PO20 .....101 K2
Lockitt Wy *LEWES* BN7 .....55 K8
Lock La *SELS* PO20 .....82 E7
Locksash Cl *SELS* PO20 .....99 E3
Locks La *RCCH* PO18 .....170 B1
Locksheath Cl *HAV* PO9 .....168 E11
Locks Hl *PTSD* BN41 .....75 G4
Lockwood Cl *BRIE/ROTT* BN2 .....78 D6
  HORS RH12 .....36 F4
Lockwood Cl *CRAWE* RH10 * 29 L1
Lockwood Crs *BRIE/ROTT* BN2 .....78 D6
Lockwood Rd *SALV* BN13 .....70 B5
Loder Gdns *SALV* BN13 .....71 H8
Loder Pl *BRI* BN1 .....76 E3
Loder Rd *BRI* BN1 .....76 E3
Lodgebury Cl *EMRTH* PO10 .....58 F5
Lodge Cl *CRAWW* RH11 .....8 C4
  EGRIN RH19 .....23 H8
  LEWES BN7 .....55 M5
  MSEA/BNM PO22 .....87 M8
  PTSD BN41 .....74 E3
Lodge Ct *BOGR* PO21 .....103 K3
  SHOR BN43 .....73 K4
Lodge Gn *PETW* GU28 .....157 K5
Lodge Hill La *HPPT/KEY* BN6 .....165 R6
Lodgelands *RHWH* RH17 .....130 E3
Lodge La *HAV* PO9 .....170 A3
  HPPT/KEY BN6 .....165 Q8
  RHWH RH17 .....146 C2
Lodge Rd *HAV* PO9 .....56 C4
Lodsworth Cl *BRIE/ROTT* BN2 * 77 L6
  HORS RH12 .....36 F4
Lodsworth Rd *BOGR* PO21 .....103 C2
Lombard St *PETW* GU28 .....139 L9
Lombardy Ri *WVILLE* PO7 .....168 A12
Lomond Av *BRI* BN1 .....52 F6
London La *RHWH* RH17 .....44 C3
London Rd *ARUN* BN18 .....64 F2
  ARUN BN18 .....66 F2
  ARUN BN18 .....175 R11
  BOGR PO21 .....2 E7
  BRI BN1 .....4 F2
  BRI BN1 .....52 D6
  BURH RH15 .....46 E6
  CRAWE RH10 .....8 F1
  CRAWE RH10 .....23 K6
  EGRIN RH19 .....23 Q4
  EPSF GU31 .....133 Q4
  FROW RH18 .....34 D5
  HFD BN5 .....163 K2
  HORL RH6 .....19 M1
  HORN PO8 .....150 E11
  HORN PO8 .....168 B7
  HORS RH12 .....10 C5
  HPPT/KEY BN6 .....165 M4
  LIPH GU30 .....118 C12
  PUL/STOR RH20 .....158 C8
  PUL/STOR RH20 .....159 J3
  PUL/STOR RH20 .....178 H2
  RHWH RH17 .....44 B2
  RHWH RH17 .....129 N1
  RHWH RH17 .....131 K5
London St *WTHG* BN11 .....12 E4
London Ter *BRI* BN1 * 4 F2
Long Acre *CRAWE* RH10 .....31 M1
Longacre Cl *LISS* GU33 .....116 D9
Longacre Crs *RHWH* RH17 .....44 C1
Longacre La *SELS* PO20 .....181 K7
Longbridge Rd *HORL* RH6 .....14 E8
Longbridge Wy *HORL* RH6 .....14 E8
Longbrook *MSEA/BNM* PO22 .....3 J6
Longchamp Cl *HORL* RH6 .....15 H6
Long Copse La *EMRTH* PO10 .....58 E7
Long Cross Hl *BOR* GU35 .....107 M4
Longdene Rd *HASM* GU27 .....109 L11
Long Down *EPSF* GU31 .....133 Q5
Longfellow Rd *WTHG* BN11 .....57 M2
Longfield Rd *EMRTH* PO10 .....125 R5
  HORS RH12 .....10 B6
Long Furlong *SALV* BN13 .....69 K8
Longfurlong La *SALV* BN13 .....69 K1
Long Hl *SWTR* RH13 .....127 L9
Longhill Cl *BRIE/ROTT* BN2 * 97 K2
Longhill Rd *BRIE/ROTT* BN2 * 97 J7
Longhurst *BURH* RH15 .....47 J7
Longhurst Rd *CRAWW* RH11 * 28 F8
Longland Av *PUL/STOR* RH20 * 159 R11
Longlands *SALV* BN13 .....71 J5
Longlands Gld *SALV* BN13 .....71 J5
Longlands Rd *EMRTH* PO10 .....58 D1
  SELS PO20 .....99 L7
Longlands Spinney *SALV* BN13 * 71 J5
Long La *ARUN* BN18 .....175 P12
  RCCH PO18 .....152 H10
Long Md *ARUN* BN18 .....65 J4
Longmead *LISS* GU33 .....116 C10
Longmead Gdns *HAV* PO9 .....57 G4
Long Meadow *SALV* BN13 .....69 J1
Longmeadow Vls *HORL* RH6 * 18 D4
Longmere Rd *CRAWE* RH10 .....29 J1
Longmoor Dr *LIPH* GU30 .....117 J4
Longmoor Rd *LIPH* GU30 .....117 K4
  LISS GU33 .....116 B1
Long Park Cnr *HPPT/KEY* BN6 .....166 A7
Longport Rd *MSEA/BNM* PO22 .....3 P4
Long Rd *PSF* GU32 .....133 P4
Longships *LHPTN* BN17 .....89 M3

Longstock Rd *HAV* PO9 .....169 J11
Longwood Av *HORN* PO8 .....168 A6
Longwood Vw *CRAWE* RH10 .....9 K3
The Loop *MSEA/BNM* PO22 .....105 H1
Loose La *LAN/SOMP* BN15 .....71 M8
Loppets Rd *CRAWE* RH10 .....9 J8
Lordings La *PUL/STOR* RH20 .....160 A6
Lordings Rd *BIL* RH14 .....141 N4
Loriners *CRAWE* RH10 .....8 C4
Lorna Rd *HOVE* BN3 .....76 C6
Lorne Rd *BRI* BN1 .....4 F1
Lotts La *LAN/SOMP* BN15 .....72 B7
Loudoun Rd *LHPTN* BN17 .....89 H4
Louisburg Rd *BOR* GU35 .....106 G3
Lovage Wy *HORN* PO8 .....150 D12
Lovedean La *HORN* PO8 .....150 B11
  HORN PO8 .....168 B4
Love La *EPSF* GU31 .....133 Q5
Loveletts *CRAWW* RH11 .....28 F4
Lovells Cl *BOGR* PO21 .....103 G3
Lover's Wk *BRI* BN1 .....76 E5
Lovers Walk Cottages
  BRI BN1 * 76 D5
Lovett Ct *FERR* BN12 * 92 B1
Loveys Rd *ARUN* BN18 .....87 L3
Lowdells Cl *EGRIN* RH19 .....23 H5
Lowdells Dr *EGRIN* RH19 .....23 J5
Lowdells La *EGRIN* RH19 .....23 H6
Lowe Cl *CRAWW* RH11 .....39 G1
Lower Barn Cl *HORS* RH12 .....36 E4
Lower Beach Rd *SHOR* BN43 .....72 E7
Lower Bere Wd *WVILLE* PO7 * 168 A10
Lower Bevendean Av
  BRIE/ROTT BN2 .....77 K4
Lower Bognor Rd *BOGR* PO21 * 103 K1
  SELS PO20 .....85 G7
Lower Chalvington Pl
  BRIE/ROTT BN2 * 5 H8
Lower Church Rd *BURH* RH15 .....46 F6
Lower Dene *EGRIN* RH19 .....23 M8
Lower Dr *STHW* BN42 .....74 D4
Lower Faircox *HFD* BN5 .....163 J4
Lower Forecourt *HORL* RH6 * 20 A2
Lower Grove Rd *HAV* PO9 .....57 H5
Lower Hanger *HASM* GU27 .....108 F11
Lower Heyshott *EPSF* GU31 .....133 P5
Lower Hone La *RCCH* PO18 .....81 M4
Lower Market St *HOVE* BN3 .....5 C8
Lower Md *EPSF* GU31 .....116 C9
  LISS GU33 .....33 L1
Lower Mere *CRAWE* RH10 .....20 B8
Lower Rd *HASM* GU27 .....109 Q7
  HAV PO9 .....56 D4
  RCCH PO18 .....172 D12
Lower Rock Gdns
  BRIE/ROTT BN2 * 5 H8
Lower Station Rd *BIL* RH14 .....142 A3
  HFD BN5 .....163 J5
  RING/NEW BN8 .....149 R7
Lower St *HASM* GU27 .....109 M11
  PUL/STOR RH20 .....158 A4
  PUL/STOR RH20 .....159 J3
Lower Tandridge Wy
  HORS RH12 .....10 B6
Lower Village *HWH* RH16 .....44 F8
Lower Wardown *EPSF* GU31 .....133 Q5
Loweswater Gdns *BOR* GU35 .....106 C4
Lowfield Heath Rd *HORL* RH6 .....18 E3
Lowfield Rd *HWH* RH16 .....124 G2
  SWTR RH13 .....124 G2
Lowfield Wy *HORL* RH6 .....19 K4
Lowlands Rd *BURH* RH15 .....47 G4
Lowther Rd *BRI* BN1 .....76 F3
  SALV BN13 .....70 E6
Loxley Gdns *SALV* BN13 * 12 A3
Loxwood *ANG/EP* BN16 .....91 G2
Loxwood Av *SALV* BN13 .....71 G8
Loxwood Farm Pl *BIL* RH14 .....122 C1
Loxwood Rd *BIL* RH14 .....112 G10
  BIL RH14 .....122 B3
  BIL RH14 .....123 J1
  CRAN GU6 .....112 G5
  HORN PO8 .....168 A3
Loxwood Wk *CRAWW* RH11 * 28 E2
Luard Ct *HAV* PO9 .....57 J4
Lucas *RHWH* RH17 .....131 N4
Lucas Cl *EGRIN* RH19 .....23 L8
Lucas Fld *HASM* GU27 .....108 H11
Lucas Gra *RHWH* RH16 .....45 G4
Lucas Rd *HORS* RH12 .....115 P9
Lucastes Av *HWH* RH16 .....44 F4
Lucastes La *HWH* RH16 .....44 F4
Lucastes Rd *HWH* RH16 .....44 F4
Lucas Wy *HWH* RH16 .....44 F4
Lucerne Av *PTSD* BN41 .....75 J4
Lucerne Cl *BOGR* PO21 .....103 K3
Lucerne Dr *CRAWE* RH10 .....30 C5
Lucerne Rd *BRI* BN1 .....76 F4
Lucking La *MSEA/BNM* PO22 .....87 J6
Lucksfield Wy *ANG/EP* BN16 .....68 F3
Lucraft Rd *BRIE/ROTT* BN2 .....53 L8
Ludlow Cl *BOGR* PO21 .....103 K3
Ludlow Ri *BRIE/ROTT* BN2 * 77 M4
Ludshott Gv *BOR* GU35 .....107 Q4
Luffs Meadow *PETW* GU28 .....139 Q4
  HFD BN5 .....163 K3
Luggs Cl *BIL* RH14 .....142 A1
Lullington Av *HOVE* BN3 .....75 L5
Lulworth Cl *CRAWW* RH11 * 8 A9
Lumley Rd *EMRTH* PO10 .....58 B4
  HORL RH6 .....14 F6
Lunce's Hl *HWH* RH16 .....47 L1
Lundy Cl *CRAWW* RH11 .....29 H6
  LHPTN BN17 .....89 M5
Lupin Cl *LHPTN* BN17 .....89 M2
Lurgashall *BURH* RH15 .....47 H8
Lustrells Rd *BRIE/ROTT* BN2 .....97 M3
Lutener Rd *MIDH* GU29 .....137 J7
Luther St *BRIE/ROTT* BN2 .....5 J5
The Luth *BIL* RH14 .....123 J12
  BIL RH14 .....140 H1
Lutman St *EMRTH* PO10 .....57 M1
Lutyens Cl *CRAWW* RH11 .....28 D5
Luxford Rd *HORS* RH12 .....36 E4
Luxford Rd *HWH* RH16 .....45 L2
Luxfords La *EGRIN* RH19 .....34 A4
Luxford Wy *BIL* RH14 .....141 N2
Lychgate Dr *HORN* PO8 .....168 C2
The Lychgates *ARUN* BN18 .....87 L1
Lye La *RCCH* PO18 .....60 E1
Lymbourn Rd *HAV* PO9 .....57 H4
Lyminster Av *BRI* BN1 .....52 F9
Lyminster Rd *ARUN* BN18 .....67 J4
  LHPTN BN17 .....67 J3
Lynchborough Rd *LIPH* GU30 .....170 L9
Lynch Down *RCCH* PO18 .....170 H11
Lynchet Cl *BRI* BN1 .....77 H3

Lynchet Down *BRI* BN1 .....77 H3
Lynchets Crs *HOVE* BN3 .....75 J2
The Lynchette *SHOR* BN43 .....73 L4
Lynchet Wk *BRI* BN1 .....77 H3
Lynchmere Av *LAN/SOMP* BN15 .....72 C5
Lyndhurst Cl *CRAWW* RH11 .....9 G4
Lyndhurst Cnr *BRIE/ROTT* BN3 * 76 C5
Lyndhurst Farm Cl *EGRIN* RH19 .....22 C5
Lyndhurst Rd *CCH* PO19 .....7 C5
  HOVE BN3 .....13 J5
  WTHG BN11 .....13 H5
Lyndum Cl *PSF* GU32 .....133 N6
Lyndum Pl *BOR* GU35 * 107 J4
Lyne Pl *HORN* PO8 .....168 C3
Lyn Rd *SALV* BN13 .....70 B7
Lynton Cl *EGRIN* RH19 .....23 M7
Lynton Cl *HORS* RH12 .....10 C3
Lyon Cl *CRAWE* RH10 .....30 B7
  HOVE BN3 .....76 C6
Lyon Cl *SWTR* RH13 .....124 G2
Lyons Rd *SWTR* RH13 .....124 H2
Lyon St *BOGR* PO21 .....2 D6
Lyon St West *BOGR* PO21 .....2 D6
Lyons Wy *SALV* BN13 .....71 K5
Lyoth La *HWH* RH16 .....45 L4
Lyric Cl *CRAWW* RH11 .....30 C5
Lysander Wy *SELS* PO20 .....63 J4
  WVILLE PO7 .....168 B9
Lyss Ct *LISS* GU33 .....116 C9
Lythe La *PSF* GU32 .....132 H4
Lytton Dr *CRAWE* RH10 .....30 C2

M

Mackerelclose *SELS* PO20 .....180 H5
Mackie Av *BRI* BN1 .....52 E7
  HPPT/KEY BN6 .....165 P4
Macklin Rd *MSEA/BNM* PO22 * 3 L4
Macleod Rd *SWTR* RH13 .....11 J7
Maddox Dr *CRAWE* RH10 .....30 C4
Madehurst Cl *ANG/EP* BN16 .....90 D5
  BRIE/ROTT BN2 * 5 M7
Madehurst Ct *CRAWW* RH11 * 28 E6
Madehurst Wy *LHPTN* BN17 .....89 J3
Madeira Av *HORS* RH12 .....10 B6
  MSEA/BNM PO22 .....3 M4
  WTHG BN11 .....13 K5
Madeira Dr *BRIE/ROTT* BN2 * 5 G3
Madeira Pde *MSEA/BNM* PO22 * 3 M4
Madeira Pl *BRIE/ROTT* BN2 .....5 G3
Madeline Rd *EPSF* GU31 .....133 N5
Madgwick La *RCCH* PO18 .....62 C4
Mafeking Rd *BRIE/ROTT* BN2 .....77 J4
Magdalene Ct *CRAWE* RH10 .....20 B8
Magdalene Rw *PSF* GU32 .....133 M6
Magellan Ter *CRAWE* RH10 * 19 M7
Magnolia Cl *SALV* BN13 .....70 A8
Magnolia Wy *HORN* PO8 .....168 D5
Magpie Cl *BOR* GU35 .....106 H7
  SWTR RH13 .....126 E4
Magpie La *SELS* PO20 .....181 J4
Magpie Rd *HORN* PO8 .....169 K4
Maidenbower Dr *CRAWE* RH10 .....30 C5
Maidenbower La *CRAWE* RH10 .....30 C5
Maiden La *CRAWW* RH11 .....29 H1
Maidment Cl *HFD* BN5 .....163 J3
Main Dr *MSEA/BNM* PO22 .....87 L2
  ARUN BN18 .....87 L2
  EMRTH PO10 .....58 D2
  RCCH PO18 .....59 G6
  RCCH PO18 .....173 M4
  STEY/UB BN44 .....100 D3
Mainstone Rd *HOVE* BN3 .....75 K6
Maismore Gdns *EMRTH* PO10 .....57 L5
Maizecroft *HORL* RH6 .....15 H5
Major Cl *BRI* BN1 .....77 G4
Major's Hl *CRAWE* RH10 .....31 M9
Malcolm Cl *BRI* BN12 .....91 K4
Malcolm Gdns *HORL* RH6 .....14 C8
Malcolm Rd *SELS* PO20 .....63 H4
Malden Pl *PUL/STOR* RH20 * 160 A12
Maldon Rd *BRI* BN1 .....76 C3
Malham Cl *CRAWE* RH10 .....30 B6
Malin Rd *LHPTN* BN17 .....89 M4
Mallard Cl *HASM* GU27 .....108 H11
  HAV PO9 .....14 F4
  HORS RH12 .....36 B4
Mallard Crs *BOGR* PO21 .....102 E6
Mallard Pl *EGRIN* RH19 .....33 L1
Mallard Rd *HAV* PO9 .....169 J8
Mallards La *SELS* PO20 .....180 H5
The Mallards *HAV* PO9 .....57 G6
Mallard Wy *EMRTH* PO10 .....58 D1
  HFD BN5 .....163 K3
Mallion's La *RHWH* RH17 .....128 A7
Mallon Dene *ANG/EP* BN16 .....90 B5
Mallory Rd *HOVE* BN3 .....76 A5
Mallow Cl *BOR* GU35 .....107 K4
  HORS RH12 .....36 D3
  WVILLE PO7 .....168 A11
Malmsbury Rd *BOR* GU35 .....106 G4
Malthouse Cl *ARUN* BN18 .....66 F3
  LAN/SOMP BN15 .....72 C5
Malthouse La *BRIE/ROTT* BN2 .....46 B6
  HPPT/KEY BN6 .....165 K1
  RCCH PO18 .....60 A2
Malthouse Mdw *LIPH* GU30 .....117 M3
Malthouse Pas *LHPTN* BN17 .....89 J3
Malthouse Rd *CRAWE* RH10 .....2 B7
  SELS PO20 .....181 L6
Malthouse Wy *LEWES* BN7 .....167 K10
The Maltings *BIL* RH14 .....124 A12
  BURH RH15 .....46 B6
  HPPT/KEY BN6 .....165 K1
  RCCH PO18 .....60 A2
Maltravers Dr *LHPTN* BN17 .....89 K5
Maltravers St *ARUN* BN18 .....66 F3
Malvern Cl *WTHG* BN11 .....94 A2
Malvern Ms *EMRTH* PO10 .....58 A4
Malvern Rd *CRAWW* RH11 .....8 D7
  LISS GU33 .....116 E11
Malvern St *HOVE* BN3 .....76 A4

Malvern Wy *BOGR* PO21 .....103 G4
Malwood Cl *HAV* PO9 .....168 H11
Manaton Cl *HWH* RH16 .....45 J5
Manchester St *BRIE/ROTT* BN2 .....4 F8
Manet Sq *MSEA/BNM* PO22 .....86 A7
Manhood La *SELS* PO20 .....101 L5
Manica Cl *BOR* GU35 .....106 C6
Manitoba Wy *SELS* PO20 .....70 B7
Manley's Hl *PUL/STOR* RH20 .....160 A12
Mann Cl *CRAWW* RH11 .....39 G1
Manning Rd *EGRIN* RH19 .....23 J7
Mannings Rd *LHPTN* BN17 .....89 H3
Mannings Cl *CRAWE* RH10 .....20 C8
Manor Av *HPPT/KEY* BN6 .....165 P4
Manor Cl *ANG/EP* BN16 .....90 E4
  BRIE/ROTT BN2 .....77 K8
  BURH RH15 .....47 J5
  CCH PO19 .....83 L2
  HASM GU27 .....108 H11
  HAV PO9 .....57 G4
  HFD BN5 .....163 L4
  HORL RH6 .....14 E6
  LAN/SOMP BN15 .....72 E6
  LAN/SOMP BN15 .....73 C7
  MSEA/BNM PO22 .....3 L4
  PUL/STOR RH20 .....160 A12
  STHW BN42 .....74 F5
  WTHG BN11 .....12 C6
Manor Ct *ANG/EP* BN16 .....90 A3
  BURH RH15 * 47 H4
  HORS RH12 * 11 L1
  LAN/SOMP BN15 .....72 C5
  PUL/STOR RH20 .....160 A12
  STHW BN42 * 74 F6
  HASM GU27 .....108 H11
Manor Crs *BRIE/ROTT* BN2 .....77 K8
  HASM GU27 .....108 H11
Manor Dr *HORL* RH6 .....14 E6
  RHWH RH17 .....44 B2
Manor Farm Cl *SELS* PO20 .....181 L5
Manor Farm La *SELS* PO20 .....181 L5
Manor Field Ct *SALV* BN13 * 71 J8
Manorfields *CRAWW* RH11 .....28 C7
Manor Flds *LIPH* GU30 .....118 A1
  SWTR RH13 .....11 M2
Manor Gdns *BRIE/ROTT* BN2 .....77 K8
  EMRTH PO10 .....58 E4
  HPPT/KEY BN6 .....164 G3
Manor Gn *BRIE/ROTT* BN2 .....77 K8
Manor Hall Rd *STHW* BN42 .....74 F5
Manor Hl *BRIE/ROTT* BN2 .....77 K7
Manor La *SELS* PO20 .....84 C7
  SELS PO20 .....181 M6
  SWTR RH13 .....126 G1
Manor Lea *WTHG* BN11 * 12 D7
Manor Lodge Rd *HAV* PO9 .....168 H8
Manor Paddock
  BRIE/ROTT BN2 .....96 D1
Manor Pde *SALV* BN13 * 70 C6
Manor Pk *BOGR* PO21 .....102 F4
Manor Pl *BOGR* PO21 .....2 D7
  BRIE/ROTT BN2 .....96 D1
Manor Rd *ANG/EP* BN16 .....90 B3
  BRIE/ROTT BN2 .....96 D1
  BURH RH15 .....47 H4
  EGRIN RH19 .....23 H7
  EMRTH PO10 .....58 E4
  HFD BN5 .....163 L4
  HORS RH12 .....36 E4
  HPPT/KEY BN6 .....164 G3
  LAN/SOMP BN15 .....72 E6
  PTSD BN41 .....75 G4
  SELS PO20 .....181 M6
  STEY/UB BN44 .....49 H3
  WTHG BN11 .....12 C6
Manor Royal *CRAWE* RH10 .....19 K8
The Manor *WTHG* BN11 * 12 C6
Manor View Ct *SALV* BN13 .....71 J8
Manor Vls *RCCH* PO18 .....60 E8
Manor Wy *BOGR* PO21 .....103 H4
  BRIE/ROTT BN2 .....77 K8
  EMRTH PO10 .....58 E4
  HFD BN5 .....163 L4
  LAN/SOMP BN15 .....72 E6
  PTSD BN41 .....75 G4
  SELS PO20 .....181 M5
  STEY/UB BN44 .....49 H3
  WTHG BN11 .....12 C6
Mansbergh Rd *CCH* PO19 .....62 D3
Mansell Rd *SHOR* BN43 .....73 L4
Manser Rd *ARUN* BN18 .....65 L4
Mansfield Cl *WTHG* BN11 .....93 M1
Mansfield Rd *HOVE* BN3 .....75 K6
  MSEA/BNM PO22 .....2 A3
  WTHG BN11 .....93 M2
Mansion Cl *BURH* RH15 .....47 H4
Mant Cl *LHPTN* BN17 .....88 C4
  PUL/STOR RH20 .....160 A12
Mantling Rd *LHPTN* BN17 .....89 J3
Manton Cl *SELS* PO20 .....100 B8
Manton Rd *BRIE/ROTT* BN2 * 77 K4
Mant Rd *PETW* GU28 .....139 L10
Maple Cl *BIL* RH14 .....123 R12
  BRIE/ROTT BN2 .....78 D6
  BURH RH15 .....47 G4
  CRAWW RH11 .....19 H8
  EMRTH PO10 .....58 A3
  HORS RH12 .....36 F4
  HWH RH16 .....45 L6
  MSEA/BNM PO22 .....87 K7
  SALV BN13 .....70 D4
Maple Crs *HORN* PO8 .....150 D7
Mapledown Cl *SWTR* RH13 .....125 Q11
Maple Dr *BURH* RH15 .....47 G4
  EGRIN RH19 .....23 M8
Maple Gdns *HOVE* BN3 .....75 J6
  MSEA/BNM PO22 .....86 B6
Maplehurst Rd *CCH* PO19 .....61 M2
  PTSD BN41 .....74 F1
  SWTR RH13 .....125 Q11
Maple Leaf *PUL/STOR* RH20 .....158 D7
Maple Leaf Dr *BOR* GU35 .....106 C6
Maple Ldg *HASM* GU27 .....119 P1
Maple Pde *ARUN* BN18 * 65 K5
  BIL RH14 .....142 A2
Maple Rd *ARUN* BN18 .....65 K5
  BIL RH14 .....142 A2
The Maples *FERR* BN12 .....91 L5
Mapletree Av *HORS* RH12 .....168 D5
Maple Wk *LAN/SOMP* BN15 .....72 A6
Maple Wy *BOR* GU35 .....107 Q3
Maple Wd *HAV* PO9 .....56 D4
Mapsons La *SELS* PO20 .....181 K5
Marama Gdns *ANG/EP* BN16 .....90 A6
Marchants Cl *ANG/EP* BN16 .....90 A6
Marchants Rd *HPPT/KEY* BN6 .....164 H3
Marchants Rd *HPPT/KEY* BN6 .....164 H3
Marchants Wy *BURH* RH15 .....46 C6
Marches Rd *HORS* RH12 .....115 N5
The Marches *HASM* GU27 .....119 L8
  HORS RH12 .....26 A4
Marchwood *CCH* PO19 .....61 M2

Marchwood Ga CCH PO19 * 61 M2
Marchwood Rd HAV PO9 .... 168 F11
Marcuse Flds RCCH PO18 .... 59 M8
Mardale Rd SALV BN13 .... 70 E7
Marden Av CCH PO19 .... 83 K2
The Mardens CRAWW RH11 .... 8 A1
Marden Wy EPSF GU31 .... 133 P6
Mardyke SHOR BN43 .... 73 J7
Mare Hill Rd PUL/STOR PO20 .... 159 N4
Maresfield Rd BRIE/ROTT BN2 ... 77 K8
Margaret Cl BOGR PO21 .... 103 K2
Margaret St BRIE/ROTT BN2 .... 5 C8
Margery Rd HOVE BN3 .... 75 J3
Marian Wy BOGR PO21 .... 3 C6
Marigolds Ldg ANG/EP BN16 * 90 A5
The Marigolds
  MSEA/BNM PO22 * 86 C4
Marina Cl EMRTH PO10 .... 58 B5
Marina Wy BRIE/ROTT BN2 .... 96 C2
Marine Av HOVE BN3 .... 75 J4
Marine Cl SELS PO20 .... 99 K7
  WTHG BN11 .... 12 A8
Marine Crs FERR BN12 .... 92 C4
Marine Dr BRIE/ROTT BN2 .... 96 C3
  BRIE/ROTT BN2 .... 97 G2
  FERR BN12 .... 91 M5
  SELS PO20 .... 99 K6
  SELS PO20 .... 181 M6
Marine Dr West BOGR PO21 .... 103 K3
  SELS PO20 .... 99 J6
Marine Gdns BRIE/ROTT BN2 .... 5 K8
  SELS PO20 .... 181 K8
Marine Pde BOGR PO21 .... 2 B9
  BRIE/ROTT BN2 .... 5 C8
  WTHG BN11 .... 12 E8
Marine Pl WTHG BN11 .... 13 J7
Mariners Cl SHOR BN43 .... 73 J8
The Mariners
  LAN/SOMP BN15 * 94 C2
Mariners Wk ANG/EP BN16 .... 90 C6
Marineside SELS PO20 .... 100 A8
Marine Sq BRIE/ROTT BN2 .... 5 K9
Marine Terrace Ms
  BRIE/ROTT BN2 .... 5 J8
Marine Vw BRIE/ROTT BN2 .... 5 H6
Marion Rd CRAWE RH10 .... 30 A6
Marisfield Pl SELS PO20 .... 181 M5
Marjoram Crs HORN PO8 .... 168 C6
Marjoram Pl SHOR BN43 .... 74 A4
Market Av CCH PO19 .... 6 E6
Market Cl MSEA/BNM PO22 .... 65 C2
Market Fld STEY/UB BN44 .... 48 C2
Market Pde HAV PO9 .... 57 G4
Market Pl BURH RH15 * 46 F7
  HWH RH16 .... 45 G4
Market Rd CCH PO19 .... 6 F5
Market Sq HORS RH12 * 10 C7
  MIDH GU29 .... 137 J10
  PETW GU28 .... 139 L9
Market St BOGR PO21 .... 2 D8
  BRI BN1 .... 4 E7
  WTHG BN11 .... 13 H6
Markfield MSEA/BNM PO22 .... 86 A7
Markham Av RDKG RH5 .... 16 B4
Markstakes Cnr
  RING/NEW BN8 .... 149 P12
Markstakes La RING/NEW BN8 .. 149 P12
Markway Cl EMRTH PO10 .... 57 L4
Markwick Ms WTHG BN11 .... 13 J4
Marlborough Cl CCH PO19 .... 7 L5
  CRAWW RH11 .... 29 H7
  HORS RH12 .... 36 C4
Marlborough Ct BOGR PO21 * ... 103 L1
Marlborough Dr BURH RH15 ..... 47 H6
Marlborough Ms BRI BN1 .... 4 C6
Marlborough Pk HAV PO9 .... 57 J2
Marlborough Pl BRI BN1 .... 4 F6
Marlborough Rd FERR BN12 .... 92 C3
  LAN/SOMP BN15 .... 94 B1
Marlborough St BRI BN1 .... 4 C6
Marlborough Wy FERR BN12 * ... 92 C3
Marldell Cl HAV PO9 .... 168 H12
Marle Av BURH RH15 .... 46 F5
Marles La BIL RH14 .... 123 R4
Marley Combe Rd HASM GU27 ... 109 J12
Marley Hanger HASM GU27 .... 119 K2
Marley La HASM GU27 .... 108 H12
Marley Wy PUL/STOR RH20 .... 160 B11
The Marlinspike SHOR BN43 ..... 73 M7
Marlow Cl CRAWE RH10 .... 8 F1
Marlow Dr HWH RH16 .... 45 L5
Marlowe Cl MSEA/BNM PO22 ..... 87 K4
Marlowe Rd SALV BN13 .... 71 K8
Marlow Rd BRIE/ROTT BN2 ..... 96 E1
Marlpit Cl EGRIN RH19 .... 23 K6
Marlpit La EMRTH PO10 .... 59 H1
  SELS PO20 .... 63 G7
Marlpit Rd EGRIN RH19 .... 42 F3
Marlpost Rd SWTR RH13 .... 125 M12
Marmion Rd HOVE BN3 .... 75 L6
Marples Wy HAV PO9 .... 56 E4
Marquis Wy BOGR PO21 .... 103 K4
Marringdean Rd BIL RH14 .... 142 A7
Marshall Av BOGR PO21 .... 2 B6
  SALV BN13 .... 70 E2
Marshall Cl MSEA/BNM PO22 ..... 65 C8
Marshall Rd CRAWE RH10 .... 30 B5
Marshalls Rw BRI BN1 .... 4 F5
Marshall Wy HOVE BN3 .... 75 L4
Marsh Barns SELS PO20 * 84 E3
Marsh Cl BOR GU35 .... 107 J6
Marsh La RCCH PO18 .... 63 M3
  RCCH PO18 .... 81 J1
  RCCH PO18 .... 172 C10
  SELS PO20 .... 84 E4
Marshwood Av WVILLE PO7 .... 168 B10
Marston Rd SALV BN13 .... 13 J1
Martha Gunn Rd
  BRIE/ROTT BN2 .... 77 J1
Martin Cl CRAWW RH11 .... 29 J1
Martindale Pl MFD/CHID GU8 * .. 110 F3
Martineau Cl BOGR PO21 .... 103 K4
Martin Rd HAV PO9 .... 57 H1
  HOVE BN3 .... 75 J4
Martins La SELS PO20 .... 82 E4
The Martins CRAWE RH10 .... 32 B1
Martlet Cl CCH PO19 .... 6 F7
Martlet Rd PETW GU28 .... 139 K10
Martlets PUL/STOR RH20 .... 159 R5
Martlets Cl HORS RH12 .... 36 B4
The Martlets ANG/EP BN16 .... 89 M6
  CRAWE RH10 .... 9 G4
  LAN/SOMP BN15 .... 72 D7
  RING/NEW BN8 .... 167 N2
  SHOR BN43 .... 73 L3
Martlets Wy FERR BN12 .... 92 B3

The Martlet HOVE BN3 .... 76 C5
Martletts Cnr HORS RH12 * 114 A10
Martlet Wy BOGR PO21 .... 102 E6
The Marts HORS RH12 .... 114 A10
Martyn Cl HFD BN5 .... 163 K4
Martyn's Cl BRIE/ROTT BN2 .... 97 K1
Martyns Pl EGRIN RH19 .... 33 M1
Marvell Cl CRAWE RH10 .... 30 B1
Marvic Ct HAV PO9 .... 168 F11
Marylands HWH RH16 .... 45 J4
Marylands Crs MSEA/BNM PO22 ... 3 H3
Masefield Crs HORN PO8 .... 168 A6
Masefield Rd CRAWW RH11 .... 28 D6
Mason Cl EGRIN RH19 .... 23 K7
Mason Rd CRAWE RH10 .... 9 G8
Masons Fld SWTR RH13 .... 126 H3
Masons Wy PUL/STOR RH20 .... 141 K12
Massetts Rd HORL RH6 .... 14 E7
Matlock Rd BRI BN1 .... 76 C4
Matthews Cl HAV PO9 .... 56 D2
Matthews Dr CRAWE RH10 .... 30 B7
Matthey Pl CRAWE RH10 .... 20 C8
Maudlin La STEY/UB BN44 .... 48 C4
Maudlyn Cl STEY/UB BN44 .... 48 D4
Maudlyn Pk STEY/UB BN44 .... 48 D4
Maudlyn Pkwy STEY/UB BN44 ... 48 C4
Mauldmare Cl BOGR PO21 .... 103 L3
Maunsell Rd CRAWE RH10 .... 30 A3
Mavis Crs HAV PO9 .... 57 G3
Maxton Wk CRAWW RH11 * 29 G7
Maxwell Rd ARUN BN18 .... 66 E4
  LHPTN BN17 .... 89 H4
Maxwell Wy CRAWE RH10 .... 19 M8
Maybridge Crs FERR BN12 .... 92 B2
Maybridge Sq FERR BN12 .... 92 B1
Maybush Dr RCCH PO18 .... 59 J6
May Cl BOR GU35 .... 107 M5
  FERR BN12 .... 92 B1
  LHPTN BN17 .... 88 C4
  MSEA/BNM PO22 .... 2 B1
  SELS PO20 .... 101 L5
May Cottages BRIE/ROTT BN2 * .. 77 H5
Maydwell Av SWTR RH13 .... 124 B9
Mayes Cl CRAWE RH10 .... 30 B4
Mayes La HORS RH12 .... 115 P8
Mayfield ANG/EP BN16 .... 90 F2
  CRAWE RH10 .... 30 C3
Mayfield Cl BOGR PO21 .... 103 M1
  BRI BN1 .... 52 F8
  SALV BN13 .... 70 F5
Mayfield Crs BRI BN1 .... 52 E8
Mayfield Rd BOGR PO21 .... 103 M1
Mayfields RHWH RH17 .... 146 D1
Mayflower Cl CRAWE RH10 .... 30 A2
Mayflower Ct HWH RH16 .... 45 J5
Mayflower Rd BOGR PO21 .... 106 F9
  HWH RH16 .... 45 J5
Mayflower Sq BRI BN1 .... 4 A3
Mayflower Wy ANG/EP BN16 .... 90 F2
Mayhouse Rd BURH RH15 .... 46 E8
Maylands Rd HAV PO9 .... 56 C3
Maynard Cl CRAWE RH10 .... 21 H5
Maynard Pl HORN PO8 .... 168 C2
Mayo Rd BRIE/ROTT BN2 .... 77 G5
Maypole La ARUN BN18 .... 65 L8
Maypole Rd EGRIN RH19 .... 23 J7
  EGRIN RH19 .... 34 D3
Mayridge SELS PO20 .... 180 H5
May Rd BRIE/ROTT BN2 .... 5 M2
May Tree Av SALV BN13 .... 70 E2
Maytree Cl ANG/EP BN16 .... 90 E1
  LAN/SOMP BN15 .... 72 A7
Maytree Wk HOVE BN3 .... 75 K4
McIndoe Rd EGRIN RH19 .... 23 J6
McIver Cl EGRIN RH19 .... 22 E5
McKerchar Cl LAN/SOMP BN15 ...72 E6
McNair Cl SELS PO20 .... 181 K5
McWilliam Rd BRIE/ROTT BN2 ... 78 B4
Meadend Cl HAV PO9 .... 169 J12
Mead La BOGR PO21 .... 3 G5
  MSEA/BNM PO22 .... 2 F2
  PUL/STOR RH20 .... 160 B11
Meadow Ap CRAWE RH10 .... 20 F6
Meadowbank BIL RH14 .... 141 J1
  PUL/STOR RH20 * 141 L12
Meadow Cl BRIE/ROTT BN2 .... 97 K2
  CRAWE RH10 .... 20 F6
  HORS RH12 .... 36 E2
  HOVE BN3 .... 76 A2
  LIPH GU30 .... 117 R1
  PTSD BN41 .... 75 G3
  SELS PO20 .... 83 M5
  STHW BN42 .... 74 F5
  WTHG BN11 .... 94 A2
Meadow Crs WTHG BN11 .... 93 M2
Meadowcroft Cl CRAWW RH11 ... 28 E4
  EGRIN RH19 .... 23 M2
Meadow Croft Cl HORL RH6 .... 20 B1
Meadow Farm La HORS RH12 .. 36 E2
Meadowfield Dr CCH PO19 .... 7 J2
Meadowland SELS PO20 .... 181 K7
Meadowlands CRAWW RH11 .... 8 C3
  HAV PO9 .... 57 H4
  HAV PO9 .... 169 K6
Meadow La BURH RH15 .... 46 E8
  HWH RH16 .... 45 L3
  LAN/SOMP BN15 .... 72 D8
  SELS PO20 .... 99 J3
Meadow Pde BRIE/ROTT BN2 * ... 97 L2
Meadow Pk ANG/EP BN16 .... 91 G4
Meadow Ri HORN PO8 .... 168 C6
Meadow Rd EMRTH PO10 .... 58 B2
  WVILLE PO7 .... 180 B2
Meadows HPPT/KEY BN6 .... 165 M4
Meadowside ANG/EP BN16 .... 68 C7
  HORL RH6 .... 15 G5
  PUL/STOR RH20 .... 160 A12
Meadowside Ct FERR BN12 * 91 M3
Meadow Sq BOGR PO21 * 99 M6
The Meadows ARUN BN18 .... 65 J4
  CCH PO19 .... 83 K2
  HOVE BN3 .... 75 H2
Meadowsweet HORN PO8 .... 168 C6
Meadow Sweet Cl SALV BN13 .... 69 M8
Meadow Ter RHWH RH17 * 40 F9
The Meadow CRAWE RH10 .... 20 F6
Meadow V BOR GU35 .... 106 H6
Meadow Vw HAV PO9 .... 56 E4
Meadowview Rd
  LAN/SOMP BN15 .... 72 C5
Meadow Wk LISS GU33 .... 116 C9
  MSEA/BNM PO22 .... 87 M4
Meadow Wy BOGR PO21 .... 103 G5

  FERR BN12 .... 91 K3
  LHPTN BN17 .... 89 L4
  LIPH GU30 .... 107 R12
  MSEA/BNM PO22 .... 85 M7
  PETW GU28 .... 139 K10
  SELS PO20 .... 63 H4
  SELS PO20 .... 64 C7
Mead Rd CRAWE RH10 .... 9 J2
  GSHT GU26 .... 109 J5
Meads Av HOVE BN3 .... 75 J4
Meads Cl HOVE BN3 .... 75 H2
The Meads BRI BN1 .... 53 J8
  EGRIN RH19 .... 33 K2
  HASM GU27 .... 109 J11
Mead Sway ARUN BN18 .... 65 J1
The Mead LIPH GU30 .... 107 Q12
  LISS GU33 .... 116 C9
  PSF GU32 .... 133 L7
Meadvale HORS RH12 .... 125 Q3
Mead Wy MIDH GU29 .... 136 H11
  HASM GU27 .... 109 J11
  WVILLE PO7 .... 168 B8
Meadway Ct SALV BN13 * 92 D1
  STHW BN42 .... 74 C5
Meadway Crs HOVE BN3 .... 75 L3
The Meadway BRIE/ROTT BN2 ... 77 L8
  HORL RH6 .... 15 H6
  SHOR BN43 .... 73 L7
Measham Cl FERR BN12 .... 91 L4
Meath Green Av HORL RH6 .... 14 E4
Meath Green La HORL RH6 .... 14 D1
Medina Pl HOVE BN3 .... 76 A8
Medina Ter HOVE BN3 .... 75 M8
Medina Vls HOVE BN3 .... 76 A8
Medlar Cl CRAWW RH11 .... 19 H8
Medmerry SELS PO20 .... 180 G5
Medmerry Hl BRIE/ROTT BN2 ... 77 K3
Medstead Rd HAV PO9 .... 57 G2
Medway CRAWE RH10 .... 31 M4
Medway Cl SALV BN13 .... 70 C6
Medway Dr EGRIN RH19 .... 33 J3
  FROW RH18 .... 34 F7
Medway Rd CRAWW RH11 .... 28 E4
Medwin Wy HORS RH12 .... 10 C6
Meeds Rd BURH RH15 .... 46 F7
Meeting House La BRI BN1 .... 4 E7
Meiros Wy PUL/STOR RH20 .... 161 J8
Melbourne Av FERR BN12 .... 92 B3
Melbourne Rd CCH PO19 .... 7 J3
  FERR BN12 .... 92 B3
Melbourne St BRIE/ROTT BN2 ... 5 J1
Melbourne Wy HORS RH12 * 36 E4
Melksham Cl SWTR RH13 .... 11 G7
Melrose Av PTSD BN41 .... 74 F4
  SALV BN13 .... 92 D1
Melrose Cl BOR GU35 .... 106 G7
  BRI BN1 .... 77 H3
  SALV BN13 .... 92 D1
Melrose Pl PUL/STOR RH20 .... 160 A10
Melton Av PUL/STOR RH20 .... 160 A10
Melton Cl PUL/STOR RH20 .... 160 A10
Melton Dr PUL/STOR RH20 .... 160 A10
Melville Rd HOVE BN3 .... 4 A1
Melville Wy FERR BN12 .... 92 B1
Mendip Cl ANG/EP BN16 .... 90 F3
Mendip Crs SALV BN13 .... 70 D6
Mendip Rd SALV BN13 .... 70 D6
Mendip Wk CRAWW RH11 .... 8 B4
Meon Cl HORN PO8 .... 150 D9
  PSF GU32 .... 133 M5
Mercer Cl CRAWE RH10 .... 30 B6
Mercer Rd BRI BN1 .... 36 B1
Mercers Md SWTR RH13 .... 145 K4
Merchant St BOGR PO21 * 2 D6
Merchistoun Rd HORN PO8 .... 168 D2
Mercury Cl BOR GU35 .... 106 H6
  CRAWW RH11 .... 28 D6
Mere Cl SELS PO20 .... 100 A8
Meredith Rd SALV BN13 .... 13 L2
Merevale BRI BN1 .... 77 G3
Mereworth Dr CRAWE RH10 .... 30 C1
Meridian Cl CRAWW RH11 .... 28 E6
Meridian Gv HORL RH6 .... 15 H5
Meridian Wy EGRIN RH19 .... 23 L6
Merle Wy HASM GU27 .... 119 K2
Merlin Cl CRAWE RH10 .... 28 D3
  HOVE BN3 .... 76 C5
Merlin Wy EGRIN RH19 .... 23 M6
  MSEA/BNM PO22 .... 87 J7
Merrion Av MSEA/BNM PO22 ..... 2 B2
Merry End MSEA/BNM PO22 ..... 87 K8
Merryfield Av HAV PO9 .... 168 E12
Merryfield Crs ANG/EP BN16 .... 68 C7
Merryfield Dr HORS RH12 .... 125 R2
  SELS PO20 .... 181 M6
Merryfield Rd EPSF GU31 .... 133 Q5
  PUL/STOR RH20 .... 160 A11
Merryfield Wy
  PUL/STOR RH20 .... 160 A11
Merryhills La BIL RH14 .... 112 H12
Merryweather Rd RCCH PO18 ... 60 A8
Merrywood La
  PUL/STOR RH20 .... 160 D9
Mersey Cl SALV BN13 .... 70 B6
Mersey Rd SALV BN13 .... 70 B6
Mersham Gdns FERR BN12 .... 92 B3
Merston Rd BRIE/ROTT BN2 ..... 78 D7
Merton Av ANG/EP BN16 .... 90 B5
Merton Cl BOGR PO21 .... 103 K1
Merton Dr LHPTN BN17 .... 89 J3
Merton Rd CRAWW RH11 .... 39 G1
  WTHG BN11 .... 13 L6
Metcalf Wy CRAWW RH11 .... 19 J7
Meteor Rd EMRTH PO10 .... 80 B2
Methuen Rd LISS GU33 .... 116 F2
Mews Ct EGRIN RH19 .... 33 L3
Mewsey Ct HAV PO9 .... 168 E10
The Mews ARUN BN18 * 67 G3
  BOGR PO21 * 2 D6
  EPSF GU31 .... 133 P6
  HAV PO9 .... 56 F1
  HORS RH12 .... 125 N1
  MFD/CHID GU8 .... 112 A4
  MSEA/BNM PO22 * 3 G5
  PUL/STOR RH20 .... 159 L3
  PUL/STOR RH20 .... 161 K9
  WTHG BN11 .... 12 E7
Mey Cl WVILLE PO7 .... 168 A10
Meyers Wd SWTR RH13 .... 144 E10
Meyners Ct HOVE BN3 .... 75 H2
Meyrick Rd HAV PO9 .... 56 E4
Michael Crs HORL RH6 .... 14 F8
Michael Cl HAV PO9 .... 56 D2
Michael Crook Cl HAV PO9 .... 56 D7
Michael Flds FROW RH18 .... 34 D7
Michelbourne Cl BURH RH15 ... 46 D8

Michel Gv ANG/EP BN16 .... 90 D4
Michell Cl HORS RH12 .... 125 R3
Micklam Cl BOGR PO21 .... 103 J3
Midas Cl WVILLE PO7 .... 56 A2
Middlefield La RCCH PO18 .... 172 E9
  SELS PO20 .... 99 H5
Middle Md STEY/UB BN44 .... 48 C1
Middle Meadow LISS GU33 .... 116 D9
Middle Onslow Cl FERR BN12 * ... 91 K2
Middle Park Wy HAV PO9 .... 56 E1
Middle Rd BRI BN1 .... 76 D4
  LAN/SOMP BN15 .... 72 C8
  SHOR BN43 .... 74 A6
  SWTR RH13 .... 144 F10
Middle St BRI BN1 .... 4 D8
  BRI BN1 .... 54 B7
  HORS RH12 .... 10 C6
  PETW GU28 .... 139 L9
  PTSD BN41 .... 75 H7
  SHOR BN43 .... 73 L6
Middleton Av HOVE BN3 .... 75 J7
Middleton Cl SALV BN13 .... 100 A7
Middleton Gdns SELS PO20 .... 63 J3
Middleton Ri BRI BN1 .... 53 K8
  HORN PO8 .... 150 E9
Middleton Rd HORS RH12 .... 125 R3
  MSEA/BNM PO22 .... 87 H4
Midhurst Dr FERR BN12 .... 91 L5
Midhurst Ri BRI BN1 .... 53 C7
Midhurst Rd HASM GU27 .... 109 L12
  HASM GU27 .... 119 L11
  LIPH GU30 .... 117 R2
  PUL/STOR RH20 .... 172 B10
Midhurst Wk HOVE BN3 .... 75 J7
Midway Rd BRIE/ROTT BN2 ..... 78 B5
The Midway MSEA/BNM PO22 .... 3 M4
Mighell St BRIE/ROTT BN2 .... 5 G6
Milbeck Cl HORN PO8 .... 168 B6
Milborne Rd CRAWE RH10 .... 30 B7
Milbury Cl FERR BN12 .... 91 L5
Milcote Av HOVE BN3 .... 75 L5
Mildmay Rd CRAWE RH10 .... 29 L1
Mile End La SELS PO20 .... 83 J3
Mile Oak Crs STHW BN42 .... 74 A4
Mile Oak Gdns PTSD BN41 .... 74 F4
Mile Oak Rd PTSD BN41 .... 74 E4
  STHW BN42 .... 74 E4
Miles Cl ARUN BN18 .... 88 A3
Milford Cl HAV PO9 .... 56 E2
Millais SWTR RH13 .... 11 L4
Millais Cl CRAWW RH11 .... 28 E7
Millais Ct SWTR RH13 .... 11 L4
Milland La LIPH GU30 .... 117 P9
Mill Av SHOR BN43 .... 73 L4
The Millbank CRAWW RH11 .... 28 E4
Mill Bay La HORS RH12 .... 10 B7
Mill Brooks RING/NEW BN8 ..... 167 N2
Mill Chase Rd BOR GU35 .... 106 H6
Mill Cl ANG/EP BN16 .... 90 C3
  CCH PO19 .... 61 G7
  EGRIN RH19 .... 33 K2
  HASM GU27 .... 108 H11
  HORL RH6 .... 14 D5
  POY/PYE BN45 .... 164 D12
  PTSD BN41 .... 75 H4
  SWTR RH13 .... 127 M10
Mill Copse Rd HASM GU27 .... 119 L1
Mill Cottages EGRIN RH19 * 33 K2
  HORS RH12 * 114 A12
Mill Ct WTHG BN11 * 12 D5
Millcroft BRI BN1 .... 52 B8
Millcroft Av STHW BN42 .... 74 D4
Millcroft Gdns STHW BN42 .... 74 D4
Millcross Rd PTSD BN41 .... 75 G4
Mill Dr HFD BN5 .... 163 K5
  HOVE BN3 .... 75 M2
Mill End EMRTH PO10 .... 58 C5
  HFD BN5 .... 163 K5
  PUL/STOR RH20 .... 159 R5
Millennium Cl LAN/SOMP BN15 .. 73 G7
Miller Rd BRI BN1 .... 76 D4
Millers Cl ANG/EP BN16 .... 90 C3
Millers Ga HORS RH12 .... 36 C3
Miller's Rd BRI BN1 .... 76 D4
The Millers ARUN BN18 .... 87 G3
Millers Wy BURH RH15 .... 46 F5
Millfarm Dr BOGR PO21 .... 102 E8
Mill Farm Rd SWTR RH13 .... 11 M2
Millfield LAN/SOMP BN15 .... 72 B6
  STEY/UB BN44 * 48 F3
  SWTR RH13 .... 143 R1
Millfield Cl ANG/EP BN16 .... 90 A6
  CCH PO19 .... 62 B5
Millfield Cottages
  BRIE/ROTT BN2 .... 5 L9
Mill Gdns SELS PO20 .... 99 L6
Mill Green Rd HWH RH16 .... 45 H3
Mill Hl SHOR BN43 .... 49 K7
Mill Hill Cl HWH RH16 .... 45 H3
  SHOR BN43 .... 73 K1
Mill Hill Dr HWH RH16 .... 45 H3
Mill Hill Gdns SHOR BN43 .... 73 K4
Mill House Gdns WTHG BN11 .... 12 B5
Millington Dr SELS PO20 .... 181 L4
Mill La ANG/EP BN16 .... 90 C3
  ARUN BN18 .... 65 J4
  ARUN BN18 .... 67 G2
  ARUN BN18 .... 174 H11
  ARUN BN18 .... 176 F3
  BOR GU35 .... 107 L4
  CCH PO19 .... 61 G7
  CRAWE RH10 .... 21 K6
  CRAWW RH11 .... 28 E1
  EGRIN RH19 .... 33 H3
  EMRTH PO10 .... 58 C1
  EPSF GU31 .... 152 E2
  HAV PO9 .... 56 F1
  HORL RH6 .... 14 C6

  HPPT/KEY BN6 .... 146 F11
  HPPT/KEY BN6 .... 165 M10
  LHPTN BN17 .... 67 J3
  LING RH7 .... 23 L1
  MFD/CHID GU8 .... 110 F6
  MFD/CHID GU8 .... 111 R5
  MIDH GU29 .... 136 D7
  MIDH GU29 .... 154 G5
  MIDH GU29 .... 155 J3
  POY/PYE BN45 .... 164 D12
  PSF GU32 .... 133 M1
  PSF GU32 .... 133 Q3
  PTSD BN41 .... 75 H4
  RHWH RH17 .... 41 H8
  RING/NEW BN8 .... 167 N2
  SALV BN13 .... 70 E3
  SELS PO20 .... 84 D4
  SELS PO20 .... 101 L6
  SELS PO20 .... 180 H6
  SHOR BN43 .... 73 K5
  SWTR RH13 .... 127 M10
  SWTR RH13 .... 144 E8
Mill Md PUL/STOR RH20 .... 161 K9
Mill Park Rd BOGR PO21 .... 102 F3
Mill Pond La RCCH PO18 .... 60 A2
Mill Pond Wy ANG/EP BN16 .... 90 E3
Mill Quay EMRTH PO10 .... 58 B6
Mill Ri BRI BN1 .... 52 B8
Mill Rd ANG/EP BN16 .... 68 C8
  ARUN BN18 .... 65 J2
  ARUN BN18 .... 67 G2
  BRI BN1 .... 52 B7
  BURH RH15 .... 47 G6
  CRAWE RH10 .... 30 A2
  EMRTH PO10 .... 58 C1
  LAN/SOMP BN15 .... 72 D5
  LISS GU33 .... 116 D8
  PTSD BN41 .... 75 G6
  PUL/STOR RH20 .... 159 R5
  RCCH PO18 .... 59 M2
  STEY/UB BN44 .... 48 B2
  WTHG BN11 .... 12 A5
Mill Road Av ANG/EP BN16 .... 90 E1
Mill Rw BRI BN1 * 4 C4
Mill Stream Meadow
  HWH RH16 .... 45 G2
The Millstream HASM GU27 .... 108 H12
Mill St BRI BN1 .... 54 B6
Millthorpe Rd HORS RH12 .... 11 J1
Mill Vale Mdw LIPH GU30 .... 117 Q10
Millview Cl BOGR PO21 .... 102 F3
Mill View Rd ARUN BN18 .... 87 L3
Mill Wy BIL RH14 .... 123 R12
  EGRIN RH19 .... 33 K2
Mill Wd BURH RH15 .... 47 G6
Millwood CRAWE RH10 .... 32 D4
Millyard Crs BRIE/ROTT BN2 ..... 78 C6
Milne Cl CRAWW RH11 .... 28 D6
Milner Rd BRIE/ROTT BN2 .... 77 H4
Milnthorpe Rd HOVE BN3 .... 75 L5
Milnwood Rd HORS RH12 .... 10 C3
Milton Av ANG/EP BN16 .... 90 A5
Milton Cl ANG/EP BN16 .... 90 A4
  LAN/SOMP BN15 .... 72 D8
Milton Crs EGRIN RH19 .... 23 H8
Milton Dr STHW BN42 .... 74 A4
Milton Mount Av CRAWE RH10 ... 30 B1
Milton Rd BRIE/ROTT BN2 .... 5 H8
  CRAWE RH10 .... 30 B2
  HORS RH12 .... 10 C3
  HWH RH16 .... 45 G4
  WTHG BN11 .... 12 E7
Milton St WTHG BN11 .... 12 E7
Mimmack Cl STEY/UB BN44 .... 48 C1
Mimosa Cl BOR GU35 .... 107 K4
Minehead Av EGRIN RH19 .... 24 A7
Minley Ct HAV PO9 .... 169 J12
The Minnels HPPT/KEY BN6 ..... 165 P6
Minsted Rd MIDH GU29 .... 136 B12
Minster Ct LHPTN BN17 * 89 H11
Minton Rd MSEA/BNM PO22 ..... 3 M5
Mint Rd LISS GU33 .... 116 E7
Misbrooks Green Rd RDKG RH5 ... 16 B4
Mistley Gdns HORL RH6 .... 14 C7
Mitchell Gdns SWTR RH13 .... 124 F2
Mitchell Rd HAV PO9 .... 56 C2
Mitchells Rd CRAWE RH10 .... 9 J3
Mixon Cl SELS PO20 .... 181 L4
Moatfield La SWTR RH13 .... 145 M5
Moat La PUL/STOR RH20 .... 159 K3
The Moat PUL/STOR RH20 .... 159 K3
Moat Rd EGRIN RH19 .... 23 K3
Moat Wk CRAWE RH10 .... 30 B2
Moat Wy FERR BN12 .... 92 B4
Mocatta Wy BURH RH15 .... 46 C4
Modena Rd HOVE BN3 .... 75 L6
Moggs Md EPSF GU31 .... 133 P6
Mole Cl CRAWW RH11 .... 29 G1
Molecomb Broadwalk
  RCCH PO18 .... 173 K8
Mole Hl WVILLE PO7 .... 168 A12
Molesworth St HOVE BN3 .... 75 L5
The Mole LHPTN BN17 .... 89 M4
Monarch Cl CRAWW RH11 .... 28 F6
  WVILLE PO7 .... 168 B10
Monarch's Wy ARUN BN18 .... 176 B8
  BRI BN1 .... 51 J7
  HAV PO9 .... 169 N8
  HORN PO8 .... 168 E4
  HOVE BN3 .... 76 A4
  PTSD BN41 .... 74 D2
  PUL/STOR RH20 .... 160 A4
  RCCH PO18 .... 170 C5
  RCCH PO18 .... 171 L5
  SALV BN13 .... 178 A11
  STEY/UB BN44 .... 48 D4
  STEY/UB BN44 .... 179 R9
Monastery La PUL/STOR RH20 ... 159 R12
Monckton Wy LEWES BN7 .... 55 K8
Monk Cl BRI BN1 .... 53 K7
Monkmead Copse
  PUL/STOR RH20 .... R7
Monkmead La PUL/STOR RH20 .. 159 Q6
Monks Av LAN/SOMP BN15 .... 72 E7
Monks Cl LAN/SOMP BN15 .... 72 D7
  RCCH PO18 .... 9 J3
Monk's Hl EMRTH PO10 .... 169 P11
Monks La RDKG RH5 .... 115 J4
Monks Orch PSF GU32 .... 133 N4
Monks Wk STEY/UB BN44 .... 49 G3

Monks Wd PSF GU32 ....133 N4
Monkwood Cl HAV PO9 ....168 E12
Monmouth St BN7 ....A6
Mons Av BOGR PO21 ....2 A3
Montacute Rd LEWES BN7 ....55 M5
Montague Cl SHOR BN43 ....74 C6
Montague Gdns EPSF GU31 ....133 R6
Montague Pl BRIE/ROTT BN2 ....5 K7
  WTHG BN11 ....13 H7
Montague Rd MIDH GU29 ....137 H7
Montague St BRIE/ROTT BN2 ....5 J8
  WTHG BN11 ....12 H7
Montagu Rd CCH PO19 ....61 G5
Montalan Crs SELS PO20 ....180 H5
Montefiore Rd HOVE BN3 ....4 A3
Monterey Dr HAV PO9 ....57 H1
Monterey Gdns BOGR PO21 ....103 M1
Monterey Pines
  MSEA/BNM PO22 ....3 M4
Montes Hl HWH RH16 ....131 J9
Monteswood La HWH RH16 ....131 J9
Montford Cl SHOR BN43 ....74 C5
Montgomeri Dr ANG/EP BN16 ......90 A2
Montgomery Dr
  MSEA/BNM PO22 ....87 J7
Montgomery Rd HAV PO9 ....57 H4
Montgomery St HOVE BN3 ....75 M6
Montier Ter PETW GU28 * 139 L7
Montpelier Crs BRI BN1 ....4 B4
Montpelier Gdns
  PUL/STOR PO20 ....178 H1
Montpelier Pl BRI BN1 ....4 A5
Montpelier Rd ANG/EP BN16 ......90 A4
  BRI BN1 ....4 A6
Montpelier St BRI BN1 ....4 B5
Montpelier Ter BRI BN1 ....4 B5
Montpelier Vls BRI BN1 ....4 B5
Montreal Rd BRIE/ROTT BN2 ....5 H5
Montreal Rd SALV BN13 ....70 F1
Montrose Cl BOR GU35 ....106 C8
  FERR BN12 ....92 B2
Monument Cha BOR GU35 ....106 H8
Monument La RCCH PO18 ....170 C10
Monument Vw BRIE/ROTT BN2 ......5 M5
Moon's La LING RH7 ....24 C2
  SWTR RH13 ....10 F8
Moor Cl BOR GU35 ....106 E6
Moorcroft Cl CRAWW RH11 ....8 B2
Moore Cl SALV BN13 ....70 A7
Moore Pl BOGR PO21 * 2 C5
Moorfield HASM GU27 ....109 J12
Moorfoot Rd SALV BN13 ....70 A4
Moorgreen Rd HAV PO9 ....168 H10
Moorhead Rd HORS RH12 ....37 G4
Moorhen Wy MSEA/BNM PO22 ......86 A7
Moorhouse La MIDH GU29 ....135 K3
The Moorings EGRIN RH19 ....22 G6
  GSHT GU26 ....108 H6
  LAN/SOMP BN15 ....72 C5
  SHOR BN43 ....74 B7
Moorland Rd CRAWE RH10 ....30 B4
Moorlands Cl GSHT GU26 ....108 H6
Moor Pk HORL RH6 * 15 C7
  WVILLE PO7 ....168 C7
Moor Park Crs CRAWW RH11 ......28 C4
Moor Pl EGRIN RH19 ....23 J7
Moor Rd HASM GU27 ....108 F12
  LISS GU33 ....116 C4
Morants Cl CCH PO19 ....7 H2
Moraunt Dr MSEA/BNM PO22 ......87 J7
Morecambe Cl CRAWW RH11 ....28 E5
Morecambe Rd BRI BN1 ....52 F7
Moreton Rd RCCH PO18 ....60 A8
Morland Av SALV BN13 ....71 K6
Morley Crs HORN PO8 ....168 B6
Morleys PUL/STOR PO20 ....161 K9
Morley St BRIE/ROTT BN2 ....4 F6
Mornington Crs HOVE BN3 ....75 J6
  MSEA/BNM PO22 ....3 M2
Mornington Man HOVE BN3 * 75 J6
Mornington Rd BOR GU35 ....106 D7
Morrell Av HORS RH12 ....36 E4
Morris Dr BIL RH14 ....141 R2
Morris Wy PUL/STOR PO20 ....159 R6
Mortimer Rd HOVE BN3 ....75 L5
  RDKG RH5 ....16 C3
Morton Cl CRAWW RH11 ....39 G1
Morton Rd EGRIN RH19 ....33 K4
Mosdell Rd PETW GU28 ....59 M5
Mosford Cl HORL RH6 ....14 E4
Moss Cl LISS GU33 ....116 D9
Mosse Gdns CCH PO19 ....61 G6
Moulsecoomb Pl
  BRIE/ROTT BN2 * 77 J3
Moulsecoomb Wy
  BRIE/ROTT BN2 ....77 K2
Mountbatten Cl CRAWW RH11 .....29 H1
Mountbatten Ct LHPTN BN17 * ...89 M3
Mount Cl CRAWE RH10 ....30 B3
Mountfields BRI BN1 ....77 H3
Mount Harry Rd LEWES BN7 ......55 M4
Mount La CCH PO19 ....6 C4
  CRAWE RH10 ....31 M5
Mount Noddy RHWH RH17 ....147 N4
Mount Pleasant ARUN BN18 ......66 F2
  BRIE/ROTT BN2 ....5 H7
  PETW GU28 * 139 L7
Mount Pleasant Rd BOR GU35 ...107 J4
The Mount BOR GU35 ....107 P3
  CRAWW RH11 ....18 A8
  HASM GU27 ....109 Q7
Mountview Rd
  LAN/SOMP BN15 ....72 C5
Mountway LAN/SOMP BN15 ....72 D4
Mountwood Rd EMRTH PO10 ....58 C4
  SELS PO20 ....181 M5
Mount Zion Pl BRI BN1 ....4 D5
Mouse La STEY/UB BN44 ....48 A1
  STEY/UB BN44 ....179 P2
Mouthey's La RCCH PO18 ....60 D3
Mowbray Dr CRAWW RH11 ....28 E5
Moyne Cl HOVE BN3 ....75 K4
Moyne Rd CRAWW RH11 ....28 E5
Muccleshell Cl HAV PO9 ....57 H1
Mulberry La RCCH PO18 * 59 M5
Muggeridge's Hl RDKG RH5 ......26 D1
Muirfield Cl CRAWW RH11 ....29 H1
Muirfield SALV BN13 ....70 D7
Mulberry Cl BRI BN1 ....76 E2
  FERR BN12 ....91 K3
  FERR BN12 ....92 B2
  HORS RH12 ....36 B4
  LAN/SOMP BN15 ....72 D7
  SHOR BN43 ....74 C4
Mulberry Ct FERR BN12 * 92 B3

Mulberry Gdns FERR BN12 ....92 B3
Mulberry La FERR BN12 ....92 B3
  HPPT/KEY BN6 ....166 A6
Mulberry Ldg ANG/EP BN16 * 90 B4
Mulberry Rd CRAWW RH11 ....19 G8
Mumford Pl CCH PO19 ....7 H8
Mundays Rw HORN PO8 ....150 D12
Munmere Wy ANG/EP BN16 ....90 D3
Munnion Rd RHWH RH17 ....130 E2
Munns Dr BURH RH15 ....47 G5
Muntham Dr SWTR RH13 ....124 H10
Murina Av BOGR PO21 ....2 A3
Murray Ct SWTR RH13 ....37 G5
Murray Rd HORN PO8 ....168 G5
  SELS PO20 ....181 J2
Murrey Ct SWTR RH13 * 37 G5
Muscliffe Ct HAV PO9 ....169 J12
Museum Hl HASM GU27 ....109 N11
Musgrave Av EGRIN RH19 ....33 K2
Mushroom Fld LEWES BN7 ....55 K8
Mustang Cl ARUN BN18 ....88 A2
Muster Gn HWH RH16 ....45 G5
Muster Gn South HWH RH16 .....45 G5
Mutton Hl LING RH7 ....23 M2
Mutton's La PUL/STOR PO20 ....160 C10
Myrtle Crs LAN/SOMP BN15 ......72 B8
Myrtle Gv BIL RH14 ....142 A2
Myrtle Gv ANG/EP BN16 ....90 D4
Myrtle Rd LAN/SOMP BN15 ....72 C8
Myrtle Ter HFD BN5 ....163 K5
Mytten Bank RHWH RH17 ....44 C3
Mytten Cl RHWH RH17 ....44 C3

N

Nab Tower La SELS PO20 ....180 H5
Nab Wk SELS PO20 ....99 L7
Nagels Cl SELS PO20 ....99 M7
Naiad Gdns MSEA/BNM PO22 .....105 J1
Naish Ct HAV PO9 ....168 D10
Naldrett Cl HORS RH12 ....11 J1
Naldretts La HORS RH12 ....113 R12
Namrik Ms HOVE BN3 ....75 M7
Nanson Rd BRI BN1 ....53 J7
Napier Rd BOGR PO21 ....168 D3
Napier Wy CRAWE RH10 ....19 L8
Nappers Wd HASM GU27 ....119 K7
Nash La RHWH RH17 ....149 L1
Nash Rd CRAWE RH10 ....29 K6
Nash Wy ARUN BN18 ....88 J4
Natal Rd BRIE/ROTT BN2 ....77 J4
Natts La BIL RH14 ....141 R2
Navarino Rd WTHG BN11 ....93 M2
Neale Cl EGRIN RH19 ....23 G6
Needlemakers CCH PO19 * 7 C4
Needles Cl HORS RH12 ....10 A8
Need's Hl SWTR RH13 ....144 D7
Nell Ball BIL RH14 ....121 P4
Nelson Cl CRAWE RH10 ....30 B4
  LAN/SOMP BN15 ....72 C5
  SELS PO20 ....63 J4
Nelson Crs HORN PO8 * 168 D2
Nelson Rd BOGR PO21 ....103 M2
  FERR BN12 ....92 C1
  HORS RH12 ....10 B3
  BRIE/ROTT BN2 ....5 G6
Nepcote La SALV BN13 ....178 H13
Nepfield Cl SALV BN13 ....178 H12
Nep Town Rd HFD BN5 ....163 K5
Neptune Cl CRAWW RH11 ....28 D5
Neptune Ct MSEA/BNM PO22 .....105 J1
Neptune Rd BOR GU35 ....106 H7
Neptune Wy LHPTN BN17 ....89 M5
Nerissa Cl WVILLE PO7 ....168 C9
Nesbitt Rd BRIE/ROTT BN2 ......77 J4
Netherfield Cl HAV PO9 ....57 H5
Netherfield Gn BRIE/ROTT BN2 ..78 E5
Netherton Cl SELS PO20 ....181 L6
  SWTR RH13 ....125 Q9
Netherwood CRAWW RH11 ....8 A8
Netley Cl CRAWW RH11 ....39 H1
Nettleton Av SELS PO20 ....63 H5
Nevile Cl CRAWW RH11 ....28 F6
Nevill Av HOVE BN3 ....75 L4
Nevill Cl HOVE BN3 ....75 M3
Nevill Crs LEWES BN7 ....55 M4
Neville Gdns EMRTH PO10 ....57 M2
Neville Rd CCH PO19 ....61 J6
  MSEA/BNM PO22 ....2 C7
Nevill Gdns HOVE BN3 ....75 M3
Nevill Pl HOVE BN3 ....75 M3
Nevill Rd BRIE/ROTT BN2 ....97 L4
  HOVE BN3 ....75 M3
  LEWES BN7 ....55 M3
Nevill Ter LEWES BN7 ....55 M4
Nevill Wy HOVE BN3 ....75 M3
Newark Pl BRIE/ROTT BN2 ....5 G4
Newark Rd CRAWE RH10 ....29 L1
New Barn BIL RH14 ....122 B11
New Barn Cl PTSD BN41 ....75 G3
  SHOR BN43 ....74 A4
New Barn Hl RCCH PO18 ....62 F1
  RCCH PO18 ....173 K12
New Barn La PUL/STOR PO20 ....159 Q5
Newbarn La BOGR PO21 ....85 L6
Newbarn Rd EPSF GU31 ....151 K2
  HAV PO9 ....56 D2
New Barn Rd SHOR BN43 ....74 A4
New Br BIL RH14 ....141 N1
Newbridge Cl HORS RH12 ......125 M2
Newbridge Rd BIL RH14 ....141 Q1
New Brighton Rd EMRTH PO10 ...58 A4
New Broadway WTHG BN11 * 12 B3
Newbury La RHWH RH17 ....44 B4
Newbury Rd CRAWE RH10 ....30 C3
New Church Rd HOVE BN3 ....75 J4
New Courtwick La LHPTN BN17 ..89 H1
New Cut ARUN BN18 ....67 G2
Newdigate Rd HORS RH12 ....27 J1
New Dorset St BRI BN1 ....4 D5
Newells Cl BRIE/ROTT BN2 ......78 D4
Newells La RCCH PO18 ....59 M3
  SWTR RH13 ....127 J7
New England Ri PTSD BN41 ......74 F1
New England Rd BRI BN1 ....4 D2
  HWH RH16 ....45 M1
  BRI BN1 ....4 E1
New Farthingdale LING RH7 .....23 M1

Newfield Rd LISS GU33 ....116 D7
  SELS PO20 ....181 N5
New Gdns LAN/SOMP BN15 * 71 L2
Newhall Cl BOGR PO21 ....103 M2
Newhall Cl HFD BN5 ....163 J10
Newham Cl STEY/UB BN44 ....48 B2
Newham La STEY/UB BN44 ....48 A3
Newhaven St BRIE/ROTT BN2 ......5 G4
Newhouse La HORS RH12 ....8 D5
  RCCH PO18 ....173 N2
Newick Rd BRI BN1 ....77 K1
Newland Rd STEY/UB BN44 ......49 G3
  WTHG BN11 ....13 H3
Newlands RHWH RH17 ....40 E8
Newlands Cl HORL RH6 ....14 E4
  HPPT/KEY BN6 ....165 P6
Newlands Crs EGRIN RH19 ....23 J7
Newlands La CCH PO19 ....61 J5
Newlands Pk CRAWE RH10 ....21 K6
Newlands Rd BRIE/ROTT BN2 ....97 M4
  CRAWW RH11 ....8 D5
  HORS RH12 ....10 C2
Newland St WTHG BN11 ....13 H3
New La EPSF GU31 ....152 E3
  HAV PO9 ....57 H1
Newlease Rd WVILLE PO7 ....168 A12
Newling Wy SALV BN13 ....70 D4
Newman Ct CRAWE RH10 ....30 B4
Newman's Gdns
  LAN/SOMP BN15 ....72 A6
Newmarket Rd BRIE/ROTT BN2 ...77 H5
  CRAWW RH10 ....9 L9
Newmarket Ter BRIE/ROTT BN2 ..77 H5
Newmer Ct HAV PO9 ....168 D11
New Moorhead Dr HORS RH12 ....37 H3
Newnham Ct HAV PO9 ....169 J12
New Pde SELS PO20 * 181 K6
  WTHG BN11 ....13 L6
New Park Rd CCH PO19 ....6 F3
New Place Rd PUL/STOR RH20 ..159 K2
Newport Dr CCH PO19 ....61 G6
Newport Ms WTHG BN11 ....94 A2
Newport Rd BURH RH15 ....46 E6
Newpound BIL RH14 ....123 M10
Newpound La BIL RH14 ....123 L11
New Rd ANG/EP BN16 ....90 D2
  BIL RH14 ....124 B11
  BOR GU35 ....106 F8
  BRI BN1 ....4 E6
  EMRTH PO10 ....58 C2
  EMRTH PO10 ....58 F5
  HASM GU27 ....109 J12
  HORN PO8 ....150 D8
  HPPT/KEY BN6 ....165 N8
  LHPTN BN17 ....89 J5
  MFD/CHID GU8 ....110 F1
  MIDH GU29 ....136 H11
  MIDH GU29 ....155 P2
  PETW GU28 ....138 F8
  RCCH PO18 ....62 F1
  RCCH PO18 ....155 Q12
  SELS PO20 ....70 B6
  SHOR BN43 ....73 L6
  STEY/UB BN44 ....49 G4
  SWTR RH13 ....125 Q9
New Salts Farm Rd SHOR BN43 ..73 P7
Newstead Hall HORL RH6 ....15 J7
New Steine BRIE/ROTT BN2 ....5 G8
New Steine Ms BRIE/ROTT BN2 ...5 G8
New St CRAWE RH10 ....10 F7
  SWTR RH13 ....13 G7
Newtimber Av FERR BN12 ....92 A2
Newtimber Dr PTSD BN41 ....74 F4
Newtimber Gdns SHOR BN43 .....73 L4
Newton Av EGRIN RH19 ....33 L3
Newton Cl HWH RH16 ....45 L2
Newton Rd CRAWE RH10 ....19 L7
  HWH RH16 ....45 L2
New Town CRAWE RH10 ....6 F5
  LAN/SOMP BN15 ....72 C7
Newtown Av BOGR PO21 ....85 M7
Newtown Rd HOVE BN3 ....76 A5
  LIPH GU30 ....117 A2
New Town PUL/STOR RH20 ....159 Q12
New Way La HPPT/KEY BN6 ......165 J7
Nicholsfield BIL RH14 ....122 G1
Nicholson Wy HAV PO9 ....56 F2
Nickleby Rd HORN PO8 ....150 C7
Nicolson Cl SELS PO20 ....63 H3
Nicolson Dr SHOR BN43 ....73 L5
Nightingale Cl CRAWW RH11 ....29 H1
  EGRIN RH19 ....33 J2
  HAV PO9 ....168 H8
  PUL/STOR RH20 ....160 B12
Nightingale Ct EMRTH PO10 .....58 C1
Nightingale La BURH RH15 .....165 N1
  CRAWE RH10 ....32 B4
  PUL/STOR RH20 ....160 B12
  RCCH PO18 ....59 H2
Nightingale Pk HAV PO9 ....57 H2
  PUL/STOR RH20 ....160 B12
Nightingale Rd BOR GU35 ......106 H7
  HAV PO9 ....10 F4
  PSF GU32 ....133 L2
Nightingales PUL/STOR RH20 ...160 A6
  SALV BN13 ....178 H10
Nightingales Cl SWTR RH13 .....11 J6
Nightingale Wk BIL RH14 ......142 A1
Nightjar Cl HORN PO8 ....168 B3
Nile St BRI BN1 ....4 E7
Nimbus Cl LHPTN BN17 ....89 M3
Ninfield Pl BRIE/ROTT BN2 .....77 K6
Niven Cl CRAWE RH10 ....30 C1
Nizells Av HOVE BN3 ....76 C5
Noahs Ark La HWH RH16 ....45 M2
Noahs Ct CRAWE RH10 * 31 M5
Noel Gn BURH RH15 ....47 G5
Noel Ri BURH RH15 ....47 G5
Nolan Rd BRIE/ROTT BN2 ....78 D6
Nonnington La HWH RH16 ....156 A4
The Nookery ANG/EP BN16 ....90 F4
Nor'Bren Av BOGR PO21 ....85 M8
Norbury Cl LAN/SOMP BN15 ......72 A5
Norbury Dr LAN/SOMP BN15 ......72 A5
Nore Crs EMRTH PO10 ....57 L4
Nore Dwn Wy RCCH PO18 ....170 B1
Nore Farm Av EMRTH PO10 ......57 L4
Noreuil Rd PSF GU32 ....133 L6
Nore Wood La ARUN BN18 ......174 H11
Norfolk Buildings BRI BN1 * 4 A6
Norfolk Cl BOGR PO21 ....2 B8

  CRAWW RH11 ....28 D7
  HORL RH6 ....14 F7
Norfolk Ct WTHG BN11 * 12 A7
Norfolk Gdns LHPTN BN17 ....89 L5
Norfolk Ms BRI BN1 ....4 A6
Norfolk Pl LHPTN BN17 ....89 L5
Norfolk Rd BRI BN1 ....4 A6
  HORS RH12 ....10 E5
  LHPTN BN17 ....89 L5
Norfolk Sq BOGR PO21 ....2 B7
  BRI BN1 ....4 A6
Norfolk St BOGR PO21 ....4 A7
  BRI BN1 ....4 A7
  WTHG BN11 ....12 A4
Norfolk Ter BRI BN1 ....4 A5
  HORS RH12 ....10 E5
Norfolk Wy MSEA/BNM PO22 .....87 M8
Norley Cl HAV PO9 ....56 F1
Norman Cl BIL RH14 ....124 B12
  BOR GU35 ....106 H6
  LHPTN BN17 ....89 L4
Norman Crs SHOR BN43 ....73 L5
Normandy Av HAV PO9 ....56 D3
Normandy Cl CRAWE RH10 ....10 A6
  EGRIN RH19 ....33 L1
Normandy Dr ANG/EP BN16 ......90 F5
Normandy Gdns HORS RH12 ......10 C8
Normandy La ANG/EP BN16 ......90 F5
Normandy Rd SALV BN13 ....12 F1
Normanhurst Cl ANG/EP BN16 ...90 F5
  CRAWE RH10 ....9 K4
Norman Rd BURH RH15 ....46 E6
  HOVE BN3 ....75 K7
Normans Ct SHOR BN43 * 73 L4
Normanton Av BOGR PO21 ....2 A8
Normanton St BRIE/ROTT BN2 .....5 J2
Norman Wy HAV PO9 ....56 D3
  MSEA/BNM PO22 ....87 L8
  STEY/UB BN44 ....48 C1
Norris Cl BOR GU35 ....106 E1
Norris Gdns HAV PO9 ....57 H5
North Av FERR BN12 ....92 D4
North Av South
  MSEA/BNM PO22 ....87 M8
North Bank HPPT/KEY BN6 ......165 M5
North Barnes La LEWES BN7 ....167 J4
North Bay EMRTH PO10 ....80 B2
North Bersted St
  MSEA/BNM PO22 ....85 M6
Northbourne Cl SHOR BN43 .....73 M5
Northbrook Cl SALV BN13 ....71 K7
Northbrook Rd SALV BN13 ......71 K7
Northcliffe Rd MSEA/BNM PO22 ..3 G4
North Cl CCH PO19 * 9 J1
  CRAWE RH10 ....9 J1
  HAV PO9 ....57 H5
  PTSD BN41 ....74 F4
North Common Rd
  RHWH RH17 ....148 G8
Northcote Gdns EMRTH PO10 .....58 F7
Northcote Rd BOGR PO21 ....103 M1
North Ct HPPT/KEY BN6 ....73 L4
Northcourt Cl ANG/EP BN16 .....90 C3
Northcourt Rd SALV BN13 ....12 F2
Northcroft HFD BN5 ....163 J4
Northdown Cl HORS RH12 ....8 C8
Northdown Ter EGRIN RH19 * 23 J6
North Dr ANG/EP BN16 ....90 E1
  BRIE/ROTT BN2 ....5 J5
Northease Cl HOVE BN3 ....75 J3
Northease Dr HOVE BN3 ....75 K2
Northease Gdns HOVE BN3 ......75 K2
North End EGRIN RH19 * 23 G6
  HPPT/KEY BN6 ....166 A5
North End Cl PETW GU28 ....139 L8
Northend La HPPT/KEY BN6 .....146 G10
North End Rd ARUN BN18 ....87 L2
Northern Crs SELS PO20 ....99 K6
North Farm Rd
  LAN/SOMP BN15 ....72 E7
Northfield SELS PO20 ....181 M6
Northfield Cl HORN PO8 ....150 D11
Northfield Ri BRIE/ROTT BN2 ...97 M3
  HOVE BN3 ....75 J1
Northfield Rd SALV BN13 ....70 F7
Northfields La SELS PO20 ......64 C5
Northfield Wy BRI BN1 ....76 F1
North Gdns BRI BN1 ....4 D2
Northgate CCH PO19 ....6 E3
Northgate Av CRAWE RH10 ....9 J1
Northgate Cl BRIE/ROTT BN2 ....97 L3
  LAN/SOMP BN15 ....72 A7
Northgate Pl CRAWE RH10 ....9 H1
Northgate Rd CRAWE RH10 ....8 F3
  HORL RH6 ....14 E8
North Ham Rd LHPTN BN17 ......89 J4
North Heath Cl HORS RH12 .....36 C4
North Heath La HORS RH12 .....36 C2
North Holmes Cl HORS RH12 ....37 G4
Northlands Av HWH RH16 ....45 H5
Northlands Cl PUL/STOR RH20 ..160 B9
Northlands Rd HORS RH12 ......36 D2
  HORS RH12 ....115 N8
North La ANG/EP BN16 ....90 A3
  ANG/EP BN16 ....91 G3
  EGRIN RH19 ....42 D4
  EPSF GU31 ....133 M12
  EPSF GU31 ....152 E1
  HORN PO8 ....150 C7
  PTSD BN41 ....74 F3
  RCCH PO18 ....155 K12
  SELS PO20 ....181 L6
  STEY/UB BN44 ....161 M11
North Md CRAWE RH10 ....29 K1
North Pallant CCH PO19 ....6 E5
North Pde BOR GU35 ....106 F3
  HORS RH12 ....10 C1
North Pl BRI BN1 ....4 F6
  LHPTN BN17 ....89 K5
North Pound ARUN BN18 ....65 J4
North Rd BRI BN1 ....76 D4
  CRAWE RH10 ....20 E6
  HORN PO8 ....150 D11
  HWH RH16 ....45 K5
  LAN/SOMP BN15 ....72 D7
  PSF GU32 ....133 N5
  PTSD BN41 ....74 F4
  RCCH PO18 ....60 B6
  SELS PO20 ....181 L6
North St BRI BN1 ....4 D6
  CCH PO19 ....6 E4

  CRAWE RH10 ....31 M5
  EDEN TN8 ....25 M3
  EMRTH PO10 ....58 A4
  EMRTH PO10 ....58 C1
  HAV PO9 ....56 E3
  HAV PO9 ....57 G4
  HORS RH12 ....10 F4
  LHPTN BN17 ....89 J2
  MIDH GU29 ....137 J9
  PETW GU28 ....139 L8
  PUL/STOR RH20 ....160 A12
  SHOR BN43 ....73 K6
  WTHG BN11 ....13 H4
North Street Ar HAV PO9 * 57 G4
North Street Qd BRI BN1 * 4 D6
North Stroud La PSF GU32 ......132 F7
Northumberland Rd
  BOR GU35 ....106 G8
Northview Rd SALV BN13 * 178 H13
North Walls CCH PO19 ....6 D4
North Wy HAV PO9 ....56 F4
  LEWES BN7 ....55 M3
  MSEA/BNM PO22 ....3 J4
  PETW GU28 ....139 K10
Northway BURH RH15 ....47 H5
  HORL RH6 ....15 L1
Northway Rd LHPTN BN17 ....89 J1
Northwood Pk CRAWE RH10 * 19 M7
Northwyke Cl MSEA/BNM PO22 ...87 H8
Northwyke Rd
  MSEA/BNM PO22 ....87 H8
Norton Cl HOVE BN3 ....76 A7
Norton Dr BRIE/ROTT BN2 ......78 C4
Norton La SELS PO20 ....64 A4
Norton Rd HOVE BN3 ....76 A7
  LAN/SOMP BN15 ....72 C8
Norway La LHPTN BN17 ....89 L2
Norway St PTSD BN41 ....74 H6
Norwich Cl BRIE/ROTT BN2 .....77 M3
Norwich Ct WTHG BN11 * 12 A7
Norwich Dr BRIE/ROTT BN2 .....77 M3
Norwich Rd CCH PO19 ....61 L5
Norwood La PETW GU28 ....156 D5
Norwood La South
  PETW GU28 ....156 D8
Novington La LEWES BN7 ....167 K8
Nowhurst La HORS RH12 ....115 K12
Nuffield Cl BOGR PO21 ....103 K2
Nugent Cl MFD/CHID GU8 ......112 A3
Nunns Fld RDKG RH5 * 16 B3
The Nurseries BOGR PO21 ......103 H2
  RHWH RH17 ....40 F8
Nursery Cl ANG/EP BN16 ....90 F5
  EMRTH PO10 ....58 A2
  HPPT/KEY BN6 ....164 G12
  HWH RH16 ....45 G4
  LAN/SOMP BN15 ....72 C5
  MSEA/BNM PO22 ....65 G7
  PTSD BN41 ....74 D1
  RDKG RH5 ....16 B4
  SHOR BN43 ....74 A5
Nursery Fld LISS GU33 ....116 B10
Nursery Gdns HORN PO8 ....168 B4
  LHPTN BN17 ....89 J2
Nurserylands CRAWW RH11 ......28 F3
Nursery La CCH PO19 ....61 G6
  HORL RH6 ....14 C7
  RHWH RH17 * 148 G8
  WTHG BN11 ....12 E7
Nursery Rd ANG/EP BN16 ....90 F1
  HAV PO9 ....57 H5
The Nursery BURH RH15 ....47 H5
Nursling Crs HAV PO9 ....168 H12
Nutbourne La PUL/STOR RH20 ..141 P11
Nutbourne Rd
  PUL/STOR RH20 ....159 P4
  SALV BN13 ....12 C1
Nutcombe La GSHT GU26 ....108 H8
Nutcroft PUL/STOR RH20 ....159 K2
Nutham La SWTR RH13 ....125 R12
Nuthatch Cl HAV PO9 ....169 J8
Nuthatch Wy CRAWE RH10 ....32 B4
Nuthurst Cl BRIE/ROTT BN2 ....77 L8
  CRAWW RH11 ....28 F2
Nuthurst Pl BRIE/ROTT BN2 ....77 L8
Nuthurst Rd SWTR RH13 ....126 F9
Nuthurst St SWTR RH13 ....126 F9
Nutley Av FERR BN12 ....92 B4
Nutley Cl BOR GU35 ....106 G7
  FERR BN12 ....92 B4
  HOVE BN3 ....75 L2
Nutley Crs FERR BN12 ....92 B4
Nutley Dr FERR BN12 ....92 B4
Nutley Rd HAV PO9 ....168 E12
Nutwick Rd HAV PO9 ....57 J2
Nye La HPPT/KEY BN6 ....166 A9
Nye Rd BURH RH15 ....47 G6
Nyes Cl HFD BN5 ....163 L4
Nyes La SWTR RH13 ....125 Q10
Nyetimber Copse
  PUL/STOR RH20 ....159 R7
Nyetimber Crs BOGR PO21 .....103 G3
Nyetimber Hl BRIE/ROTT BN2 ...77 K3
Nyetimber La BOGR PO21 ......102 F3
  PUL/STOR RH20 ....159 Q6
Nyetimber Ml BOGR PO21 ......102 F3
The Nyetimbers BOGR PO21 ....102 F3
Nyewood Gdns BOGR PO21 ....2 B6
Nyewood La BOGR PO21 ....2 A5
Nyewood Pl BOGR PO21 ....2 A8
Nymans Cl HORS RH12 ....36 F2
Nymans Ct CRAWE RH10 ....2 A6
Nyton Rd RCCH PO18 ....63 M3
  SELS PO20 ....64 B5

O

Oakapple Cl CRAWW RH11 ....29 G8
  SWTR RH13 ....145 K4
Oakapple Rd STHW BN42 ....74 C4
Oak Av CCH PO19 ....6 B2
  PUL/STOR RH20 ....160 E10
Oak Bank HWH RH16 ....45 J2
Oak Cl BRI BN1 ....76 D2
  CCH PO19 ....6 B2
  CRAWE RH10 ....20 E6
  MFD/CHID GU8 ....110 F7
  MSEA/BNM PO22 ....86 D7
  SALV BN13 ....70 D4
  SWTR RH13 ....143 Q2
Oak Cottages HASM GU27 ......108 H11
Oak Ct CRAWE RH10 * 19 J7
Oak Cft EGRIN RH19 ....33 M1

Oakcroft Gdns LHPTN BN17...89 L2
Oakdale Rd HWH RH16...45 J6
Oak Dell CRAWE RH10...30 B2
Oakdene Av PTSD BN41...74 D2
Oakdene Cl PTSD BN41...74 D2
Oakdene Crs PTSD BN41...74 D2
Oakdene Gdns PTSD BN41...74 D1
Oakdene Ri PTSD BN41...74 D1
Oakdene Wy PTSD BN41...74 D1
Oak End ARUN BN18...66 D3
　PUL/STOR RH20...160 A6
Oakenfield BURH RH15...46 E4
Oakfield BIL RH14...121 D2
Oakfield Av SELS PO20...99 L6
Oakfield Cl HWH RH16...45 K2
Oakfield Ct HAV PO9...169 J12
Oakfield Rd SELS PO20...99 L6
　SWTR RH13...145 K4
Oakfields CRAWE RH10...30 C2
　RDKG RH5...114 H1
Oakfield Wy EGRIN RH19...23 L6
Oak Gv BIL RH14...122 H1
　MSEA/BNM PO22...86 B7
Oak Hall Pk BURH RH15...47 C8
Oakhanger Rd BOR GU35...106 D4
Oakhaven CRAWE RH10 *...8 E7
Oakhill Rd BOR GU35...107 H4
　SWTR RH13...10 F5
Oakhurst GSHT GU26...108 G3
　HFD BN5...163 K3
　HPPT/KEY BN6...146 E12
　MIDH GU29...136 C9
Oakhurst Dr WVILLE PO7...168 B9
Oakhurst Gdns ANG/EP BN16...90 D3
　EGRIN RH19...23 H7
Oakhurst La BIL RH14...112 F11
　HWH RH16...45 L6
Oakhurst Ms SWTR RH13 *...11 M1
Oaklands BIL RH14...142 A2
　HASM GU27...109 M10
　HORL RH6...15 H6
　RHWH RH17...130 E1
　SWTR RH13...11 C6
Oaklands Cl SWTR RH13...126 F11
Oaklands La MIDH GU29...154 H11
Oaklands Rd HAV PO9...57 H4
　HWH RH16...45 C4
　PSF GU32...133 M5
Oaklands Wy CCH PO19...6 E2
Oak La HORS RH12...125 P2
Oak Lees HWH RH16 *...45 L1
Oakleigh Cl WTHG BN11...93 M1
Oakleigh Rd HORS RH12...11 K1
　WTHG BN11...93 M1
Oakley Cl EGRIN RH19...34 A2
Oakley Gdns ANG/EP BN16...90 F5
Oakley Rd BOR GU35...106 C4
　HAV PO9...168 E12
Oak Little SWTR RH13...144 E10
Oak Meadow SELS PO20...82 D8
Oakmeadow Cl EMRTH PO10...58 A4
Oakmead Rd BURH RH15...46 E8
Oakmont Dr HORN PO8...168 A7
Oak Park Dr HAV PO9...57 H2
Oak Rd CRAWW RH11...8 D5
　HORN PO8...150 D8
　SWTR RH13...125 P12
Oakroyd Cl BURH RH15...47 H4
Oaks Cl HORS RH12...37 G3
　SELS PO20...64 C7
Oaks Coppice HORN PO8...168 B3
Oakshott Dr HAV PO9...168 H12
Oakside La HORL RH6...15 H5
The Oaks ANG/EP BN16...90 D4
　BOGR PO21...103 K2
　BURH RH15...46 B5
　EGRIN RH19...33 M1
　HFD BN5 *...163 L11
　HWH RH16...45 H4
　HWH RH16...45 M5
　MFD/CHID GU8 *...110 C5
Oaktree Cl BOGR PO21...102 E3
Oak Tree Cl BOR GU35...107 N5
　EGRIN RH19 *...23 H6
Oak Tree Dr EMRTH PO10...57 M1
　EMRTH PO10...58 A1
　LISS GU33...116 D9
Oak Tree Farm RCCH PO18...59 J4
Oak Tree La HASM GU27...108 G11
　MFD/CHID GU8...112 A4
　SELS PO20...64 C8
Oak Tree Rd BOR GU35...106 F8
Oak Tree Wy SWTR RH13...11 K2
Oakvale PUL/STOR RH20...159 R6
Oak Wk HORS RH12...27 L7
Oak Wy CRAWE RH10...29 K1
Oakway SWTR RH13...126 H2
Oakwood SWTR RH13...144 F10
Oakwood Av HAV PO9...56 C2
Oakwood Cl BURH RH15...47 C7
　MIDH GU29...136 C10
　SELS PO20...63 J3
Oakwood Dr ANG/EP BN16...90 F1
Oakwood Flats HWH RH16 *...45 G5
Oakwood Gdns BOGR PO21...2 C4
Oakwood Rd BURH RH15...47 C7
　HORL RH6...15 C5
　HWH RH16...45 C5
Oates Wk CRAWE RH10...9 J9
Oathall Av HWH RH16...45 J5
Oathall Rd HWH RH16...45 J4
　HORL RH6...15 C5
Oatlands CRAWW RH11...28 F4
Oberon Cl WVILLE PO7...168 B9
Oberon Wy CRAWW RH11...28 C4
Ocean Cl FERR BN12...91 K5
Ocean Dr FERR BN12...91 K5
Ocean Pde FERR BN12...91 K4
Ockenden La RHWH RH17...40 C7
Ockenden Wy HPPT/KEY BN6...165 M6
Ockley Ct ANG/EP BN16...2 D7
Ockley Hl HPPT/KEY BN6...165 P5
Ockley La BURH RH15...165 G2
　HPPT/KEY BN6...165 P5
Ockley Rd BOGR PO21...2 D7
Ockley Wy HPPT/KEY BN6...165 P5
Octavius Ct WVILLE PO7...168 C8
Offham Rd LEWES BN7...55 M3
Offington Av SALV BN13...71 G6
Offington Ct SALV BN13...71 H7
Offington Dr SALV BN13...71 G6
Offington Gdns SALV BN13...70 F6
Offington La SALV BN13...70 F7
Okehurst La BIL RH14...123 R9

Okehurst Rd BIL RH14...123 P7
Old Arundel Rd RCCH PO18...62 E3
Old Bakery Gdns CCH PO19...7 H6
Old Barn Cl BOGR PO21...102 E3
Old Barn Dr RDKG RH5...16 C3
Old Barn Wy STHW BN42...74 F4
Old Boat Wk BRI BN1...53 G6
Old Br PUL/STOR RH20...159 J3
Old Bridge Rd RCCH PO18...60 B6
Old Brighton Rd (North)
　CRAWW RH11...39 H2
Old Brighton Rd (South)
　CRAWW RH11...39 H2
Old Brighton Rd South
　HORL RH6...19 K5
Old Broyle Rd CCH PO19...61 H3
Old Buddington La
　MIDH GU29...136 H7
Oldbury Cl HORS RH12...36 F2
Old Coastguards
　MSEA/BNM PO22...3 K7
Old Convent EGRIN RH19 *...23 K7
Old Copse Rd HAV PO9...57 H3
Old Cottage Cl SELS PO20...63 H4
Old Court Cl BRI BN1...76 E1
Old Crawley Rd HORS RH12...37 H1
Old Denne Gdns HORS RH12...10 C8
Olde Place Ms BRIE/ROTT BN2...97 L4
Older Wy ANG/EP BN16...68 C7
Old Farm Cl BOGR PO21...103 J3
　RHWH RH17...45 K7
Old Farm La EMRTH PO10...58 B5
Old Farm Rd BRI BN1...52 E8
　SELS PO20...181 J5
Old Farm Wy CHAM PO6...56 A6
Oldfield Crs STHW BN42...74 C6
Oldfield Rd HORL RH6...14 E8
The Old Flour Ml HPPT/KEY PO10 *...58 C6
Old Forge Cl HORS RH12...27 L8
Old Fort Rd SHOR BN43...73 M7
Old Glebe HASM GU27...119 L7
The Old Granary RCCH PO18 *...63 J1
Old Guildford Rd HORS RH12...125 N1
Old Haslemere Rd HASM GU27...109 M12
Old Holbrook HORS RH12...36 D1
Old Hollow CRAWE RH10...30 E1
Old Horsham Rd CRAWW RH11...8 B7
Oldhouse La HAV PO9...170 A3
　PUL/STOR RH20...142 D10
　SELS PO20...101 G6
　SWTR RH13...142 E6
Old House La SWTR RH13...143 L3
Old House Ms HORS RH12 *...10 C5
Oldlands Av HPPT/KEY BN6...165 P5
　RHWH RH17...40 E8
Oldlands Wy MSEA/BNM PO22...86 D6
Old London Rd BRI BN1...52 D8
　PUL/STOR RH20...158 C7
　PUL/STOR RH20...178 H1
Old Manor Cl CRAWW RH11...28 F1
Old Manor Farm HAV PO9 *...56 C4
Old Manor House Gdns
　MSEA/BNM PO22...87 G3
Old Manor Rd ANG/EP BN16...90 A4
Old Market Av CCH PO19...6 E5
Old Market Sq STEY/UB BN44 *...48 C2
Old Martyrs CRAWW RH11...19 J8
Old Mead Rd LHPTN BN17...67 H8
Old Mill Cl BRI BN1...52 D8
Old Mill Dr PUL/STOR RH20...160 A12
Old Mill La EPSF GU31...133 Q4
Old Millmeads HORS RH12...36 B4
Old Mill Pl HASM GU27...109 J10
　PUL/STOR RH20...159 L4
The Old Ml ARUN BN18 *...67 G2
Old Orchards CRAWE RH10...30 C3
Old Parish La BRIE/ROTT BN2...78 C5
Old Park Cl RHWH RH17...44 D3
Old Park La RCCH PO18...82 B3
Old Pl BOGR PO21...103 K3
Old Point MSEA/BNM PO22...105 K1
Old Printing House Sq
　ARUN BN18 *...67 G2
The Old Quarry HASM GU27...119 J1
Old Rectory Cl EMRTH PO10...58 C1
Old Rectory Ct
　MSEA/BNM PO22 *...3 L4
Old Rectory Dr SELS PO20...64 D6
Old Rectory Gdns
　MSEA/BNM PO22...3 L4
　STHW BN42...74 C6
Old Rectory Rd CHAM PO6...56 A5
The Old Rectory
　MSEA/BNM PO22...3 L5
Old Rd EGRIN RH19...33 L1
Old Salts Farm Rd
　LAN/SOMP BN15...72 F8
Old School Cl SELS PO20...100 C1
Old School Ct HWH RH16...45 J6
Old School Ms MSEA/BNM PO22...3 L3
Old School Pl BURH RH15...46 E7
Old School Rd LISS GU33...116 C9
The Old School
　PUL/STOR RH20...158 D3
Old Shoreham Rd BRI BN1...4 B2
　LAN/SOMP BN15...73 H4
　SHOR BN43...73 J5
　STHW BN42...74 E5
The Old Stables
　MSEA/BNM PO22 *...3 M1
Old Station Cl CRAWE RH10...31 M2
Old Station Wy BOR GU35...106 D4
Old Steine BRI BN1...4 F7
Old Stocks SALV BN13...178 H11
The Old Theatre CCH PO19 *...6 E4
Old Wickham La HWH RH16...45 G2
Old Wickhurst La HORS RH12...125 N4
Oldwick Mdw RCCH PO18...172 C12
Old Worthing Rd ANG/EP BN16...91 G3
Old Yard Cl SWTR RH13...144 F10
Olive Rd HOVE BN3...75 M4
Oliver Rd HORS RH12...125 N4
Olivers Meadow SELS PO20...64 C6
Oliver Whitby Rd CCH PO19...6 A2
Olivia Cl WVILLE PO7...168 B8
Olivier Cl BRIE/ROTT BN2...5 K4
Olivier Rd CRAWE RH10...30 C4
Onslow Dr FERR BN12...91 K3
Onslow Rd HOVE BN3...76 A4
Ontario Cl HORL RH6...15 M7
　SALV BN13...70 B7
Ontario Gdns SALV BN13...70 B7
Ontario Wy LIPH GU30...117 G9
Openfields BOR GU35...107 M5
Ophir Rd WTHG BN11...93 M2

Orange Rw EMRTH PO10...58 A5
Orchard Av CCH PO19...6 D2
　HOVE BN3...75 M4
　LAN/SOMP BN15...72 D6
　SALV BN13...70 F8
　SELS PO20...181 L7
Orchard Cl BOGR PO21...2 B7
　EPSF GU31...152 H1
　FERR BN12...91 K2
　HFD BN5...163 L11
　HORL RH6...14 E5
　HORN PO8...168 D3
　HWH RH16...45 G1
　MIDH GU29...153 L1
　PETW GU28...139 L10
　RHWH RH17...149 J2
　SELS PO20...71 G8
　SHOR BN43...73 K5
　STHW BN42...74 E5
Orchard Cnr HWH RH16...45 L4
Orchard Crs ARUN BN18...64 F2
Orchard Dell PUL/STOR RH20...160 B3
Orchard Gdns ANG/EP BN16...90 C3
　CCH PO19...6 D3
　HOVE BN3...76 A4
　SELS PO20...64 C8
Orchard Gv HORN PO8...168 A6
Orchard Hl HORS RH12...113 R10
Orchard La EMRTH PO10...58 B5
　SELS PO20...81 M6
Orchard Pl ARUN BN18...67 G5
Orchard Rd ANG/EP BN16...90 F3
　BURH RH15...46 D7
　HAV PO9...57 G5
　HOVE BN3...75 M4
　SWTR RH13...11 H7
Orchard Side SELS PO20...83 L5
The Orchards CRAWW RH11...28 C4
Orchard St CCH PO19...6 D3
　CRAWW RH11...8 E3
The Orchard BOGR PO21...103 H4
　HASM GU27...109 J12
　HORL RH6 *...14 F6
　SHOR BN43...37 G5
Orchard Wy ARUN BN18...64 F2
　BURH RH15...46 E6
　EGRIN RH19...23 K8
　HPPT/KEY BN6...164 G3
　HWH RH16...45 G1
　LAN/SOMP BN15...72 D6
　MIDH GU29...137 J9
　MSEA/BNM PO22...2 C2
　MSEA/BNM PO22...65 G7
　PUL/STOR RH20...159 K2
　RHWH RH17...128 E9
Orchid Pk HWH RH16...45 M5
Orchid Vw BRI BN1...53 H7
Orde Cl CRAWE RH10...20 C8
Oriel Cl CRAWE RH10...20 B8
Oriel Ct ANG/EP BN16...65 G7
Oriental Pl BRI BN1...4 A7
Orient Rd LAN/SOMP BN15...73 H4
Orkney Ct SALV BN13...70 A8
Orme Rd WTHG BN11...12 E3
Ormesby Crs CRAWE RH10...20 A4
Ormesby Wk CRAWE RH10...30 A5
Ormonde Av CCH PO19...7 H5
Ormonde Wy SHOR BN43...73 J7
Orpen Pl SELS PO20...181 M6
Orpen Rd HOVE BN3...76 C4
Orpington Rd EPSF GU31...133 M7
Osborn Crs CCH PO19...61 K5
Osborne Cl LAN/SOMP BN15...72 B7
　WVILLE PO7...168 B10
Osborne Dr LAN/SOMP BN15...72 B7
Osborne Rd BRI BN1...76 E3
　PSF GU32...133 N5
Osborne Vls HOVE BN3...76 A8
Osmonde Cl SALV BN13...12 F2
Osmond Rd HOVE BN3...4 A3
Osprey Gdns MSEA/BNM PO22...86 B6
Osprey Quay EMRTH PO10...58 C6
Ostlers Vw BIL RH14...141 R2
Otard Cl SELS PO20...181 L6
Otford Cl CRAWW RH11...39 H1
Othello Dr WVILLE PO7...168 B9
Ottawa Dr LIPH GU30...117 R2
Otterbourne Crs HAV PO9...168 E12
Otterbourne Pl EGRIN RH19 *...23 G8
Otter Cl CCH PO19...61 K5
Otway Cl CRAWW RH11...28 E5
Otway Rd CCH PO19...61 L4
Oulton Wk CRAWE RH10...30 A5
Outerwyke Av MSEA/BNM PO22...3 M1
Outerwyke Gdns
　MSEA/BNM PO22...3 M1
Outerwyke Rd MSEA/BNM PO22...3 L4
Outram Rd MSEA/BNM PO22...83 M4
Oval La SELS PO20...181 L8
The Oval LISS GU33...116 C9
　SALV BN13...70 A8
　SALV BN13...178 H10
Oval Waye FERR BN12...91 K5
Overdale Pl BOR GU35 *...106 G8
Overdale Wk BOR GU35...106 G8
Overdene CRAWW RH11...28 F3
Overdown Ri PTSD BN41...74 E1
Overhill STHW BN42...74 D4
Overhill Cl BRI BN1...52 D8
Overhill Dr BRI BN1...52 D8
Overhill Gdns BRI BN1...52 D8
Overhill Wy BRI BN1...52 D7
Overmead SHOR BN43...73 M4
Overstrand Av ANG/EP BN16...90 B6
Over St BRI BN1...4 E4
Overton Crs HAV PO9...168 E12
Overton Shaw EGRIN RH19...23 K6
Ovingdean Cl BRIE/ROTT BN2...78 B2
Ovingdean Rd BRIE/ROTT BN2...97 J1
Oving Rd CCH PO19...7 J4
Oving Ter CCH PO19 *...7 K4
Owen Cl BURH RH15...46 E5
Owers Cl BURH RH15...46 E5
Owers Wy SELS PO20...99 K6
Owlbeech Wy SWTR RH13...37 G5
Owletts CRAWE RH10...30 C4
Owlscastle Cl CRAWE RH10...30 C4
Owlsbury Gv HAV PO9...168 C12

Oxen Av SHOR BN43...73 L5
Oxford Cl SELS PO20...99 L6
　BRI BN1...4 F7
Oxford Ct BRI BN1...4 F7
Oxford Dr BOGR PO21...103 K2
Oxford Ms HOVE BN3...76 B6
Oxford Pl BRI BN1...4 E5
Oxford Rd CRAWE RH10...29 G7
　SWTR RH13...10 F6
　WTHG BN11...13 G4
Oxford St BOGR PO21...2 A8
　BRI BN1...4 E5
Oxford Ter STEY/UB BN44 *...48 C2

P

Pacific Wy SELS PO20...181 L8
Packham Wy BURH RH15...46 E8
Paddock Cl HASM GU27...119 K8
　SALV BN13...12 C1
Paddock Fld BRI BN1 *...54 A8
Paddock Gdns EGRIN RH19...23 K2
Paddock Gn ANG/EP BN16...90 D3
Paddockhall Rd HWH RH16...45 G4
Paddockhurst La RHWH RH17...41 J5
Paddockhurst Rd CRAWE RH10...31 H7
　CRAWW RH11...28 A7
Paddock La SELS PO20...181 K6
The Paddocks HWH RH16...44 E6
　LAN/SOMP BN15...72 E8
　LEWES BN7...166 H4
　STEY/UB BN44...49 G2
The Paddock BOR GU35...107 M4
　CRAWE RH10...30 C3
　GSHT GU26...108 D5
　HASM GU27...109 K9
　HOVE BN3...75 K6
　LHPTN BN17...67 H7
　MSEA/BNM PO22...3 E3
　SHOR BN43...73 J4
Paddock Wy HASM GU27...109 R7
　LIPH GU30...107 Q12
　PSF GU32...133 L7
　SALV BN13...178 H11
Padnell Av HORN PO8...168 C7
Padnell Rd HORN PO8...168 C6
Padwick Rd HAV PO9...57 H3
Padwicks Fld PUL/STOR RH20...158 B2
Pages La BIL RH14...140 F7
Paget Cl SWTR RH13...11 C9
Pagewood Cl CRAWE RH10...30 C5
Pagham Cl EMRTH PO10...58 B5
Pagham Gdns HISD PO11...98 A3
Pagham Rd BOGR PO21...102 E5
　SELS PO20...84 F8
Pain's Flat RHWH RH17...46 C1
Palace Pl BRI BN1...4 F6
Palatine Rd FERR BN12...92 B1
Paling Wy HASM GU27...119 K8
The Pallant FERR BN12...92 A1
　HAV PO9...57 G4
Pallingham Dr CRAWE RH10...30 B6
Pallingham La BIL RH14...140 E7
Palma Ct WTHG BN11 *...12 C1
Palm Ct SALV BN13...70 D6
Palmeira Av HOVE BN3...76 B7
Palmeira Sq HOVE BN3...76 B8
Palmer Cl HORL RH6...14 E4
　PUL/STOR RH20...160 C11
Palmer Pl ANG/EP BN16...68 D7
　CRAWE RH10...30 B6
Palmers Field Av CCH PO19...62 A5
Palmer's Rd EMRTH PO10...58 A4
Palmerston Av FERR BN12...92 B3
Palmers Wy SALV BN13...71 J4
Pangdean La HPPT/KEY BN6...46 B6
Pangdene Cl BURH RH15...46 C8
Pankhurst Av BRIE/ROTT BN2...5 K4
Pannell Cl EGRIN RH19...23 J8
Pannells Ash BIL RH14...122 D2
Pannett BURH RH15...46 D5
Pantiles BOR GU35...107 C4
The Pantiles BRIE/ROTT BN2...91 K4
Panton Cl EMRTH PO10...57 M2
Parade Man ANG/EP BN16...90 F5
The Parade ANG/EP BN16...90 F5
　BOGR PO21 *...2 D7
　BOGR PO21...102 E7
　BRI BN1 *...76 A1
　CRAWE RH10...9 H1
　EGRIN RH19 *...23 G6
　HORS RH12 *...125 R2
　HOVE BN3...75 K3
Paradise La EMRTH PO10...58 C1
Parchment St CCH PO19...6 D2
The Parchment HAV PO9...57 G4
Parham Cl ANG/EP BN16...90 A5
　BRIE/ROTT BN2...5 L6
　LHPTN BN17...89 J3
　SALV BN13...70 E4
Parham Rd CRAWW RH11...28 E2
　SALV BN13...70 E4
Parish La CRAWE RH10...39 L3
Park Av HOVE BN3...75 K6
　HPPT/KEY BN6...165 N6
　SELS PO20...181 M6
　SHOR BN43...73 M4
　WTHG BN11...13 K3
Park Cl BRI BN1...46 K8
　BURH RH15...46 K8
　HASM GU27...109 Q8
　HOVE BN3...75 K6
　PTSD BN41...74 F6
　SALV BN13...70 F6
Park Copse SELS PO20...181 P4
Park Crs BRIE/ROTT BN2...5 H2
　BRIE/ROTT BN2...97 L4
　EMRTH PO10...57 L4
　FROW RH18...34 F7
　MIDH GU29...136 H9
　PTSD BN41...74 F6
　SELS PO20...181 N5
Park Crescent Pl
　BRIE/ROTT BN2 *...5 H2
Park Crescent Rd
　BRIE/ROTT BN2...5 G2
Park Crescent Ter
　BRIE/ROTT BN2...5 H2
Park Dr ANG/EP BN16...90 C3
　ARUN BN18...87 M3
　FERR BN12...91 L3

MSEA/BNM PO22...87 J8
Park East HWH RH16 *...45 J7
Parker Cl CRAWE RH10...30 C4
Parker Ct PTSD BN41...75 G3
Park Farm Cl HORS RH12...36 C2
Parkfield HORS RH12...10 D3
Parkfield Av HAV PO9...103 G2
Parkfield Cl CRAWW RH11...28 E5
Parkfield Ct SALV BN13...12 A2
Parkfield Rd SALV BN13...12 A2
Parkfield Wy HWH RH16...44 E6
Park Hl BRIE/ROTT BN2...5 H6
Park House Farm Wy HAV PO9...168 D12
Parkhurst Gv HORL RH6...14 D5
Parkhurst Rd HORL RH6...14 D5
Parklands SHOR BN43...74 B5
Parklands Av BOGR PO21...2 B5
　FERR BN12...92 C4
　HORN PO8...168 B4
Parklands Rd CCH PO19...6 C3
　HPPT/KEY BN6...165 N6
Park La ARUN BN18...65 H1
　EMRTH PO10...169 Q9
　HASM GU27...119 L7
　HAV PO9...57 G5
　HORN PO8...168 D2
　HWH RH16...130 C7
　MFD/CHID GU8...109 P2
　PUL/STOR RH20...160 G8
　RCCH PO18...173 N12
　SELS PO20...64 A7
　SELS PO20...181 M4
　STHW BN42...74 C6
　SWTR RH13...126 F11
　SWTR RH13...144 D5
　WVILLE PO7...168 D5
Parklawn Av HORL RH6...14 E4
Park Mnr BRI BN1 *...76 C2
Parkmore Ter BRI BN1...4 D1
Park Pde HAV PO9...56 F1
　HWH RH16...45 H5
Park Pl ARUN BN18...65 H2
　HORS RH12...10 D7
Park Ri HORS RH12...10 A2
　HOVE BN3...75 K2
　PETW GU28...139 L7
Park Rd ARUN BN18...87 M2
　BOGR PO21...2 B9
　BRI BN1...53 K8
　BRIE/ROTT BN2...97 L4
　BURH RH15...46 E6
　EGRIN RH19...23 J8
　EGRIN RH19...23 K3
　EMRTH PO10...58 E4
　FROW RH18...34 F7
　HASM GU27...109 M13
　HFD BN5...163 K5
　HORS RH12...45 G5
　HWH RH16...45 G5
　MSEA/BNM PO22...J7
　PETW GU28...139 L9
　PSF GU32...133 N6
　RCCH PO18...173 J11
　RHWH RH17...128 C2
　SELS PO20...181 N5
　SHOR BN43...73 M4
　SWTR RH13...124 C3
　WTHG BN11...13 J3
Park Rd North HAV PO9...56 F1
Park Rd South HAV PO9...57 G1
Park Road Ter BRIE/ROTT BN2...5 H6
Parkside BOGR PO21...2 F4
　CRAWE RH10...9 G4
　HAV PO9...57 G5
　HPPT/KEY BN6...165 M5
　SHOR BN43...73 M4
　WTHG BN11 *...13 J4
Parkside Av LHPTN BN17...89 L4
Parkside Ms HORS RH12...10 E5
Park Sq BRIE/ROTT BN2...96 E2
The Parks PTSD BN41...74 F2
Park St BOR GU35...106 G6
　BRI BN1...54 B7
　BRIE/ROTT BN2...5 H7
　HORS RH12...10 E5
　SWTR RH13...124 F2
Park Ter BOGR PO21...2 B9
Park Ter East SWTR RH13...10 E7
Park Ter West SWTR RH13...10 E7
The Park BRIE/ROTT BN2...97 M4
Park Vw CRAWW RH11...8 E5
　HORL RH6...14 F6
　HWH RH16...45 H5
Park View Ct ANG/EP BN16...90 D3
Park View Gdns EGRIN RH19...23 J8
Park View Rd HOVE BN3...76 A4
Park View Ter BRI BN1...76 D5
Parkway BOGR PO21...103 M2
Park Wy CRAWE RH10...30 B1
　HAV PO9...56 F4
　HORS RH12...10 D4
　MIDH GU29...137 L7
　STHW BN42...74 E5
Park Way SWTR RH13...74 E5
The Parkway ANG/EP BN16...90 C4
Park West HWH RH16 *...45 J7
Parnell Cl CRAWE RH10...30 C5
Parochial Ms BRIE/ROTT BN2 *...4 F5
Parochial Ter BRIE/ROTT BN2 *...4 F5
Parrock La HRTF TN7...35 H5
Parry Cl SWTR RH13...37 G5
Parry Dr ANG/EP BN16...90 A4
Parsonage Cl PSF GU32...133 M5
Parsonage Est EPSF GU31...134 H5
Parsonage Rd HFD BN5...163 K4
　HORS RH12...10 F1
Parsonage Wy HORS RH12...11 G1
Parsons Cl ANG/EP BN16...90 F1
　HASM GU27...109 M5
　HORL RH6...10 F1
Parsons Gn HASM GU27...109 M5
Parson's Hl ARUN BN18...67 G2
Parsons La GSHT GU26...108 F3
Parsons Wk ARUN BN18...67 G2
Parthings La HORS RH12...125 Q5
Partridge Green Rd
　SWTR RH13...144 H10
Partridge La HORS RH12...17 K7
　RDKG RH5...17 L1
Passfield Rd LIPH GU30...107 M9
Passfield Wk HAV PO9...169 J12
Passingham Wk HORN PO8...168 B5
Paston Pl BRIE/ROTT BN2...5 L9
Pasture Hill Rd HWH RH16...45 G5

The Pasture CRAWE RH10 .... 30 B3
Patcham By-Pass BRI BN1 .... 52 D7
Patcham Gra BRI BN1 .... 52 D8
Patchdean BRI BN1 .... 52 D8
Patching Cl CRAWW RH11 ...... 28 C2
  FERR BN12 .... 92 A1
Patchings SWTR RH13 .... 11 J4
Paterson Dr LISS GU33 .... 116 F3
Paterson Wilson Rd
  LHPTN 89 K4
Pathfield CRAWE RH10 .... 9 J2
Pathfield Rd HORS RH12 .... 114 A10
Pathfield Rd HORS RH12 .... 114 A10
Pathfields Cl HASM GU27 ...... 109 N10
Path Link CRAWE RH10 .... 9 J2
Patricia Av FERR BN12 .... 92 A4
Patricia Cl FERR BN12 .... 92 C4
Patrick's Cl LISS GU33 .... 116 D9
Patrington Cl CRAWW RH11 ... 28 F6
Patterdale Cl CRAWW RH11 .... 8 B9
Pavilion Buildings BRI BN1 ..... 4 E7
Pavilion Cl HPPT/KEY BN6 .... 165 M4
Pavilion Pde BRIE/ROTT BN2 .. 4 F6
  WTHG BN11 .... 13 H7
Pavilion St BRIE/ROTT BN2 .... 4 F7
The Pavilions CRAWW RH11 ... 39 H3
Pavilion Wy EGRIN RH19 .... 33 K1
Pax Cl CRAWW RH11 .... 28 D5
Paxmead Crs SALV BN13 .... 71 J7
The Paymaster General's Rbt
  CRAWE 9 L4
Payne Av HOVE BN3 .... 75 L5
Payne Cl BOGR PO21 .... 102 F5
  CRAWE 30 C1
Paynesfield RHWH RH17 .... 146 D2
Paythorne Cl STHW BN42 ...... 74 C4
Paythorne Dro HFD BN5 .... 163 Q12
Payton Dr BURH RH15 .... 46 F7
Peace Cl BRI BN1 .... 77 H4
Peacemaker Cl CRAWW RH11 .. 28 D5
Peace Rd MIDH GU29 .... 155 T9
The Peacheries CCH PO19 ..... 7 H6
Peachey Rd SELS PO20 .... 181 K7
Peacock Cl CCH PO19 .... 62 B5
Peacock La BRI BN1 .... 76 D1
Peacock's HI SWTR RH13 ...... 126 H11
Peak La ANG/EP BN16 .... 91 H5
Peak Rd HORN PO8 .... 150 B8
The Peak HAV PO9 .... 169 K7
Pears Gv EMRTH PO10 .... 58 C5
Pearson Rd ARUN BN18 .... 66 E3
  CRAWE 30 A3
Pearsons Retreat WTHG BN11 *.. 94 A2
Pear Tree Cl BOR GU35 .... 107 J5
Peartree Cl BURH RH15 .... 46 D6
Pear Tree HI REDH RH1 * 14 F1
Pear Tree Rd BOR GU35 .... 107 J4
Peary Cl HORS RH12 .... 36 C3
Pease Cft EPSF GU31 .... 152 E2
Pebble Wk LHPTN RH17 .... 89 M2
Peckhams Copse La SELS PO20 .. 84 C2
Peeks Brook La HORL RH6 ..... 15 L7
Peel Cl LHPTN RH17 .... 89 H3
Peel Rd BRIE/ROTT BN2 .... 96 E1
Peerley Cl SELS PO20 .... 99 M7
Peerley Rd SELS PO20 .... 99 M7
Pegasus Cl HASM GU27 .... 108 G12
Pegasus Wy EGRIN RH19 ...... 23 M6
Pegler Wy CRAWW RH11 .... 8 E4
Pegwell Cl CRAWW RH11 ...... 28 E5
Pelham Cl BOR GU35 .... 106 C3
Pelham Ct CRAWW RH11 ...... 29 C5
  HORS RH12 * 10 A6
Pelham Dr CRAWW RH11 ...... 28 E7
Pelham Pl CRAWW RH11 ...... 29 C7
Pelham Rd HWH RH16 .... 45 K3
  SALV BN13 .... 70 E8
Pelham Sq BRI BN1 .... 4 F5
Pelham St BRI BN1 .... 4 F4
Pelham Ter EMRTH PO10 ...... 58 B5
Pellbrook Rd LEWES BN7 ...... 55 M2
Pelleys La SELS PO20 .... 83 L4
Pemberton Cl LAN/SOMP BN15 *.. 72 D2
Pembley Gn CRAWE RH10 ..... 21 K6
Pembroke Av FERR BN12 .... 92 E3
  HOVE BN3 .... 75 M7
Pembroke Crs HOVE BN3 ...... 75 M6
Pembroke Gdns HOVE BN3 ... 75 M7
Pembroke Rd CRAWE RH10 ... 20 D8
Pembroke Wy BOGR PO21 .... 103 K2
Pembury Cl HWH RH16 .... 45 L6
  SALV BN13 .... 13 G2
Pembury Rd HAV PO9 .... 57 H5
  SALV BN13 .... 13 G1
Pendeen Gdns LHPTN BN17 .. 67 H8
Pendean BURH RH15 .... 46 H8
Pende Cl LAN/SOMP BN15 .... 72 C5
Pendine Av WTHG BN11 .... 93 M2
Pendragon Cl HOVE BN3 * 75 M5
Penfold La ANG/EP BN16 ...... 90 D5
Penfold Rd CRAWE RH10 ...... 30 A7
  SALV BN13 .... 71 K8
Penfolds Pl ARUN BN18 .... 66 F3
Penfold Wy STEY/UB BN44 .... 48 C3
Penhill Rd LAN/SOMP BN15 .. 72 E8
Penhurst Pl BRIE/ROTT BN2 .. 77 L7
Penhurst Pl HAV PO9 .... 56 C7
Penk Rdg HAV PO9 .... 56 A5
Penland Cl HWH RH16 .... 45 G2
Penland Rd HWH RH16 .... 45 G3
Penland's Cl STEY/UB BN44 .. 48 C3
Penlands Ri STEY/UB BN44 ... 48 C3
Penlands V STEY/UB BN44 .... 48 B3
Penlands Wy STEY/UB BN44 .. 48 C3
Penleigh Cl LAN/SOMP BN15 .. 72 E8
Pennant Hills HAV PO9 .... 56 C3
Penn Cl CRAWW RH11 .... 19 J8
  MSEA/BNM PO22 .... 87 K8
Penn Ct CRAWW RH11 * 28 E5
Penn Crs HWH RH16 .... 45 K4
Pennels Cl LIPH GU30 .... 117 Q11
Pennerly Ct HAV PO9 .... 168 G12
Penner Rd HAV PO9 .... 56 E10
Pennine Cl CRAWW RH11 ..... 8 A3
Penns Ct STEY/UB BN44 .... 48 C3
Penns Pl EPSF GU31 .... 134 A6
Penns Rd PSF GU32 .... 133 M5
Pennycord Cl SELS PO20 ...... 181 L8
Pennycress Av SALV BN13 .... 69 M8
Pennyfields MSEA/BNM PO22 *.. 87 H8
Penny La EMRTH PO10 .... 58 C5
Penryn Dr BOR GU35 .... 107 R4
Pensfold La HORS RH12 .... 114 B12
Penshurst Cl CRAWE RH10 ... 30 C2

Penstone Pk LAN/SOMP BN15 .. 72 C7
Pentere Rd HORN PO8 .... 168 B3
Pentland Rd SALV BN13 .... 70 D6
Penton Ct HAV PO9 .... 169 J11
Penwarden Wy RCCH PO18 ... 60 B6
Penwith Dr HASM GU27 .... 108 H12
Penwood Gn HAV PO9 .... 169 J12
Peperham Rd HASM GU27 ..... 109 M9
Peper Harow HORN PO8 .... 168 C3
Peppard Rd CRAWE RH10 ..... 30 C5
Pepper Dr BURH RH15 .... 46 E8
Peppering La ARUN BN18 ...... 176 H9
Pepperscoombe La
  STEY/UB BN44 .... 48 F2
Peppersgate SWTR RH13 ...... 127 M10
Peppers Yd HORS RH12 * 10 F4
Perche Ct MIDH GU29 * 136 G11
Perching Dro HFD BN5 .... 163 R12
Percival Ter BRIE/ROTT BN2 .. 5 M9
Percy Rd HORS RH12 .... 10 B3
Percy Ter PETW GU28 * 139 L9
Peregrine Rd LHPTN BN17 .... 89 L3
Perimeter Rd East HORL RH6 .. 20 L3
Perimeter Rd North HORL RH6 .. 14 D8
Perimeter Rd South HORL RH6 .. 19 L4
Periwinkle Cl BOR GU35 .... 107 K4
Perrots Cl STEY/UB BN44 ...... 48 B3
Perry Av EGRIN RH19 .... 23 K6
Perryfield La SWTR RH13 ...... 127 P11
Perryfield Rd CRAWW RH11 ... 8 E4
Perryfields BURH RH15 .... 46 D5
Perrylands HORL RH6 .... 18 E2
Perrylands La HORL RH6 .... 15 L7
Perrymount Rd HWH RH16 .... 45 H4
Perry Wy BOR GU35 .... 107 N5
Perseus Rd WVILLE PO7 .... 56 A2
Perth Cl CRAWW RH11 .... 19 J8
Perth Wy HORS RH12 .... 11 K1
Pescott's Cl SELS PO20 .... 82 D8
Peskett Cl SWTR RH13 .... 125 J10
Peterborough Rd CRAWE RH10 .. 29 K7
Peterhouse Cl BOGR PO21 .... 103 L1
Peter Rd LAN/SOMP BN15 .... 94 B1
Petersfield La HORL RH6 .... 150 F6
Petersfield Rd BOR GU35 ...... 106 F8
  EPSF GU31 .... 133 H11
  HAV PO9 .... 57 G2
  LISS GU33 .... 106 E12
  LISS GU33 .... 116 B4
  MIDH GU29 .... 136 G9
Peter's La SELS PO20 .... 180 C5
Peters Rd SELS PO20 .... 180 G5
Peter Weston Pl CCH PO19 ... 7 G5
Petlands Gdns HWH RH16 ..... 45 J6
Petlands Rd HWH RH16 .... 45 H6
Pett Cl BRIE/ROTT BN2 .... 77 L7
Petts Cl SWTR RH13 .... 181 L4
Petworth Av FERR BN12 .... 92 B5
Petworth Ct CRAWW RH11 .... 28 E6
  MSEA/BNM PO22 .... 3 L1
Petworth Dr BURH RH15 .... 46 F5
  HORS RH12 .... 36 E2
Petworth Rd BIL RH14 .... 141 J1
  BRI BN1 .... 53 D7
  HASM GU27 .... 109 N12
  MFD/CHID GU8 .... 110 H5
Pevensey Cl CRAWE RH10 .... 30 B4
Pevensey Gdn WTHG BN11 ... 12 A7
Pevensey Rd BOGR PO21 ...... 103 L1
  BRIE/ROTT BN2 .... 5 J1
  SWTR RH13 .... 125 G12
  WTHG BN11 .... 12 E4
Peverel Rd CRAWE RH10 ...... 28 D4
  SALV BN13 .... 12 A2
Peveril Cl LAN/SOMP BN15 ... 71 M7
Peveril Rd LAN/SOMP BN15 .. 71 M7
Philip Rd WVILLE PO7 .... 168 A12
Philips Crs BOR GU35 .... 107 N4
Phillips Cl BOR GU35 .... 107 N4
  HORS RH12 .... 30 A8
Philliswood La RCCH PO18 .... 153 M11
Phoenix Cl CCH PO19 .... 6 F7
  LHPTN BN17 .... 89 G5
Phoenix Crs STHW BN42 .... 74 C5
Phoenix La EGRIN RH19 .... 34 D3
Phoenix Ri BRIE/ROTT BN2 ... 5 G4
Phoenix Ri BRIE/ROTT BN2 ... 5 G4
Phoenix Wy STHW BN42 .... 74 C5
Phrosso Rd WTHG BN11 .... 92 E4
Pickers Gn HWH RH16 .... 45 K1
Pickers La REDH RH1 .... 15 K1
Pickhurst La PUL/STOR RH20 .. 141 J10
Pickhurst Rd MFD/CHID GU8 .. 110 H6
Pickwell La RHWH RH17 .... 146 C1
Picton St BRIE/ROTT BN2 ..... 5 J2
Picts La SWTR RH13 .... 127 L12
Pierces La HWH RH16 .... 44 F7
Pier Rd LHPTN BN17 .... 89 J5
Piers Secombe Cl
  PUL/STOR RH20 .... 158 E8
Pigbush La BIL RH14 .... 112 G10
Pigeonhouse La ANG/EP BN16 .. 90 D5
Pigeon Pass CRAWE RH10 .... 32 B4
Piggery Hall La SELS PO20 .... 99 L4
The Pike PUL/STOR RH20 ..... 178 H3
Pilgrims Cl SALV BN13 .... 12 B2
Pilgrims Trail SALV BN13 * 12 A3
Pilgrims Wk SALV BN13 .... 12 A3
Pilgrims Wy BOGR PO21 .... 103 G4
  BOR GU35 .... 107 M4
Piltdown Rd BRIE/ROTT BN2 .. 77 L7
Pinckards MFD/CHID GU8 ..... 110 H4
Pine Bank GSHT GU26 .... 108 H5
Pine Cl BIL RH14 .... 123 R12
  CRAWH RH10 .... 19 H8
  MIDH GU29 .... 137 J12
  PUL/STOR RH20 .... 160 E10
Pine Gdns HORL RH6 .... 14 F7
Pine Gv CCH PO19 .... 61 H4
  EGRIN RH19 .... 23 G6
  HAV PO9 .... 57 H4
Pineham Copse HWH RH16 ... 45 J5
Pinehill Rd BOR GU35 .... 106 H7
Pinehurst BURH RH15 .... 46 F8
  HORS RH12 .... 10 D2
Pinehurst Cl WVILLE PO7 ...... 168 D7
Pinehurst Pk BOGR PO21 ...... 103 J1
Pines Av SALV BN13 .... 71 J6
Pines Rd LIPH GU30 .... 117 M1
Pine Shaw CRAWE RH10 .... 30 B2
Pines Rd LIPH GU30 .... 117 M1
The Pines ANG/EP BN16 .... 90 E1
  ARUN BN18 .... 87 L2
  BRIE/ROTT BN2 * 5 G3
  HORS RH12 .... 37 H4
  HPPT/KEY BN6 * 164 G2

HWH RH16 .... 45 L5
Pinetops HORS RH12 * 37 H5
Pine Tree Gdns HORN PO8 .... 168 B7
Pine Trees HPPT/KEY BN6 .... 165 L4
Pine Trees Cl ANG/EP BN16 .. 68 E6
Pinetrees Cl CRAWE RH10 .... 21 G6
Pine Vw BOR GU35 .... 107 Q3
Pine View Cl HASM GU27 ..... 109 M9
Pine Wk BOGR PO21 .... 103 J1
  LISS GU33 .... 116 D7
Pine Way Cl EGRIN RH19 ...... 33 K2
Pinewood Av HAV PO9 .... 56 C2
Pinewood Cl ANG/EP BN16 ... 90 F3
  HORS RH12 .... 125 N2
Pinewood Ct MIDH GU29 ..... 137 K11
Pinewood Gdns BOGR PO21 .. 103 M2
Pinewood Wy HWH RH16 ...... 45 G7
  MIDH GU29 .... 136 H12
Pinfold Cl BRIE/ROTT BN2 .... 78 D7
Pinkhurst La SWTR RH13 ...... 125 K3
Pinks La SELS PO20 .... 100 C3
Pinland Rd SWTR RH13 .... 144 E12
Pipers Cl HOVE BN3 .... 75 J1
Pipers End SWTR RH13 .... 124 H2
Pipers La PETW GU28 .... 120 G6
Pipers Md HORN PO8 .... 150 B8
Pipers Cl BOR GU35 .... 100 C2
Pitcroft La EPSF GU31 .... 133 N12
The Pitcroft CCH PO19 .... 62 B5
Pitfold Av HASM GU27 .... 108 G11
Pitfold Cl HASM GU27 .... 108 H11
Pit Rd HPPT/KEY BN6 .... 164 H4
Pitsham La MIDH GU29 .... 136 G12
Pitsham Wd MIDH GU29 .... 136 G11
Pitt Gdns BRIE/ROTT BN2 .... 78 C5
Place Crs WVILLE PO7 .... 168 A12
Plainfields Cl CCH PO19 .... 61 L3
Plainwood Cl CCH PO19 .... 61 L3
Plaistow Cl BRIE/ROTT BN2 .. 77 L7
Plaistow Rd BIL RH14 .... 122 B10
  BIL RH14 .... 122 C5
  MFD/CHID GU8 .... 111 J12
Plaitford Gv HAV PO9 .... 56 D1
Plantain Crs CRAWW RH11 ... 28 F7
Plantation Cl SALV BN13 .... 70 E6
Plantation Ri SALV BN13 .... 70 F6
Plantation Rd LISS GU33 .... 116 B9
The Plantation ANG/EP BN16 .. 90 F4
  PUL/STOR RH20 .... 159 Q12
  SALV BN13 .... 70 E7
Plantation Wy BOR GU35 ...... 106 D9
  PUL/STOR RH20 .... 159 R12
The Plat HORS RH12 .... 125 R3
Platts Meadow BIL RH14 .... 141 K1
The Platt HWH RH16 .... 45 L4
  LING RH7 .... 23 H1
Plaw Hatch La EGRIN RH19 .. 43 K4
Playden Cl BRIE/ROTT BN2 ... 96 D1
Plaza Pde WTHG BN11 * 12 F7
Pleasant La EMRTH PO10 ..... 80 E4
Plough Cl CRAWW RH11 .... 28 E1
Plough La HORS RH12 .... 29 H4
Plover Cl CRAWW RH11 .... 29 H1
  MSEA/BNM PO22 .... 86 A6
  SELS PO20 .... 99 M7
Plovers Rd HORN PO8 .... 168 B3
  SWTR RH13 .... 11 K3
Plumer Rd LISS GU33 .... 116 F2
Plummerden La HWH RH16 ... 130 H7
Plumpton Bostall LEWES BN7 .. 166 E11
Plumpton Gv WVILLE PO7 ..... 168 C8
Plumpton La LEWES BN7 ...... 166 H9
Plumpton Rd BRIE/ROTT BN2 .. 5 L4
Plumtree Cross La SWTR RH13 .. 125 P9
Plymouth Av BRIE/ROTT BN2 .. 77 J4
Pockford Rd MFD/CHID GU8 .. 111 J5
Polecat La SWTR RH13 .... 126 B8
Poles La CRAWW RH11 .... 44 C2
Polestub La RHWH RH17 ...... 44 C2
Poling Cl FERR BN12 .... 92 A1
Poling St ARUN BN18 .... 67 M7
Pollards CRAWW RH11 .... 28 D8
Pollard's HI SWTR RH13 .... 11 J5
Pollard's HI SWTR RH13 .... 143 R4
Polperro Cl FERR BN12 .... 91 K4
Pomper La HPPT/KEY BN6 .... 146 H11
Pond Cl BIL RH14 .... 122 G1
  BIL RH14 .... 141 R1
Pond Copse La BIL RH14 ...... 112 G12
Pondcroft Rd HWH RH16 ...... 45 L2
Pondfield Rd HORS RH12 ...... 114 A9
Pond La HORN PO8 .... 150 C7
Pond Ms SALV BN13 * 70 C7
Pond Ri PUL/STOR RH20 ...... 160 B4
Pond Rd BOR GU35 .... 107 P5
  SELS PO20 .... 100 A8
  SHOR BN43 .... 73 L6
Pondside HWH RH16 .... 44 F6
Pondtail Cl HORS RH12 .... 36 C3
Pondtail Copse HORS RH12 ... 36 C3
Pondtail Dr HORS RH12 .... 36 C3
Pondtail Pk HORS RH12 .... 36 C3
Pondtail Rd HORS RH12 .... 36 B3
Pond Wy EGRIN RH19 .... 24 A8
Pond Wood Rd CRAWE RH10 .. 29 M1
Pookbourne La
  HPPT/KEY BN6 .... 146 F8
Pook HI MFD/CHID GU8 .... 110 D6
Pook La HAV PO9 .... 57 J5
  RCCH PO18 .... 172 D12
Pool Va BRI BN1 .... 4 D3
Popes Md HASM GU27 .... 109 M10
Popham Ct HAV PO9 .... 168 D11
Poplar Av HOVE BN3 .... 75 K2
Poplar Cl BRI BN1 .... 77 H1
  CRAWW RH11 .... 19 H8
  HOVE BN3 .... 75 K2
Poplar Rd SALV BN13 .... 70 B8
The Poplars ARUN BN18 .... 87 M1
  BRIE/ROTT BN2 * 5 G3
  SWTR RH13 .... 11 G4
Poplar Wy MIDH GU29 .... 136 H12
The Poplers HPPT/KEY BN6 .. 165 P2
Poppy Cl LHPTN BN17 .... 89 M2
  SWTR RH13 .... 11 K3
Porchester Cl SWTR RH13 .... 125 R11
Portfield Av CCH PO19 .... 52 F7
Portfield Wy CCH PO19 .... 7 L1
Port Hall Av BRI BN1 .... 76 D5
Port Hall Ms BRI BN1 .... 76 D5
Port Hall Pl BRI BN1 .... 76 D5

Port Hall Rd BRI BN1 .... 4 B1
Port Hall St BRI BN1 .... 76 D5
Portland Av HOVE BN3 .... 75 K6
Portland Cl LHPTN BN17 .... 89 M3
Portland Ms BRIE/ROTT BN2 *.. 5 K9
Portland Rd BURH RH15 .... 46 E6
  EGRIN RH19 .... 33 K1
  HOVE BN3 .... 75 J6
  WTHG BN11 .... 13 G6
Portland's Cl PSF GU32 .... 133 Q4
Portland Sq LISS GU33 .... 116 C9
  WTHG BN11 * 13 G6
Portland St BRI BN1 .... 4 D5
Portland Vw HOVE BN3 .... 75 J6
Portsmouth La HWH RH16 .... 45 J4
Portsmouth Rd GSHT GU26 .. 109 K5
  HORN PO8 .... 168 D3
  LIPH GU30 .... 117 Q4
Portsmouth Wood Cl
  HWH RH16 .... 45 J1
Portswood Rd HAV PO9 .... 168 E11
Portway STEY/UB BN44 .... 48 B3
Post Horn La FROW RH18 ..... 34 D8
Posthorses PUL/STOR RH20 .. 161 K9
Post Office La SELS PO20 ..... 84 C4
Post Vw PUL/STOR RH20 ...... 178 B1
Potash Ter HAV PO9 * 56 F7
The Potteries HPPT/KEY BN6 *.. 47 M8
Potters Cft SWTR RH13 .... 11 M8
Potters Fld LISS GU33 .... 116 D9
Potters Gn SWTR RH13 .... 145 K3
Potters La BURH RH15 .... 46 E8
Potters Md LHPTN BN17 .... 89 H3
Potters Pl HORS RH12 .... 10 C5
Pottery La RCCH PO18 .... 59 J6
Pouchlands BRIE/NEW BN8 .. 167 M3
Poulner Cl HASM GU27 .... 108 D11
Poulner Ct HAV PO9 .... 168 D11
Poulter's La SALV BN13 .... 71 G7
Pound Cl BIL RH14 .... 112 C12
  BOR GU35 .... 107 N4
  PETW GU28 .... 139 L10
Pound Farm Rd CCH PO19 ... 7 J4
Poundfield La BIL RH14 .... 122 C2
Pound Hill Pl CRAWE RH10 ... 30 B3
Pound La STEY/UB BN44 .... 49 G3
  SWTR RH13 .... 126 H3
  SWTR RH13 .... 143 N9
  SWTR RH13 .... 145 J5
Pound Pl PETW GU28 * 139 L9
Pound Rd ARUN BN18 .... 65 J4
  SELS PO20 .... 99 G4
Pound St PETW GU28 .... 139 L9
The Pound BURH RH15 .... 46 E5
Pound Wy ANG/EP BN16 ...... 68 F8
Povey Cross Rd HORL RH6 .... 14 D8
Poveys Cl BURH RH15 .... 46 C6
Powell Cl HORL RH6 .... 14 D5
Powis Gv BRI BN1 .... 4 B5
Powis Rd BRI BN1 .... 4 B5
Powis Sq BRI BN1 .... 4 B5
Powis Vls BRI BN1 .... 4 B5
Poynes Rd HORL RH6 .... 14 D4
Poynings Dr HOVE BN3 .... 75 L2
Poynings Rd CRAWW RH11 ... 28 C4
Poynter Rd HOVE BN3 .... 75 M5
Poyntz Cl CCH PO19 .... 83 L2
Pratton Av LAN/SOMP BN15 .. 72 C6
Prawn Cl SELS PO20 .... 181 J5
Premier Pde LISS GU33 .... 116 F2
Prescott Gdns BURH RH15 * .. 46 F6
Preston Av HOVE BN3 .... 76 C2
Preston Circ BRI BN1 .... 4 E1
Preston Dra BRI BN1 .... 76 E3
Preston Gra BRI BN1 .... 76 D4
Preston Hall Ms ANG/EP BN16 *.. 90 E3
Preston Paddock ANG/EP BN16 .. 90 E3
Preston Park Av BRI BN1 .... 76 D4
Preston Rd BRI BN1 .... 4 D1
Preston St BRI BN1 .... 4 B7
Preston Village Ms BRI BN1 * .. 76 D4
Prestonville Rd BRI BN1 .... 4 A3
Prestwick Cl CRAWW RH11 ... 28 C4
Prestwick La HASM GU27 ..... 109 R7
  MFD/CHID GU8 .... 110 D5
Prestwood Cl CRAWW RH11 .. 19 G8
Prestwood La CRAWW RH11 .. 18 B7
Pretoria Av MIDH GU29 .... 136 M9
Pretoria Cl LISS GU33 .... 116 F3
Pretoria Rd MIDH GU29 .... 136 H10
Price Wy RHWH RH17 .... 130 E2
Priest Croft Cl CRAWW RH11 .. 28 F5
Priestlands Cl HORL RH6 .... 14 E5
Priestley Wy CRAWE RH10 .... 19 M7
  MSEA/BNM PO22 .... 87 J8
Prime Cl ARUN BN18 .... 65 J4
Primrose Av HAV PO9 .... 56 C3
Primrose Cl BURH RH15 .... 46 C5
  CRAWW RH11 .... 29 G6
Primrose Copse HORS RH12 .. 36 C3
Primrose La FROW RH18 .... 34 F8
  LISS GU33 .... 116 H9
Primula Rd BOR GU35 .... 106 H6
Prince Albert St BRI BN1 .... 4 D7
Prince Av LAN/SOMP BN15 ... 73 G8
Prince Charles Rd LEWES BN7 .. 57 H4
Prince Edward's St HAV PO9 .. 57 G4
Prince George's St HAV PO9 .. 57 G4
Prince of Wales Cl
  WVILLE PO7 .... 168 B10
Prince Regent's Cl
  BRIE/ROTT BN2 .... 96 D1
Princes Av HOVE BN3 .... 75 M7
Princes Cl BOR GU35 .... 106 C3
Prince's Crs BRI BN1 .... 75 J6
  HOVE BN3 .... 75 M7
Princes Cft BOGR PO21 .... 102 F4
Prince's Dr RCCH PO18 .... 172 K9
  WVILLE PO7 .... 168 B8
Prince's Pl BRI BN1 .... 4 E7
Prince's Rd BRI BN1 .... 77 G5
  PSF GU32 .... 133 L5
Princess Anne Rd HORS RH12 .. 114 A11
Princess Av BOGR PO21 .... 103 M3
  SALV BN13 .... 92 G2
Princess Ct HWH RH16 .... 45 J2
Princess Gdns HORN PO8 ..... 168 C2
Princess Margaret Rd
  HORS RH12 .... 114 A10
Princes Sq HOVE BN3 .... 75 M7
Princess Rd CRAWW RH11 ... 8 C4
Prince's St BRI BN1 .... 4 E7
Prince's Ter BRIE/ROTT BN2 .. 96 D1
Prince William Cl SALV BN13 .. 70 C1
Prings La SWTR RH13 .... 127 J9

Prinsep Rd HOVE BN3 .... 75 M5
Prinsted La EMRTH PO10 ..... 58 E6
Priors Acre RCCH PO18 .... 63 J2
Priors Dean Crs HAV PO9 ..... 56 C1
Priorsdean Crs HAV PO9 .... 56 C1
Priors Leaze La RCCH PO18 .. 59 H4
Priors Rd BURH RH15 .... 46 F8
  CCH PO19 .... 61 H5
  FROW RH18 .... 43 M3
  HPPT/KEY BN6 .... 165 M4
The Priory BRI BN1 * 52 D8
Priory Wy HWH RH16 .... 45 J5
Privet Rd BOR GU35 .... 107 K4
Prochurch Rd HORN PO8 ...... 168 C5
Proctor Cl CRAWE RH10 .... 30 D5
The Promenade EMRTH PO10 .. 58 A6
Prospect Cl HAV PO9 .... 169 J12
Prospect Pl CRAWW RH11 .... 56 F4
  HAV PO9 .... 56 F4
  WTHG BN11 .... 13 G7
Providence Pl BRI BN1 .... 4 E3
Providence Ter CRAWE RH10 *.. 31 M5
  WTHG BN11 .... 13 G5
The Providence CCH PO19 .... 6 D3
Pruetts La LISS GU33 .... 116 C12
Pryors La BOGR PO21 .... 103 C9
Puckshott Wy HASM GU27 .... 109 N9
Pudding La HORL RH6 .... 18 D1
Puffin Hil CRAWE RH10 .... 32 B4
Puffin Rd CRAWW RH11 * 28 C4
Pulborough Cl BRIE/ROTT BN2 .. 77 L6
Pulborough Rd
  PUL/STOR RH20 .... 159 Q11
Pulborough Wy
  MSEA/BNM PO22 .... 87 J7
Pulens Crs EPSF GU31 .... 133 R5
Pulens La EPSF GU31 .... 133 Q5
Pump La HORN PO8 .... 168 B4
Punch Copse Rd CRAWE RH10 .. 9 K2
Punches La SELS PO20 .... 84 C8
Purbeck Pl LHPTN BN17 .... 89 H4
Purbrook Wy HAV PO9 .... 56 C1
  WVILLE PO7 .... 56 A1
Purcell Rd CRAWW RH11 ...... 28 E6
Purley Cl CRAWW RH11 .... 30 C6
The Purrocks PSF GU32 .... 133 N4
Purton Rd HORS RH12 .... 10 B2
Putmans La EPSF GU31 .... 134 C11
Puttick Cl PUL/STOR RH20 ... 160 B11
Puttocks Cl HASM GU27 .... 108 G12
Pyecombe Cl CRAWW RH11 .. 8 C4
Pyecombe St POY/PYE BN45 .. 164 H11
Pyle Cl HORN PO8 .... 168 B5
Pyrford Cl BOGR PO21 .... 103 G5

Q

The Quadrangle SALV BN13 ... 178 H12
  HPPT/KEY BN6 .... 165 P5
Quail Cl HORS RH12 .... 36 C2
Quail Wy HORN PO8 .... 168 B3
Quakers La HWH RH16 .... 45 K4
Quantock Cl CRAWW RH11 ... 8 A3
  SALV BN13 .... 70 C5
Quantock Rd SALV BN13 ...... 70 C5
The Quantocks LHPTN BN17 .. 89 J5
Quarely Rd HAV PO9 .... 168 D11
The Quarries SWTR RH13 ..... 127 J3
Quarry Bank Rd BRI BN1 ...... 77 G3
Quarry Cl BURH RH15 .... 47 J6
  HORS RH12 .... 36 E3
Quarry HI HWH RH16 .... 44 F3
Quarry La EGRIN RH19 .... 23 H4
Quarry Ri EGRIN RH19 .... 23 M6
Quarry Wy SWTR RH13 .... 125 Q12
Quarterbrass Farm Rd
  HORS RH12 .... 36 C2
The Quashetts SALV BN13 .... 13 H2
Quayside LHPTN BN17 .... 89 C4
Quebec Cl HORL RH6 .... 15 M6
  LIPH GU30 .... 117 R2
Quebec Rd BRIE/ROTT BN2 .. 5 H5
Queen Alexandra Av HOVE BN3 *.. 75 M2
Queen Anne's Dr HAV PO9 .... 56 D3
Queen Caroline Cl HOVE BN3 *.. 75 M2
Queen Elizabeth Av
  HOVE BN3 .... 46 E7
Queen Elizabeth Rd
  HORS RH12 .... 114 A10
Queen Mary Av HOVE BN3 ... 75 M7
Queen's Av CCH PO19 .... 7 K3
Queensbury Ms BRI BN1 .... 4 B7
Queens Crs BURH RH15 .... 46 E5
  HORN PO8 .... 168 D2
Queensdown School Rd
  BRI BN1 .... 77 H2
Queens Dr HPPT/KEY BN6 .... 165 N5
Queens Flds East BOGR PO21 .. 103 L1
Queens Flds West BOGR PO21 .. 103 L1
Queen's Gdns BRI BN1 .... 4 E5
  CCH PO19 .... 6 C9
  HOVE BN3 .... 76 B8
Queens Ga HORL RH6 .... 19 M1
Queens Ms ARUN BN18 .... 67 G3
Queensmead BOGR PO21 ..... 102 E5
Queens Pde LAN/SOMP BN15 *.. 72 E7
  SWTR RH13 * 10 E7
Queen's Park Rd BRIE/ROTT BN2 .. 5 H6
Queen's Park Ter
  BRIE/ROTT BN2 .... 5 K5
Queen's Pl BRI BN1 .... 4 D6
  SHOR BN43 .... 73 L6
Queen Sq BRI BN1 .... 4 D6
Queen's Rd BRI BN1 .... 4 D5
  EGRIN RH19 .... 23 K8
  HORL RH6 .... 14 F6

Ryecroft La *PUL/STOR* RH20 .... 160 A12
Ryecroft Meadow *SWTR* RH13 .. 126 H3
Ryecroft Rd *RHWH* RH17 .... 146 D2
Rye Farm La *SWTR* RH13 .... 125 K11
Ryefield Cl *EPSF* GU31 .... 133 R6
Ryelands *CRAWW* RH11 .... 28 F4
  HORL RH6 * 15 H5
Ryelands Dr *BRIE/ROTT* BN2 ..... 77 J2
Ryersh La *RDKG* RH5 .... 16 B2
Ryst Wood Rd *FROW* RH18 .... 35 G7

S

Sabre Rd *EMRTH* PO10 .... 80 B2
Sachel Court Rd *CRAN* GU6 ...... 112 E6
Sack La *MSEA/BNM* PO22 .... 86 E4
Sackville Rd *EGRIN* RH19 .... 23 H6
Sackville Crs *SALV* BN13 .... 13 K1
Sackville Gdns *HOVE* BN3 .... 75 L7
Sackville La *EGRIN* RH19 .... 23 G6
Sackville Rd *HOVE* BN3 .... 75 M7
  SALV BN13 .... 13 J2
Sackville Wy *SALV* BN13 .... 13 K2
Saddle La *SELS* PO20 .... 181 K5
Saddler Rw *CRAWE* RH10 .... 8 F9
Saddlers Cl *BURH* RH15 .... 47 J8
Saddlers Scarp *GSHT* GU26 ..... 108 D5
Saddlescombe Rd
  POY/PYE BN45 .... 51 J1
The Sadlers *RCCH* PO18 .... 62 C4
Sadler St *BOGR* PO21 .... 2 D8
Sadlers Wk *EMRTH* PO10 .... 58 B5
Sadler Wy *BRIE/ROTT* BN2 ...... 77 L7
Saffron Cl *CRAWW* RH11 .... 28 F6
  SHOR BN43 .... 74 B4
The Saffrons *BURH* RH15 .... 46 D4
Sage Cl *WVILLE* PO7 .... 168 B11
St Agnes Pl *CCH* PO19 .... 7 G4
St Agnes Rd *EGRIN* RH19 .... 23 K7
St Alban's Rd *HWH* RH16 .... 57 H1
St Andrew Cl *HORN* PO8 .... 150 D11
St Andrews *HORL* RH6 * 15 C7
St Andrew's Cl *FERR* BN12 ...... 91 K3
  SELS PO20 .... 63 H7
St Andrews Ct *CCH* PO19 * 6 E3
St Andrews Gdns *SALV* BN13 * .. 12 A1
St Andrews Rd *BOR* GU35 .... 106 E7
  BRI BN1 .... 76 F4
  BURH RH15 .... 47 H5
  CHAM PO6 .... 56 A5
  CRAWW RH11 .... 28 C4
  PTSD BN41 .... 75 C6
  SALV BN13 .... 92 E1
St Annes HI *MIDH* GU29 .... 137 J10
St Annes Rd *CRAWE* RH10 ...... 20 D5
St Ann's HI *MIDH* GU29 .... 137 J10
St Ann's Rd *HORN* PO8 .... 168 D2
St Anselm's Rd *SALV* BN13 ...... 12 C2
St Anthony's Wk *BOGR* PO21 .. 103 J2
St Anthony's Wy *ANG/EP* BN16 .. 90 C3
St Aubin Cl *CRAWW* RH11 * 28 E7
St Aubins Rd *FERR* BN12 .... 91 L5
St Aubyns *HOVE* BN3 .... 75 M7
St Aubyn's Crs *PTSD* BN41 ...... 75 H6
St Aubyn's Md *BRIE/ROTT* BN2 .. 97 M4
St Aubyn's Rd *PTSD* BN41 .... 74 F6
  PTSD BN41 .... 75 H6
St Aubyns South *HOVE* BN3 ..... 75 M8
St Augustine Cl *RHWH* RH17 ... 149 J2
St Augustine Rd *LHPTN* BN17 ... 89 K5
St Austins *GSHT* GU26 * 108 G6
St Bartholomews Cl *CCH* PO19 * .. 6 H4
St Bernards Ct *LAN/SOMP* BN15 .. 72 D8
St Blaises Rd *BRI* BN1 .... 63 H1
St Botolph's Rd *WTHG* BN11 ... 12 C3
St Brelades Rd *CRAWW* RH11 .. 28 E7
St Catherines *CRAWE* RH10 ..... 20 B8
  LHPTN BN17 .... 89 J5
St Christopher's Cl *CCH* PO19 .. 61 H7
  HASM GU27 * 109 K11
  HORS RH12 .... 10 D2
St Christopher's Rd
  HASM GU27 .... 109 K11
  HAV PO9 .... 56 D2
St Clares Av *HAV* PO9 .... 168 E10
St Clare's Cl *BOGR* PO21 .... 85 M7
St Clement Rd *CRAWW* RH11 ... 28 E7
St Cuthmans Cl *BRIE/ROTT* BN2 .. 77 K7
St Cuthman's Rd
  STEY/UB BN44 .... 162 C12
St Cyriacs *CCH* PO19 .... 6 D3
St David's Rd *HORN* PO8 .... 150 D10
St Dunstan's Rd *SALV* BN13 ...... 12 A3
St Edmunds Cl *CRAWW* RH11 ... 19 J3
St Edmund's Rd *HWH* RH16 ...... 45 J6
St Edward's Cl *EGRIN* RH19 ...... 23 H8
St Elmo Rd *SALV* BN13 .... 12 C2
St Flora's Cl *LHPTN* BN17 * 89 L4
St Flora's Wy *LHPTN* BN17 ...... 89 L4
St Francis Cl *HWH* RH16 .... 45 K7
St Francis Pl *HAV* PO9 .... 56 F2
St Gabriels Rd *BIL* RH14 .... 142 A1
St Georges *HORL* RH6 * 15 G7
St George's Av *HAV* PO9 .... 57 H4
St Georges Cl *HORL* RH6 .... 15 G6
  SELS PO20 .... 181 M5
St Georges Ct *CRAWE* RH10 ..... 8 F1
St George's Dr *CCH* PO19 .... 83 L2
St George's Gdns *HORS* RH12 .. 11 H2
  WTHG BN11 * 13 L5
St George's La *HPPT/KEY* BN6 .. 165 J4
St George's Ms *BRI* BN1 .... 4 F5
St George's Pl *BRI* BN1 .... 4 F5
  HPPT/KEY BN6 .... 165 J4
St George's Rd *BRIE/ROTT* BN2 .. 5 K8
St Georges Wk *SELS* PO20 .... 64 G6
  SWTR RH13 .... 144 E10
  WTHG BN11 * 13 L4
St George's Ter *BRIE/ROTT* BN2 .. 5 J8
St Giles Cl *SHOR* BN43 .... 74 A5
St Giles Wy *HORN* PO8 .... 150 D11
St Helen's Crs *HOVE* BN3 .... 75 J2
St Helen's Dr *HOVE* BN3 .... 75 J1
St Helen's Rd *BRIE/ROTT* BN2 .. 5 L2
St Helier Cl *CRAWW* RH11 .... 28 F7
St Helier Rd *FERR* BN12 .... 91 L5
St Heliers Av *HOVE* BN3 .... 75 K6
St Hilda Av *HORN* PO8 .... 150 D11
St Hilda's Cl *CRAWE* RH10 * ... 20 B8
  HORL RH6 .... 15 G6
St Hill Rd *EGRIN* RH19 .... 33 G3
St Hubert Rd *HORN* PO8 .... 150 D11

St Hugh's Cl *CRAWE* RH10 .... 20 B8
St Itha Cl *SELS* PO20 .... 181 L7
St Itha Rd *SELS* PO20 .... 181 L7
St Ives *CRAWE* RH10 * 30 B2
St James Av *LAN/SOMP* BN15 .. 72 D5
St James' Rd *HORN* PO8 .... 150 D9
St James' Rd *CCH* PO19 .... 7 J3
  EGRIN RH19 .... 23 J8
  EMRTH PO10 .... 58 A4
St James's Av *BRIE/ROTT* BN2 .. 5 H8
St James's Cl *SELS* PO20 .... 82 D8
St James's Pl *BRI* BN1 .... 4 F7
St James's St *CCH* PO19 .... 7 J3
St James's St *BRI* BN1 .... 4 F7
  BRIE/ROTT BN2 .... 5 G8
St James's Street Ms
  BRIE/ROTT BN2 .... 5 G7
St Joan Cl *CRAWW* RH11 .... 19 J8
St John Bank *RING/NEW* BN8 .. 167 N1
St John Cl *SWTR* RH13 .... 11 J7
St John's Av *BURH* RH15 .... 46 C6
  FERR BN12 .... 92 C4
St John's Cl *BOGR* PO21 .... 103 L1
  FERR BN12 .... 92 B4
  MIDH GU29 * 136 H10
  SELS PO20 .... 64 C7
St John's Crs *HORS* RH12 .... 125 P2
St Johns Ms *BRIE/ROTT* BN2 * .. 5 J8
St John's Pl *BRIE/ROTT* BN2 ..... 5 J8
  HOVE BN3 .... 76 B7
St Johns Rd *BURH* RH15 .... 46 F6
  CRAWW RH11 .... 8 D4
  EGRIN RH19 .... 23 K7
  EMRTH PO10 .... 58 D7
  HAV PO9 .... 56 D1
  HOVE BN3 .... 76 B8
  HWH RH16 .... 45 H6
St John's St *CCH* PO19 .... 6 F5
St Joseph's Cl *HOVE* BN3 .... 75 M5
St Josephs Wy *HWH* RH16 ...... 45 M5
St Julians Cl *SHOR* BN43 .... 74 B6
St Julian's La *SHOR* BN43 .... 74 B6
St Keyna Av *HOVE* BN3 .... 75 J7
St Lawrence Av *SALV* BN13 ...... 12 C1
St Lawrence Wy
  HPPT/KEY BN6 .... 164 H2
St Leodegar's Wy *SELS* PO20 .. 83 M4
St Leonard's Av *HOVE* BN3 ...... 75 H7
St Leonards Dr *CRAWE* RH10 .... 9 M8
St Leonard's Gdns *HOVE* BN3 .. 75 J7
St Leonard's Rd
  BRIE/ROTT BN2 * 5 J1
  HOVE BN3 .... 75 H7
  SWTR RH13 .... 11 H9
St Louie Cl *STHW* BN42 .... 74 F5
St Luke's Cl *LAN/SOMP* BN15 .. 94 A1
St Luke's Rd *BRIE/ROTT* BN2 .... 5 K4
St Luke's Ter *BRIE/ROTT* BN2 ... 5 K4
St Malo Cl *FERR* BN12 .... 91 L5
St Margarets *BRIE/ROTT* BN2 * .. 97 M4
St Margaret's Av *EGRIN* RH19 .. 23 K3
St Margaret's Pl *BRI* BN1 .... 4 B7
St Margaret's Rd *EGRIN* RH19 .. 23 L6
St Margarets Ter *MIDH* GU29 * .. 137 K8
St Mark's Crs *LAN/SOMP* BN15 .. 94 A1
St Mark's La *HORS* RH12 .... 36 D3
St Mark's St *BRIE/ROTT* BN2 .... 96 D1
St Martin's Cl *RHWH* RH17 ..... 128 C2
St Martin's La *LHPTN* BN17 * 89 J4
St Martin's Pl *BRIE/ROTT* BN2 .. 5 H2
St Martins Rd *LHPTN* BN17 ...... 89 J4
St Martin's Sq *CCH* PO19 .... 6 E4
St Martin's St *BRIE/ROTT* BN2 .. 5 H1
  CCH PO19 .... 6 E4
St Mary Magdalene St
  BRIE/ROTT BN2 .... 5 H1
St Mary's Cl *BIL* RH14 .... 142 A1
  LAN/SOMP BN15 .... 71 M6
  LHPTN BN17 .... 89 L4
  MSEA/BNM PO22 .... 2 E2
  PUL/STOR RH20 .... 159 K3
  RCCH PO18 .... 172 B10
  SHOR BN43 .... 73 L6
St Mary's Dr *ANG/EP* BN16 ...... 90 A4
  CRAWE RH10 .... 30 A1
St Marys Gdn *CCH* PO19 .... 6 E3
St Mary's Gdns *HORS* RH12 ..... 11 H2
  LHPTN BN17 .... 89 K4
St Marys Gate Ms *ARUN* BN18 * .. 66 F2
St Marys Meadow *ARUN* BN18 .. 87 L2
St Mary's Pl *BRIE/ROTT* BN2 ..... 5 J8
St Mary's Rd *LISS* GU33 .... 116 C9
  RCCH PO18 .... 63 H1
  SHOR BN43 .... 73 L6
St Mary's Rd West *BURH* RH15 .. 46 D5
St Mary's Sq *BRIE/ROTT* BN2 .... 5 M9
St Mary's Wy *LHPTN* BN17 * 89 K4
St Matthew's Rd *WTHG* BN11 ... 12 E4
St Maur's Rd *FERR* BN12 .... 91 K3
St Michaels Cl *PETW* GU28 ..... 120 F6
St Michael's Ct *WTHG* BN11 .... 12 C6
St Michael's Pl *BRI* BN1 .... 4 B5
St Michaels Rd *EGRIN* RH19 ..... 23 K7
  HAV PO9 .... 56 D2
  PTSD BN41 .... 75 G6
  WTHG BN11 .... 12 C6
St Michaels Wy *HORN* PO8 .... 150 D11
St Nicholas' La
  MSEA/BNM PO22 .... 87 L8
St Nicholas Rd *BRI* BN1 .... 4 D5
  HAV PO9 .... 56 D1
  PTSD BN41 .... 75 G6
  RCCH PO18 .... 172 B10
St Nicolas La *SHOR* BN43 .... 73 J5
St Osmund Rd *FERR* BN12 ...... 91 J3
St Pancras *CCH* PO19 .... 6 F4
St Pancras Gn *LEWES* BN7 ...... 55 J8
St Patrick's La *LISS* GU33 ...... 116 F8
St Patrick's Rd *HOVE* BN3 .... 75 M6
St Paul's Av *LAN/SOMP* BN15 .. 94 A1
St Paul's Cl *HWH* RH16 .... 45 J4
St Paul's Gdns *CCH* PO19 .... 6 D2
St Paul's Rd *CCH* PO19 .... 6 D2
St Paul's St *BRIE/ROTT* BN2 ..... 5 H1
St Peter's *CCH* PO19 .... 6 D3
St Peters Cl *BOGR* PO21 .... 103 K1
  SWTR RH13 .... 145 K4
St Peter's Crs *SELS* PO20 .... 181 L5
St Peters Market *CCH* PO19 * 6 E5
St Peter's Pl *BRI* BN1 .... 4 F4
  LAN/SOMP BN15 * 94 A1
St Peters Rd *BURH* RH15 .... 46 F6
  CRAWW RH11 .... 28 F7
  PSF GU32 .... 133 N6

PTSD BN41 .... 75 G6
St Peter's Sq *EMRTH* PO10 ...... 58 A5
St Peter's St *BRI* BN1 .... 4 F4
St Philips Ms *HOVE* BN3 .... 75 L6
St Raphael's Rd *WTHG* BN11 ... 92 E4
St Richards Cl *FERR* BN12 .... 92 B2
St Richard's Dr *CRAWE* RH10 * .. 9 K3
St Richards Ms *CRAWE* RH10 * .. 9 K3
St Richard's Rd *PTSD* BN41 ...... 75 H6
  SELS PO20 .... 64 D6
St Richard's Wy *BOGR* PO21 ... 103 J2
St Roche's Cl *RCCH* PO18 ...... 172 C10
St Sampson Rd *CRAWW* RH11 .. 28 E7
St Stephens Cl *HASM* GU27 .... 109 M10
St Swithun's Cl *EGRIN* RH19 * .. 23 L8
St Theresas Cl *HAV* PO9 .... 56 D2
St Thomas Dr *BOGR* PO21 ..... 102 E5
St Valerie Rd *WTHG* BN11 ...... 12 B7
St Vincent Cl *CRAWE* RH10 ..... 30 C4
St Vincent Crs *HORN* PO8 ...... 168 C3
St Wilfreds Cl *SELS* PO20 .... 181 N5
St Wilfreds Rd *BURH* RH15 ..... 47 G5
  SALV BN13 .... 13 J1
St Wilfreds Vw *SELS* PO20 * ... 181 J7
St Wilfrid Rd *CCH* PO19 .... 61 J6
St Wilfrids Rd *BURH* RH15 ...... 47 G5
St Wilfrid's Wy *HWH* RH16 ...... 45 K5
St Winefride's Rd *LHPTN* BN17 .. 89 K5
St Winifred's Cl *BOGR* PO21 ...... 2 B8
Sake Ride La *HFD* BN5 .... 145 N12
Salehurst Rd *CRAWE* RH10 ...... 30 D3
Salet Wy *WVILLE* PO7 .... 168 C8
Salisbury Rd *CRAWE* RH10 ...... 29 L7
  HOVE BN3 .... 76 B3
  WTHG BN11 .... 13 G5
Salisbury Wy *CCH* PO19 .... 61 L4
Salt Box Cl *SWTR* RH13 .... 125 J11
Saltdean Cl *CRAWE* RH10 .... 8 E9
Salterns Rd *CRAWE* RH10 .... 30 B6
Saltham La *SELS* PO20 .... 84 D4
Salthill La *CCH* PO19 .... 61 G6
Salthill Rd *CCH* PO19 .... 61 G6
The Saltings *HAV* PO9 .... 57 G7
  LAN/SOMP BN15 .... 72 A9
  LHPTN BN17 .... 89 M3
  SELS PO20 .... 100 D1
  SHOR BN43 .... 73 J6
Saltings Wy *STEY/UB* BN44 ..... 48 F3
Salvia Cl *WVILLE* PO7 .... 168 B11
Salvington Cl *SALV* BN13 .... 70 C4
Salvington Gdns *SALV* BN13 ... 70 C7
Salvington HI *SALV* BN13 .... 70 D4
Salvington Rd *CRAWW* RH11 ... 28 C4
  SALV BN13 .... 70 D6
Samaritan Cl *CRAWW* RH11 ..... 28 D5
Samphire Cl *CRAWW* RH11 ...... 28 C5
Samphire Dr *SALV* BN13 .... 69 M8
Sampsons Dr *SELS* PO20 .... 63 H6
Sanctuary Ct
  PUL/STOR RH20 * 159 M7
Sanctuary La *PUL/STOR* RH20 .. 160 F12
Sandeman Wy *SWTR* RH13 ...... 11 H9
Sandfield Av *LHPTN* BN17 .... 89 J1
Sandgate La *PUL/STOR* RH20 .. 160 D11
Sandgate Rd *BRI* BN1 .... 63 K3
Sandhawes HI *EGRIN* RH19 ..... 23 M5
Sandheath Rd *GSHT* GU26 ..... 108 F2
Sandhill La *CRAWE* RH10 .... 32 B3
  PUL/STOR RH20 .... 178 H2
Sandhills Rd *SWTR* RH13 .... 125 J10
Sandhurst Av *BRIE/ROTT* BN2 .. 78 C4
Sandleford Rd *HAV* PO9 .... 168 E10
Sandlewood Cl *HORN* PO8 ...... 150 D8
Sandown Av *FERR* BN12 .... 92 B5
Sandown Cl *FERR* BN12 .... 92 B4
Sandown Rd *BRIE/ROTT* BN2 ... 5 L2
  STHW BN42 .... 74 E5
Sandpiper Cl *CRAWW* RH11 .... 28 C5
Sandridge La *HWH* RH16 .... 130 C8
Sandringham Cl *HOVE* BN3 ..... 75 M2
  SELS PO20 .... 100 A8
Sandringham Ct
  LAN/SOMP BN15 * 72 E8
Sandringham Dr *HOVE* BN3 ..... 75 M2
Sandringham Ms *SALV* BN13 ... 70 C6
  SALV BN13 * 71 J7
Sandringham Rd *CCH* PO19 .... 7 K5
  CRAWW RH11 .... 29 G7
  PSF GU32 .... 133 N5
Sandringham Wy *BOGR* PO21 .... 2 A4
Sandrock *HASM* GU27 .... 109 M11
  MIDH GU29 .... 136 C9
Sandrocks Wy *HWH* RH16 ...... 45 H7
Sandsbury La *PSF* GU32 .... 133 J4
Sands La *HFD* BN5 .... 163 K11
The Sands *BOR* GU35 .... 106 D7
Sandwich Rd *WTHG* BN11 ...... 92 E4
Sandy Cl *EPSF* GU31 .... 133 R6
Sandygate La *SWTR* RH13 ...... 127 L6
Sandy La *CRAWE* RH10 .... 31 M1
  EGRIN RH19 .... 23 K8
  EGRIN RH19 .... 42 D3
  GSHT GU26 .... 109 J7
  HASM GU27 .... 108 F10
  HASM GU27 .... 109 P8
  HFD BN5 .... 163 J5
  LISS GU33 .... 116 H10
  PUL/STOR RH20 .... 158 B3
  PUL/STOR RH20 .... 158 B8
  PUL/STOR RH20 .... 160 E12
  RCCH PO18 .... 60 C1
Sandymount Av
  MSEA/BNM PO22 .... 2 B2
Sandymount Cl
  MSEA/BNM PO22 .... 2 C1
Sandy Point Cl *SELS* PO20 ...... 180 H5
Sandy Point La *SELS* PO20 ...... 180 H5
Sandy Rd *BOGR* PO21 .... 102 F6
Sandy V *HWH* RH16 .... 45 G7
San Feliu *EGRIN* RH19 .... 24 A7
Sangers Dr *HORL* RH6 .... 14 E7
Sanyhils Av *BRI* BN1 .... 52 E6
Sapphire Cl *WVILLE* PO7 .... 168 B10
Sapphire Rdg *WVILLE* PO7 ..... 168 B10
Sarel Wy *HORL* RH6 .... 15 G4
Sargent Cl *CRAWE* RH10 .... 29 L7
Sarisbury Cl *MSEA/BNM* PO22 .... 3 M3
Sark Cl *CRAWW* RH11 .... 28 F7
Sark Gdns *FERR* BN12 .... 91 L5
Satinwood Cl *MSEA/BNM* PO22 . 87 K7
Saturn Cl *CRAWW* RH11 .... 28 D7
Saucelands La *SWTR* RH13 ..... 142 C9
Saunders Cl *CRAWE* RH10 ...... 30 A3
Saunders HI *BRI* BN1 .... 53 J6

Saunders Park Ri
  BRIE/ROTT BN2 .... 77 H4
Saunders Park Vw
  BRIE/ROTT BN2 .... 77 H4
Savernake Wk *CRAWE* RH10 ..... 9 K9
Savile Crs *BOR* GU35 .... 106 H6
Saville Gdns *BIL* RH14 .... 142 A2
Savill Rd *HWH* RH16 .... 45 K1
Sawyers Cl *BURH* RH15 .... 47 J8
Saxby Cl *MSEA/BNM* PO22 ...... 65 G8
Saxby Rd *BURH* RH15 .... 46 C5
Saxifrage Wy *SALV* BN13 .... 69 M8
Saxley *HORL* RH6 .... 15 H5
Saxley Ct *HAV* PO9 .... 168 E11
Saxon Cl *ANG/EP* BN16 .... 91 G2
  BIL RH14 .... 124 A12
  BOGR PO21 .... 102 E5
  HORN PO8 .... 150 D9
Saxon Crs *HORS* RH12 .... 10 A1
Saxon Rd (East) *RCCH* PO18 ... 59 L3
Saxon Rd (West) *RCCH* PO18 ... 59 J3
Scarborough Rd *BRI* BN1 .... 76 C4
School Cl *BURH* RH15 .... 46 E7
  HORS RH12 .... 36 F5
  PUL/STOR RH20 .... 158 F10
  STHW BN42 .... 74 D6
School Dell *RCCH* PO18 .... 59 M7
School HI *ARUN* BN18 .... 174 H12
  HORS RH12 .... 115 Q9
  PUL/STOR RH20 .... 160 A12
  SALV BN13 .... 178 H11
School La *ARUN* BN18 .... 66 F3
  BIL RH14 .... 142 B1
  EGRIN RH19 .... 34 C3
  EMRTH PO10 .... 58 A5
  EMRTH PO10 .... 58 C1
  EMRTH PO10 .... 169 Q12
  FROW RH18 .... 34 E7
  LISS GU33 .... 116 C9
  MFD/CHID GU8 .... 110 G5
  MIDH GU29 .... 136 C8
  PETW GU28 .... 138 A6
  POY/PYE BN45 .... 165 K11
  PSF GU32 .... 133 P3
  PUL/STOR RH20 .... 157 L9
  PUL/STOR RH20 .... 158 B3
  PUL/STOR RH20 .... 177 R1
  PUL/STOR RH20 .... 178 H3
  RCCH PO18 .... 59 G6
  RCCH PO18 .... 152 C11
  RHWH RH17 .... 131 R5
  SELS PO20 .... 64 B3
  SELS PO20 .... 181 K5
  STEY/UB BN44 .... 48 C2
  STEY/UB BN44 .... 162 C12
  SWTR RH13 .... 143 M8
School Ri *BRIE/ROTT* BN2 .... 77 K7
School Rd *ARUN* BN18 .... 176 F2
  BIL RH14 .... 123 K12
  BOR GU35 .... 106 G5
  GSHT GU26 .... 108 E6
  HASM GU27 .... 109 J12
  HAV PO9 .... 56 F4
  HOVE BN3 .... 75 L6
  STEY/UB BN44 .... 48 F5
Scory Cl *CRAWW* RH11 .... 28 C5
Scotland La *HASM* GU27 .... 109 M12
Scotlands Cl *HASM* GU27 .... 109 L12
Scotlands Dr *HASM* GU27 .... 109 L12
Scotland St *BRIE/ROTT* BN2 ..... 5 H5
Scotney Cl *SALV* BN13 .... 70 A4
Scotney Ct *HAV* PO9 .... 169 J11
Scott Rd *CRAWE* RH10 .... 9 J9
  HOVE BN3 .... 75 L6
Scott St *BOGR* PO21 .... 2 C8
Scratchface La *HAV* PO9 .... 56 D3
  WVILLE PO7 .... 56 A1
Scratchings La *PETW* GU28 ..... 121 M8
Sea Av *ANG/EP* BN16 .... 90 C4
Seabrook Cl *BOGR* PO21 .... 103 J2
Sea Cl *FERR* BN12 .... 92 D3
  MSEA/BNM PO22 .... 105 K1
Seacourt Cl *BOGR* PO21 .... 103 J2
Seadown Pde
  LAN/SOMP BN15 * 72 A8
Sea Dr *FERR* BN12 .... 91 L5
  MSEA/BNM PO22 .... 105 J1
Seafield Av *FERR* BN12 .... 92 C5
Seafield Cl *SELS* PO20 .... 99 L7
Seafield Rd *ANG/EP* BN16 .... 90 B6
  ANG/EP BN16 .... 90 E5
  HOVE BN3 .... 76 A8
Seafields *EMRTH* PO10 .... 57 M5
  SELS PO20 .... 180 A1
Seafield Wy *SELS* PO20 .... 99 M7
Seaford Rd *CRAWW* RH11 ...... 28 F8
  HOVE BN3 .... 75 H7
Sea Gv *SELS* PO20 .... 181 J7
Seagull Cl *SELS* PO20 .... 180 H4
Seagull La *EMRTH* PO10 .... 58 A4
Seahaven Gdns *SHOR* BN43 .... 73 H4
Sea La *ANG/EP* BN16 .... 90 E5
  ANG/EP BN16 .... 91 J3
  BOGR PO21 .... 102 E5
  FERR BN12 .... 91 J3
  FERR BN12 .... 92 B4
  MSEA/BNM PO22 .... 87 K8
Sea Lane Cl *ANG/EP* BN16 ...... 90 E4
Sea Lane Gdns *FERR* BN12 ...... 91 J3
Seal Rd *SELS* PO20 .... 181 K8
Seal Sq *SELS* PO20 .... 181 K8
Seaman's Gn *RDKG* RH5 .... 16 C1
Seamill Park Av *WTHG* BN11 ... 94 B2
Seamill Park Crs *WTHG* BN11 .. 94 A2
Seamill Wy *WTHG* BN11 .... 94 A2
Sea Pl *FERR* BN12 .... 92 C5
Searle's Vw *HORS* RH12 .... 36 F4
Sea Rd *ANG/EP* BN16 .... 89 J1
  ANG/EP BN16 .... 90 F5
  MSEA/BNM PO22 .... 3 K7
Sea-saw Wy *BRIE/ROTT* BN2 ... 77 L6
Seaside *ANG/EP* BN16 .... 90 E8

Seaside Cl *LAN/SOMP* BN15 .... 72 E8
Seaside Rd *LAN/SOMP* BN15 ... 72 E8
Seaton Cl *LHPTN* BN17 .... 89 J1
Seaton La *LHPTN* BN17 .... 89 J1
Seaton Pk *LHPTN* BN17 .... 89 J1
Seaton Rd *LHPTN* BN17 .... 89 J1
Seaview Av *ANG/EP* BN16 .... 90 F5
  ANG/EP BN16 .... 91 J5
Seaview Ct *LAN/SOMP* BN15 ... 94 C1
Seaview Rd *ANG/EP* BN16 .... 90 E5
  BRIE/ROTT BN2 .... 78 A5
Sea View Rd *WTHG* BN11 .... 12 C8
Sea View Wy *BRIE/ROTT* BN2 .. 78 C4
Seaward Dr *SELS* PO20 .... 99 H4
Seawaves Cl *ANG/EP* BN16 ...... 90 F4
Sea Wy *BOGR* PO21 .... 102 E5
  MSEA/BNM PO22 .... 88 A8
  MSEA/BNM PO22 .... 105 J1
Sebastian Gv *WVILLE* PO7 ..... 168 B9
Sebastopol Rd *MFD/CHID* GU8 .. 110 C1
Second Av *EMRTH* PO10 .... 58 E5
  HAV PO9 .... 57 J3
  HOVE BN3 .... 76 B8
  LAN/SOMP BN15 .... 72 D7
  MSEA/BNM PO22 .... 105 G1
  SALV BN13 .... 71 J6
  SELS PO20 .... 100 A8
  SELS PO20 .... 100 E4
Sedbury Rd *LAN/SOMP* BN15 .. 72 B5
Seddon Cl *CCH* PO19 .... 7 J1
Sedgefield Cl *CRAWE* RH10 ..... 30 D2
Sedgewick Cl *CRAWE* RH10 .... 30 B3
Sedgwick La *SWTR* RH13 ...... 126 D5
Sefter Rd *BOGR* PO21 .... 103 G1
Sefton Av *BOGR* PO21 .... 103 J2
Sefton Cl *SALV* BN13 .... 70 C7
Sefton Rd *PTSD* BN41 .... 74 C2
Selangor Av *EMRTH* PO10 .... 57 L4
Selba Dr *BRIE/ROTT* BN2 .... 78 B5
Selborne Av *HAV* PO9 .... 168 E12
Selborne Pl *PSF* GU32 .... 133 P4
Selborne Pl *HOVE* BN3 .... 76 B6
  LHPTN BN17 * 89 K5
Selborne Rd *HOVE* BN3 .... 76 B7
  LHPTN BN17 .... 89 K5
  WTHG BN11 .... 13 L3
Selborne Wy *ANG/EP* BN16 ..... 90 E4
  BOR GU35 .... 106 D7
Selbourne Cl *CRAWE* RH10 ..... 20 C7
Selbourne Rd *HAV* PO9 .... 56 F4
Selby Cl *HWH* RH16 .... 45 H6
Selden La *SALV* BN13 .... 69 G4
  SALV BN13 .... 70 E7
Selden Pde *SALV* BN13 * 70 E6
Selden Rd *WTHG* BN11 .... 13 L4
Selden's Ms *SALV* BN13 .... 70 E7
Selden's Rd *SALV* BN13 .... 70 E7
Selham Cl *BRI* BN1 .... 53 J7
  CCH PO19 .... 61 M2
  CRAWW RH11 .... 28 F2
Selham Dr *BRI* BN1 .... 53 J7
Selham Pl *BRI* BN1 * 53 J7
Selhurst Cl *ANG/EP* BN16 .... 90 D4
Selhurstpark Rd *RCCH* PO18 .. 173 N5
Selhurst Rd *BRIE/ROTT* BN2 .... 78 D7
Selkirk Cl *SALV* BN13 .... 92 D1
Selmeston Pl *BRIE/ROTT* BN2 .. 77 L7
Selsey Cl *BOGR* PO21 .... 103 M3
Selsey Cl *BRI* BN1 .... 53 K7
  HISD PO11 .... 98 A3
  SALV BN13 .... 70 E8
Selsey Rd *CCH* PO19 .... 83 K2
  CRAWW RH11 .... 28 F7
  SELS PO20 .... 83 K6
  SELS PO20 .... 101 K3
Selsfield Dr *BRIE/ROTT* BN2 .... 77 J2
Selsfield Rd *CRAWE* RH10 .... 31 M7
  EGRIN RH19 .... 42 B2
  RHWH RH17 .... 42 A8
Selway La *LHPTN* BN17 .... 89 L3
Selwyn Av *LHPTN* BN17 .... 89 J2
Selwyn Cl *BOGR* PO21 .... 103 L1
  CRAWE RH10 .... 20 B8
Semley Rd *BRI* BN1 .... 76 F4
  HPPT/KEY BN6 .... 165 M5
Sentinel Cl *WVILLE* PO7 .... 168 C8
Sequoia Pk *CRAWW* RH11 .... 8 E7
Sergison Cl *HWH* RH16 .... 44 F4
Sergison Rd *HWH* RH16 .... 45 G4
Serrin Wy *HORS* RH12 .... 36 C4
Service Rd *HORL* RH6 .... 19 M2
Servite Cl *BOGR* PO21 .... 2 A5
Setfords Fld *RING/NEW* BN8 ... 149 P12
Sevelands Cl *BRIE/ROTT* BN2 .. 77 L6
Sevenfields *BURH* RH15 .... 46 B5
Seventh Av *LAN/SOMP* BN15 .. 72 C5
Severals Rd *MIDH* GU29 .... 136 E9
Severn Rd *CRAWE* RH10 .... 30 B4
Seville St *BRIE/ROTT* BN2 .... 5 J2
Sewill Cl *HORL* RH6 .... 18 E2
Seymour Cl *BOR* GU35 .... 107 R5
  CRAWW RH11 .... 28 F7
Seymour St *BRIE/ROTT* BN2 ..... 5 L9
Shackleton Rd *CRAWE* RH10 .... 9 M8
Shadwells Cl *LAN/SOMP* BN15 .. 72 E6
Shadwells Rd *LAN/SOMP* BN15 .. 72 E6
Shaftesbury Av *FERR* BN12 ..... 92 D2
Shaftesbury Pl *BRI* BN1 .... 5 H5
Shaftesbury Rd *ANG/EP* BN16 .. 90 B5
  BRI BN1 .... 5 J2
  CRAWE RH10 .... 30 C5
Shakespeare Av *FERR* BN12 ..... 92 D2
Shakespeare St *HOVE* BN3 ...... 75 M5
Shalbourne Crs *SELS* PO20 .... 100 B8
Shaldon Rd *HAV* PO9 .... 169 J11
Shalesbrook La *FROW* RH18 .... 34 F8
Shamrock Cl *CCH* PO19 .... 7 H1
  FERR BN12 .... 60 B8
Shandon Gdns *SALV* BN13 ...... 71 J7
Shandon Rd *SALV* BN13 .... 71 J7
Shandon Wy *SALV* BN13 .... 71 J7
Shandys Cl *HORS* RH12 .... 125 P4
Shanklin Rd *BRIE/ROTT* BN2 .... 5 K1
Shardcroft Av *LHPTN* BN17 ..... 89 H5
Shardeloes Rd *ANG/EP* BN16 .. 68 E7
Sharon Cl *CRAWE* RH10 .... 30 A9
Sharps Rd *HAV* PO9 .... 169 J12
Sharpthorne Cl *CRAWW* RH11 .. 28 A3
Sharpthorne Crs *PTSD* BN41 ... 75 H4
Shaves Wood La
  HPPT/KEY BN6 .... 164 B7
Shaves Wood Rd
  HPPT/KEY BN6 .... 164 B8
Shaw Cl *MSEA/BNM* PO22 ...... 87 M8
Shawfield Rd *HAV* PO9 .... 57 H5

Shawford Gv HAV PO9 ...... 168 D12
Shaw's La SWTR RH13 ...... 143 N1
Shaws Rd CRAWE RH10 ...... 9 J1
Shear Hl EPSF GU31 ...... 133 Q4
Shearwater Dr CHAM PO6 ...... 56 A6
  MSEA/BNM PO22 ...... 86 B7
Sheddington Cl BURH RH15 ...... 46 F5
Sheepbell Cl PTSD BN41 ...... 75 G2
Sheepdown Cl PETW GU28 ...... 139 M10
Sheepdown Dr PETW GU28 ...... 139 L10
Sheepfair LEWES BN7 ...... 55 M3
Sheep Fold Av ANG/EP BN16 ...... 90 D3
Sheep La MIDH GU29 ...... 137 J9
Sheep Pen La STEY/UB BN44 ...... 48 C2
Sheep St PSF GU32 ...... 133 N6
Sheep Wk BRIE/ROTT BN2 ...... 97 L4
Sheepwash La RCCH PO18 ...... 172 C12
  SELS PO20 ...... 99 J2
Sheffield Cl CRAWE RH10 ...... 30 A2
Shelby Rd SALV BN13 ...... 70 B7
Sheldon Cl CRAWE RH10 ...... 30 C4
Sheldon Ct WTHG BN11 ...... 12 C7
Shellbridge Rd ARUN BN18 ...... 65 K1
Shelldale Av PTSD BN41 ...... 75 G6
Shelldale Crs PTSD BN41 ...... 75 G6
Shelldale Rd PTSD BN41 ...... 75 G5
Shelley Cl CRAWE RH10 ...... 30 B1
Shelley Dr HORS RH12 ...... 125 M2
  EGRIN RH19 ...... 23 J8
  HORS RH12 ...... 10 B3
  HOVE BN3 ...... 75 L6
  WTHG BN11 ...... 12 E6
Shelley Ldg LHPTN BN17 * 89 L5
Shelley Rd BOGR PO21 ...... 103 J2
Shelleys Ct SWTR RH13 * 11 M3
Shell La RHWH RH17 ...... 41 H8
Shellys Ct SWTR RH13 * 11 M3
Shenfield Wy BRI BN1 ...... 77 G3
Shenstone HWH RH16 ...... 45 L1
Shepherd Cl CRAWE RH10 ...... 8 F9
Shepherdsgrove La
  EGRIN RH19 ...... 24 E4
  HRTF TN7 ...... 35 J8
Shepherds La PETW GU28 ...... 138 A6
Shepherds Md BURH RH15 ...... 46 E5
  SALV BN13 ...... 70 D2
Shepherds Wk HPPT/KEY BN6 ...... 165 M4
Shepherds Wy HORS RH12 ...... 36 F4
  LIPH GU30 ...... 118 A2
  RING/NEW BN8 ...... 167 M2
Sheppard Wy PTSD BN41 ...... 74 F2
Sheppey Cl CRAWW RH11 ...... 29 C6
Sheppeys HWH RH16 ...... 45 C7
Sheraton Wk CRAWW RH11 * 29 G8
Sherborne Cl HOVE BN3 ...... 75 J2
Sherborne Cl CCH PO19 ...... 6 A4
Sherbourne La SELS PO20 ...... 180 H5
Sherbourne Rd HOVE BN3 ...... 75 J2
Sherbourne Wy HOVE BN3 ...... 75 J2
Sherbrooke Cl SALV BN13 ...... 70 C4
Sherfield Av HAV PO9 ...... 168 H12
Sheridan Cl EGRIN RH19 ...... 23 H8
Sheridan Rd SALV BN13 ...... 71 J8
Sheridan Ter HOVE BN3 ...... 75 M5
Sherlock Av CCH PO19 ...... 6 A1
Shermanbury Dr
  PUL/STOR RH20 ...... 159 R11
Shermanbury Gra
  SWTR RH13 * 144 H11
Shermanbury Rd SALV BN13 ...... 12 D2
  SWTR RH13 ...... 144 F10
Sherrington Rd BRIE/ROTT BN2 ...... 78 E5
Sherwood Cl LISS GU33 ...... 116 D6
  MSEA/BNM PO22 ...... 2 A1
Sherwood Dr HWH RH16 ...... 44 F4
Sherwood Rd MSEA/BNM PO22 ...... 2 A4
Sherwood Wk CRAWE RH10 ...... 9 K9
Shetland Cl CRAWE RH10 ...... 30 D2
Shetland Cl SALV BN13 ...... 70 A8
Shillinglee Rd MFD/CHID GU8 ...... 110 G12
Shingle Rd SHOR BN43 ...... 73 M7
Shingle Wk SELS PO20 ...... 99 L7
Shinwell Wk CRAWW RH11 * 29 G7
Shipfield BOGR PO21 ...... 103 L3
Shipleybridge La HORL RH6 ...... 20 E4
Shipley Ct LIPH GU30 ...... 117 Q2
Shipley Paygate SWTR RH13 ...... 143 N8
Shipley Rd BRIE/ROTT BN2 ...... 78 D6
  CRAWW RH11 ...... 28 F3
  SWTR RH13 ...... 143 P6
Ship St BRI BN1 ...... 4 D7
  EGRIN RH19 ...... 33 K1
  SHOR BN43 ...... 73 K6
Ship Street Gdns BRI BN1 * 4 D7
Shipton Green La SELS PO20 ...... 100 A2
Shire Cl WVILLE PO7 ...... 168 C8
Shire Pde CRAWE RH10 * 30 C2
Shire Pl CRAWE RH10 * 30 C2
Shirley Av HOVE BN3 ...... 76 A3
Shirley Cl ANG/EP BN16 ...... 90 C5
  BOGR PO21 ...... 102 F5
  SALV BN13 ...... 71 G4
  SHOR BN43 ...... 74 B5
Shirley Dr HOVE BN3 ...... 76 B4
  MSEA/BNM PO22 ...... 86 F7
  SALV BN13 ...... 71 G6
Shirley Rd HOVE BN3 ...... 76 B5
Shirleys Gdn MSEA/BNM PO22 ...... 3 M2
Shirley St HOVE BN3 ...... 76 A6
Sholing Ct HAV PO9 ...... 168 E11
Shooting Fld STEY/UB BN44 ...... 48 C1
Shopfield Cl ANG/EP BN16 ...... 90 B3
Shopham Br PETW GU28 ...... 157 M3
Shop La RCCH PO18 ...... 172 D12
Shopsdam Rd LAN/SOMP BN15 ...... 94 E1
Shopwhyke Rd SELS PO20 ...... 62 D6
Shorecroft BOGR PO21 ...... 103 L4
Shoreham By-Pass PTSD BN41 ...... 74 F1
  SHOR BN43 ...... 73 L3
Shoreham Rd CRAWE RH10 ...... 30 B6
  HFD BN5 ...... 163 K10
  STEY/UB BN44 ...... 49 G5
Shore Rd RCCH PO18 ...... 81 M2
  SELS PO20 ...... 99 K2
Shoreside Wk SELS PO20 ...... 99 J5
Short Cl CRAWW RH11 ...... 29 J1
Short Furlong LHPTN BN17 ...... 89 L4
Short Gallop CRAWE RH10 * 30 C2
Shortgate Rd BRIE/ROTT BN2 ...... 77 L1
Shorts Cl HWH RH16 ...... 45 H6
Shortsfield Cl HORS RH12 ...... 36 B4
Shotterfield Ter LISS GU33 ...... 116 D4

Shottermill HORS RH12 ...... 36 F2
Shottermill Pk HASM GU27 * 108 H10
Shotters BURH RH15 ...... 46 D8
Shovelstrode La EGRIN RH19 ...... 24 D7
Shripney La MSEA/BNM PO22 ...... 86 A5
Shripney Rd MSEA/BNM PO22 ...... 2 E1
Shrubbs Dr MSEA/BNM PO22 ...... 87 L8
Sidehill Dr PTSD BN41 ...... 74 E3
Sideways La HORL RH6 ...... 14 B8
Sidlaw Ter BOGR PO21 ...... 2 F7
Sidlesham Cl HISD PO11 ...... 98 A3
Sidlesham La SELS PO20 ...... 82 E8
Silchester Dr CRAWW RH11 ...... 8 A8
Silkin Wk CRAWW RH11 * 29 G8
Sillwood Pl BRI BN1 ...... 4 A6
Sillwood Rd BRI BN1 ...... 4 A6
Sillwood St BRI BN1 ...... 4 A7
Sillwood Ter BRI BN1 ...... 4 A6
Silver Birch Cl LISS GU33 ...... 116 D9
Silver Birch Dr
  MSEA/BNM PO22 ...... 87 K7
  SALV BN13 ...... 70 B8
Silver Birches HFD BN5 ...... 163 L10
  HWH RH16 ...... 45 K5
Silverdale HPPT/KEY BN6 ...... 165 Q6
  PUL/STOR RH20 ...... 158 D8
  WTHG BN11 * 94 A3
Silverdale Av HOVE BN3 ...... 76 C6
Silverdale Cl BOGR PO21 ...... 102 F5
Silverdale Dr LAN/SOMP BN15 ...... 72 B8
Silverdale Rd BURH RH15 ...... 47 C7
  HOVE BN3 ...... 76 C6
Silver Gld PUL/STOR RH20 ...... 160 B7
Silver La BIL RH14 ...... 142 A2
Silverlea Gdns HORL RH6 ...... 15 H7
Silverlock Cl CCH PO19 ...... 7 J1
Silverlock Pl EMRTH PO10 * 169 Q12
Silverston Av BOGR PO21 ...... 103 M3
Silvertrees EMRTH PO10 ...... 58 A3
Silver Wy SELS PO20 ...... 100 B8
Silverwood CRAWE RH10 * 21 L6
  PUL/STOR RH20 ...... 159 Q6
Silverwood Copse
  PUL/STOR RH20 ...... 159 Q6
Silverwood Ct ANG/EP BN16 * 90 B4
Sinclair Cl CRAWE RH10 ...... 30 D5
Sincox La SWTR RH13 ...... 142 H11
Singleton Cl BOGR PO21 ...... 103 C4
  FERR BN12 ...... 91 L2
Singleton Crs FERR BN12 ...... 91 L2
Singleton Gdns HORN PO8 ...... 150 E9
Singleton Rd BRI BN1 ...... 52 D2
  HORS RH12 ...... 125 N2
Sinnocks PUL/STOR RH20 ...... 160 B4
Sir George's Pl STEY/UB BN44 ...... 48 D2
Siskin Av CRAWE RH10 ...... 32 B4
Siskin Cl HORS RH12 ...... 36 D4
Siskin Gv WVILLE PO7 ...... 168 B11
Sissinghurst Cl CRAWE RH10 ...... 30 C2
Six Acres CRAWW RH11 ...... 29 H8
Six Acres Cl SWTR RH13 ...... 125 J11
Skeyne Dr PUL/STOR RH20 * 159 K3
Skiff La BIL RH14 ...... 122 G10
Skinners La SWTR RH13 ...... 143 R1
Skipton Wy HORL RH6 ...... 15 G4
Skylarks BIL RH14 ...... 141 R2
Skylark Vw HORS RH12 ...... 36 C2
Slade La EPSF GU31 ...... 134 F5
Slattsfield Cl SELS PO20 ...... 181 M6
Slaugham Ct CRAWW RH11 ...... 28 B3
Slaugham La RHWH RH17 ...... 128 B5
Sleets Rd HORS RH12 ...... 125 P2
Slider's La UCK TN22 ...... 131 Q11
Slimbridge Rd BURH RH15 ...... 46 E6
Slindon Bottom Rd ARUN BN18 ...... 64 F1
Slindon Cl HORN PO8 ...... 150 E8
Slindon Gdns HAV PO9 ...... 57 G5
Slindon Rd SALV BN13 ...... 71 J7
Slinfold Cl BRIE/ROTT BN2 ...... 5 M7
The Slipe ARUN BN18 ...... 64 F6
Slipper MI EMRTH PO10 * 58 B6
Slipper Rd EMRTH PO10 ...... 58 B6
Sloe Cl CCH PO19 ...... 7 J2
Slonk Hill Rd SHOR BN43 ...... 73 M4
Sloop La RHWH RH17 ...... 131 M12
Sloughbrook Cl HORS RH12 ...... 36 E3
Sloughgreen La RHWH RH17 ...... 128 G8
Slugwash La RHWH RH17 ...... 148 E8
Smallcroft LHPTN BN17 ...... 89 H4
Smallcutts Av EMRTH PO10 ...... 58 E4
Smallfield Rd HORL RH6 ...... 15 G6
Smallham HORL RH6 ...... 15 G6
Smalls Md CRAWW RH11 ...... 8 D4
Smeeds Cl EGRIN RH19 ...... 23 M6
Smee La RCCH PO18 ...... 62 C4
Smithbarn SWTR RH13 ...... 11 L4
Smithbarn Cl HORL RH6 ...... 15 G5
Smith Cl CRAWE RH10 ...... 8 F7
Smithers Hill La SWTR RH13 ...... 143 L9
Smith La EMRTH PO10 ...... 58 E4
The Smithy SWTR RH13 ...... 145 K4
Smock Aly PUL/STOR RH20 ...... 160 B7
Smokyhouse La PETW GU28 ...... 138 A12
Smolletts EGRIN RH19 ...... 33 H1
Smugglers End RHWH RH17 ...... 128 D1
Smuggler's La RCCH PO18 ...... 81 M4
  RDKG RH5 ...... 115 P2
  STEY/UB BN44 ...... 49 G3
  SWTR RH13 ...... 124 G10
Smugglers Wk FERR BN12 ...... 92 D4
Smugglers Wy SWTR RH13 ...... 125 J11
Snapes Rd PUL/STOR RH20 ...... 160 C10
Snednore LEWES BN7 ...... 55 L8
Snell Hatch CRAWW RH11 ...... 8 A3
Snipe La HASM GU27 ...... 119 K4
Snowberry Crs HAV PO9 ...... 57 J2
Snowdrop Cl CRAWW RH11 ...... 28 F7
  LHPTN BN17 ...... 90 A2
Snowdrop La HWH RH16 ...... 45 M5
Snowflakes La HWH RH16 ...... 130 G11
Snow Hl CRAWE RH10 ...... 21 L4
Snowhill La CRAWE RH10 ...... 21 L4
Soane Cl CRAWW RH11 ...... 28 D5
Soberton Rd HAV PO9 ...... 56 F2
Soldridge Cl HAV PO9 ...... 169 J11
Solent Cl LHPTN BN17 ...... 89 M2
Solent Rd HAV PO9 ...... 56 F4
  SELS PO20 ...... 99 L2
Solent Wy EMRTH PO10 ...... 58 A6
  HAV PO9 ...... 57 K6
  HAV PO9 ...... 57 K6
  SELS PO20 ...... 181 K8

Solway Av BRI BN1 ...... 52 E6
Solway Cl LHPTN BN17 ...... 89 M4
Somborne Dr HAV PO9 ...... 168 G12
Somergate HORS RH12 ...... 125 Q3
Somerhill Av HOVE BN3 ...... 76 C6
Somerhill Rd HOVE BN3 ...... 76 C6
Somerley La SELS PO20 ...... 100 C4
Somerset Av SALV BN13 ...... 106 G6
Somerset Cl SALV BN13 ...... 70 F8
Somerset Gdns BOGR PO21 ...... 2 D3
Somerset Rd ANG/EP BN16 ...... 91 G3
  FERR BN12 ...... 91 L5
Somerset St BRIE/ROTT BN2 ...... 5 J7
Somerstown CCH PO19 ...... 6 D2
Somerton Gn MSEA/BNM PO22 ...... 3 K2
Somerville Dr CRAWE RH10 ...... 20 B8
Sompting Av SALV BN13 ...... 71 J8
Sompting By-Pass SALV BN13 ...... 71 K6
Sompting Cl BRIE/ROTT BN2 ...... 77 L6
Sompting Rd BRIE/ROTT BN2 ...... 77 K6
Sonnet Wy WVILLE PO7 ...... 168 C9
Sopers PUL/STOR RH20 * 159 K1
Sopers La STEY/UB BN44 ...... 48 A6
Sopley Cl HAV PO9 ...... 169 J11
Sorrel Cl CRAWW RH11 ...... 28 F7
  WVILLE PO7 ...... 168 B11
Sorrel Rd HORS RH12 ...... 36 D4
South Acre EPSF GU31 ...... 152 E2
Southall Av BRIE/ROTT BN2 ...... 77 J4
Southampton St BRIE/ROTT BN2 ...... 5 J4
South Av BOGR PO21 ...... 103 K2
  BRIE/ROTT BN2 ...... 5 J6
  FERR BN12 ...... 92 D4
  HPPT/KEY BN6 ...... 164 H4
South Bank CCH PO19 ...... 6 D8
  HPPT/KEY BN6 ...... 165 M6
South Bay EMRTH PO10 ...... 80 B2
South Beach SHOR BN43 * 73 L7
Southbourne Av EMRTH PO10 ...... 58 C5
Southbrook CRAWW RH11 ...... 29 H8
Southbrook Cl HAV PO9 ...... 57 G5
Southbrook Rd HAV PO9 ...... 57 G6
  RCCH PO18 ...... 59 M2
South Cl BURH RH15 ...... 46 D6
  CRAWE RH10 ...... 9 J1
  HAV PO9 ...... 57 H5
Southcote Av SELS PO20 ...... 99 K6
Southcourt Cl ANG/EP BN16 ...... 90 D3
Southcourt Rd SALV BN13 ...... 12 F3
Southdean Cl MSEA/BNM PO22 ...... 87 L8
Southdean Dr MSEA/BNM PO22 ...... 87 L8
Southdown Av BRI BN1 ...... 76 F4
  LEWES BN7 ...... 55 M5
  PTSD BN41 ...... 75 H5
Southdown Cl CCH PO19 ...... 7 J1
  CCH PO19 ...... 62 A5
  HORS RH12 ...... 36 F4
  HWH RH16 ...... 45 K4
  MIDH GU29 ...... 136 G11
Southdown Ms BRIE/ROTT BN2 ...... 5 J7
Southdown Pl BRI BN1 ...... 76 F4
Southdown Rd BOGR PO21 ...... 2 C7
  BRI BN1 ...... 76 F4
  HORN PO8 ...... 150 D10
  PTSD BN41 ...... 74 F3
  SHOR BN43 ...... 73 L4
  STHW BN42 ...... 74 D6
South Downs LEWES BN7 ...... 166 H4
South Downs Wy ARUN BN18 ...... 174 H3
  ARUN BN18 ...... 176 G4
  BRIE/ROTT BN2 ...... 78 E1
  EPSF GU31 ...... 152 H4
  HFD BN5 ...... 50 E3
  HORN PO8 ...... 150 D2
  HPPT/KEY BN6 ...... 165 M11
  HPPT/KEY BN6 ...... 165 K9
  LEWES BN7 ...... 54 F5
  LEWES BN7 ...... 78 E1
  LEWES BN7 ...... 79 H1
  PETW GU28 ...... 156 D9
  PSF GU32 ...... 150 A3
  PUL/STOR RH20 ...... 175 L2
  PUL/STOR RH20 ...... 177 K3
  PUL/STOR RH20 ...... 179 J5
  SHOR BN43 ...... 50 A3
  STEY/UB BN44 ...... 48 B6
  STEY/UB BN44 ...... 49 H5
  STEY/UB BN44 ...... 179 M5
Southdown Ter STEY/UB BN44 * 48 C2
Southdown View Cl SALV BN13 ...... 71 L8
Southdown View Rd
  SALV BN13 ...... 71 L8
Southdown View Wy
  SALV BN13 ...... 71 K7
Southdown Wy
  PUL/STOR RH20 ...... 160 C10
South Dr ANG/EP BN16 ...... 90 C2
  BURH RH15 ...... 46 D6
  FERR BN12 ...... 91 K5
  MSEA/BNM PO22 ...... 87 H8
Southern Ga CCH PO19 ...... 6 C6
Southern Rd BOR GU35 ...... 106 G4
  SELS PO20 ...... 181 L1
Southey Rd WTHG BN11 ...... 12 E7
South Farm Rd SALV BN13 ...... 71 H8
Southfield Rd SALV BN13 ...... 71 J8
Southfields Cl CCH PO19 ...... 83 C2
Southfields Rd LHPTN BN17 ...... 89 L4
Southgate CCH PO19 ...... 6 C6
Southgate Av CRAWE RH10 ...... 9 H5
Southgate Dr CRAWE RH10 ...... 8 E7
Southgate Pde CRAWE RH10 ...... 8 E7
Southgate Wy CRAWE RH10 ...... 8 E7
South Gv PETW GU28 ...... 139 L10
South Holmes Rd SWTR RH13 ...... 37 G5
South Hurst BOR GU35 ...... 106 G8
Southlands EGRIN RH19 ...... 33 K4
Southlands Av HORL RH6 ...... 14 F5
Southlands La PUL/STOR RH20 ...... 160 B6
Southlands Pk MIDH GU29 ...... 136 H12
South La ARUN BN18 ...... 176 C6
  EMRTH PO10 ...... 58 F2
  EPSF GU31 ...... 151 L4
  HORN PO8 ...... 150 C7
  HORN PO8 ...... 151 J4
  PETW GU28 ...... 138 G10
Southleigh Rd EMRTH PO10 ...... 58 A2
  HAV PO9 ...... 57 J4
South Ldg LAN/SOMP BN15 ...... 72 B6
South Lodge Cl BURH RH15 ...... 46 E5
Southmoor La HAV PO9 ...... 56 A6
Southmount BRIE/ROTT BN2 ...... 77 G4
Southon Cl PTSD BN41 ...... 74 E2

Southover Pl BRIE/ROTT BN2 ...... 5 G3
Southover Rd BOGR PO21 ...... 2 C7
Southover St BRIE/ROTT BN2 ...... 5 J7
South Pallant CCH PO19 ...... 6 C7
South Pde HORL RH6 * 14 C5
South Pas LHPTN BN17 ...... 89 L5
South Pier Rd HORL RH6 ...... 19 M2
South Rd BRI BN1 ...... 76 D4
  HORN PO8 ...... 150 D12
  HWH RH16 ...... 45 K5
  LIPH GU30 ...... 117 K4
South Road Ms BRI BN1 ...... 76 D4
Southsea Av FERR BN12 ...... 92 D3
Southside PUL/STOR RH20 ...... 159 L3
South Strd ANG/EP BN16 ...... 90 F5
South St BRI BN1 ...... 4 E7
  CCH PO19 ...... 6 B7
  EMRTH PO10 ...... 58 A5
  HAV PO9 ...... 57 G4
  HORS RH12 ...... 10 C6
  HPPT/KEY BN6 ...... 166 A6
  LAN/SOMP BN15 ...... 94 D1
  MIDH GU29 ...... 137 J10
  PTSD BN41 ...... 74 F4
  RHWH RH17 ...... 44 B4
  SALV BN13 ...... 12 B2
  SWTR RH13 ...... 144 F10
  WTHG BN11 ...... 13 H7
South Ter LHPTN BN17 ...... 89 L5
South Vw ANG/EP BN16 ...... 91 G5
  HPPT/KEY BN6 ...... 166 A4
  LEWES BN7 * 166 H4
Southview HFD BN5 * 163 L11
South View Cl CRAWE RH10 ...... 21 K6
Southview Cl SHOR BN43 ...... 74 B6
Southview Dr WTHG BN11 ...... 12 A4
Southview Gdns WTHG BN11 ...... 12 A4
  WTHG BN11 ...... 92 B3
Southview Rd BOR GU35 ...... 107 G4
  MSEA/BNM PO22 ...... 105 G1
  STHW BN42 ...... 74 D5
South View Ter HFD BN5 ...... 163 L11
Southwark Cl CRAWW RH11 ...... 29 C7
Southwark Wk BOGR PO21 ...... 103 K2
Southwater Cl BRIE/ROTT BN2 ...... 5 L5
  CRAWW RH11 ...... 28 F3
  FERR BN12 ...... 92 A2
Southwater St SWTR RH13 ...... 125 K10
South Wy BOGR PO21 ...... 85 M8
  LEWES BN7 ...... 55 M4
Southway BURH RH15 ...... 46 C6
  LHPTN BN17 ...... 89 L5
Southways Av SALV BN13 ...... 71 K7
Southways Pk CRAWE RH10 * 19 J6
Southwick Cl EGRIN RH19 ...... 23 J7
Southwick Sq STHW BN42 ...... 74 D6
Southwick St STHW BN42 ...... 74 D5
Southwold Cl SALV BN13 ...... 70 D4
South Woodlands BRI BN1 ...... 76 D1
The Spain PSF GU32 ...... 133 M6
Sparks Ct LHPTN BN17 ...... 89 L4
Spark's La RHWH RH17 ...... 129 M7
Sparrow Dr HORN PO8 ...... 168 A5
Sparrow Wy BURH RH15 ...... 46 C6
Sparsholt Cl HAV PO9 ...... 168 D12
Sparshott Rd SELS PO20 ...... 181 L8
Spartan Cl EMRTH PO10 ...... 80 B2
Spatham La HPPT/KEY BN6 ...... 166 C3
Spats La BOR GU35 ...... 107 N1
Spear Hl PUL/STOR RH20 ...... 161 K6
Speedwell Cl SALV BN13 ...... 69 M8
Speedwell Wy HORS RH12 ...... 36 D4
Spencer Av HOVE BN3 ...... 75 J2
Spencer Rd EMRTH PO10 ...... 57 M1
  LAN/SOMP BN15 ...... 72 C8
Spencers Pl HORS RH12 ...... 10 A1
Spencers Rd CRAWW RH11 ...... 8 D5
  HORS RH12 ...... 10 B4
Spencer St BOGR PO21 ...... 2 E5
Spey Cl SALV BN13 ...... 70 B5
Spicers Cl BURH RH15 ...... 46 E4
Spierbridge Rd
  PUL/STOR RH20 ...... 159 R11
Spiers Wy HORL RH6 ...... 15 G7
Spindle Cl HAV PO9 ...... 57 K2
Spindle Warren HAV PO9 ...... 57 K2
Spindle Wy CRAWE RH10 ...... 9 J5
Spinnaker Cl LHPTN BN17 ...... 89 M4
Spinnaker Vw HAV PO9 ...... 56 B2
Spinnals Gv STHW BN42 ...... 74 C6
Spinney Cl CRAWE RH10 ...... 32 B1
  HORS RH12 ...... 37 G3
  HPPT/KEY BN6 ...... 165 K4
  SELS PO20 ...... 181 K5
Spinney La PUL/STOR RH20 ...... 159 R6
  SELS PO20 ...... 81 M7
Spinney North
  PUL/STOR RH20 ...... 159 L3
The Spinney ANG/EP BN16 ...... 90 F5
  BOGR PO21 ...... 103 K2
  CRAWW RH11 ...... 8 B7
  GSHT GU26 ...... 108 D5
  HASM GU27 ...... 108 G12
  HORL RH6 ...... 14 F4
  HORN PO8 ...... 168 B3
  HOVE BN3 ...... 76 B2
  HPPT/KEY BN6 ...... 165 N4
  HWH RH16 ...... 45 G4
  PUL/STOR RH20 ...... 159 L3
  SELS PO20 ...... 81 M7
Spinney Wk MSEA/BNM PO22 ...... 65 G7
Spitalfield La CCH PO19 ...... 7 H2
Spital Rd LEWES BN7 ...... 55 M4
Spithandle La STEY/UB BN44 ...... 161 N12
Spode La EDEN TN8 ...... 25 M1
Spooners Rd HORS RH12 ...... 11 L1
Springate Rd STHW BN42 ...... 74 E5
Springbank CCH PO19 ...... 61 G4
Spring Cl CRAWW RH11 ...... 8 B7
Spring Copse CRAWE RH10 ...... 21 H6
Springfarm Rd HASM GU27 ...... 108 H12
Springfield BOGR PO21 ...... 102 F3
  EGRIN RH19 ...... 23 J5
Springfield Av ANG/EP BN16 ...... 90 D4
  HAV PO9 ...... 56 C3
  RCCH PO18 ...... 172 C10
  RHWH RH17 ...... 146 D1
  SELS PO20 ...... 82 B6
Springfield Crs HORS RH12 ...... 10 B5

Springfield La HORS RH12 ...... 38 A5
Springfield Pk HORS RH12 * 10 B5
Springfield Park Rd HORS RH12... 10 B5
Springfield Rd BRI BN1 ...... 76 F5
  CRAWW RH11 ...... 8 D5
  HORS RH12 ...... 10 C5
Spring Gdns BRI BN1 ...... 4 D6
  CRAWE RH10 ...... 30 D5
  EMRTH PO10 ...... 58 A5
  PUL/STOR RH20 ...... 160 H11
Spring La HPPT/KEY BN6 ...... 165 M9
  HWH RH16 ...... 130 E8
  SWTR RH13 ...... 124 F2
Spring Meadow FROW RH18 ...... 34 B4
  MIDH GU29 * 136 H11
Spring Plat CRAWE RH10 ...... 30 B3
Spring Plat Ct CRAWE RH10 * 30 B3
Spring St BRI BN1 ...... 4 A4
Spring V HORN PO8 ...... 168 C5
Spring Wy EGRIN RH19 ...... 23 M5
Springwell HAV PO9 ...... 57 G4
Springwood Av WVILLE PO7 ...... 168 A11
Spronkett's La RHWH RH17 ...... 145 R1
Sproule Cl ARUN BN18 ...... 88 A3
Sproutes La SWTR RH13 ...... 142 F9
Spruce Av BOR GU35 ...... 106 G6
  WVILLE PO7 ...... 168 B10
Spurgeon Cl CRAWW RH11 ...... 8 D2
Spur Rd CCH PO19 ...... 7 L6
Spy La BIL RH14 ...... 122 H1
Squadron Dr SALV BN13 ...... 70 A7
Square Dr HASM GU27 ...... 119 L4
The Square CRAWE RH10 ...... 8 E4
  EMRTH PO10 ...... 58 C2
  EPSF GU31 ...... 152 E1
  LIPH GU30 ...... 117 Q3
  MSEA/BNM PO22 ...... 65 G7
  PSF GU32 ...... 133 N6
  SALV BN13 * 71 J8
Squires Cl CRAWE RH10 ...... 31 M1
Squirrel Cl CRAWW RH11 ...... 19 G8
Squirrel Rdg CRAWE RH10 * 32 A2
Squirrels Copse
  PUL/STOR RH20 ...... 160 F10
Stable Cl CRAWE RH10 ...... 30 C6
Stable Fld MSEA/BNM PO22 ...... 88 A4
Stable La SALV BN13 ...... 178 H11
Stable Rd BOR GU35 ...... 106 F3
Stacey Cl HAV PO9 ...... 168 E10
Stackfield Rd CRAWW RH11 ...... 28 D4
Stafford Rd BRI BN1 ...... 4 B1
  CRAWW RH11 ...... 18 F8
  PSF GU32 ...... 133 N4
Staffords Cl ANG/EP BN16 ...... 90 A3
Staffords Pl HORL RH6 ...... 15 G7
Stafford Wy HPPT/KEY BN6 ...... 165 P6
Stag Cl HFD BN5 ...... 163 K3
Stagelands CRAWW RH11 ...... 29 G1
Stagshorn Rd HORN PO8 ...... 168 D2
Stairbridge La RHWH RH17 ...... 146 F5
Stakers La SWTR RH13 ...... 143 R1
Stakes Hill Rd WVILLE PO7 ...... 56 A1
Stalham Wy MSEA/BNM PO22 ...... 3 L1
Stallard Cl EMRTH PO10 ...... 57 M4
Stall House La PUL/STOR RH20... 141 N10
Stammers Hl HFD BN5 ...... 50 E2
Stanbridge La CRAWW RH11 ...... 28 D4
Stanbridge Rd HAV PO9 ...... 57 J2
Stanbrok Cl BOGR PO21 ...... 103 K2
Stanbury Cl RCCH PO18 ...... 60 A6
Standean Cl BRI BN1 ...... 53 L2
Standen Cl EGRIN RH19 ...... 22 F6
Standen Pl HORS RH12 ...... 36 F2
Standford Hl BOR GU35 ...... 107 K8
Standford La BOR GU35 ...... 107 K6
Standgrove Pl RHWH RH17 ...... 130 D3
Standinghall La CRAWE RH10 ...... 30 F5
Stane St BIL RH14 ...... 124 A12
  BIL RH14 ...... 141 R3
  PUL/STOR RH20 ...... 159 K1
  RCCH PO18 ...... 62 D4
  RCCH PO18 ...... 63 G2
  SWTR RH13 ...... 124 E4
Stane Street Cl
  PUL/STOR RH20 ...... 159 K1
Stanford Av BRI BN1 ...... 76 F5
  HPPT/KEY BN6 ...... 165 M5
Stanford Cl HOVE BN3 ...... 76 B4
  HPPT/KEY BN6 ...... 165 M5
  MSEA/BNM PO22 ...... 2 F2
Stanford Cottages
  SWTR RH13 * 126 D5
Stanford Ct HAV PO9 ...... 169 J12
Stanford Orch HORS RH12 ...... 115 Q10
Stanford Rd BRI BN1 ...... 76 D5
Stanford Sq WTHG BN11 ...... 13 J6
Stanford Ter HPPT/KEY BN6 * 125 N2
Stanford Wy HORS RH12 ...... 125 N2
Stan Hl HORL RH6 ...... 18 B7
Stanhope Rd LHPTN BN17 ...... 89 K3
  WTHG BN11 ...... 13 G4
Stanier Cl CRAWE RH10 ...... 30 A4
Stanley Av PTSD BN41 ...... 74 E2
Stanley Cl BOGR PO21 ...... 2 E5
  CRAWE RH10 ...... 9 H2
Stanley Rd BRI BN1 ...... 4 F2
  EMRTH PO10 ...... 58 B5
  LHPTN BN17 ...... 89 J2
  PTSD BN41 ...... 74 E2
  WTHG BN11 ...... 13 H3
Stanley St BRIE/ROTT BN2 ...... 5 J5
Stanley Wk SWTR RH13 ...... 10 E6
Stanmer Av BRIE/ROTT BN2 ...... 77 H5
Stanmer Park Rd BRI BN1 ...... 76 F3
Stanmer St BRI BN1 ...... 77 G3
Stanmer Vls BRI BN1 ...... 77 G2
Stanovr Gdns BOGR PO21 ...... 103 L5
Stanover Rd MSEA/BNM PO22 ...... 86 F6
Stansfield Cl ANG/EP BN16 * 90 C3
Stanstead Crs BRIE/ROTT BN2 ...... 78 E4
Stansted Crs HORS RH12 ...... 169 J11
Stanswood Rd HAV PO9 ...... 168 E11
Stanton Dr CCH PO19 ...... 61 L2
Stanway Cl BRIE/ROTT BN2 ...... 78 E7
Staplands Dr BRIE/ROTT BN2 * 78 E7
Staplefield Rd RHWH RH17 ...... 128 F6
  RHWH RH17 ...... 129 K9
Staple La RCCH PO18 ...... 172 C9
Staples Barn HFD BN5 ...... 163 L4
Staples Barn La HFD BN5 ...... 163 L4
Staples Hl SWTR RH13 ...... 144 E10

204 Sta - Tes

Stapleton Ct BOGR PO21 103 J2
Stapley Rd HOVE BN3 75 J5
Star Cl SWTR RH13 11 L2
Starina Gdns WVILLE PO7 168 C9
Starling Cl BURH RH15 46 C6
Star Rd SWTR RH13 144 F11
Station Ap BOGR PO21 * 2 D6
BRI BN1 54 A7
CCH PO19 6 D6
EMRTH PO10 * 58 A4
HORL RH6 15 G6
HORS RH12 27 L8
HPPT/KEY BN6 165 M5
MFD/CHID GU8 110 E1
PUL/STOR RH20 158 H3
RDKG RH5 16 A4
RHWH RH17 131 K2
Station Approach Rd
HORL RH6 * 20 A1
Station Cl LEWES BN7 166 H4
SWTR RH13 10 F5
Station Hl CRAWE RH10 30 A2
Station La MFD/CHID GU8 110 D1
Station Pde ANG/EP BN16 * 90 D3
LAN/SOMP BN15 * 72 D8
WTHG BN11 * 12 B3
Station Rd ANG/EP BN16 90 C3
ARUN BN18 67 J4
BIL RH14 122 G2
BIL RH14 142 A1
BOGR PO21 2 D6
BOR GU35 106 F4
BRI BN1 76 C2
BURH RH15 47 G7
CRAWE RH10 8 F5
CRAWE RH10 32 A1
EGRIN RH19 23 J8
EGRIN RH19 42 F3
EPSF GU31 133 N5
FROW RH18 34 E6
HFD BN5 163 J4
HORL RH6 15 G6
HORS RH12 36 A1
HORS RH12 113 Q7
HORS RH12 114 A10
LEWES BN7 166 H3
LIPH GU30 117 Q3
LISS GU33 116 C9
MIDH GU29 136 G10
PETW GU28 139 K11
PSF GU32 133 M5
PUL/STOR RH20 158 H3
RCCH PO18 60 B6
RHWH RH17 131 M4
RING/NEW BN8 149 P6
STEY/UB BN44 48 D2
STHW BN42 74 D6
SWTR RH13 10 F5
SWTR RH13 125 N6
SWTR RH13 144 F3
SWTR RH13 145 K3
WTHG BN11 13 H3
Station St BRI BN1 4 E4
Station Wy CRAWE RH10 8 F5
Staunton Rd HAV PO9 56 F4
Staunton Wy EPSF GU31 151 K4
HAV PO9 56 D5
HAV PO9 56 F2
HORN PO8 150 H5
Stavely Gdns CCH PO19 61 L2
Stean Furlong LHPTN BN17 89 H2
Stedham La MIDH GU29 136 D6
Steele Cl PUL/STOR RH20 160 B4
Steels La RCCH PO18 59 K8
Steep Cl SALV BN13 178 H12
Steepdown Rd
LAN/SOMP BN15 72 B5
Steep La SALV BN13 178 H12
Steeple Vw SALV BN13 70 F8
Steepways GSHT GU26 108 E3
Steeres Hl HORS RH12 27 H2
Steers La CRAWE RH10 20 B5
Steine Gdns BRIE/ROTT BN2 4 F7
Steine La BRI BN1 4 E7
Steine St BRIE/ROTT BN2 4 F8
Stein Rd EMRTH PO10 58 E3
Stemp Dr BIL RH14 141 R1
Stempswood Wy
MSEA/BNM PO22 65 G7
The Stennings EGRIN RH19 23 H6
Stephen Cl CRAWW RH11 19 J8
HORN PO8 168 C7
Stephenson Dr EGRIN RH19 33 L3
Stephenson Pl CRAWE RH10 30 A3
Stephenson Wy CRAWE RH10 9 M4
Stephens Rd BRI BN1 77 G3
Stepney Cl CRAWE RH10 30 B5
Sterling Buildings HORS RH12 * 10 C6
Sterling Pde ANG/EP BN16 * 90 B4
Sterling Pk CRAWE RH10 * 20 A6
Sternway LHPTN BN17 89 M4
Stevenage Rd CRAWW RH11 28 D7
Stevenson Rd BRIE/ROTT BN2 5 K7
Stewards Ri ARUN BN18 66 E4
Steyne Gdns WTHG BN11 13 J6
Steyne St BOGR PO21 2 D7
The Steyne BOGR PO21 2 D8
WTHG BN11 13 J6
Steyning Av HOVE BN3 75 L2
Steyning By-Pass
STEY/UB BN44 48 E4
Steyning Cl CRAWE RH10 29 K1
FERR BN12 92 A2
LAN/SOMP BN15 72 C5
Steyning Crs PUL/STOR RH20 159 R11
Steyning Rd BRIE/ROTT BN2 97 L4
SHOR BN43 49 H8
SWTR RH13 144 B6
Steyning Ter HAV PO9 * 57 G3
Steyning Wy MSEA/BNM PO22 86 D6
Stile Gdns HASM GU27 109 J11
Stillers MFD/CHID GU8 * 110 G5
Stipenhoke HFD BN5 * 163 L5
Stirling Av WVILLE PO7 168 A10
Stirling Cl BURH RH15 47 H5
CRAWE RH10 30 A4
Stirling Court Rd BURH RH15 47 H5
Stirling Pl HOVE BN3 75 M7
Stirling Rd CCH PO19 6 F6
Stirling Wy BOGR PO21 103 K3
EGRIN RH19 24 A6
SWTR RH13 11 H5
Stirrup Wy CRAWE RH10 30 C2
Stoatley Hollow HASM GU27 109 K9
Stoatley Ri HASM GU27 109 K9
Stoatley River HASM GU27 109 K9
Stockbridge Cl HAV PO9 169 J12
Stockbridge Gdns CCH PO19 6 B9
Stockbridge Pl CCH PO19 * 6 C9
Stockbridge Rd CCH PO19 6 D8
Stockcroft Rd RHWH RH17 40 F8
Stocker Rd BOGR PO21 2 A9
Stockfield HORL RH6 * 15 G5
Stockheath La HAV PO9 56 F2
Stockheath Rd HAV PO9 56 F1
Stockheath Wy HAV PO9 57 G2
Stocklands Cl RHWH RH17 44 C1
Stocks Cl HORL RH6 15 G7
Stocks Flds STEY/UB BN44 * 161 N12
Stocks La RCCH PO18 62 A1
SELS PO20 99 M7
Stocks Md PUL/STOR RH20 178 H3
Stockwell Rd EGRIN RH19 33 K3
Stodham La LISS GU33 116 B11
LISS GU33 134 B1
Stoke Abbott Rd WTHG BN11 13 G5
Stoke Rd ARUN BN18 176 D7
Stokes Cl CRAWE RH10 30 B6
Stoneage Cl MSEA/BNM PO22 86 B7
Stonebridge Ct HORS RH12 * 125 R3
Stonechat Cl EPSF GU31 133 R7
Stonechat Rd HORN PO8 168 B3
Stone Cl SALV BN13 70 E7
Stonecourt Cl HORL RH6 15 H6
Stonecroft Cl HOVE BN3 75 K1
Stonecrop Cl CRAWW RH11 28 F6
Stonecross La HWH RH16 130 G6
Stonecross Rd BRIE/ROTT BN2 77 L1
Stonedene Cl BOR GU35 107 Q5
FROW RH18 35 G7
Stonefield Cl CRAWE RH10 8 F6
Stonefields ANG/EP BN16 90 B4
Stonefield Wy BURH RH15 46 E4
Stonehall La RHWH RH17 129 Q2
Stoneham Cl PSF GU32 133 L5
Stoneham Pk PSF GU32 133 L5
Stoneham Rd HOVE BN3 75 L6
Stone Hatch CRAN GU6 112 H6
Stonehill Crs BOGR PO21 103 G2
Stonehill Pk BOR GU35 107 Q5
Stonehill Rd BOR GU35 107 R5
Stonehouse La SWTR RH13 144 G5
Stonehouse Rd LIPH GU30 118 A1
Stonehurst Ct BRIE/ROTT BN2 5 L4
Stonehurst Rd SALV BN13 70 E8
Stone La SALV BN13 70 E7
Stoneleigh Av BRI BN1 52 E7
Stoneleigh Cl BRI BN1 52 E7
EGRIN RH19 23 L7
Stonepark Dr FROW RH18 34 F7
Stonepit La HFD BN5 162 G4
Stonepound Rd
HPPT/KEY BN6 165 M5
Stoners Cl HORL RH6 19 J1
Stonery Cl PTSD BN41 74 F3
Stonery Rd PTSD BN41 74 F3
Stone Sq HAV PO9 57 G1
Stone St BRI BN1 4 B6
Stoney Bottom GSHT GU26 108 F6
Stoneybrook HORS RH12 125 Q4
Stoney Hl PETW GU28 * 139 K12
Stoney La RHWH RH17 40 F4
SELS PO20 180 C1
SHOR BN43 74 B5
Stoney Stile Cl BOGR PO21 103 H4
Stoney Stile La BOGR PO21 103 H4
Stopham Cl SALV BN13 70 F8
Stopham Rd CRAWE RH10 30 B6
PUL/STOR RH20 158 F4
Stor Meadow PUL/STOR RH20 160 A11
Storrington Cl HOVE BN3 75 K3
RCCH PO18 61 G6
Storrington Ri SALV BN13 70 E1
Storrington Rd HORN PO8 150 E8
PUL/STOR RH20 178 E1
Story Rd CCH PO19 7 J2
Stour Cl EPSF GU31 133 M7
SALV BN13 70 B5
Stour Rd SALV BN13 70 B5
Stovolds Hl CRAN GU6 112 D1
Strand Cl CRAWE RH10 30 C5
Strand Pde FERR BN12 92 D1
The Strand BRIE/ROTT BN2 96 F2
FERR BN12 91 K5
FERR BN12 92 A2
Strand Wy MSEA/BNM PO22 105 G1
Strange Gdn BOGR PO21 103 K4
Stratford Pl BOGR PO21 * 2 C6
Stratford Rd WVILLE PO7 168 B9
Strathfield Cl HWH RH16 45 J5
Strathmoor Gdns MIDH GU29 137 J8
Strathmore Cl SALV BN13 92 D1
Strathmore Rd CRAWW RH11 18 F8
SALV BN13 92 D1
Stratton Ct MSEA/BNM PO22 3 H3
Strawberry La
PUL/STOR RH20 160 E9
Strawson Ct HORL RH6 14 E5
Stream Cl RCCH PO18 * 60 A8
Stream La PUL/STOR RH20 159 Q4
Stream Pk EGRIN RH19 22 F6
Streat Bostall HPPT/KEY BN6 166 F10
Streat La HPPT/KEY BN6 166 F1
HPPT/KEY BN6 166 F8
Streel's La PETW GU28 121 L8
Street End La SELS PO20 101 K2
Street End Rd SELS PO20 101 K2
Streetfield Rd SWTR RH13 124 G2
Street Hl CRAWE RH10 30 D4
Street La RHWH RH17 130 D1
The Street ANG/EP BN16 90 B4
ARUN BN18 65 K5
BIL RH14 121 R3
EPSF GU31 152 D2
HORL RH6 18 D2
HPPT/KEY BN6 164 D3
HPPT/KEY BN6 166 C9
LAN/SOMP BN15 72 D5
LEWES BN7 55 K8
MIDH GU29 136 D8
PUL/STOR RH20 159 P3
PUL/STOR RH20 160 E6
PUL/STOR RH20 176 B2
PUL/STOR RH20 178 G3
RCCH PO18 63 J2
RDKG RH5 16 C3
RHWH RH17 146 D3
SALV BN13 69 K4
SELS PO20 81 L6
SHOR BN43 73 J4
STEY/UB BN44 48 E3
SWTR RH13 124 G1
SWTR RH13 145 K3
Stretch Hl PUL/STOR RH20 140 B12
Stretham La HFD BN5 163 K9
Strettington La RCCH PO18 62 F2
Strettons Copse LIPH GU30 117 Q10
Strickland Cl CRAWW RH11 28 D4
Stride Cl CCH PO19 7 J4
Stringer Wy BRI BN1 76 E2
Strood Ga RHWH RH17 148 F8
Strood La HORS RH12 115 M10
Strouden Ct HAV PO9 168 E10
Stroud End PSF GU32 133 J5
Stroud Green Dr BOGR PO21 85 M8
Stroudley Cl CRAWE RH10 30 A4
Stroudwood Rd HAV PO9 57 H2
Strudgate Cl CRAWE RH10 30 A5
Stuart Cl CRAWE RH10 30 B4
WTHG BN11 13 M2
Stuart Wy EGRIN RH19 33 L2
Stubbington Av BOR GU35 106 F8
Stubcroft La SELS PO20 100 A6
Stubfield HORS RH12 125 R2
Stubpond La LING RH7 22 C2
Stumblemead RHWH RH17 40 F8
Stumblets CRAWE RH10 30 B2
Stumps La RCCH PO18 82 B1
Sturges Rd BOGR PO21 2 C6
Sturt Av HASM GU27 109 J12
Sudbury Cl BOGR PO21 103 H4
Sudeley Pl BRIE/ROTT BN2 5 M9
Sudeley St BRIE/ROTT BN2 5 L8
Sudeley Ter BRIE/ROTT BN2 5 L8
Sudley Gdns BOGR PO21 2 F6
Sudley Rd BOGR PO21 2 E6
Suffolk Cl HORL RH6 14 F7
Suffolk St HOVE BN3 75 L5
Sugar La RHWH RH17 131 L4
Sugden Rd WTHG BN11 13 L3
Sugworth Cl HWH RH16 45 G2
Sullington Cl BRIE/ROTT BN2 77 L1
Sullington Copse
PUL/STOR RH20 160 B11
Sullington Gdns SALV BN13 70 E1
Sullington Hl CRAWW RH11 8 E8
Sullington La PUL/STOR RH20 178 C2
Sullington Md HORS RH12 125 P2
Sullington Wy SHOR BN43 73 M5
Sullivan Dr CRAWW RH11 28 D7
Sultan Rd EMRTH PO10 58 A4
Summer Cl PTSD BN41 74 F6
Summerdale Rd HOVE BN3 75 J3
Summerdown Cl SALV BN13 70 A8
Summerfield Rd SELS PO20 99 H3
Summerfields SALV BN13 178 H11
Summerhill Cl HWH RH16 45 H2
MSEA/BNM PO22 87 J7
Summerhill Dr HWH RH16 45 J2
MSEA/BNM PO22 87 H7
Summerhill Gra HWH RH16 45 J2
Summerhill La HWH RH16 45 J2
Summerhill Rd HORN PO8 168 B6
Summerlands Wk HAV PO9 * 169 J12
Summer La BOGR PO21 102 E4
Summerlea Cl ANG/EP BN16 90 A2
Summerlea Gdns
LHPTN BN17 * 89 K4
Summerley Cnr
MSEA/BNM PO22 * 105 G1
Summerley La
MSEA/BNM PO22 87 G8
Summersdale Rd CCH PO19 61 M4
Summersdeane STHW BN42 74 E4
Summersvere Cl CRAWE RH10 19 M8
Sumner Rd EPSF GU31 133 L12
Sumners RHWH RH17 130 D2
Sun Brow HASM GU27 109 J12
Sunbury Cl BOR GU35 106 H6
Sundale La MSEA/BNM PO22 87 K8
Sunderland Cl SELS PO20 63 J3
Sunderland Ms ANG/EP BN16 * 90 C4
Sunderton La HORN PO8 150 D8
Sundew Cl CRAWW RH11 28 F7
Sunflower Cl LHPTN BN17 89 M1
Sun Inn Rd MFD/CHID GU8 112 A4
Sunneymead Cl SELS PO20 181 L7
Sunningdale Ct CRAWW RH11 8 E7
FERR BN12 * 92 B2
Sunningdale Gdns
MSEA/BNM PO22 86 A6
SELS PO20 * 99 J6
Sunningdale Rd SALV BN13 70 C7
Sunninghill Av HOVE BN3 75 K3
Sunninghill Cl HOVE BN3 75 K3
Sunny Av CRAWE RH10 31 M1
Sunnybox La ARUN BN18 65 J1
Sunny Cl FERR BN12 92 D4
Sunnycroft Cl RHWH RH17 148 H3
Sunnydale Av BRI BN1 52 F7
Sunnydale Cl BRI BN1 52 F7
Sunnyheath HAV PO9 56 F1
Sunnyhill Cl CRAWE RH10 31 M1
Sunnymead CRAWE RH10 * 32 A1
CRAWW RH11 8 E3
Sunnymead Cl
MSEA/BNM PO22 87 M8
Sunnymead Dr SELS PO20 181 M7
Sunnyside Cl ANG/EP BN16 90 F1
Sunnyside Rd BOR GU35 107 R5
Sunny Wy RCCH PO18 60 A8
Sunnywood Dr HWH RH16 45 G6
Sun Park Cl BOGR PO21 85 M7
Sunset La PUL/STOR RH20 159 R8
Sunte Av HWH RH16 45 J2
Sunte Cl HWH RH16 45 H2
Sunvale Av HASM GU27 108 G11
Sunvale Cl HASM GU27 108 G11
Sunwood Rd HAV PO9 168 E12
Surrenden Cl BRI BN1 76 E1
Surrenden Crs BRI BN1 76 E2
Surrenden Holt BRI BN1 76 E2
Surrenden Pk BRI BN1 76 F2
Surrenden Ri CRAWW RH11 39 H1
Surrenden Rd BRI BN1 76 E2
Surrey St ARUN BN18 66 F3
BRI BN1 4 D4
LHPTN BN17 89 J5
WTHG BN11 12 F7
Surrey Whf ARUN BN18 67 G3
Surry St SHOR BN43 73 L6
Sussex Border Pth BRI BN1 50 F4
BRI BN1 52 A5
CRAWE RH10 32 C2
EDEN TN8 25 H1
EGRIN RH19 23 M8
EGRIN RH19 24 C4
EGRIN RH19 33 M4
EMRTH PO10 58 B2
EMRTH PO10 80 A2
EPSF GU31 134 C12
HASM GU27 110 E12
HASM GU27 119 Q4
HAV PO9 169 N9
HFD BN5 50 F3
HORL RH6 19 H1
HORL RH6 20 D1
HORN PO8 151 K9
HORN PO8 169 L2
HORS RH12 27 H2
HORS RH12 113 K9
LIPH GU30 117 R4
LISS GU33 117 J7
MFD/CHID GU8 111 R11
POY/PYE BN45 51 L3
PTSD BN41 50 D7
RDKG RH5 114 H4
RHWH RH17 131 N1
Sussex Ct HWH RH16 * 45 H6
Sussex Dr BOGR PO21 102 F4
Sussex Gdns ANG/EP BN16 90 A3
EPSF GU31 133 N7
RHWH RH17 45 L6
Sussex Gv SELS PO20 100 B8
Sussex Hts BRI BN1 * 4 B7
Sussex Ms BRIE/ROTT BN2 96 D1
Sussex Pl BOGR PO21 * 2 F7
BRIE/ROTT BN2 5 G5
Sussex Rd EPSF GU31 133 P7
HOVE BN3 76 A8
HWH RH16 45 H6
LAN/SOMP BN15 73 H8
WTHG BN11 13 H4
Sussex Sq BRIE/ROTT BN2 96 D1
Sussex St BOGR PO21 2 E7
BRIE/ROTT BN2 5 G6
LHPTN BN17 89 J3
Sussex Ter BRIE/ROTT BN2 5 G5
MIDH GU29 * 136 H10
Sussex Wy BURH RH15 46 D5
Sussex Whf SHOR BN43 * 74 A7
Sutherland Cl ANG/EP BN16 90 A5
BOGR PO21 2 C7
BOR GU35 106 G8
Sutherland Rd BRIE/ROTT BN2 5 K7
Sutton Av ANG/EP BN16 90 B5
Sutton Cl BRIE/ROTT BN2 78 D4
MSEA/BNM PO22 3 K1
Sutton Fld BOR GU35 106 F8
Swainsthorpe Cl HWH RH16 45 J6
Swaledale Cl CRAWW RH11 8 C9
Swallow Cl HAV PO9 57 J3
Swallowfield Cl SWTR RH13 126 H4
Swallow Field Copse
SWTR RH13 125 R10
Swallow Rd CRAWW RH11 29 H1
Swallows Cl LAN/SOMP BN15 73 H8
Swallows Green Dr
SALV BN13 70 B8
Swallows La SWTR RH13 161 Q1
The Swallows LHPTN BN17 * 89 J5
Swallow St CRAWE RH10 32 B4
Swallowtail Rd HORS RH12 36 D3
Swan Barn Rd HASM GU27 109 N11
Swanborough Dr
BRIE/ROTT BN2 77 L6
Swanborough Dro LEWES BN7 79 L2
Swanborough Hollow
LEWES BN7 79 M1
Swanborough Pl
BRIE/ROTT BN2 77 L6
Swanbourne Cl
LAN/SOMP BN15 72 E5
Swanbourne Rd LHPTN BN17 89 J2
Swan Cl EMRTH PO10 58 B6
PUL/STOR RH20 159 R11
RING/NEW BN8 167 P2
SWTR RH13 125 R11
Swan Cnr PUL/STOR RH20 159 J3
Swan Ct PUL/STOR RH20 * 159 J3
Swandean Cl SALV BN13 70 D5
Swan Dene BOGR PO21 102 E6
Swanfield Dr CCH PO19 7 J2
Swan La HORL RH6 18 E2
Swanmore Rd HAV PO9 168 E10
Swann Cl BURH RH15 47 J6
Swann Wy HORS RH12 125 P2
Swansea Gdns BOGR PO21 2 B8
Swans Ghyll FROW RH18 34 D6
Swan St PSF GU32 133 M6
Swan Vw PUL/STOR RH20 159 K3
Swan Wk HORS RH12 * 10 C6
Swarraton Rd HAV PO9 57 H2
Sway Ct HAV PO9 * 169 J12
Swaythling Rd HAV PO9 168 E11
Sweetbriar Gdns WVILLE PO7 168 A12
Sweetlands HPPT/KEY BN6 165 P4
Swift Cl BURH RH15 46 B6
HORN PO8 168 B2
Swift La CRAWW RH11 29 J1
Swift Rd EMRTH PO10 80 B2
Swift Wy LHPTN BN17 89 H1
Swillage La SALV BN13 68 F4
Swinburn Gdns HORN PO8 168 A5
Swindon Rd HORS RH12 10 A2
Swiss Gdns SHOR BN43 73 K6
Swissland Hl EGRIN RH19 23 K3
Sword Cl HORN PO8 150 C8
Sycamore Av HORS RH12 37 H4
Sycamore Cl ANG/EP BN16 90 E1
BRIE/ROTT BN2 78 D5
CRAWW RH11 19 H8
HORN PO8 150 D8
PTSD BN41 75 H2
Sycamore Dr EGRIN RH19 23 M8
Sycamore Rd
MSEA/BNM PO22 86 B6
Sydmonton Ct HAV PO9 169 J11
Sydney Rd BOR GU35 106 G6
HWH RH16 45 H3
Sydney St BRI BN1 4 E5
Syers Rd LISS GU33 116 C9
Syke Cluan Cl
MSEA/BNM PO22 65 G7
Sylvan Cl HWH RH16 45 L5
Sylvan Rd CRAWE RH10 9 L8
LAN/SOMP BN15 72 A7
Sylvan Vw WVILLE PO7 168 A12
Sylvan Wy BOGR PO21 2 A7
Sylvester Wy HOVE BN3 75 H2
Sylvia Cl BOGR PO21 102 F4
Symbister Rd PTSD BN41 75 H6
Syresham Gdns HWH RH16 45 H5

T

Tabard Ga BOGR PO21 103 G4
Tack Lee Rd ARUN BN18 87 L2
Tagdell La HORN PO8 168 A1
Talbot Cl HAV PO9 56 E3
Talbot Crs BRI BN1 53 J7
Talbot La HORS RH12 10 D7
Talbot Rd HAV PO9 56 E2
LHPTN BN17 89 H4
Tallis Cl CRAWW RH11 28 E6
Tall Oaks HWH RH16 45 L4
Tall Trees EGRIN RH19 * 33 L1
Talman Cl CRAWW RH11 * 28 D4
Tamar Av SALV BN13 70 B5
Tamar Cl CRAWE RH10 30 B4
SALV BN13 70 B6
Tamar Down WVILLE PO7 168 B10
Tamarisk Cl MSEA/BNM PO22 86 B7
WVILLE PO7 168 B12
Tamarisk Wk SELS PO20 99 L7
Tamarisk Wy ANG/EP BN16 90 D5
FERR BN12 91 L5
Tamar Wy SELS PO20 63 J3
Tamplin Ter BRIE/ROTT BN2 5 G4
Tamworth Rd HOVE BN3 75 L6
Tanbridge Pk HORS RH12 10 A7
Tanbridge Pl HORS RH12 10 A8
Tandridge Rd HOVE BN3 75 K7
Tangle Oak EGRIN RH19 22 D5
Tangley Wk HAV PO9 * 169 J12
Tangmere Gdns BOGR PO21 103 J3
Tangmere Rd BRI BN1 52 F7
CRAWW RH11 28 E3
SELS PO20 62 E6
Tankerdale La LISS GU33 133 R1
The Tanneries HAV PO9 * 56 F4
Tanners Cross HWH RH16 44 F7
Tanners Fld RHWH RH17 47 M4
Tanners La HASM GU27 109 M10
Tanners Md RHWH RH17 128 F4
Tannery Cl CCH PO19 6 A5
SWTR RH13 124 F2
Tansy Cl WVILLE PO7 168 B11
Tansy Md PUL/STOR RH20 159 Q11
Tanyard Av EGRIN RH19 33 M1
Tanyard Cl CRAWE RH10 30 B6
SWTR RH13 11 G8
Tanyard La STEY/UB BN44 48 B2
Tanyard Wy HORL RH6 15 G5
Tarbery Crs HORN PO8 168 D2
Tarham Cl HORL RH6 14 D4
Tarmount La SHOR BN43 73 L6
Tarner Rd BRIE/ROTT BN2 5 H6
Tarn Ri HORN PO8 150 D11
Tarn Rd GSHT GU26 108 G6
Tarragon Wy SHOR BN43 74 B4
Tarrant Gdns HAV PO9 56 E2
Tarrant Sq ARUN BN18 * 67 G2
Tarrant St ARUN BN18 67 G3
Tarrant Whf ARUN BN18 67 G3
Tarring Ga SALV BN13 * 12 B1
Tarring Rd WTHG BN11 12 C3
Tasman Cl ANG/EP BN16 90 C5
Tasman Wy SALV BN13 70 B6
Tate Crs BURH RH15 46 E4
Tates Wy HORS RH12 114 A10
Taunton Rd BRIE/ROTT BN2 77 L4
Taunton Wy BRIE/ROTT BN2 77 M4
Tavern Ct HASM GU27 119 L7
Taverner Pl CCH PO19 7 G8
Tavistock Down BRI BN1 77 H3
Tavistock Gdns HAV PO9 57 J4
Tavy Cl SALV BN13 70 B7
Tavy Rd SALV BN13 70 B7
Taw Cl SALV BN13 70 C6
Taylors Cl BOR GU35 107 J4
Taylors Fld MIDH GU29 136 H11
Taylors La BOR GU35 107 J4
RCCH PO18 82 B1
Taylors Ri MIDH GU29 136 H11
Taylor Wk CRAWW RH11 8 D3
Teal Cl HORN PO8 168 B2
HORS RH12 36 B4
Teal La SELS PO20 181 J5
Teasel Cl CRAWW RH11 29 G6
Teazle Cl EPSF GU31 133 R7
Teesdale CRAWW RH11 8 D9
Teg Cl PTSD BN41 75 H3
Telconia Cl BOR GU35 107 R5
Telegraph La EPSF GU31 152 H3
Telegraph St BRIE/ROTT BN2 5 J8
Telford Pl CRAWE RH10 9 H5
Telgarth Rd FERR BN12 91 K5
Telham Ct CRAWW RH11 * 28 E6
Tempest Av WVILLE PO7 168 B10
Templars Cl MSEA/BNM PO22 87 J7
The Templars SALV BN13 71 K6
Temple Cl CRAWE RH10 30 C4
Temple Gdns HOVE BN3 4 A4
Temple Gv BURH RH15 46 C5
Temple La RDKG RH5 16 D3
Temple Rd LISS GU33 116 D7
Templesheen Rd
MSEA/BNM PO22 88 A8
Temple St BRI BN1 4 A6
Tenacre Cl CCH PO19 62 B5
Ten Acres WTHG BN11 93 M2
Tenantry Down Rd
BRIE/ROTT BN2 77 K6
Tenantry Rd BRIE/ROTT BN2 77 J5
Tennis Rd HOVE BN3 75 K7
Tennyson Av ANG/EP BN16 89 M4
Tennyson Cl CRAWE RH10 30 A1
HORS RH12 36 D3
Tennyson Ri EGRIN RH19 23 H8
Tennyson Rd BOGR PO21 103 M2
WTHG BN11 12 F5
Tennyson's La HASM GU27 119 P1
Terminus Ml CCH PO19 * 6 C6
Terminus Pl BRI BN1 4 D3
LHPTN BN17 89 J4
Terminus Rd BRI BN1 4 D3
CCH PO19 6 D7
LHPTN BN17 89 H4
Terminus St BRI BN1 4 D4
Tern Rd CRAWW RH11 28 C4
The Terrace ARUN BN18 * 67 K4
FERR BN12 * 92 B3
LAN/SOMP BN15 94 D1
Terringes Av SALV BN13 70 D8
Terry Rd CRAWW RH11 29 G8
Terwick La EPSF GU31 135 P9
Test Cl EPSF GU31 133 M8
Testers Cl SWTR RH13 143 R2

Test Rd LAN/SOMP BN15 .... 72 A7
Testwood Rd HAV PO9 .... 168 E12
Teville Ga WTHG BN11 .... 13 G3
Teville Pl WTHG BN11 .... 12 F3
Teville Rd WTHG BN11 .... 12 F3
Thackeray Rd SALV BN13 .... 13 L1
Thakeham Cl ANG/EP BN16 .... 91 G2
FERR BN12 .... 91 M3
Thakeham Copse
PUL/STOR RH20 .... 160 E11
Thakeham Dr FERR BN12 .... 91 M3
Thakeham Rd PUL/STOR RH20 .. 160 C11
Thalassa Rd WTHG BN11 .... 94 A2
Thames Cl BRIE/ROTT BN2 .... 5 H6
LHPTN BN17 .... 89 M5
Thames Wy SALV BN13 .... 70 C6
The Thatch Ct
LAN/SOMP BN15 * 72 E5
Thatcher Cl CRAWE RH10 .... 8 E9
Thatchers Cl BURH RH15 .... 47 J8
HORL RH6 .... 15 G4
HORS RH12 .... 11 G1
Thatchway Cl LHPTN BN17 .... 89 J3
The Thatchway ANG/EP BN16 .... 68 D8
ANG/EP BN16 .... 90 C5
Theatre La CCH PO19 .... 6 E5
Thelton Av HORS RH12 .... 125 N2
Theobalds Rd BURH RH15 .... 47 H3
Thesiger Cl WTHG BN11 .... 93 M2
Thesiger Rd WTHG BN11 .... 93 M1
Theydon Cl CRAWE RH10 .... 9 L7
Thicket La RCCH PO18 .... 174 A12
Third Av HAV PO9 .... 57 H3
HOVE BN3 .... 76 A8
LAN/SOMP BN15 .... 72 D6
MSEA/BNM PO22 .... 105 G1
SALV BN13 .... 71 J6
SELS PO20 .... 100 A8
SELS PO20 .... 100 D5
Thirlmere Cl BOR GU35 .... 106 G4
Thirlmere Crs LAN/SOMP BN15 .... 72 A8
Thirlmere Rd CRAWW RH11 .... 28 C5
Thirlmere Wy MSEA/BNM PO22 .. 87 G8
Thistledown HORN PO8 .... 168 C4
Thistledowne Gdns
EMRTH PO10 .... 58 C5
Thistledown V BIL RH14 * 122 E1
Thistle Wy SWTR RH13 .... 125 R10
Thistledown V BIL RH14 .... 122 E1
Thompson Rd BRI BN1 .... 77 H4
MSEA/BNM PO22 .... 87 L8
Thomson Cl SALV BN13 .... 70 A7
Thorgate Rd LHPTN BN17 .... 89 G2
Thornbush Crs PTSD BN41 .... 75 G2
Thorn Cl EPSF GU31 .... 133 R7
Thorncroft Rd LHPTN BN17 .... 89 L3
Thorndean Dr RHWH RH17 .... 128 E10
Thorndean Rd BRIE/ROTT BN2 .... 77 J2
Thornden SWTR RH13 .... 145 K3
Thorndene Av BOGR PO21 .... 2 A5
Thorndyke Cl CRAWE RH10 .... 30 C4
Thorney Dr SELS PO20 .... 181 J7
Thorney Old Pk EMRTH PO10 .... 80 E4
Thorney Rd EMRTH PO10 .... 58 C8
Thornham La EMRTH PO10 .... 58 C7
Thornhill Av BRI BN1 .... 52 F6
Thornhill Cl HOVE BN3 .... 75 K3
Thornhill Ri PTSD BN41 .... 74 F1
Thornhill Vw GSHT GU26 * 108 G6
Thornhill Wy PTSD BN41 .... 74 F2
Thornhurst BURH RH15 .... 47 H8
Thorn Rd WTHG BN11 .... 12 E7
Thornscroft STEY/UB BN44 .... 48 C1
Thornton Cl HORL RH6 .... 14 D6
Thornton Meadow BIL RH14 .... 141 J1
Thornton Pl HORL RH6 .... 14 D6
Threals Copse PUL/STOR RH20 .. 160 B8
Threal's La PUL/STOR RH20 .... 160 B7
Three Acres HORS RH12 .... 125 R4
Three Bridges Rd CRAWE RH10 .... 9 J4
Three Gates La HASM GU27 .... 109 N10
Threestile Rd HORS RH12 .... 115 Q8
Thresher Cl WVILLE PO7 .... 168 D8
Thrusloes BOGR PO21 .... 103 L2
Thruxton Rd HAV PO9 .... 168 D12
Thurlow Rd WTHG BN11 .... 13 K3
Thurne Wy HORS RH12 .... 114 A10
Thyme Cl SHOR BN43 .... 74 B4
Ticehurst Cl CRAWE RH10 .... 30 D3
Ticehurst Rd BRIE/ROTT BN2 .... 77 L8
Tichborne Gv HAV PO9 .... 168 E12
Tichborne St BRI BN1 .... 4 E6
Tideway LHPTN BN17 .... 89 M5
Tidworth Rd HAV PO9 .... 57 G1
Tidy St BRI BN1 .... 4 E5
Tilbury Pl BRIE/ROTT BN2 .... 5 G6
Tilbury's Cl BOR GU35 .... 106 G6
Tilbury Wy BRIE/ROTT BN2 .... 5 H5
Tile Barn La SELS PO20 .... 100 B4
Tilers Cl BURH RH15 .... 47 J6
Tilford Rd GSHT GU26 .... 109 J4
HORN PO8 .... 168 A3
Tilgate Cl BRIE/ROTT BN2 .... 5 L5
Tilgate Dr CRAWE RH10 .... 29 K8
Tilgate Forest Ldg
CRAWW RH11 * 39 H5
Tilgate Pde CRAWE RH10 .... 29 K6
Tilgate Pl CRAWE RH10 .... 29 K6
Tilgate Wy CRAWE RH10 .... 9 G9
Tilletts La HORS RH12 .... 115 P9
Tillinghurst La RHWH RH17 .... 41 L7
Tillington Gdns HORN PO8 .... 150 E9
Tillington Rd PETW GU28 .... 139 K10
Tillotson Cl CRAWE RH10 .... 30 C4
Tillstone Cl BRIE/ROTT BN2 .... 77 J3
Tillstone St BRIE/ROTT BN2 .... 5 H7
Tilmore Gdns PSF GU32 .... 133 N4
Tilmore Rd PSF GU32 .... 133 N4
Tiltwood Dr CRAWE RH10 .... 22 B8
Timber Cl SALV BN13 .... 70 B8
Timber Ct HORS RH12 .... 10 C3
Timberham Farm Rd HORL RH6 .. 19 J1
Timberlands CRAWW RH11 .... 29 G8
PUL/STOR RH20 .... 160 B11
Timberlea Cl PUL/STOR RH20 .... 161 K9
Timberleys LHPTN BN17 .... 89 L2
Timber Ml SWTR RH13 .... 125 Q11
Timbermill Ct HASM GU27 .... 109 J11
The Timbers SWTR RH13 .... 126 H3
Timsbury Crs HAV PO9 .... 56 F2
Tindal Cl BURH RH15 .... 47 J6
Tinghall BOGR PO21 .... 103 K2
Tinsley Cl CRAWE RH10 .... 19 M8
Tinsley Gn CRAWE RH10 .... 20 A6
Tinsley La CRAWE RH10 .... 19 M8
Tinsley La North CRAWE RH10 .... 20 A6
Tinsley La South CRAWE RH10 .... 29 M1
Tintern Cl BRI BN1 .... 77 G4
Tintern Rd CRAWW RH11 .... 28 F5
Tinwood La RCCH PO18 .... 173 P12
Tipper La EPSF GU31 .... 152 E2
Tisbury Rd HOVE BN3 .... 76 B7
Tisted Ct HAV PO9 * 169 J12
Titchfield Cl BURH RH15 .... 47 J8
Titch Hl LAN/SOMP BN15 .... 71 M1
Tithe Barn Cl BOGR PO21 .... 103 H4
Tithe Barn Wy BOGR PO21 .... 103 G4
Tithe Gn ANG/EP BN16 .... 90 A4
Tithe Orch EGRIN RH19 .... 22 D5
Titian Rd HOVE BN3 .... 75 L6
Titmus Dr CRAWE RH10 .... 29 L6
Titnore La FERR BN12 .... 69 M7
Titnore Wy SALV BN13 .... 69 M8
Titus Gdns WVILLE PO7 .... 168 B9
Tivoli Crs BRI BN1 .... 76 C4
Tivoli Crs North BRI BN1 .... 76 C3
Tivoli Pl BRI BN1 .... 76 C3
Tivoli Rd BRI BN1 .... 76 C3
Toat La PUL/STOR RH20 .... 140 H10
Toddington La LHPTN BN17 .... 89 J1
Toddington Pk LHPTN BN17 .... 89 K1
Todds Cl HORL RH6 .... 14 D4
Todmore LISS GU33 .... 116 C2
Toftwood Cl CRAWE RH10 .... 30 B4
Tollgate Hl CRAWW RH11 .... 39 H1
Tollgate La RHWH RH17 .... 44 B1
Tollhouse Cl CCH PO19 .... 6 C5
Tomtit Crs CRAWE RH10 .... 32 B4
Tomtits La FROW RH18 .... 34 D8
Tongdean Av HOVE BN3 .... 76 B2
Tongdean La BRI BN1 .... 76 C1
Tongdean Ri BRI BN1 .... 76 B1
Tongdean Rd HOVE BN3 .... 76 A2
Toomey Rd STEY/UB BN44 .... 162 C12
Topaz Gv WVILLE PO7 .... 168 C9
Top Rd ARUN BN18 .... 174 H12
EGRIN RH19 .... 42 E4
Top St RHWH RH17 .... 146 D1
Torberry Dr EPSF GU31 .... 133 Q7
Tor Cl WVILLE PO7 .... 56 A2
Torcross Cl BRIE/ROTT BN2 .... 77 K5
Toronto Cl SALV BN13 .... 70 C7
Toronto Dr HORL RH6 .... 15 M7
Toronto Ter BRIE/ROTT BN2 .... 5 H5
Torrance Cl HOVE BN3 .... 75 L5
Torridge Cl SALV BN13 .... 70 B7
Torrington Cl BOR GU35 * 107 K4
Tortington Mnr ARUN BN18 * 66 D6
Torton Hill Rd ARUN BN18 .... 66 F3
Tor Wy EPSF GU31 .... 133 P6
Tote La MIDH GU29 .... 136 D3
Totland Rd BRIE/ROTT BN2 .... 5 L2
Tottington Dr HFD BN5 .... 163 K11
Tottington Wy SHOR BN43 .... 74 A4
Tower Cl CCH PO19 .... 6 D3
EGRIN RH19 .... 23 J7
HORL RH6 .... 14 E6
Tower Ct EGRIN RH19 * 23 K7
Tower Gdns HAV PO9 .... 57 G7
Towergate BRI BN1 .... 76 D3
Tower Hl SWTR RH13 .... 125 R5
Tower House Cl RHWH RH17 .... 44 B2
Tower Rd BRIE/ROTT BN2 .... 5 J4
GSHT GU26 .... 108 H5
HORS RH12 .... 37 M1
LAN/SOMP BN15 .... 72 C8
LIPH GU30 .... 117 Q1
WTHG BN11 .... 13 J4
Towers Rd STEY/UB BN44 .... 49 G3
Tower St CCH PO19 .... 6 D3
EMRTH PO10 .... 58 B5
Town Barn Rd CRAWW RH11 .... 8 D3
Town Cross Av BOGR PO21 .... 2 C5
Town Hall Rd HAV PO9 .... 57 H4
Town La PSF GU32 .... 133 Q4
RCCH PO18 .... 172 F4
Town Md CRAWW RH11 .... 8 E2
Town Quay ARUN BN18 * 67 G2
Townsend Crs LHPTN BN17 .... 89 L3
Tozer Wy CCH PO19 .... 7 H4
Trafalgar Cl EMRTH PO10 .... 58 E5
Trafalgar Ct BRI BN1 .... 4 F4
Trafalgar Ga BRIE/ROTT BN2 .... 96 E2
Trafalgar La BRI BN1 .... 4 E5
Trafalgar Pl BRI BN1 .... 4 E4
Trafalgar Ri HORN PO8 .... 150 C8
Trafalgar Rd HORS RH12 .... 10 C2
PTSD BN41 .... 75 G5
Trafalgar St BRI BN1 .... 4 E4
Trafalgar Ter BRI BN1 * 4 E4
Tramway Cl SELS PO20 .... 83 L5
Treadcroft Dr HORS RH12 .... 36 D4
Treadwheel Rd HORN PO8 .... 168 H3
Tredcroft Rd HOVE BN3 .... 76 A3
Tree Av HASM GU27 .... 109 J9
Treemans Rd (Lewes Rd)
RHWH RH17 .... 131 M6
Treetops SWTR RH13 .... 143 Q2
Tree Tops Cl BRIE/ROTT BN2 .... 78 D5
Treeview CRAWW RH11 .... 29 H8
Trefoil Cl HORS RH12 .... 36 D4
WVILLE PO7 .... 168 A10
Trefoil Crs CRAWW RH11 .... 28 F7
Tregarth Rd CCH PO19 .... 61 M3
Treharne Cl SALV BN13 .... 70 C6
Treloar Rd HISD PO11 .... 98 A4
Trendle Gn BOGR PO21 .... 103 L2
Trenear Cl SWTR RH13 .... 11 G6
Trent Cl CRAWW RH11 .... 28 E5
LAN/SOMP BN15 .... 72 B7
Trent Rd FERR BN12 .... 92 D3
Tretawn Gdns SELS PO20 .... 181 M7
Trevanne Plat CRAWE RH10 .... 30 C2
Trevelyan Pl HWH RH16 * 45 H4
Treveor Cl WTHG BN11 .... 12 F5
Treyford Cl BRIE/ROTT BN2 .... 78 D4
CRAWW RH11 .... 28 E3
Triangle Cottages RHWH RH17 .. 128 D1
Triangle Rd HWH RH16 .... 45 H6
Triangle Wy BURH RH15 .... 46 C4
Trig St RDKG RH5 .... 16 D1
Trimmers Wd GSHT GU26 .... 108 G3
Trinity Cl CRAWE RH10 .... 30 B1
Trinity Rd HPPT/KEY BN6 .... 164 H3
Trinity St BRIE/ROTT BN2 .... 5 H2
Trinity Wy BOGR PO21 .... 103 L1
LHPTN BN17 .... 89 L5
Tripp Hl PUL/STOR RH20 .... 158 A6
Tristram Cl LAN/SOMP BN15 .... 71 M6
Triton Pl MSEA/BNM PO22 .... 87 H8
Trojan Wy WVILLE PO7 .... 56 A2
Troon Cl CRAWW RH11 .... 28 C4
Trosnant Rd HAV PO9 .... 56 F3
Trotton Cl CRAWE RH10 .... 30 B6
Trotton Rd EPSF GU31 .... 135 N9
Trout La SWTR RH13 .... 143 K1
Trout Rd HASM GU27 .... 108 H11
Troymede RHWH RH17 .... 40 F8
True Blue Prec LHPTN BN17 .... 89 J2
Truggers RHWH RH17 .... 128 C1
Truleigh Cl BRIE/ROTT BN2 .... 78 E6
Truleigh Dr PTSD BN41 .... 74 F1
Truleigh Rd STEY/UB BN44 .... 49 G3
Truleigh Wy SHOR BN43 .... 73 M4
Trundle Cl RCCH PO18 .... 172 B11
Trundle Md HORS RH12 .... 36 B4
Trundle View Cl
MSEA/BNM PO22 .... 65 G7
Truro Cl CCH PO19 .... 61 L4
Truro Ct WTHG BN11 * 12 A7
Truro Crs BOGR PO21 .... 103 K2
Trusler's Hill La
HPPT/KEY BN6 .... 164 A5
Tryndel Wy MSEA/BNM PO22 .... 105 G1
Tudor Av EMRTH PO10 .... 57 M1
Tudor Cl BRIE/ROTT BN2 * 97 L3
CCH PO19 .... 61 L3
CRAWE RH10 .... 30 C4
EGRIN RH19 .... 33 L2
GSHT GU26 .... 108 G7
HOVE BN3 .... 75 L3
MSEA/BNM PO22 .... 87 J8
PUL/STOR RH20 .... 159 N4
SALV BN13 .... 178 H11
Tudor Dr SELS PO20 .... 64 C5
STEY/UB BN44 .... 48 F2
Tudor Gdns BURH RH15 .... 46 E5
Tudor Village PUL/STOR RH20 .. 160 F10
Tufts Fld MIDH GU29 .... 136 G11
Tufts Meadow MIDH GU29 .... 136 H11
Tuggles Plat HORS RH12 .... 115 P10
Tulip Ct HORS RH12 * 10 D2
Tulip Gdns HAV PO9 .... 56 D3
Tullett Rd CRAWE RH10 .... 30 A7
Tulls La BOR GU35 .... 107 L7
Tunbridge Crs LIPH GU30 .... 107 Q12
Tunbridge La LIPH GU30 .... 107 Q11
Tunnmeade CRAWW RH11 .... 28 D4
Tunsgate STEY/UB BN44 .... 48 C2
Tunworth Ct HAV PO9 .... 169 J12
Tuppenny La EMRTH PO10 .... 58 D5
Turkey La BURH RH15 .... 47 G6
Turnbull Rd CCH PO19 .... 7 G3
Turner Ct EGRIN RH19 .... 23 M6
Turner Rd SALV BN13 .... 71 K7
Turners Cl SWTR RH13 .... 143 R1
Turners Hill Rd CRAWE RH10 .... 21 L7
CRAWE RH10 .... 30 D3
EGRIN RH19 .... 32 F4
Turners Md MIDH/CHID GU8 .... 110 H6
PUL/STOR RH20 .... 159 Q11
Turners Mill Cl HWH RH16 * 45 G2
Turners Mill Rd HWH RH16 .... 45 G3
Turner Wy BURH RH15 .... 46 E5
SELS PO20 .... 181 M6
Turnpike Cl CCH PO19 .... 83 K2
Turnpike Pl CRAWW RH11 .... 29 J1
Turnpike Rd ARUN BN18 .... 176 G3
Turnpike Wy PUL/STOR RH20 .. 161 K9
Turret House Ms
MSEA/BNM PO22 * 3 L4
Turtledove Av CRAWE RH10 .... 32 B4
Turton Cl BRIE/ROTT BN2 .... 5 L7
Tuscan Av MSEA/BNM PO22 .... 87 L8
Tuscany Gdns CRAWE RH10 .... 29 K1
Tuscany Wy WVILLE PO7 .... 168 C9
Tushmore Av CRAWE RH10 .... 19 K8
Tushmore Ct CRAWE RH10 * 29 K1
Tushmore Crs CRAWE RH10 .... 19 K8
Tushmore La CRAWE RH10 .... 29 K1
Tussock Cl CRAWW RH11 .... 28 F5
Tuxford Cl CRAWE RH10 .... 30 B5
Tweed La CRAWW RH11 .... 18 E8
Twineham Cl BRIE/ROTT BN2 .... 77 L6
Twineham La HPPT/KEY BN6 .... 146 B12
Twitten Cl STHW BN42 .... 74 D6
Twitten La EGRIN RH19 .... 22 D5
Twittenside STEY/UB BN44 * 49 G4
Twittens Wy HAV PO9 .... 57 G4
The Twitten BURH RH15 .... 47 G5
CRAWW RH11 .... 8 B3
HPPT/KEY BN6 .... 164 D3
STHW BN42 .... 74 D6
Twitten Wy SALV BN13 .... 12 B1
Two Barns La RCCH PO18 .... 172 A12
Two Mile Ash Rd SWTR RH13 .... 125 J10
Two Ways BIL RH14 .... 122 H1
Twyford Cl SALV BN13 .... 70 D7
Twyford Gdns SALV BN13 .... 70 D7
Twyford Rd BRI BN1 .... 53 J7
SALV BN13 .... 70 D7
Twyhurst Ct EGRIN RH19 .... 23 J6
Twyne Cl CRAWW RH11 .... 28 E5
Twyner Cl HORL RH6 .... 15 H5
Tye La ARUN BN18 .... 65 K4
Tylden Wy HORS RH12 .... 36 E3
Tyler Rd CRAWE RH10 .... 8 F9
Tyler's Gn HWH RH16 .... 44 E4
Tylston Meadow LIPH GU30 .... 107 Q12
Tyndalls GSHT GU26 .... 109 J5
Tyne Cl CRAWE RH10 .... 30 B4
SALV BN13 .... 70 B6
Tyne Wy BOGR PO21 .... 103 J2
The Tynings LAN/SOMP BN15 .... 72 D8
Tythe Barn RHWH RH17 .... 146 D2
Tythe Barn Rd SELS PO20 .... 181 L7

U

Uckfield Cl BRIE/ROTT BN2 .... 77 L7
Ullswater Cl BOR GU35 .... 106 G4
Ullswater Dr LHPTN BN17 .... 89 M2
Ullswater Gv MSEA/BNM PO22 .... 87 G7
Ullswater Rd LAN/SOMP BN15 .... 72 A8
Underdown Rd STHW BN42 .... 74 D5
Underhill La HPPT/KEY BN6 .... 165 M9
Undermill Rd STEY/UB BN44 .... 49 G3
Underwood Cl CRAWE RH10 .... 32 A1
Underwood Rd HASM GU27 .... 109 J10
Union Pl WTHG BN11 .... 13 H5
Union Ri LISS GU33 .... 116 G3
Union Rd BRIE/ROTT BN2 .... 5 G3
HAV PO9 .... 56 F4
Union St BRI BN1 .... 4 E7
Updown Hl HWH RH16 .... 44 F7
Upfield HORL RH6 .... 14 F8
Upfield Cl HORL RH6 .... 14 F8
Uphill Wy SELS PO20 .... 83 M5
Uplands Av SALV BN13 .... 70 E4
Uplands Cl HASM GU27 .... 109 N9
Uplands Rd BRI BN1 .... 77 H3
HAV PO9 .... 169 K7
Uppark Gdns HORS RH12 .... 36 E3
Uppark Wy MSEA/BNM PO22 .... 87 J7
Upper Abbey Rd
BRIE/ROTT BN2 .... 5 L8
Upper Bedford St
BRIE/ROTT BN2 .... 5 J8
Upper Bere Wd WVILLE PO7 .... 168 A11
Upper Bevendean Av
BRIE/ROTT BN2 .... 77 K4
Upper Bognor Rd BOGR PO21 .... 2 F5
Upper Boundstone La
LAN/SOMP BN15 .... 72 C6
Upper Brighton Rd
LAN/SOMP BN15 .... 72 A6
Upper Chalvington Pl
BRIE/ROTT BN2 .... 77 K8
Upper Cl FROW RH18 .... 34 E7
Upper Dr ANG/EP BN16 .... 91 G5
The Upper Dr HOVE BN3 .... 76 B5
Upperfield MIDH GU29 .... 137 J7
Upper Forecourt HORL RH6 .... 20 A2
Upper Gardner St BRI BN1 .... 4 E5
Upper Gloucester Rd BRI BN1 .... 4 D4
Upper Hamilton Rd BRI BN1 .... 4 B1
Upper Heyshott EPSF GU31 .... 133 P6
Upper High St WTHG BN11 .... 13 J3
Upper Hollingdean Rd BRI BN1 .. 77 G4
Upper Kingston La STHW BN42 .. 74 C4
Upper Lewes Rd BRIE/ROTT BN2 .. 5 G2
Upper Market St HOVE BN3 .... 76 C8
Upper Mt HASM GU27 .... 109 Q8
LISS GU33 .... 116 B10
Upper North St BRI BN1 .... 4 B5
Upper Park Pl BRIE/ROTT BN2 .... 5 H6
Upper Rock Gdns
BRIE/ROTT BN2 .... 5 H7
Upper St James's St
BRIE/ROTT BN2 .... 5 H8
Upper St Johns Rd BURH RH15 .. 46 F6
Upper School Dr HASM GU27 .... 109 J12
Upper Shoreham Rd
SHOR BN43 .... 73 K5
Upper Station Rd HFD BN5 .... 163 J4
Upper St PUL/STOR RH20 .... 158 A2
Upper Sudeley St
BRIE/ROTT BN2 .... 5 L8
Upperton Rd PETW GU28 .... 138 G7
Upper Wardown EPSF GU31 .... 133 Q5
Upper Wellington Rd
BRIE/ROTT BN2 .... 5 J2
Upper West Dr FERR BN12 .... 91 K4
Upper West La
LAN/SOMP BN15 .... 72 D6
Upper Winfield Av BRI BN1 .... 52 E7
Upton Av STHW BN42 .... 74 D4
Upton Cl HAV PO9 .... 168 E10
Upton Gdns SALV BN13 .... 92 E1
Upton Rd CCH PO19 .... 6 C8
SALV BN13 .... 92 E1
Upways Cl SELS PO20 .... 181 L4
Ursula Av SELS PO20 .... 181 K7
Ursula Av North SELS PO20 .... 181 K7
Ursula Sq SELS PO20 .... 181 K8

V

Vachery La CRAN GU6 .... 113 N1
Vale Av BRI BN1 .... 52 D6
SALV BN13 .... 70 E3
Valebridge Cl BURH RH15 .... 47 H3
Valebridge Dr BURH RH15 * 47 H4
Valebridge Rd BURH RH15 .... 47 H4
Vale Dr HORS RH12 .... 10 A5
SALV BN13 .... 70 E3
Vale Gdns PTSD BN41 .... 75 G6
Valencia Rd WTHG BN11 .... 12 B3
Valentine Cl SALV BN13 .... 71 G6
Valentine Ct WVILLE PO7 .... 168 B9
Valentine Dr BURH RH15 .... 46 D5
Valentines Gdns BOGR PO21 .... 103 H3
Valentines Lea PETW GU28 .... 120 F5
Valerie Cl PTSD BN41 .... 75 G3
Vale Rd HWH RH16 .... 45 G7
PTSD BN41 .... 75 H6
The Vale BRIE/ROTT BN2 .... 78 D8
HORN PO8 .... 150 D12
Valetta Pk EMRTH PO10 .... 57 M5
Valetta Rd EMRTH PO10 .... 80 E4
Vale Wk SALV BN13 .... 70 E3
Valewood Cl SWTR RH13 .... 124 G12
Vale Wood La GSHT GU26 .... 108 F5
Valewood La SWTR RH13 .... 124 H12
Valewood Rd HASM GU27 .... 119 M1
Valiant Rd EMRTH PO10 .... 80 E4
Vallance Cl BURH RH15 .... 46 D5
Vallance Gdns HOVE BN3 .... 75 M7
Vallance Rd HOVE BN3 .... 75 M7
Valley Cl BRI BN1 .... 76 B1
Valley Dr BRI BN1 .... 76 B1
Valley Gdns SALV BN13 .... 70 F4
Valley Park Dr HORN PO8 .... 150 E10
Valley Rd LAN/SOMP BN15 .... 72 B5
LEWES BN7 .... 55 M5
PTSD BN41 .... 74 F3
Valley Side LIPH GU30 .... 107 Q12
Vanbrugh Cl CRAWW RH11 .... 28 D6
Vancouver Cl SALV BN13 .... 70 C7
Vancouver Ct HORL RH6 .... 15 M6
Vancouver Dr CRAWW RH11 .... 19 J8
Vancouver Rd SALV BN13 .... 70 B7
Van Dyck Pl MSEA/BNM PO22 .... 85 M7
Van Gogh Pl MSEA/BNM PO22 .... 86 A7
Vanguard Wy EGRIN RH19 .... 24 F6
Vann Bridge Cl HASM GU27 .... 119 K7
Vanners CRAWE RH10 * 9 G1
Vann Rd HASM GU27 .... 119 K7
Vanzell Rd MIDH GU29 .... 137 K8
Varey Rd SALV BN13 .... 70 A7
Varna Rd BOR GU35 .... 106 H6
Varndean Cl BRI BN1 .... 76 D2
Varndean Dr BRI BN1 .... 76 D2
Varndean Gdns BRI BN1 .... 76 D2
Varndean Holt BRI BN1 .... 76 E2
Varndean Rd BRI BN1 .... 76 D2
Varsity Rd EMRTH PO10 .... 80 E4
Vauxhall Wy PSF GU32 .... 133 M6
Velyn Av CCH PO19 .... 7 G4
Venice Cl WVILLE PO7 .... 168 B9
Ventnor Vls HOVE BN3 .... 76 A7
Venus La BOGR PO21 .... 102 D6
Veras Wk PUL/STOR RH20 .... 160 F12
Verbania Wy EGRIN RH19 .... 24 A8
Verbena Crs HORN PO8 .... 168 C5
Verdley Pl HASM GU27 .... 119 M10
Vere Rd BRI BN1 .... 4 F1
Vermont Dr ANG/EP BN16 .... 90 F4
Vermont Wy ANG/EP BN16 .... 90 F4
Verner Cl BOR GU35 .... 107 M5
Vernon Av BRIE/ROTT BN2 .... 78 B4
Vernon Cl ANG/EP BN16 .... 90 B4
HORS RH12 .... 11 L1
Vernon Gdns BRI BN1 .... 4 B4
Vernon Ter BRI BN1 .... 4 B4
Veronica Cl ANG/EP BN16 .... 90 F5
Veronica Wy BRIE/ROTT BN2 .... 5 H8
Verwood Rd HAV PO9 .... 169 J11
Viaduct Rd BRI BN1 .... 4 E2
Via Ravenna CCH PO19 .... 6 A5
Via Ravenna Rbt CCH PO19 .... 6 B6
Vicarage Cl HORS RH12 .... 38 B3
Vicarage Flds SALV BN13 .... 70 C6
Vicarage Gdns GSHT GU26 .... 108 F6
Vicarage La ANG/EP BN16 .... 90 E4
BRIE/ROTT BN2 .... 97 L4
HASM GU27 .... 109 J11
HORL RH6 .... 14 E5
MSEA/BNM PO22 .... 3 K5
PETW GU28 .... 138 A7
RDKG RH5 .... 16 C3
RHWH RH17 .... 149 J2
STEY/UB BN44 .... 48 C2
Vicarage Rd CRAWE RH10 .... 31 M2
Vicarage Ter BRIE/ROTT BN2 .... 97 L4
Vicars Cl CCH PO19 .... 6 D5
Victoria Av BURH RH15 .... 46 D6
MIDH GU29 .... 137 K8
Victoria Cl BURH RH15 .... 46 E7
HORL RH6 .... 14 F6
MIDH GU29 * 136 H10
Victoria Dr BOGR PO21 .... 2 B8
Victoria Gdns BURH RH15 .... 46 E7
LHPTN BN17 * 89 J5
SELS PO20 .... 64 C6
Victoria Gv HOVE BN3 .... 76 B7
Victoria Ms BOGR PO21 * 2 D4
BRIE/ROTT BN2 * 97 L4
Victoria Park Gdns WTHG BN11 .. 12 E4
Victoria Pl BRI BN1 .... 4 B5
Victoria Rd BOGR PO21 .... 2 B8
BRI BN1 .... 4 B5
BURH RH15 .... 46 E7
CCH PO19 .... 7 L3
CRAWW RH11 .... 8 D4
EMRTH PO10 .... 57 M4
HORL RH6 .... 14 F6
HWH RH16 .... 45 J6
PTSD BN41 .... 75 G5
RHWH RH17 .... 40 F8
SHOR BN43 .... 73 K6
STHW BN42 .... 74 C6
WTHG BN11 .... 12 F4
Victoria Rd South BOGR PO21 .... 2 B9
Victoria St BRI BN1 .... 4 B5
SWTR RH13 .... 10 E6
Victoria Vls ARUN BN18 * 87 M2
Victoria Wy BURH RH15 .... 46 E7
EGRIN RH19 .... 33 L2
LIPH GU30 .... 117 Q1
Victor Rd EMRTH PO10 .... 80 E4
Victory Av HORN PO8 .... 168 B3
Victory Ms BRIE/ROTT BN2 .... 96 F2
Victory Rd HORS RH12 .... 10 B3
Views Pth HWH RH16 * 45 L5
The View BOGR PO21 .... 102 F5
Viking Wy HORN PO8 .... 150 D10
The Village Barn BRI BN1 .... 52 D6
Village Cl PTSD BN41 .... 75 G3
Village St PSF GU32 .... 133 Q3
Village Wy BRI BN1 .... 54 B7
Villiers Cl BRIE/ROTT BN2 .... 78 D5
Vinall Gdns HORS RH12 .... 125 N1
Vincent Cl LAN/SOMP BN15 .... 72 C7
SWTR RH13 .... 11 J6
Vincent Rd SELS PO20 .... 181 J7
Vine Pl BRI BN1 .... 4 C5
Vineries Cl SALV BN13 .... 70 F7
The Vineries BURH RH15 .... 47 J6
Vines Cross Rd BRIE/ROTT BN2 .. 77 L6
Vine St BRI BN1 .... 4 F5
Viney Cl PUL/STOR RH20 .... 161 J8
Vinnetrow Rd CCH PO19 .... 7 M8
SELS PO20 .... 84 D2
Vinson Rd LISS GU33 .... 116 D9
Viscount Dr BOGR PO21 .... 103 G5
Vivienne Cl CRAWW RH11 .... 19 J8
Vowels La EGRIN RH19 .... 32 C7
Vulcan Cl CRAWW RH11 .... 29 H7
Vulcan Rd EMRTH PO10 .... 80 E4

W

Waddington Cl CRAWW RH11 .... 28 F6
Wade Court Rd HAV PO9 .... 57 H5
Wade End SELS PO20 .... 181 J5
Wade La HAV PO9 .... 57 H6
The Wadeway SELS PO20 .... 181 J5
The Wadeys BIL RH14 .... 141 R1
Wadham Cl CRAWE RH10 .... 20 B8
Wadhurst Cl BOGR PO21 .... 2 A4
Wadhurst Dr FERR BN12 .... 92 A3
Wadhurst Ri BRIE/ROTT BN2 .... 77 L8
Wadlands Brook Rd
EGRIN RH19 .... 23 J4
The Wad SELS PO20 .... 99 G4
Wagg Cl EGRIN RH19 .... 23 M8
Waggoners Wy GSHT GU26 .... 108 D6
Waggoners Wells Rd
GSHT GU26 .... 108 D7
Wagtail Cl HORS RH12 .... 36 B2
Wagtail Rd HORN PO8 .... 168 B3
Wain End HORS RH12 .... 36 C4
Wainwrights CRAWE RH10 .... 8 E9
Wakefield Rd BRIE/ROTT BN2 .... 5 G1
Wakefield Wy BOGR PO21 .... 103 K1
Wakefords Wy HAV PO9 .... 169 J11
Wakehams Green Dr
CRAWE RH10 .... 20 C8
Wakehurst Dr CRAWE RH10 .... 8 F9
Wakehurst La RHWH RH17 .... 130 D1
Wakehurst Ms HORS RH12 .... 125 Q4
Wakehurst Pl ANG/EP BN16 .... 90 B4
Wakestone La PUL/STOR RH20 .. 140 B8

Walberton Cl MSEA/BNM PO22 ..... 3 M2
Walburton Wy HORN PO08 ... 150 E9
Waldegrave Rd BRI BN1 ..... 76 E3
Walden Gdns HORN PO08 ... 168 D6
Walders Rd ANG/EP BN16 ..... 89 M3
Waldron Av BRI BN1 ..... 53 J7
Waldron Pl BRI BN1 * 53 J7
Waldshut Rd LEWES BN7 ..... 55 M2
Walesbeech CRAWE RH10 ..... 9 M6
Walhatch Cl FROW RH18 ..... 34 E7
Walker Rd CRAWE RH10 ..... 30 A5
The Walkway ANG/EP BN16 ..... 90 F1
Wallace Av WTHG BN11 ..... 92 E3
Wallace Ms WTHG BN11 * 92 E4
Wallace Pde FERR BN12 * 92 E3
Wallace Rd ANG/EP BN16 ..... 90 B3
Wallage La CRAWE RH10 ..... 31 J3
Walldown Rd BOR GU35 ... 106 H8
The Walled Gdn BIL RH14 ... 112 C10
Wallfield BOGR 103 L4
Wall Hill Rd EGRIN RH19 ..... 34 C4
Wallis Ct CRAWE RH10 * 19 L7
Wallis Wy BURH RH15 ..... 46 D5
  SWTR RH13 ..... 11 M2
Wallner Crs MSEA/BNM PO22 ..... 87 H8
Walmer Cl SWTR RH13 ... 125 R11
Walmer Crs BRIE/ROTT BN2 * 77 M4
Walmsleys Wy SELS PO20 ... 180 B1
Walnut Av ANG/EP BN16 ..... 90 A4
  CCH PO19 ..... 6 B3
Walnut Cl BRI BN1 ..... 76 D2
Walnut La CRAWW RH11 ..... 19 G8
Walnut Ldg SALV BN13 * 12 E2
Walnut Pk HWH RH16 ..... 45 L5
The Walnuts HORS RH12 * 10 C2
Walnut Tree Dr EMRTH PO10 ..... 58 F2
Walnut Tree Wy SALV BN13 ..... 70 D8
Walpole Av FERR BN12 ..... 92 C3
Walpole Rd BRIE/ROTT BN2 ..... 5 K8
Walpole Ter BRIE/ROTT BN2 ..... 5 L7
Walsham Cl MSEA/BNM PO22 ..... 1 K1
Walsingham Rd HOVE BN3 ..... 75 L3
Walters Gn LHPTN BN17 * 67 J8
Waltham Park Rd
  PUL/STOR RH20 ... 158 C12
Walton Av BOGR PO21 ..... 3 C4
Walton Bank BRI BN1 ..... 53 K8
Walton Cl SALV BN13 ..... 70 E7
Walton Dr SWTR RH13 ..... 37 H5
Walton Heath CRAWE RH10 ..... 30 C1
Walton La RCCH PO18 ..... 60 B8
Walton Ldg SALV BN13 ..... 70 E7
Walton Rd BOGR PO21 ..... 2 F7
Walwyn Cl SELS PO20 ... 100 D1
Wanderdown Cl
  BRIE/ROTT BN2 ..... 97 K1
Wanderdown Dr
  BRIE/ROTT BN2 ..... 97 K1
Wanderdown Rd
  BRIE/ROTT BN2 ..... 97 J1
Wanderdown Wy
  BRIE/ROTT BN2 ..... 97 K1
Wandle Cl CRAWE RH10 ..... 30 B4
Wandleys Cl SELS PO20 ..... 64 F3
Wandleys Dr SELS PO20 ..... 64 F4
Wandleys La SELS PO20 ..... 64 F4
Wansford Wy
  MSEA/BNM PO22 ... 105 H1
Wantage Cl CRAWE RH10 ..... 30 B6
Wantley Hill Est HFD BN5 ... 163 L3
Wantley La PUL/STOR RH20 ... 160 B11
Wantley Rd SALV BN13 ..... 70 F4
Wappingthorn Farm La
  STEY/UB BN44 * 162 D7
Warble Heath Cl RCCH PO18 ... 172 C11
Warbler Cl HORN PO08 ..... 168 B2
Warblers Wy MSEA/BNM PO22 ..... 86 A6
Warbleton Cl BRIE/ROTT BN2 ..... 77 K8
Warblington Av HAV PO9 ..... 57 J4
Warblington Rd EMRTH PO10 ..... 57 M6
Warbrook Ct HAV PO9 ... 169 J12
Warburton Cl EGRIN RH19 ..... 23 M8
Ward Crs EMRTH PO10 ..... 58 B2
Warden Ct RHWH RH17 ..... 44 C3
Warelands BURH RH15 ..... 46 E8
Warenne Rd HOVE BN3 ..... 75 H2
Warleigh Rd BRI BN1 ..... 4 F1
Warltersville Wy HORL RH6 ..... 15 H8
Warmdene Av BRI BN1 ..... 52 E7
Warmdene Rd BRI BN1 ..... 52 E7
Warmdene Wy BRI BN1 ..... 52 E7
Warminghurst Cl
  PUL/STOR RH20 ... 161 J3
Warner Cl CRAWE RH10 ..... 30 D7
Warner Rd SALV BN13 ..... 13 L1
  SELS PO20 ..... 181 J7
Warner's La SELS PO20 ... 180 H5
Warnford Crs HAV PO9 ... 168 E12
Warnham Cl FERR BN12 ..... 92 C4
Warnham Court Ms
  HORS RH12 * ... 114 H5
Warnham Ms FERR BN12 * 92 H4
Warnham Ri BRI BN1 ..... 52 F8
Warnham Rd CRAWE RH10 ..... 9 M8
  FERR BN12 ..... 92 C3
  HORS RH12 ..... 36 A4
  HORS RH12 ..... 10 N1
Warninglid La SWTR RH13 ... 127 N5
The Wedges WTHG BN11 ... 124 G8
Warren Av BRIE/ROTT BN2 ..... 78 B4
Warren Cl BOR GU35 ... 106 D7
  BRIE/ROTT BN2 ..... 78 A5
  EGRIN RH19 ..... 22 D6
  SALV BN13 ..... 71 G6
Warren Crs ANG/EP BN16 ..... 90 E3
Warren Cft PUL/STOR RH20 ... 159 G12
Warren Dr CRAWW RH11 ..... 28 F2
  LEWES BN7 ..... 55 M5
  SWTR RH13 ... 125 R10
Warren Farm La CCH PO19 ..... 61 L3
Warren Farm Pl SALV BN13 ..... 70 F5
Warren Gdns SALV BN13 ..... 71 G4
Warren La RING/NEW BN8 ... 149 H5
Warren Ri BRIE/ROTT BN2 ..... 78 A5
Warren Rd BRIE/ROTT BN2 ..... 77 K6
  BRIE/ROTT BN2 ..... 78 A5
  LISS GU33 ... 116 D6
  LISS GU33 ... 116 C9
  SALV BN13 ..... 70 F5
Warren Side EPSF GU31 ... 152 E3
The Warren BURH RH15 ..... 47 H8
  FERR BN12 ..... 91 L5
Warren Wy BRIE/ROTT BN2 ..... 78 C5
  MSEA/BNM PO22 ..... 65 G7
  RING/NEW BN8 ... 149 G5
Warrenwood RING/NEW BN8 ... 149 R5
Warrington Cl CRAWW RH11 ..... 28 D7

Warrior Cl PTSD BN41 ..... 75 G3
Warrs Hill La RING/NEW BN8 ... 149 P4
Warsash Cl HAV PO9 ... 168 F11
Warwick Gdns WTHG BN11 ..... 13 J8
Warwick La WTHG BN11 * 13 J6
Warwick Mt BRIE/ROTT BN2 * 5 J8
Warwick Pl MSEA/BNM PO22 ..... 87 J8
  WTHG BN11 ..... 13 K5
Warwick Rd WTHG BN11 ..... 13 K6
Warwick St WTHG BN11 ..... 13 H6
Wasdale Cl HORN PO08 ... 150 D11
Washford La BOR GU35 ... 107 J5
Washington Bostal
  PUL/STOR RH20 ... 178 H4
Washington Rd CRAWW RH11 ..... 28 D6
  EMRTH PO10 ..... 58 A4
  HORN PO08 ..... 168 E3
  HRH16 ..... 45 J4
  PUL/STOR RH20 ... 178 D1
  STEY/UB BN44 ... 179 N2
Wassand Cl CRAWE RH10 ..... 9 M3
Waterbury Rd RHWH RH17 ... 131 L3
Waterdyke Av STHW BN42 ..... 74 D6
Waterfield Cl SWTR RH13 ..... 11 H4
Waterfield Gdns CRAWW RH11 ..... 28 D5
Waterford Gdns LHPTN BN17 ..... 88 D4
Waterhall Rd BRI BN1 ..... 52 B7
Waterlands La HORS RH12 ... 114 H9
Water La ANG/EP BN16 ..... 69 H6
  LHPTN BN17 ..... 89 J3
  PUL/STOR RH20 ... 160 C11
  SWTR RH13 ... 161 M12
Water Lea CRAWE RH10 ..... 9 M6
Waterloo Rd HAV PO9 ..... 57 G4
  MSEA/BNM PO22 ..... 3 C4
Waterloo Sq BOGR PO21 ..... 2 D7
Waterloo St HOVE BN3 ..... 76 C8
Waterman Cl BOR GU35 ... 107 J7
The Waterplat CCH PO19 ..... 62 B5
Waters Edge BOGR PO21 ..... 103 K4
  PUL/STOR RH20 ... 158 H4
Waters Edge Gdns
  EMRTH PO10 ..... 58 A5
Watersedge Gdns SELS PO20 ..... 99 M4
Watersfield Rd SALV BN13 ..... 71 G8
Waterside EGRIN RH19 ..... 24 A8
  HORL RH6 ..... 14 F4
  BOR GU35 ... 106 H5
  CRAWW RH11 ..... 28 D5
Waterside Dr CRAWE RH10 ..... 83 L2
The Waterside LHPTN BN17 * 89 H4
Waterstone Cl SELS PO20 ..... 81 M6
Waterworks Rd FROW RH18 ..... 34 E5
Waterworks Rd PSF GU32 ... 133 P3
Watery La CCH PO19 ..... 6 F9
  RCCH PO18 ... 170 H12
Watling Cl STHW BN42 ..... 74 D6
Watling Rd STHW BN42 ..... 74 D6
Watson Cl CRAWE RH10 ..... 30 B6
Watson Wy SELS PO20 ..... 64 C6
Waveney Wk CRAWE RH10 ..... 30 A5
Waverley Cl HORS RH12 * 10 A6
Waverley Crs BRI BN1 ..... 77 G4
Waverley Rd ANG/EP BN16 ..... 90 B4
  BOGR PO21 ..... 103 M1
Wavertree Rd FERR BN12 ..... 92 C2
Wayfarer's Wk EMRTH PO10.. 57 M6
Wayfield Av HOVE BN3 ..... 75 L4
Wayfield Cl HOVE BN3 ..... 75 K4
Waykeham Wy BURH RH15 ..... 47 H7
Wayland Av BRI BN1 ..... 76 B1
Wayland Hts BRI BN1 ..... 76 B1
Wayside BRI BN1 ..... 52 C7
  CRAWW RH11 ..... 28 D5
  LAN/SOMP BN15 * 72 J8
  RDKG RH5 * 16 C3
Wayside Av SALV BN13 ..... 70 C6
Wayside Cottages SWTR RH13 . 127 J6
The Way ANG/EP BN16 ..... 90 F5
Weald Av HOVE BN3 ..... 75 L4
Weald Cl HPPT/KEY BN6 ... 164 C13
  SWTR RH13 ..... 11 G9
Weald Dr CRAWE RH10 ..... 9 L6
Weald Drive Rbt CRAWE RH10 ..... 9 K5
Weald Dyke SHOR BN43 ..... 73 L7
Wealden Wy HWH RH16 ..... 45 G5
Wealdon Cl SWTR RH13 ... 143 J9
Weald Ri HWH RH16 ..... 45 H6
Weald Rd BURH RH15 ..... 46 D6
The Weald EGRIN RH19 ..... 23 L6
Wear Cl SALV BN13 ..... 70 B6
Weare St RDKG RH5 ... 115 M2
Wear Rd SALV BN13 ..... 70 B6
Weatherhill Cl HORL RH6 ..... 15 L6
Weatherhill Rd HORL RH6 ..... 15 M6
Weaver Cl CRAWW RH11 * 28 D4
Weavers Cl BURH RH15 ..... 47 J8
  MIDH GU29 ... 137 J7
Weavers Down LIPH GU30 * ... 117 L2
Weavers Gn HAV PO9 ..... 57 K2
Weavers Hi ANG/EP BN16 ..... 68 F7
Weavers Ring ANG/EP BN16 ..... 68 F7
Webb Cl BOGR PO21 ..... 102 F6
  CRAWW RH11 ..... 29 G8
Weddell Rd CRAWE RH10 ..... 9 J9
Wedgewood Rd MSEA/BNM PO22.. 3 M5
Welbrook CRAWE RH10 ..... 9 L9
Welbeck Av HOVE BN3 ..... 75 K7
Welbeck Cl BURH RH15 ..... 47 J5
Welbeck Dr BURH RH15 ..... 47 J5
Welchwood Cl HORN PO08 ... 168 A3
Welesmere Rd BRIE/ROTT BN2 .. 97 M2
The Welkin HWH RH16 ..... 45 L1
Welland Cl SALV BN13 ..... 70 C5
Welland Rd SALV BN13 ..... 70 C5
Well Copse La HORN PO08 ... 150 D12
Wellcroft Cottages
  HPPT/KEY BN6 ... 164 D4
Weller Cl CRAWE RH10 ..... 30 C4
Wellesley Av FERR BN12 ..... 92 C3
Wellfield EGRIN RH19 ..... 34 B2
Wellgreen La LEWES BN7 ..... 55 L8
Wellhouse La BURH RH15 ... 165 Q2
Well House Rd
  PUL/STOR RH20 * ... 161 K8
Wellingham La SALV BN13 ..... 70 D1
Wellingham Wy HORS RH12.. 28 D7
Wellington Av BOR GU35 ... 106 C7
Wellington Cl CRAWE RH10 ..... 20 D8
  HORN PO08 ... 168 E3
Wellington Gdns SELS PO20 ... 181 L5
Wellington Rd BOGR PO21 ..... 2 B7
  BRIE/ROTT BN2 ..... 5 H2
  CCH PO19 ..... 61 M4
  HORS RH12 ..... 10 E6
  PTSD BN41 ..... 75 G7
Wellington St BRIE/ROTT BN2 ..... 5 J3
Wellington Town Rd
  EGRIN RH19 ..... 23 J6
Wellington Wy HORL RH6 ..... 14 E4
Well La HASM GU27 ... 109 N11
  MFD/CHID GU8 * ... 110 C1
  MIDH GU29 ... 154 H1
Well Meadow HAV PO9 ... 168 F11
Wellow Cl HAV PO9 ..... 56 E2
Wells Cl BOGR PO21 ..... 102 E6
Wells Cl HORS RH12 ... 125 Q3
  LEWES BN7 ... 166 H3
Wells Ct WTHG BN11 * 12 A7
Wells Crs BOGR PO21 ..... 103 J2
  CCH PO19 ..... 61 L4
Wellsfield SELS PO20 ..... 99 H4
Wells Lea EGRIN RH19 ..... 23 J6
Wells Meadow EGRIN RH19 ..... 23 J6
Wells Rd CRAWE RH10 * 29 K7
Welwood Cl SWTR RH13 ..... 37 G5
Welyn Cl CRAWW RH11 ..... 28 D6
Wembley Av LAN/SOMP BN15 .. 72 C7
Wembley Gdns
  LAN/SOMP BN15 ..... 72 C7
Wembury Pk LING RH7 ..... 22 D1
Wenban Rd WTHG BN11 ..... 13 G6
Wenceling Cottages
  LAN/SOMP BN15 ..... 73 H8
Wendover Rd HAV PO9 ..... 56 F3
Wendy Rdg ANG/EP BN16 ..... 90 A3
Wenlock Cl CRAWW RH11 ..... 28 F5
Wensleydale CRAWE RH10 ..... 29 H6
Wensley Gdns EMRTH PO10 ..... 58 A3
Wentworth Cl
  MSEA/BNM PO22 ..... 65 G6
  SALV BN13 ..... 70 E5
Wentworth Ct ANG/EP BN16 * .. 90 F4
Wentworth Dr CRAWE RH10 ..... 30 C2
  HORN PO08 ... 168 C2
Wesermarsch Rd HORN PO08.. 168 B5
Wesley Cl CRAWW RH11 ..... 28 D6
  HORL RH6 ..... 14 F4
Wessex Av BOGR PO21 ..... 2 A3
  SELS PO20 ..... 99 M6
Wessex Rd HORN PO08 ... 150 E10
West Ashling Rd RCCH PO18 ..... 59 K2
West Av BOGR PO21 ..... 103 L2
  CRAWE RH10 ..... 29 L1
  LAN/SOMP BN15 ..... 72 F8
  MSEA/BNM PO22 ..... 87 L7
West Bank ARUN BN18 * 65 M8
West Beach Pk South
  LHPTN BN17 * 89 H5
West Beach Rd SHOR BN43 ..... 73 J8
Westbourne Av EMRTH PO10 ..... 58 B3
  SALV BN13 ..... 13 G2
Westbourne Cl EMRTH PO10 ..... 58 B3
Westbourne Gdns HOVE BN3 ..... 75 M7
Westbourne Pl HOVE BN3 ..... 75 M7
Westbourne Rd EMRTH PO10 ..... 58 B3
Westbourne St HOVE BN3 ..... 75 M6
Westbourne Vls HOVE BN3 ..... 75 L7
West Bracklesham Dr
  SELS PO20 ..... 99 M8
Westbrook FROW RH18 * 34 D6
West Brook Cl RCCH PO18 ..... 59 M8
Westbrooke WTHG BN11 ..... 13 G5
Westbrook Cl HORN PO08 ... 168 B3
West Brook Fld RCCH PO18 ..... 59 M8
Westbrook Wy STHW BN42 ..... 74 E6
West Broyle Dr CCH PO19.. 61 H3
West Buildings WTHG BN11 ..... 12 F7
West Burton La
  PUL/STOR RH20 ... 157 R12
West Chiltington La BIL RH14.. 142 C7
  BIL RH14 ... 142 K4
  SWTR RH13 ... 124 H7
West Chiltington Rd
  PUL/STOR RH20 ... 159 N5
  PUL/STOR RH20 ... 160 A9
  PUL/STOR RH20 ... 160 D4
West Cl HASM GU27 ... 119 L2
  MSEA/BNM PO22 ..... 87 J8
  PTSD BN41 ..... 75 H4
West Common HWH RH16 ..... 45 J2
West Common Dr HWH RH16 ..... 45 K2
Westcott Cl CRAWW RH11 ..... 39 H1
Westcourt Pl SALV BN13 ..... 12 F2
Westcourt Rd SALV BN13 ..... 12 F3
Westcroft SELS PO20 ... 181 J7
Westdean Rd SALV BN13 ..... 71 G8
Westdene Dr BRI BN1 ..... 52 B8
West Dr ANG/EP BN16 ..... 90 C1
  BOGR PO21 ..... 103 H4
  BRIE/ROTT BN2 ..... 5 H4
  FERR BN12 ..... 91 K5
  MSEA/BNM PO22 ..... 87 M8
West End La HASM GU27 ... 110 C9
  HFD BN5 ... 162 F6
West End Wy LAN/SOMP BN15.. 94 C1
Westgate Cl FERR BN12 ..... 91 L3
Westgate Ms BRIE/ROTT BN2.. 64 C6
Westgate Rd BRIE/ROTT BN2.. 77 K1
Westgate St SELS PO20 ..... 64 C7
Western Av EMRTH PO10 ..... 58 B1
Western Cl LAN/SOMP BN15 .. 94 B1
Western Esp PTSD BN41 ..... 75 F7
Western Ldg LAN/SOMP BN15 *.. 72 B6
Western Pde EMRTH PO10 ..... 57 M6
Western Pl WTHG BN11 ..... 12 E7
Western Rd BOR GU35 ... 106 F3
  BURH RH15 ..... 46 E6
  HAV PO9 ..... 56 F3
  HPPT/KEY BN6 ... 164 G3
  HWH RH16 ..... 45 J6
  LAN/SOMP BN15 ..... 94 B1
  LHPTN BN17 ..... 89 K5
  LISS GU33 ... 116 C9
  SELS PO20 ... 181 L7
  SHOR BN43 ..... 73 K6
Western Rd North
  LAN/SOMP BN15 ..... 72 B7
Western Rw WTHG BN11 ..... 12 F7
Western St BRI BN1 ..... 76 B8
Western Ter BRI BN1 ..... 4 B6
  LAN/SOMP BN15 * 71 L4
Westfield MSEA/BNM PO22.. 86 A6
Westfield Av ANG/EP BN16 ..... 90 F5
Westfield Cl BRI BN1 ..... 76 F1

Westfield Crs BRI BN1 ..... 52 F8
Westfield Rd CRAWW RH11 ..... 8 B4
West Front Rd BOGR PO21 ... 102 E7
West Furlong La
  HPPT/KEY BN6 ... 164 H4
Westgate CCH PO19 ..... 6 B4
West Ga LEWES BN7 ... 166 H3
West Green Dr CRAWW RH11 ..... 8 C3
West Gun Copse Rd
  SWTR RH13 ... 125 N8
Westhampnett Rd CCH PO19 ..... 7 J1
West Head LHPTN BN17 ..... 89 L5
West Hi EGRIN RH19 ..... 23 K3
  EGRIN RH19 ..... 33 J1
  RHWH RH17 ..... 130 B1
  SALV BN13 ..... 70 D3
West Hill Cl SALV BN13 * 70 D3
Westhill Dr BURH RH15 ..... 46 D6
West Hill Pl BRI BN1 ..... 4 C4
West Hill Rd BRI BN1 ..... 4 C4
West Hill St BRI BN1 ..... 4 C4
West Hoathly Rd EGRIN RH19.. 33 H6
Westingway BOGR PO21 ... 103 M2
Westlake Cl SALV BN13 ..... 70 E8
Westland Av SALV BN13 ..... 12 B2
Westlands ANG/EP BN16 ..... 89 M3
  FERR BN12 ..... 91 J4
Westland's Copse La
  PETW GU28 ... 138 E5
Westlands La SELS PO20 ..... 82 C3
Westlands Rd HWH RH16 ..... 45 L4
  SELS PO20 ..... 83 M5
West La EGRIN RH19 ..... 33 J1
  LAN/SOMP BN15 ..... 72 D7
Westleas HORL RH6 ..... 14 D4
West Leigh EGRIN RH19 ..... 33 L2
Westloats Gdns BOGR PO21 ..... 2 B4
  BOGR PO21 * 85 M8
Westloats La BOGR PO21 ..... 85 M8
West Mare La PUL/STOR RH20. 159 N4
West Md ANG/EP BN16 ..... 90 D5
West Meade RCCH PO18 ..... 61 H7
Westmead Rd CCH PO19 ..... 61 H7
West Meads HORL RH6 ..... 15 H4
West Meads Dr BOGR PO21 ..... 85 L8
Westminster Dr BOGR PO21 ... 103 J2
Westminster Rd CRAWE RH10.. 30 B4
Westmorland Dr
  MSEA/BNM PO22 ..... 87 G7
Westmount Cl STHW BN42 ..... 74 C5
Weston La PSF GU32 ... 133 J9
  RCCH PO18 ... 170 G12
Weston Rd EPSF GU31 ... 133 P6
Westons Hi SWTR RH13 ... 125 L8
West Onslow Cl FERR BN12 * 91 K2
West Pallant CCH PO19 ..... 6 E5
West Pde HORN PO08 ... 168 A5
  WTHG BN11 ..... 12 A8
West Park Crs BURH RH15 ..... 46 C5
Westpark La FERR BN12 ..... 92 D3
West Park Rd CRAWE RH10 ..... 21 L6
  LING RH7 ..... 22 B1
  RHWH RH17 ... 128 C2
West Preston Ms
  ANG/EP BN16 * 90 D4
West Ridings ANG/EP BN16 ..... 90 D5
West Rd EMRTH PO10 ..... 57 M5
  POY/PYE BN45 ... 164 E11
  PTSD BN41 ..... 74 F6
West Sands La SELS PO20 ... 180 H5
West Stoke Rd CCH PO19 ..... 61 J3
West Strd SELS PO20 ..... 98 F5
West St BIL RH14 ... 141 K1
  BOGR PO21 ..... 2 D8
  BRI BN1 ..... 4 D7
  BRIE/ROTT BN2 ..... 97 L4
  BURH RH15 ..... 46 E6
  CCH PO19 ..... 6 C5
  CRAWW RH11 ..... 8 E5
  EGRIN RH19 ..... 33 K1
  EMRTH PO10 ..... 58 A5
  HASM GU27 ... 109 M11
  HAV PO9 ..... 56 F4
  HORS RH12 ..... 10 B4
  HPPT/KEY BN6 ... 165 R6
  LAN/SOMP BN15 ..... 71 M6
  MIDH GU29 ... 137 J10
  PTSD BN41 ..... 75 H4
  PUL/STOR RH20 ... 159 R12
  SELS PO20 ... 181 J7
  SHOR BN43 ..... 73 K6
  WTHG BN11 ..... 12 F7
West Tyne SALV BN13 ..... 70 C8
Westup Rd RHWH RH17 ... 129 M1
West Vw BOR GU35 * ... 106 E8
  HOVE BN3 * 76 B5
  HWH RH16 ..... 45 J6
West View Dr ARUN BN18 ..... 87 L3
West View Gdns EGRIN RH19.. 33 K1
West View Rd BOR GU35 ... 107 R5
Westview Ter SALV BN13 ... 178 H11
West Walberton La ARUN BN18 .. 65 H3
Westward Cl RCCH PO18 ..... 60 B8
Westward La PUL/STOR RH20. 159 R7
West Wy CCH PO19 ..... 61 H4
  CRAWE RH10 ..... 9 L2
  HOVE BN3 ..... 75 J3
  LAN/SOMP BN15 ..... 72 F8
  SALV BN13 ..... 13 G2
  SWTR RH13 ... 124 G2
Westway CRAWE RH10 ..... 20 A2
  HORL RH6 ..... 14 A2
  LHPTN BN17 ..... 89 J3
  MSEA/BNM PO22 ..... 2 F3
Westway Cl PTSD BN41 ..... 74 D1
Westway Gdns PTSD BN41 ..... 74 D1
Westways HAV PO9 ..... 56 D1
Westwood Cl EMRTH PO10 ..... 58 B2
Wetherdown EPSF GU31 ... 133 P6
Weycombe Rd HASM GU27 ... 109 M9
Weydown Rd HASM GU27 ... 109 L10
Wey Hl HASM GU27 ... 109 K11
Weyhill HASM GU27 ... 109 L10
Weylands Cl LIPH GU30 ... 107 R12
Weyland Cl LIPH GU30 * ... 118 A1
Wey Lodge Cl LIPH GU30 * ... 118 A1
Wey South Pth CRAN GU6 ... 112 D7
  PUL/STOR RH20 ... 140 E9
Weysprings HASM GU27 ... 109 J10
Whaddon Ct HAV PO9 ... 168 D11
Wharf Rd HOVE BN3 ..... 75 J7
The Wharf MIDH GU29 ... 137 J10
Wheatcroft LHPTN BN17 ..... 89 H2
Wheatear Dr EPSF GU31 ... 133 R7
Wheatfield Rd SELS PO20 ... 181 M5

Wheatfield Wy BRIE/ROTT BN2.. 77 L2
  HORL RH6 ..... 15 G5
Wheatsheaf Cl BURH RH15 ..... 46 D3
  HORS RH12 ..... 36 D4
Wheatsheaf La RHWH RH17 ..... 44 D3
Wheatsheaf Rd HFD BN5 ... 163 M1
Wheatstone Cl CRAWE RH10.. 20 A6
Wheelbarrow Castle
  MIDH GU29 ... 137 K7
Wheeler Ct HWH RH16 * 45 J7
Wheeler Rd CRAWE RH10 ..... 30 A5
Wheelers La HORL RH6 ..... 15 M7
Wheelers Wy EGRIN RH19 ..... 22 D6
Wheelwright La BURH RH15 ..... 47 J8
Wheelwrights HASM GU27 ... 119 L3
  PUL/STOR RH20 ... 160 B4
Wheelwrights La GSHT GU26 ... 108 D5
Wherwell Ct HAV PO9 ... 169 J12
Whichelo Pl BRIE/ROTT BN2 ..... 5 J4
Whichers Cl HAV PO9 ... 169 J9
Whichers Gate Rd HAV PO9 ... 169 J9
Whippingham Rd
  BRIE/ROTT BN2 ..... 5 K1
Whippingham St
  BRIE/ROTT BN2 ..... 5 K1
Whistler Av CCH PO19 ..... 61 M4
Whistler Cl CRAWE RH10 ..... 29 L6
White Av LISS GU33 ... 116 F3
Whitebeam Cl HORN PO08 ... 168 D4
White Beam Ri HORN PO08 ... 150 D8
Whitebeam Rd SALV BN13 ..... 70 B8
Whitebeam Wy
  MSEA/BNM PO22 ..... 87 K7
  SELS PO20 ..... 63 J4
Whitechimney Rw
  EMRTH PO10 ..... 58 C2
White City MIDH GU29 ... 136 H10
Whitecroft ANG/EP BN16 * 90 B4
Whitecross St BRI BN1 ..... 4 F4
White Dirt La HORN PO08 ... 150 D10
Whitegates Cl RING/NEW BN8.. 167 N2
Whitehall Dr CRAWW RH11 ..... 28 D3
Whitehall Pde EGRIN RH19 * 23 K8
White Hart Cl HORS RH12 ..... 10 C2
Whitehaven HORN PO08 ... 168 B3
Whitehawk Cl BRIE/ROTT BN2.. 77 K7
Whitehawk Crs BRIE/ROTT BN2.. 77 K8
Whitehawk Hill Rd
  BRIE/ROTT BN2 ..... 5 M7
Whitehawk Rd BRIE/ROTT BN2.. 77 M7
Whitehawk Wy BRIE/ROTT BN2.. 77 L7
Whitehill Rd BOR GU35 ... 107 K8
Whitehorse Rd HORS RH12 ..... 37 G3
White Horses Wy LHPTN BN17.. 89 M4
Whitehouse Gdns PSF GU32 ... 133 M4
White House Pl SALV BN13 ..... 70 D5
White Ladies Cl HAV PO9 ..... 57 H4
Whitelands HWH RH16 ..... 45 J6
  MSEA/BNM PO22 ..... 3 M1
Whitelea Rd LHPTN BN17 ..... 89 J3
Whitelot Cl STHW BN42 ..... 74 D4
Whitelot Wy STHW BN42 ..... 74 D3
Whitely Hl CRAWE RH10 ..... 30 E8
Whiteman's Cl RHWH RH17 ..... 44 B1
Whitemans Gn RHWH RH17 ..... 44 A1
Whiterock Pl STHW BN42 ..... 74 E6
White's Cl HPPT/KEY BN6 ... 164 H2
Whites Cottages SWTR RH13 *. 126 D6
Whiteside Cl CCH PO19 ..... 7 G2
Whites La HASM GU27 ... 118 H10
White St BRIE/ROTT BN2 ..... 5 G7
White Styles Rd
  LAN/SOMP BN15 ..... 72 A7
Whitethorn Dr BRI BN1 ..... 76 A1
Whitethroat La RHWH RH17 ... 129 K3
Whiteway Cl BRIE/ROTT BN2 ..... 97 L3
Whiteways MSEA/BNM PO22.. 85 M7
Whiteways Cl LHPTN BN17 ..... 89 J3
  MSEA/BNM PO22 ..... 85 M7
Whitfield Cl HASM GU27 ... 109 M8
  MSEA/BNM PO22 ..... 3 G2
Whitfield Rd HASM GU27 ... 109 M9
Whitley Cl EMRTH PO10 ... 169 Q12
Whitley Rd HORN PO08 ... 168 A3
Whitmoor Vale Rd GSHT GU26.. 108 C2
Whitmore V GSHT GU26 ... 108 C3
Whitmore Vale Rd GSHT GU26. 108 A5
Whitmore Wy HORL RH6 ..... 14 C5
Whitsbury Rd HAV PO9 ... 168 H12
Whittingham Gdns BRI BN1 ..... 76 C2
Whittington College
  EGRIN RH19 ..... 22 F5
Whittington Ct EMRTH PO10 ..... 58 A5
Whittington Rd CRAWE RH10 ..... 29 J8
Whittle Wy CRAWE RH10 ..... 19 M5
Whitworth Rd CRAWW RH11 ..... 19 J6
Whyke Cl CCH PO19 ..... 7 H8
Whyke Ms CCH PO19 ..... 7 H4
Whyke Rd CCH PO19 ..... 7 H4
Whylands Av SALV BN13 ..... 70 C5
Whylands Cl SALV BN13 ..... 70 C5
Whylands Crs SALV BN13 ..... 70 C5
Whytings SWTR RH13 ... 126 A3
Wick Cl MSEA/BNM PO22 ..... 87 G3
The Wickets BURH RH15 ..... 46 E4
Wick Farm Rd LHPTN BN17 ..... 89 H3
Wickham Cl HORL RH6 ..... 14 E5
  HWH RH16 ..... 45 H2
Wickham Dr HPPT/KEY BN6 ... 165 L4
Wickham Hl HPPT/KEY BN6 ... 165 K5
Wickham La LEWES BN7 ... 167 P7
Wickham Wy HWH RH16 ..... 45 H2
Wickhurst Cl PTSD BN41 ..... 74 C1
Wickhurst La HORS RH12 ... 125 P3
Wickhurst Ri PTSD BN41 ..... 74 D1
Wickhurst Rd PTSD BN41 ..... 74 C1
Wick La MIDH GU29 ... 137 K5
  MSEA/BNM PO22 ..... 87 G3
Wickor Cl EMRTH PO10 ..... 58 B3
Wickor Wy EMRTH PO10 ..... 58 A2
Wicks Rd BIL RH14 ... 141 K1
Wick St LHPTN BN17 ..... 89 J2
Widdicombe Wy
  BRIE/ROTT BN2 ..... 77 K3
Widewater Cl LAN/SOMP BN15. 73 H4
Widewater Ct SHOR BN43 * 73 J2
Widgeon La SELS PO20 ... 180 H5
Widgeon Wy HORS RH12 ..... 36 B4
Wield Cl HAV PO9 ..... 56 D1
Wigan Crs HAV PO9 ..... 56 C3
Wight Wy SELS PO20 ... 181 L8
Wigmore Cl BRI BN1 ..... 77 G4
Wigmore Rd SALV BN13 ..... 71 J7
Wilberforce Cl CRAWW RH11 ..... 39 H1
Wilberforce Wy SWTR RH13 ... 125 R9
Wilbury Av HOVE BN3 ..... 75 L6

Wilbury Crs HOVE BN3 .... 76 C6
Wilbury Gdns HOVE BN3 .... 76 B5
Wilbury Gv HOVE BN3 .... 76 B7
Wilbury Rd HOVE BN3 .... 76 B7
Wilbury Vls HOVE BN3 .... 76 B6
Wilby Av STHW BN42 .... 74 D4
Wildacre CI BIL RH14 .... 122 E2
Wildbrooks CI PUL/STOR RH20 .. 159 L3
Wilderness Ri EGRIN RH19 .... 23 M4
Wilderness Rd HPPT/KEY BN6 .. 164 H3
The Wilderness HWH RH16 .... 45 L1
Wilderwick Rd EGRIN RH19 .... 23 M2
Wildgoose Dr HORS RH12 .... 125 Q2
Wild Orchid Wy SWTR RH13 .... 125 K10
Wild Park CI BRIE/ROTT BN2 .... 77 K2
Wildwood La CRAN GU6 .... 112 H4
Wilfrid Rd HOVE BN3 .... 75 J5
Wilkins CI HORN PO8 .... 150 C7
Wilkinson CI ANG/EP BN16 .... 90 F1
    BRIE/ROTT BN2 .... 97 L2
Willard Wy PUL/STOR RH20 .... 161 J8
Willett CI PETW GU28 .... 156 C6
Willetts Wy BIL RH14 .... 122 G2
William Allen La HWH RH16 .... 45 L4
William Morris Wy
    CRAWW RH11 .... 39 G1
William Olders Rd
    ANG/EP BN16 .... 90 F1
Williamson Cl HASM GU27 .... 109 Q8
Williams Rd RCCH RH18 .... 60 B6
    SHOR BN43 .... 74 A5
William St BOGR PO21 .... 2 E6
    BRIE/ROTT BN2 .... 4 F6
    PTSD BN41 .... 75 G6
Williams Wy CRAWE RH10 .... 9 G5
Willingdon Rd BRIE/ROTT BN2 .. 77 K4
Willow Av ANG/EP BN16 .... 90 D4
Willowbed Av CCH PO19 .... 7 J8
Willowbed Dr CCH PO19 .... 7 J8
Willow Brean HORL RH6 .... 14 D5
Willow Brook LHPTN BN17 .... 89 H2
    MSEA/BNM PO22 .... 87 M8
Willowbrook Av SALV BN13 .... 13 M1
Willowbrook Wy
    HPPT/KEY BN6 .... 165 P6
Willow CI BOR GU35 .... 106 H6
    BRIE/ROTT BN2 .... 78 D5
    CRAWE RH10 .... 29 K1
    EGRIN RH19 .... 23 J6
    HAV PO9 .... 57 H4
    HPPT/KEY BN6 .... 164 G2
    LAN/SOMP BN15 .... 73 H8
    LIPH GU30 .... 118 A2
    PUL/STOR RH20 .... 160 A7
    STEY/UB BN44 .... 48 D1
Willow Cnr HORL RH6 .... 18 C2
Willow Ct HORL RH6 * 15 C3
    WTHG BN11 .... 12 A4
Willow Crs SALV BN13 .... 70 B8
Willowdale CI PSF GU32 .... 132 C3
Willowdene CI HAV PO9 .... 56 C1
Willow Dr BIL RH14 .... 142 A1
Willow Gdns EMRTH PO10 .... 58 C1
    HPPT/KEY BN6 .... 164 H2
    LIPH GU30 .... 118 A2
Willowhale Av BOGR PO21 .... 103 J3
Willowhayne Av ANG/EP BN16 .. 90 F5
Willowhayne CI ANG/EP BN16 .. 90 F5
Willowhayne Crs ANG/EP BN16 .. 90 F5
Willow Md EGRIN RH19 .... 33 L1
Willow Pk HWH RH16 .... 45 L5
Willow Rdg CRAWE RH10 .... 31 M6
Willow Rd HORS RH12 .... 37 G4
    LISS GU33 .... 116 C9
The Willows ANG/EP BN16 .... 90 C4
    ARUN BN18 * 66 D8
    BIL RH14 .... 141 R2
    BRIE/ROTT BN2 * 5 G1
    BURH RH15 .... 47 G4
    LAN/SOMP BN15 * 72 D8
    MFD/CHID GU8 .... 110 F5
    PUL/STOR RH20 .... 158 H4
    PUL/STOR RH20 * 159 R12
    SALV BN13 * 178 H11
    SELS PO20 .... 181 L5
Willow Tree Av HORN PO8 .... 168 C7
Willow Wy BOGR PO21 .... 103 C8
    HPPT/KEY BN6 .... 164 H1
    PUL/STOR RH20 .... 161 J9
Wills Cl ARUN BN18 .... 88 A3
Wilman Gdns BOGR PO21 .... 103 J3
Wilmington CI BRI BN1 .... 52 E8
    CRAWW RH11 .... 39 G1
    HPPT/KEY BN6 .... 165 N6
Wilmington Pde BRI BN1 .... 52 E8
Wilmington Wy BRI BN1 .... 52 E8
    HWH RH16 .... 45 K4
Wilmot Rd SHOR BN43 .... 74 B5
Wilson Av BRIE/ROTT BN2 .... 96 E1
Wilson CI CCH PO19 .... 61 G4
    CRAWE RH10 .... 30 C6
Wilson Ct ARUN BN18 .... 88 A3
Wilsons Rd BOR GU35 .... 107 G4
Wilton CI ANG/EP BN16 .... 90 A2
    SELS PO20 .... 100 A8
    SWTR RH13 .... 144 F10
Wilton Dr ANG/EP BN16 .... 90 A2
    HORN PO8 .... 168 B4
Wilverley Av HAV PO9 .... 57 H1
Wimblehurst Rd HORS RH12 .... 10 D2
Wimland HI HORS RH12 .... 27 J7
Wimland Rd HORS RH12 .... 27 H5
Wimlands La HORS RH12 .... 27 J6
Wincanton CI CRAWE RH10 .... 30 C3
Wincanton Wy WVILLE PO7 .... 168 C8
Winchelsea Gdns WTHG BN11 .. 12 A8
Winchester Dr CCH PO19 .... 61 L5
Winchester Rd ANG/EP BN16 .. 90 D3
    CRAWE RH10 .... 29 K7
    PSF GU32 .... 132 C3
    PSF GU32 .... 133 L5
    WTHG BN11 .... 12 D6
Winchester St BRI BN1 .... 4 E1
The Winches SWTR RH13 * 38 B3
Winchfield Crs HAV PO9 .... 56 D1
Wincombe Rd BRI BN1 .... 76 C4
Winden Av CCH PO19 .... 7 H5
Windermere Ct FERR BN12 * 92 A3
Windermere Crs LAN/SOMP BN15 72 C6
Windermere Rd BOR GU35 .... 106 G4
    HWH RH16 .... 45 J5
Windlesham Av HOVE BN3 .... 4 A4
Windlesham CI PTSD BN41 .... 74 F4
Windlesham Gdns
    ANG/EP BN16 .... 90 F3

BRI BN1 .... 4 B4
    SHOR BN43 .... 73 L4
Windlesham Rd BRI BN1 .... 4 B4
    SHOR BN43 .... 73 L5
Windmill SELS PO20 .... 63 J4
Windmill Av HPPT/KEY BN6 .... 165 N6
Windmill CI ANG/EP BN16 .... 90 F1
    BOGR PO21 .... 103 G4
    HORL RH6 .... 15 C6
    HORN PO8 .... 150 D8
    HOVE BN3 .... 75 L3
    PUL/STOR RH20 .... 161 K8
    STEY/UB BN44 .... 49 G3
    SWTR RH13 .... 11 L3
Windmill Copse
    PUL/STOR RH20 .... 160 A11
    SELS PO20 .... 99 L6
Windmill Ct CRAWE RH10 .... 29 J1
    SELS PO20 .... 99 L6
Windmill Dr ANG/EP BN16 .... 90 C3
    BOR GU35 .... 107 G3
    BRI BN1 .... 52 B7
    BURH RH15 .... 46 F5
Windmill Fld RCCH PO18 .... 59 M8
Windmill La EGRIN RH19 .... 23 J6
    EGRIN 34 B2
    HFD BN5 .... 163 J6
Windmill Platt RHWH RH17 .... 128 D1
Windmill Rd LHPTN BN17 .... 89 J6
    STHW BN42 .... 74 D4
Windmill St BRIE/ROTT BN2 .... 5 H8
Windmill Ter BRIE/ROTT BN2 .... 5 H5
Windmill Vw BRI BN1 .... 52 A5
Windover Crs LEWES BN7 .... 55 M3
Windrum CI HORS RH12 .... 125 Q5
Windrush CI CRAWW RH11 .... 28 E5
    SALV BN13 .... 70 F5
Windsor CI ANG/EP BN16 .... 90 A2
    BOGR PO21 .... 103 K1
    CRAWW RH11 .... 29 H7
    HOVE BN3 .... 75 M2
    HWH RH16 .... 45 H7
    SWTR RH13 .... 125 R12
Windsor Dr ANG/EP BN16 .... 90 A2
    SELS PO20 .... 99 K6
Windsor PI EGRIN RH19 .... 33 M1
Windsor Rd BOR GU35 .... 107 G4
    CCH PO19 .... 7 K5
    PSF GU32 .... 133 N6
    SELS PO20 .... 181 L7
    WTHG BN11 .... 13 M4
Windsor St BRI BN1 .... 4 D6
Windsor Wk BOR GU35 .... 107 G4
Windsor Wy LAN/SOMP BN15 .. 73 G7
Windward CI LHPTN BN17 .... 89 M4
Windways MFD/CHID GU8 .... 112 A2
Windyridge CRAWW RH11 .... 28 F4
Wineham La HFD BN5 .... 145 Q10
Winfield Av BRI BN1 .... 52 E7
Winfield CI BRI BN1 .... 52 E8
    PTSD BN41 .... 74 F2
Winfield Wy EMRTH PO10 .... 58 A1
Wingle Tye Rd BURH RH15 .... 165 P1
Winguard Wy CCH PO19 .... 6 E7
Winkfield Rw HORN PO8 .... 168 B4
Winkhurst Wy BURH RH15 .... 47 J8
Winkton CI HAV PO9 .... 56 E2
Winnet Wy SWTR RH13 .... 125 R11
Winnipeg CI LIPH GU30 .... 117 R2
Winscombe Av HORN PO8 .... 168 B7
Winslade Rd HAV PO9 .... 168 E12
Winston CI BOGR PO21 .... 85 L7
Winston Crs BOGR PO21 .... 85 L7
Winston Rd LAN/SOMP BN15 .. 94 B2
Winterbourne HORS RH12 .... 36 C2
Winterbourne CI LEWES BN7 .. 55 M5
    SALV BN13 .... 70 A8
Winterbourne La LEWES BN7 .. 55 M5
Winterbourne Rd CCH PO19 .... 61 M3
Winterbourne Wy SALV BN13 .. 70 A8
Winterfold CRAWE RH10 .... 9 L9
Winter Gdns CRAWW RH11 .... 8 D6
The Winter Knoll LHPTN BN17 .. 89 L4
Winterpit CI SWTR RH13 .... 127 J3
Winterpit La SWTR RH13 .... 127 J3
Winters La MIDH GU29 .... 137 K6
Winterslow Dr HAV PO9 .... 168 F11
Winterton Ct SWTR RH13 .... 10 F6
Winterton Ldg LHPTN BN17 * .. 89 K4
Winterton Wy SHOR BN43 .... 74 A7
Winton CI WTHG BN11 .... 13 G5
Winton Rd PSF GU32 .... 133 N6
Wire Mill La LING RH7 .... 22 D1
Wisborough Ct CRAWW RH11 .. 28 E6
Wisborough Gdns BIL RH14 .... 141 L11
Wisborough La
    PUL/STOR RH20 .... 160 B12
Wisden Av BURH RH15 .... 46 D4
Wisteria Dr BOR GU35 .... 106 G7
Wisteria Gdns HAV PO9 .... 57 J1
Wiston Av CCH PO19 .... 6 B9
    SALV BN13 .... 71 G8
Wiston CI SALV BN13 .... 71 G8
Wiston Ct CRAWW RH11 .... 28 E6
Wiston Rd BRIE/ROTT BN2 .... 77 L6
Wiston Wy BRIE/ROTT BN2 .... 77 L6
Witchampton CI HAV PO9 * 168 H12
Withdean Av BRI BN1 .... 76 C3
    FERR BN12 .... 92 A5
Withdean Ct BRI BN1 .... 76 C2
Withdean Court Av BRI BN1 .... 76 C2
Withdean Crs BRI BN1 .... 76 C2
Withdean Ri BRI BN1 .... 76 C2
Withdean Rd BRI BN1 .... 76 C2
Wither DI HORL RH6 .... 14 D5
Witherslack CI BOR GU35 .... 107 G5
Withey Brook HORL RH6 .... 14 C8
Withey Mdw HORL RH6 .... 14 C8
Withy Bush BURH RH15 .... 46 D5
Withypitts CRAWE RH10 .... 31 M6
Withypitts East CRAWE RH10 .. 31 M6
Wittcomb Ter BOR GU35 * 106 F8
Wittering Rd HISD PO11 .... 98 A3
Wivelsfield Rd HWH RH16 .... 45 H7
Woburn PI BRI BN1 .... 53 L8
Woburn Rd CRAWW RH11 .... 28 F5
Wode CI HORN PO8 .... 150 D10
Woelfs CI PUL/STOR RH20 * 161 K8
Wold CI CRAWW RH11 .... 28 E5
Woldhurstlea CI CRAWW RH11 .. 28 E5
Wolfmere La LISS GU33 .... 116 D3
Wolseley Rd BRI BN1 .... 53 J7
    PTSD BN41 .... 74 F5
Woisey CI BOGR PO21 .... 103 K4
Wolstenbury Rd ANG/EP BN16 .. 90 B2
Wolstonbury CI CRAWW RH11 .. 8 D7

Wolstonbury Rd HOVE BN3 .... 4 A2
Wolstonbury Wy BURH RH15 .. 47 G6
Wolverstone Dr BRI BN1 .... 77 H3
Wolverton CI HORL RH6 .... 14 E8
Wolverton Gdns HORL RH6 .... 14 E7
Wolverton Rd HAV PO9 .... 168 F12
Wolves HI RDKG RH5 .... 16 B5
Wonston CI HAV PO9 .... 169 K11
Woodard Rd LAN/SOMP BN15 .. 72 E6
Woodards Vw SHOR BN43 .... 73 J8
Woodberry La HAV PO9 .... 169 L8
Woodborough CI SELS PO20 .. 100 B7
Woodbourne Av BRI BN1 .... 76 E1
Woodbourne CI LISS GU33 .... 116 D9
Woodbridge Ct HORS RH12 * .. 36 F4
Woodbridge Pk ANG/EP BN16 .. 90 F4
Woodbury Av EGRIN RH19 .... 34 A1
    HAV PO9 .... 57 G5
    PSF GU32 .... 133 M4
Woodbury Rd EGRIN RH19 .... 34 A1
Woodbury Gv HORN PO8 .... 168 A4
Wood CI REDH RH1 .... 14 F1
Woodcock HI EGRIN RH19 .... 22 E3
Woodcot Crs HAV PO9 .... 168 H11
Woodcote HORL RH6 .... 15 G5
Woodcote La LHPTN BN17 .... 67 J8
    PUL/STOR RH20 .... 140 E12
Woodcote Rd FROW RH18 .... 34 D7
Woodcourt CRAWW RH11 .... 29 H8
Woodcrest Rd BURH RH15 .... 46 E8
Woodcroft BRI BN1 .... 76 B3
Woodcroft La HORN PO8 .... 168 A4
Woodcroft Rd CRAWW RH11 .. 28 C5
Woodcutters RHWH RH17 .... 149 J2
Woodale La BIL RH14 .... 124 D12
Wood End HORS RH12 .... 37 H4
Woodend RCCH PO18 .... 171 K12
Woodend CI CRAWE RH10 .... 29 M1
Woodfield SWTR RH13 .... 125 P12
Woodfield CI BOGR PO21 .... 102 F6
    CRAWE RH10 .... 9 H1
    SELS PO20 .... 63 J4
Woodfield Park Rd
    EMRTH PO10 .... 58 C5
Woodfield Rd CRAWE RH10 .... 9 H2
    HORS RH12 .... 114 A10
Woodgate CI SELS PO20 .... 64 C8
Woodgate Meadow
    LEWES BN7 .... 166 H2
Woodgate Pk SELS PO20 .... 64 C8
Woodgate Rd SELS PO20 .... 64 C8
Woodgates CI SWTR RH13 .... 11 H4
Woodgreen Av HAV PO9 .... 56 E3
Woodhall CI RHWH RH17 .... 44 C2
Woodhatch SWTR RH13 .... 125 Q11
Woodhayes HORL RH6 .... 15 G5
Woodhorn La SELS PO20 .... 63 J6
Woodhouse CI HOVE BN3 .... 75 K6
Woodhouse La HAV PO9 .... 169 K5
    HORN PO8 .... 168 H3
Woodhouse Rd HORN PO8 .... 168 G2
    HOVE BN3 .... 75 K6
Wooding Gv CRAWW RH11 .... 29 G8
Woodington CI HAV PO9 .... 168 H11
Woodland Av BURH RH15 .... 47 H5
    HOVE BN3 .... 75 M2
    SALV BN13 .... 70 E4
Woodland CI BIL RH14 .... 124 B7
    BURH RH15 .... 47 H5
    HOVE BN3 .... 76 A3
    SWTR RH13 .... 37 G5
Woodland Dr CRAWE RH10 .... 32 A1
    HOVE BN3 .... 76 A3
Woodland La SWTR RH13 .... 38 A6
Woodland Rd SELS PO20 .... 181 K8
Woodlands CRAWE RH10 .... 30 C1
    HOVE BN3 .... 76 B3
Woodlands Av ANG/EP BN16 .. 90 B4
    EMRTH PO10 .... 57 M2
Woodlands CI ANG/EP BN16 .. 68 F6
    BIL RH14 * 124 A7
    CRAWE RH10 .... 32 A2
    HPPT/KEY BN6 .... 165 M5
    SALV BN13 .... 69 L4
Woodlands La CCH PO19 .... 6 C1
    HASM GU27 .... 109 J10
    LISS GU33 .... 116 E11
    RCCH PO18 .... 170 C7
Woodlands Pk ARUN BN18 * .. 87 L2
Woodlands Rd EGRIN RH19 .... 23 M5
    HWH RH16 .... 45 J5
    LHPTN BN17 .... 89 K5
    MSEA/BNM PO22 .... 86 A7
The Woodlands BOR GU35 .... 106 G8
    BRI BN1 .... 52 D8
Woodlands Wk BRIE/ROTT BN2 .. 97 J1
Woodland Wy BRI BN1 .... 76 E1
    SWTR RH13 .... 11 M2
Wood La HFD BN5 .... 163 L11
Woodlark Gdns EPSF GU31 .... 133 R6
Woodlea Rd SALV BN13 .... 12 A2
Woodleigh CI HAV PO9 .... 57 K2
Woodleigh Rd BURH RH15 .... 47 H5
Woodmancote La EMRTH PO10 .. 58 F1
Woodmancote Rd SALV BN13 .. 12 C1
Woodmans HI CRAWW RH11 .. 29 H8
Woodpecker CI BOR GU35 .... 106 G7
    HAV PO9 .... 57 J4
Woodpecker Crs BURH RH15 .. 47 G4
Woodpecker La
    PUL/STOR RH20 .... 160 B12
Woodpecker Rd PETW GU28 .. 139 L10
Woodpecker Wy CRAWE RH10 .. 32 B3
    SALV BN13 .... 70 B8
Wood Ride HWH RH16 .... 45 G6
Woodridge CI HWH RH16 .... 45 K6
Wood Rd GSHT GU26 .... 108 G3
Woodroyd Av HORL RH6 .... 14 E7
Woodroyd Gdns HORL RH6 .... 14 E8
Woodruff Av HOVE BN3 .... 76 A3
Woodsedge WVILLE PO7 .... 168 B12
Woods Hill CI EGRIN RH19 .... 23 J7
Woods Hill La EGRIN RH19 .... 23 J7
Woodside MSEA/BNM PO22 .... 65 G7
    SWTR RH13 .... 37 G5
Woodside Av BRI BN1 .... 76 C3
Woodside CI BOR GU35 .... 106 G6
    PUL/STOR RH20 .... 160 B11
    SWTR RH13 .... 145 J9

Woodside Crs BOR GU35 .... 106 G6
    HORL RH6 .... 15 M6
Woodside Pk BOR GU35 .... 106 G6
Woodside Rd CRAWE RH10 .... 29 L1
    MFD/CHID GU8 .... 110 F5
    SALV BN13 .... 12 D2
Woodsland CI HPPT/KEY BN6 .. 165 M5
Woodsland Rd HPPT/KEY BN6 .. 165 M5
Woodslands HORL RH6 .... 15 G5
Woodstock CI EGRIN RH19 .... 23 H7
    MSEA/BNM PO22 .... 2 B1
Woodstock Av HORN PO8 .... 168 B4
Woodstock La CRAWE RH10 .. 36 C4
Woodstock Gdns BOGR PO21 .. 103 L3
Woodstock Rd HAV PO9 .... 56 D3
Wood St BOGR PO21 .... 2 A8
    EGRIN RH19 .... 23 J8
Woods Wy FERR BN12 .... 92 B2
Woodview CI BRI BN1 .... 53 J7
Woodview SHOR BN43 .... 73 L4
Woodview Ct SHOR BN43 * 73 L4
Woodville Rd HAV PO9 .... 56 C3
Woodwards CRAWW RH11 .... 29 G8
Woodwards CI SELS PO20 .... 47 G8
Woolbeding La MIDH GU29 .... 136 E6
Woolborough CI CRAWE RH10 .. 9 L1
Woolborough La CRAWE RH10 .. 19 L8
    CRAWE RH10 * 29 M1
    REDH RH1 .... 15 L1
Woolborough Rd CRAWE RH10 .. 8 F2
Wooldridge Wk LHPTN BN17 .. 88 C4
Wool La MIDH GU29 .... 137 J10
Woolmer CI HAV PO9 .... 169 J12
Woolmer Hill Rd HASM GU27 .. 108 F10
Woolmer La LIPH GU30 .... 107 R9
Woolmer Rd LISS GU33 .... 116 C2
Woolmer St EMRTH PO10 .... 57 M1
Woolner Av PSF GU32 .... 133 N5
The Woolstaplers CCH PO19 .... 6 D4
Woolston Rd HAV PO9 .... 168 D11
Woolven CI BURH RH15 .... 46 D8
Woolvens Rw HFD BN5 .... 163 L4
Wophams La SELS PO20 .... 83 H6
Worcester Ct WTHG BN11 * 12 A7
Worcester Rd CCH PO19 .... 61 L4
    CRAWE RH10 .... 29 K7
Worcester Vls HOVE BN3 .... 75 H6
Wordsworth CI CRAWE RH10 .. 30 A1
Wordsworth Gdns
    MSEA/BNM PO22 .... 87 J7
Wordsworth PI HORS RH12 .... 36 D2
Wordsworth Ri EGRIN RH19 .... 23 H8
Wordsworth Rd WTHG BN11 .. 12 D6
Wordsworth St HOVE BN3 .... 75 M6
Worms La MSEA/BNM PO22 .... 87 H6
Worsted La EGRIN RH19 .... 34 A2
Worthing Rd ANG/EP BN16 .... 90 B7
    HORS RH12 .... 10 B7
    LHPTN BN17 .... 89 K2
    SWTR RH13 .... 10 A9
    SWTR RH13 .... 125 Q11
    SWTR RH13 .... 143 R2
    SWTR RH13 .... 161 P2
Worthing Road Picts HI
    SWTR RH13 .... 126 A1
Worth Park Av CRAWE RH10 .. 30 B2
Worth Rd CRAWE RH10 .... 30 B3
Worth Wy CRAWE RH10 .... 30 B4
    CRAWE RH10 .... 30 B4
Worthy Ct HAV PO9 * 169 J12
Wray CI EGRIN RH19 .... 34 C3
Wraysbury Park Dr
    EMRTH PO10 .... 58 A1
Wren CI HORS RH12 .... 36 C2
    PUL/STOR RH20 .... 159 J3
Wren Ct CRAWE RH10 * 29 K6
Wren Crs MSEA/BNM PO22 .... 86 A7
Wrenfield PI BOGR PO21 .... 2 C8
Wren St CRAWE RH10 .... 32 B4
Wrexham Gv HORN PO8 .... 150 C10
Wright CI CRAWE RH10 * 30 A7
Wrotham HI MFD/CHID GU8 .. 111 R6
Wroxham Wk CRAWE RH10 .... 30 A5
Wroxham Wy MSEA/BNM PO22 .. 3 K1
Wyatt CI BIL RH14 .... 141 J1
Wyatts La RHWH RH17 .... 131 N4
Wyberlye Rd BURH RH15 .... 46 F5
Wychperry Rd HWH RH16 .... 45 G4
Wychwood BIL RH14 .... 122 E2
Wychwood CI BOGR PO21 .... 103 K4
Wychwood Gdns WTHG BN11 .. 94 A2
Wychwood Wk BOGR PO21 .... 103 K4
Wyde Feld BOGR PO21 .... 103 L3
Wye CI CRAWW RH11 .... 39 H1
Wyeford CI HAV PO9 .... 169 J11
Wyke Av WTHG BN11 .... 13 J6
Wykeham CI STEY/UB BN44 .... 48 C2
Wykeham Rd WTHG BN11 .... 12 E5
Wykeham Ter BRI BN1 * 4 C6
Wykeham Wy BURH RH15 .... 47 H7
Wyke La North
    MSEA/BNM PO22 .... 87 H8
Wykwood LIPH GU30 .... 118 A1
Wylde Green La LISS GU33 .... 116 D8
Wylds La PSF GU32 .... 133 K9
Wyncombe CI PUL/STOR RH20 .. 158 C2
Wyndham CI HORN PO8 .... 168 C5
Wyndham Lea
    PUL/STOR RH20 .... 159 R7
Wyndham Rd PETW GU28 .... 139 L10
Wyndham St BRIE/ROTT BN2 .. 5 H8
Wynlea CI CRAWE RH10 .... 31 M1
Wynnes Ms HOVE BN3 .... 75 M6
Wynnstay BURH RH15 * 47 G7
Wysemead HORL RH6 .... 15 H5
The Wyshe POY/PYE BN45 .... 165 K11
Wythering CI BOGR PO21 .... 102 E6
Wythwood HWH RH16 .... 45 H8
Wyvern CI SELS PO20 .... 63 K4
Wyvern Wy BURH RH15 .... 47 H6

Yaldhurst Ct HAV PO9 .... 169 J11
Yapton La ARUN BN18 .... 65 L5
Yapton Rd MSEA/BNM PO22 .. 65 J8
Yardlea CI HAV PO9 .... 169 J8
Yardley St BRI BN1 .... 4 F1
Yarmouth CI CRAWE RH10 .... 9 M7
Yarrow CI HORS RH12 .... 36 D4
Yately CI HAV PO9 .... 168 F12
Yattendon Rd HORL RH6 .... 15 G6
Yeoman Rd SALV BN13 .... 70 A8

Yeomans Acre BOGR PO21 .... 103 L2
Yeomans Fld RCCH PO18 .... 59 J4
Yeomans La LIPH GU30 .... 117 P1
Yeomans PI BOR GU35 .... 107 M4
Yeoman Wy SALV BN13 .... 92 A1
Yewens MFD/CHID GU8 .... 110 G4
Yew La EGRIN RH19 .... 23 G6
The Yews HORN PO8 .... 168 C2
Yew Tree CI HORL RH6 .... 14 F4
    MSEA/BNM PO22 .... 2 B1
Yewtree CI SWTR RH13 .... 145 K3
Yew Tree PI LISS GU33 .... 116 D9
Yew Tree Rd HORL RH6 .... 18 D2
Yoells Crs HORN PO8 .... 168 A3
Yoells La HORN PO8 .... 168 A3
York Av EGRIN RH19 .... 33 M1
    HOVE BN3 .... 4 A4
York Cha CCH PO19 .... 61 L3
York CI BOR GU35 .... 106 G7
    PSF GU32 .... 133 L6
    SWTR RH13 .... 11 K3
    SWTR RH13 .... 125 R12
York Gdns LHPTN BN17 .... 89 J4
York Gv BRI BN1 .... 4 E3
York HI BRI BN1 .... 4 E3
Yorkhurst HI RCCH PO18 .... 155 J12
York PI BRI BN1 .... 4 F4
York Rd BOGR PO21 .... 2 E7
    BURH RH15 .... 46 C7
    CCH PO19 .... 7 J6
    CRAWE RH10 .... 29 K7
    HOVE BN3 .... 4 A6
    LHPTN BN17 .... 89 J4
    SELS PO20 .... 181 L8
    WTHG BN11 .... 13 J6
York Vls BRI BN1 .... 4 E3
Yorkwood LISS GU33 .... 116 C9
Youngsmere CI BRI BN1 .... 53 G7

Zeus La WVILLE PO7 .... 56 A2
Zion Gdns BRI BN1 .... 4 D6

36 On the Quay Hotel
  EMRTH PO10 .... 58 A5
Abbotsford Special School
  BURH RH15 .... 46 E3
ACE Primary Department
  BRI BN1 .... 76 D3
Aids Positive Underground
  Theatre
  BRIE/ROTT BN2 .... 5 J7
Albourne CE Primary School
  HPPT/KEY BN6 .... 164 D3
Aldingbourne Primary
  School
  SELS PO20 .... 64 C7
Aldrington House Hospital
  HOVE BN3 .... 75 L7
Alexander House Hotel
  CRAWE RH10 .... 32 B4
Alias Hotel Seattle
  BRIE/ROTT BN2 .... 96 E2
All England Jumping Course
  RHWH RH17 .... 146 E9
Allman Business Park
  SELS PO20 .... 83 G7
All Saints CE Primary
  School
  HORS RH12 .... 36 E3
Amberley CE First School
  ARUN BN18 .... 176 F2
Amberley Railway
  ARUN BN18 .... 176 E4
Amberley Working
  Museum
  ARUN BN18 .... 176 E5
Amesbury School
  GSHT GU26 .... 108 H8
Amey Industrial Estate
  PSF GU32 .... 133 M6
AMF Bowling
  CRAWW RH11 .... 8 E3
  WTHG BN11 .... 13 G7
The Angel Hotel
  MIDH GU29 .... 137 J9
Aquarena Swimming Pool
  WTHG BN11 .... 13 K6
Archway Theatre
  HORL RH6 .... 14 F7
The Arden Foot & Health
  Clinic
  BRIE/ROTT BN2 .... 4 F7
Ardingly College & Ardingly
  College Junior &
  Pre-Preparatory School
  RHWH RH17 .... 130 C3
Ardington Hotel
  WTHG BN11 .... 13 J6
Ardmore School
  WTHG BN11 .... 13 G5
Arthur Griffiths Clinic
  BOGR PO21 .... 102 F6
Arts Centre
  HAV PO9 .... 57 G4
Arun Business Park
  MSEA/BNM PO22 .... 3 G2
Arundale Preparatory School
  PUL/STOR RH20 .... 159 L3
Arundel Castle
  ARUN BN18 .... 67 G2
Arundel CE Primary School
  ARUN BN18 .... 66 D3
Arundel & District Hospital
  ARUN BN18 .... 66 F2
Arundel FC
  ARUN BN18 .... 67 H2
Arun Fitzalan Swimming Pool
  ARUN BN18 .... 67 H3
Arun House
  HORS RH12 .... 10 E4
Arun Indoor Bowling Club
  BOGR PO21 .... 103 M2
Arun Leisure Centre
  MSEA/BNM PO22 .... 3 J3
Arun Retail Park
  MSEA/BNM PO22 .... 86 D7
Arunside Primary School
  HORS RH12 .... 125 R3
Arun Vale Infant School
  LHPTN BN17 .... 89 J3
Arun Yacht Club
  LHPTN BN17 .... 89 J5
Ashdown Forest Golf Club
  FROW RH18 .... 34 E8
Ashdown Forest
  Health Centre
  FROW RH18 .... 34 D6
The Ashdown Hospital
  HWH RH16 .... 45 G3
Ashdown House School
  FROW RH18 .... 35 J5
Ash Grove Industrial Park
  MSEA/BNM PO22 .... 86 C6
Ashington CE Primary School
  PUL/STOR RH20 .... 161 J8
Ashton Park School
  ANG/EP BN16 .... 90 E4
  PUL/STOR RH20 .... 141 P8
Ashurst CE Primary School
  STEY/UB BN44 .... 162 C4
Ashurst Wood Primary School
  EGRIN RH19 .... 34 D3
Ashwyn Business Centre
  BURH RH15 .... 46 F4
Assembly Hall
  WTHG BN11 .... 13 G5
Astra Business Centre
  REDH RH1 .... 14 F2
Atlas Medical Centre
  HORL RH6 .... 19 M2
Avalon Health Centre
  ANG/EP BN16 .... 90 C3
The Avenue Surgery
  BURH RH15 .... 46 E7
Aviation Trading Estate
  HPPT/KEY BN6 .... 164 D6
Avisford Park Golf Club
  ARUN BN18 .... 65 K4
Avocet Industrial Estate
  BURH RH15 .... 46 D7
Avocet Trading Estate
  BURH RH15 .... 46 D7
Balcombe CE Primary School
  RHWH RH17 .... 40 E7
Baldwins Hill Primary School
  EGRIN RH19 .... 23 H6
Balfour J & I School
  BRI BN1 .... 76 E2

Baliffscourt Hotel & Health Spa
  LHPTN BN17 .... 88 D7
Band Stand
  HORS RH12 .... 10 D6
Barncroft Infant School
  HAV PO9 .... 56 E1
Barncroft Junior School
  HAV PO9 .... 56 D1
Barnham Medical Centre
  MSEA/BNM PO22 .... 65 G6
Barnham Primary School
  MSEA/BNM PO22 .... 65 G7
Bartons Infant School
  MSEA/BNM PO22 .... 86 A7
Beachcroft Hotel
  MSEA/BNM PO22 .... 3 K6
Beach Hotel
  WTHG BN11 .... 12 E8
Beacon Hill CP School
  GSHT GU26 .... 108 F3
Beaver Industrial Estate
  LIPH GU30 .... 117 R3
Bedales School
  PSF GU32 .... 133 N4
Bellerbys College
  HOVE BN3 .... 76 B6
Bell Tower Industrial Estate
  BRIE/ROTT BN2 .... 96 E1
Benfield Junior School
  PTSD BN41 .... 75 H5
Ben Turner Industrial Estate
  CCH PO19 .... 7 M4
Berkeley Hotel
  WTHG BN11 .... 12 F7
Best Western Roundabout
  Hotel
  PUL/STOR RH20 .... 159 R7
Bevendean Primary School
  BRIE/ROTT BN2 .... 77 L3
Bewbush Community Primary
  School
  CRAWW RH11 .... 28 D6
Bewbush Leisure Centre
  CRAWW RH11 .... 28 E7
Bewbush Medical Centre
  CRAWW RH11 .... 28 D6
Bewhurst County First School
  CRAWW RH11 .... 28 E6
Bidbury J & I School
  HAV PO9 .... 56 E3
Bignor Roman Villa & Museum
  PUL/STOR RH20 .... 157 N11
Billingshurst Junior School
  BIL RH14 .... 142 A2
  SALV BN13 .... 69 J5
Binswood View Business
  Centre
  BOR GU35 .... 106 A3
Birches Industrial Estate
  EGRIN RH19 .... 22 F6
The Birch Hotel
  RHWH RH17 .... 45 K6
Birchwood Grove Primary
  School
  BURH RH15 .... 47 H8
Birdham Primary School
  SELS PO20 .... 82 D8
Bishop Luffa School
  CCH PO19 .... 61 J6
Bishops Palace
  CCH PO19 .... 6 C4
Bishop Tufnell CE J & I School
  MSEA/BNM PO22 .... 87 H7
Black Down (NT)
  HASM GU27 .... 120 A3
Blackmoor Golf Club
  BOR GU35 .... 106 D8
Blackthorns Primary School
  HWH RH16 .... 45 K3
Blackwell Primary School
  EGRIN RH19 .... 23 K6
Blatchington Mill School
  HOVE BN3 .... 75 M3
Blatchington Mill School &
  Sixth Form College
  HOVE BN3 .... 75 M4
Bleach's Yard Industrial
  Estate
  LIPH GU30 .... 117 R3
Bluebell Railway
  EGRIN RH19 .... 42 E5
  RHWH RH17 .... 131 K6
  UCK TN22 .... 131 Q11
Bognor Lawn Tennis Club
  BOGR PO21 .... 103 M1
Bognor Regis Community
  College
  BOGR PO21 .... 85 M8
Bognor Regis Golf Club
  MSEA/BNM PO22 .... 86 F7
Bognor Regis Museum
  BOGR PO21 .... 2 D8
The Bognor Regis Retail Park
  MSEA/BNM PO22 .... 86 C6
Bognor Regis Town FC
  BOGR PO21 .... 103 M2
Bognor Regis Yacht Club
  BOGR PO21 .... 2 B9
Bognor RFC
  BOGR PO21 .... 2 B3
Bohunt Manor
  LIPH GU30 .... 117 Q2
Bohunt School
  LIPH GU30 .... 117 Q1
Bolney CE Primary School
  RHWH RH17 .... 146 D3
Bolney Grange
  Industrial Park
  RHWH RH17 .... 146 G7
Bookers Vinyard
  RHWH RH17 .... 146 C2
Booth Museum of Natural
  History
  HOVE BN3 .... 76 C5
Borde Hill Garden
  HWH RH16 .... 129 R7
Bordon Infant School
  BOR GU35 .... 106 F5
Bordon Trading Estate
  BOR GU35 .... 106 D4
Borers Business Park
  CRAWE RH10 .... 21 H6
Bosham Abbey
  RCCH PO18 .... 81 M1
Bosham CP School
  RCCH PO18 .... 60 B8

Bosham FC
  RCCH PO18 .... 60 B8
Bosham Sailing Club
  RCCH PO18 .... 81 M1
Bosmere Junior School
  HAV PO9 .... 57 G4
Bourne Community College
  EMRTH PO10 .... 58 D4
Bowling Alley
  BRIE/ROTT BN2 .... 96 E2
Boxgrove CE Primary School
  RCCH PO18 .... 63 J1
Bramber Castle
  STEY/UB BN44 .... 48 E3
Bramber Road First School
  SALV BN13 .... 71 K7
Brambletye School
  EGRIN RH19 .... 34 B4
Brantridge School
  RHWH RH17 .... 128 F4
Braybon Business Park
  BURH RH15 .... 46 D7
Breaky Bottom Vineyard
  LEWES BN7 .... 79 M6
Bridge Industrial Estate
  HORL RH6 .... 15 G6
Bridge Medical Centre
  CRAWE RH10 .... 9 M3
Bridge Road Business Park
  HWH RH16 .... 45 H2
Brighton Business Centre
  BRI BN1 .... 4 F2
The Brighton Centre
  BRI BN1 .... 4 C7
Brighton College of
  Technology
  BRI BN1 .... 4 D1
  BRIE/ROTT BN2 .... 5 G3
Brighton County Court
  BRI BN1 .... 4 F6
Brighton Fishing Museum
  BRI BN1 .... 4 D8
Brighton General Hospital
  BRIE/ROTT BN2 .... 5 M3
Brighton & Hove Albion FC
  (Withdean Stadium)
  BRI BN1 .... 76 C2
Brighton & Hove Golf Club
  BRI BN1 .... 51 J6
Brighton & Hove Greyhound
  Stadium
  HOVE BN3 .... 75 M4
Brighton & Hove High School
  HOVE BN3 .... 76 B5
Brighton & Hove High School
  GDST
  BRI BN1 .... 4 E7
Brighton Hove & Sussex
  VI Form College
  HOVE BN3 .... 4 A1
Brighton Media Centre
  BRI BN1 .... 4 D7
Brighton Museum & Art Gallery
  BRI BN1 .... 4 F6
Brighton Pier
  BRIE/ROTT BN2 .... 4 F9
Brighton Racecourse
  BRIE/ROTT BN2 .... 77 K6
Brighton RFC
  BRI BN1 .... 52 A7
Brighton Youth Centre
  BRIE/ROTT BN2 .... 5 H7
British Engineerium-Museum
  of Steam & Mechanical
  Antiquities
  HOVE BN3 .... 76 A3
Broadbridge Business Centre
  RCCH PO18 .... 60 A6
Broadbridge Heath Retail
  Park
  HORS RH12 .... 125 P2
Broadbridge Heath Stadium
  HORS RH12 .... 125 P3
Broadfield East First School
  CRAWW RH11 .... 29 H7
Broadfield Health Centre
  CRAWW RH11 .... 29 G7
Broadlands Business Campus
  HORS RH12 .... 26 B5
  HORS RH12 .... 38 A1
Broadmarsh Business &
  Innovation Centre
  HAV PO9 .... 56 D5
Broadwater CE F & M School
  SALV BN13 .... 71 H8
Broadwater Industrial
  Estate
  SALV BN13 .... 71 L7
Broadwater Manor School
  SALV BN13 .... 71 J8
Broadwater & Worthing
  Cemetery
  SALV BN13 .... 71 H8
Brookers Road Industrial
  Estate
  BIL RH14 .... 142 B2
Brookfield Hotel
  EMRTH PO10 .... 57 L4
Brookham School
  LIPH GU30 .... 118 B3
Brooklands Trading Estate
  SALV BN13 .... 12 D3
The Brook School
  CRAWE RH10 .... 30 B6
Brookside Industrial Estate
  ANG/EP BN16 .... 90 B2
Broxhead Trading Estate
  BOR GU35 .... 107 J3
Buchan Country Park
  RCCH PO18 .... 28 D8
Buckingham Middle School
  SHOR BN43 .... 73 L5
Burgess Hill Clinic
  BURH RH15 .... 46 F7
Burgess Hill Golf Club
  BURH RH15 .... 46 D3
Burgess Hill School for Girls
  BURH RH15 .... 47 G7
Burgess Hill Town FC
  BURH RH15 .... 47 G4
Buriton Business Park
  EPSF GU31 .... 133 K10
Buriton Primary School
  EPSF GU31 .... 133 L12
Burleigh Infant School
  CRAWE RH10 .... 32 A1

Burstow Lodge Business
  Centre
  HORL RH6 .... 15 C8
Burstow Primary School
  HORL RH6 .... 15 M6
Bury CE First School
  PUL/STOR RH20 .... 176 A2
Butser Ancient Farm
  PSF GU32 .... 150 H8
Butter Market
  CCH PO19 .... 6 E4
Camelsdale County First
  School
  HASM GU27 .... 109 J12
Cardinal Newman School
  HOVE BN3 .... 76 C5
Carlton Hill Primary School
  BRIE/ROTT BN2 .... 5 G6
Carrier Business Park
  CRAWE RH10 .... 30 A2
Castledean School
  BRI BN1 .... 77 H3
Catherine Corbett Clinic
  HAV PO9 .... 57 G3
Catherington CE Controlled
  Infant School
  HORN PO8 .... 150 C12
Cavendish Hotel
  WTHG BN11 .... 12 F8
Centenary Industrial Estate
  BRI BN1 .... 77 G4
Central CE Junior School
  CCH PO19 .... 6 C3
Central Industrial Estate
  HAV PO9 .... 56 F4
Central Sussex College
  CRAWE RH10 .... 9 H4
Central Sussex College
  (East Grinstead Campus)
  EGRIN RH19 .... 23 K8
Centre of Arts
  CCH PO19 .... 6 E4
Chailey Heritage School
  RING/NEW BN8 .... 149 M6
Chailey School
  RING/NEW BN8 .... 167 N2
Chanctonbury Leisure
  Centre
  PUL/STOR RH20 .... 159 Q11
Chanctonbury Ring
  STEY/UB BN44 .... 179 L4
Chantry Industrial Estate
  PUL/STOR RH20 .... 178 B1
Chapel Royal
  BRI BN1 .... 4 E7
Charlwood Place
  HORL RH6 .... 18 D1
Charlwoods Industrial
  Estate
  EGRIN RH19 .... 23 K6
Charlwood Village Infant
  School
  HORL RH6 .... 18 E2
Charter Medical Centre
  HOVE BN3 .... 76 C6
Chartham Park Golf Club
  EGRIN RH19 .... 23 H3
Chase Community Hospital
  BOR GU35 .... 106 G3
Chesswood Middle School
  WTHG BN11 .... 13 K2
Chesworth Junior School
  SWTR RH13 .... 11 H4
Chichester Airfield
  RCCH PO18 .... 62 B1
Chichester Cathedral
  CCH PO19 .... 6 D5
Chichester College
  ANG/EP BN16 .... 90 E4
  CCH PO19 .... 6 B5
  PUL/STOR RH20 .... 141 N8
Chichester College of Arts,
  Science & Technology
  BOGR PO21 .... 2 E7
  CCH PO19 .... 6 E4
Chichester College of
  Technology
  CCH PO19 .... 6 B4
Chichester Crematorium
  CCH PO19 .... 7 K1
Chichester District Museum
  CCH PO19 .... 6 F4
Chichester Festival Theatre
  CCH PO19 .... 6 E1
Chichester Golf Club
  SELS PO20 .... 83 M8
Chichester High School
  for Boys
  CCH PO19 .... 6 D8
Chichester High School
  for Girls
  CCH PO19 .... 6 C8
  CCH PO19 .... 6 E7
Chichester Lawn Tennis &
  Squash Club
  CCH PO19 .... 6 F2
Chichester Nuffield Hospital
  CCH PO19 .... 61 L4
Chichester Priory Park Cricket
  & Hockey Club
  CCH PO19 .... 6 F3
Chichester RFC
  CCH PO19 .... 61 M5
Chichester Yacht Club
  SELS PO20 .... 82 E6
Chiddingfold Golf Club
  MFD/CHID GU8 .... 110 C8
Chidham Parochial Primary
  School
  RCCH PO18 .... 59 K7
Child Clinic
  BRIE/ROTT BN2 .... 4 F6
Christchurch Medical Centre
  HAV PO9 .... 57 K2
Christ's Hospital Infirmary
  SWTR RH13 .... 125 P7
Christ's Hospital School
  SWTR RH13 .... 125 N8
The Christ's Hospital Sports
  Centre
  SWTR RH13 .... 125 N7
Churchers College
  EPSF GU31 .... 133 P5
Churchers College Junior
  Department
  PSF GU32 .... 133 M6

Churchill Square Shopping
  Centre
  BRI BN1 .... 4 C7
Cissbury Ring
  SALV BN13 .... 179 L12
Cisswood House Hotel
  SWTR RH13 .... 127 K6
City Business Centre
  CCH PO19 .... 6 E7
  SWTR RH13 .... 10 E7
The City Business Centre
  CRAWW RH11 .... 19 J7
City College of Brighton
  & Hove
  BRI BN1 .... 4 F4
City Fields Business Park
  SELS PO20 .... 63 J3
Clair Hall Cinema
  HWH RH16 .... 45 H4
Clanfield Junior School
  HORN PO8 .... 150 C6
Clapham & Patching CE
  Primary School
  SALV BN13 .... 69 K4
Clarence Road School
  SWTR RH13 .... 10 F7
Clarks Industrial Estate
  HOVE BN3 .... 76 A5
Clayton Tunnel
  POY/PYE BN45 .... 165 K10
Clayton Windmills
  HPPT/KEY BN6 .... 165 M10
The Clockhouse Business
  Centre
  MIDH GU29 .... 137 J9
Coldean Primary School
  BRI BN1 .... 53 J6
Colgate Primary School
  SWTR RH13 .... 38 B3
Colhook Industrial Park
  PETW GU28 .... 121 J12
The College of Richard Collyer
  HORS RH12 .... 10 E2
The College of St Barnabas
  LING RH7 .... 23 L1
Comfort Inn
  LHPTN BN17 .... 67 J5
Community & Adult Education
  Centre
  HORL RH6 .... 14 D6
Community Mental Health
  Centre
  BURH RH15 .... 46 F5
Compton & Up Marden CE
  School
  RCCH PO18 .... 152 C11
Conifers School
  MIDH GU29 .... 137 K8
Connaught Theatre & Cinema
  WTHG BN11 .... 13 H5
Conway Court Clinic
  HOVE BN3 .... 76 A5
Coombe Road Primary School
  BRIE/ROTT BN2 .... 77 J4
The Copthorne Business Centre
  CRAWE RH10 .... 21 G6
Copthorne CE Junior School
  CRAWE RH10 .... 21 G6
Copthorne Fairway Infant
  School
  CRAWE RH10 .... 21 G6
Copthorne Golf Club
  CRAWE RH10 .... 21 H6
Copthorne Hotel
  CRAWE RH10 .... 20 F7
Copthorne Hotel & Resort
  Effingham Park
  CRAWE RH10 .... 21 L5
Copthorne Junior School
  CRAWE RH10 .... 21 G6
Copthorne Preparatory School
  CRAWE RH10 .... 21 K6
Copthorne Squash Club
  CRAWE RH10 .... 20 F7
Corn Exchange Theatre
  BRI BN1 .... 4 E6
Cornfield School
  LHPTN BN17 .... 89 K2
Cosmic Cycle
  HORS RH12 .... 10 B6
Cottesmore Golf &
  Country Club
  CRAWW RH11 .... 38 D2
Cottesmore St Marys RC
  Primary School
  HOVE BN3 .... 76 C5
Cottesmore School
  CRAWW RH11 .... 38 E1
County Mall Shopping Centre
  CRAWE RH10 .... 9 G4
County Oak Retail Park
  CRAWW RH11 .... 19 J7
County Record Office
  CCH PO19 .... 6 C4
The Courtlands Hotel
  HOVE BN3 .... 76 B7
Court Meadow Special
  School
  RHWH RH17 .... 44 D1
Cowdray Park Golf Club
  MIDH GU29 .... 137 L8
Crawley College Annexe
  CRAWW RH11 .... 8 D2
Crawley Down CE School
  CRAWE RH10 .... 32 A1
Crawley Down Health Centre
  CRAWE RH10 .... 31 M1
Crawley Health Clinic
  CRAWW RH11 .... 9 G3
Crawley Hospital
  CRAWW RH11 .... 8 C3
The Crawley Lawn Tennis Club
  CRAWE RH10 .... 30 A1
Crawley Leisure Centre &
  Athletics Arena
  CRAWE RH10 .... 9 K5
Crawley Museum
  (Goffs Park House)
  CRAWW RH11 .... 8 B6
Crawley RFC
  CRAWW RH11 .... 18 F7
Crawley Town FC
  CRAWW RH11 .... 29 H7
The Crookhorn Community
  School
  WVILLE PO7 .... 56 A1

Crosspost Industrial Estate
RHWH RH17 .... 146 C4
Crouchers Country Hotel & Restaurant
SHOR BN43 .... 83 H5
Cyril Richings Business Centre
SHOR BN43 .... 74 A6
David Lloyd Health & Fitness Centre
BRIE/ROTT BN2 .... 96 D2
Davigdor Infant School
HOVE BN3 .... 76 C7
Davison CE High School for Girls
WTHG BN11 .... 13 M3
D-Day Museum
SHOR BN43 .... 73 J6
Deacon Trading Estate
SALV BN13 .... 71 L8
Dean Farm Golf Club
BOR GU35 .... 106 E1
Deepdene School
HOVE BN3 .... 75 J6
Dell Quay Sailing Club
SELS PO20 .... 82 F3
Denmans Garden
ARUN BN18 .... 64 D2
Denvale Trade Park
CRAWE RH10 .... 9 H5
Desmond Anderson Primary School
CRAWE RH10 .... 29 J7
The De Vere Grand Hotel
BRI BN1 .... 4 B7
Devil's Dyke
BRI BN1 .... 51 H2
Dharma School
BRI BN1 .... 52 F7
Ditcham Park School
EPSF GU31 .... 151 N5
Ditchling St Margarets CEP School
HPPT/KEY BN6 .... 166 J1
Ditton Place School
RHWH RH17 .... 128 H1
Doll House Museum
PETW GU28 .... 139 L10
Dolphin House Clinic for Adults
BRI BN1 .... 4 E6
Dolphin Industrial Estate
SHOR BN43 .... 74 C4
Dolphin Leisure Centre
HWH RH16 .... 45 G3
Dome Cinema
WTHG BN11 .... 13 J7
Dorset House School
PUL/STOR RH20 .... 176 C2
Downlands Business Park
SALV BN13 .... 71 K5
Downlands School
HPPT/KEY BN6 .... 165 N6
Downsbrook Middle School
SALV BN13 .... 71 K8
Downsbrook Trading Estate
SALV BN13 .... 71 K7
Downs Crematorium
BRIE/ROTT BN2 .... 77 J5
Downs Infant School
BRI BN1 .... 76 F5
Downs Junior School
BRI BN1 .... 76 F4
Downs Park School
PTSD BN41 .... 75 G3
Downview CP School
MSEA/BNM PO22 .... 3 K1
Drayton House
SELS PO20 .... 62 E8
Driving Test Centre
CRAWW RH11 .... 8 D4
The Dr Jan De Winter Clinic for Cancer Prevention Advice
BRI BN1 .... 4 E7
Duke of York's Premier Picture House Cinema
BRI BN1 .... 4 E2
Dunannie School
PSF GU32 .... 133 M3
Duncton CE First School
PETW GU28 .... 156 G6
Dunhurst School
PSF GU32 .... 133 M3
Dunnings Squash Club
EGRIN RH19 .... 33 K3
Dunsfold Aerodrome
CRAN GU6 .... 112 E4
Durrington First School
SALV BN13 .... 70 D6
Durrington Health Centre
SALV BN13 .... 70 C7
Durrington High School
SALV BN13 .... 70 D8
Eagle Trading Estate
BIL RH14 .... 142 A2
Easebourne CE Primary School
MIDH GU29 .... 137 L7
East Brighton Golf Club
BRIE/ROTT BN2 .... 96 E1
East Court
EGRIN RH19 .... 23 L7
Eastgate CE Primary School
SELS PO20 .... 64 D6
East Grinstead Health Clinic
EGRIN RH19 .... 23 K7
East Grinstead Sports Club
EGRIN RH19 .... 33 H4
Eastmead Industrial Estate
RCCH PO18 .... 172 B10
East Preston CP School
ANG/EP BN16 .... 90 F3
East Street Medical Centre
LHPTN BN17 .... 89 J4
East Wittering Business Centre
SELS PO20 .... 99 M5
East Wittering CP School
SELS PO20 .... 99 L6
East Worthing Industrial Estate
SALV BN13 .... 71 L8
Eaton Place Surgery
BRIE/ROTT BN2 .... 5 M9
Ebernoe Common National Nature Reserve
PETW GU28 .... 121 L10

The Edge Sports Centre
HASM GU27 .... 108 C9
Edward Bryant CP School
BOGR PO21 .... 2 E6
Effingham Park Golf Club
CRAWE RH10 .... 21 L5
The Elizabeth Johnson Organisation
LIPH GU30 .... 107 L9
Ellscott Park
SELS PO20 .... 100 E1
Elm Grove County First School
WTHG BN11 .... 92 E2
Elm Grove Primary School
BRIE/ROTT BN2 .... 5 K2
Emerson College
FROW RH18 .... 35 G6
Emsworth Museum
EMRTH PO10 .... 58 A5
Emsworth Primary School
EMRTH PO10 .... 57 M4
English Bowling Association
WTHG BN11 .... 13 K5
English Martyr Catholic Primary School
FERR BN12 .... 70 C8
Enterprise Industrial Estate
HORN PO8 .... 168 D1
Environment Agency
WTHG BN11 .... 13 H6
Estcots CP School
EGRIN RH19 .... 23 M8
Evolution Health Centre
BRI BN1 .... 4 B5
Fairfield Infant School
HAV PO9 .... 57 H3
Fairfield Medical Centre
PETW GU28 .... 139 L10
Fairlight Primary School
BRIE/ROTT BN2 .... 5 J1
Fairway Trading Estate
BRIE/ROTT BN2 .... 77 K1
Falmer High School
BRI BN1 .... 53 M8
Farlington School
HORS RH12 .... 115 L11
Farney Close School
RHWH RH17 .... 146 E3
Faygate Business Centre
HORS RH12 .... 27 L8
Felbridge Primary School
EGRIN RH19 .... 22 E5
Felpham Community College
MSEA/BNM PO22 .... 3 K2
Felpham & Middleton Health Centre
MSEA/BNM PO22 .... 87 J8
Felpham Sailing Club
MSEA/BNM PO22 .... 3 L6
Fernhurst Primary School
HASM GU27 .... 119 L7
Ferring CE Primary School
FERR BN12 .... 91 L3
Ferring FC
FERR BN12 .... 91 K3
Field Place First School
FERR BN12 .... 92 C1
Findon Manor Hotel
SALV BN13 .... 178 H11
Firsland Park Estate
HPPT/KEY BN6 .... 146 A12
Fishbourne CE Primary School
CCH PO19 .... 61 G7
Fishbourne Roman Palace
CCH PO19 .... 61 G7
Fishers Farm Park
BIL RH14 .... 123 L11
Fishersgate First School
PTSD BN41 .... 74 F6
Fishing Club House
FROW RH18 .... 34 A6
Fittleworth CE First School
PUL/STOR RH20 .... 158 B2
Flansham Business Centre
MSEA/BNM PO22 .... 87 G6
Flora McDonald Junior School
LHPTN BN17 .... 89 H3
The Fold School
HOVE BN3 .... 75 J6
Fonthill Lodge School
EGRIN RH19 .... 33 H1
Fontigarry Farm Business Park
REIG RH2 .... 14 B1
Fontwell Medical Centre
ARUN BN18 .... 64 F2
Fontwell Park Racecourse
ARUN BN18 .... 64 E3
Ford Airfield Industrial Estate
ARUN BN18 .... 88 A2
Ford Lane Business Park
ARUN BN18 .... 88 C1
Fordwater Special School
CCH PO19 .... 61 M4
Forest Row Business Park
FROW RH18 .... 34 E6
Forest Row CE Infant School
FROW RH18 .... 34 E7
Forest Row CE Primary School
FROW RH18 .... 34 E7
The Forest School
SWTR RH13 .... 11 K8
The Forest Shopping Centre
BOR GU35 .... 106 H6
Forge Wood Industrial Estate
CRAWE RH10 .... 20 A7
Forum House Business Centre
CCH PO19 .... 6 F5
Fowlers Business Centre
SWTR RH13 .... 145 K4
Foxbridge Golf Club
BIL RH14 .... 122 D4
French Business Communications
PUL/STOR RH20 .... 160 D11
Freshbrook County First School
LAN/SOMP BN15 .... 72 D7
Freshfield Industrial Estate
BRIE/ROTT BN2 .... 5 K6
Friary Hall
CRAWE RH10 .... 8 F5
Friends of Arundel Castle CC
ARUN BN18 .... 66 F1
Front Lawn Junior School
HAV PO9 .... 168 G12

Funpark
LHPTN BN17 .... 89 J6
Funtington CP School
RCCH PO18 .... 60 A2
Garcia Trading Estate
SALV BN13 .... 92 E2
Gardner Arts Centre Cinema
BRI BN1 .... 53 M6
The Gattons Infant School
BURH RH15 .... 46 D6
Gatwick Gate Industrial Estate
HORL RH6 .... 19 K4
Gatwick Industrial Estate
HORL RH6 .... 18 E3
Gatwick Manor Golf Club
CRAWE RH10 .... 19 K6
Gatwick Medical Centre
HORL RH6 .... 20 A2
Gatwick Moat House Hotel
HORL RH6 .... 14 D8
Gatwick Park Hospital
HORL RH6 .... 14 D7
Gatwick Worth Hotel
CRAWE RH10 .... 30 E2
Gemini Business Centre
HOVE BN3 .... 75 M5
Genesis Business Centre
SWTR RH13 .... 11 J3
George Gale & Co Brewery
HORN PO8 .... 168 E2
George II Statue
BRI BN1 .... 4 E6
Georgian Gardens CP School
ANG/EP BN16 .... 90 C3
Georgian House Business Centre
BRIE/ROTT BN2 .... 4 F7
Georgian House Hotel
HASM GU27 .... 109 N10
Gerald Daniel Sailing Club
RCCH PO18 .... 81 K3
Gerrard House Business Centre
ANG/EP BN16 .... 90 E3
Gerston Business Park
PUL/STOR RH20 .... 177 R1
Ghyll House Farm Estate
SWTR RH13 .... 126 C8
Gilmans Industrial Estate
BIL RH14 .... 142 A3
The Glade Infant School
BOGR PO21 .... 85 M8
Glebe Middle School
STHW BN42 .... 74 C6
Glenhurst School
HAV PO9 .... 57 H4
Glenwood School
EMRTH PO10 .... 57 M4
Goldstone Primary School
HOVE BN3 .... 75 K4
Goldstone Retail Park
HOVE BN3 .... 76 A5
Goodwood Country Park
RCCH PO18 .... 173 L5
Goodwood Motor Circuit
RCCH PO18 .... 62 C2
Goodwood Racecourse
RCCH PO18 .... 173 J6
Gordon Centre
BOGR PO21 .... 2 C7
Goring CE First School
FERR BN12 .... 92 B3
Goring CC
FERR BN12 .... 91 M3
Gossops Green Clinic
CRAWW RH11 .... 28 E5
Gossops Green Community Primary School
CRAWW RH11 .... 28 F4
Graffham First School
PETW GU28 .... 156 A7
The Grange Leisure Centre
MIDH GU29 .... 136 H10
Granville Hotel
BRI BN1 .... 4 B7
Gravetye Manor Hotel
EGRIN RH19 .... 42 D1
Graylingwell Hospital
CCH PO19 .... 61 M4
Grayshott CE Primary School
GSHT GU26 .... 108 E6
Grayshott Clinic
GSHT GU26 .... 108 E5
Grayswood CE Aided Infant School
HASM GU27 .... 109 Q7
Great Ballard School
RCCH PO18 .... 174 C10
Greatham Primary School
LISS GU33 .... 116 C3
Great Walstead School
HWH RH16 .... 131 J11
Green Field Effective Education
EGRIN RH19 .... 23 J8
Greenfields School
FROW RH18 .... 34 B8
Greenway School
HORS RH12 .... 10 A3
Greywell Shopping Centre
HAV PO9 .... 168 G12
Guildbourne Shopping Centre
WTHG BN11 .... 13 J6
The Guildhall
CCH PO19 .... 6 F3
Halsford Park Primary School
EGRIN RH19 .... 23 G7
Ham Bridge Trading Estate
SALV BN13 .... 93 M1
Hambrook Business Centre
RCCH PO18 .... 59 J1
Ham Business Centre
SHOR BN43 .... 73 M6
Hamilton Lodge School
BRIE/ROTT BN2 .... 5 L7
Ham Manor Golf Club
ANG/EP BN16 .... 90 C1
Hammerwood Park
EGRIN RH19 .... 25 H7
Hampers Common Industrial Estate
PETW GU28 .... 139 L7
Hamsey Primary School
RING/NEW BN8 .... 167 R9

Handcross Park School
RHWH RH17 .... 39 J7
Handcross Primary School
RHWH RH17 .... 39 H8
Hangdown Mead Business Park
EGRIN RH19 .... 42 F4
Hangleton County J & I School
HOVE BN3 .... 75 K3
Hapstead Business Centre
RHWH RH17 .... 130 E1
Harbour Park
LHPTN BN17 .... 89 J6
Harlands Primary School
HWH RH16 .... 45 G2
Haslemere Hall
HASM GU27 .... 109 M10
Haslemere Hospital & Health Centre
HASM GU27 .... 109 N10
Haslemere Museum
HASM GU27 .... 109 N10
Hassocks Golf Club
HPPT/KEY BN6 .... 165 M4
Hassocks Infant School
HPPT/KEY BN6 .... 165 N5
Havant Business Centre
HAV PO9 .... 56 E5
Havant Leisure Centre
HAV PO9 .... 57 G2
Havant Museum
HAV PO9 .... 57 H4
Havant Retail Park
HAV PO9 .... 56 C4
Havant RFC
HAV PO9 .... 56 E3
Havant Sixth Form College
HAV PO9 .... 56 F2
Havant War Memorial Hospital
HAV PO9 .... 56 F3
Havant & Waterlooville FC
HAV PO9 .... 168 H12
The Hawthorns First School
SALV BN13 .... 70 B8
The Hawth Theatre, Cinema & Conference Complex
CRAWE RH10 .... 9 J5
Hayward Business Centre
HAV PO9 .... 57 J2
Haywards Heath College
HWH RH16 .... 45 G3
Haywards Heath FC
HWH RH16 .... 45 K5
Haywards Heath Golf Club
HWH RH16 .... 130 C8
Haywards Heath Hospital
HWH RH16 .... 44 F4
Haywards Heath RFC
RHWH RH17 .... 44 A1
Hazel Cottage Clinic
BRIE/ROTT BN2 .... 78 B5
Hazelwick School
CRAWE RH10 .... 29 M1
Hazelwood Trading Estate
SALV BN13 .... 13 L1
The Health Centre
BIL RH14 .... 123 J12
Heath Business Centre
REDH RH1 .... 15 G2
Heene CE First School
WTHG BN11 .... 12 E4
Heene Community Centre
WTHG BN11 .... 12 D6
The Henfield Business Park
HFD BN5 .... 163 M8
Henfield & District Leisure Centre
HFD BN5 .... 163 K3
Herbert Hone Clinic
BRIE/ROTT BN2 .... 5 M9
Herbert Shiner School
PETW GU28 .... 139 L10
The Herne Farm Leisure Centre
EPSF GU31 .... 133 P5
The Herne Junior School
EPSF GU31 .... 133 P5
Herons Dale School
SHOR BN43 .... 74 C4
The Herons Swimming & Fitness Centre
HASM GU27 .... 109 J11
Heron Way Primary School
SWTR RH13 .... 11 J7
Hertford Junior School
BRI BN1 .... 77 H2
Heyworth Primary School
HWH RH16 .... 45 H4
The Hickstead Hotel
RHWH RH17 .... 146 F8
Hickstead International Arena
RHWH RH17 .... 146 E9
Highcroft Industrial Estate
HORN PO8 .... 168 D1
Highdown Hill
FERR BN12 .... 69 K8
Highfield School
LIPH GU30 .... 118 B3
Hill Barn Golf Club
SALV BN13 .... 71 H5
Hillcrest School
SWTR RH13 .... 124 F1
Hill's Cemetery
HORS RH12 .... 125 Q3
Hillside Industrial Estate
HORN PO8 .... 168 D1
Hillside Special School
PTSD BN41 .... 74 F3
Hilltop Primary School
CRAWW RH11 .... 8 D8
Hilton Park Hotel
RHWH RH17 .... 44 D5
The Hindhead Golf Club
GSHT GU26 .... 108 E3
HM Prison
LEWES BN7 .... 55 M4
Hobbs Industrial Estate
LING RH7 .... 22 C2
Holbrook Primary School
HORS RH12 .... 36 C2
Holbrook Recreation Centre
HORS RH12 .... 36 D2
Holiday Village
BOGR PO21 .... 3 H6
Hollingbury Castle
BRI BN1 .... 77 H1

Hollingbury Industrial Estate
BRI BN1 .... 53 G6
Hollingbury Park Golf Club
BRI BN1 .... 77 G1
Hollybush Business Centre
HORL RH6 .... 20 E5
Hollycombe Primary School
LIPH GU30 .... 117 R9
Hollycombe Steam Collection
LIPH GU30 .... 118 B6
Hollywood Bowl
CRAWE RH10 .... 8 E1
Holmbush First School
SHOR BN43 .... 74 C4
Holmbush Industrial Estate
MIDH GU29 .... 136 H11
The Holme Primary School
BOR GU35 .... 107 L3
Holtye Golf Club
EDEN TN8 .... 25 L6
Holy Cross Hospital
HASM GU27 .... 109 J10
Holy Gate Cactus Gardens
PUL/STOR RH20 .... 161 K6
Holy Trinity CE (A) Primary School
RHWH RH17 .... 44 C2
Holy Trinity CE Primary School
SWTR RH13 .... 127 M6
The Holy Trinity CE School
CRAWW RH11 .... 28 C3
Home Farm Business Centre
BRI BN1 .... 77 J2
Honeybridge Park
SWTR RH13 .... 161 P4
Horley Anderson Centre
HORL RH6 .... 14 D6
Horley Health Centre
HORL RH6 .... 14 F6
Horley Infant School
HORL RH6 .... 14 F6
Horndean CE Junior School
HORN PO8 .... 168 D2
Horndean FC
HORN PO8 .... 168 D2
Horndean Health Centre
HORN PO8 .... 168 E2
Horndean Infant School
HORN PO8 .... 168 D2
Horndean Technology College
HORN PO8 .... 168 C2
Horsham Arts Centre
HORS RH12 .... 10 D3
Horsham Cricket & Sports Club
HORS RH12 .... 10 B8
Horsham FC
SWTR RH13 .... 10 E8
Horsham Golf & Fitness Club
SWTR RH13 .... 125 R7
Horsham Hospital
HORS RH12 .... 10 D3
Horsham Museum
HORS RH12 .... 10 C7
Horsham Trading Estate
SWTR RH13 .... 11 G3
Horsham YMCA FC
SWTR RH13 .... 10 E8
Horsted Keynes Industrial Estate
RHWH RH17 .... 131 L2
Hotel du Vin
BRI BN1 .... 4 D7
Hotel Ibis
CRAWE RH10 .... 19 K6
Hove Business Centre
HOVE BN3 .... 76 A5
Hove General Hospital
HOVE BN3 .... 75 M6
Hove Medical Centre
HOVE BN3 .... 75 K3
Hove Museum & Art Gallery
HOVE BN3 .... 75 M6
Hove Park School
HOVE BN3 .... 75 M4
Hove Polyclinic
HOVE BN3 .... 75 L4
Hove RFC
HOVE BN3 .... 76 A4
Hubbard School
EGRIN RH19 .... 23 K8
Huffwood Trading Estate
BIL RH14 .... 142 A2
SWTR RH13 .... 144 F10
Hulbert Junior School
WVILLE PO7 .... 168 A11
Hurstpierpoint College
HPPT/KEY BN6 .... 165 J1
Hurstpierpoint Preparatory School
HPPT/KEY BN6 .... 165 J1
Hurstwood Park Hospital
RHWH RH17 .... 45 K7
The Hyde Business Park
BRIE/ROTT BN2 .... 77 L4
Ifield Community College
CRAWW RH11 .... 28 F2
Ifield Golf & Country Club
CRAWW RH11 .... 28 C3
Iford & Kingston CE Primary School
LEWES BN7 .... 55 L8
Imberhorne Business Centre
EGRIN RH19 .... 23 J4
Imberhorne School
EGRIN RH19 .... 23 G7
The Imber Sports Centre
EGRIN RH19 .... 23 J6
Imperial Hotel
HOVE BN3 .... 76 B8
Independent Business Park
EGRIN RH19 .... 22 F6
Ingfield Manor School
BIL RH14 .... 124 B7
The Inglenook Hotel
BOGR PO21 .... 102 F3
Innkeeper's Lodge
BRI BN1 .... 52 D7
HAV PO9 .... 169 J9
Intensive School of English
BRI BN1 .... 4 D6
Itchenor Sailing Club
SELS PO20 .... 81 M6

Itchingfield Primary School
  SWTR RH13 .... 125 K7
Ivydene Industrial Estate
  EGRIN RH19 .... 34 C2
James Searle Industrial Estate
  HORS RH12 .... 11 H1
Jessie Younghusband Primary
School
  CCH PO19 .... 61 L5
Jikack Industrial Estate
  HPPT/KEY BN6 .... 46 A5
Jolesfield CE Primary School
  SWTR RH13 .... 144 F9
Jubilee Hall Clinic
  CRAWE RH10 .... 9 M3
K-Bis Theatre School
  BRI BN1 .... 76 D3
Kelvin Business Centre
  CRAWE RH10 .... 19 L8
Kemptown Brewery
  BRIE/ROTT BN2 .... 5 J8
Kenwood Business Park
  HAV PO9 .... 57 H2
King Alfred Leisure Centre
  HOVE BN3 .... 75 M8
King Business Centre
  HPPT/KEY BN6 .... 146 D12
King Edward VII Hospital
  MIDH GU29 .... 136 G3
Kingley Vale National Nature
Reserve
  RCCH PO18 .... 171 M8
Kings Court School
  HORN PO8 .... 150 B12
Kingsham Primary School
  CCH PO19 .... 6 F8
The Kings Hotel
  BRI BN1 .... 4 A7
Kingsmanor Community
College
  SHOR BN43 .... 74 B5
Kings Road Industrial Estate
  HASM GU27 .... 109 K11
Kingston Buci First School
  SHOR BN43 .... 74 A5
Kingsway Hotel
  WTHG BN11 .... 12 E7
King's Windmill
  SWTR RH13 .... 143 M9
The Knoll Business Centre
  HOVE BN3 .... 75 J5
Komedia
  BRI BN1 .... 4 E5
Laburnum Grove Junior School
  MSEA/BNM PO22 .... 2 C1
Lady Bee Marina Industrial
Estate
  PTSD BN41 .... 74 D7
Ladycross Business Park
  LING RH7 .... 24 B2
Lancastrian Infant School
  CCH PO19 .... 6 C2
Lancing Business Centre
  LAN/SOMP BN15 .... 72 B8
Lancing College
  LAN/SOMP BN15 .... 72 F3
Lancing College Chapel
  LAN/SOMP BN15 .... 73 G3
Lancing Health Centre
  LAN/SOMP BN15 .... 72 D7
Landerry Industrial Estate
  SELS PO20 .... 181 K5
The Lanes
  BRI BN1 .... 4 E7
Langley Green Primary School
  CRAWW RH11 .... 29 H1
Langrish House Hotel
  PSF GU32 .... 132 D6
Langrish Primary School
  PSF GU32 .... 132 H6
Langshott County Infant
School
  HORL RH6 .... 15 H4
Langshott Manor Hotel
  HORL RH6 .... 15 J4
The Lansdown Place Hotel
  HOVE BN3 .... 76 C8
The Laurels County First
School
  SALV BN13 .... 70 A7
Lavant CE Primary School
  RCCH PO18 .... 172 B11
Lavant House Rosemead
  RCCH PO18 .... 172 B12
The Lavinia Norfolk Centre
  ANG/EP BN16 .... 90 E2
Lawn Tennis Club
  HORL RH6 .... 14 E6
Lawson Hunt Industrial Park
  HORS RH12 .... 125 N1
Leechpool Lane Primary
School
  SWTR RH13 .... 11 M2
Leonardslee Lakes &
Gardens
  SWTR RH13 .... 127 M9
Lewes Victoria Hospital
  LEWES BN7 .... 55 M4
Lillies Caravan Park
  MSEA/BNM PO22 .... 65 H8
Limeburners
  BIL RH14 .... 141 P1
Limeburners (Camping)
  ANG/EP BN16 .... 68 F5
Limes Business Centre
  HORL RH6 .... 18 E3
Lindfield Junior School
  HWH RH16 .... 45 L2
Lindfield Medical Centre
  HWH RH16 .... 45 L1
Lindfield Primary School
  HWH RH16 .... 45 K2
Lineside Industrial Estate
  LHPTN BN17 .... 89 G3
Liphook CE Junior School
  LIPH GU30 .... 117 P1
Liphook Golf Club
  LIPH GU30 .... 117 P6
Liphook Infant School
  LIPH GU30 .... 117 P1
Liss Business Centre
  LISS GU33 .... 116 B8
Liss J & I School
  LISS GU33 .... 116 D10
Littlegreen School
  RCCH PO18 .... 152 B9

Littlehampton Community
School
  LHPTN BN17 .... 89 K3
Littlehampton Golf Club
  LHPTN BN17 .... 89 H5
Littlehampton Health Centre
  LHPTN BN17 .... 89 K5
Littlehampton Hospital
  LHPTN BN17 .... 89 K4
Littlehampton Museum
  LHPTN BN17 .... 89 K4
Littlehampton Swimming
Centre
  LHPTN BN17 .... 89 L6
Littlehampton Town FC
  LHPTN BN17 .... 89 J4
Littlehampton Tutorial Unit
  LHPTN BN17 .... 89 K3
Littlehaven Infant School
  HORS RH12 .... 36 E4
Littlemead School
  SELS PO20 .... 62 F6
Local Education Office
  HAV PO9 .... 57 G2
London-gatwick Airport
  HORL RH6 .... 19 L2
London Meed CP School
  BURH RH15 .... 46 F8
Longhill High School
  BRIE/ROTT BN2 .... 97 K1
Longley Industrial Estate
  BRI BN1 .... 4 E2
Longley Trading Estate
  CRAWE RH10 .... 9 G5
Look & Sea! Visitor Centre
  LHPTN BN17 .... 89 H5
Lowfield Heath Industrial
Estate
  HORL RH6 .... 19 K4
Loxwood Primary School
  BIL RH14 .... 122 H1
Ludshott Common (NT)
  GSHT GU26 .... 108 B6
Lurgashall Vineyard
  PETW GU28 .... 120 A9
Lyminster County Infant
School
  LHPTN BN17 .... 89 J2
Lyndhurst First School
  WTHG BN11 .... 13 M3
Lyons Farm Estate
  SWTR RH13 .... 125 K3
Lythe Hill Hotel & Spa
  HASM GU27 .... 110 A12
Mackley Industrial Estate
  HFD BN5 .... 163 L11
Maidenbower First & Middle
School
  CRAWE RH10 .... 30 C5
Maidenbower Junior School
  CRAWE RH10 .... 30 C5
Mainline Business Centre
  LISS GU33 .... 116 C9
Malt House Trading Estate
  SHOR BN43 .... 74 A6
Manhood Community College
  SELS PO20 .... 181 K5
Mannings Heath Golf Club
  SWTR RH13 .... 127 K2
Manor Farm Business Centre
  POY/PYE BN45 .... 164 E12
Manor Field Primary School
  BURH RH15 .... 47 H5
Manorfield Primary School
  HORL RH6 .... 14 E6
Manor Green College
  CRAWW RH11 .... 28 F1
Manor Green Primary School
  CRAWW RH11 .... 19 J7
Manor Hall County Middle
School
  STHW BN42 .... 74 D5
Manor Hall First School
  STHW BN42 .... 74 E6
Manor House Hospital
  HOVE BN3 .... 75 M6
Manor Sports Ground Pavilion
  SALV BN13 .... 71 J8
March CE Primary School
  RCCH PO18 .... 62 D4
Marchwell Industrial Estate
  CCH PO19 .... 62 A4
Marine Clinic
  BRIE/ROTT BN2 .... 97 M4
Market Cross
  CCH PO19 .... 6 E4
Marlborough Business Centre
  LAN/SOMP BN15 .... 94 B1
Marlipins Museum
  SHOR BN43 .... 73 K7
Marriott Goodwood Park
Hotel & Country Club
  RCCH PO18 .... 173 J11
Martlets Trading Estate
  FERR BN12 .... 92 B2
Matform Business Centre
  CCH PO19 .... 6 A6
Meadowbrook Industrial
Centre
  CRAWE RH10 .... 19 M8
Meadow Road Industrial
Estate
  WTHG BN11 .... 94 A1
The Meadow School
  BOR GU35 .... 107 H4
The Meads Primary School
  EGRIN RH19 .... 33 N4
Meath Green Infant School
  HORL RH6 .... 14 E4
Meath Green Junior School
  HORL RH6 .... 14 E4
Mechanical Music &
Doll Collection
  CCH PO19 .... 7 L2
The Medmerry Primary School
  SELS PO20 .... 181 K5
Meridian Shopping Centre
  HAV PO9 .... 57 G4
Michael Ayres Junior School
  BOGR PO21 .... 85 M8
Michael Hall School
  FROW RH18 .... 34 C8
Middle Park Medical Centre
  HAV PO9 .... 56 D1
Middle Street Primary School
  BRI BN1 .... 4 D7

Middleton Business Park
  MSEA/BNM PO22 .... 87 K7
Middleton Medical Centre
  MSEA/BNM PO22 .... 87 L8
Midhurst CE Primary School
  MIDH GU29 .... 136 G10
Midhurst Grammar School
  MIDH GU29 .... 136 H9
Midhurst Intermediate School
  MIDH GU29 .... 137 K7
Mid Sussex Golf Club
  HPPT/KEY BN6 .... 166 C4
Mile Oak Clinic
  PTSD BN41 .... 74 E2
Mile Oak Primary School
  PTSD BN41 .... 74 E2
Millais School
  SWTR RH13 .... 11 J6
Mill Chase Community School
  BOR GU35 .... 107 J6
Mill Green Industrial Estate
  BURH RH15 .... 45 H3
The Mill Primary School
  CRAWW RH11 .... 28 F3
Mill Road Industrial Estate
  PTSD BN41 .... 75 G6
The Millstream Hotel &
Restaurant
  EPSF PO18 .... 59 M8
Mill View Hospital
  HOVE BN3 .... 75 K4
Milton Mount Primary School
  CRAWE RH10 .... 30 A1
Minerva Studio Theatre Cinema
  CCH PO19 .... 6 E1
Minerva Theatre
  CCH PO19 .... 6 E1
Modern Mould Business Centre
  LHPTN BN17 .... 89 G3
Modern Moulds Business
Centre
  LAN/SOMP BN15 .... 94 B1
Montague Shopping Centre
  WTHG BN11 .... 13 H6
Montessori House for Children
  BRI BN1 .... 76 F4
Morley Street Health Centre
  BRIE/ROTT BN2 .... 5 G5
Moulscoomb Clinic
  BRIE/ROTT BN2 .... 77 K2
Moulsecoomb Health Clinic
  BRIE/ROTT BN2 .... 77 K2
Moulsecoomb Primary School
  BRIE/ROTT BN2 .... 77 K2
Mowden School
  HOVE BN3 .... 76 C4
National Nature Reserve
  EPSF GU31 .... 132 G12
Natural Health Centre
  CCH PO19 .... 6 D7
Nest Business Park
  HAV PO9 .... 57 J1
Newhouse Farm Business
Centre
  HORS RH12 .... 37 H2
Newick House School
  BURH RH15 .... 47 H8
Newick House Special School
  BURH RH15 .... 47 G8
Newlands Health Clinic
  HWH RH16 .... 45 H5
New Life School
  EGRIN RH19 .... 23 J7
New Park Film Centre Cinema
  CCH PO19 .... 6 F3
New Venture Theatre
  BRI BN1 .... 4 A6
Nightingale Industrial Estate
  HORS RH12 .... 10 F3
Norfolk Arms Hotel
  ARUN BN18 .... 67 G2
Northbourne Medical Centre
  SHOR BN43 .... 73 M5
Northbrook College Sussex
  FERR BN12 .... 92 A1
  HWH RH16 .... 45 G5
  SALV BN13 .... 71 J8
  WTHG BN11 .... 13 H5
Northbrook Trading Estate
  SALV BN13 .... 71 K7
Northchapel Primary School
  PETW GU28 .... 120 F6
Northgate Primary School
  CRAWE RH10 .... 29 K1
North Heath Lane Industrial
Estate
  HORS RH12 .... 36 C3
North Heath Primary School
  HORS RH12 .... 36 C4
North Lancing First & Middle
School
  LAN/SOMP BN15 .... 72 D5
Northlands Business Park
  HORS RH12 .... 115 M5
Northlands Wood Primary
School
  HWH RH16 .... 45 L6
North Lodge Industrial Park
  LIPH GU30 .... 118 A5
North Mundham Primary
School
  SELS PO20 .... 84 C3
Northolmes Junior School
  HORS RH12 .... 36 F4
North Terminal
  HORL RH6 .... 19 K1
Nyewood CE J & I School
  BOGR PO21 .... 103 M1
Nymans Garden (NT)
  RHWH RH17 .... 128 E2
Oakendene Industrial
Estate
  SWTR RH13 .... 145 N4
Oakfield Middle School
  LAN/SOMP BN15 .... 72 C6
Oakgrove College
  SALV BN13 .... 70 D8
Oakhurst Business Park
  SWTR RH13 .... 125 Q11
Oaklands Business Centre
  WTHG BN11 .... 92 E2
Oaklands Catholic School
  WVILLE PO7 .... 168 A12
Oakmeeds Community
College
  BURH RH15 .... 46 F7

Middleton Business Park
The Oaks Primary School
  CRAWE RH10 .... 9 K9
Oakwood Industrial Park
  CRAWE RH10 .... 19 M8
Oakwood School
  HORL RH6 .... 15 G6
  RCCH PO18 .... 60 E3
Oakwood Sports Centre
  HORL RH6 .... 15 H6
Oathall Community College
  HWH RH16 .... 45 J3
Ockenden Manor Hotel
  RHWH RH17 .... 44 B3
Odeon Cinema
  BOGR PO21 .... 3 J6
  BRI BN1 .... 4 C7
Old Barn Theatre
  CRAWW RH11 .... 28 E1
Old Darlington Mushroom
Farm Industrial Estate
  ANG/EP RH16 .... 68 F8
Old Ship Hotel
  BRI BN1 .... 4 D7
Old Thorns Hotel, Golf &
Country Club
  LIPH GU30 .... 117 L2
The Old Tollgate Restaurant
& Hotel
  STEY/UB BN44 .... 48 E3
Old Town Hall
  HORS RH12 .... 10 C7
Open University
  EGRIN RH19 .... 23 K8
Orchard Business Centre
  REDH RH1 .... 14 F1
The Orchards Comm Middle
School
  FERR BN12 .... 92 C1
The Orchards Shopping
Centre
  HWH RH16 .... 45 H5
Oriel High School
  CRAWE RH10 .... 8 F3
Orion Cinema
  BURH RH15 .... 46 F6
Our Lady of Lourdes RC
Primary School
  BRIE/ROTT BN2 .... 97 L3
Our Lady of Sion Junior
School
  WTHG BN11 .... 13 G5
Our Lady of Sion School
  WTHG BN11 .... 12 F6
Our Lady Queen of Heaven CP
School
  CRAWW RH11 .... 29 G1
Ouse Valley Viaduct
  RHWH RH17 .... 129 R5
Ovingdean Hall School
  BRIE/ROTT BN2 .... 97 J1
Padnell Infant School
  HORN PO8 .... 168 B6
Padnell Junior School
  HORN PO8 .... 168 C6
Pagham CC
  BOGR PO21 .... 102 F4
Pagham FC
  BOGR PO21 .... 102 F4
Pagham Harbour
(Nature Reserve)
  BOGR PO21 .... 102 F6
Pagham Yacht Club
  BOGR PO21 .... 102 F6
Palatine School
  FERR BN12 .... 70 C2
Pallant House & Art Gallery
  CCH PO19 .... 6 E5
Palmers Road Industrial Estate
  EMRTH PO10 .... 58 B4
Parham House & Gardens
  PUL/STOR RH20 .... 159 L12
Park Community School
  HAV PO9 .... 168 D12
Park House Primary School
  HAV PO9 .... 168 D12
Parkland Business Centre
  LAN/SOMP BN15 .... 94 C1
Parklands Community School
  CCH PO19 .... 6 A3
Park Recreation Centre
  HORS RH12 .... 10 D5
Park View Leisure Centre
  HOVE BN3 .... 75 K6
Parsonage Business Park
  HORS RH12 .... 11 C1
Passfield Mill Business Park
  LIPH GU30 .... 107 L8
Patcham High School
  BRI BN1 .... 52 E7
Patcham House Special
School
  BRI BN1 .... 52 D7
Patcham Infant School
  BRI BN1 .... 52 D7
Patcham Junior School
  BRI BN1 .... 52 E7
The Pavilion Clinic
  BRI BN1 .... 4 B6
Pavilion Retail Park
  BRIE/ROTT BN2 .... 77 H3
Pavilions in the Park
  HORS RH12 .... 10 D4
Pavilion Theatre
  BRI BN1 .... 4 E6
  WTHG BN11 .... 13 H7
Paxhill Park Golf Club
  HWH RH16 .... 130 H9
Paxton Business Centre
  HOVE BN3 .... 75 J5
Peacock Industrial Estate
  HOVE BN3 .... 75 C6
Pelham Court Business Centre
  CRAWW RH11 .... 29 G2
Pennthorpe School
  HORS RH12 .... 113 R10
The Peter Gladwin Primary
School
  PTSD BN41 .... 75 G3
Petersfield Business Park
  PSF GU32 .... 133 L6
Petersfield Community
Hospital
  PSF GU32 .... 133 M6
Petersfield Golf Club
(new course)
  LISS GU33 .... 133 R1

Petersfield Golf Club
(old course)
  EPSF GU31 .... 133 P8
Petersfield Infant School
  PSF GU32 .... 133 N6
Petersfield RFC
  EPSF GU31 .... 134 A5
The Petersfield School
  PSF GU32 .... 133 M7
Petersfield Swimming Pool
  EPSF GU31 .... 133 P6
Petersfield Town FC
  EPSF GU31 .... 133 P5
Petersgate Infant School
  HORN PO8 .... 150 D9
Petworth CE Primary School
  PETW GU28 .... 139 L10
Petworth Cottage Museum
  PETW GU28 .... 139 L9
Petworth House & Park (NT)
  PETW GU28 .... 139 L9
Petworth Industrial Estate
  PETW GU28 .... 139 L7
Philpots Manor School
  EGRIN RH19 .... 42 B4
Picturedome Cinema
  BOGR PO21 .... 2 C6
Piggott's Business Park
  WTHG BN11 .... 12 F4
Piries Place
  HORS RH12 .... 10 D6
Plaistow & Kirdford Primary
School
  BIL RH14 .... 122 A2
Plumpton College
  LEWES BN7 .... 166 G9
Plumpton Primary School
  LEWES BN7 .... 167 J4
Plumpton Racecourse
  LEWES BN7 .... 166 H5
Pool Valley Coach Station
  BRI BN1 .... 4 F8
Portfield Community School
  CCH PO19 .... 7 J3
Portfield FC
  CCH PO19 .... 7 K2
Portfield Retail Park
  CCH PO19 .... 7 L2
Portland Business Park
  HOVE BN3 .... 75 K6
Portland Road Trading Estate
  HOVE BN3 .... 75 J5
Portslade Community College
  STHW BN42 .... 74 E3
Portslade Health Centre
  PTSD BN41 .... 75 G6
Portslade Sixth Form Centre
  PTSD BN41 .... 74 F4
Pound Hill Infant School
  CRAWE RH10 .... 30 B2
Pound Hill Junior School
  CRAWE RH10 .... 30 B2
Prebendal School
  CCH PO19 .... 6 C4
Premier Travel Inn
  ARUN BN18 .... 67 J4
  BRI BN1 .... 4 D7
  CCH PO19 .... 6 C7
  CRAWE RH10 .... 19 K6
  CRAWW RH11 .... 8 A6
  EGRIN RH19 .... 22 F5
  HAV PO9 .... 56 C4
  HORL RH6 .... 14 E8
  HORS RH12 .... 10 F4
  MSEA/BNM PO22 .... 86 C4
The Prependal School
  CCH PO19 .... 6 E3
Preston Manor
  BRI BN1 .... 76 D4
Preston Park Clinic
  BRI BN1 .... 76 F4
Preston Park Hotel
  BRI BN1 .... 76 D3
Priests House
  EGRIN RH19 .... 42 D3
Prince Regent Swimming
Complex
  BRI BN1 .... 4 E6
Princes Marine Hotel
  HOVE BN3 .... 75 M7
The Princess Royal Hospital
  HWH RH16 .... 45 J7
The Princess Arts Centre
  HWH RH16 .... 45 J6
Priory Lane Arcade
  CCH PO19 .... 6 E2
Priory (ruins)
  RCCH PO18 .... 63 J1
Pulborough Brooks RSPB
Nature Reserve
  PUL/STOR RH20 .... 159 M6
Pyecombe Golf Club
  POY/PYE BN45 .... 165 L11
Quality Hotel
  BRI BN1 .... 4 C7
Quarry Lane Industrial
Estate
  CCH PO19 .... 7 K7
Queen Alexandra Hospital
Home
  WTHG BN11 .... 12 D6
Queen Elizabeth Country
Park
  HORN PO8 .... 150 H2
Queen Elizabeth II Silver
Jubilee School
  SWTR RH13 .... 11 K7
Queensdown School
  BRI BN1 .... 77 H2
Queens Inclosure Primary
School
  WVILLE PO7 .... 168 B8
Queen Victoria Hospital
  EGRIN RH19 .... 23 L6
Queen Victoria Statue
  HOVE BN3 .... 76 B8
Quell Farm Industrial Estate
  PUL/STOR RH20 .... 158 P9
Rake Business Park
  LISS GU33 .... 116 H9
Rake CE First School
  LISS GU33 .... 117 J8
Ramada Hotel
  CRAWE RH10 .... 29 M1
Regent Business Centre
  BURH RH15 .... 46 D7

Regis Centre & Alexandra
  Theatre
  BOGR PO21 .... 2 E8
Riders J & I School
  HAV PO9 .... 168 E12
Rikkyo School in England
  HORS RH12 .... 113 L9
Ritz Cinema
  HORS RH12 .... 10 E5
Riverbank Business Centre
  SHOR BN43 .... 73 J6
Riverside Business Centre
  SHOR BN43 .... 73 L6
Riverside Industrial Estate
  LHPTN BN17 .... 89 G4
Riverside School
  WVILLE PO7 .... 56 A2
RNIB
  HOVE BN3 .... 76 C7
Rock & Bowl Bowling Alley
  EGRIN RH19 .... 23 K8
Roedean School
  BRIE/ROTT BN2 .... 97 G2
Roffey Park Institute
  HORS RH12 .... 37 L3
Roffey Social & Sports Club
  HORS RH12 .... 36 F4
Rogate CE Primary School
  EPSF GU31 .... 135 J5
Rose Green County Infant
  School
  BOGR PO21 .... 103 H3
Rose Green County Junior
  School
  BOGR PO21 .... 103 G2
The Rotherfield Sports
  Ground
  MIDH GU29 .... 137 J7
Rottingdean FC
  BRIE/ROTT BN2 .... 97 L2
Roussillon Barracks
  CCH PO19 .... 61 M4
Rowfant Business Centre
  CRAWE RH10 .... 31 K3
Rowland's Castle Golf Club
  HAV PO9 .... 169 J7
Royal Ashdown Forest
  Golf Club
  FROW RH18 .... 34 F8
Royal George Clinic
  BURH RH15 .... 46 D6
The Royal Hotel
  BOGR PO21 .... 2 D8
The Royal Junior School
  GSHT GU26 .... 108 G8
Royal Pavilion
  BRI BN1 .... 4 E7
The Royal Pavilion Townhouse
  Hotel
  BRI BN1 .... 4 A7
The Royal School
  HASM GU27 .... 109 L7
Royal & Sun Alliance Sports
  Club
  HORS RH12 .... 36 D3
Royal Sussex County Hospital
  BRIE/ROTT BN2 .... 5 L8
RSPCA HQ
  HORS RH12 .... 10 C7
Rudford Industrial Estate
  ARUN BN18 .... 88 C3
Rudgwick Medical Centre
  HORS RH12 .... 113 R10
Rudgwick Primary School
  HORS RH12 .... 114 A10
Rudyard Kipling CP School
  BRIE/ROTT BN2 .... 78 D6
Rumboldswhyke CE Infant
  School
  CCH PO19 .... 7 J6
Rusper Golf Club
  RDKG RH5 .... 17 H5
Rusper Primary School
  HORS RH12 .... 27 H2
Rustington Community
  Primary School
  ANG/EP BN16 .... 90 A3
Rustington Retail Park
  ANG/EP BN16 .... 90 C2
Rustington Trading Estate
  ANG/EP BN16 .... 90 B2
Rutherford Way Industrial
  Estate
  CRAWE RH10 .... 19 M6
The Rydon Community School
  PUL/STOR RH20 .... 160 C11
Sackville Community College
  EGRIN RH19 .... 23 M8
Sackville Trading Estate
  HOVE BN3 .... 75 M5
Saddlers Walk Shopping Centre
  CCH PO19 .... 6 F4
St Albans CE Primary School
  HAV PO9 .... 57 H2
St Andrews CE First & Middle
  School
  CRAWE RH10 .... 9 M7
St Andrews CE High School
  for Boys
  SALV BN13 .... 13 J1
St Andrews CE Primary School
  HOVE BN3 .... 76 A1
  SWTR RH13 .... 126 F8
St Anthonys School
  CCH PO19 .... 61 L5
St Aubyns School
  BRIE/ROTT BN2 .... 97 M4
St Augustines CE Primary
  RHWH RH17 .... 149 J2
St Bartholomews CE Primary
  School
  BRI BN1 .... 4 E3
St Bartholomews Primary
  School
  HASM GU27 .... 109 M9
St Bartholomews Tutorial
  College
  BRI BN1 .... 4 E7
St Bernadettes RC Primary
  School
  BRI BN1 .... 76 D3
St Catherine's Hospice
  CRAWE RH10 .... 8 F7
St Catherines RC School
  LHPTN BN17 .... 89 J3

St Christophers School
  HOVE BN3 .... 75 L7
St Edmunds School
  GSHT GU26 .... 108 G6
St Faith Clinic
  BRIE/ROTT BN2 .... 96 D1
St Francis of Assisi Primary
  School
  CRAWE RH10 .... 9 G4
St Georges Hall
  CCH PO19 .... 7 H6
St Giles CE Primary School
  RHWH RH17 .... 131 H5
St Hill Manor
  EGRIN RH19 .... 33 H5
St Hugh's Monastery
  SWTR RH13 .... 145 J7
St Ives School
  HASM GU27 .... 109 P9
St James CE Primary School
  EMRTH PO10 .... 58 A3
  PUL/STOR RH20 .... 158 D7
St James Industrial Estate
  CCH PO19 .... 7 K2
St John Ambulance Station
  CCH PO19 .... 7 H4
St Johns Catholic Primary
  School
  HORS RH12 .... 125 R4
St Johns Primary School
  Rowlands Castle
  HAV PO9 .... 169 J9
St John the Baptist Primary
  School
  SALV BN13 .... 178 G11
St John the Baptist RC Primary
  School
  BRIE/ROTT BN2 .... 5 L6
St Josephs Business Park
  HOVE BN3 .... 75 M5
St Josephs RC Primary School
  BRI BN1 .... 77 G4
  HWH RH16 .... 45 H5
St Josephs Trading Estate
  HOVE BN3 .... 75 L5
St Lawrence CE Primary
  School
  HPPT/KEY BN6 .... 164 H3
St Leonards Community Infant
  School
  SWTR RH13 .... 10 F6
St Lukes Swimming Pool
  BRIE/ROTT BN2 .... 5 K4
St Lukes Terrace Junior School
  BRIE/ROTT BN2 .... 5 K5
St Margarets CE Primary School
  CRAWW RH11 .... 8 A1
St Margarets Convent of Mercy
  Junior School
  MIDH GU29 .... 136 H9
St Margarets Primary School
  ANG/EP BN16 .... 68 E6
St Marks CE Primary School
  BRIE/ROTT BN2 .... 96 D1
  RHWH RH17 .... 128 C4
St Martins CE Primary School
  SELS PO20 .... 101 J5
St Mary Magdalen Primary
  School
  BRI BN1 .... 4 B5
St Marys CE First School
  PUL/STOR RH20 .... 178 G3
St Marys CE Primary School
  EGRIN RH19 .... 23 J7
  HORS RH12 .... 10 C8
  LHPTN BN17 .... 88 D5
  MFD/CHID GU8 .... 110 G6
  PUL/STOR RH20 .... 159 K2
St Marys Hospital (Almhouses)
  CCH PO19 .... 6 E4
St Marys RC Primary School
  BOGR PO21 .... 2 F7
  PTSD BN41 .... 75 G6
  WTHG BN11 .... 12 E5
St Mary's Slindon CE Primary
  School
  ARUN BN18 .... 65 J1
St Nicholas & St Mary CE First
  & Middle School
  SHOR BN43 .... 73 M5
St Pauls Catholic College
  HWH RH16 .... 45 J4
St Pauls CE Primary School
  BRI BN1 .... 4 C5
St Peters Catholic Primary
  School
  EGRIN RH19 .... 23 H7
  SHOR BN43 .... 73 M5
  WVILLE PO7 .... 168 A12
St Peters CE Primary School
  HFD BN5 .... 163 J3
  RHWH RH17 .... 130 D1
  RING/NEW BN8 .... 149 P9
  SWTR RH13 .... 145 J3
St Peters Infant School
  PTSD BN41 .... 75 G6
St Peters Medical Centre
  BRI BN1 .... 4 F3
St Philip Howard Catholic
  High School
  MSEA/BNM PO22 .... 64 F7
St Philips Catholic Primary
  School
  ARUN BN18 .... 66 F2
St Richards Hospital
  CCH PO19 .... 7 G1
St Richards RC Primary
  School
  CCH PO19 .... 6 E6
St Robert Southwell Primary
  School
  HORS RH12 .... 36 F3
St Thomas Mores RC Primary
  School
  HAV PO9 .... 56 E2
St Wilfrids Catholic Primary
  School
  BURH RH15 .... 46 E6
St Wilfrids CE Primary School
  HWH RH16 .... 45 K6
St Wilfrids RC Primary School
  ANG/EP BN16 .... 68 G7
St Wilfrids RC School
  CRAWW RH11 .... 8 B6
Salfords Industrial Estate
  REDH RH1 .... 14 F1

Sandhurst School
  WTHG BN11 .... 13 L5
Satellite Business Village
  CRAWE RH10 .... 19 K7
Scott Broadwood CE Infant
  School
  RDKG RH5 .... 16 C3
Seaford College
  PETW GU28 .... 156 D8
Seal CP School
  SELS PO20 .... 181 L6
Sea Life Centre
  BRIE/ROTT BN2 .... 4 F8
Selsey Business Centre
  SELS PO20 .... 181 K6
Selsey Country Club
  SELS PO20 .... 181 K3
Selsey CC
  SELS PO20 .... 181 K6
Selsey Golf Club
  SELS PO20 .... 181 K3
Selsey Health Centre
  SELS PO20 .... 181 K5
Selsey Indoor Market
  SELS PO20 .... 181 K6
The Seven Dials Medical
  Centre
  BRI BN1 .... 4 C4
Seymour First & Middle School
  CRAWW RH11 .... 29 G7
Sharps Copse Primary School
  HAV PO9 .... 169 J12
Sharpthorne Tunnel
  EGRIN RH19 .... 42 F4
Sheddingdean Business Centre
  BURH RH15 .... 46 E4
Sheddingdean Primary School
  BURH RH15 .... 46 F4
Sheet CP School
  PSF GU32 .... 133 Q3
Shelley Primary School
  HORS RH12 .... 125 N2
Ship & Anchor Marina
  ARUN BN18 .... 66 D8
The Ship Hotel
  CCH PO19 .... 6 E3
Shipley CE Primary School
  SWTR RH13 .... 143 L8
Shopwhyke Industrial Centre
  CCH PO19 .... 7 M3
Shoreham Airport
  SHOR BN43 .... 73 H6
Shoreham Beach First School
  SHOR BN43 .... 73 M7
Shoreham College
  SHOR BN43 .... 74 C6
Shoreham FC
  PTSD BN41 .... 75 G6
Shoreham First School
  SHOR BN43 .... 73 K5
Shoreham Health Centre
  SHOR BN43 .... 73 L6
Shottermill Infant School
  HASM GU27 .... 109 J10
Sidlesham CP School
  SELS PO20 .... 101 J5
Sidlesham FC
  SELS PO20 .... 101 L5
Singing Hills Golf Course
  HPPT/KEY BN6 .... 164 C7
Singleton CE Primary School
  RCCH PO18 .... 172 G2
Slindon College
  ARUN BN18 .... 174 G12
Slindon Common (NT)
  ARUN BN18 .... 65 J2
Slindon Wood (NT)
  ARUN BN18 .... 64 F2
Slinfold CE Primary School
  SWTR RH13 .... 124 G1
Slinfold Park Golf &
  Country Club
  SWTR RH13 .... 124 E3
Snowhill Business Centre
  CRAWE RH10 .... 21 M5
Sofitel
  HORL RH6 .... 19 L1
Somerhill Junior School
  HOVE BN3 .... 76 C7
Somerset Hospital
  PETW GU28 .... 139 L9
Sompting Abbots Sch
  LAN/SOMP BN15 .... 71 M5
South Bersted CE Primary
  School
  MSEA/BNM PO22 .... 2 D2
South Bersted Industrial
  Estate
  MSEA/BNM PO22 .... 2 E1
Southbourne County J & I
  School
  EMRTH PO10 .... 58 F5
South Downs College
  WVILLE PO7 .... 56 B2
Southdowns Country Hotel
  EPSF GU31 .... 135 M9
South Downs Health Clinic
  BRI BN1 .... 4 D4
Southfields Industrial Estate
  RCCH PO18 .... 60 A7
Southgate Magistrates Court
  CCH PO19 .... 6 E6
Southgate Primary School
  CRAWE RH10 .... 8 F8
South Lodge Hotel
  SWTR RH13 .... 127 L10
South of England
  Showground
  RHWH RH17 .... 41 M8
South Terminal
  HORL RH6 .... 19 M2
Southwater Business Park
  SWTR RH13 .... 125 Q12
Southwater Country Park
  SWTR RH13 .... 143 Q1
Southwater Junior School
  SWTR RH13 .... 125 Q11
Southwick Business Centre
  STHW BN42 .... 74 D6
Sovereign Business Centre
  BURH RH15 .... 46 D7
Special Support Facility
  CCH PO19 .... 7 J3
The Spread Eagle Hotel &
  Health Spa
  MIDH GU29 .... 137 J10

Spring Copse Business Park
  SWTR RH13 .... 124 E2
Springfield First School
  SALV BN13 .... 13 K1
Springfield Industrial Estate
  RHWH RH17 .... 47 L4
Stakes Hill Infant School
  WVILLE PO7 .... 168 A11
Stammerham Business Centre
  HORS RH12 .... 26 D2
Standen (NT)
  EGRIN RH19 .... 33 J5
Stanford Infant School
  BRI BN1 .... 76 D5
Stanford Road Junior School
  BRI BN1 .... 4 C1
Stanley Deason Leisure Centre
  BRIE/ROTT BN2 .... 77 L8
Stansted House
  HAV PO9 .... 169 R8
Star Road Industrial Estate
  SWTR RH13 .... 144 E11
Star Road Trading Estate
  SWTR RH13 .... 144 F10
Station Approach Industrial
  Estate
  PUL/STOR RH20 .... 158 H3
Station Road Industrial
  Estate
  SWTR RH13 .... 125 Q12
Staunton Country Park
  HAV PO9 .... 168 F7
Staunton Park Community
  School
  HAV PO9 .... 169 J10
Stedham CP School
  MIDH GU29 .... 136 C8
Steep School
  PSF GU32 .... 133 M2
The Stepping Stone School
  GSHT GU26 .... 109 J6
Steyning Athletic Club
  STEY/UB BN44 .... 48 B2
Steyning Grammar Upper
  School
  STEY/UB BN44 .... 48 C1
Steyning Health Centre
  STEY/UB BN44 .... 48 C2
Steyning St Andrews CE
  Primary School
  STEY/UB BN44 .... 48 C1
Steyning Sports Centre
  STEY/UB BN44 .... 48 B1
Steyning Town FC
  STEY/UB BN44 .... 48 C1
Stonelands School
  HOVE BN3 .... 76 A7
Storrington First School
  PUL/STOR RH20 .... 159 R11
Storrington Lawn Tennis Club
  PUL/STOR RH20 .... 159 R12
Suffolk House Hotel &
  Restaurant
  CCH PO19 .... 6 F4
Summersea Community
  Primary School
  LHPTN BN17 .... 90 A2
Sumners Ponds Fishery &
  Campsite
  SWTR RH13 .... 124 H11
Sundridge School
  HORN PO8 .... 168 A7
The Surrey & Sussex
  Crematorium
  CRAWE RH10 .... 20 C6
Sussex County CC
  HOVE BN3 .... 76 B6
Sussex English Language
  School
  WTHG BN11 .... 13 G6
Sussex Eye Hospital
  BRIE/ROTT BN2 .... 5 L8
Sussex House Business Park
  HOVE BN3 .... 75 L5
Sussex Manor Business Park
  CRAWE RH10 .... 19 M7
Sussex Nuffield Hospital
  BRIE/ROTT BN2 .... 78 B5
  HOVE BN3 .... 75 L7
Sussex Police & Register Office
  SALV BN13 .... 70 C8
The Sussex Toy &
  Model Museum
  BRI BN1 .... 4 E4
Swandean Hospital
  SALV BN13 .... 70 C5
Swandean School of English
  WTHG BN11 .... 12 F5
The Swan Inn Hotel
  MFD/CHID GU8 .... 110 H6
Swan Walk Shopping Centre
  HORS RH12 .... 10 C6
Swedish Folk High School
  PTSD BN41 .... 75 G5
Swedish School
  CRAWE RH10 .... 9 K8
Sweetwoods Park Golf Club
  EDEN TN8 .... 25 M5
Sydney West Sports Centre
  BURH RH15 .... 46 E5
TA Centre
  CRAWE RH10 .... 9 G2
  HORS RH12 .... 10 D7
Tanbridge House School
  HORS RH12 .... 125 Q3
Tanbridge Retail Park
  HORS RH12 .... 10 A6
Tangmere Military Aviation
  Museum Trust
  SELS PO20 .... 63 J4
Tangmere Primary School
  SELS PO20 .... 63 J3
The Tanneries Industrial Estate
  HAV PO9 .... 56 F4
Taro Leisure Centre
  PSF GU32 .... 134 A6
Tavistock & Summerhill School
  HWH RH16 .... 45 J2
Templars County Infants
  School
  LAN/SOMP BN15 .... 72 A7
Temple Bar Business Park
  RCCH PO18 .... 62 F2
Terminus Road Industrial
  Estate
  CCH PO19 .... 6 A7

Thakeham First School
  PUL/STOR RH20 .... 160 E6
Theatre Royal
  BRI BN1 .... 4 E6
Thistle Hotel
  BRI BN1 .... 4 E8
  HORL RH6 .... 14 F4
Thomas A Becket First School
  SALV BN13 .... 70 F8
Thomas A Becket Middle
  School
  SALV BN13 .... 71 G8
Thomas Bennett Community
  College
  CRAWE RH10 .... 29 J6
Thornberry Middle School
  LAN/SOMP BN15 .... 72 E8
Thorney Island Airfield
  EMRTH PO10 .... 80 D3
Thorney Island Primary School
  EMRTH PO10 .... 80 B2
Three Bridges Community
  Centre
  CRAWE RH10 .... 9 L2
Three Bridges CC
  CRAWE RH10 .... 9 L4
Three Bridges FC
  CRAWE RH10 .... 9 M4
Three Bridges First School
  CRAWE RH10 .... 9 L2
Three Bridges Junior School
  CRAWE RH10 .... 9 K3
Ticehurst Clinic
  HOVE BN3 .... 75 M7
Tilgate Forest Business Centre
  CRAWW RH11 .... 29 J8
Tilgate Forest Golf Centre
  CRAWE RH10 .... 29 M7
Tilgate Park
  CRAWE RH10 .... 29 L8
Timberlaine Industrial Estate
  CCH PO19 .... 7 J6
Timberlaine Trading Estate
  SALV BN13 .... 71 L8
Toat Monument
  PUL/STOR RH20 .... 141 J9
Tobias School of Art
  EGRIN RH19 .... 33 J3
Torah Academy
  HOVE BN3 .... 75 M7
Touch for Health Centre
  BOGR PO21 .... 2 B6
The Towers Convent School
  STEY/UB BN44 .... 49 H4
Town Hall Museum &
  Art Gallery
  WTHG BN11 .... 13 H5
Toyshorse International
  Stud Farm
  BIL RH14 .... 123 R1
Trafalgar County Infant School
  HORS RH12 .... 10 B2
Travelodge
  ARUN BN18 .... 64 F2
  BIL RH14 .... 124 B9
  BRI BN1 .... 76 E5
  EMRTH PO10 .... 57 M3
  HORL RH6 .... 19 K4
  LHPTN BN17 .... 89 G4
  LIPH GU30 .... 107 N12
  RHWH RH17 .... 146 F8
The Triangle
  BURH RH15 .... 46 C5
Tristar Business Centre
  SWTR RH13 .... 144 F11
Trosnant Primary & Infant
  School
  HAV PO9 .... 56 F2
Turners Hill CE Primary School
  CRAWE RH10 .... 31 M6
Twineham CE Primary School
  RHWH RH17 .... 146 B9
Tyes Cross
  EGRIN RH19 .... 43 H3
UGC Cinema
  BRIE/ROTT BN2 .... 96 E2
  CRAWE RH10 .... 8 F1
Unicorn Trading Estate
  HASM GU27 .... 109 L10
University College Chichester
  CCH PO19 .... 6 F1
University of Brighton
  BRI BN1 .... 53 M8
  BRI BN1 .... 77 H3
  BRIE/ROTT BN2 .... 4 F6
University of Chichester
  (Bognor Regis Campus)
  MSEA/BNM PO22 .... 3 G5
University of Sussex
  BRI BN1 .... 54 A6
University of Sussex Sports
  Centre
  BRI BN1 .... 53 M7
Uplands Special School
  BRI BN1 .... 77 H3
Uppark (NT)
  EPSF GU31 .... 152 C5
Upper Beeding Primary School
  STEY/UB BN44 .... 48 F3
Vale First & Middle School
  SALV BN13 .... 70 E3
Valley Farm Business Park
  HPPT/KEY BN6 .... 146 C12
Varndean College
  BRI BN1 .... 76 E2
Varndean School
  BRI BN1 .... 76 F2
Vicarage Lane Clinic
  HASM GU27 .... 109 J11
Victoria Cottage Hospital
  EMRTH PO10 .... 58 A4
Victoria Industrial Estate
  BURH RH15 .... 46 C7
Victoria Road Trading
  Estate
  PTSD BN41 .... 75 H5
Vinalls Business Centre
  HFD BN5 .... 163 K5
Vinnetrow Farm Business
  Centre
  SELS PO20 .... 84 D2
Volks Electric Railway
  BRIE/ROTT BN2 .... 5 H9
Wakehurst Place & Millennium
  Seed Bank (NT)
  RHWH RH17 .... 41 L6

Walberton & Binsted CE
Primary School
ARUN BN18 .... **65** K4
Wallands Primary School
LEWES BN7 .... **55** M3
Walstead Cemetery
HWH RH16 .... **130** G11
Warblington Secondary
School
HAV PO9 .... **57** J4
Warden Park School
RHWH RH17 .... **44** D4
War Memorial Hospital
MSEA/BNM PO22 .... **2** D3
Warner Farm Touring Park
SELS PO20 .... **181** J4
Warnham CE Primary School
HORS RH12 .... **115** Q9
Warninglid Primary School
RHWH RH17 .... **128** B7
Warren Park Primary School
HAV PO9 .... **168** E10
Waterfield First School
CRAWW RH11 .... **28** D5
Waterhall Golf Club
BRI BN1 .... **51** M7
Water Lane Industrial Estate
PUL/STOR RH20 .... **160** C10
Waterlooville Golf Club
HORN PO8 .... **168** C7
Watersmead Business Park
LHPTN BN17 .... **89** H1
Waterworks Cottages
HOVE BN3 .... **75** M3
Wattlehurst Farm
HORS RH12 .... **115** R2
Waytefield Clinic
BRI BN1 .... **76** E3
Weald & Downland Open Air
Museum
RCCH PO18 .... **172** A2
The Weald School
BIL RH14 .... **142** A2
Wedglen Industrial Estate
MIDH GU29 .... **136** G10

Welfare Clinic
HOVE BN3 .... **75** K3
Wessex Superbowl
HAV PO9 .... **56** C4
West Bank Fort
LHPTN BN17 .... **89** J6
West Blatchington Junior
School
HOVE BN3 .... **75** L1
Westbourne CP School
EMRTH PO10 .... **58** C1
Westbourne House School
SELS PO20 .... **62** E6
West Chiltington Community
School
PUL/STOR RH20 .... **160** B4
West Chiltington Golf Club
PUL/STOR RH20 .... **160** A3
West Dean CE Primary School
RCCH PO18 .... **172** B4
West Dean College
RCCH PO18 .... **172** D3
West Dean Gardens
RCCH PO18 .... **172** D3
Westdene Primary School
BRI BN1 .... **52** B8
Westergate Community
School
SELS PO20 .... **64** D6
Westfield Industrial Estate
HORN PO8 .... **168** E2
Westgate Leisure Centre
CCH PO19 .... **6** C5
West Green First School
CRAWW RH11 .... **8** C2
West Hill Community Hall
BRI BN1 .... **4** D3
West Hoathly CE Primary
School
EGRIN RH19 .... **42** B1
Westholme Clinic
FERR BN12 .... **92** C3
Westholme Clinic
WTHG BN11 .... **12** E6

West Hove Golf Club
HOVE BN3 .... **75** H3
West Hove Junior School
HOVE BN3 .... **75** L6
West Lavington CE First
School
MIDH GU29 .... **137** K11
West Park CE Controlled
School
FERR BN12 .... **92** C3
West Pier (Derelict)
BRI BN1 .... **4** B8
West Sands Leisure Centre
SELS PO20 .... **180** H6
West Sussex College of Design
WTHG BN11 .... **13** H5
West Sussex Golf Club
PUL/STOR RH20 .... **159** P7
West Sussex School of English
STEY/UB BN44 .... **48** C2
West Wittering Parochial
Primary School
SELS PO20 .... **99** G4
Weydown Industrial Estate
HASM GU27 .... **109** M10
Weyford Infant School
BOR GU35 .... **107** J5
Weyford Junior School
BOR GU35 .... **107** J5
Whitehawk Clinic
BRIE/ROTT BN2 .... **77** L8
Whitehawk Primary School
BRIE/ROTT BN2 .... **77** K7
Whitehill Cemetery
BOR GU35 .... **107** K6
White Rose Touring Park
LHPTN BN17 .... **67** J8
Whitestyles Middle School
LAN/SOMP BN15 .... **72** A7
Whytemead First School
SALV BN13 .... **71** K8
Wickbourne Infant School
LHPTN BN17 .... **89** H3
Wick FC
LHPTN BN17 .... **89** J1

Wigmore AFC
SALV BN13 .... **71** J6
Wigmore Trading Estate
SALV BN13 .... **71** L8
Wildfowl Reserve
LEWES BN7 .... **79** C2
The Wildwood Golf Club
CRAN GU6 .... **112** H7
William Penn Primary
.... School
SWTR RH13 .... **142** H7
The Willows First School
LAN/SOMP BN15 .... **72** D6
Windlesham House School
PUL/STOR RH20 .... **178** F6
Windmills Junior School
HPPT/KEY BN6 .... **165** P6
Windmill Theatre & Cinema
LHPTN BN17 .... **89** J6
Windsor Hotel
WTHG BN11 .... **93** M3
Winston Business Centre
LAN/SOMP BN15 .... **72** B8
Winterpick Business Park
HFD BN5 .... **145** Q12
Wisborough Green Primary
School
BIL RH14 .... **123** K12
Wispers School
HASM GU27 .... **109** M8
Wiston Business Park
PUL/STOR RH20 .... **160** H11
Witterings Health Centre
SELS PO20 .... **99** K6
Wivelsfield Primary School
RHWH RH17 .... **47** L3
Woodingdean Primary
School
BRIE/ROTT BN2 .... **78** B5
Woodlea Primary School
BOR GU35 .... **106** G8
Woodruff Business Centre
CCH PO19 .... **6** A6
Woods Mill Nature Reserve
HFD BN5 .... **163** L9

Woodvale Brighton
Crematorium
BRIE/ROTT BN2 .... **5** M1
Woolmer Hill Athletics Track
HASM GU27 .... **108** G9
Woolmer Hill Technology
College
HASM GU27 .... **108** G10
Worthing Athletics Track
FERR BN12 .... **92** D2
Worthing College
SALV BN13 .... **92** D2
Worthing Crematorium
SALV BN13 .... **178** F9
Worthing FC
SALV BN13 .... **12** D2
Worthing Golf Club
SALV BN13 .... **71** G4
Worthing High School
SALV BN13 .... **12** E1
Worthing Hospital
WTHG BN11 .... **13** J3
Worthing Pavilion Bowling
Club
SALV BN13 .... **12** D3
Worthing Pier
WTHG BN11 .... **13** J7
Worthing Priority Care
ANG/EP BN16 .... **90** C4
Worthing RFC
ANG/EP BN16 .... **91** G1
Worthing & Southlands
Hospital
SHOR BN43 .... **74** A5
Worth School
CRAWE RH10 .... **31** G8
WWT Arundel
ARUN BN18 .... **67** H1
Wyndham Business Park
MIDH GU29 .... **136** G10
Yapton CE Primary School
MSEA/BNM PO22 .... **87** L1
Yattendon School
HORL RH6 .... **14** F5

Acknowledgements

Schools address data provided by Education Direct.

Petrol station information supplied by Johnsons

One-way street data provided by © Tele Atlas N.V. Tele Atlas

Garden centre information provided by

Garden Centre Association 🌸 Britains best garden centres

Wyevale Garden Centres 🌳

The statement on the front cover of this atlas is sourced, selected and quoted
from a reader comment and feedback form received in 2004

How do I find the perfect place?